HISTORY + FOR EDEXC

RELIGION AND THE STATE

in early modern Europe

ROBIN BUNCE
CHRISTINE KNAACK
SARAH WARD

DYNAMIC LEARNING

HODDER
EDUCATION
AN HACHETTE UK COMPANY

Every effort has been made to trace all copyright holders, but if any have been inadvertently overlooked the Publishers will be pleased to make the necessary arrangements at the first opportunity.

Although every effort has been made to ensure that website addresses are correct at time of going to press, Hodder Education cannot be held responsible for the content of any website mentioned in this book. It is sometimes possible to find a relocated web page by typing in the address of the home page for a website in the URL window of your browser.

Hachette UK's policy is to use papers that are natural, renewable and recyclable products and made from wood grown in sustainable forests. The logging and manufacturing processes are expected to conform to the environmental regulations of the country of origin.

Orders: please contact Bookpoint Ltd, 130 Milton Park, Abingdon, Oxon OX14 4SB. Telephone: (44) 01235 827720. Fax: (44) 01235 400454. Email education@bookpoint.co.uk Lines are open from 9 a.m. to 5 p.m., Monday to Saturday, with a 24-hour message answering service. You can also order through our website: www.hoddereducation.co.uk

© Robin Bunce, Sarah Ward and Christine Knaack

First published in 2015 by

Hodder Education,

An Hachette UK Company

Carmelite House

50 Victoria Embankment

London EC4Y 0DZ

www.hoddereducation.co.uk

Impression number   10 9 8 7 6 5 4 3 2 1

Year   2019 2018 2017 2016 2015

Cover photo © The Art Archive / Alamy

Illustrations by Integra Software Services

Typeset in 10/12.5pt Bembo Std Regular by Integra Software Services Pvt. Ltd., Pondicherry, India

Printed in Italy

A catalogue record for this title is available from the British Library.

ISBN 978 1 471 837579

CONTENTS

INTRODUCTION

History + for Edexcel A level: Religion and the state in early modern Europe supports Edexcel's Route B. Specifically, it supports the following papers:

- Paper 1B: England, 1509–1603: authority, nation and religion
- Paper 2B.1: Luther and the German Reformation, c1515–55
- Paper 2B.2: The Dutch Revolt, c1563–1609

About the course

Your overall A level History course for the Edexcel Specification includes three externally examined papers and coursework. If you are studying AS History, there are two externally examined papers. The papers are:

- Paper 1: Breadth study with interpretations (AS and A level)
- Paper 2: Depth study (AS and A level)
- Paper 3: Themes in breadth with aspects in depth (A level only)

This book covers the breadth study with interpretations 'England, 1509–1603: authority, nation and religion' and two depth studies of which you must study one: 'Luther and the German Reformation, c1515–55' or 'The Dutch Revolt, c1563–1609'.

How to use this book

This book had been designed to help you develop the knowledge and skills necessary to succeed in Paper 1 and Paper 2.

The book divides into three main parts, dealing with Paper 1, Paper 2.1 and Paper 2.2 respectively. The structure of each part parallels the structure of the specification. Therefore:

- Paper 1 has four themes, each divided into three chapters, and a final section dealing with the historical interpretation, again divided into four chapters. Each theme and historical interpretation begins with a **Big Picture**, setting the scene for the material which follows.
- Paper 2 starts with a big picture overview of the whole period and then is divided into four chapters dealing with the four key topics of the specification.

Each chapter begins with an overview of the theme, topic or interpretation discussed to set it in context and ends with either a chapter summary or conclusion to help with revision of the key points included in the chapter. Summary diagrams at the end of chapters should also help with revision.

There are a series of other features throughout the book to help aid your understanding of the period and develop your essay writing skills.

Essay writing skills

Essay technique sections at the end of chapters help develop essay writing skills. These include how to:

- focus on the question
- structure your answer
- deploy detail
- analyse
- create and sustain a balance argument.

Where necessary, they also show how to approach the sources and extracts that accompany some examination questions.

Practice questions provide exam-style questions so that you can practise answering questions related to the different topic and themes that you study.

Help with note making

On pages ix–xi there are a series of note-making styles, which you can use as you work through the book. These are designed to ensure that your note making is clear, and sets you up to revise for the exam.

Note it down activities appear throughout the book, to guide your note taking. They sometimes refer back to the note-making styles outlined at the beginning of the book.

Work together

The book also contains Work together activities. These consist of activities designed to help you work with a partner to check your understanding of the topics as you go along.

Extended reading

In addition to the traditional textbook narrative, this book contains five specially commissioned essays from practising academic historians. These address the historical interpretation: Was there a general crisis of government in the last years of Elizabeth I's reign, 1589–1603? The essays are designed to introduce the historical debate in a way that is directly related to the exam.

Recommended reading

You can find recommended reading sections throughout the book. These are designed to point you in the direction of both classic works on the subject and examples of more recent historical writing.

About the exam

The A level exam

The A level comprises three papers and coursework. Paper 1 and Paper 2 are examined at the same time, as part of the same route. Paper 1 is worth 30 per cent of the total A level and Paper 2 is worth 20 per cent. Paper 3 is examined separately and is worth 30 per cent, with the coursework making up the final 20 per cent of marks. This section looks at Paper 1 and Paper 2, as these are the papers this book supports.

Paper 1

The Paper 1 exam paper is divided into three parts: Section A, Section B and Section C. The different sections will test different skills and aspects of the history you have studied.

Sections A and B test your knowledge of the period 1509–88. The questions test your breadth of knowledge of four key themes:

- Monarchy and government, 1509–88
- Religious changes, 1509–88
- State control and popular resistance, 1509–88
- Economic, social and cultural change, 1509–88

Section C tests your depth of knowledge regarding a key historical debate: Was there a general crisis of government in the last years of Elizabeth I's reign, 1589–1603?

Sections A and B

Sections A and B test the breadth of your knowledge, and each section requires you to write an essay. In both Section A and B you have to answer one question from a choice of two.

Section A of the exam paper contains two questions, of which you are required to complete one. Questions in

Section A will test the breadth of your knowledge by focusing on at least ten years.

Section B of the exam paper also contains two questions, of which you are required to complete one. Questions in Section B will test the breadth of your knowledge by focusing on at least one-third of the period you have studied: 26 years.

Neither Section A nor B requires you to read or analyse either sources or extracts from the work of historians.

Section A and B questions require you to deploy a variety of skills. The most important are focus on the question, selection and deployment of relevant detail, analysis and, at the highest level, prioritisation.

Questions in Section A and B will focus on one of the following concepts:

- cause
- consequence
- change/continuity
- similarity/difference
- significance.

Therefore, the questions will typically begin with one of the following stems:

- How far …
- How accurate is it to say …
- To what extent …
- How significant …
- How successful …

Section C

Section C of the exam paper is different to Sections A and B. While Section A and B test your own knowledge, Section C tests your own knowledge and your ability to analyse and evaluate interpretations of the past in the work of historians. Therefore, Section C contains two extracts from the work of historians. Section C of the exam contains one compulsory question.

Section C focuses on an interpretation related to the following controversy:

Was there a general crisis of government in the last years of Elizabeth I's reign, 1589–1603?

It looks at the following aspects of the potential crisis:

- the significance of threats to national security from Spain and Ireland
- the extent of faction at court and the succession issue
- the importance of growing conflicts with parliament and the session of 1601
- the importance of harvest failures in the 1590s and the growth of social distress.

Section C tests your ability to analyse and evaluate different historical interpretations in the light of your own knowledge. Therefore, it tests a variety of skills including:

- Identifying the interpretation.
- Writing a well-structured essay.
- Integrating own extracts with own knowledge.
- Reaching an overall judgement.

Paper 2

Paper 2 is a depth paper. This means that the questions will test your knowledge of short periods of history.

Luther and the German Reformation, c1515–55's key topics are:

- Conditions in early sixteenth-century Germany
- Luther's early challenge to the Catholic Church, 1517–20
- Development of Lutheranism, 1521–46
- The spread and survival of Lutheranism, 1521–55

The Dutch Revolt, c1563–67's key topics are:

- Origins of the Dutch Revolt, c1563–67
- Alva and Orange, 1567–73
- Spain and the reconquest, 1573–84
- Securing the independence of the United Provinces, 1584–1609

The Paper 2 exam is divided into two sections. Section A is a source question while Section B requires you to write an essay from your own knowledge.

Section A

In the A level paper questions in Section A require you to analyse two primary sources. They will typically be phrased in the following way:

How far could the historian make use of Sources 1 and 2 together to investigate [x]?

You are required to use the sources, your own knowledge and the information given about the sources. You might consider the following:

- What the sources would tell the historian about the topic.
- How nature, origin and purpose could give the historian more information about the critical stance of the author, as well as some evidence about usefulness.
- How you can use your knowledge of the historical context to support or develop inferences made from the sources, and to either confirm the accuracy or limitations of information within them or to note limitations and challenge the accuracy of the sources.
- What you could say about the two sources in combination.

Section B

You should answer questions in Section B in the form of an essay. The questions could focus on the following concepts:

- cause
- consequence
- change/continuity
- similarity/difference
- significance.

The questions could begin with the following question stems:

- How far …
- How accurate is it to say …
- To what extent …

The AS level exam

The AS level comprises two papers. Paper 1 is worth 60 per cent of the total AS level and Paper 2 is worth 40 per cent.

Paper 1

The AS exam tests all of the same content as the A level exam, and is structured in exactly the same way. However, there are differences between the two exams:

Section A and B

There are three key differences between A level and the AS in Sections A and B.

- **Wording**: The wording of AS level questions will be less complex than the wording of A level questions. Specifically, there are likely to be fewer adjectives or qualifying phrases in the question. For example:

A level question	AS level question
How accurate is it to say that popular pressure was the fundamental reason for the religious changes of the period 1547–63?	To what extent was popular pressure the main reason for the religious changes of the period 1547–63?

- **Focus**: Section A questions can focus on a more limited range of concepts at AS than at A level. Specifically, at AS level Section A questions can only focus on **cause** and **consequences** (including success and failure), whereas A level questions can focus on a wider variety of concepts.
- **Mark scheme**: The A level mark scheme has five levels, whereas the AS level mark scheme only has four. This means that full marks are available at AS for an analytical essay, whereas sustained analysis is necessary for full marks at A level.

Section C

Section C of the AS exam focuses on the same aspects of the same debate:

Was there a general crisis of government in the last years of Elizabeth I's reign, 1589–1603?

As in the A level exam you have to answer one compulsory question based on two extracts. The AS level exam is different from the A level exam in the following ways:

- **The question**: The AS level question is worded in a less complex way than the A level question. For example:

A level	AS level
In the light of differing interpretations, how convincing do you find the view that the last years of Elizabeth's reign were destabilised by factional strife at court? To explain your answer, analyse and evaluate the material in both extracts, using your own knowledge of the issues.	Historians have different views about whether there was a general crisis of government in the last years of Elizabeth I's reign. Analyse and evaluate the extracts and use your knowledge of the issues to explain your answer to the following question. How far do you agree with the view that, during the last ten years of Elizabeth's reign, English government was destabilised by factionalism?

- **The extracts**: At AS the extracts will be slightly shorter and you may get extracts taken from textbooks as well as the work of historians. In this sense the extracts at AS level should be slightly easier to read and understand.
- **The mark scheme**: The A level mark scheme has five levels, whereas the AS level mark scheme only has four. This means that full marks are available at AS for an analytical essay, whereas sustained analysis is necessary for full marks at A level.

Paper 2

The AS exam tests all of the same content as the A level exam, and is structured in a similar way. However, there are differences between the two exams:

Section A

Section A of the AS exam is structured in a different way to the A level exam. In essence, Section A at AS tests the same skills as Section A at A level, but over two questions rather than one.

The AS Section A is divided into Part (a) and Part (b).

Part (a)

Part (a) contains one compulsory question related to a single source. Part (a) asks you to consider how the source is of value to a historian who is engaged in a specified enquiry. For example, the question might ask:

> **Why is Source 1 valuable to the historian for an enquiry into the sale of indulgences in early sixteenth-century Germany?**

The question requires you to reach a judgement about the ways in which Source 1 is valuable. In that sense the question is not primarily about looking for the ways in which the source is unreliable. Examiners are looking for the following skills:

- Detailed contextual knowledge that explains the meaning of relevant points made by the source.
- Valid inferences.
- An overall judgement about the value of the source related to valid criteria.

Part (b)

Part (b) contains one compulsory question related to a single source. Part (b) asks you to consider how much weight to give a source for a specified enquiry. Therefore, Part (b) requires you to consider the value and the limits of the source.

Part (b) tests your ability to:

- comprehend and analyse source material
- use historical knowledge to weigh the value of the source
- reach a judgement, based on valid criteria, about the value of the source.

Section B

Section B of the AS exam tests the same content knowledge as Section B of the A level exam. Section B comprises three questions, of which you must complete one.

Paper 2 Section B questions are very similar to Paper 1 Section B questions (see page vii). The key difference relates to the period on which the question focuses. Paper 2 examines your knowledge of depth. Therefore Section B questions can focus on a single event or a single year. Alternatively they might focus on the whole chronology of the course, in this case c1515–55. For example, Paper 2, Section B questions could ask:

> **Why did Lutheranism survive in the years 1521–55?**

NOTE TAKING

Good note taking is really important. Your notes are an essential revision resource. What is more, the process of making notes will help you understand and remember what you are reading.

How books work

Most books are written as clearly as possible. Therefore, writers use a variety of techniques to help you learn.

Authors often break up their work into key points (the most important ideas and themes) and supporting evidence (the details that support the key points). Key points are usually general statements. For example, a key point might be 'Dynasty was all important to Henry VIII, and remained so for his heirs. This made the issue of the succession absolutely central to politics', while the supporting evidence might be a list of detailed examples that indicate the key point is correct.

How to make notes

Most note-making styles reflect the distinction between key points and supporting evidence. Below is advice on a variety of different note-taking styles. Throughout each section in the book are note-making activities for you to carry out.

Hints and tips

The important thing is that you understand your notes. Therefore, you don't have to write everything down, and you don't have to write in full sentences.

While making notes you can use abbreviations:

Full text	Abbreviation
Mary, Queen of Scots, was a Catholic and (at the time) heir to the throne.	MQS = RC, heir to throne.

You can use arrows instead of words:

Full text	Arrow
Increased	↑
Decreased	↓

You can use mathematical notation:

equals	=
plus, and	+, &
because	∵
therefore	∴

Here's an example:

Text	Notes
Dudley was widely unpopular because of his closeness to the Queen and influence over her.	Dudley = v. unpopular Closeness to QE & influence over her

Note-making styles

There are a large number of note-making styles. You can find examples of four popular styles below. All of them have their strengths, it is a good idea to try them all and work out which style suits you.

The examples below are of notes taken from Chapter 1 on pages 4–32.

Style 1: Bullet points

Bullet points can be a useful method of making notes because:

- They encourage you to write in note form, rather than in full sentences.
- They help you to organise your ideas in a systematic fashion.
- They are easy to skim read later.
- You can show relative importance visually by indenting less important, or supporting points.

1 Scan the section before you read it in depth. Identify headings (points of explanation). Significantly, you should try looking for the key points in the first sentence of each paragraph. On your page of notes, set the key points out in sections.
2 Now read carefully through the section. Write supporting points or points of evidence under the relevant headings.

The end result should look like this.

The Spanish marriage

- Mary determined to rule.
- Not personally interested in marriage but knew needed heir for kingdom.
- Chose Philip II of Spain. Marriage treaty prevented Philip II from governing role.
- Philip II absent in Spain, only visited once after 1556.

Style 2: The 1:2 method

The 1:2 method is a variation on bullet points. The method is based on dividing your page into two columns: the first for the main point, the second for supporting detail. This allows you to see the structure of the information clearly.

1 Divide your page like this:

Key points	Supporting detail

2 Write the key points in the left-hand section.
3 Write the supporting detail in the right-hand section.

The end result should look like this:

Key points	Supporting detail
Spanish marriage	<ul><li>Mary determined to rule.</li><li>Followed same coronation procedure as predecessors.</li><li>Not personally interested in marriage but knew needed heir for kingdom.</li><li>Chose Philip II of Spain.</li><li>Marriage treaty prevented Philip from governing role.</li><li>Philip II absent in Spain, only visited once after 1556.</li></ul>

Style 3: Spider diagrams

Spider diagrams or mind maps can be a useful method of making notes because:

- They will help you to categorise factors: each of the main branches coming from the centre should be a new category.
- They can help you see what is most important: often the most important factors will be close to the centre of the diagram.
- They can help you see connections between different aspects of what you are studying. It is useful to draw lines between different parts of your diagram to show links.
- They can also help you with essay planning: you can use them to quickly get down the main points and develop a clear structure in response to an essay question.

1 Draw a circle in the middle of your piece of paper. It should be large enough to contain the section title.
2 Scan the section and identify headings. Draw lines out from your central circle – remember to leave plenty of room between them so that you can fit in all of your notes.
3 Read through the section carefully. Write supporting points or points of evidence under the relevant headings.

The end result should look like this.

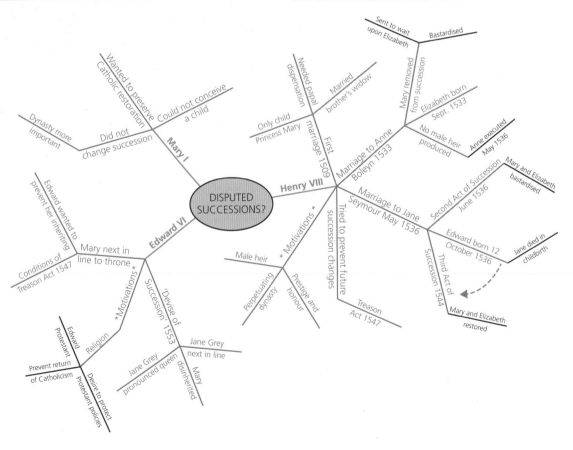

Style 4: Index cards

Index cards are particularly useful when you are revising for your exam, or when you are planning your essays.

Revision

Index cards are small, and therefore they encourage you to prioritise, by forcing you to note down only the most important information.

Essay planning

You can use index cards to help plan essays in the following way. First, select all of the cards that are relevant to your essay. Arrange the cards in order to develop a structure for your essay. Rearranging the cards can also help work out the best structure for your essay.

1 Scan through the section. Identify either themes or important sub-sections. Use a different index card for each sub-section. On one side of each index card write:
   - the title of the main section in the top left corner in one colour
   - the title of the sub-section that you are currently reading about in the middle of the index card, in another colour

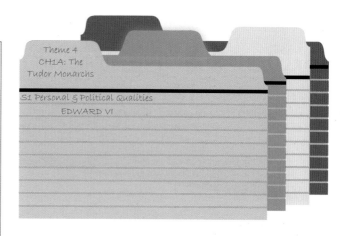

Theme 4
CH1A: The
Tudor Monarchs

S1 Personal & Political Qualities
        EDWARD VI

2 Now read the section carefully. On the back of each index card bullet point the relevant notes.

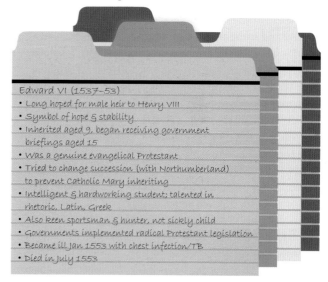

Edward VI (1537–53)
- Long hoped for male heir to Henry VIII
- Symbol of hope & stability
- Inherited aged 9, began receiving government briefings aged 15
- Was a genuine evangelical Protestant
- Tried to change succession (with Northumberland) to prevent Catholic Mary inheriting
- Intelligent & hardworking student; talented in rhetoric, Latin, Greek
- Also keen sportsman & hunter, not sickly child
- Governments implemented radical Protestant legislation
- Became ill Jan 1553 with chest infection/TB
- Died in July 1553

3 You can punch a hole in the corner of the cards, and tag-tie the cards for each section together.

Theme 1 Monarchy and government, 1509–88

The Big Picture

The Tudor monarchs changed the religious and political landscape of the country they ruled. They were strong-willed and stubborn in their desire to achieve their aims – whether the aim was an annulment of a childless marriage or the restoration of Catholicism to England and Wales. Dynastic concerns were central to their motivations. Their religious faith drove them to make hugely significant changes to the way that the country worshipped and the environment they worshipped in, whether that was to advance Protestantism or restore Catholicism. The succession was disputed or amended several times in the sixteenth century. For Henry VIII this was a function of the need to produce a male heir to succeed him, whereas for Edward VI the issue was the religion of those next in line to the throne. Gender was not central to their motivations. While Mary was the first regnant queen, her gender was more of an issue in relation to her marriage and the question of an heir rather than regarding her ability to rule. Mary's husband Philip II of Spain did not have a role in government and she ruled alone. Similar questions about marriage and succession resurfaced regularly for Elizabeth I, but she was also able to use her gender as an advantage during her long reign.

The role of parliament changed between 1509 and 1588. It was vital in securing Henry VIII's annulment and the break from Rome. Henry worked together with parliament in achieving his aims and in altering the political and religious situation irrevocably. This was the high point of parliament's influence in the Tudor period, and by Elizabeth I's rule this was beginning to wane. The Crown found new ways to control parliament and the majority of MPs wanted to work with the Queen. There were conflicts between Queen and parliament, but also co-operation.

The principal secretaries and ministers of this period included some well-known figures like Thomas Wolsey, Thomas Cromwell and Lord Burghley. They advised the monarchs, executed their policies and demands, and negotiated difficult situations with political cunning and skill. The monarchs, parliaments and ministers interacted throughout the period 1509–88, creating a political and religious situation that was very different at the end of the period to the beginning.

In this theme you will consider the following:
→ **The Tudor monarchs:**
   The personal and political attributes of the monarchs, the disputed successions, and the role of gender in Mary's and Elizabeth's reigns.
→ **The changing role of parliament:**
   Henry VIII's parliaments before 1529, from 'King and Parliament' to 'King-in-Parliament', and the growing confidence of parliament under Elizabeth.
→ **The principal servants of the Crown:**
   The powers exercised by leading ministers, the influence of Wolsey, Cromwell and Burghley, and changes to the structure of government.

TIMELINE

1485	Henry VII's victory at the Battle of Bosworth Field; Tudor dynasty established
1509	Henry VII died; Henry VIII ascended to the throne
1509 June	Henry VIII married Catherine of Aragon by papal dispensation
1510	Henry VIII's first parliament summoned
1512	Parliament restricted the use of benefit of clergy to ordained members of the priesthood
1513	Henry VIII called a parliament to fund the invasion of France
1516 February	Mary born
1518	The Treaty of London
1520 17–24 June	The Field of Cloth of Gold
1523	Henry VIII called a parliament to grant taxes
1529	Fall of Cardinal Thomas Wolsey
1529–36	The 'Reformation Parliament' met
1531	Mary banned from seeing her mother by Henry VIII
1533	Henry VIII married Anne Boleyn
1533 September	Elizabeth born
1534 November	The Act of Supremacy passed
1536 January	Anne Boleyn miscarried a male child
1536 May	Anne Boleyn was executed; Henry VIII married Jane Seymour
1536 June	Second Act of Succession passed
1537 12 October	Edward VI born
1540	Fall of Thomas Cromwell
1544	Mary and Elizabeth reinstated in the succession in the Third Act of Succession
1547	The Treason Act passed under Henry VIII
1547 28 January	Death of Henry VIII; Edward VI ascended to the throne
1552	Edward VI began to receive detailed governmental briefings
1553 May	The Duke of Northumberland's son, Guildford Dudley, married Jane Grey
1553 6 July	Death of Edward VI
1553 10 July	Jane Grey proclaimed queen
1553 19 July	Jane Grey deposed by Mary I; Mary proclaimed queen
1554 July	Mary I married Philip II of Spain
1558 17 November	Death of Mary I; Elizabeth I became queen
1559	Elizabeth's first parliament met; Elizabeth I's speech to parliament about marriage
1563	Parliament petitioned Elizabeth to marry following her illness
1568	Mary, Queen of Scots, arrived in England
1571	William Strickland proposed a bill to further reform the Prayer Book; William Cecil created Lord Burghley
1572	Burghley appointed Lord High Treasurer
1578	Elizabeth considered marriage to the Duke of Anjou
1586	Anthony Cope presented a revised Puritan version of the Prayer Book and a bill for reform to the religious laws
1587 February–March	Anthony Cope imprisoned in the Tower of London for an attack on Elizabeth's prerogative
1603	Death of Elizabeth I

1a: The Tudor monarchs

Overview

Sixteenth-century England and Wales experienced huge religious, political, social and economic change. This was, to a large degree, influenced by the country's monarchs. The Tudor monarchs who ruled England and Wales from 1485 to 1603 were all determined individuals who were prepared to make enormous changes in the lives of their people in order to achieve their goals. They would not have seen this as selfish – particularly in religious matters where there was a strong sense from Edward VI onwards of attempting to do the best for the English people and to save them from eternal damnation. The monarch, it was believed, was put on the throne to rule in the best interests of their people. All of the rulers in this period shared some common characteristics. They were determined to rule rather than be ruled by their advisers. They were strong-minded, if not stubborn. Dynastic loyalty determined their behaviour in most cases, unless (like Edward VI) religion over-ruled that. They had varying interests and preoccupations, and religion was an important determinant of their behaviour.

Dynasty was vital to Henry VIII and remained so for his heirs. This made the issue of the succession absolutely central to politics. The succession changed three times under Henry VIII and again under Edward VI. Mary I avoided the temptation to do this, but feared the impact of Elizabeth's Protestantism. Disputed successions brought instability among the political classes and the ordinary people as well as for the royal family. Succession had clear implications for the future of the dynasty. Gender has been frequently explored in relation to Elizabeth I, but it was also a significant point for discussion for Mary too. She was the first queen regnant, the first queen to rule as a monarch in her own right. While their gender did not affect their determination or ability to rule, it did cause more questions to be raised about marriage and children. It could also be used to their advantage, particularly by Elizabeth I.

This chapter explores the Tudor monarchs, their priorities, personalities and political qualities through the following sections:

1 *Personal and political qualities* looks at each of the Tudor monarchs as rulers and people. It examines their personal attributes and political aptitude.
2 *Disputed successions?* examines the extent to which Tudor successions were disputed. It looks at the causes and implications of disputed successions.
3 *The significance of gender for Mary and Elizabeth* discusses these two reigning queens and the impact of their gender on their rule. It explores the theory of the king's two bodies and the reactions of different people to the prospect of a female 'king'.

Note it down

Begin your collection of index cards here using the method on page xi. For each monarch create two cards. One will be for their personal qualities; the other for their political abilities. Write their name and the years that they reigned for on the front of the card. On the back write brief notes about these aspects for each monarch.

This chapter also contains some complicated political, theoretical and social concepts. The best note-taking method to use here would be the 1:2 method (see page x). In the left-hand column write the important headings or points and in the right-hand column make notes on the content that relates to them.

1 Personal and political qualities

As might be expected, the personal qualities and political abilities of the Tudor monarchs were very different. Their upbringings, interests and priorities varied greatly and these had an impact on how the country was ruled. Their personalities had an effect on how government operated as well as how they related to people around them, including future heirs to the throne and close family.

Note it down

Create a spider diagram (see page x) for the different political and personal characteristics of the monarchs. First, read the section carefully and identify common characteristics. Note them on your diagram.

Henry VIII (1491–1547)

Henry VIII inherited the throne from his father, Henry VII, in 1509. Henry VIII was not originally meant to inherit the throne, but his elder brother Prince Arthur died in 1502 shortly after marrying Catherine of Aragon. This meant that Henry became king on his father's death. Henry VII was not a **hereditary** monarch, however, and had seized the throne in 1485 after his victory over Richard III at the **Battle of Bosworth Field**. This meant that the Tudor **dynasty** was still very new. This provides part of the explanation for Henry's complete preoccupation with an heir: the dynasty needed to be strongly established and look stable for it to continue, and avoid the fate of Richard III. Henry was determined that his family would continue to rule the country and was prepared to take extreme measures in order to achieve that. He wanted to extend royal authority and power over institutions and regions within the British Isles, and this was interwoven with his personal and dynastic objectives.

Henry was firmly in control of his government. He was no mere figurehead but a king who was very determined to achieve his main aims and ideals. His ministers, Thomas Wolsey and subsequently Thomas Cromwell, did not rule on his behalf. They did carry out royal policy once it was decided but Henry played a key role in the decisions. Even when away on a **royal progress** Henry kept in communication with London, keen to be up to date with all matters. Henry had a decisive influence on important issues such as war, the **Royal Supremacy**, and the **theology** of his new Church of England. He did listen to his advisors, however, and the court could make an impact on his decisions.

When young, Henry was handsome and athletic. Henry was extremely interested in theology. He loved music, dance, hunting and chivalric ideals. He was highly educated and energetic – a symbol of renewal and change. Indeed Henry's reign was to see significant religious, political and social change. Henry was able but not as intelligent as he believed himself to be. Historian John Guy has described him as having a 'second-rate mind with what looks suspiciously like an inferiority complex'. As the years went on Henry became increasingly egotistical, demanding, self-righteous and sometimes morbid. He suffered increasing ill-health and became erratic and unpredictable. Throughout his reign Henry wanted to conquer more territory, especially in France, and was obsessed with **chivalry** and honour. Honour was an important concept in Europe in this period, not just an empty word but a concept that could start expensive wars and battles over supremacy.

Edward VI (1537–53)

Edward VI was the male heir that Henry had longed for since his first marriage, born to Henry and Jane Seymour (Henry's third wife) in 1537. He was a symbol of hope and stability during his father's life and of change at the beginning of his own reign. Edward's birth made life at court easier for his half-sisters and put an end to Henry's frantic search for a solution to his dynastic problems. Inheriting the throne in 1547 at only 9 years old, Edward laboured under heavy expectations. As he was under the age of 18 years old, a regent was appointed to govern for him. Initially this was Edward Seymour, Earl of Somerset (see page 6), but after a coup in 1549,

▲ The family of Henry VIII, painted in about 1545. From left to right: Mary, Edward, Henry, Jane Seymour, Elizabeth. What does this contemporary painting tell the historian about the relative importance of Henry's children? What can it say about Henry's own image?

Edward Seymour, 1st Duke of Somerset (c1500–52)

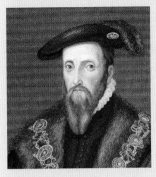

Edward Seymour was born to a noble family and from early youth was involved in court and royal affairs. He was a member of the household of Princess Mary from 1514, aged 14. He received titles and positions from Henry VIII after his sister Jane Seymour married the King in 1536. Seymour's nephew Edward became king on the death of Henry VIII in 1547. Seymour became Lord Protector (a kind of **regent** to Edward) and created himself Duke of Somerset in 1547. Through political skill, manipulation and bribes, Somerset gathered much more power and authority than was ever intended in Henry VIII's will. The will stipulated a Regency Council rather than one man having such power. He was a skilled soldier, waging a successful war against the independent kingdom of Scotland and defending English territories such as Boulogne-sur-Mer against the French. During the **protectorate** this put an enormous financial burden on the English nation. Somerset fell following the rebellions of 1549, which were seen as a failure of government despite Somerset's popularist proclamations against **enclosure**. Correctly fearing a coup, Somerset seized Edward VI and withdrew to Windsor Castle, but was arrested by the Regency Council on 11 October 1549. He was initially released and restored to the Privy Council in 1550 but was executed for felony in January 1552 after plotting against his successor's rule.

John Dudley, 1st Duke of Northumberland (1504–53)

John Dudley was the eldest son of Edmund Dudley, a councillor to Henry VII who was executed by Henry VIII in 1510 as a scapegoat for his father's financial policies. John Dudley was restored to his estates in 1512. He was brought up by a guardian, Sir Edward Guildford, whose daughter Jane he married in 1525. He was father to their 13 children and was believed to be a diligent and highly involved parent. Dudley took part in Wolsey's diplomatic ventures in 1521 and 1527, fought in the 1523 invasion of France and was knighted for his actions. He was close to Henry VIII, being appointed as a knight of the body in 1524. Dudley was intelligent as well as being a skilled sportsman, excelling at archery, jousting and wrestling. Dudley was a member of evangelical circles in the 1530s and led one of the King's armies against the Pilgrimage of Grace in 1536. He became Viscount Lisle after the death of his stepfather in 1542. He fought in the wars against Scotland and was Lord Admiral in the wars against France. Dudley was one of the leading **evangelical reformers** at court, and this stood him in good stead for Edward's rule. He was not an enemy of Somerset and, indeed, was his second-in-command in Scotland. He was involved in the brutal repression of Kett's rebellion in 1549. As Somerset's fall was plotted, Dudley managed to consolidate his power on the Regency Council, effectively replacing Somerset in 1549. He took the title Lord President of the Regency Council and repressed Somerset's attempts to re-establish his power. He was less autocratic than Somerset and more prepared to work with the Council. He encouraged Edward VI to take an increasing role in government as he got older and established practical measures to attempt to deal with the problem of poverty. He was created Duke of Northumberland in 1551. Northumberland promoted evangelical Protestants to positions within the Church, and advanced the Protestant Reformation despite its widespread unpopularity. He brought an end to Somerset's costly wars. Northumberland played a key role in Edward's attempt to change the succession, a role that was to bring about his rapid fall on the accession of Mary I. His efforts in favour of Jane Grey (his daughter-in-law) led to his trial and execution in August 1553. Northumberland's attempts to secure Mary's intervention in his favour (including converting back to Catholicism) were fruitless.

John Dudley, Earl of Northumberland, took over. He took the title of Lord President of the Regency Council to differentiate himself from Somerset. Although in the early years of Edward's reign the policies of his government were created by others, such as Lord Protector Somerset, Edward himself soon became involved personally. This was particularly the case in religious policy. During 1552, aged 15 years, Edward started to receive detailed briefings on the government's financial crisis. He began to directly participate in government from May of that year. The boldest policy of Edward's reign, the attempt to change the succession in favour of Jane Grey, has generally been assumed to be Protector Northumberland's. It is impossible to tell whose idea it originally was but drafts of the document show Edward's personal hand in working out the details involved. Edward was genuinely evangelical and his involvement in this is most likely a demonstration of his religious belief overcoming his dynastic loyalty.

In terms of his personal qualities, Edward was an intelligent and hardworking student. An archive of Edward's writings still survives, and demonstrates his abilities in **rhetoric** and argument; Latin and Greek. He made thorough notes on sermons that he heard, showing his deep personal **piety** and interest in religious matters. Edward has been portrayed in the past, particularly in popular culture and literature, as a sickly child because of his early death. This was not the case. Like his father, he was a keen sportsman and enjoyed hunting and military displays. His illness in his last months did not define Edward as a person or ruler. His writings also demonstrate that he was committed to evangelical Protestantism. He translated scriptural passages into French as a gift for Protector Somerset in 1548 and between December 1548 and August 1549 wrote a treatise on the papal supremacy. He concluded that the Pope was the 'son of the devil, a bad man, an Antichrist and abominable tyrant'. Edward's governments were to implement some of the most radical religious changes of the sixteenth century. The question of how Edward would have ruled had he lived longer is an intriguing one, but impossible to answer. He fell ill in late January 1553 with a chest infection or tuberculosis. In late May his condition worsened significantly, and he died in July.

Mary I (1516–58)

Mary had a difficult and unstable upbringing. In her earliest years she was the **heir apparent**, with all the luxuries and benefits that such a status brought. She received a **classical humanist education** and was intended to be **betrothed** to a European prince. This childhood was disrupted because of Henry VIII's determination to produce a male heir. Her status and future became increasingly uncertain, especially after Henry's desire to divorce her mother, Catherine of Aragon, became known. After 1531 Henry banned Mary from seeing her mother, and declared Mary **illegitimate** after he married Anne Boleyn in 1533. Mary was removed to Hatfield to wait upon her half-sister Elizabeth. Mary's health declined in these years, and was to remain poor for the rest of her life. Her situation began to improve after the birth of Edward. She was reinstated in the succession by 1544 and this was confirmed by Henry's will. When Henry died Mary was 31 years old. Her subsequent battles with her half-brother Edward concerning her religion upset her greatly, and nearly brought the kingdom to the brink of war with the **Holy Roman Empire**.

Mary succeeded to the throne finally at 37 years old, overcoming Edward and Northumberland's plan to remove her from the succession and place Jane Grey on the throne. She was understandably embittered by her treatment since childhood and (unlike Edward) was not well prepared by her father or advisers for the role she was about to assume. She was generous and amiable but also stubborn. During her reign she suffered from depression, anxiety, **neuralgia**

Lady Jane Grey (1536–54)

Lady Jane Grey was of noble birth and was a first cousin once removed of Edward VI. She was the eldest daughter of Henry Grey, 1st Duke of Suffolk, and his wife Lady Frances Brandon. Her mother was the youngest daughter of Mary Tudor, Queen of France, whose father was Henry VII. She received a humanist education in Latin, Greek, Hebrew and Italian. Her father was a Protestant and (particularly after her Protestant upbringing) she followed in his footsteps. She was sent to live in the household of Edward VI's uncle Thomas Seymour and Henry VIII's widow Catherine Parr in February 1547. She was chief mourner at Catherine Parr's funeral in 1548. Jane was engaged to the Duke of Northumberland's son, Guildford Dudley, in spring 1553 and they were married in May of that year. As Edward VI lay dying in 1553 the succession was changed by him and Northumberland so that Jane Grey would succeed him on the throne. This was to avoid the Catholic Mary becoming queen. The King died on 6 July 1553 and Jane was informed that she was queen. She was proclaimed queen on 10 July, refusing to allow her husband to be king and taking residence in the Tower of London. After a brief armed struggle, however, and a popular rising in favour of Mary, the forces of Northumberland were defeated. Mary I entered London in procession on 3 August 1553. Jane and Guildford Dudley were charged with high treason and tried in London on 13 November. All of the defendants were found guilty and sentenced to death but it was reported that Jane's life was to be spared. If that was true, Thomas Wyatt's rebellion changed that and Jane was beheaded on 12 February 1554.

and **phantom pregnancies**. Mary was unsurprisingly untrusting towards other people and placed her faith in Catholicism instead. She was an extremely devoted Catholic throughout her life. She also tended to favour Spaniards more than Englishmen for her closest advisers – she had been very close to her Spanish mother and she found Spaniards more help than Englishmen. This drove her into a controversial and unpopular match with Philip II of Spain in 1554 – one that she insisted on despite her English advisers' opinions. Religion was not the sole focus of Mary's policy despite her infamous reputation. She certainly was determined to restore Catholicism to England, and in her short five years of rule she experienced a reasonable level of success in this. But she continued also to reform government, attempted to increase trade and respond to problems like poverty.

Once Mary succeeded to the throne she was determined to rule as a monarch rather than a **consort**, issuing commands and orders with authority and determination. She was very aware of her royal status. Mary was a dutiful monarch and was earnest about her role. She was not temperamentally suited or intelligent enough to understand the complexities that faced her in government but she was a dedicated ruler. Mary was astute enough, however, to realise that she needed capable advisers and that she needed to consult and listen to them in order to help her rule. She gathered advisers who were experienced in government, from both Catholic and Protestant faiths. Mary's reputation as a woman and ruler has suffered over the centuries but in recent times she has been somewhat rescued from her label 'Bloody Mary' and seen in a much more nuanced light.

Elizabeth I (1533–1603)

Elizabeth, too, suffered during the 1530s from Henry VIII's determination to achieve his dynastic goals. Like Mary she was excluded from the succession after her early life as a royal princess and termed a 'bastard'. In terms of her political concerns Elizabeth followed her father Henry VIII and sister Mary I in strictly protecting her royal prerogative. As with Mary, Elizabeth was determined to rule England rather than letting others rule for her. It was extremely difficult for her advisers to change her mind. That said, she did not have as many ideological preconceptions as Mary did. She was a moderate Protestant but was not dogmatic like Edward. Her own worship included traditional elements as well as reformed ones. The religious settlement now known as the Elizabethan settlement was a compromise that in some ways reflected her own religious beliefs (see page 48). Elizabeth operated shrewdly in the field of international diplomacy. One political weakness of Elizabeth was that she hesitated when important decisions needed to be made. This made life extremely difficult for her councillors but was caused by a cautious attitude to political and financial decisions. This caution could on other occasions be very useful.

Elizabeth I was intelligent and hardworking. She was educated and accomplished. She spoke French, Italian and Spanish and read Latin. She played the **virginal**, danced and hunted skilfully. Elizabeth enjoyed plays and **masques**, and went on long royal progresses around her realm. On the other hand, Elizabeth was vain and jealous within her personal relationships. She could be sharp-tongued and, when crossed, had an appalling temper. It is extremely difficult to discern Elizabeth's own ideas or beliefs. Few writings survive that are indisputably hers, written accounts of her by contemporaries are largely very flattering or propagandistic and her behaviour was always determined by her knowledge that she was effectively performing for an audience. As such we do not know her true attitudes on important issues like that of marriage. Elizabeth knew the power of images, and was careful to nurture and control her own image as queen of England.

2 Disputed successions?

There was only one succession in the period 1509–88 that was disputed after the death of the previous monarch. This was the succession of Jane Grey. There were, however, disputes about who would succeed to the throne during the lifetime of two other monarchs. The **line of succession** was changed at least three times during the reign of Henry VIII, as his daughters Mary and Elizabeth were successively **bastardised** and later **legitimised**. Edward VI, towards the end of his short life, also attempted to amend the succession in favour of the Protestant Grey family. This meant removing his sisters from the line of succession and amending the intentions of his father Henry VIII.

Note it down

Use bullet points to take notes on this section. Think about the following questions:

- Why was it necessary for Henry VIII to change the line of succession?
- What were Edward VI's motives for trying to change the succession?
- How was Mary I able to triumph?
- Why did Mary I not change the succession?

Henry VIII and the line of succession

For Henry, it was essential to produce a male heir. Henry wanted to make sure that his dynasty survived and the only surefire way to achieve that was to produce a son who could inherit the throne. This is absolutely crucial in understanding Henry's actions towards his two daughters, Mary and Elizabeth.

Henry VIII's first marriage

Henry VIII had married Catherine of Aragon on 11 June 1509, made possible by a **papal dispensation**. According to Church law, a man could not marry his brother's widow. Catherine had previously been married to Henry's elder brother Arthur, who died five months after he married Catherine in 1501 (see page 5). Mary was born on 18 February 1516 but after this, although Catherine was able to get pregnant, she suffered miscarriage and stillbirth every time. This became a theological problem for Henry. He began to see the situation as God's judgement against him. He thought that the cause of this was his marriage to his brother's widow. He wanted the Pope to overturn the dispensation and annul the marriage, allowing him to marry again. 1532 saw the beginning of the process whereby Henry broke with Rome and achieved Royal Supremacy (see page 38). This culminated with the Act of Supremacy in November 1534, which established the Church of England. This allowed Henry to obtain an annulment of his marriage to Catherine and to marry Anne Boleyn, which he did in January 1533.

The birth of Princess Elizabeth and the downfall of Anne Boleyn

Princess Elizabeth was born in September 1533. This meant that a new succession was needed because if the marriage of Henry to Catherine was not legitimate, neither were the children that came from it. Princess Mary was removed from the succession and called a bastard. She was sent to join her sister's household, to wait upon her. This was a severe blow to a girl brought up as a royal princess, with a strong awareness of the implications of that status. Henry hoped that Elizabeth's birth at the beginning of the marriage was just the first of many, including (of course) a son. In order to achieve that he had made unprecedented

changes to the religious and political life of England. Henry's hopes for his marriage to Anne Boleyn were not to be fulfilled. Anne was outspoken and actively attempted to achieve further religious reform. She made interventions in politics and religious causes which Henry heartily disapproved of. More importantly, Anne had been unable to produce a male heir. Her political enemies also plotted against her, advancing Jane Seymour as a more suitable and submissive candidate for queen. On 29 January 1536 Anne miscarried a male child, and by May 1536 she was dead, executed by the King for treason and adultery.

The birth of an heir and the impact on the succession

Only ten days later, on 30 May 1536, Henry VIII married Jane Seymour. This led to the Second Act of Succession, given royal assent in June 1536. This meant that both Mary and Elizabeth were bastardised and removed from the line of succession. On 12 October 1537 Henry's only legitimate son, Edward, was born. Although the birth killed his mother it secured the Tudor dynasty. Eventually, the birth of an heir to Henry led to an improvement in the situation of Mary and Elizabeth. Now that the King had a healthy son to inherit the throne it seems that Mary and Elizabeth were seen as less of a threat. In 1544, therefore, the Third Act of Succession was passed through parliament. This restored Mary and Elizabeth to the succession, albeit with certain conditions, and by doing so recognised their legitimacy. Henry VIII attempted to ensure against any change to this by also instituting the Treason Act of 1547. This Act made it treason to change the Act of Succession. The King's will, last amended in 1547 on his deathbed, confirmed the succession as passing through Edward, Mary and Elizabeth.

Edward VI and the Protestant succession

Edward VI inherited the throne on the death of his father in 1547. He was strongly Protestant (see page 7). He aimed to protect and advance Protestantism in England rather than to obey his father's last will and testament and maintain the hybrid form of Catholic worship established by Henry. He and his advisers had attempted to persuade Mary to change her religion from Catholicism

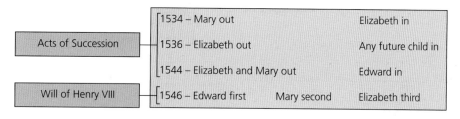

Acts of Succession	1534 – Mary out		Elizabeth in
	1536 – Elizabeth out		Any future child in
	1544 – Elizabeth and Mary out		Edward in
Will of Henry VIII	1546 – Edward first	Mary second	Elizabeth third

▲ Figure 1: Henry VIII and the succession

to Protestantism. They failed, and as Edward became increasingly ill he tried to prevent England returning to Catholicism by removing Mary from the succession. His adviser and regent Northumberland also had reasons for wanting Mary's removal – his repressive policies towards Catholics (see page 43) meant that he was sure to suffer reprisals if Mary were to come to the throne.

A 'device' was created in order to overturn Henry VIII's will and the Third Act of Succession of 1544. Edward aimed to disinherit both Mary and Elizabeth. The Crown would now pass to the male descendants of Henry VIII's younger sister, Mary. Right at the end of Edward's life, however, there were no male descendants of this line for the Crown to pass to. This meant that Jane Grey would become queen according to Edward's device. Once again, this benefited Northumberland. His son Guildford Dudley had married Jane Grey in May 1553. When Edward died on 6 July 1553 his death was kept a secret while the succession was secured and on 10 July 1553 Jane Grey was proclaimed queen in London.

Jane Grey vs Mary

Only nine days after Lady Jane Grey was proclaimed queen she fell from power. Mary acted decisively in the role of queen from the point of Edward's death on

6 July. She asserted her right to the throne in a letter to the Privy Council in London and sent copies to various towns and important individuals. This had a galvanising effect in drawing supporters to Mary's side. Support came from common people as well as from the gentry. The countryside rose in support of Mary and by 13 July towns like Norwich had proclaimed her queen. Northumberland left London to deal with the threat and in his absence Jane Grey's government crumbled. Northumberland surrendered after Mary's proclamation as queen on 19 July. She entered London on 3 August.

This did not entirely solve the problem of the succession. Henry VIII's final will demanded that the Crown would pass to Elizabeth unless Mary had issue. This meant that Mary needed to marry and produce children as soon as possible in order to consolidate her rule. It also, therefore, explains her determination on this score.

Consequences of disputed successions

The causes of the disputed successions discussed in this section are relatively clear – understandable anxiety about the future of dynasty; religious concerns; political imperative. The consequences are important to consider

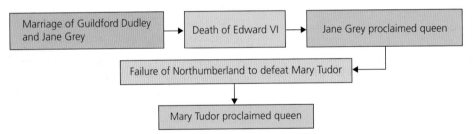

▲ Figure 2: Lady Jane Grey and the succession crisis, 1553

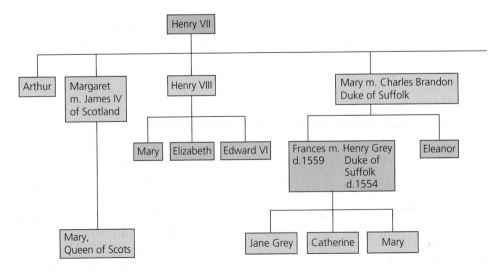

▲ Figure 3: Claimants to the English throne

too, however, as the issue of the royal succession was at some key moments important in determining policy in other areas. These consequences include:

- creating factions at crucial moments
- bastardising individuals who would become monarchs in the future, with important psychological and legal consequences
- introducing instability in government towards the end of a monarch's reign.

3 The significance of gender for Mary and Elizabeth

Jane Grey, acceding to the throne in 1553, should have been the first **queen regnant** of England but her rule was cut short before she was crowned. This means that it was Mary who was the first woman to rule England in her own right. She was followed by Elizabeth I. Women had ruled England before this point but they tended to rule on behalf of their husband or son, or, like Queen Matilda (who ruled from April–November 1171), have their rule disputed and then ended. Before the Tudor period, therefore, women had ruled as consorts or had not ruled at all. Many aspects of a monarch's role were seen as exclusively male, for example being military leaders and heads of the Church. This led to several issues: Would a woman rule as well as a man? What difficulties could a foreign marriage cause to a reigning queen's rule? How should a reigning queen's husband be treated? What about those responsibilities that were seen as the preserve of males?

Even though Jane Grey's rule was extremely short, even she did not give up all her authority to advisers. She at first resisted attempts to proclaim her queen, and then decided that her husband, Guildford Dudley, would be a royal duke and not a king. In short, Jane was prepared to rule and not act as a puppet to her male advisers and husband. At their accession neither Mary nor Elizabeth was married, and their royal status and education had prepared them to some degree to rule. So how much difference did their gender make to Mary and Elizabeth? What kinds of difference existed and what were the consequences of those differences?

Note it down

This section includes some difficult terms. Create an index card for each one, and remember to look up any terms you don't understand in the glossary or a dictionary. Put the term on the front, and a definition on the back. Also explain how this is relevant to the topic.

Women in the Tudor period

Before thinking about gender in relation to the reigning queens of the Tudor period it is important to consider how women were treated and portrayed in Tudor society more generally. This is necessary to contextualise the treatment and behaviour of the queens. Women in Tudor England have been portrayed in the past as simply subordinated, restricted, and dominated in every aspect of their lives by men. More recently, historians have shown how the picture was more complicated in reality. Some women exercised

'The queen's two bodies'

The 'queen's two bodies' is a difficult concept but one that is extremely helpful in explaining the legal and theoretical justifications for allowing women to rule as kings. Historians of gender have argued that concepts of kingship were strongly linked to gender. There was a **legal fiction** in the early modern period that depicted the monarch as having two bodies – a natural, earthly, fallible body and a theoretical 'royal' body. The second, known as the body politic, continued after the death of the natural body, passing to the next in line to the throne. This helped to make successions smoother legally and less unstable. Historians such as Cynthia Herrup believe that the words used to describe ideal qualities of kingship (even by monarchs themselves) were both male and female, no matter the gender of the current reigning monarch. Ideal monarchs were brave and peace loving; economical

and bountiful; unyielding and tender. Monarchs were 'nursing fathers' to their subjects, whether they themselves were male or female. This makes Elizabeth I's claim to be both man and woman to her subjects both more credible and less exceptional – it was part of the theoretical image of all early modern monarchs in their political body. As Herrup has said, the key to a successful reign was to balance male and female qualities. So while it was true that for the sake of social order and hierarchy a male monarch was preferred by early modern people, it was not as bad as it has been portrayed in the past. There were early modern writers who argued on behalf of female kings – on the basis of the 'two bodies', of royal blood, providence and God's will. The Elizabethan bishop John Aylmer even argued that femininity as a quality was a weakness, but not one necessarily linked to biological gender.

remarkable independence and power, others survived or managed their position with more agency than had previously been thought. It is certainly true that women enjoyed less power and had fewer options available to them than men – at every level of society. Men had great power within the household as well as economically. Women could, however, inherit landed estates and manage households. Popular culture, such as ballads, plays and sermons, demonstrated anxiety about women going against social order and becoming disorderly. On the other hand popular culture praised pious and modest women who knew their place.

In Elizabeth's reign particularly it seems that there were worries about the moral standards and the extent to which women were subverting them. While the main focus of such ballads and plays was the behaviour of women, it actually reflected more on the reputation of the men who were meant to keep them in control. Men who failed to control their wives were seen as pathetic and emasculated.

More women in this period were portrayed in portraits, participated in print discussions of new ideas and genres. They attended plays, ran businesses and took part in litigation to defend their property. Women made decisions about their own religious belief and practice, either to remain Catholic in defiance of Elizabethan statutes or to become godly and commit to hearing sermons and reading the scriptures. This was certainly no age of women's rights but it was far from universally the case that women were entirely subordinated and repressed.

Queen Mary I

Mary I was the first woman to reign in her own name as a monarch of England. Ordinary women had for generations either been forced through economic

circumstance or had chosen to go beyond normal roles. Yet political culture at an elite level assumed that females were inherently limited in their abilities and in their authority. Even Mary's cousin Charles V wrote to her very shortly after she acceded to the throne to advise her of the constraints that she should face as a female ruler. These assumptions would have been simply intolerable for a male monarch – especially Mary's father Henry VIII. Mary addressed this head on in a speech to her **Privy Council**. She asked them to assist her in her rule, reminding them of their oaths and speaking of her determination to fulfil her responsibilities. It is not known whether Mary was putting on a strategic performance in order to win over the Privy Council or whether she believed genuinely that women needed the help of men in order to carry out extraordinary roles. If Mary was acting strategically, she clearly realised that it was helpful on occasion to use 'female frailties' to achieve political objectives.

The Spanish marriage

Yet Mary was also determined to rule rather than be the puppet of male advisers. In her coronation ceremony she followed the same procedure and wore the same costume as her male predecessors. Mary received the symbols of the powers of kingship, which included the orb and sceptre. Like a king, she was anointed and the crown of England placed upon her head. Indeed Mary herself was known to say that she had no personal interest in marriage but was married to her kingdom. The question of her marriage was a matter for her to decide, and rather than choosing the 'safe' English candidate she decided to marry Philip II of Spain in July 1554 – an unpopular choice but her own to make. When she did marry Philip, English parliaments had no difficulty separating Mary as a wife from Mary as a ruler. The marriage treaty actually prevented Philip from having any say in the running

Wyatt's rebellion, 1554

Mary announced her intention to marry Philip of Spain on 15 January 1554 but it was widely known before this announcement. It was not a popular match. This was not because of Philip's religion but because the kingdom to which Philip was heir spread across so much of Europe already. Habsburg territory included the Low Country, Milan, Naples, Sicily and the New World. Wyatt's rebellion aimed to prevent the marriage. It was led by Sir Thomas Wyatt, a gentleman with a hatred of the Spanish and their government. The conspirators included the Duke of Suffolk, the Earl of Devon and Lord Thomas Grey. The leaders of the rebellion (Suffolk, Wyatt, Sir James Croft and Sir Peter

Carew) planned to raise men in their four counties and then they would all converge on London. They would replace Mary with Elizabeth, who would then marry the Earl of Devon. In the event, only Wyatt in Kent was able to raise a substantial force. Although it proved more difficult to put down the revolt than had been assumed, Mary was able to rouse London in her support. Her army defeated the rebels on the outskirts of London. Wyatt was arrested, tortured and beheaded. His body was quartered. His fellow rebels were either exiled or executed. The Wyatt family lost their title and lands, only having them restored by Elizabeth on her accession.

of government. Mary was the sole ruler of England. Practically, Philip's political influence was diminished by his absence. He became king of Spain in 1556 and after that visited Mary only once, aiming to persuade her to join him in waging war against France.

An heir to the throne

On the other hand, once Mary was married the dynastic and religious pressure on her to have a child was extreme. A child would guarantee the succession and keep England Catholic. Philip's absences in Spain did not improve Mary's chances of conceiving a child but the principal judgement made was against Mary's constitution and health. People spoke of her 'hysterical' symptoms preventing her from getting pregnant – signs of 'feminine weakness'. When it appeared she was pregnant, four months after the wedding, there was great celebration. Yet months later it became clear that Mary I had suffered a phantom pregnancy. Unlike other women suffering the same affliction, for Mary there were political as well as personal implications. The phantom pregnancy publically humiliated Mary and raised questions about the stability of her rule. In January 1558 Mary announced she was pregnant again, but once again this was not the case. By spring 1558 it appears that Mary had accepted that she would not produce an heir. Although she knew the consequences were most likely to be a return to Protestantism, Mary did not alter the succession as her brother had. Mary respected dynasty and blood – meaning her half-sister's succession was unfavourable but inevitable. By August 1558 Mary was dead, the victim of a flu epidemic, and it was indeed Elizabeth who became queen.

Elizabeth I, 'the virgin queen'

Although Jane Grey and Mary I had ruled as regnant queens before her, it is Elizabeth I whose gender has featured most prominently in discussions of her reign. The prospect of Elizabeth's succession was also received with much less anxiety than Mary's. Most of those who had spoken against women rulers when Mary came to the throne were anti-Catholic Protestant reformers, such as John Knox, and Elizabeth's loyalty to the Protestant religion assuaged most of those anxieties. In fact, several writers (probably opportunistically) took this chance to praise female rulers and defend their abilities against earlier critics like Knox. These writers included John Aylmer and John Bale.

Elizabeth and female rule

Elizabeth did have to contend throughout her reign with the idea that in ruling, she would lose her femininity by exercising authority over men. There was an idea that this would make her incapable of motherhood, one of the essences of femininity. People also feared that women in general would assert themselves over men if women ruled. This would upset the social order, and is one reason why Elizabeth insisted throughout her reign on the exclusivity of her royal blood. Her royal blood set her apart from other women and formed a barrier between her actions and those of others. Theoretical concepts like the 'two bodies' (see page 11) aided with this, particularly in political and intellectual circles. Elizabeth's speeches sometimes made use of this ambiguous gendered language where she referred to her weak female body as well as more stereotypically male aspects like courage and leadership.

The question of marriage

The question of Elizabeth's marriage was another important area in which her gender and its impact was discussed. Many different historians have argued about Elizabeth's suitors, her desire to get married and her reasons for not doing so. As with Mary, there were very good reasons for Elizabeth to get married – to produce an heir, to uphold the Protestant religion, to stabilise the succession and prevent further disputes. Elizabeth had many different suitors. Early on in her reign they included Philip II of Spain, Eric XIV of Sweden and Archduke Charles of Austria. She informed all of those who approached her in 1559 and 1560 that at the moment she was remaining single. In a speech to parliament in February 1559 she responded to those who had petitioned her to marry that at this point in time she wanted to remain single but had an open mind to marriage in the future. She promised that when she did choose a husband it would be for the good of the country.

For a few years after 1560 she did, it appears, consider marriage. She wished to avoid questions of the succession and felt that it may be her duty. Robert Dudley was seen as one candidate but ultimately Elizabeth decided against it.

When she fell ill in October 1562 with smallpox it became clear how much instability the Queen's death would cause. She had no named successor and no favourable heir. As a consequence parliament once again petitioned her to marry in 1563 or to clarify the succession in law. Elizabeth conceded that 'as a prince' she should marry, even though as an individual she was not inclined to. Negotiations with the Habsburgs for a marriage to Archduke Charles of Austria lasted until 1567 but came to nothing. In summer 1578, aged 45, Elizabeth once again considered marriage. She opened negotiations with Francis, Duke of Anjou, brother of King Henry III of France. This was a political choice, a way to resolve problems arising from the Dutch Revolt.

Robert Dudley (1532–88) and Elizabeth I

Robert Dudley was the son of the Duke of Northumberland, who was Edward VI's Lord President of the Regency Council (see page 6). He first met Elizabeth in the royal classroom when they were children. Their friendship was to last the rest of their lives.

In Mary's reign, Dudley is said to have sold some of his land in order to help Elizabeth financially, despite struggling himself. Dudley's fortunes changed greatly when Elizabeth came to the throne in 1558. He was made master of the horse, a prestigious position with frequent access to the Queen, and arranged many of her events and amusements. He was a horseman and athlete, intelligent and handsome. This gave rise to many rumours that Elizabeth and Dudley were lovers. This can never be proven, but it is certain that they had an affectionate relationship and were close friends. The death of Dudley's wife in circumstances that appeared suspicious led to accusations of murder against Dudley. It was said that Dudley had murdered his wife so that he could marry Elizabeth. This is unlikely, and the rumours meant that no marriage could take place even if both parties had wished for it. Dudley was widely unpopular because of his closeness to the Queen and influence over her. After a long and successful political and military career Dudley died in 1588. Elizabeth was reportedly grief-stricken at the loss, and locked herself away.

The English hoped that this would persuade Anjou not to get involved in the Netherlands. There seems to have been a genuine attempt at courtship, but this potential marriage proved very unpopular with the ordinary people and with her Council. By November 1581 the negotiations had foundered. Despite the romanticism of Elizabeth's marriage question to generations of historians and fiction writers, it appears clear that she made a conscious choice as a ruler to remain single.

Virgin queen

Elizabeth's use of her status as a virgin was politically astute. It allowed her to become almost the embodiment of the kingdom, sacrificing her married state to rule the country. After 1578 Elizabeth began to be celebrated as a virgin queen. Her celibacy and virginity became symbols of the country's power. It was celebrated in poems and portraits. This became known as the cult of Gloriana and will be discussed on page 137.

Conclusion

The Tudor monarchs ruled England and Wales during a period of great change. They all had strong personalities and their policies reflected their political and religious concerns and interests. During Henry VIII's reign the question of the succession was of vital importance, and the changes in the succession reflected this as Henry sought desperately to produce a male heir to continue the dynasty. Following this struggle religion played a significant part in disputed successions. The sixteenth century also saw the first two regnant queens of England and Wales. Mary I and Elizabeth I ruled the country as monarchs rather than consorts.

For both Mary and Elizabeth, their gender could be a problem and an advantage. There were ways in which their femininity could be used in order to secure their aims and objectives. On the other hand, being a woman created expectations of marriage and motherhood that to some extent were problematic for them as rulers. Although there is no doubt that there was a preference for male monarchs, the political nation was able to work with these queens regnant. Legal fictions such as the two bodies of the monarch gave a justification for female rule.

Work together

Practise using the knowledge you have gained from this section. Work with another person. Read through your notes very carefully. Now put them away, and taking it in turns, describe the personal and political qualities of the monarchs you have read about. When you have finished, read over the notes again. What did you miss?

Significance of gender for Mary and Elizabeth

- Women were not as entirely repressed and subordinated as has been assumed in the past
- There were legal and theoretical concepts that justified female rule
- Mary I was England's first regnant queen
- She was determined to rule in her own right
- She chose her husband herself, despite opposition to the Spanish marriage
- She was unable to conceive an heir but did not try to change the succession and dynasty was crucially important to her
- Elizabeth was also determined to rule
- She resented discussion of her marriage and seems to eventually have made a conscious decision to remain single
- She used the image of the 'virgin queen' to her advantage

Personal and political qualities

- Henry VIII prioritised dynasty
- He governed firmly and had a decisive influence on key issues
- He was interested in theology, music, dancing and hunting
- He was obsessed with chivalry
- Edward VI became king aged 9 years old
- He began to receive governmental briefings aged only 15
- He played a significant part in the attempt to change the succession
- Edward was an intelligent and hardworking student
- Mary was determined to rule
- She was also focused on dynasty
- Mary was strongly Catholic and made restoring Catholicism a priority
- She married Philip of Spain in the face of strong opposition
- Elizabeth was shrewd politically, although could be indecisive
- Elizabeth was intelligent, educated and hard working
- She enjoyed music, dancing and masques

THE TUDOR MONARCHS

Disputed successions

- Henry VIII received a papal dispensation to marry Catherine of Aragon, but the marriage did not produce a male heir
- When he married Anne Boleyn, Mary was declared illegitimate and Elizabeth became heir to the throne
- After Anne Boleyn's execution, Henry's marriage to Jane Seymour finally produced a male heir, Edward, in 1536
- Although both Mary and Elizabeth were declared illegitimate in 1536, they were returned to the succession after Edward's birth
- Edward VI tried to remove Mary from the succession and make Jane Grey queen, but this did not succeed ultimately as Mary had popular support and regained the throne

▲ Summary diagram: The Tudor monarchs

Recommended reading

Helen Castor, *She-Wolves: The Women Who Ruled England Before Elizabeth* (London, 2010).

This is a fascinating account of female rulers of England. The final chapter, 'New Beginnings', explores Mary I's rule.

Susan Doran, 'The Queen' in Susan Doran and Norman Jones (editors), *The Elizabethan World* (Routledge, 2011), pages 35–58.

This chapter in this excellent book on different aspects of Elizabeth's England deals specifically with the Queen. It is a very good summary of Elizabeth as a person and queen, examining key aspects of her image and rule.

John Guy, *Tudor England* (OUP, 1988).

This is a good, accessible narrative account of the lives and reigns of the Tudor monarchs.

Diarmaid MacCulloch, *The Boy King: Edward VI and the Protestant Reformation* (University of California Press, 2002).

Chapter 1 provides an interesting account of Edward's personality, upbringing and his growing responsibility in government.

Robert Tittler, *The Reign of Mary I* (Longman, 1991).

This is a good short account of Mary I's reign. Chapters 1 (on Mary's background and upbringing) and 3 (on her accession and government) are particularly relevant for this chapter.

Essay technique: Understanding the question

Section A and B questions require you to deploy a variety of skills. The most important are focus on the question, selection and deployment of relevant detail, analysis and, at the highest level, prioritisation. The introduction to this book (page vi) gives more detail about Section A and B questions.

Section A and B questions for AS level are different from that of A level, and some guidance about this is given on pages vii–viii. However, you will need to develop very similar skills for the AS exam, therefore the activities will help with the AS exams as well. There are also some AS-style questions to practise at the end of chapters.

In order to answer the question successfully you must understand how the question works. Below is a typical question.

The question is written precisely in order to make sure that you understand the task. Each part of the question has a specific meaning:

'How significant', like other stems such as 'How far', indicates that you are required to evaluate the extent of something, rather than giving a yes or no answer.

How significant was religion in succession disputes from 1534 to 1558?

This sets out the subject that you must address.

The dates define the period you should consider.

Overall, *all* Section A and B questions ask you to make a judgement about the extent of something, in a specific period. In order to focus on the question you must address all three elements. The most common mistakes come from misunderstanding or ignoring one of these three elements.

Activity: What should a good answer look like?

Having read the advice on Section A and B questions, complete the following activity:

1 Make a bullet-point list of the skills that you need to do well in this type of essay.
2 Number the skills in order of their difficulty, so the easiest skill to demonstrate is 1, and the hardest 4.
3 Try and work out what a good essay would look like. Specifically note down your thoughts about the following questions:
   – Roughly, how many paragraphs should the essay have?
   – Which skills should you deploy in which sections of the essay?
   – How should you structure the different types of paragraphs?

TIP: Don't just guess, use the advice in this section to try and figure out what a good essay should look like.

Work together

Having completed these activities, swap them with a partner. Consider:

1 Did you agree on which skills were easiest to demonstrate and which skills were hardest? How did each of you make this judgement?
2 Did you agree on the number of paragraphs in the essay?
3 How did you and your partner make the judgement about the number of paragraphs you should write?
4 If you had different reasons for the judgement, whose reasons were better and why?
5 Did you agree on where the different skills should be used?
6 Were your reasons for locating skills in different parts or throughout the essay as good as your partner's reasons?
7 Did you agree on how to structure each paragraph?
8 Can your partner justify their thoughts on how to structure a paragraph?

Use this discussion as a basis for further notes on how to approach the question. For advice on the structure of the essay see page 22.

1b: The changing role of parliament

Overview

Parliament is one of England's most important political institutions. During the Tudor era, this institution underwent significant changes. These changes shaped parliament, helping it evolve into today's institution. These changes were primarily undertaken during the reigns of two Tudor monarchs, Henry VIII and Elizabeth I. This section will examine the theme of the changing role of parliament by examining the following topics:

1 *Henry VIII's parliaments before 1529*, which describes the policies introduced early in Henry's reign.
2 *From 'King and Parliament' to 'King-in-Parliament'*, which examines an important shift in the way power was conceived during Henry VIII's reign.
3 *The growing confidence of parliament under Elizabeth*, which explores how parliament matured into a modern political institution during Elizabeth's reign.

Note it down

Create an annotated timeline for this chapter, which includes many dates specific to the topic of parliaments. On one side of the page write the dates, and on the other side note the event and some brief details about it – for example, what the parliament was called for, or what it achieved.

1 Henry VIII's parliaments before 1529

In the sixteenth century, parliament met only when the monarch summoned it. A number of years could pass between meetings of parliament. In the 24 years of Henry VII's reign, for example, parliament was only in session for just over a year and a half. Parliament served two key purposes when Henry VIII became king in 1509. First, parliament met when monarchs needed to raise taxes. Parliament played no role in the day-to-day governing of the country. It represented the entire population of the kingdom. When laws were created in parliament, it meant that the entire population consented to them. This was especially important regarding taxes. Taxes could not be raised unless they received parliamentary consent. The second purpose that parliament served was to complete the kingdom's business. In this role, parliament would meet in order to create legislation that would be beneficial to the kingdom. This could include new laws that regulated import duties or laws mandating improvements to roads or towns.

Henry VIII's earliest parliaments dealt with a variety of different matters. His first parliament was summoned in 1510. This parliament focused on introducing reforms that reversed some of his father's unpopular policies. The parliaments of 1512 and 1515 dealt with religious

reforms. A 1512 Act restricted the use of **benefit of clergy** to ordained members of the priesthood. This parliament was also asked to raise money in order to fund Henry's 1513 invasion of France. In 1515, additional legislation reaffirmed benefit of clergy. Parliament was not summoned again until 1523. Henry had gone to war with France again in 1522. The parliament that met in 1523 agreed to pay a tax in order to finance the loan the King had taken out to finance this war. Henry's earliest parliaments, therefore, followed the model of creating legislation that would benefit the people and that parliament alone could assent to taxation.

2 From 'King and Parliament' to 'King-in-Parliament'

The parliament that Henry VIII summoned to meet beginning in 1529 was one of the longest-running parliaments in history. This parliament first met in 1529, and was not adjourned until 1536, meeting in seven separate sessions during these seven years. This long parliament is today known as the 'Reformation Parliament' because the legislation it passed focused on the idea of reformation. This parliament led to the break with Rome, the foundation of the Church in England, and revolutionary changes in social policy. The Reformation Parliament also introduced a different way to think about the relationship between the Crown and parliament. This change can be described as a movement from following the principle of 'King and Parliament' to favouring the idea of 'King-in-Parliament'.

'King and Parliament'

What was the concept of 'King and Parliament'? Parliament had not historically been the executive body at the heart of government. Historian David Loades described parliament's original purpose as 'a means of communication between the king and his subjects'. It met irregularly, when called by the king. The main reason for this was to grant taxes so that the king could wage war. Because of its role as a means of communication, it was also an important way that people could petition the king on public or private matters. Finally, parliament was a High Court. The House of Lords was the highest court in the land, and its judgements could not be challenged in any other court. Parliament could **impeach** people, and could declare them guilty of offences like **treason**. If so, the convicted person would not be able to appeal to any other court. Despite this, the king had the final say. No measure in parliament could be passed without the king's approval. The king was not obliged to call parliament, and there was no legal requirement for him to do so. As long as he could manage to govern the kingdom without needing extra money, he did not need to summon a parliament to meet.

Parliament was sometimes viewed as a counterbalance to the king's power, granting approval to his legislation. This was different to other European countries. In France, for example, the king could simply impose laws and taxes as he wished. The English saw the French king's power to impose his will on the people so freely as tyrannical. The great medieval political theorist, Sir John Fortescue, described England as a 'royal and political' kingdom. This meant that the Crown and the people were bound together in a political partnership. Before the Reformation Parliament, however, it was a partnership in which the king had much more power. This is why the term 'King and Parliament' is sometimes used. Although the king and the parliament did interact, the king could operate without parliament, and could govern without recourse to parliament for a long time. Rather than parliament, the king's Council was the body at the centre of government, and carried out the monarch's decisions. Parliament approved laws that the king made, but the king could use his prerogative while parliament was not in session. In Henry VII's reign parliament was only summoned once in 12 years. Despite this, the House of Commons was the main representative assembly of the kingdom, and election to it was a matter of prestige. Henry VIII called parliaments more regularly than his father. Parliament sat in 1510, 1512, 1515, 1523 and 1529. During those years, parliament operated as it traditionally had, and did not exceed its traditional powers.

'King-in-Parliament'

The Reformation Parliament (1529-36) brought about great changes in virtually every aspect of English social life. These changes included the ways in which the monarch and the people were understood to interact with each other. As with many other aspects of political, social, and religious change in the sixteenth century, the change from 'King and Parliament' began with Henry VIII's 'Great Matter'. Henry had tried to achieve an annulment of his marriage to Catherine of Aragon through diplomacy with the Pope, but it had not worked. The Archbishop of Canterbury, William Warham, was also not prepared to co-operate. Henry turned to parliament instead as a way to achieve his aims (see page 38). According to Loades, Henry VIII used management and persuasion to force through the measures that would lead to the break from Rome and the establishment of the Royal Supremacy. This would bring huge additional power to the King, particularly in the sphere of religion. Parliament, in passing these measures, conferred this power on the King.

After that point, the powers of parliament and the King increased. Working together, they dissolved the monasteries, confiscated Church land, and wrought enormous changes in the religious landscape of the country. In doing this, the assumptions about parliament's sphere changed. Parliament was no longer there to approve taxes or to act as a court, but was competent to make decisions about all different matters. Its powers would continue to evolve, and parliamentarians increasingly felt able to challenge the monarch's **prerogative** from Elizabeth I onwards – although generally not successfully. This was a huge change from the situation before 1529, however, and marked a move from a system where the king operated largely independently with the aid of his Council, calling parliament largely for taxes (King and Parliament) to one where he worked with (or 'in') parliament. Henry argued in doing this that he had just reclaimed power from the Pope, stolen from English kings over the centuries. It gave the English monarchy more authority and power, but also created a more powerful institution in parliament. Law-making after the Reformation Parliament required the monarch to act together with the two Houses of Parliament. Together 'King-in-Parliament' became the supreme **legislative** authority in the kingdom.

3 The growing confidence of parliament under Elizabeth

Elizabeth's relationship with her parliaments was rather complicated. Elizabeth and her parliaments worked together to rule the kingdom. It is important to remember, however, that the Queen was still responsible for summoning parliaments. Parliament was not constantly in session during Elizabeth's reign but was called in order to vote for taxation and to create new laws. Elizabeth called ten parliaments over the course of her reign and they met for an average of less than ten weeks. The first met immediately after her accession in January 1559.

During Elizabeth's reign, parliament was more directly involved in some of the kingdom's important decisions. The influence and importance of parliament had increased over the period since the 1530s, when they had been asked to pass a huge range of legislation, particularly in relation to the Reformation (see page 17). The approval of parliament made new legislative measures more authoritative, handing them a stamp of approval from the nation's political representatives. This made parliament more assertive. The precise constitutional relationship between Elizabeth and her parliaments was complicated and disputed (see page 179).

Note it down

Create a spider diagram (see page x) to take notes on the different issues that Elizabeth and her parliaments argued about. Also note areas and reasons for co-operation. Put 'Elizabeth and her parliaments' in the centre of the diagram and use the headings as 'legs'.

The religious settlement

In the 1560s, the religious settlement is an example of this parliamentary involvement and assertiveness. In the 1530s, parliament had approved a statutory law declaring that Henry VIII was the Supreme Head of the Church in England (see page 38). His ministers, particularly Thomas Cromwell and Thomas Cranmer, devised and implemented the policies that shaped the Church in the 1530s and 1540s. In the 1560s, however, even the terminology applied to the monarch was questioned. Elizabeth's title was the 'Supreme Governor' of the Church. Parliament took an active role in creating the policies and documents that served as the foundation of the Church. They negotiated with the Queen and her Privy Council in order to develop the Church that they wanted in the kingdom. Historian John Neale claimed that there was a sizeable and organised Puritan opposition pushing for, and achieving, a more Protestant settlement. This has since been disproved – only 22 of the group Neale

Key debate
Neale and the rise of parliament

In the 1950s the historian John Neale, in his book *Elizabeth I and her Parliaments*, was responsible for the view that parliament gained in confidence during Elizabeth's reign, creating conflict between the House of Commons and the Queen. He particularly emphasised the role played by Puritan MPs, depicting them as a form of organised opposition. In this narrative, these advances laid the way for later challenges to the monarchy by parliaments under the Stuarts. Historians have disputed Neale's version of events since the 1970s and 1980s, and continue to refine their view of parliament in this period. Geoffrey Elton was one of the first to argue that Neale's interpretation was wrong, followed by Michael Graves and Norman Jones. They argue that Neale misinterpreted the evidence and that parliament was actually not on the rise in this period. According to these historians there was no attempt to act as an organised opposition to the Queen, they did not withhold subsidies in exchange for their demands being met, and they did not attack the royal prerogative. Instead, parliaments supported the Queen and worked with her during her long reign.

identified were certainly Protestants, and the presence of at least 20 Catholics in this parliament was ignored by Neale. Elizabeth needed parliament's approval for her religious policies because she wanted its co-operation in financial matters, but this didn't necessarily mean that it was able to manipulate her or ignore royal prerogative. That said, parliament's powers to grant taxes to the monarch were vital at the beginning of Elizabeth's reign because the ordinary revenue of the Crown was simply not enough to govern the country.

Further religious reform

Elizabeth did protest at some matters raised in **bills** by Puritans aiming for further religious reform along Protestant lines. She objected to such bills in 1566, 1571 and 1586–87 because she believed that such matters were an issue for royal prerogative, not for parliament to discuss. Generally this led to these bills being abandoned, though sometimes it took time. One issue that kept returning to parliament was that of the Book of Common Prayer. Puritan MPs thought it was too much of a compromise, and wanted further reform of the Prayer Book. William Strickland proposed a bill to that effect in 1571, and Anthony Cope presented a revised Puritan version of the Prayer Book and a bill for reform to the religious laws to the Speaker of the House of Commons in 1586. For what Elizabeth saw as an attack on her prerogative, Cope was imprisoned in the Tower of London for a month from February to March 1587. This did not dissuade Puritan MPs, however, and Puritan attempts to push for further reforms continued until the end of Elizabeth's reign (see page 69).

Marriage and the succession

Elizabeth also resisted any discussion in parliament of the question of her marriage. MPs were concerned that the succession was not settled and that it was possible that a Catholic may inherit should Elizabeth fail to marry. She told parliament that they should not presume to ask her to marry. In 1566 Elizabeth dissolved parliament early after both Houses tried to withhold subsidies until Elizabeth settled the succession. She ordered parliament to stop discussing the matter but MPs continued, in defence of the free speech of parliament. Elizabeth withdrew her order but still refused to settle the succession as MPs wanted her to. She dissolved parliament a year early instead. The arrival of Mary, Queen of Scots, in England in 1568 exacerbated the issue. She was a Catholic and (at the time) heir to the throne. Catholic plots in Mary's favour continued until her execution in 1587, and the succession issue featured in parliamentary discussions even beyond that point.

Co-operation and control

Many MPs shared Elizabeth's view of parliament's role during her reign. Their priorities were their local interests. They prioritised legislation that would benefit their constituents and regions, and were largely happy to pass laws proposed by the government. The vast majority of them did not claim that Elizabeth should listen to unsolicited advice on matters outside of their ordinary purview. Many did not want to prolong their stay in London, aiming to conclude business quickly and harmoniously and return home to their counties. Others wanted to please the Queen and gain political favour rather than annoy her with unwanted advice. It is certainly not proven that there was any more conflict between Elizabeth and her parliaments than that experienced by previous monarchs.

When Elizabeth did want to control the MPs in parliament she had plenty of ways to do so, for example:

- Threatening to remove troublesome MPs from their prized local offices.
- The Crown was directly in control of the election of some MPs, and could use noble supporters to control others – so the Crown had some control over who would be nominated as MP.
- The Privy Council and Elizabeth's ministers used **patronage** to ensure that their supporters handled matters in parliament to Elizabeth's liking.

▲ A drawing of Elizabeth and her parliament. This image dates from 1682 – nearly 100 years after the period discussed above. What does it tell us about the position of the monarch within parliament? What impact might its date have on its value as evidence?

- The Queen had the power to use certain laws (for example those against **sedition**) to forbid discussion of particular matters.
- Elizabeth used her personal charm and tact to exert influence, as well as losing her temper when matters did not go her way.

Conclusion

The institution of parliament changed a lot in the sixteenth century. From being an occasional body that was called to grant taxes up to 1529 it became more of a partner to the monarch by Elizabeth's reign. It became more important from 1529 because Henry VIII needed parliament's approval in his quest to annul his marriage to Catherine of Aragon. By the end of the period it seems that the monarch had the upper hand once again.

Henry VIII's parliaments before 1529

- Parliament met only when summoned – years could pass without parliament sitting
- They were called when the monarch needed taxes and to create legislation
- Henry VIII's first parliament was called because he needed taxes
- Parliaments in 1512 and 1515 were for religious reforms

THE CHANGING ROLE OF PARLIAMENT

The growing confidence of parliament under Elizabeth

- Parliament negotiated with the Queen and Privy Council to create the new religious policies
- Elizabeth resisted the calls of a Puritan minority in parliament for further religious reform
- Most MPs wanted to co-operate with the Crown, to reform their constituencies and gain favour with the Queen
- The Queen used tact and charm to manage parliament, as well as political patronage

From 'King and Parliament' to 'King-in-Parliament'

- Magna Carta aimed to prevent kings from becoming tyrants
- Parliament was seen as a counterbalance to the monarch's power
- Parliament had to agree to legislation
- The Crown and parliament were a political partnership
- The Reformation Parliament was especially influential
- They helped Henry to break with Rome

▲ Summary diagram: The changing role of parliament

Recommended reading

Michael A. R. Graves, *Tudor Parliaments: The Crown, Lords and Commons, 1485–1603* (Routledge, 1985).

Gives details about this important institution and the changes it endured over the course of the Tudor period.

John Lotherington (editor), *The Tudor Years* (Hodder, 2003).

Chapter 8, 'Elizabeth I: The Government of England', is extremely useful on the debates between historians and the behaviour of Elizabeth's parliaments.

www.tudors.org/as-a2-level/tudor-parliaments/

This is a detailed article on Tudor parliaments, designed especially for A level students covering this topic. It covers the nature and function of parliament, parliament and privilege, and relations between the Crown and parliament.

Essay technique: Focus and structure

All of your examined essays will be judged on how far they focus on the question, and on the quality of their structure. The better your focus and the clearer your structure, the better your chance of exam success.

Focus of the question

First, you must identify the focus of the question. Imagine you are answering the following question:

> **How far does religion explain parliament's changing influence in the years 1529–88?**

The question has two parts:
- religion
- parliament's changing influence in the years 1529–88.

Essentially, the question asks you to explain parliament's changing influence, therefore that is the primary focus of the question. However, you must evaluate the importance of religion too: this is the secondary focus of your essay.

Structuring your essay

Your essay should be made up of three or four paragraphs, each addressing a different factor which helps to explain parliament's changing influence from 1529 to 1588. One of these paragraphs has to explain the factor stated in the question: religion. Therefore, your essay plan should look something like this:

- Paragraph 1 [Stated factor]: Religion in the period 1529–88.

- Paragraph 2: Changes to common law.

- Paragraph 3: Financial needs of the monarch.

- Paragraph 4: Questions over the succession.

It's a good idea to deal with the stated factor first, otherwise you may run out of time and then miss the opportunity to deal with this important part of the question. Once you've dealt with the stated factor, deal with the other factors in order of their importance; write about the most important factor first.

In addition to your three or four main points, you should begin your essay with a clear introduction and end with a conclusion (see pages 74–75) that contains a focused summary of your essay.

The example above is a causation question, which asks you to consider how far a stated factor caused a specific process. Significantly, not all questions deal with cause, and not all questions have an obvious stated factor. Nonetheless, you will need to consider a range of themes in any essay you write. Therefore, you should always begin by thinking of the three or four main topics you want to discuss, and these should be the basis of your essay.

Paper 1 England, 1509–1603: authority, nation and religion

Writing a focused introduction

Having made your plan it is important you write a focused essay. One way of doing this is to use the wording of the question to help write your answer. For example, the first sentence of your essay could look like this:

Clear focus ———• Religion explains the changing influence of parliament in the years 1529–88 *to a great extent.* •——— Answers 'How far'

This sentence has a clear focus on the question by addressing 'how far' religion explains the changing influence of parliament. In this sense, the first sentence provides a focused answer to the whole question.

Focus throughout the essay

A second way of maintaining focus is to begin each paragraph with a clear point, which both refers to the primary focus of the question and links it to a factor.

For example, you could begin your third paragraph with the following point:

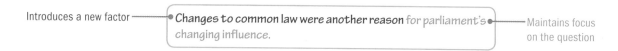

Introduces a new factor ———• **Changes to common law were another reason** *for parliament's* •——— Maintains focus *changing influence.* on the question

This sentence clearly introduces a new factor – changes to common law – while maintaining focus on the question.

Summary

- Work out the primary and secondary focus of the question.
- Plan your essay with a series of factors that focus on the question.
- Use the words in the question to formulate your answer.
- Return to the primary focus of the question at the beginning of every paragraph.

Question practice

Sections A and B of the Paper 1 exam examine your knowledge in breadth. Therefore, you will need to read beyond this chapter in order to fully answer these sample questions.

1 How far did religion affect Elizabeth I's relationships with her parliaments in the period 1558 to 1588?

2 To what extent were succession concerns the main issue facing parliaments from 1529 to 1588?

Activity

Having looked over your notes for Chapter 1b:

- Make a bullet-point list of the big themes that you could use to answer Question 1.
- Make a bullet-point list of the other information that you would need to include to answer Question 1.

1c: The principal servants of the Crown

Overview

Monarchs were expected to be wise, capable and just. They shaped the way their kingdom was perceived at home and overseas. Above all else, rulers were to dispense justice throughout their realms and to defend their people from foreign hostilities. However, it was impossible for individual rulers to understand everything that happened in every area of the kingdom all at once. They were aided in their decision-making processes by a number of knowledgeable experts. In this section, we will examine the theme of the principal servants of the Crown by exploring the following topics:

1 *The powers of leading ministers*, which highlights the primary ministers within Tudor government and explains their role in the government.
2 *The influence of Wolsey, Cromwell and Burghley*, which focuses on three of the most important government servants during the sixteenth century.
3 *Changes to the structure of government*, which identifies the key institutional changes that took place over the course of the sixteenth century.

Note it down

This chapter also includes some very important political figures. Create index cards for Wolsey, Cromwell and Burghley (see page xi). Remember to take notes on their key actions and policies, as well as their long-term significance.

1 The powers of leading ministers

The Tudor monarchs were capable rulers who governed a large and diverse kingdom. In order to rule efficiently, they relied on officials and minsters in the countryside, at embassies in foreign countries and at court. These officials gathered and analysed information, and they advised the monarch about policy decisions. Advising the monarch was the primary role of these ministers: the monarch relied on their opinions about every political and financial matter that arose. They explained events to the monarch and recommended a specific action. However, it is important to remember that the course of action that would be undertaken remained the monarch's decision alone. It was therefore crucially important that the monarch received accurate information and the best advice possible. The leading ministers were entrusted with ensuring that the monarch could make the right decisions.

There were a number of government ministers within the Tudor court. The most important minister was the Lord Chancellor (see Table 1). The Lord Chancellor acted as the monarch's representative in parliament. He was responsible for opening and closing parliamentary sessions. The Principal Secretary, or Secretary of State, was another critically important role (see Table 2 on page 25). The Secretaries were responsible for handling the monarch's correspondence, reading and responding to letters and messages sent to the monarch. The Secretaries were knowledgeable about current affairs in the kingdom and overseas. They often advised their rulers about policy direction. As a result, they had to be reliable and discreet, or they could jeopardise the kingdom's stability.

Table 1: Lord Chancellors

1509	William Warham, Archbishop of Canterbury
1515	Cardinal Thomas Wolsey
1529	Sir Thomas More
1533	Thomas Audley, Lord Audley
1544	Thomas Wriothesley
1547	Thomas Wriothesley, Earl of Southampton
	William Poulet, Lord St John
	Richard Rich, Lord Rich
1552	Thomas Goodricke, Bishop of Ely
1553	Stephen Gardiner, Bishop of Winchester
1556	Nicholas Heath, Archbishop of York
1558	Sir Nicholas Bacon
1579	Sir Thomas Bromley
1587	Sir Christopher Hatton
1591	William Cecil, Lord Burghley

Table 2: Principal Secretaries

1500–16	Thomas Rothall
1516–26	Richard Pace
1526–29	William Knight
1529–34	Stephen Gardiner
1534–40	Thomas Cromwell
1540–43	Thomas Wriothesley
1540–43	Sir Ralph Sadler
1543–48	Sir William Paget
1544–57	Sir William Petre
1548–49	Sir Thomas Smith
1549–50	Nicholas Wotton
1550–53	Sir William Cecil
1553	Sir John Cheke
1553–58	Sir John Bourne
1557–58	John Boxall
1558–72	Sir William Cecil
1572–77	Sir Thomas Smith
1573–90	Sir Francis Walsingham
1577–81	Thomas Wilson
1586–87	William Davison
1590–1612	Sir Robert Cecil

2 The influence of Wolsey, Cromwell and Burghley

Three of the best-known ministers of this period were Thomas Wolsey, Thomas Cromwell, and William Cecil, Lord Burghley. Wolsey and Cromwell served Henry VIII; Burghley first served Edward VI before rising to prominence as Elizabeth I's Principal Secretary. These three men shared many things in common, including dedication to their service to the Crown and a background in law. Each of these men helped shape and implement policy during their respective monarchs' reigns, and each contributed to the growing centralisation of the state that took place over the course of the early modern period.

Note it down

To help you remember the policies of Wolsey, Cromwell and Cecil, copy and complete the following table as you go along:

	Wolsey	Cromwell	Burghley
Religion			
Foreign policy			
Governmental changes			

Thomas Wolsey (1473–1530)

Thomas Wolsey came from a humble background in Ipswich. His father was likely a butcher but Wolsey was able to attend grammar school and Magdalen College School. He studied theology at Magdalen College, Oxford. He served the court as a royal **almoner** under Henry VII and survived the changes the new King made in courtly personnel. He was selected to be the new King's almoner in 1509. He became a member of Henry VIII's Council in 1510. Wolsey was ambitious and recognised that his own fortunes were tied to the King's. He hoped to one day become Pope. Henry selected him to be Archbishop of York in 1514. He became a cardinal and Henry's Lord Chancellor in 1515. He started construction on Hampton Court Palace after these appointments. Wolsey became one of Henry VIII's most important advisers. He was not opposed to reform of the Church, dissolving corrupt monasteries in 1524 and 1527. Wolsey relied on the King's favour for the maintenance of his power. He lacked popularity at court and had made enemies with his financial policies. Wolsey's failure to obtain an annulment of Henry's marriage to Catherine of Aragon led to his downfall. He was arrested in 1529 and stripped of his offices, powers and lands. He was accused of treason and ordered to London, but fell ill on the journey from York. Wolsey died at Leicester on 29 November 1530.

Thomas Wolsey

When Henry VIII ascended the throne, he removed many of his father's principal ministers. These men were widely unpopular because the common understanding was that they were responsible for encouraging Henry VII to become greedy and to stop financial support of institutions and talented individuals. Henry VIII's reign ushered in a new era. He was a young king, and he brought new talent and energy to the court through the ministers he selected to advise and support him during the early stages of his reign. Thomas Wolsey was one of the best and brightest at the young king's new court. With time, he became one of the most powerful men in the kingdom, second only to the King.

Wolsey believed that Henry needed to show that he was a powerful and important figure on the international political stage. He advised the young Henry to support famous scholars and artists from other parts of Europe and to invite them to the court. These activities helped to elevate England's prestige and enhance its reputation among Europe's powerful and elite. Wolsey worked hard for the kingdom, usually resolving the day-to-day tasks of business and administration while the young king took on more interesting activities, like hunting and jousting. Wolsey even managed Henry's 1513 invasion of France.

As the King's minister, Wolsey has a complex reputation. His enemies complained that he abused authority by taking too much authority on himself. He was known for being calculating and ruthless, but Wolsey was ambitious and creative in politics. He often looked for political opportunities. He wanted to adopt a policy of regular taxation to fund the Crown, but this did not work. Wolsey was responsible for patronage. He controlled official information, selected the King's personnel, and was the adviser that the King listened to the most. If the King suggested a royal policy, Wolsey was responsible for working out the details to make the policy work. His policies often received the approval of the rest of the Council. Ultimately though, it was the King's responsibility to make decisions. Henry was likely to follow Wolsey's advice but he was still responsible for making his own choices.

Religion

Wolsey encouraged the King in pursuing his personal religious interests. When the German reformer Martin Luther published tracts questioning the integrity of the Roman Catholic Church, Henry personally responded by publishing a tract of his own in 1521. He consulted Wolsey as he drafted his *Assertion of the Seven Sacraments*. It was originally written in Latin under the title *Assertio septum sacramentum*. This text used scriptural examples to argue that Luther's religious ideals were heretical. Henry's efforts in protecting the Church from people like Luther earned him the title 'Defender of the Faith' from the appreciative Pope.

Treaty of London

Wolsey was instrumental in two other important international endeavours pursued by Henry. The first was the 1518 Treaty of London. Henry and other European princes came to believe that they could prevent war if they worked together to pursue peace. England, France, the Holy Roman Empire, the Netherlands and Spain signed a peace agreement with each other and the papacy. In all, around 20 states, encompassing all of Europe, agreed to the treaty. These groups were all afraid of the threat posed by the powerful Ottoman Empire. They agreed that they would not attack each other, and that all would come to the aid of one if attacked. This treaty was a significant non-aggression pact. Wolsey had encouraged Henry to pursue peace rather than war, and the treaty was a result of Wolsey's work. It significantly raised Henry's profile, and England was seen as one of the three major powers as a result of his efforts to achieve peace through the treaty.

The Field of Cloth of Gold

The second important international endeavour Wolsey helped Henry with was the Field of Cloth of Gold. England's primary rival was France. Like England, France had a new king. Francis I was similar to Henry in many ways: both were young, handsome, and respected for their physical and intellectual prowess. They regarded each other as competitors and were curious about each other. They had become allies through the Treaty of London, though they had not yet personally met.

The Field of Cloth of Gold was the Kings' opportunity to meet each other in friendship. They would confirm the conditions of the 1518 treaty at the Field. Both sides hoped the Field would result in lasting friendship between England and France. The two kings, along with their wives and enormous entourages, met near Calais from 17 to 24 June 1520. This meeting was a magnificent display of wealth and power. The Field combined elements of a tournament – feasting, hunting, jousting – with a lavish political summit. Henry and Francis attended religious services together, exchanged gifts, and attended masques. The Field of Cloth of Gold was one of the most important achievements of Henry's reign and Wolsey's time in office. Though the initiatives established ultimately failed when England and France went to war in 1522, the Field helped to secure Henry's reputation as a powerful prince.

▲ The Field of Cloth of Gold painted c1545. What might be the purpose of this image? What impression does it give of the event and of the importance of the figures depicted?

Wolsey's downfall

In June 1529, Wolsey and Cardinal Campeggio were selected to preside over the trial in London that would decide the fate of Henry's marriage to Catherine of Aragon. The Queen argued that she could not receive a fair trial in London (see page 37), and Campeggio declared that the case would appear before the Pope's courts in Rome. This was a disastrous decision for Henry, and led to Wolsey's downfall. Henry was angry. He seized some of Wolsey's lands and sent him to York. Wolsey was eventually charged with treason. He almost certainly would have been found guilty of this crime and executed, but Wolsey died as he travelled to London to face these charges in 1530.

Wolsey's legacy

Wolsey helped Henry settle into his role as king on his accession. He reformed the Court of **Star Chamber**, transforming it from an **appeals court** to a court where plaintiffs could bring cases directly before the King. He taught Henry to think beyond his kingdom and to consider his role within Christendom. Henry's international prestige was elevated as a result of Wolsey's peace initiatives and because he encouraged the King to support talented artists and scholars from all over Europe.

Thomas Cromwell

Thomas Cromwell was Wolsey's successor as Henry's chief minister. He was enormously influential and held a huge number of positions. His rise to power was meteoric and his political survival over the years remarkable.

Securing the Tudor dynasty

When Cromwell became Lord Chancellor, Henry's most important objective was securing the dynasty by producing a male heir. Henry had determined that the only way this would be possible was to divorce Catherine and find a new queen to take her place. However, divorce was very difficult according to Church law, and the King would need a special dispensation from the Pope allowing a divorce to take place. The problem of obtaining a divorce from Catherine became known as the King's **'Great Matter'** (see page 36). One of Cromwell's chief responsibilities was finding a solution to this problem. The solution that he and a large number of scholars working with him devised was to break with the Roman Catholic Church. The scholars and propagandists working with Cromwell argued that ancient kings of England had been secular governors but they were also rulers of the Church in England. They argued that the King should take up his rightful role as the Supreme Head of the Church in England. The Act of Supremacy (see page 38), ratified in 1534, declared that the King would do just that. The Roman Catholic Church had lost its way and fallen into errors, Cromwell argued. It was the King's responsibility to ensure that the Church in England was free from sin and heresy. The English Reformation had begun.

The King's Vicegerent

In 1536, Cromwell was given the role of the King's **Vicegerent** in spiritual and ecclesiastical matters. This meant that the King was the Church's supreme head

Thomas Cromwell (c1485–1540)

Thomas Cromwell was born around 1485 in Putney, Surrey. He was not of noble birth, but was the son of a man who had been a blacksmith, cloth merchant and innkeeper. While he was a young man, Cromwell left England and travelled to continental Europe. He visited France, the Low Countries and Italy, though little information remains about what exactly he did there. It is said that he was a mercenary soldier, fighting for the French at the Battle of Garigliano on 28 December 1503, though there is no definitive proof of this. In Italy he worked for a Florentine banker and later lived among English merchants in the Low Countries. Some records indicate that he was in Rome in 1514, and documents in the Vatican archives suggest that he was an agent for the Archbishop of York there. He was an MP in 1520, was sent on embassies to Rome on the behalf of the town of Boston in 1517 and 1518, and he was elected a member of Gray's Inn in 1524. From 1516 to 1530 he was a member of Wolsey's household. He became Wolsey's chief servant, and feared that he would fall alongside his master. He avoided this fate. By 1529 Cromwell was elected MP for Taunton. He was appointed to the King's Privy Council by the final weeks of 1530. He was to hold numerous offices in the King's services, including Chancellor of the Exchequer, Steward of the Duchy of Lancaster, and Master of the Rolls. He succeeded in helping the King have his marriage to Catherine of Aragon annulled but fell after the failure of Henry's marriage to Anne of Cleves. He was condemned as a traitor and executed on 28 July 1540, the same day as Henry's marriage to Catherine Howard.

but that Cromwell was the King's deputy in religious matters. Cromwell worked with Thomas Cranmer, the Archbishop of Canterbury, to set the doctrine of the Church in England. Together, they devised the official policies and wrote the foundational texts for the Church. These included a statement of faith (the Ten Articles of 1536), a ban on the cult of the saints and on pilgrimages and the requirement that every parish own a copy of the Bible in English so that ordinary parishioners had access to it. Cromwell also investigated the monasteries and began closing them. These measures were unpopular with large numbers of the King's subjects. They even prompted the largest rebellion faced by a Tudor monarch, the Pilgrimage of Grace of 1536 (see page 95). The rebels were openly hostile to Cromwell, demanding his removal from power. The King defended Cromwell and the other men the rebels named. He argued that it was his right to select his own advisers, and that ordinary subjects had no say in the matter.

Key debate

Elton's 'revolution in government' theory

G. R. Elton, one of the most influential and important historians of Tudor government and politics, put forward a new theory about Henry VIII's reign in 1953. He argued that England experienced a 'revolution in government' during the 1530s. Elton presented the idea that political conditions lent themselves to a new way to govern the realm which involved a shift in the way the kingdom was administered. Government grew substantially during this decade, and became increasingly bureaucratic in nature. Another change that Elton identified was a decline in the importance of the royal household and an increase in the importance of parliament and formal ministers. He believed that Cromwell was the most important figure in the process. He credited Cromwell as the mastermind behind the creation of the Privy Council, the divorce, the Royal Supremacy and new government agencies. Elton argued that England entered the Tudor age as a firmly medieval monarchy but had become a recognisably modern state by the end of the dynasty.

Elton's ideas have been challenged by a number of historians. One important book addressing these questions was *Revolution Reassessed*, edited by Christopher Coleman and David Starkey and published in 1986. The essays in this book examined aspects of Elton's argument and added nuance to things they found. For example, John Guy's essay suggested that the Privy Council experienced a natural evolution during this period, and that it adapted to meet the changing needs of government. For Guy, this was a natural change rather than a deliberate break. Starkey's essay found that the royal household remained an important route for access to the monarch. It remained a vibrant place of politics long after Elton had believed it was in decline. Other historians have challenged Cromwell's influence.

Cromwell's fall

Cromwell was one of the most important men in England throughout the 1530s, but everything changed in 1540. The pace of the religious reforms Cromwell and Cranmer had helped to introduce in England were slowing. Almost without warning, Cromwell lost favour with the King. Historians have been unable to identify a conclusive reason for Henry's abrupt turn against his trusted minister. However, there is evidence to suggest that the King's attitude changed as a result of Cromwell's part in the Cleves marriage and because he fell under the influence of religious conservatives at court. Cromwell had arranged the marriage between Henry and his fourth wife, Anne of Cleves. The marriage was strategically valuable because it forged a bond between England and a prominent Protestant family in Europe, but Henry was disgusted by his new wife when he met her in person. The marriage was never consummated and was quickly annulled. Henry blamed Cromwell for the marriage's failure. Meanwhile, Cromwell's enemies were gaining influence over the King at court. The most powerful of his enemies were Thomas Howard, Duke of Norfolk, and Stephen Gardiner, the Bishop of Winchester. On 10 June 1540, Cromwell was arrested during a meeting in the Privy Chamber. Days earlier, he had been given the title Earl of Essex. He was accused of encouraging heresy and contemplating treason. His enemies used his ambition against him, claiming that Cromwell wanted to make himself more powerful than the King. He was executed on 28 July 1540.

Cromwell's legacy

Cromwell's importance rests in his ability to organise. He is often credited with creating the **Royal Supremacy** and prompting a revolution in government. This view on his legacy has been challenged in recent years, but it is important to observe that the King had relied on Cromwell in numerous circumstances over the course of the 1530s. He was the King's Principal Secretary, drafted parliamentary legislation and policy and was granted enormous powers in order to bring about religious reform. His religious initiatives forever changed the religious landscape in England, laying the foundations for the English Church. The King would never again rely so heavily on one individual to guide him in policy, as he had on Wolsey and Cromwell. After 1540, Henry used the Privy Council as the means through which policy was conceived and implemented.

William Cecil, Lord Burghley

William Cecil, created Lord Burghley by Elizabeth in February 1571, was Elizabeth's closest adviser. Unlike Wolsey and Cromwell, he had not been a part of the Church hierarchy before taking on his important role in Elizabeth's government. Instead, he was a faithful Protestant reformer and scholar of the common law. Another difference between Burghley and his two most famous predecessors was that the Cecil family had connections to court. His grandfather had been yeoman of the guard to Henry VII, an elite group of soldiers who served as the King's personal bodyguard. This role would have placed Cecil's grandfather into an important

---

William Cecil, Lord Burghley (1520–98)

William Cecil was the only son of Richard Cecil, a Lincolnshire landowner and gentleman. He went to school locally at Stamford and then to university, studying at St John's College, Cambridge. He met the eminent scholars Roger Ascham and John Cheke, marrying Cheke's sister Mary in 1541. Cecil's son from this marriage, Thomas, was a future politician and Earl of Exeter. Mary died in 1543 and he married Mildred Cooke three years later – another highly educated lady. Cecil began his career in the service of the Duke of Somerset. He became an MP around 1543. He was imprisoned in November 1549 in the Tower of London upon Somerset's fall but was released after less than three months. Cecil signed Edward VI's 'Devise for the Succession' in 1549 but was later to claim to Mary I that he had been forced to. Cecil continued to sit as an MP in Mary's parliaments but gained no great position until Elizabeth's reign, whereupon he became her most trusted adviser. Cecil held many important positions under Elizabeth, including Lord Treasurer and Secretary of State. He died in 1592, to be succeeded by his son Robert (his eldest son by his second marriage) as the Queen's most trusted adviser. Cecil was an intelligent man, a conscientious parent and was interested in **genealogy** and heraldry in his spare time. He was an amateur architect and horticulturalist. He was also ruthless, cunning and could be unprincipled when his aims demanded it.

and trusted position at court. Both his father and his grandfather served at Henry VIII's court. Elizabeth selected Cecil to be the surveyor of her estates in 1550 and he therefore became one of her most trusted advisers. Many of the men who had been prominent at Edward's court became members of Elizabeth's Privy Council, including Cecil.

Cecil was one of the most important figures in Elizabeth's court. She had known him for years before her accession. He helped her to make a smooth transition to power and served as her secretary of state. In 1572, she selected him to serve as lord treasurer when that office became vacant. Although Burghley was Elizabeth's trusted adviser, he did not have the same independence in the role as Wolsey or Cromwell. Instead, Burghley was obliged to carry through Elizabeth's decisions, a task made difficult by the Queen's indecisiveness.

Burghley and religious policy

One of the most important policies that Burghley developed at the beginning of Elizabeth's reign was the restoration of the Royal Supremacy. Burghley was a Protestant, and believed that English religious issues were best handled by the English themselves rather than the papacy. Religion thus shaped the kingdom's foreign policy during Burghley's tenure as Elizabeth's secretary. The Queen preferred neutrality whenever possible but England was sometimes compelled to intervene, and so with

Burghley's guidance, England supported Protestant causes in Europe. The government did what it could to help Protestants in France during its wars of religion. England also provided support to the Dutch during their revolt against Roman Catholic Spain, even providing a governor to rule over them. Religion, therefore, helped to shape the foreign policy decisions made by Burghley and other governmental figures.

In addition to foreign policy matters, religion was essential to the development of domestic policy during Elizabeth's reign. The question of religion was one of the key problems that needed to be resolved in Elizabeth's reign. Burghley and other members of the Privy Council worked closely with parliament to restore the Royal Supremacy and the forms of Protestant worship that had been introduced in Edward VI's reign. The other key domestic policy problem that Burghley worked on was the question of the royal succession. Elizabeth was unmarried and had no children when she became queen. Burghley made recommendations about potential husbands for Elizabeth. He desperately tried to make Elizabeth either marry or name a successor in order to provide political stability in the event of her untimely death.

3 Changes to the structure of government

Over the course of the sixteenth century, England's government was transformed. The centralisation of government was one of the most important achievements of the period. This was brought about through changes in the way that the role of parliament was understood. There were changes in the localities as well. For example, Henry VII restored an earlier system of councils in the localities. The Council in **the Marches** and Wales and the Council of the North were used as bases for royal authority in areas that were somewhat hostile to Tudor rule. These were revitalised again by Henry VIII and in the 1560s by Elizabeth following the revolt of the northern earls (see page 101). In the 1540s, parliament passed legislation that extended the English common law system to Wales. This meant that England and Wales shared the same legal system for the first time. Many historians argue that the changes in government brought about during this period changed the country from a backwards place into a kingdom that was more or less a modern state. Over the course of this period, England's government experienced four key changes that led to greater centralisation:

- Parliament was regarded as the most important political institution.
- The government became increasingly bureaucratised.

Burghley and the Privy Council

The Privy Council was established by Henry VIII in 1540. Before this there had been informal groups of nobles and gentlemen who advised the monarch but Henry established it as an institution. Under Henry there were initially 19 members, although this later expanded. Their principal role was to advise the King and execute policy. Elizabeth reduced the Council back to 19 members, selecting reliable and competent men to act for her as professional administrators. Most of Elizabeth's first Privy Council had prior experience of administration. The Council was the Queen's most important source of advice and, as such, it helped to shape national policy. They made the kingdom's important decisions. They issued orders to Justices of the Peace, commissioners and other deputies in the counties. They administered the Queen's finances. Throughout the political process, Burghley thought through the implications of the options that the Privy Council could take. His final recommendations were based on the analyses that he made. During the time that Burghley was Principal Secretary, the role was transformed from that of a powerful man to the spokesperson for a group of powerful advisers.

- The Privy Council became a formalised institution.
- Religion was determined by the secular authorities.

Conclusion

The sixteenth century witnessed the growing importance of administrators and advisers in helping the monarchs to rule. Wolsey, Cromwell and Burghley all helped to shape policy and aided the monarch in making important decisions. When the monarch had made their own decisions (with or without advice) these men attempted to help the monarch achieve their aims. Cromwell, for example, aided Henry VIII in achieving the annulment of his marriage to Catherine of Aragon. They were all ruthless politicians who survived as long as they did by using their political instincts to avoid harm. They helped to shape the positions they held, such as Principal Secretary, and the institutions they belonged to, like the Privy Council. In a period when the Crown's control extended beyond politics to religion, able politicians were needed to support and advise the monarch.

Work together

With your partner, consider the relative impact of Wolsey, Cromwell and Burghley. Individually, read pages 25–30 again carefully and, if necessary, undertake your own research in order to decide who made the most significant impact in the period 1509–88. If you differ, discuss why. Give your reasons and explain why you think the others are less important.

The influence of Wolsey, Cromwell and Burghley

- Wolsey believed in the importance of diplomacy, enhancing the King's and country's prestige
- He was calculating, ruthless and ambitious, but politically creative
- Wolsey encouraged the King to follow his own religious interests
- He was instrumental in the 1518 Treaty of London and the Field of the Cloth of Gold
- He fell from power when unable to secure the papal dispensation
- Cromwell solved the problem of the King's marriage
- He worked closely with the King on his religious policies, e.g. the dissolution of the monasteries
- He fell because of the Anne of Cleves marriage and changing religious climate
- Burghley was a Protestant reformer and lawyer who was Elizabeth I's closest adviser
- Religion helped shape his foreign policy advice
- He tried to persuade Elizabeth to either marry or name her successor
- He was instrumental in the Privy Council

Powers of leading ministers

- The Crown relied on officials to govern
- They advised the monarch, explained events and recommended actions
- The Lord Chancellor was the King's representative in parliament
- The Principal Secretary handled the monarch's correspondence and advised on policy direction
- They had to be reliable and discreet

THE PRINCIPAL SERVANTS OF THE CROWN

Changes to the structure of government

- Parliament became much more important as a political institution
- The Privy Council was formally established and gained in power
- Religion was governed by the secular authorities
- Government became more administrative and bureaucratised

▲ Summary diagram: The principal servants of the Crown

Recommended reading

John Guy, 'Thomas Wolsey, Thomas Cromwell and the Reform of Henrician Government', Chapter 2 in *The Reign of Henry VIII: Politics, Policy and Piety*, edited by Diarmaid MacCulloch (Macmillan, 1995).

Provides a concise and clear comparison of Henry VIII's influential two ministers.

Natalie Mears, 'The Council', Chapter 4 in *The Elizabethan World*, edited by Susan Doran and Norman Jones (Routledge, 2011 and 2014).

Provides an overview of the development of the Privy Council. This essay also addresses themes including foreign relations and the queen's gender.

S. J. Gunn, *Early Tudor Government, 1485–1558* (Palgrave Macmillan, 1995).

This book provides a clear introduction to the huge topic of government in Tudor England. It also presents the research against the backdrop of contemporary European monarchs.

Essay technique: Deploying detail

As well as focus and structure (see page 22) your essay will be judged on the extent to which it includes accurate detail. Detailed essays are more likely to do well than essays which are vague.

What is detail?

Essentially, correct dates, proper names and statistics are all examples of detail. You can also increase the level of detail in your essays by using correct technical vocabulary: words like 'Privy Council' or 'secretary of state' that you have learned whilst studying this chapter.

How to use detail

You should use detail to support the points that you are making. The main points provide the overall structure for the essay, the details help prove the points that you are making.

Imagine you are answering the following question:

> **How accurate is it to say that Thomas Cromwell was the most influential minister in the period 1529–88?**

You might want to make the point that Cromwell introduced reforming policies. You could support this by referring to the dissolution of the monasteries. Specifically, you could refer to the number of monasteries dissolved, the wealth confiscated and the monks and nuns ejected.

Activity: Adding detail

Here is a plan in answer to the question opposite:

- Break from Rome/King's 'Great Matter'.
- Dissolution of the monasteries.
- Reforming policies.
- Wolsey's diplomatic triumph, for example the Field of Cloth of Gold.
- Wolsey raised the profile of the English court through the universities and patronage.
- Burghley consolidated control over finances and the council into the secretaryship.

Using your notes from the previous chapter, find at least three pieces of detail to support each of these points.

Try and select a variety of types of detail: if possible make sure you use statistics, dates, the names of people and organisations, and technical vocabulary.

Question practice

1 Was religion the main reason for Henry VIII's break from Rome? Explain your answer. **AS**
2 How far did Elizabeth I successfully control parliament in the period 1566–88? Explain your answer. **AS**
3 How accurate is it to say that the importance and role of parliament changed fundamentally in the period 1509–88?
4 How accurate is it to say that the power and authority of the monarch expanded dramatically in the period 1509–88?

Theme 2 Religious changes, 1509–88

The Big Picture

The religious situation in England and Wales changed almost immeasurably between 1509 and 1588. Religious traditions, practices and festivities that had been pivotal to parishes over hundreds of years were abolished. The emphasis of worship changed from a visual culture to a written culture. The head of the Church and the position of the Church in relation to the state both altered forever. Everyone from the nobles to agricultural labourers was affected by these changes. The changes did not happen in a linear way. Religion in the later years of Henry VIII's reign was still recognisably Catholic. This changed to an evangelical reforming policy under Edward VI, and back to Catholicism again under Mary. Elizabeth I attempted a compromise but it was one that favoured Protestantism over traditional religion. There was also a remarkable degree of continuity, however, particularly in the religious lives of ordinary people. Depending on where they were in the country, the religious services experienced by most people may well have altered little until Elizabeth's reign. Her success was due to longevity as well as compromise, and the changes she introduced were gradually accepted.

Catholicism was the only official religion from 1509 to 1534. Throughout the rise of the Reformation in continental Europe, England remained firmly traditional in its religious faith. Yet Henry VIII's 'Great Matter' was to disrupt this. Catholics were persecuted under Edward and restored under Mary. However, Catholicism was to suffer again under Elizabeth despite the compromises on some aspects of ritual and music. Catholics who refused to conform to Elizabeth's Church of England were branded 'recusants'. Gradually they were frozen out of positions of influence in local and national government. This did not stop a significant minority from remaining openly Catholic. It also created a new group of 'church papists', those who seemed to conform but practised Catholicism in secret. The persecution of Catholics increased after the papal bull excommunicated Elizabeth in 1570. After this laws against Catholics were made much more severe, but despite this most Catholics remained loyal subjects of the Queen – a fact obscured by several unsuccessful Catholic plots in Elizabeth's reign.

Religious reformers or evangelicals gradually became known as 'Protestants' after 1541. They wanted a reformed or renewed Church with a focus on the scriptures as the word of God. Protestants desired a Church with less ritual, generally aimed to remove religious images, and wanted a plainer fabric of the Church. Early reformers in England were influenced by figures such as Martin Luther and Ulrich Zwingli. They were seen as heretics and punished if discovered. Anne Boleyn's influence did much to change this, as did Henry VIII's need to produce a male heir. Although Henry did not favour radical Protestantism, the education he gave to his heir, Edward, meant that this was the direction taken from 1547. While Protestantism was promoted by Elizabeth it was not enough for some, more radical, reformers. They became an opposition group, pressing for further change, and are now known as 'Puritans'. Due to of their outspoken opposition they were also persecuted by the regime.

In this theme you will consider the following:
→ **The Tudor monarchs and religious change:**
   The changes made by the Tudor monarchs to the religion of England.
→ **Catholicism and its survival:**
   Popular attitudes to Catholicism, the extent of religious changes from 1529 to 1536, the extent to which Catholicism survived in the regions, Catholic recusancy and the Jesuit missions and the role of the Catholic nobility.
→ **Protestantism and Puritanism:**
   Protestant influences in England from 1509 to 1547, Protestantism in the reign of Edward VI, and the growth and significance of Puritanism in Elizabeth I's reign.

TIMELINE

1509 June	Henry VIII married Catherine of Aragon
1531	The clergy agreed that Henry VIII could hold the title 'Supreme Head' of the English Church
1532 August	Thomas Cranmer became Archbishop of Canterbury
1533	The Act against Appeals to Rome passed
1533 March	Henry's marriage to Catherine of Aragon declared unlawful, his secret marriage to Anne Boleyn declared valid
1534	Act of Supremacy
1535	*Valor Ecclesiasticus* – comprehensive survey and valuation of Church lands
1536	Act against the Authority of Rome passed
1536	The Ten Articles reducing the number of sacraments
1536–40	The dissolution of the monasteries
1536–37	Pilgrimage of Grace
1538	Visitations and a limited iconoclastic campaign undertaken by Thomas Cromwell
1539	Act of Six Articles
1543	Act for the Advancement of True Religion
1547	Iconoclastic campaigns by evangelical reformers
1547 November	Act of Six Articles, the King's Book, heresy laws, treason laws and the Act for the Advancement of True Religion all repealed by Edward VI's first parliament
1547	Laws approved dissolving chantries
1548	Cornish rebellion
1548 February	More iconoclastic policies introduced, including destruction of images, lime washing of parish churches
1549 February	First Act of Uniformity, First Prayer Book
1549 June	Prayer Book rebellions
1549 November	Edward VI's third parliament passed three bills for destruction of religious books, removal of shattered images, commission to reform ordinations
1552	Second Act of Uniformity, Second Book of Common Prayer
1553 January	Church commissioners ordered to seize all valuables from parish churches
1553 October	Mary I's first parliament, repealed reforming legislation
1554 April–May	Mary's second parliament, approved Spanish marriage but not heresy laws or punishments for non-attendance at church
1554 November	Cardinal Pole restored England to papal obedience
1556 March	Cranmer executed for heresy
1559 January	Elizabeth I's first parliament refused to reinstate the Royal Supremacy and Second Prayer Book
1559	New religious legislation passed, including the Act for Supremacy and the Act of Uniformity. Recusancy fines introduced
1563	The Thirty-Nine Articles of Religion agreed
1569	The revolt of the northern earls
1570 April	Pope Pius V excommunicated Elizabeth I
1571	Ridolfi plot
1574	Missionary priests started to come to England from the Continent
1580	Jesuit priests began to come to England
1581	Anti-Catholic legislation. Penalties for recusancy hugely increased, Catholic priests subject to treason laws
1581 November	Edmund Campion executed
1583	Babington plot
1585–85	Throckmorton plot
1587	Execution of Mary, Queen of Scots

2a: Tudor monarchs and religious change

Overview

The period 1509–88 witnessed some incredibly significant changes to religion in England and Wales implemented by the Tudor monarchs. After the break from the Catholic Church under Henry VIII, England and Wales saw a stricter Protestantism in the brief rule of Edward VI, then an attempt at a return to Catholicism under Mary I and finally moderate Protestantism under Elizabeth. Although these changes stemmed from the personal decisions, beliefs and policies of the individual monarchs, they were to affect the lives of everyone. They ensured that centuries-old practices, rituals and traditions were meant to be abandoned or changed. The practice of religion affected more than just the spiritual life of ordinary people. Traditional festive calendars had formed the basis for people's seasons, work practices and much more.

Some of these changes were more successful and ultimately had more effect than others. It is important to note that while orders were given and laws made to change religious practice, that didn't mean that the changes necessarily took place everywhere. Catholicism remained strong in parts of the country. Even where Protestantism had been enthusiastically accepted Catholicism did not instantly die out. People were not always open about their feelings towards religious changes. It is believed that many outwardly conformed to the changes but in private they thought and worshipped differently. The desire of the authorities for greater religious uniformity as well as security explains some of the compromises allowed under Elizabeth. The Elizabethan settlement of 1559 was one such compromise. Elizabeth was also prepared to allow translations of the Bible and religious materials into Welsh in order to encourage the Welsh to accept Protestantism and thus secure their loyalty to the state.

This chapter examines religious change by Tudor monarchs through the following sections:

1 *Henry VIII and the end of papal power in England* explores the motivations, context and events of Henry VIII's break from Rome, as well as the consequences of that change for religion in England.

2 *Religious changes under Edward* looks at the changes made by Edward VI in favour of evangelical reform. These were enormous changes to religious practices and the fabric of churches.

3 *Religious changes under Mary* discusses the Catholic restoration under Mary, the role of Cardinal Pole in that restoration, and the impact of the policies. It also looks at the persecutions under Mary and how they fit into the Catholic restoration.

4 *The Elizabethan compromise of 1558–63* examines religious policy in the early years of Elizabeth's reign, and the desire for a more permanent (and largely Protestant) religious settlement.

Note it down

This is a long chapter with many significant dates, events, and policies. Begin your note taking with the 1:2 method (see page x). Put the name of the monarch in the left-hand column, and the policies/events in the right-hand column. Remember the aim is not to copy everything but to select the most important information, such as the causes, main events and consequences of (for example) a policy. You should also begin an annotated timeline here – construct this like a normal timeline but alongside the dates summarise the main events.

1 Henry VIII and the end of papal power in England

Writers, **polemicists** and historians have held different views as to the reasons why Henry VIII opted to change the course of religion in England, breaking from Rome and the Pope. Contemporary Catholic writers thought that it was caused by Henry's desire to divorce Catherine of Aragon and marry Anne Boleyn – he was lustful and immoral. Henry himself claimed that his marriage to Catherine was causing him agonies of conscience. He said he knew that the marriage was wrong, and went against the Bible. This made him feel so guilty and meant that God's judgement was against him. Modern historians such as Richard Rex, John Guy and Susan Brigden agree that the need for an heir was in fact the most pressing reason for the whole situation. Henry knew that for the Tudor **dynasty** to be stable he needed a male heir, and his marriage to Catherine had not produced one. The need for a royal annulment led directly to the Act of Supremacy in 1534 – had the Pope, Clement VII, agreed to an annulment there would have been no break from Rome.

Catherine of Aragon and the English throne

Before examining the **'Great Matter'** that was eventually to lead to the break from Rome, it is necessary to look at the context to this period. Catherine of Aragon and Henry VIII were married in 1509 very soon after he succeeded to the throne. Catherine had been married previously, to Henry's brother Arthur, Prince of Wales. Arthur and Catherine had been **betrothed** since she was three years old and they married in November 1501 when she was 15. The marriage was short lived, however, because Arthur died only six months later in April 1502, aged 15. The marriage was the result of Henry VII's diplomacy drive with Spain. He wanted this alliance with the Habsburgs to continue and so aimed for Catherine to marry his second son, Henry.

Church doctrine taught that the marriage of a widow to the deceased husband's brother was forbidden because of the closeness of the family relationship. It was possible to be awarded **papal dispensation** for such a marriage, however, and this is exactly what Henry VII did. Henry VII obtained a papal dispensation from Pope Julius II, although he chose not to organise the marriage immediately. In fact, Henry and Catherine were not married for another seven years, as Henry looked around for better candidates.

The issue of the papal dispensation and Catherine's earlier marriage would not have come to the fore had the union with Henry produced a male heir. After 15 years of marriage the only surviving child was Princess Mary. Several other children had lived only briefly, including at least one boy. Henry VIII came to see this as a judgement on the marriage and began to explore ways of ending it.

Theological arguments

When Henry VIII first began to doubt his marriage he turned to the Bible to find justifications to support his ideas. There were two key biblical texts that supported his position. Leviticus 18:16 said 'Thou shalt not uncover the nakedness of thy brother's wife: it is thy brother's nakedness.' This he interpreted to mean that sexual relations with his brother's wife was a form of incest. Leviticus 20:21 said 'If a man shall take his brother's wife, it is an unclean thing: he hath uncovered his brother's nakedness: and they shall be childless.' The implications of this text were even more worrying – that the absence of an heir was God's judgement on a sinful and unlawful marriage.

Initially secretly, Henry looked at ways to annul his marriage. This meant ridding himself of the papal dispensation that his father had been granted so that Henry could marry Catherine. He chose to do this not by trying to find loopholes in the dispensation but by arguing that the Pope was wrong to grant the dispensation to begin with. Henry's argument was that it was not in the power of the Pope to grant a dispensation for such a serious breach of divine law. Henry and Cardinal Wolsey asked the theologian and Bishop of Rochester John Fisher for his opinion on the matter of whether the prohibition in Leviticus was part of **natural law**. If it was, then it would not be in the power of the Pope to give such permission.

Unfortunately for Henry, Fisher found that it could not definitely be seen as natural law because in other parts of the Bible (specifically in the book of Deuteronomy) it explicitly supported marrying a brother's widow. Fisher argued that it was so controversial that it was the Pope's place to decide the answer, and given that the preceding pope had made the dispensation, asking the Pope's decision was unlikely to produce a favourable outcome. Just as Henry's position was looking doubtful, Robert Wakefield, a theologian and former protégé of Fisher's, came up with a solution to get around Fisher's argument. Wakefield argued that the command that Fisher identified in the book of Deuteronomy only applied if the first marriage had not been consummated. If the marriage had been consummated, then Leviticus still applied. Unfortunately for Henry, Queen Catherine insisted that it had not. The theological argument lasted for six years and was only resolved when Henry and his advisers found more drastic solutions.

Diplomatic efforts

Initially, Henry VIII and Cardinal Wolsey tried to use diplomacy to end Henry's marriage to Catherine of Aragon. The English bishops Stephen Gardiner and Edward Foxe were sent as royal ambassadors to Pope Clement VII in Rome in 1528. Their mission was to get the Pope's permission for the hearing on the King's marriage to be held in England, presided over by Wolsey. Obviously this was the scenario that was most likely to result in the King achieving his aims.

Charles V and Henry VIII's 'Great Matter'

Pope Clement VII was in a difficult position at that time. In May 1527 the Holy Roman Emperor, Charles V, had invaded Rome and imprisoned the Pope. This meant the Pope was very much under Charles' control, however unwillingly. Charles V was Catherine of Aragon's nephew and, therefore, was strongly opposed to the divorce. Aside from Catherine's hurt feelings, he also had to consider that it would be dishonourable to his family and possibly beneficial to his enemies, the French. At this time the concept of honour was vitally important. Dishonour to one's family was damaging to reputation and status – not something that could be tolerated by the Holy Roman Emperor. An annulment may have benefited the French because Henry was considering a marriage alliance with the French royal family should his attempt to escape his current marriage succeed. The Emperor and the French royal family had been engaged in a long-running series of wars (the Habsburg-Valois Wars, 1494–1559) and for the aunt of the Emperor to be thrown over for the French king's family would be extremely damaging.

Problems facing the Pope

This meant that the Pope was stuck in the middle of two powerful rulers who were both determined to have their own way. He was also reluctant to grant Henry's request because of the manner of his objection to the marriage. His argument that popes did not have the authority to grant dispensations in such a case challenged papal authority. Given events happening elsewhere in Europe, especially the German Reformation, Clement did not want to give any more credit to such challenges. It is likely that, as Catherine was such a pious and devout wife and Catholic, Clement felt that her case had more justice. He was also aware later on that Henry wished to pursue a relationship with Anne Boleyn. As Anne's sister, Mary, had previously been Henry's mistress and had borne him a child, Henry would need another papal dispensation to marry as, in law, this meant they were too closely related.

Clement VII's decision

So Clement did not grant exactly what Henry wished. Instead, he allowed a **papal legate**, Cardinal Campeggio, to go to England to try the case alongside Wolsey. Campeggio first attempted to avoid a court hearing by persuading Catherine to become a nun. If she were to agree to this, Catherine would become a bride of God and Henry would be freed from his marital obligations to her. There is no doubt this would have been agreeable to Henry, Wolsey, Campeggio and the Pope. It was not agreeable, however, to Catherine. She refused, arguing that she served God in the role of a good and devoted wife, not as a nun. This made the court hearing inevitable, and Catherine caused further problems once it began by protesting against the fairness and legitimacy of the court. She sent an appeal to the Pope in Rome, saying that there would be no fair trial in England and asking for the proceedings to be revoked. Her success in achieving this meant that the hearings came to an end, and with them the career of Wolsey.

Henry VIII and Anne Boleyn

Anne Boleyn was charming and witty, attracting Henry VIII's attention when she was a maid of honour to Queen Catherine. She was educated and persuasive, with a strong personality. Anne's sister Mary was one

Anne Boleyn (c1501–36)

Anne Boleyn was the daughter of diplomat Sir Thomas Boleyn and Elizabeth, the daughter of the Duke of Norfolk. From 1513 she was a lady-in-waiting to the Archduchess Margaret in the Netherlands, and then from 1514 she was a lady-in-waiting at court of France, to Queen Mary – King Henry VIII's younger sister. After that she served Queen Claude of France for seven years.

It was during this period that she developed her interest in reformed religion, literature and philosophy and absorbed the etiquette and culture of the French court. Anne returned to England in 1522, initially to marry her Irish cousin the Earl of Ormond, and when those plans failed she was appointed lady-in-waiting to Catherine of Aragon. Her experience, style and education in France made her even more attractive at court. She was also described as a charming and attractive woman. Anne became betrothed to Lord Henry Percy by 1523, though Cardinal Wolsey was quick to end this betrothal by early 1524, partly because Percy's father did not approve of the match. Henry VIII began to pursue Anne from early 1526, and so began the rollercoaster period from pursuit, to marriage, queenship, and execution for Anne Boleyn.

of Henry's previous mistresses, and had borne him a child. Unlike her sister, Anne refused to become a royal mistress. By Easter 1527 Henry was begging her, but she would only consent to becoming his queen. It seems that Henry did eventually promise to marry Anne because by January 1533 she was found to be pregnant. Clearly this made the matter of the royal divorce more urgent. Henry married Anne in a secret ceremony on 25 January 1533.

The expediency of pregnancy was not the only influence that Anne Boleyn had upon the nature of religious affairs in England under Henry VIII. Anne was educated in France and, while there, had been exposed to the ideas of Christian humanism. These ideas had convinced her that **evangelical reform** was necessary in England. This included the translation of the Bible into English, a process prohibited specifically to date. She used her influence with the King and at court to protect reformers. Anne encouraged the King to read the works of evangelical reformers such as William Tyndale in the hope that he too would be converted to the cause. She was instrumental in the fall of Cardinal Wolsey and her faction at court was deeply involved in the promotion of radical solutions to the problem of the King's first marriage.

The Act of Supremacy and the break from Rome

Henry's predicament became increasingly desperate, and the plans to address it more radical. From late 1530 we see evidence that the King's supporters began to question the very authority of popes over kings in their own territories. This argument steadily grew in strength and in September 1530 Henry told the Pope's representative that the Pope could not summon him to Rome for a hearing about his marriage because the Pope did not have the authority to do so – only kings had control in their own territories, not popes. From October 1530 Henry created and consulted a committee made up of lawyers and clergymen to see if he could get a dispensation from the English parliament to divorce Catherine, circumnavigating the Pope entirely. A lot of material was gathered around this time and during these discussions that was to be central to the doctrine of **Royal Supremacy** as implemented a few years later.

The Royal Supremacy

The resulting idea, the Royal Supremacy, was that the king was *both* head of the state and head of the Church. This was a completely new idea. Existing Protestant writings supported it no more than Catholic ones did – even in the middle of the German Reformation. This isn't to say that kings of England had always obeyed the pope – they hadn't, but if they had disobeyed the pope they faced sanctions, such as **excommunication** or **papal interdict**. At the time that the doctrine was formed, Henry was trying to assert control over the clergy who had taken Catherine's side in the argument. These included bishops, influential figures who Henry needed to either silence or persuade. Henry undertook a complex set of manoeuvres to gain royal control over the Church courts. Through threats and manipulation the clergy were put on the defensive. By 1531 they had agreed that Henry could have the title 'Supreme Head' of the English Church. The changes did not stop there, and by May 1532 a conference of the clergy had agreed that the Church was subservient to the Crown in matters of law. Around the same time another **bill** was put before parliament. This became the Act in Restraint of Annates, and was an attempt to strong-arm the Pope into approving Henry's actions. If the Pope refused, by May 1533 the 'annates', the payments of the English Church to Rome, would come to an end and the papacy would lose valuable income as well as spiritual control over an important territory.

Cranmer as Archbishop

The death in August 1532 of the aged and inflexible Archbishop of Canterbury, William Warham, meant that a more agreeable candidate could replace him. That candidate was Thomas Cranmer, a reformer who had been previously favourable to the King. The Pope confirmed Cranmer as Archbishop. In September 1532 Thomas Cromwell had already drafted the bill against appeals to Rome – this would forbid appeals to the Pope (such as Catherine's) and mean that any hearing on the King's marriage would happen in England. This was passed as an Act in 1533. The Church was instructed to declare that consummated marriages to a brother's widow were unlawful, and papal dispensations invalid. The coast was clear for a trial, presided over by Cranmer and bound to be in the King's favour. Henry's marriage was declared unlawful by 23 May 1533 and his secret marriage to Anne Boleyn declared valid. This led to the altering of the succession and the oath to uphold the succession (see page 9). The new Act of Treason was used to prosecute those who refused to take the oath, including Fisher and Thomas More. Both were dead by July 1535, executed for their refusal and convicted of treason. The Act of Supremacy itself, defining Henry VIII's power as Supreme Head of the Church, was passed by parliament in 1534. The final step in the break from Rome was the Act against the Authority of Rome, passed in 1536. The King had achieved his aims. Despite this, his path towards this was neither inevitable nor, at any stage, clear.

Thomas Cranmer (1489–1556)

Thomas Cranmer was born into a minor gentry family in Nottinghamshire. He went to Cambridge in 1503, and was elected to a fellowship at Jesus College in c1510. He had to leave this job when he married, but after his wife died in childbirth he returned. Cranmer entered the Church at this point, becoming an eminent theologian. From 1520 he belonged to a group of academics who discussed the ideas emerging from Luther's Reformation in Germany. This group were to lead the Reformation in England, and included William Tyndale and Thomas Bilney. Through a chance meeting in 1529, Cranmer became involved in Henry VIII's divorce controversy. He was commissioned to write a thesis arguing for the King and defending his arguments with reference to scripture. He married again in 1532 to the daughter of a minor German reformer. He was appointed Archbishop of Canterbury in the same year and ruled in favour of Henry VIII's annulment of his marriage to Catherine of Aragon. He promoted the publication of an English Bible and took a leading role in Edward VI's reforming policies. It was technically his involvement in Edward's plan to change the succession that led to charges of treason being brought against him by Mary I, although his staunch Protestantism would most likely have led to the same result. Cranmer was executed by burning on 21 March 1556.

Consequences of the changes

The legal and religious changes described above had far-reaching consequences:

- Remaining loyal to the Pope and traditional Catholicism became illegal.
- The King's power expanded greatly into new areas such as the Church and ecclesiastical matters.
- The King replaced the Pope at the top of the Church hierarchy. As he was resident in England rather than far away in Rome he was able to enforce policies much more forcefully and consistently.
- It enabled the financial exploitation of the Church by the monarchy, including the diversion of payments like **'first fruits'** to the King rather than the Pope and a new annual tax of revenues.
- This led to the *Valor Ecclesiasticus* of 1535, a comprehensive survey and valuation of Church assets. It was needed to impose the above taxes accurately but also revealed the wealth of the Church to a monarchy that was perpetually stretched for money.
- The most dramatic aspect of Henry's 'Reformation' was the dissolution of the monasteries from 1536–40, an enormous and systematic money-gathering exercise that used the need to reform the monasteries as little more than an excuse for confiscating their wealth.

What was religion under Henry after 1534?

Under Henry VIII the English Church did not make a quick journey from Catholicism to Protestantism. In fact, most traditional Catholic practices remained in place. Some key changes were made, and this must have seemed extremely significant at the time, but in comparison to Edward's policies Henry VIII's religion was very much like traditional Catholicism.

- Defined by the Act of Six Articles 1539.
- Denial of **transubstantiation** defined as heresy.
- Lutheran doctrine of justification by faith alone banned.
- Clerical marriage banned.
- Monasteries dissolved, monks and nuns allowed to repudiate their vows and re-join society.
- Doctrine of **purgatory** abandoned, pilgrimages banned, great shrines, for example Walsingham, destroyed.
- Vernacular scripture approved in form of Great Bible.

2 Religious changes under Edward

Edward had been educated to rule (see page 7) and took the responsibility very seriously. He had studied the scriptures, made notes on the sermons he heard and tried to apply these lessons to his role as king. Edward was an evangelical reformer by inclination and education. He wanted to introduce 'true religion' to his kingdom and reform government and society to remove abuses, for example of the poor. His biblical role model was Josiah, a young king in the Old Testament. He had destroyed **idols** and set up 'true religion' in his kingdom. For Edward to emulate Josiah he would have to make religious changes in England on evangelical lines. His political and spiritual advisers were instrumental in making this happen.

A godly vanguard?

Evangelical reformers knew that the Council set up to rule on behalf of the boy king included evangelicals. As a result, they hoped for a kingdom newly inspired by godly reformation of the Church and of religious worship. They produced tracts and ballads that decried the mass and called for the destruction of images. In 1548 alone 31 tracts appeared that opposed the Catholic mass. They also published many evangelical books calling for greater reform. Out of 394 books published while Somerset was in power (see below), 159 were published by reformers. Evangelicals preached radical sermons that cried out against every aspect of the traditional faith.

Even before government policies regarding religious reform were implemented religious radicals took matters into their hands. Evangelical zealots pulled down religious images, destroyed statues and shrines. In places where they had control they changed the fabric of churches. They whitewashed the interior of churches to remove wall paintings that had terrified, instructed and exhorted generations of worshippers. They removed **rood screens** that were seen as forming an inappropriate barrier between God and the worshippers. They put up the **royal arms** and messages from scripture instead. In reformed Christianity the focus was the 'word of God' – the scriptures of the Bible. Images were seen as false idols, distracting people from the proper worship of God. They aimed to remove the mass, which they also saw as false worship. This created huge tensions in areas where such **iconoclasm** was widespread, largely in London and the south-east, leading to threats of violence against reformers from those who did not agree with them.

Protector Somerset and the evangelical cause

Edward Seymour, Edward VI's uncle, became Lord Protector of the realm and governor of the king's person shortly after the death of Henry VIII. He created himself Duke of Somerset after assuming the role of Lord Protector (see page 6). Somerset and his wife were both evangelicals. They had protected fellow evangelicals during the last years of Henry's reign and after his death became a focus for returning exiles such as John Hooper, Thomas Becon and William Turner. When Somerset became Lord Protector he listened to evangelical reformers' ideas about how to create a Christian commonwealth. He allowed radical reformers to publish books by Luther, Tyndale and Wycliffe (for example) that were previously banned under Henry VIII.

Religious policy under Somerset

Compared to the actions of evangelical zealots outside government, the reforms undertaken by Somerset and the Regency Council were cautious and gradual.

Somerset's early legislation, 1547

The 1538 injunctions of Thomas Cromwell were reintroduced and the clergy were encouraged to use Cranmer's 'homilies'. These were pre-prepared sermons on reforming lines, issued in July 1547. Henry VIII's Act of Six Articles was passed in June 1539 as part of the King's retreat from reforming principles. It reinforced heresy laws and made it clear that Catholic doctrine was the basis of the English Church, not reformed Protestantism. This Act was repealed in Edward's first parliament on 4 November 1547. The Act that was used to repeal the Act of Six Articles also revoked the **King's Book** of 1543, the heresy laws, treason laws, and the **Act for the Advancement of True Religion** of 1543. This repeal made it easier to silence opposition from traditional clergy like Bishop Stephen Gardiner. It must be clarified that the Royal Supremacy was not repealed – in fact it was vital to Somerset and Edward's reforms, giving them the authority to act against Catholic religious practice in the English Church.

Instructions were given for visitations like those imposed by Thomas Cromwell in 1538. The visitors were obedient servants or fervent Protestants, and strictly enforced the destruction of images and other traditional practices now seen as **superstitious**. Sermons were to be preached, pulpits installed in parish churches, and key parts of the services to be in English only.

Laws against chantries

After this, a raft of radical Protestant legislation was passed by parliament. In 1547 parliament approved a law dissolving chantries. Chantries were funds that people paid into in order that they would spend less time in purgatory, the state between heaven and hell that souls were sent to before they reached their final destination.

Purgatory and prayers for the souls of the dead were now seen as superstitious. This scheme was begun by Henry VIII as a way to bring more money into the treasury rather than having purely religious motives. The government confiscated the property and funds of **chantry chapels**. While the money was also useful in Edward's reign – especially for Somerset's wars – the motives given in the legislation were much more explicitly religious.

They referred to men's 'Ignorance of their very true and perfect salvation through the death of Jesus Christ, and … devising and fantasising vain opinions of purgatory and masses satisfactory to be done for them which be departed.' Chantry chapels were physically eliminated from church buildings, a significant change to the buildings themselves.

Edwardian iconoclasm

Further iconoclastic policies were introduced from 11 February 1548. This was a radical demand. The Regency Council demanded that all of the images in churches and depictions of saints in stained-glass windows be destroyed. Lime washing of the interior of parish churches was demanded. The purpose of this was to destroy wall paintings. For generations these had taught the illiterate key Bible stories and parables, in order to inspire and terrify them into behaving religiously. After a few years most parishes gave in to these demands, as well as (in 14 parishes) removing their mediaeval stone altars. Yet while the idea was that the people should consult the scriptures instead of superstitious images, this was difficult for many people in most places. It relied on a level of literacy that simply was not there. Festive traditions and ceremonies were also banned. From January 1548 four seasonal ceremonies were forbidden. Candlemas candles, ashes on Ash Wednesday, palms on Palm Sunday and the ceremony of **Creeping to the Cross** on Good Friday had all been important markers within the English calendar. They were also ways that ordinary people could express their devotion to the Church.

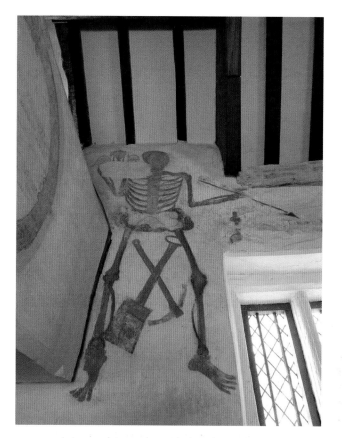

▲ A wall painting of a skeleton, at Llangar Church in Denbighshire. What impact could the destruction of these images have had on the parish church and the congregation? How would the experience of religion have changed for ordinary people?

Iconoclasm

'Iconoclasm' refers to a movement or to incidents where religious images are destroyed, usually in violent outbreaks. It can also refer to hostility to religious images more generally. It was a feature of the Reformation across Europe from c1522 and tended to happen either when Reformation movements were becoming stronger (like under Edward VI of England, from 1549 to 1553) or when it was under attack. Protestant reformers disliked religious images because they believed that people were encouraged to worship the images instead of focusing on God and his words in the Bible. For them the word of God in the Bible was much more important, and the images an evil distraction of the Catholic Church.

Protestant uniformity and the Prayer Book

In Edward's next parliament (24 November 1548–14 March 1549) attempts were made to produce a new and uniform Protestant service that would replace the traditions that were now banned and would instill new loyalty to the Protestant Church. Thomas Cranmer was authorised to prepare a Common Prayer book. The parliament were keen to avoid unrest caused by new developments, so avoided building radical **theology** into the prayer book. Prior to this all preaching had been banned so that official and approved measures could be put in place. The Prayer Book was enforced by the First Act of Uniformity, and those deviating from it could be punished. It was extremely difficult to enforce this Act, however, because the wording of the prayer book was so open.

The Book of Common Prayer, 1549

There had been a **litany** in English (rather than the traditional Latin) since 1544 in response to Henry VIII's command for English prayers to be sung in public processions to pray for his success in his invasion of France. This was composed by Cranmer from a range of sources and was revised in 1547. Controversially, it included the phrase praying for protection from 'the tyranny of the Bishop of Rome, and all his detestable enormities'. A new English 'Order of Communion' appeared early in Edward VI's reign, and it seemed logical for an English prayer book to follow. The Book of Common Prayer published in 1549 was largely written by Cranmer and a committee of 12 bishops and learned men appointed in 1548. It set out the daily offices, readings for Sundays and holy days, and other important services such as communion and baptism. The calendar at the front only commemorated the saints' days of Jesus, the New Testament saints and All Saints' Day. The daily offices of the medieval Catholic Church were reduced to two - matins and evensong. Each service was to include whole chapters of biblical scripture, in keeping with the Protestant concentration on scripture rather than ceremony and images. It was made compulsory to use the Prayer Book in all parishes. It led to the Prayer Book rebellions and Princess Mary refused to use it in her private chapel.

The First Act of Uniformity was followed by more legislation. In February 1549 clerical marriage was allowed, and approximately 20 per cent of priests took the opportunity to get married. This was often for practical reasons rather than because they supported the Reformation, but it did give them a stake in the Reformation in the future. Despite all the changes, however, certain traditional characteristics and practices still remained a feature of the English Church:

- Traditional **vestments** were still used.
- Still rails around altar for priest alone instead of communion table for all.
- Candles on the altar.
- Prayers for the dead.

Somerset and the enclosure riots

Somerset's evangelical advisers advised him to deal with greedy landlords, who they blamed for causing rural poverty through **enclosure**. This led to a commission on enclosure to be set up on 1 June 1548 and a proclamation in April 1549 to enforce laws against enclosure. While it might seem like this was economic legislation, it was inspired by religious views on the causation of distress – evangelicals argued that the greed of landlords in enclosing the commons was part of the Devil's work, the Devil encouraging the love of money and self-love. The Christian people were trampled by such greed and policies were needed to redress that.

The commissions, however, had unintended consequences. In spring and late summer of 1549 there were widespread riots and rebellions. Evangelicals were horrified that at least some of the riots proclaimed themselves to be in the name of the 'commonwealth', previously an evangelical religious term. Kett's rebellion in 1549, based outside Norwich, was motivated by opposition to the religious changes implemented by gentry supporters of religious reform (see page 99). These rebels opposed the abolition of traditional religious practices that they treasured and they rose up to defend them against the government and the evangelical gentry.

The aftermath of the rebellions was to lead to a conspiracy to remove Protector Somerset. Although he had gained popular support from some for his religious stance and attempt to improve the lot of the poor, there were many more who disagreed with his policies on both of those issues. Somerset was replaced by the Duke of Northumberland.

Northumberland and religious policy

Writers and historians have doubted the Duke of Northumberland's commitment to reformed Protestantism. The Duke of Northumberland's desperate conversion back to Catholicism shortly before his execution by Mary I was one reason for this. In fact Northumberland was part of the circle of court evangelicals in the mid-1520s and didn't celebrate mass after the death of Henry VIII. During his time in power he allowed radicals like John Knox to preach at court and appointed John Hooper as Bishop of Gloucester.

Religious legislation from 1549

The march of reformation continued under Northumberland. Conservative clergy were removed, and more legislation was passed to reform the Church. Parliament sat again from 4 November 1549 and passed three religious bills. These contained orders for the following:

- Destruction of missals and other religious books.
- Shattered images were to be removed from churches.
- A commission was set up to reform ordinations.

This process continued in 1550. A new service book was produced for the ordination of new priests. This ordinal showed that some minor positions within the Church had been removed, making it less hierarchical. It also promoted preaching of the gospel, a distinctly Protestant preoccupation.

Changes to the fabric of the Church

Nicholas Ridley, as the new Bishop of London, ordered altars to be taken out of the parish churches in his diocese and communion tables put in their place. Altars were seen as superstitious, and did not reflect the way that reformers believed the congregation should interact with God. By the end of the year this had been enforced in other dioceses around the country.

On 3 March 1551 the Council demanded the confiscation of church plate. Little happened until April 1552 when inventories were ordered to be drawn up in every parish. In January 1553 new church commissioners were ordered to seize all valuables from parish churches except the church linen, bells and chalices. Everything else of high value was sent to London. Less valuable metals were melted down locally and the profits transferred to the capital.

The Second Act of Uniformity, 1552

The final major piece of religious legislation in Edward's reign came in 1552. This was the Second Act of Uniformity. It enforced the newly produced and more radical Second Book of Common Prayer. It required everyone to attend church on Sundays and instructed justices of the peace to prosecute those who didn't use the new Book of Common Prayer.

The Second Book of Common Prayer of 1552 was radical for the following reasons:

- It renamed church services. The service previously known as matins was changed to morning prayer and that previously known as evensong became evening prayer. This replaced 'Catholic' Latin names with English ones.

- The Eucharist or mass became known as Holy Communion or the Lord's Supper.
- Vestments were largely abolished.
- Singing was discouraged – much church music was lost in this period (see page 134).
- The doctrine of transubstantiation was excluded.

The Articles of Faith

It was intended that the Articles of Faith would also have been in place by this point. They were drafted by Thomas Cranmer but were returned to him for revisions in 1552. The final draft was composed of 42 articles, of a distinctly reforming nature. This would have been a statement of the position and beliefs of the English Church under Edward. They were never imposed in Edward's reign because in February 1553 he became ill. Edward died on 6 July 1553. The articles were not forgotten, however, and would form the basis for the Thirty-Nine Articles under Elizabeth.

Edward's reign had been traumatic for Catholics. Some went into exile abroad, while others meticulously noted down the names of those destroying the images and fabric of parish churches. These notes became very useful in prosecuting such people in Mary's reign. Conservative bishops had been removed from their positions, replaced by radicals. Priests were allowed to marry and familiar services completely changed. It must have seemed to many as if the religious world had been turned upside down.

The impact of diplomacy

Somerset could not appear too radical due to the considerations of international diplomacy. England did not want to turn foreign allies against her, such as the Holy Roman Emperor Charles V. He was Princess Mary's cousin and could have intervened in Somerset's military campaigns or waged war against England if provoked. The First Book of Common Prayer was left deliberately open to interpretation so that Somerset could reassure Charles V that the reforms were not radical. The need to appease Charles to this level ended when Northumberland, Somerset's replacement, concluded the Treaty of Boulogne with the French on 24 March 1550. This gave England a new ally and meant that they didn't rely so much on the Holy Roman Empire. It did not mean that Northumberland or Edward could completely ignore Charles, however, as he continued to keep a watchful eye over the treatment of Princess Mary and the question of her being allowed to practise her faith.

3 Religious changes under Mary

Henry VIII's Act of Supremacy of 1534 and the rest of the legislation around it had fundamentally changed the position and beliefs of the English Church. Henry's Church, however, still stuck to many of the basic foundations of Catholicism (see page 39). During his son Edward VII's reign the situation changed significantly and rapidly. Within only six years, absolutely fundamental changes were made to the liturgy, fabric and hierarchy of the Church. Throughout all of this turbulent period Mary had remained constant and faithful to the Catholic Church. She was as zealous for Catholicism as Edward was for evangelical Protestantism. It should not be surprising, therefore, that Mary fought hard to re-implement the practices of the Catholic Church in England from her accession in 1553. She, and from 1554 her adviser Cardinal Pole, instituted a drive for re-Catholicisation that included repeals of Edwardian legislation, changes to Church personnel, censorship, persecution and education. The popular image of 'Bloody Mary' is a very narrow one even in a consideration of her policies on religion.

Note it down

Mary tried to restore the English Church to Catholicism, meaning that a lot of Edward's changes were reversed. Create a table like the one below to help you keep track of the religious changes.

Policy/changes	Edward VI	Mary I
Bishops		
Clerical marriage		
Church fabric		
Religious legislation		
Church lands		

1553: the early stages of Catholic restoration

When Mary defeated Jane Grey's forces and gained the throne in July 1553 it was unclear what her religious policy would be. She had both Protestants and Catholics on her Privy Council and seemed initially inclined towards a more tolerant policy than had perhaps been expected. Her reasons for this are clarified to some extent in Mary's proclamation of 18 August 1553. In it she promised that heretics (in this case Protestants) would not be prosecuted.

She condemned the diversity of opinion regarding religion – for her Catholicism was the only true faith – but felt that persecution simply would not be necessary as most people were Catholic at heart. In Mary's eyes, people had been beguiled into converting during Edward's reign because it was the ruling orthodoxy. Now that she was on the throne, these people would return voluntarily to Catholicism.

Legally, there were measures that needed to be taken to restore the Catholic faith to England. The heresy laws needed to be reinstated and this required the approval of parliament. Without them, Mary could not legally persecute those she saw as heretics even if she wanted to. England also needed to be returned and accepted formally into the Catholic Church again, and absolved of its sins since the 1530s. This could not be done without a papal legate who needed to be appointed to Rome and to travel to England.

While persecution was both undesirable and illegal at this early stage, it was possible for Mary to take action in other areas. These included changing the personnel of the Church, making it a requirement once more for priests to be unmarried, and calling a parliament to repeal Edward's religious legislation.

Mary's early moves towards Catholic restoration

- **The removal of evangelical bishops:** Seven Protestant bishops were removed by Mary. Four of these, Cranmer, Ridley, Hooper and Latime, were imprisoned. Further to this, Cranmer, Ridley and Latimer were forced to debate their ideas and beliefs with Catholic theologians. The intention of this was to show how wrong-headed they were and to humiliate them in the face of the superior learning and doctrines of their Catholic counterparts. This didn't quite work as expected, particularly in the case of Ridley. He managed to defeat 33 Catholic theologians in debate, which proved to Mary the degree of challenge that was facing her as she attempted to reintroduce Catholicism.
- **All priests were required to be celibate:** As explained on page 42, approximately 20 per cent of clergy had married after the First Act of Uniformity in February 1549. These clergy (around 2,000 in number) were now deprived of their livings because in Catholicism priests are required to be unmarried and celibate. These clergy were mostly in the more enthusiastically Protestant areas in London and the south-east. This clearly caused a shortage of clerical manpower as it took some time to train and recruit new, suitable priests to replace them.
- **Repeal of Protestant legislation:** Mary's first parliament sat in October 1553. It had clear objectives as regards the laws passed in Edward's reign. This parliament, therefore, repealed the First and Second

Prayer Books of 1549 and 1552 and the Acts of Uniformity that went with them. It repealed the legislation regarding clerical marriage, communion in both kinds and Cranmer's Forty-Two Articles. This was not unopposed, with a significant number of MPs voting against it, but did succeed in passing through parliament. Mary's second parliament sat from April to May 1554. They were more defiant, refusing to re-enact Henry VIII's Act of Six Articles (see page 39) or institute punishments for non-attendance at court. Neither parliament dealt with the legislation surrounding the Royal Supremacy, which meant that legally Mary was still Supreme Head of the English Church.

Other problems still remained for Mary's government to ponder. The question of Church lands was perhaps the most problematic. Upon the dissolution of the monasteries from 1536 to 1540, their lands had been granted to Henry's supporters or sold to the nobility and gentry. This meant that any move by the Church to reclaim these lands would be highly unpopular with a group of people whose support Mary desperately needed. They were both Protestant and Catholic, and were responsible for much of the government in the localities.

Pole and the re-Catholicisation of England

Cardinal Pole, Mary's cousin, was chosen to be the papal legate responsible for returning England to the Catholic fold. He arrived in November 1554 at a time when Mary's third parliament was sitting. This parliament was due to repeal the Act of Attainder against Pole instituted by Henry VIII because of Pole's opposition to Henry's divorce. It also was prepared to abandon the Royal Supremacy. This same parliament revived the fifteenth-century heresy laws and repealed all legislation against the papacy enacted since the rule of Henry VIII.

On 30 November 1554, Pole began by absolving England and restoring it to papal obedience. The legislative efforts of parliament meant that he was safe and legally able to operate fully as papal legate. He began by addressing the need to reconstitute the Church hierarchy, improve people's understanding of the faith and recreate the fabric of the Church as it had been before Edward. His strategies were systematic, thorough and designed for the long term, and it is important to remember this when attempting a critique of Pole's efforts.

Pole's policies

Pole undertook the following:

- **Bishops:** The surviving bishops removed by Edward – Gardiner, Bonner and Tunstall – were returned to

their offices. New bishops were appointed to replace the reformers removed by Mary in 1553.

- **Seminaries:** Fourteen were set up in order to train new priests to replace those ejected by Mary in 1553. This needed time to take effect, however, even with Pole's efforts to increase capacity at the universities by founding two new colleges at Oxford (Trinity and St John's).
- **Clerical discipline:** Pole wanted to create a less ignorant, better educated and disciplined clergy. He urged his bishops to be role models and good examples of spiritual discipline for their clergy. In this field he had some success, and likely would have achieved more over a longer period. The Twelve Decrees instituted at the **synod** of 1555 commanded residence from the clergy, and ideally **pluralism** would have ended. The manpower shortage meant that an end to pluralism was not possible.
- **Finance:** The Church was impoverished and suffering material decay. Pole made it a priority for his bishops to undertake audits and visitations in an attempt to improve finances.
- **New books:** Pole attempted to produce books to counteract the Protestant Bible. These were intended to instruct people in the Catholic faith, such as the **Catechism**, Catholic New Testament and a *Book of Homilies*.
- **Church fabric:** This refers to attempts to restore Catholic features in church buildings. Rood screens, altars and images reappeared, the mass was worshipped again and the necessary equipment reclaimed or purchased. It is probable that much of this had been hidden or was recoverable, particularly in remote or conservative areas.

Current historical scholarship indicates that these measures did have an effect, and that the restoration of Catholic features to parish churches was particularly successful within such a short amount of time. The restoration of Catholicism was intended to be a long-term process. Nobody had the benefit of hindsight to realise that the reign would be short and the return of Protestantism nigh. These positive administrative moves may well, over a longer period of time, have aided in the restoration of a strong and healthy Catholic Church in England.

Church lands: a difficult question

The question of Church lands remained a thorny one. This was one piece of reforming legislation that was not repealed, and was left unresolved until January 1555. The Pope clearly desired the return of the lands to the Church, as did Pole. Intense negotiation by Philip and Mary did soften Pole's stance, however, and in January 1555 Pole conceded that the lands acquired by laymen after the dissolution of the monasteries would remain in the hands of their current owners. This passed through parliament as legislation and received royal assent on 16 January 1555.

Pole's appointment was to be short lived. He was well respected, highly educated, efficient and very organised as an administrator. He had been abroad for nearly 20 years, however, and did not comprehend (to begin with) the level of change that had happened while he was away. This meant he had unrealistic expectations of what others under him could achieve, and how long it would take them. He failed to understand the degree to which the new ideas and practices had become embedded. He was not an inspirational leader for his clergy and his preference to avoid working with the laity until the problems with the hierarchy were sorted out seemed to confirm that the Catholic Church was remote from the people of the country. Pole became Archbishop of Canterbury after Cranmer's execution for heresy in 1556 but only a year later was summoned back to Rome, his authority removed by a new and hostile pope. Although Pole has been seen in England as an inflexible defender of Catholicism, to the new Pope Paul IV he was too close to being a reformer himself and advocated too many compromises with Protestant groups across Europe.

Persecution, execution and exile

The persecution and execution of Protestants has become one of the defining features of Mary's reign. This is partly because of the number of executions (around 300 Protestants were burned by Mary, compared to two religious radicals under Edward and 12 under Henry VIII) but also because of the nature of the victims – 50 women, and the majority of humble origin. Clearly the numbers were high in comparison to the two preceding monarchs. Yet it is important to remember that the modern horror at the barbaric punishments of the past was not the reason for the opposition at the time. Capital punishment was accepted by Protestants and Catholics as an appropriate method to deal with crime. After the revolt of the northern earls against Elizabeth in 1569 approximately 700 people were sentenced to hang, and the death sentence could be handed down in ordinary circumstances for what now seem like minor offences. The numbers executed also pale into insignificance compared to the anti-Protestant campaigns in continental Europe. Opposition to the burnings was also aided by an extraordinarily successful propaganda campaign by exiled Protestants such as John Foxe. While exiled in Switzerland, Foxe produced his *Acts and Monuments* (better known as Foxe's *Book of Martyrs*) which memorialised anti-Protestant persecution in highly sensationalist terms. It was published in 1563 after the restoration of Protestantism under Elizabeth I. This history of the victors subsequently was highly influential in determining future impressions of Mary's rule as barbaric and doomed to fail as a result of God's judgement.

Cardinal Reginald Pole (1500–58)

Reginald Pole was born into a noble family. His mother was of royal blood. He was a great-nephew of Edward IV and Richard III, and a great-grandson of the 16th Earl of Warwick. He was educated at Charterhouse and his education was partly paid for by Henry VIII. Pole attended Oxford and graduated with his BA in 1515. He was sent to Italy by the King in February 1521 and established a household at Padua where he became friends with a notable group of Renaissance scholars. He corresponded with Pope Clement VII and Erasmus, and returned to England in 1527 to continue his studies. Possibly in order to avoid being drawn into the King's 'Great Matter'

Pole left again in 1529 to study in Paris. Pole felt unable to support the King in his drive to achieve an annulment, but left for the Continent again in 1532 with Henry's blessing. Pole's relationship with the King broke down further while abroad, as he again wrote encouraging Henry not to move further from the Catholic Church. Pole was appointed cardinal in December 1536 and was nominated papal legate to England. This enraged Henry VIII. Pole was sent by the Pope to the Emperor to organise an embargo against Henry in 1539. Pole's family were arrested in 1538 on charges of treason for corresponding with Pole. His mother was executed in 1541. Pole was involved in negotiations to unify the Church in 1540 and 1541, and was seen as a conciliator who wished to compromise on many issues with Protestant reformers – somewhat contrary to his later reputation in England. Mary I's accession led to Pole's return to England and appointment as Archbishop of Canterbury in 1556. After spearheading the Catholic restoration he died during an influenza epidemic in London in 1558, only 12 hours after Mary I's death.

The burnings of Protestants, 1555–58

The executions took place between February 1555 and Mary's death in 1558. Most were of Protestants who refused to conform to the new heresy laws or worship according to the Catholic rite. They were charged with heresy and burned publically as a consequence. There is no doubt that the burnings elicited strong emotions from the watching public. The earliest victims were popular preachers such as Rowland Thomas, executed 9 February 1555. The most well known were the former bishops Ridley, Latimer and Cranmer. Ridley and Latimer died on Broad Street in Oxford on 16 October 1555, with Cranmer following on 21 March 1556. Cranmer had recanted previously and should normally have been spared but was made an example of by Mary, leading him to repudiate all his recantations on the day of his execution. It is probable that the courage of the better known 'martyrs' encouraged the other, more humble, prisoners to maintain their position and suffer death by burning. They saw themselves as God's chosen, with their reward coming to them shortly in heaven. The policy does seem to have been counter-productive in the short term in alienating even moderates from the regime. The executions themselves were highly emotional events and the authorities apprentices, from attending. It helped to prevent unity in the kingdom and, although nobody knows what the result would have been had the regime lasted longer, it damaged the government's attempts to bring England into a state of religious uniformity.

Protestant exiles

From January 1554 approximately 788 reformers chose to go abroad into exile during Mary's reign. Most of them went to cities in Protestant countries such as Switzerland and some of the states in the **Holy Roman Empire**. These included Basle, Frankfurt, Strasbourg and Zurich. A few went to Huguenot cities in France such as Rouen and Caen, while a few others went to the Venetian Republic. In contrast to those executed back home in England, these people were not largely of humble status – such people could not afford to travel overseas. There were two nobles (Francis, Earl of Bedford and Katherine, Duchess of Suffolk) but the biggest group were Protestant gentry. Other groups included clergy, theology students and merchants. John Foxe is perhaps the most well-known Protestant cleric who took refuge abroad, writing his famous *Acts and Monuments* while in Switzerland. A significant number were women (approximately 125) and there were 146 children and 45 servants – indicating that some whole families moved abroad to be able to practise their faith without persecution. This had implications for future theological discussions as English reformers mixed with more theologically advanced continental reformers.

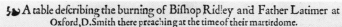

The burning of bishops Latimer and Ridley, from an illustration in John Foxe's *Book of Martyrs*. What impression does this source give of the burnings of Latimer and Ridley? What are the problems with using a source with such Protestant intentions and what useful information does it contain?

Protestants remaining in England worshipped in secret, establishing underground networks to organise Protestant services. As Catholics would under Elizabeth, they worshipped in private houses and sympathetic inns. Some Protestant preachers, such as George Eagles, chose to continue preaching openly but risked arrest and execution through doing so. They communicated with many of those connected or related to the Marian exile, keeping them up to date on matters at home while receiving ideas and news in return.

Impact of Mary's religious policies

Posterity has judged Mary harshly as regards her religious policies – hindsight means that many writers and historians from all periods since 1558 saw hers as an unfulfilled reign whose policies were unsuccessful. Yet they were intended to be long term and methodical. Neither Mary nor her advisers could foresee the short length of the reign and it is impossible to judge long-term policies on the evidence of the short term. In fact, there were good reasons to expect that many were sympathetic to Mary's religious policies. There was a widespread and heartfelt religious conservatism in many areas of England and Wales. The traditional Catholic practices and rituals were familiar to many and were maintained in remote areas despite changes instructed in London. A large group of people clearly conformed to whatever was asked of them in purely legal terms, but maintained a range of other beliefs in private. There is strong evidence that people responded positively to the policies around Church fabric and the re-Catholicisation of parish churches. The burnings were unpopular and counterproductive but did not occur throughout the kingdom. Their impact has possibly been exaggerated by Protestant **polemicists** and their evidence used as the basis for historical accounts.

Mary's attempts to re-establish monasteries in the kingdom were clearly unsuccessful as were other aspects of policy that relied on zeal and enthusiasm. Pole was not an inspirational leader and much more time was needed to replace ejected priests with those educated at the newly established seminaries. Other aspects of Catholic religiosity were difficult to renew. Mary's reign was brief but her policies were remarkably successful.

4 The Elizabethan compromise of 1558–63

Queen Elizabeth herself was educated as a Protestant by her tutor Roger Ascham, worshipped as a Protestant and was generally expected, even by Mary I, to restore Protestantism to England. She was a believer in the theology of Thomas Cranmer, Archbishop under Henry VIII and Edward VI and author of the two Books of Common Prayer published in Edward's reign in 1549 and 1551. Elizabeth was not, however, a radical reformer. She held some beliefs and maintained some practices that were closer to traditional Catholicism. This included the use of candles, an altar rather than a communion table, a crucifix in the chapel, and sacred music in services. Elizabeth was also only too aware that most English people were not reformers. She wanted to create a Church that would be open to as many people as possible within a broadly Protestant framework, a unifying rather than dividing Church.

Note it down

To help you in assessing Elizabeth's reign in relation to religious change, divide your paper into two. On the left-hand side note aspects of Elizabeth's religious policy that would have appealed to Protestants. On the right, note those that were intended to compromise with Catholics. How far was the Elizabethan compromise truly a compromise on the basis of your notes?

Early attempts to prevent religious disorder

As with Mary and her desire to reintroduce Catholicism in 1553, Elizabeth could not act to restore Protestantism without legislation being passed in parliament. She needed to reinstate the Royal Supremacy and introduce the Second Book of Common Prayer (1552) as first steps towards this restoration of reformed religion. She needed to do this for the same reasons as Mary did – to legalise the prosecution of the religious opposition, to legitimise the change, and to formalise the form that the religious settlement would take.

Elizabeth was well aware of the actions of evangelical zealots at the beginning of Edward's reign. On their own initiative and prior to legislation being enacted, they destroyed images and altars and preached radical sermons. It also led to localised unrest between them and the majority Catholic population. The Queen wanted to prevent similar unrest. On 28 December 1558 she took immediate measures to try to avoid radical preachers antagonising a largely Catholic population. She silenced all preachers until parliament had met and religion was settled. Perhaps understandably this did not quiet the fears of Catholics, either clergy or laypeople. It was a very delicate line that Elizabeth had to tread. The changes of the last 20 years meant that some sections of the population would be anxious and unsettled no matter what the religious settlement.

The Elizabethan compromise: the legislative programme

Elizabeth's first parliament assembled in January 1559. She aimed to reinstate the Royal Supremacy and the Second Prayer Book. In this parliament she was unsuccessful. The House of Commons was willing to support the measures but the Lords was not. This was because the Catholic bishops and lords did not want the changes to happen, in particular the return of the Book of Common Prayer. Obviously Elizabeth could not let the House of Lords hold her religious programme to ransom. Her government took the following actions:

- Arresting and imprisoning two of the leading Catholic bishops. The aim was to intimidate the rest of the Catholics in the House of Lords.
- A rigged theological disputation was organised between Catholic and Protestant theologians. It was designed to make the Catholics look obstructive and lose them support.

The government returned to parliament in spring 1559 with a new set of legislation that was intended to be less offensive to the Catholic party. The measures are summarised in Table 1.

This was passed by both Houses of Parliament, though this was by only a margin of three votes. Had the two Catholic bishops not been imprisoned and the Abbot of Westminster absent, this vote would not have been passed.

Elizabeth knew that if the reforms appeared too radical then conservative sections of the population would reject them. She and her government took a great deal of care in how the changes were presented. This was not represented as a new Church but as reforms to the old one. Definitions were kept vague and ambiguous so that it would be acceptable to as many people as possible. Church ceremonies and rituals were maintained to a moderate degree and there was no stipulation that sacred music and ornaments should go. This made it possible that many conservatives could remain inside the Church of England. Many of the Catholic clergy chose to stay within the Church and this may have persuaded their congregation to stay too. Those who refused to meet the stipulations of the Elizabethan compromise were punished. Stubborn Catholic bishops were deprived of their office, and Protestant bishops appointed in their place. Only 300 clergymen decided to refuse the oath and also lost their positions. This effectively removed hardcore Catholic clergymen from the Church and made it easier for the new changes to settle in and be accepted.

This moderate approach to Catholics did not last through the entirety of Elizabeth's reign. The **recusancy** laws that formed part of the Act of Uniformity of 1559 resulted in a range of punishments for those Catholics who persistently refused to attend Church of England services. They were initially threatened with imprisonment and a fine imposed of 12 shillings. Yet as the political and international climate changed this approach was hardened. Catholic plots and the presence of Mary, Queen of Scots until her death in 1587 led to higher fines and harsher punishments for **recusants** in England. From 1570 onwards the term 'recusant' was applied to those who refused to attend Church and further restrictions were placed on Catholics in laws passed in 1593.

Table 1: 1559 legislation

Legislation	For Catholics	For Protestants
Bill for Supremacy Introduced so that the Queen would have control of the Church. Included an oath of loyalty to be taken by clergy. It repealed Mary's heresy laws and established the Commission for Ecclesiastical Causes to impose order and uniformity in religion.	The Queen didn't take the title 'Supreme Head' – Catholics saw the Pope as head of the Church and this was designed to ease their consciences.	Radicals like John Knox did not like the idea of anyone, let alone a woman, ruling the Church as 'head' of the Church as they believed only God was head of the Church.
The Uniformity Bill The 1552 Prayer Book was imposed again for use in all churches. Those not using it would be imprisoned. Church attendance was enforced. Heavy fines were introduced for those speaking out against the Prayer Book.	The Prayer Book was modified so that it allowed for a broad interpretation of the doctrine of transubstantiation that would be more acceptable to Catholics. Words abusing the Pope were deleted from a sequence of prayers called the Litany.	The Prayer Book was a centrepiece of English Protestantism and was vital in imposing Protestant discipline in England.

The injunctions and visitations of 1559

The royal injunctions of 1559 were a set of instructions to the clergy. They laid out what was to be taught, how the clergy should operate and also what restrictions there were upon them. The clergy had to teach the Royal Supremacy and argue against the Pope being head of the Church. Processions and pilgrimages were banned and the clergy had to ensure they did not take place. They demanded that every parish church should buy a copy of the Bible in English rather than keeping the Latin Bible and a copy of a book by Erasmus called *The Paraphrases of the Gospels.* Erasmus was a **humanist** and highlighted problems within the Catholic Church but he remained Catholic himself. With the exception of the purchase of Erasmus' book, these were measures against explicitly 'Catholic' practices. On the other hand, there was some continuity with traditional Catholic practice, such as kneeling while at prayer, bowing at the name of Jesus and that the clergy should wear vestments. These stipulations were not favoured by radical Protestants.

The injunctions also had restrictions on demands of Protestant reformers, however, specifically preaching. Every preacher had to be licensed by the authorities. This meant that the authorities had control over who could preach and under what circumstances. In order to gain a licence a clergyman had to have a MA degree. As the teachings of the universities (at that point only Oxford and Cambridge) were also to a large extent controlled by the government, this meant that it would be difficult for radical preachers to preach legally.

These injunctions were enforced via a series of visitations, like those of Thomas Cromwell in 1538 and of Edward's government. While the injunctions were relatively moderate, the men chosen to enforce them on the visitations tended to be aggressively Protestant. This led to iconoclasm, and the destruction of equipment, images and vestments judged to be Catholic. These visitors also examined the clergy on their beliefs, checking that they were compatible with the Act of Uniformity. As a result, over 400 clergymen resigned or were ejected from their livings between 1559 and 1564.

The Thirty-Nine Articles of Religion, 1563

In 1559 Elizabeth appointed Matthew Parker, former chaplain to Anne Boleyn and a moderate Protestant, as Archbishop of Canterbury. It was he who was to determine the direction of the doctrine of the new Church of England as agreed at the Convocation of the Church in 1563. These Thirty-Nine Articles acted as a statement of the doctrine of the Church. They were largely based on Cranmer's Forty-Two Articles from 1552. They outlined what the Church stood for in relation to Catholicism and more radical Protestantism. Like the Act of Uniformity, they tried to appeal to the widest possible group of people and accommodated some requirements of both faiths. There was concern in 1563 at the frustration of radical Protestants who wanted the reforms to go a lot further, to keep pace with changes in continental Europe. Elizabeth did not intend for this to happen. The Thirty-Nine Articles set out the boundaries within which religion was intended to operate in England from that point forward.

How influential was the Elizabethan compromise on the religious situation in England?

The Elizabethan compromise was of vital importance in determining the future direction of religion in England. It caused great discontent amongst radicals – both Protestant and Catholic – who felt that it did not meet their demands. These groups became alienated from the mainstream Church and were open to prosecution under the Act of Uniformity. For most people, however, there was enough of traditional worship left for them to conform in some way. It is not known how genuinely 'Protestant' a nation it created. As intended, there was enough room within the legislation for fairly traditionalist worship to continue despite key doctrinal changes. One recent and influential idea is that of historian Alexandra Walsham, who argues that as well as stubborn Catholic recusants there were also 'Church papists'. These were people who conformed on the surface and who met the stipulations of the law, but who maintained varying degrees of Catholic practice in private. An examination of correspondence, wills and other manuscript evidence indicates strong support for this idea. As the very point of this approach was to avoid detection by the law (and the penalties imposed by the recusancy laws) it is very hard to gauge the size of this group. They were reviled by both the Catholic Church and Protestant reformers – by Catholics because they were not ideologically and morally strong enough to resist conforming, and by Protestants because their conformity was not real.

Catholic recusancy

As the older, formerly Catholic, priests died out and were replaced with young and enthusiastic Protestant clergy, the parishes across England and Wales were consistently ministered to in a more reformed fashion. Slowly but surely traditional practices in many places either died out or became more anachronistic. This drove some to exclude themselves from the Church but many had got used to it and now saw it as a symbol of the nation – something to differentiate England from the countries across the seas, something to be proud of and support in its own right. Events such as the Spanish Armada and, more generally, the enmity with Spain aided in the creation of an anti-Catholic tradition. Encouraged by the government as a way to ensure political loyalty, this antipopery tended to depict Catholics as a danger to the populace and as potential traitors. There is no doubt that this captured the popular imagination at times of crisis, even as many people were apparently able to differentiate 'Catholics' as the enemy from their relatives or local gentry who continued to worship according to the Catholic faith.

In any case, the Elizabethan compromise became (for good or ill) the foundation of the Church of England as it still is today. Its ambiguity enabled many to feel able to stay within the Church, and it could be seen as a strength that so many different views have co-existed within the one organisation for hundreds of years. On the other hand, its openness has also been a problem. It has often been argued that in trying to be everything to everyone, the Church of England was satisfying nobody entirely. The ambiguities caused conflicts between different wings of the Church in Elizabeth's time and ever since. It is difficult to argue, however, that the Elizabethan compromise was not extremely significant as a turning point in the religious, political and social history of England and Wales.

Conclusion

The people of England and Wales experienced huge changes from the 1530s through to the 1560s. Although the impact on religious practices in parishes around the country varied greatly, the demands of the government (whether for Protestant or Catholic policies) would have been known and experienced by most people. The beliefs and desires of the Tudor monarchs had a significant impact on these religious changes, and were often a driving force behind radically varying religious policies. Although the Elizabethan compromise was an attempt to put an end to divisions and disputes about religion, it did not work for all. Nevertheless, it did embed some of the Protestant policies that had made

a fleeting appearance in Edward VI's reign. Religion in England and Wales changed permanently after Elizabeth's reign.

Work together

Work with the timeline at the beginning of the theme (page 34) or with your own if you have made one. In pairs, take it in turns to explain each event in the timeline. Explain why the event happened, what the main events were and what the consequences were. If there are any that you can't remember, note them down and revise them together.

Recommended reading

Susan Brigden, *New Worlds, Lost Worlds: The Rule of the Tudors 1485–1603* (Penguin, 2001).

There is much in this accessible and interesting book that will be of use to students of this module, but Chapters 4, 6 and 7 have much relevant and valuable material on religious changes in the period.

John Guy, *Tudor England* (OUP, 1988).

Chapter 5 is an excellent summary of the events leading up to the break from Rome.

Ronald Hutton, *The Rise and Fall of Merry England: the Ritual Year, 1400–1700* (OUP, 1994).

This is a fascinating read as a whole, but Chapter 1 is particularly useful regarding English religion and ritual before 1540.

John Lotherington (editor), *The Tudor Years* (Hodder, 2002).

Chapters 6 and 7 are very worthwhile for looking at religious policy in the reigns of Edward VI and Mary I. Chapter 15 is excellent for the religion of the people of England.

Richard Rex, *Henry VIII and the English Reformation* (Palgrave Macmillan, 2006).

Chapter 1 is a useful exploration of the divorce and the Royal Supremacy.

Henry VIII and papal control in England

- Henry VIII was desperate to have a male heir to continue the dynasty
- After 15 years of marriage to Catherine, his brother's widow, he only had one daughter, Mary
- He hunted for theological arguments to support the end of this marriage
- He tried to use diplomacy with the Pope, but the Pope was facing his own political problems
- Anne Boleyn's pregnancy made the situation more urgent and more drastic solutions were sought
- The Royal Supremacy was the solution, making Henry VIII head of Church and state
- This meant appeals to Rome would be forbidden and the marriage was declared unlawful at trial
- Although a lot about religious practice remained the same, there were some changes relating to transubstantiation, monasteries and removal of scripture

The Elizabethan compromise of 1558–63

- Elizabeth I was a moderate Protestant who also maintained some traditional practices
- In order to pass measures restoring the Royal Supremacy and prayer books, she had to remove Catholic bishops and amend the legislation
- The Acts of Uniformity, Prayer Book and Royal Supremacy were introduced
- The rules for worship were kept ambiguous so some traditional practices could remain
- The recusancy laws were introduced within the Act of Uniformity to punish Catholics
- Visitations happened in 1559 to enforce the legislation
- The Thirty-Nine Articles were adopted as a statement of doctrine

TUDOR MONARCHS AND RELIGIOUS CHANGE 1509–88

Religious changes under Mary I

- Mary was a staunch Catholic and aimed to restore Catholicism
- Early on she removed evangelical bishops, made celibacy a requirement for priests again and repealed Edward's Protestant legislation
- After Pole returned in 1554 he introduced reforms to seminaries, clerical discipline and Church finance
- Pole attempted to restore the Church fabric to as it was before Edward's changes
- Church lands were not recovered because the government needed the support of the gentry
- Some Protestants went into exile, while some radicals who remained in England were burned as traitors
- The restoration seems to have been fairly successful given Mary's short reign

Religious changes under Edward VI

- Reformers started implementing radical changes even before the government did
- Early legislation repealed Henry VIII's heresy and treason laws
- Iconoclasm was introduced, chantries were banned and priests were allowed to marry
- Through the two Acts of Uniformity (1549 and 1552) and the Books of Common Prayer, Protestant worship was enforced
- There were changes to the fabric of the Church, which increased as the period progressed
- Some Catholics went into exile

▲Summary diagram: Tudor monarchs and religious change

Question practice

1 Was religion the main motive for Edward VI's attempt to change the succession? Explain your answer. **AS**

2 How successful were efforts to introduce Protestantism to England from 1549–88? Explain your answer. **AS**

3 How far was popular pressure the most fundamental reason for the religious changes of the period 1547–63?

4 How far were the religious policies of the monarchs responsible for the rebellions in the period 1536 to 1569?

2b: Catholicism and its survival

Overview

For a long time the history of the Reformation in England and Wales focused on the political interventions of the monarchs in the mid-sixteenth century. The impact of these interventions on ordinary people was not explored to the same extent. It was assumed that there was a straightforward journey from Catholicism to Protestantism, with an associated rise of anti-Catholicism. Research since the 1970s has contradicted this simplistic story. It has demonstrated that there was not just a binary choice of Catholicism and Protestantism in this period but that the choice should instead be seen as a spectrum. Some people remained wedded to Catholicism in every way, becoming known as **recusants**. They were supported from the 1570s by missionary priests or **Jesuits**, and by the Catholic nobility. During Elizabeth's reign the distribution of Catholics became more limited. Certain areas in the north, south-west, Wales and the borders sustained more numerous Catholic communities for a longer time, although there were pockets distributed across the country even then.

Others became radical Protestant reformers and wanted more religious change. Most of the population was somewhere in between these two positions. Many conformed outwardly to the religious changes ordered by the government but remained attached to traditional practices and continued them in secret, particularly early on in the period. Others picked and chose elements from either tradition. Religious practices also varied in different areas of the country, with Catholicism remaining strong in some areas even into the seventeenth century. The story of Catholicism in England is complex but fascinating.

This chapter examines Catholicism and its survival through the following sections:

1 *Popular attitudes to Catholicism* explores the attitudes of the majority of the population to Catholics and Catholic worship under the Tudor monarchs. It looks at how and when attitudes changed.

2 *The extent of religious changes 1529–36* examines how far religion changed under Henry VIII from traditional orthodox Catholicism to reformed Protestantism.

3 *The survival of Catholicism in the regions* looks at the extent to which Catholicism remained strong in regions outside London and the south-east. It also looks specifically at Wales, for which policies were especially constructed in Elizabeth's reign in relation to its religious preferences.

4 *Recusancy and Jesuit missions in Elizabeth's reign* explores the changing strategies of Catholics after the 1570s. It examines the impact of missionary priests sent to look after and re-convert English people to Catholicism.

5 *The role of the Catholic nobility* looks at the way that some members of Catholic elites supported fellow Catholics, sheltered priests and occasionally took part in rebellions in support of Catholicism.

1 Popular attitudes to Catholicism

In the popular imagination of recent times Catholicism was seen as a foreign faith – not relevant to or part of what it meant to be English. This is testament to the success of Protestant policies and propagandists since the time of Henry VIII. At times of crisis, like the Spanish Armada (1588), English Civil War (1642–47) and **Glorious Revolution** (1688), Catholics were portrayed as the enemy – and English or Welsh Catholics as possible traitors and betrayers. Yet this would have been unimaginable in 1509 and implausible to all but a minority until the reign of Elizabeth I. This section explores changing attitudes and responses to Catholicism from Henry VIII to Elizabeth I.

> ### Note it down
>
> Make notes on the following questions as you read through this chapter:
> - How did the population experience the Catholic Church before 1534?
> - How did people respond to the changes made by Henry VIII?
> - Why did the changes cause such fear and uncertainty?
> - What was the response to the Catholic restoration?
> - How did Elizabeth's reign change this situation?

The Catholic Church in England before the Act of Supremacy

Late medieval **piety** was vibrant, not decaying or drastically unpopular. In fact, this is one of the big questions that historians still grapple with – why, given the vibrancy of the Church and the unwanted nature of the Reformation, did it become such a success in the longer term? Religious culture in England before the Reformation was festive, rich and lively. Processions, images, pilgrimages and rituals were central to the everyday lives of ordinary people. Their seasons were defined by the Church rituals such as Creeping to the Cross at Easter and the processions on local or national saints' days. These traditions were not forced upon people or signs of blind conformity. People chose to celebrate some aspects of late medieval Catholicism more than others, depending on where they lived. Local traditions and practices ensured that there was no uniform approach, no matter how much the Church would have liked it. Most parishioners seem to have been satisfied with their local clergy and there are minimal signs of **anticlericalism** except where specific priests were deemed to have behaved badly.

Yet critical voices were being raised – **evangelical reformers** criticised aspects of traditional Christianity and called for a different approach (see page 40). The challenge raised by these voices, particularly after they achieved influence in the late 1520s, was to be profound and long-lasting for those who still held traditional beliefs.

Popular responses to the Henrician Reformation

In political and legislative terms the Reformation began with Henry VIII's Act of Supremacy of 1534 and associated legislation in the mid-1530s (see page 38). There were evangelical reformers operating in England in the 1520s but they were very few in number and were frequently imprisoned and persecuted as heretics (see page 66). Henry VIII's 'Great Matter' and his relationship with Anne Boleyn was to change all of that. The King's adoption of some reforming theology and practices within the English Church, his attacks on the papacy and the break from Rome all led to reformers enjoying a period of importance and favour. Yet this did not mean that the majority of the population of England and Wales was affected significantly by the changes. Even the King saw his new Church as a balance between Catholicism and reform, with the emphasis more on Catholic practices.

The reforms led to much confusion and uncertainty in English parishes – it was unclear to many what was now allowed, and what was not. Purgatory had been abandoned as a doctrine, but that did not stop most people continuing to fear it. An iconoclastic campaign in 1538, although limited compared to its equivalent under Edward, caused fear and bewilderment. Relics were seized, such as the piece of the noose which hanged Judas from Caversham in Berkshire. The pagan image of Dderfel Gadarn was confiscated from Llandderfel in Meirionedd and taken to London, then used to kindle the fire that burned a Franciscan friar, Friar Forest, in May 1538. These images of beauty and piety belonged to the community and their loss was felt sincerely. Their replacement by the English Bible was simply insufficient due to the high levels of illiteracy that rendered it irrelevant to many. There was also trauma experienced at the orders to abandon beliefs that had conferred comfort and hope. With short life expectancy and the potential terror of hell, the abolition of doctrines of purgatory and the removal of the saints who they believed could intercede in their favour meant that a safety net had been removed. One other royal injunction that caused widespread dissatisfaction was that of 1536 that restricted the number of holy days. Besides increasing the number of working days this also affected some local seasonal customs and festive culture.

The Pilgrimage of Grace

The Pilgrimage of Grace (late 1536 to early 1537) provides some evidence of popular feeling at the religious changes instituted under Henry VIII. This Yorkshire rising, alongside a slightly earlier Lincolnshire rebellion, was a protest against Henry's religious policies (see pages 95–97). Specifically, the rebels were angry about the break with Rome and the dissolution of the monasteries, alongside economic and political grievances related to poor harvests and the royal divorce. The local monasteries were important religious centres as well as being central to the local economy. Ordinary people worshipped and worked for the monasteries and they were correctly apprehensive about the sale of Church lands to the nobility and gentry. Recently, historians such as Andy Wood have argued that it was the ordinary people who were the force behind these risings. If so, this indicates that the relatively minor changes under Henry (as compared to Edward's reforms) still caused considerable opposition.

This indicates that during the reign of Henry VIII Catholicism was still the religious choice of the majority of England. It was identified with familiar and popular practices, rituals and beliefs and was not yet alienated from the people. In some areas of London and the south-east this began to change but, in general, Catholicism remained strong on the eve of the Edwardian Reformation.

Catholics during the Edwardian Reformation

The reign of Edward VI was an opportunity for evangelical reformers to create a new society; to reform worship (as they thought) to bring the word of God to England and Wales; to cleanse the kingdom of the 'corruptions' of Rome. Through a series of legislation (see pages 39–43) Somerset, the Regency Council and Northumberland completely remodelled the practices and fabric of the English Church. There is little to suggest that these reforms had widespread popular support. Many more changes were made by Edward's governments than by those of Henry VIII. The changes were also more far-reaching. They assaulted elements central to English Catholic worship including the use of images, the liturgy, clerical marriage and the appearance and furniture of parish churches. These changes were carried out via legislation. This meant that they were legally enforceable, so anyone maintaining traditional Catholic practices was open to prosecution. The surviving evidence (a very small percentage of the whole) does suggest that many parishes obeyed the government's instructions, at least on the surface. Since the vast majority of the clergy were the same as before the changes it is unlikely that every parish changed the way that it worshipped; this would certainly have been possible in more remote areas.

In the south-east of England and in London there were spontaneous outbreaks of iconoclasm in 1547, attacking images and altars (see page 68). Some of the revolts also had evangelical overtones and made evangelical demands. This indicates that there was some popular feeling behind the Protestant measures introduced by Somerset, but they were still the actions of a minority rather than widespread across England. On the other hand, there were also rebellions against the reforming religious policies. There was a serious rebellion in Cornwall in 1548 caused by the injunctions to list all possessions of parish churches – people feared that confiscation of property they saw as belonging to those communities would be next. In June 1549 the county rebelled again, alongside Devon, in response to the introduction of the First Prayer Book, aiming to defend their traditional religion. They saw it as an attack on local culture as well as on the religion that formed a vital part of that (see pages 98–99). From this it must be assumed that popular attitudes towards Catholicism (or traditional religion, as it was mostly likely seen by most people) were generally either positive or neutral.

A return to Catholicism: Mary I

Edward's reign had lasted only six years but it was long enough to cause significant damage to the Catholic Church in England. The effect on traditional festivities, Church fabric and aspects of belief was significant. The evidence is, however, that it was not a popular Reformation. The grassroots evidence of Catholic restoration after 1553 is impressive, as is the fact that there were very many more professed Catholics by the time of Mary's death than there were convinced Protestants when she came to the throne in 1553. Unlike Henry and Edward, Mary faced no large-scale regional revolts about religion. Wyatt's rebellion of 1554 was concerned specifically with the Spanish marriage rather than the restoration of Catholicism (see page 12). The seasonal festivities of early Tudor England returned under Mary I, seemingly spontaneously. Many parishes were quick to purchase new equipment to celebrate the mass and obeyed the drive to re-Catholicise the English Church. Wealthy **patrons** and the devout donated religious books and equipment for churches, and shrines were rebuilt through donations. This does not suggest that there was a widespread movement away from Catholicism under Edward. As many Protestants did under Mary, Catholics had seemingly conformed under Edward only to return to their preferred form of worship when it was no longer forbidden.

It is true that some English people were convinced by the policies and preaching during Edward's reign. They were mostly based in the south-east of England and in London. They were spread across all social groupings. These evangelical reformers were clearly anti-Catholic, although it seems they were generally able to live within communities of those who did not agree with them unless they were conspicuous or clearly broke the law.

Changing attitudes to Catholicism under Elizabeth

The English Church of the 1560s retained many aspects of traditional religion as well as of reformed Protestantism (see page 50). In many places traditional rituals and cultural events continued, such as the tolling of bells for the souls of the dead and mystery plays at Corpus Christi in towns like Chester and York. Images and altars were not quick to disappear, and the physical reforms of parish churches took a long time to be complete (if they ever were in some places). The ambiguity of the Elizabethan compromise in 1559 gave a lot of room for manoeuvre. Changes were also slow because people were unsure if there would be a return to Catholicism after Elizabeth's death because she was single and the succession was uncertain. The monarch and the people were seemingly in tune in the 1560s. Elizabeth was keen to encourage Protestantism but not at the expense of unity and stability.

From 1570 this situation began to change. The political and international situation was gradually altering, making it more and more difficult for people not to take sides in the fight between Catholicism and Protestantism – particularly in continental Europe. Confessional identities were sharpened by the more reformed Thirty-Nine Articles of 1563, the Council of Trent in 1564 and most of all by the papal bull of 1570. This papal bull declared Elizabeth a heretic and absolved all her subjects from obedience to her. This increased the government's fear of Catholics and also provided challenges for Catholic subjects who wanted to obey the Pope – who should they stay loyal to?

The impact of Catholic plots

A number of Catholic plots (however unsuccessful) also hardened attitudes. The 1569 revolt of the northern earls, aiming to restore Catholicism, led to its leaders being executed and several prominent participants fleeing to Paris and exile. Scottish Catholic supporters of Mary, Queen of Scots, also stayed in Paris. This worried Elizabeth's regime and increased suspicion of Catholics at home in England. The Ridolfi plot in 1571 tried to replace Elizabeth with Mary, and led to further distrust. The Babington plot of 1583 and the Throckmorton plot of 1585–86 provoked even more anti-Catholic feeling, as these also aimed to assassinate Elizabeth and replace her with the Catholic Mary, Queen of Scots. Mary was finally executed by Elizabeth in 1587. Government suspicion of its Catholic subjects alienated many of them from the regime, especially as they were increasingly removed from local and national government posts that their families had occupied for decades. It also encouraged more general anti-Catholic feeling among the population. As the Church of England increasingly became a symbol of the English nation, attacks on it and the Queen became unpopular and unpatriotic. Although this didn't necessarily mean that Catholics were ostracised in local communities, it did increase tensions and make it harder for them to practise openly.

Anti-Catholic legislation

This was worsened by the anti-Catholic legislation introduced from 1581. After the Jesuits and missionary priests began to enter England secretly with the aim of re-converting people to Catholicism, laws were passed to render this treason (see page 61). In the same legislation financial penalties for **recusancy** were hugely increased, from 12 shillings to £20 pounds – a huge sum in the 1580s. Local officials were instructed to find and prosecute Catholics,

confiscating their religious equipment and arresting their priests. The relative tolerance of the 1560s had passed, and anti-Catholicism was the order of the day. This did not mean that all English people suddenly became anti-Catholic. Most people had some Catholic relatives, there were still pockets of Catholicism around the country and ideals of kinship and neighbourliness meant that Catholic people still formed part of local communities. It did become less safe and less acceptable to be Catholic, however, and those harbouring priests risked execution for treason. As more people became convinced Protestants, that risk increased.

2 The extent of religious changes 1529–36

Religious causes played their part in the break from Rome and the Act of Supremacy, but the main cause was Henry's need for a male heir (see page 9). The religious laws made by Henry in the period 1529–36 related to the King's power in relation to the Church and to the clergy. Not many aspects of the legislation in this period related to changes in religious worship itself. The most significant change was the abolition of purgatory. Thomas Cromwell's injunctions of 1536 took a moderate stand against images in churches and religious pilgrimages. The number of holy days was also reduced, and that induced popular resentment because of the effect that it had on working practices and seasonal customs. The 'Ten Articles', also of 1536, reduced the number of sacraments from seven to three, causing confusion about the impact of it in churches. The clergy were instructed to preach in favour of the changes and against the Pope. All these changes were enforced systematically by visitations, such as those organised by Cromwell in 1538, to ensure that royal religious policy was carried out. There was relatively little large-scale resistance to these changes, but there was widespread discontent. Only the most stubborn were severely punished – but this still led to over 300 people being executed as a result of the treason laws between 1532 and 1540 in relation to the Royal Supremacy.

Despite this, religious worship itself changed little in the period 1529–36. Henry's Act of Six Articles enforced traditional heresy laws against radical reformers and the form of worship remained Catholic. Churchwardens' accounts and other parish sources tell us that most of the traditional rituals and ornaments remained up until the end of Henry's reign. Parishes continued to buy traditional religious equipment such as vestments, altar cloths and crucifixes. While there were significant changes to the government of the Church and for the clergy, Catholicism remained the basis of religious worship in England during 1529–36.

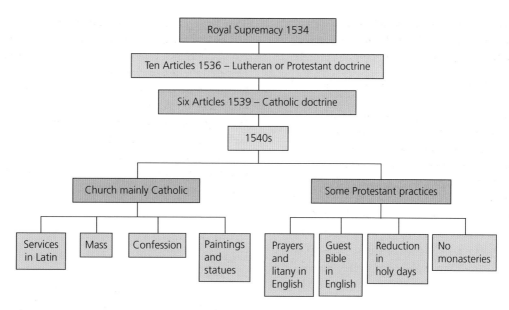

▲ Figure 1: Henry VIII's religious legacy

3 The survival of Catholicism in the regions

Throughout the majority of the period 1509–1603 the survival of Catholicism was not confined to 'the regions' – the majority of the population maintained their loyalty and affection for traditional conservative religious practices. Indeed the pro-Catholic risings in Yorkshire and Lincolnshire in the Pilgrimage of Grace, as well as in Cornwall and Devon in 1548 and 1549, are evidence of the strength of feeling about religious belief in these areas. It is true, however, that Catholic communities survived much longer outside London and the south-east once Protestantising measures had taken effect in Elizabeth's reign. These regions also maintained a more vibrant and consistent Catholic culture that was to last, to some degree, into the seventeenth century and beyond.

'The regions'

So what is meant by 'the regions'? Generally it is a term used to describe parts of England and Wales that are far away from London. These include Yorkshire, Lancashire, Cornwall, Devon and the counties of Wales. Radical reformers and later Puritans saw these areas as the 'dark corners' of the land – where the light of 'true religion' had not shone. They retained strong Catholic communities and beliefs for longer, and once the majority of the population had joined the Church of England they remained highly religiously conservative. In the north of England former monks and nuns served parishes using the Catholic rite, and these parishes were later to remain centres of illegal

Catholicism. Radical Protestantism had little chance or popular following in these parts of the country.

Outward conformity vs recusancy

As has been explained, there was not just a stark choice of Catholicism or Protestantism from 1536 onwards. Many chose to conform outwardly with stipulations about Protestant worship, while maintaining strong sympathy for traditional religion. Some believed that this outward conformity was wrong and hypocritical. They maintained their Catholic beliefs outwardly, worshipped illegally in private chapels and houses, and refused to attend Church of England services. They continued to go on pilgrimages and educate their children in the Catholic faith. These people were known as 'recusants' from the 1570s onwards, and were increasingly harassed with fines and imprisonment as fears about foreign Catholic enemies and Catholic plots continued. These were exacerbated by actual risings like that of the northern earls in 1569 (see page 101) and the Ridolfi plot in 1571, which had the aim of restoring Catholicism. Lancashire, the North Riding of Yorkshire, parts of Worcestershire and Monmouthshire remained strongholds of Catholicism for at least 200 years afterwards.

Catholic worship was easier in more remote areas as it was difficult for the authorities in London to find out what exactly what was happening in every parish, especially those far away from the capital. This made it less difficult for whole villages or areas to remain broadly Catholic, sustaining themselves through networks of fellow believers. Gentry houses (especially those with secret or private chapels) were often used as venues for worship, and these services included more humble people as well as the gentry themes. As measures against Catholics became ever more restrictive these networks increased in importance – and became a fixation of the government in the process, representing a possible threat in terms of plots and rebellions.

Catholicism and religious conservatism in Wales

The Elizabethan government was particularly afraid of the survival of Catholicism in Wales. The Welsh had been extremely reluctant to abandon traditional Catholic beliefs and practices and stubbornly refused to change. This was particularly worrying for central government due to the geographical position of Wales and its long coastline. The fear was that, should Wales remain Catholic, it would open England up to Spanish invasions – presumably because Wales would aid their Catholic co-religionists. This led the government to take drastic action to ensure that the Welsh did convert. Although the Welsh language had been forbidden in the courts and all officials had to (in theory) be able to speak English since the Act of Union in 1536, the English government sponsored the translation of the Bible into Welsh. The New Testament was translated by William Salesbury and published in 1567, with Bishop William Morgan's translation of the whole Bible following in 1588. Translating the Bible into the vernacular was an important part of Protestant ideology but this had been avoided by English governments who, above all, wanted uniformity. While the translations and accommodation of the Welsh language seem like common sense today, they were radical in the mid-sixteenth century. No other part of the British Isles was granted the same exception.

This was a sensible move. Well over 80 per cent of the population of Wales spoke only Welsh. English preaching and written materials would have no use or appeal to them. Alongside this, Welsh humanists nurtured and encouraged origin myths about the Church of England representing a return to the original **Celtic Church**. These myths encouraged the Welsh to think of the English Church as their Church, as the Church of the ancient Britons, as the Welsh were sometimes referred to. Gradually this does seem to have worked, and by the seventeenth century the Welsh were so loyal to the Church (albeit a very conservative form of it) that they were prepared to fight to preserve it and the monarchy in the civil wars that broke out in 1642. It also was important in preserving the Welsh language.

This did not mean that Catholicism died out, more that the numbers reduced. Worship in most areas of Wales continued to be extremely traditional and conservative. Images and crucifixes survived in Wales even in Church of England worship well beyond the Elizabethan era. Some cults of saints continued to be popular, such as that of St Beuno at Clynnog Fawr on the Lleyn peninsula. His cult remained active as late as 1589. In reports to the Archbishop of Canterbury in 1567 the Bishop of Bangor reported the use of candles, altars, relics and processions in remote parts of his diocese. The candlelit dawn service known as 'plygain' persisted in North Wales, and is still held in places today. North Wales was home to many holy wells, including the famous shrine at Holywell known as St Winifred's Well. This was a great pilgrimage centre and drew Catholics from across England and Wales to seek medical cures and ask the saint for her blessing. It was the subject of hostile reports from successive bishops over the years, and was of enough concern for the Privy Council to issue instructions to destroy it on several occasions from the reign of Henry VIII onwards. Welsh religion and the survival of Catholicism in the principality remained a concern long after the death of Elizabeth.

4 Recusancy and Jesuit missions in Elizabeth's reign

From 1570 the Catholic Church made increasingly organised efforts to bring England back to Catholicism. The most significant effort was that to send missionary priests and Jesuits to persuade the English people to re-join the Catholic faith, and to do so openly. 'Church papists' were no good to the Catholic Church – they didn't want people who practised the religion in secret but those who were openly and proudly Catholic. This was because they believed the compromise of partial conformity with the Protestant Church was sinful and hypocritical, but it was also encouraging to others if a significant population declared themselves to be Catholic. From 1574 missionary priests were sent from the Continent upon a religious mission to England, followed in 1580 by their rivals the Jesuits.

> ### Note it down
> Create a spider diagram (see page x) for this section. Label the 'legs' as follows: aims of the missionary priests and Jesuits; threat posed by missions; government response to the missionary priests' and Jesuits' arrival. Now make notes using these themes to help structure your thoughts on this section.

Missionary priests

From 1574 onwards missionary priests came to England in order to convert people back to the Catholic faith. They mostly came from the seminary at Douai in the Netherlands, founded in 1568 by Cardinal William

Allen. It was set up to establish an English mission to serve the surviving Catholic families among the nobility and gentry and to reconvert the English people. These were secular priests rather than Jesuits, who didn't appear until 1580. Elizabeth's government saw this as a serious threat. This was partly because they wanted to maintain Protestantism as the religion of the country, aiming to convert people to Protestantism rather than losing them to Catholicism again. The missionary priests were also seen as a threat because, although the priests themselves were English, they came from abroad and could be seen as a threat to the state. They were trained for the purpose of converting souls, had studied the Bible in detail in order to be able to debate with Protestants, and had been instructed in effective preaching. They were able to offer confession to those who had been unable to do so for a number of years. The missionary priests were impressively educated and committed individuals who aimed to do three things:

- To minister to existing recusant families.
- To convert people back to Catholicism.
- To encourage those who were wavering or undecided to explicitly choose and admit their choice to be Catholic.

The numbers of missionary priests were not high. The first four came over in 1574. By 1580 there were approximately 100 more, but considering the size of the country and the number of parishes this was a very small number indeed. It is nearly impossible to judge the impact of the missionary priests. The scale of their task is unknown – for example, how far had England really strayed from Catholicism? As their actions were intended to be secret it is impossible to know how far they succeeded in their mission.

The impact of international secular and religious politics

The government's response was not just to the threat of a relatively small group of Catholic priests. Missionary priests were a threat on the basis that they could convert members of the population or persuade others to remain Catholic. Pope Pius V excommunicated Elizabeth I in a papal bull on 17 April 1570. This meant that Elizabeth's Catholic subjects were freed from their allegiance to her, in theory meaning that she was at more risk from extreme Catholics who may have wanted to assassinate her in order to bring back Catholicism. Pope Gregory XIII, who succeeded Pius in May 1572, took further measures to restore England to Catholicism. He encouraged Philip II, King of Spain, to invade England. Cardinal William Allen was invited to Rome in 1576 to advise the Pope about the plausibility of an invasion from the Spanish Netherlands. In 1579 another English exile, Nicholas Sander, was asked to invade Ireland in order to cause problems for Elizabeth there.

None of these plans by the Pope achieved anything significant in terms of restoring Catholicism in England. In fact, in some senses they were extremely unhelpful for English Catholics and the priests sent to serve them. This is because the missionary priests claimed to be uninterested in politics – thus depicting themselves as unthreatening to the English state. But this was made implausible by the Pope's plans, and in any case was unlikely to have been believed even if true – religion and politics were intimately linked throughout this period. This led to the severe punishments meted out to Catholic priests and recusants in Elizabeth's reign. Priests were seen as foreign agents who were a political and religious threat to the Queen and the state more broadly.

The Jesuit missions

The Jesuits were founded in order to convert people to Catholicism. Known for their fanaticism and zeal for the Catholic faith, they worked to make converts in areas where Christianity was previously unknown, like India and Japan. They also operated extremely successfully within underground networks and were not unwilling to die as martyrs for their faith. This is partly why governments were so afraid of their presence. In England, like the missionary priests, it was generally Englishmen who were sent on the mission because it was felt (probably correctly) that people would respond much better to one of their own countrymen. Englishmen would also be more aware of the historical, political and social context that surrounded their mission. The first two Jesuits arrived in 1580.

Robert Persons

Robert Persons was a fellow of Balliol College, Oxford, who left for the Continent after being forced to resign from his post in 1574 because of his religious views. He joined the Jesuits in July 1575 and was sent to England in 1580. He

The Jesuit Order

The Jesuit Order was founded in 1534 by Ignatius of Loyola (now St Ignatius of Loyola), a Spanish soldier who experienced a religious conversion after being wounded in battle. The Order was approved of by Pope Paul III in September 1540. The Jesuits laid particular emphasis on missionary work and absolute obedience to the Pope. They played a prominent role in the Catholic Counter-Reformation, with education being another key focus of the Order. They aimed to stop the spread of Protestantism and to return people to the communion of the Catholic Church. It was the missionary and educational role of the Jesuit Order which led to the arrival of Jesuit priests in England.

began with a tour of the Midlands and the West Country. Persons was an excellent organiser. He began to build a network of safehouses for missionary priests, which would protect them from some of the dangers of their role. Despite efforts to extend the network, these were largely in the south and east of England. As missionaries they were expected to travel around the country in a way that was simply not typical in this period. Strangers were easily identified in towns and villages and there were strong **vagrancy** laws that discouraged wandering between places (see page 87). This made missionary priests extremely vulnerable to discovery and capture. Even the safehouses did not make the situation a lot safer – if local officials were zealous Protestants or if there was a national crisis that prompted officials to act more conscientiously, local gentry houses would be searched and priests located. This was especially the case if the gentry family that lived there were known Catholics. Persons was also instrumental in producing and printing Catholic propaganda materials such as pamphlets and setting up a secret printing press at Stonor Park in Oxfordshire. Persons was effective but was forced to flee to Europe in 1581 after the arrest and execution of his colleague Edmund Campion.

Edmund Campion

Edmund Campion had also been a fellow at Oxford, at St John's College. He had led a theological debate in front of Elizabeth I in 1566 and became a deacon in the Church of England in 1564. It became increasingly clear that his opinions were not orthodox, however, and he left for Ireland in 1569. By 1571, after being hunted as a Catholic, he left Ireland for Douai. He left Douai for Rome in 1573, joining the Jesuits. He taught at the Jesuit College in Prague for six years as a professor of **rhetoric** and philosophy but was called to take part in the English mission in 1580. When he arrived, Campion issued a declaration to demonstrate that he was not there for political purposes, called the 'Challenge to the Privy Council'. This made his life more difficult as the government became even more determined to track him down. He travelled as a wandering priest in Berkshire, Oxfordshire, Northamptonshire and Lancashire. He wrote another pamphlet, *Decem Rationes* (Ten Reasons). This explained reasons why the Church of England was invalid. It was printed at Persons' printing press at Stonor Park in 1581. This further increased the heat on both Campion and Persons. He was finally arrested in Berkshire on 14 July 1581. Campion was imprisoned in London, tortured on the rack and made to dispute with Protestant theologians. Campion was tried on 20 November 1581.

He was found guilty and **hanged, drawn and quartered** on 1 December at Tyburn alongside two other priests – Fathers Ralph Sherwin and Alexander Briant. Sherwin had been ministering in London and Briant in Somerset.

The fate of Campion did not dissuade other Jesuits from making the journey to England. Jesuits expected difficult conditions and danger on their mission, particularly in a hostile country like England. Future leaders of the Jesuit mission in England made sure that incoming priests were sent to staunch Catholic families where there was less chance of betrayal. They could then undertake the mission with a little more safety.

▲ An engraving of the executed Jesuit priest Edmund Campion, produced by Catholics in 1631. What does the background to the picture say about Catholic feelings towards such priests and those who executed them?

The government's response to the missionary priests and Jesuits

The government acted decisively to remove the threat of, firstly, the missionary priests. They instructed Justices of the Peace (see page 82) to identify and prosecute any recusants in their areas. Perhaps unsurprisingly this was not especially successful – in areas with large recusant populations the local officials were often either related to or connected to local recusants, so were not keen to report them. Bishops, as local representatives of the Church, were also required to identify and report back to the Archbishop on the numbers of recusants in their dioceses. This began in 1577 and was still continuing at the end of the seventeenth century. These two measures were intended to monitor recusants and to use intimidation to encourage them to conform to the Church of England. A third measure was intended to remove the problem. The first execution of a missionary priest, Cuthbert Mayne, was in November 1577 using legislation not originally intended for that specific purpose. He had been ministering to Catholic families in the religiously conservative county of Cornwall. One more priest, John Nelson, and a Douai seminary student, Thomas Sherwood, were executed in 1578.

It was the arrival of the Jesuits in 1580 that galvanised the government into creating new legislation specifically to deal with the problem of missionising Catholic priests. In 1581 parliament passed a law making it an act of treason to reconcile anyone to the Catholic Church. More legislation was passed in 1585, parliament decreeing that all priests trained abroad should leave the country within 40 days on pain of death. Between 1581 and 1586 30 priests were executed and 50 were put in prison. This did not put off such dedicated missionaries, however, as a further 179 priests arrived in the same period. In 1588, 21 priests were put to death and 57 more between 1596 and 1603. Lay people who sheltered priests or let them live in their houses would also lay themselves open to charges of treason. The government wanted to isolate Catholics and, by opening the community to more serious prosecution, increase divisions among them. If the legislation was intended to wipe out the Catholic mission and the Catholic lay community, it certainly did not work. Men continued to leave England, train abroad, and return as missionary priests or Jesuits. Executed priests became martyrs for their faith, recusants became better at concealing their worship, and communities of both faiths continued not to report all their Catholic inhabitants. The Catholic problem was one that governments faced for a long time after Elizabeth's death.

5 The role of the Catholic nobility

The Catholic nobility and gentry were important in several ways during the upheavals of the sixteenth century:

- While in positions of power they aimed to influence the monarch towards Catholicism or traditional religious practices.
- They played a prominent role in uprisings and rebellions in favour of Catholicism.
- They protected and sheltered fellow Catholics and, after 1574, missionary and then Jesuit priests in their houses and used their local influence.

The nobility and Catholic rebellions

The majority of rebellions in this period had strongly religious causes. The Lincolnshire rising and Pilgrimage of Grace in 1536, the Prayer Book rebellion and Kett's rebellion of 1549 and the revolt of the northern earls of 1569 all had a strong element of religious discontent (see pages 95–102). The Catholic nobility played a role in most of these rebellions, most notably the Pilgrimage of Grace and the revolt of the northern earls. They were also involved in plots against Queen Elizabeth's life, such as the Ridolfi plot of 1571 and the Babington plot of 1586. The Catholic nobles were extremely powerful. They owned huge areas of land, especially in the north of England. They could demand their tenants and servants to follow them, so could command a large armed following.

The role of the nobility and gentry in the regions

The gentry were not as rich or influential as the nobles but there were many more of them and they were important in their local areas. Under Elizabeth Catholic gentry and noble families suffered greatly – financially, socially and physically. They were fined increasingly heavily, sometimes to the ruin of their fortunes. They were excluded from political offices that brought social status. If they were found to be plotting or sheltering priests, they could be arrested and executed. Yet for some this strengthened their resolve and became part of their identity as an excluded community. While many were loyal to the Queen and the state this loyalty was increasingly questioned. Sir Thomas Tresham of Rushton in Northamptonshire was one good example of a gentleman who suffered financially and socially for his religion, but whose piety and devotion remained extremely strong in the face of persecution. Other loyal Catholic gentry families included the Bedingfields of Oxburgh in Norfolk, the Mostyns of Talacre in Flintshire and the Meynells of North Kilvington in Yorkshire.

While the nobility and gentry took risks sheltering priests, the priests in return prioritised ministering to their communities rather than in more public settings. This made sense for several reasons – gentry financial support, the central role they played in local and regional communities, and the ability to use their houses and private chapels for worship. In the seventeenth century some families (for example the Mostyns of Talacre) allowed the Jesuits to establish schools in their houses in order to spread the word.

Conclusion

Catholicism changed from the orthodox religion of England and Wales to a persecuted faith in the space of only a few years from Mary's to Elizabeth's reign. Though Henry VIII did abolish purgatory and institute some iconoclasm, and Edward VI aimed to completely obliterate Catholic worship, most people remained loyal to Catholicism until the reign of Elizabeth. As Elizabeth's policies settled in, this changed. After the papal bull in 1570 Catholics were more at risk than ever before. This did not stop all Catholics practising, however, and recusants and Church papists continued their loyalty to the Catholic Church in private.

Work together

Work in a pair to create a chart that explores continuity and change in this section. Draw a table with three columns like the one below. Together, work through the section and identify the elements of continuity and change in relation to the treatment and behaviour of Catholics. Remember to include dates in your notes, for example if a period of continuity came to an end in 1570, then note this down. If a change happened in 1549, put that in the table.

Aspect of Catholic behaviour and treatment	Continuity	Change
Traditional Catholic practices protected and promoted.	Most continued until the reign of Edward VI in 1547.	Break from Rome meant Catholicism no longer official religion (final break 1536). Some iconoclasm in 1538. Doctrine of purgatory abandoned in 1534.
Most people were loyal to traditional Catholic religion.	Largely until the reign of Elizabeth (from 1558), when it gradually changed.	

Recommended reading

John Bossy, *The English Catholic Community, 1570–1850* (Darton, Longman & Todd, 1979).

The classic text on English Catholics.

Eamon Duffy, *The Stripping of the Altars: Traditional Religion in England, 1400–1580* (Yale University Press, 2005).

This is a prize-winning and highly influential account of the impact of the Reformation on the English Church. Part II contains a compelling exploration of this impact under all of the monarchs in this period.

Eamon Duffy, *The Fires of Faith: Catholic England under Mary Tudor* (Yale University Press, 2009).

This book specifically covers Catholicism under Mary I. Its coverage of the Catholic Restoration in Chapter 1 and Cardinal Pole in Chapter 2 would both be very useful.

Richard Rex, *Henry VIII and the English Reformation* (Palgrave Macmillan, 2006).

Chapter 3 is particularly useful regarding popular religion during Henry VIII's rule.

Robert Tittler, *The Reign of Mary I* (Longman, 1991).

Chapter 5 contains a highly accessible summary of the Catholic restoration.

Popular attitudes to Catholicism

- The late medieval Church was not unpopular and included a rich and vibrant festive culture
- The iconoclastic campaign of 1538 and the dissolution of the monasteries (1536–40) caused fear, bewilderment and rebellion
- There were iconoclastic outbreaks under Edward VI, but these were by a minority and largely confined to the south-east
- Parishes were quick to adopt Mary's reforms and the Catholic restoration
- Mary faced no large-scale regional revolts, unlike Henry VIII and Edward VI
- Attitudes began to change more under Elizabeth's long rule
- The political and international situation began to change, with Catholic countries threatening England
- Catholic plots increased tensions
- Anti-Catholic legislation from 1581 made it more dangerous and less acceptable to be Catholic

The role of the Catholic nobility and gentry

- The nobility and gentry were powerful in their territories and could be influential at court
- Some Catholic nobles became involved in the many Catholic plots of the period
- Persecution sometimes strengthened their resolve and became part of their identity
- Many were loyal to the Queen but their loyalty was increasingly questioned
- Gentry financial and practical support meant that priests often prioritised their needs

CATHOLICISM AND ITS SURVIVAL

Extent of religious changes 1529–36

- The changes from 1529 to 1536 were mostly about the King's power in relation to the Pope, Church and clergy
- The abolition of purgatory was a significant change, as were the Injunctions of 1538
- The changes caused widespread discontent
- But religious worship changed little and some of Henry's legislation specifically enforced traditional Catholic worship

Recusancy and Jesuit missions in Elizabeth's reign

- The papal bull of 1570 said that English Catholics didn't owe allegiance to the Queen anymore as she was a heretic
- The Catholic Church made increasing efforts to reconvert English people, including sending missionary priests (from 1570) and Jesuits (from 1580)
- Missionary priests came to minister to Catholic families and convert people back to Catholicism. Their numbers were small
- Jesuits aimed to convert people also. They were not unwilling to die as martyrs
- The government took severe measures against these priests because they saw them as a foreign and religious threat
- It led to legislation, making it treason to try and convert people to Catholicism
- Recusant laws were made more severe

The survival of Catholicism in the regions

- Survival of Catholicism not confined to the regions for most of the period
- Some people appeared to conform but worshipped as Catholics in secret when it was banned – makes it hard to assess the numbers of Catholics
- It was harder to track Catholic activity further from London

▲ Summary diagram: Catholicism and its survival

Essay technique: Analysis

In Sections A and B of the exam your essays are judged on their focus and structure (see page 22), the extent to which they include relevant detail (see page 16), and the extent to which they are analytical. Therefore, having made a relevant point and supported it with accurate detail you should conclude each paragraph with analysis.

Analysis is a term that covers a variety of high level skills including explanation and evaluation. In essence, analysis means breaking down something complex into smaller parts. Therefore, a clear structure, which breaks down a complex question into a series of paragraphs, is the first step towards writing an analytical essay.

The purpose of explanation is to account for why something happened, or why something is true or false. Therefore, an explanatory statement requires two parts: a **claim** and a **justification**. For example, imagine you are answering the following question:

> **How far do you agree that Catholicism was the dominant religion in England and Wales between 1536 and 1562?**

You might want to argue that, on the contrary, Protestantism made significant gains in this period. Having made this point, and supported it with relevant detail, you can then explain how this answers the question. For example, you could conclude your paragraph like this:

Claim ———— Protestantism, therefore, made significant gains in the period 1536–62 *because* one Protestant king (Edward VI) and several Protestant ministers made far-reaching religious reforms and preachers had the chance to legitimately convert people to their faith.

———— Relationship
———— Justification

The first part of this sentence is the claim, the second part justifies the claim. 'Because' is a very important word to use when writing an explanation, as it shows the relationship between the claim and the justification.

Activity: Claim and justification

Here is a plan in answer to the question above:

- Catholicism was the religion of most of the people in this period.
- There were rebellions against several key reforms and for Catholicism.
- The reforms were enforced by a minority of evangelicals in power.
- Significant religious reforms were implemented by Protestants which were difficult to fully reverse.
- A significant and vocal minority were converted to Protestantism, and because they were influential this finally led to Protestant political dominance.

Using your notes from the previous chapter:

1 Write a paragraph about either how Catholicism was dominant because it was the religion of the majority in this period, or about the influential Protestant minority. Make sure the paragraph:
   - begins with a clear point that clearly focuses on the question
   - develops the point with at least three pieces of accurate detail
   - concludes with explanation: a claim and a justification.

2 Write a conclusion to the essay in which you weigh up at least two factors and reach a judgement about how far Catholicism was the dominant religion in England and Wales in the period 1536–62.

2c: Protestantism and Puritanism

Overview

Until Henry VIII made his first moves towards introducing some aspects of reformed religion Protestantism was considered heretical. One of the earliest groups who were to share some of the beliefs of Protestants was the Lollards. They were a radical group inspired by the theologian John Wycliffe. Wycliffe had been condemned as a heretic in 1415 and his followers were increasingly persecuted and burnt as heretics in the centuries following. This makes the religious changes from 1529 to 1603 even more incredible. Diarmaid MacCulloch has described the Protestant Reformation as 'a howling success', summarising it as 'an act of state which made possible the growth of popular Protestantism'. Considering the status of proto-Protestant groups in the early years of Henry VIII's reign this transformation was remarkable. Evangelical reformers had a period of influence in Henry's reign from the 1520s to the mid-1530s but their heyday was under Edward VI as evangelical reform became the guiding light of the government's religious policy. By the end of Elizabeth's reign much of the ritual, practices and fabric of popular pre-Reformation had been destroyed, including masses, penances, purgatory and pilgrimages.

'Puritan' originated as a term of abuse for the more radical Protestants. It is important to remember that, although 'evangelical reformers', 'Protestants' and 'reformers' are all used as umbrella terms for the religious believers who differed from Catholicism; they were not one united group. Beliefs differed widely on a number of issues, and reformers disagreed as to how far reform needed to go. Those who held more radical beliefs became known as 'Puritans'. They made the clearest impact from Elizabeth's reign onwards, pressing unsuccessfully for further religious change. They believed the Reformation had not gone far enough, and this drove them into opposition against the government.

This chapter examines Protestantism and Puritanism through the following sections:

1 *Protestant influences in England, 1509–47* explores the early stages in the development of English Protestantism. It examines the earliest evangelical reformers and significant reforming influences from the Continent. It also discusses Anne Boleyn's influence.

2 *Protestantism under Edward VI* looks at Edward VI's religious policies and their impact in England.

3 *The growth and significance of Protestantism under Elizabeth I* discusses the evolution of Protestantism in Elizabeth's reign. It looks at the impact of those policies on the people of England and Wales. Additionally, it identifies and explores some more extreme Protestants who became opposed to Elizabeth's policies.

1 Protestant influences in England, 1509–47

Due to the limited nature of Henry VIII's changes to worship and religious practice, Protestantism was only truly established in England after 1547 when Edward VI ascended to the throne. Before this, however, there had been evangelical activity in England from the 1520s. Some of the earliest support for the Reformation came from merchants and lawyers. Merchants in particular came into contact with evangelical ideas when trading with cities in Germany where the Reformation had begun. A minority of academics, clergymen and gentry also developed reforming sympathies, and they were naturally drawn together in encouragement and support. In the 1520s and until the mid-1530s the influence of the reformers grew. Their ideas suited the King's needs (although that does not necessarily mean his motives were entirely cynical) and it has been argued that Anne Boleyn was herself a powerful advocate of evangelical reform at court both before and after her marriage. It became easier, although still illegal, to publish heretical books from the 1530s and reformers had created strongholds in London that were impossible for conservatives to entirely undermine.

The Lollards: early reformers

The Lollards originated at the end of the fourteenth century. They were persecuted as heretics and were showing signs of a revival in England in the early sixteenth century. The Catholic Church in England began to hunt for them again and found them still existing in secret networks and communities, largely based in London, the south-east, Coventry and Bristol. Lollards worshipped in private houses and shared many characteristics with the reformers that emerged in the first decade of the sixteenth century. They shared an emphasis on reading the scriptures and on the translation of the Bible into English. They doubted transubstantiation and believed the veneration of images and crucifixes was wrong. The Lollards were a very small minority group who were seen as dangerous heretics to be justly persecuted. Yet soon some of their central beliefs, corresponding as they did with evangelical reform, would be promoted by kings and governments – it was this, rather than persecution, which caused Lollardy to die out.

Erasmus, Colet and reform from 1509–25

Desiderus Erasmus, a clergyman and writer, was a **humanist**. He wrote a highly influential book, *The Handbook of a Christian Soldier*, in 1504. He wanted to renew and reform the Catholic Church, believing that it had become corrupt and sinful. He called for education, and an end to the reliance on ceremonies. He visited Oxford and Cambridge at the turn of the century. John Colet thought similarly, and also wanted to renew the Church through an understanding of the gospels. Colet founded St Paul's school in 1509 and it was to produce the next generation of evangelical reformers who came to prominence in the 1520s and 1530s. Both of these men were orthodox Catholics who wanted renewal rather than being reformers, but they contributed to the development of evangelical thought. Thomas Cromwell was inspired by Erasmus' translation of the New Testament, published in 1516. This translation led

to calls for further change – for translations into English, and for it to be available to many more people. The calls for change came from many people, but included William Tyndale and Martin Luther. Tyndale believed so strongly in the importance of Christians experiencing the word of God in their own language that he translated the New Testament into English himself and published it in 1525. Luther initially objected to a papal campaign for indulgences in 1519 but his thinking rapidly developed. Luther's ideas formed the basis of the German Reformation and the challenge to the Catholic Church across Europe.

Ironically, Henry VIII was a vocal opponent of Luther and the threat he believed Lutheranism posed to the Church. In fact, Henry was awarded the title 'Defender of the Faith' by the Pope after a defence of the sacraments written by him was published in July 1521. But Lutheranism soon gained converts in England. They attempted to gain converts to their cause by preaching and using their knowledge of the Bible to persuade people of their convictions.

Who were the first evangelical reformers?

Luther's ideas spread first among Germans. German merchants traded with England and London merchants traded with German cities. Trade routes, therefore, were one of the most important conduits for reformed thought. Clergymen and scholars at Oxford and Cambridge Universities were also early adopters of Lutheran ideas. They were educated enough to read the Latin translations of Luther's works, and their role was to dispute and consider new ideas. The ideas were most enthusiastically taken up by students but some established scholars were convinced too. Hugh Latimer, Bishop of Worcester under Henry VIII, chaplain to Edward VI and Protestant martyr, was a fellow of Clare College and a university chaplain when he was converted by Thomas Bilney in 1524. Bilney converted Latimer after he had heard Latimer speak against the new ideas of the Reformation in a theological debate.

Bilney was to be one of the first martyrs of the English Reformation, executed in Norwich on 19 August 1531 for persistently preaching against the veneration of relics and saints, as well as pilgrimages. On most points, Bilney was an orthodox Catholic but his preaching was deemed too radical by Wolsey for him to be allowed to continue.

From the mid-1530s the English evangelicals built relationships with important Swiss reformers such as Heinrich Bullinger of Zurich. The Reformation in Switzerland had taken a slightly different turn to that in Germany, and their enthusiasm for humanism more easily mirrored English concerns. Thomas Cranmer and Heinrich Bullinger were friendly correspondents from 1536, leading to student exchanges between Zurich and Oxford. When royal policy turned against the reformers again in 1539, it was to Switzerland that Protestant exiles fled. They would do so again during Mary's reign.

Historian Susan Brigden has described the early reform movement as a 'protest movement' – putting up the early modern equivalent of fly posters, going on the run, sheltering fellow reformers, rescuing others from prison, singing forbidden radical ballads, destroying images and preaching without a licence. Yet this was not a mass movement. The numbers of evangelicals in the early days were very small indeed, and they were confined to a limited area of the country. Although this included London, it is very unlikely that they would have triumphed and increased in numbers to the extent they did without royal support.

The influence of Anne Boleyn

Anne Boleyn has been seen as a strong evangelical influence on the King and at court. Historians' opinions on the religious beliefs of Anne Boleyn differ greatly. Maria Dowling and Eric Ives argue that she was a devout evangelical who aimed to foster reform at the English court and beyond. Ives argued that it was Anne who pushed Henry VIII into asserting his supremacy over the Church. George Bernard and Reitha Warnicke disagree. They both believe she was very conventional in her religious beliefs. Her apparent contribution to reform was praised heavily by John Foxe in his *Acts and Monuments*, and by her chaplain William Latimer in his account of her life. It must be remembered, on the other hand, that both of these accounts were written to promote Protestantism in Elizabeth's reign and functioned as reformist propaganda. Given the limited amount of evidence available about Anne, her life and beliefs, it is very difficult to judge exactly what kind and level of influence she had in relation to religion. It does seem, however, that she did support evangelical reform to some extent and that she herself held some reforming beliefs.

Anne Boleyn's links to reformers

Anne was certainly linked to well-known reformers such as Edward Foxe, Nicholas Shaxton, Hugh Latimer and William Barlow. She lent money to Latimer and Shaxton when they needed it to pay for their promotion to bishop. Anne Boleyn, when queen, presented evangelical reformers like Edward Crome to well-paid ecclesiastical livings. She intervened on behalf of reformers like Thomas Garrett who were accused of heresy and appointed another clergyman, William Betts, implicated in the same heresy case, as her chaplain. She was patron to Thomas Cranmer, Archbishop of Canterbury after the death of William Warham in 1532. In Europe Anne Boleyn was recognised as a reformer. She was heavily involved in the successful diplomatic efforts to save a French reformer called Nicholas Bourbon and bring him over to England. After he arrived Anne employed him as a schoolmaster.

Ownership of reformist books

Anne was also regarded as someone influential for reformers to turn to. An evangelical petitioner accused of owning banned religious books wrote to her in 1530 asking for help. She gave financial aid to a promoter of Tyndale's English New Testament in 1534 and supported the evangelical Thomas Patmore when he was accused of heresy in 1530. Anne owned reformist books herself, including a Tyndale *New Testament* and two early French reforming books. Five of her religious books were Bibles – as the private reading of the scriptures in the vernacular was very much a reforming preoccupation this is a strong indication of her beliefs. Her reformist sympathies were most probably fostered during her time at the French court, as her religious beliefs seem to correspond most with the early French humanist reformers. Thomas Cranmer himself wrote to the King acknowledging and praising Anne's love for the Gospel in May 1536.

When discussing the early days of reform it is not possible to identify a solid group of people who all believed the exact same thing. Reforming ideas were changing and developing rapidly, and there was no established orthodoxy in the same way as there was to a greater degree in Catholicism. In this kind of religious environment people supported each other who didn't necessarily agree on every theological matter – especially while their broad principles were counted as heretical. So while Anne Boleyn may not have agreed entirely with the people (like Bourbon, Latimer or Cranmer) she supported, the reformers had to form a loose network of support in order to help spread their ideas and avoid prosecution.

Evangelical reformers, the court and Henry VIII

Evangelical preachers like Latimer, John Bale and Thomas Cromwell were extremely useful to Henry VIII when he needed support and justification for the break from Rome. They were enthusiastic about the policy of Royal Supremacy because it meant rejecting the dominance of the Pope in Rome. Perhaps they believed that this would lead to an increased concentration on the scriptures – a centrally important aspect of reformed religion. Henry was using them to show that his policy was religiously acceptable. He himself rejected most aspects of evangelical theology and maintained a loyalty to most of the features of traditional Catholic worship. Yet the evangelicals were not just exploited by Henry. He gave them a platform to preach openly to many interested people. This gave them the chance to gain converts and support among powerful and influential people at court and in the Church. Thomas Cromwell had reforming sympathies, and even after the death of Anne Boleyn his religious policies tended towards Protestant reform. They included the dissolution of the monasteries, which was religiously satisfactory to Cromwell as well as being financially profitable for the Exchequer. He also supported iconoclasm and from 1538 the English Bible was enforced for every parish.

Yet Henry would only allow reform to go so far. Soon it became clear that some radical reformers wanted to go a lot further than others, and began to attack aspects of the Catholic faith that Henry himself held dear. This led to a governmental crackdown on reform. New injunctions would implement severe penalties for religious offences. Henry's fears were also partly political. The spread of reform across England was causing divisions and dissent in local communities, and had the potential to be problematic for the government. With that in mind, further reform was suppressed from the end of 1538, and the persecution of Protestants began afresh.

2 Protestantism under Edward VI

The reign of Edward VI was the first chance for evangelical reformers to achieve their aims, and create the kind of Reformation that they wanted. And reformers knew what they wanted to achieve even before any legislation was passed.

Iconoclasm before legislation

Reformers pulled down images in London as soon as Edward's accession was announced in January 1547. It must be noted that this does not mean that the entire population of London were ever reformers, merely that there was a vociferous minority who were prepared to take action there to achieve their religious aims. By September iconoclasm was far advanced in the areas where there were significant numbers of reformers, such as London, Norfolk, Essex and Suffolk. There was iconoclasm in Norwich and Cambridge in September 1547 and in October of that year the parishioners of Great St Mary's in Cambridge chose to sell their silver crucifix. Protestant propagandists encouraged such behaviour and urged the government to go further and quicker with its religious policies. Targets included the mass and altars in parish churches. Indeed, when the reforming policies were introduced, it seems that they were obeyed in the majority of parishes – especially where visitations enforced them strictly. Walls were whitewashed, images

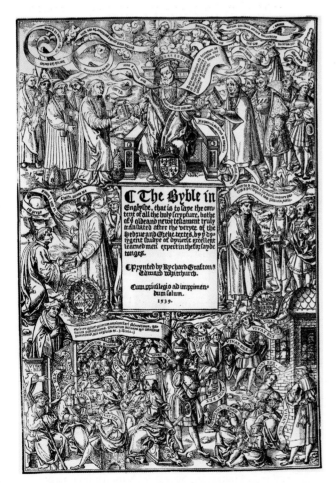

▲ The title page of the Great Bible, 1539. The title page was commissioned from Holbein's apprentices by Thomas Cromwell and shows Henry presenting the Bible to Cranmer and Cromwell. What impression was Henry VIII trying to give in this image, which was at the front of the Great Bible?

and statues confiscated and destroyed, altars replaced and the equipment of Catholic worship given up for confiscation. This did vary regionally, with the north of the country lagging behind even in compliance to these orders. But it seems that while the people of England would obey the government's commands for the destruction of the old order, they were less keen to embrace the new one.

Popular support for the Edwardian Reformation

While there were clear regional variations in enthusiasm for the Edwardian Reformation, it is fair to say that there is little evidence of widespread popular positive support for it. The Swiss reformer Martin Bucer criticised the English Reformation for its destructiveness, and this is to a great extent a fair criticism. Due to an extreme shortage of evangelical clergy, the kind of preaching that might have persuaded more people of the positive spiritual benefits of the Reformation was simply not available in the vast majority of places. The other pillar of Protestantism, education, was little help due to low literacy levels and the limited number of schools. Church attendance at the new English services was reduced in many places. It was hard to persuade parishes to spend their money on the new English Bible or Erasmus' *Paraphrases* (see page 50). There is little sign that an enthusiastic Protestant culture sprung up in England aside from in its heartlands in the south-east, and even that was tempered somewhat by the cautious and somewhat non-committal gentry. Wales showed very little sign at all of adopting the new Protestant practices and the Edwardian government did virtually nothing to attempt to persuade them. This is one reason why Elizabeth's Church of England experienced more of a struggle in Wales than anywhere else.

Evangelical Protestants no doubt made numerous converts during Edward's reign. When Mary came to the throne over 800 of them left for exile on the Continent. Mary's restoration of Catholicism was successful on a number of levels (see page 45). This included the conversion of Protestant reformers back to Catholicism. Historian Eamon Duffy has described a 'rapid collapse' in the evangelical community, their leaders bemoaning the speed with which believers even in strong evangelical towns like Norwich returned to Catholicism. He quotes Nicholas Ridley, who while in prison wrote of his suspicions that even the elites who had supported the Edwardian Reformation 'were never persuaded in their hearts'.

3 The growth and significance of Protestantism under Elizabeth I

During previous periods of Protestant reform the majority of the people conformed reluctantly, demonstrating little enthusiasm for the changes imposed under Henry VIII or Edward VI. Yet by the end of Elizabeth's reign England could finally perhaps be called a Protestant country. Protestantism became once again the religion of the English Church. It was enforced by bishops in visitations of their dioceses and, through judicious use of compromise and persuasion, became largely adopted by the English (and eventually Welsh) people. The settlement of the Church of England in 1563 did a lot to achieve this. Elizabeth herself practised a moderate and, in some ways, conservative form of Protestantism. It allowed for compromise on some familiar traditional practices that made it less alarming and alien to ordinary people. It also had much more time to embed itself – Elizabeth's reign of 45 years allowing for the recruitment and training of Protestant clergy and for the enforcement of Protestant religious practices to take effect. The majority of the people got used to the changes and, with the Church of England becoming identified with the country itself, became protective and proud of it. Many became genuine enthusiasts for the Church and for Protestantism, responding to preaching and Protestant propaganda as well as persuasion by family, friends and acquaintances.

Not all of the population felt that way, however, and there were visible minorities on both ends of the religious spectrum who felt dissatisfied with the Elizabethan settlement. The response of the Catholics has already been discussed on pages 58–61. A form of Protestant opposition also developed, and would press for further changes and a greater degree of religious reform throughout Elizabeth's reign. This group became known as 'Puritans', a term of abuse for the more extreme Protestants. This was not one united movement and there were different types of Puritans, but what they had in common was a feeling that the Elizabethan Settlement involved too much compromise with Catholicism. They had felt great hope at the beginning of Elizabeth's reign, believing that true and 'godly' religion would be established. They wanted a pure and reformed Church. Elizabeth did not provide that, for reasons of personal belief and political awareness.

The 'godly' – Puritan opposition in Elizabethan England

It must first be noted that not all Puritans pressed actively for further change. Some groups of Puritans co-existed peacefully within the Church of England. Their beliefs were obviously different to their neighbours', to some degree, and they lived and behaved in a way that marked them out. But they were not necessarily antagonistic to the Church of England or vocal in calling for further change. Presbyterians did call for a different Church system – they thought the hierarchy of archbishops and bishops was too Catholic, and wanted a system of ministers and church elders instead. The system they wanted would be a national system with regional and national synods, or meetings, convened. Each church would send representatives and, together, decisions would be made that would affect the whole Church. This was radically different to the existing system and it was not clear where the Queen would fit into it. Some Puritans, known as 'Separatists', went even further still. They did not think there should be any national system, and wanted individual congregations to be able to determine their own doctrine. The number of Separatists was always extremely small in Elizabeth's reign.

Elizabeth's archbishops and the Puritans

Elizabeth appointed three Archbishops of Canterbury from 1558 to 1603, and two of these had significant but opposing approaches to Puritan groups.

Grindal and the Puritans

Edmund Grindal was appointed Archbishop of Canterbury on 26 July 1575 after the death of the previous Archbishop, Matthew Parker. Parker had been severe on Protestant nonconformists but Grindal had different sympathies. He had been one of Edward VI's chaplains, had gone into exile in Strasbourg during Mary's reign, and tended to be more 'godly' than many others who were senior in the Church hierarchy. He was a conforming Puritan. Grindal soon faced a challenge that was to effectively cut short his career – he argued with the Queen. In 1577 he was suspended by the Queen for disobedience, for refusing to put an end to 'prophesyings' when ordered to in 1576. These were exercises by which new preachers practised and honed their preaching skills in front of an audience. There were 'moderators' there, experienced preachers who would give their view on the sermons they heard, offering advice for improvement. The Queen saw these meetings as being Presbyterian (which was not necessarily the case), and as being a threat to uniformity in the Church. Grindal consulted his bishops, founded that 10 out of 15 bishops agreed with the existence of prophesyings, and wrote to Elizabeth to defend the meetings. In doing so, he informed the Queen of the limits of her power, reminded her that she was 'a mortal creature' and, therefore, thoroughly enraged her. He was placed under virtual house arrest, suspended from most of his powers and was only reconciled to the Queen in 1582, shortly before his death in 1583.

Whitgift and the godly

The next Archbishop, John Whitgift, had no such godly leanings. He particularly valued obedience and uniformity and launched an attack on the Puritan movement. In 1583 Whitgift introduced the Three Articles. These were imposed on all clergy and were intended to enforce uniformity on all clergymen within the Church of England. He used a binding oath to administer the articles – a measure only previously taken in civil law, and one taken extremely seriously. His approach was extremely divisive, and he was advised to moderate it by the Privy Council. The privy council had been written to by gentry who supported the clergy affected by these measures. The Three Articles demanded that:

- every clergyman accept the Royal Supremacy
- every clergyman accept the Book of Common Prayer and ordinal that stipulated that episcopacy was the only proper government for the Church
- every clergyman agree that the Thirty-Nine Articles (see page 50) were also correct.

After the Privy Council had asked that the oath be modified most reluctant clergy did agree to the Three Articles. It did drive some out of the Church of England and into either Presbyterianism or Separatism, however, as they no longer felt that their opinions would be tolerated.

Table 1: Archbishops of Canterbury

Term in office	Archbishop of Canterbury
1503–32	William Warham
1533–55	Thomas Cranmer
1556–58	Cardinal Reginald Pole
1559–75	Matthew Parker
1575–83	Edmund Grindal
1583–1604	John Whitgift

Presbyterians in the reign of Elizabeth

The first influential Presbyterian to speak out was Thomas Cartwright. He was a professor of Divinity at the University of Cambridge, and embarked in 1570 on a series of lectures. In them he argued that the hierarchy of archbishops, bishops, deans and archdeacons should be abolished, and a system of Church elders be brought in instead. He also thought that the minister should be elected by the congregation. This was revolutionary, and because it implied that the monarch could not be Supreme Governor, it led to Cartwright being sacked from his position and leaving England for Switzerland in 1570. Cartwright's lectures did not lead to a strong Presbyterian movement developing.

John Field, a clergyman deprived of his living in 1572 for his failure to conform fully to the Prayer Book and other demands of the Church, was the next to advocate Presbyterianism loudly. He did so in two printed manifestoes published in 1572, in which he argued that the best system of Church government was a Presbyterian one. He wrote that bishops were the enemies of true Christianity and that the Prayer Book was an 'unperfect book' with material picked out from 'that popish dunghill' the Mass Book. He said that public baptism was 'full of childish and superstitious toys' and that kneeling at communion was 'popish idolatry'. Perhaps unsurprisingly considering the venom in these pamphlets, Field was imprisoned for a year as a result. Field was to resurface again in the 1580s, attempting to exploit discontent at

Archbishop Whitgift's strict measures against Puritan nonconformity. He launched a national survey to establish grievances against the bishops, hoping (unsuccessfully) to influence future parliaments to pass legislation in support of Presbyterians.

In the 1584 parliament Dr Peter Turner attempted to introduce a bill that would establish a Presbyterian system – this was vetoed immediately by the Queen. The Presbyterians in parliament tried again in the 1586–87 parliament. In February 1587 one of the Puritan MPs, Anthony Cope, offered for discussion a bill that would replace the Prayer Book with the Genevan Prayer Book, which included a Presbyterian form of Church government (see pages 19–20). The bill had little chance of passing. It threatened the influence of the gentry who made up the majority of parliament and was unsupported even by other Puritans. The government attacked the bill anyway and imprisoned Cope and several supporters, but there is little evidence that this was even necessary. Presbyterianism was not strong in most areas of England and did not constitute a significant threat to the Church hierarchy.

The Separatists

The Separatists were more radical than the Presbyterians. They completely denied that the Church and nation were associated and united. This seemed like disloyalty to the Elizabethan regime and the group were persecuted heavily. There were very few Separatists, they were a loose rather than a united group, and they lacked powerful supporters due to their absence of support for the idea of a national Church governed by the authority of the Crown. The most important group of Separatists were the Brownists, named after their founder Robert Browne. In 1582 he wrote a pamphlet entitled *Treatise of Reformation without tarrying for any*. In it he argued that people should not wait for further reformation to be carried out by the government or authority. He argued that the Church of England was corrupt and infested with Catholic superstition. Browne had already left the country by the time he published this treatise, but it became an offence to distribute it. In 1583 two men, John Copping and Elias Thacker, were hanged for distributing it. Browne himself returned to England in 1583 and conformed to the Church of England but his followers chose new leaders. In 1593 an Act was passed in parliament that strongly linked church attendance with loyalty to the regime. Continued worship as Separatists was punishable by death.

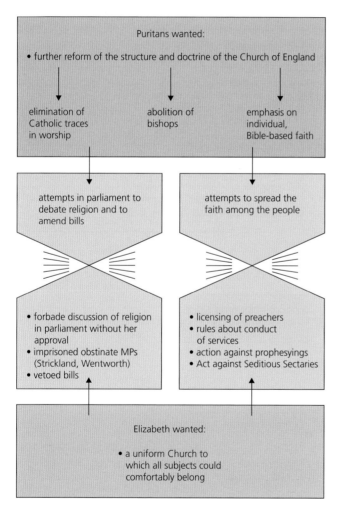

▲ Figure 1: Summary of royal efforts to contain Presbyterianism in the 1570s and 1580s

Conclusion

Protestantism, or evangelical reform, in some ways both began and ended this period as a movement of opposition. Although Elizabeth's Church of England was a Protestant Church, more extreme Protestants moved into opposition and were punished for it. Between the death of Henry VIII and the accession of Elizabeth the position of Protestants see-sawed. They were promoted by Edward VI and persecuted by Mary I. In the end a compromise was made that pleased most, but not all, of the people.

Work together

The status of evangelical reformers changed a lot in this period. Work together to produce a graph that demonstrates when their status altered and how. At the far left of the horizontal axis write the date at the beginning of the period (1509) and at the far right write the end of the period (1588). In between put the dates advancing in periods of ten years. At the top of the vertical axis write a heading, for example 'Degree of evangelical influence'. Now read through your notes and complete the graph.

▼ Summary diagram: Protestantism and Puritanism

The growth and significance of Protestantism under Elizabeth

- Through the Elizabethan Compromise in 1563 and Elizabeth's long and stable rule, Protestantism became the religion of most people
- Protestantism became associated with England's identity against foreign Catholic threats
- Some Protestants thought this did not go far enough and they pushed for further change. They became known as Puritans
- Presbyterians wanted a national system of elders and ministers, not bishops and Archbishops
- Separatists wanted a Church with no national system, but individual choice
- Archbishop Grindal was a conforming Puritan who refused to put an end to practices the Queen disliked. He was suspended from most of his powers
- Archbishop Whitgift took a severe approach to Puritan groups, using an oath to enforce uniformity
- In the 1584 parliament, Turner attempted to introduce a bill to establish a Presbyterian system but the Queen vetoed it
- Another attempt in 1587 was also put down by the government
- Separatists were persecuted and from 1593 Separatism was punishable by death

Protestant influences in England, 1509–47

- The Lollards were now considered as proto-Protestants. They were persecuted as heretics
- Erasmus, the humanist, influenced English theologians when he visited
- Martin Luther's ideas came to England via merchants and academics
- He converted academics and churchmen like Hugh Latimer and Thomas Bilney
- From the 1530s English reformers made contact with Swiss theologians, providing a refuge when Mary I was persecuting Protestants
- Anne Boleyn was linked to prominent reformers like Latimer, Barton and Foxe. She was patron to Thomas Cranmer
- Evangelical preachers were useful to Henry VIII when he tried to justify the break from Rome

PROTESTANTISM AND PURITANISM

Protestantism under Edward VI

- Enthusiastic radicals began iconoclastic attacks as soon as Edward VI's succession was announced
- This continued in areas where there were significant numbers of reformers, like London, Norfolk and Essex
- The was little widespread popular support for the Edwardian Reformation
- There was a shortage of evangelical clergy and education was little help
- Mary's reign saw a rapid collapse in numbers of evangelicals

Recommended reading

Patrick Collinson, *The Elizabethan Puritan Movement* (Clarendon Press, 1990).

This book would be particularly useful for those looking for an in-depth examination of the Puritan movement in Elizabeth's reign.

David Loades, *Essays on the Reign of Edward VI* (Headstart History, 1994).

Chapter 2 is an especially fine summary of the approach of Edward and his government to the Protestant Reformation.

John Lotherington (editor), *The Tudor Years* (Hodder, 2002).

Chapter 9, on Elizabeth and religion, contains an extremely useful summary of the Puritans and the opposition they posed in Elizabeth's reign.

Diarmaid MacCulloch, *The Boy King: Edward VI and the Protestant Reformation* (Palgrave, 2001).

While most of this book is extremely complex, Chapter 1 includes a very useful exploration of those involved in the Edwardian Reformation, not least the character of Edward VI himself.

Diarmaid MacCulloch, *The Later Reformation in England, 1547–1603* (Palgrave Macmillan, 2001).

This book includes in Chapter 2 a very good summary of Edwardian religion policies. It also looks at Protestant radicals in opposition in Chapter 9.

Essay technique: Overall judgement

In addition to focus and structure (see page 22), the level of relevant detail (see page 16), and analysis (see page 64), your exam essays will be assessed on how far you reach a supported overall judgement. The clearer and better supported your judgement, the better your mark is likely to be.

The mark scheme distinguishes between five levels of judgement (this is a summary – the full mark scheme can be found on Edexcel's website):

Level 1 (LOW)	No overall judgement.
Level 2	Stated overall judgement, but no support.
Level 3	Overall judgement is reached, with weak support.
Level 4	Overall judgement is reached, and supported.
Level 5 (HIGH)	Overall judgement is reached, and supported by consideration of the relative significance of key factors.

This section looks at reaching and supporting an overall judgement. Dealing with the relative significance of key factors is discussed at the end of Chapter 4c (see pages 140–41).

Reaching an overall judgement

The conclusion of your essay should reach an overall judgement. This judgement should reflect the overall argument of your essay.

Imagine you are answering the following question:

> **How far do you agree with the view that the personal beliefs of the Tudor monarchs were the most significant reason for religious change in the period 1536–62?**

Your essay plan might look like this:
- **Paragraph 1: Personal beliefs**
- **Paragraph 2: Dynastic reasons**
- **Paragraph 3: Political stability**
- **Paragraph 4: Economic needs**

Your essay argues that in the period 1536–62 the personal beliefs of the monarchs *were* the main reason for religious change. This remained constant but other factors were important in parts of the period, such as dynastic reasons, political stability and economic needs. This argument should be reflected in your overall judgement. Therefore, the first line of your conclusion might look like this:

Establishes that you are reaching your overall judgement.

The judgement distinguishes between the most significant and less significant reasons. It has the beginnings of a sophisticated and balanced judgement.

> **In conclusion**, the personal beliefs of the Tudor monarchs were the most significant reason for religious change across the period 1536–62. **Other reasons were important but less consistently so.**

The words of the question are used to answer the question – ensuring a clear focus.

This is a good start, because an overall judgement has been reached that reflects the argument of the essay. But so far the overall judgement has only weak support.

Supporting your overall judgement

In order to get into the higher levels it is important to support your overall judgement. This can be achieved by backing up your judgement with a summary of the key points of your essay. For example, the overall judgement you have just read could be improved by adding the following summaries of your argument:

This summary supports the judgement about the most significant factor.

> **In conclusion, the personal beliefs of the Tudor monarchs were the most significant reason for religious change across the period 1536–62.** Indeed Henry VIII, Edward VI, Mary I and Elizabeth I all made religious changes due to their own religious convictions. The abolition of purgatory, production of the 1549 and 1552 Prayer Books, the attempts to restore Catholicism by Mary and the Elizabethan settlement provide evidence of this. **Other reasons were important but were less consistently so.** Political stability was a concern of Henry VIII and Elizabeth I. Dynastic reasons were primarily a concern of Henry VIII before the birth of Edward in 1537. Therefore, despite the additional reasons which were each important for particular monarchs, the most significant reason for religious change across the period was the personal beliefs of the Tudor monarchs.

This supports the judgement about the other factors.

The final sentence provides a summary overall judgement.

This conclusion is an example of high level work because it reaches an overall judgement and supports it with material that reflects the rest of the essay.

Activity: Writing an overall judgement

Here is a plan in answer to the question:

How successful were moves to spread Protestantism within England and Wales from 1559 to 1585?

- Paragraph 1: Elizabethan settlement – largely successful in the long term.
- Paragraph 2: Changes to Church fabric – moderately successful.
- Paragraph 3: Royal injunctions and visitations – broadly successful.
- Paragraph 4: Recusancy and other anti-Catholic laws – partially successful.

Using your notes from the previous chapter:

1 Write two summary sentences that state an overall judgement about the ways in which moves to spread Protestantism succeeded and the ways in which they failed.
2 Support these with a summary overview of the successes and failures.
3 Write a final sentence that summarises your judgement.

Theme 3 State control and popular resistance, 1509–88

The Big Picture

Local government became much more standardised under the Tudors, with stronger links between the localities and central government. Long established offices and bodies, such as Lord Lieutenant, the Council in the Marches and Wales, and the Council of the North, were made more powerful and permanent. New offices were created, for example that of Deputy Lieutenant. The role of Justice of the Peace was expanded and numbers increased greatly. These roles bound the nobility and gentry to the Crown in loyalty by giving them position and status, while providing the Crown with more strength and control in the regions. Political and religious unrest made this particularly important but it was also a sign of the Crown's desire to expand its authority and power.

Poverty was one problem that made a strengthened and standardised government necessary. It was a moral, religious and political problem, something for all parts of society to worry about. Remedies for poverty addressed the 'undeserving' and 'deserving' poor separately. The 'undeserving' poor who begged without the required licence were punished through whipping, branding and being put in the stocks. After 1572 repeated vagrancy would be punished with hanging. The 'respectable' poor were allowed licences to beg, and collections were made to aid them. There were charities set up to help the poor, usually from bequests in the wills of wealthy people. From

1598 the government passed more legislation to try and deal with poverty. Even so, the poor in the Tudor period faced an extremely difficult situation with very little safety net. Even those not called 'undeserving' were very vulnerable to any form of economic crisis.

It was not just the poor who constituted the resistance to Tudor rule. Popular resentment was more widespread. There were many different specific causes of the popular resistance of the sixteenth century. Despite this, common themes of religious resentment, economic distress and political resistance were all present. The rebellions involved the nobility, gentry, yeomenry and agricultural labourers – a broad cross-section of society. There were serious popular rebellions under Henry VIII, Edward VI and in the earlier years of Elizabeth I's reign. By the end of the period popular resistance had declined greatly. A more stable period under Elizabeth I, better economic conditions and stern action taken against previous rebellions may have caused this. Plots against the Crown became increasingly confined to small groups with religious and political aims.

By 1588 central and local government was strengthened and stabilised, and popular unrest was on the wane. This did not mean that the government of England and Wales was without problem – poverty remained a severe issue, for example. Nevertheless, many of the institutions set up or altered under the Tudor monarchs survived as the backbone of local government for many years afterwards, and some still remain today.

In this theme you will consider the following:
→ **Tudor control of the country:**
   The Council in the Marches and Wales and the Council of the North, the role of the nobility in maintaining control, the increasing power of the Justices of the Peace and the Lord Lieutenants under Elizabeth.
→ **The state and the poor:**
   The reasons for the growth of poverty, the punishment of beggars and vagrants, the importance of charities

and how local authorities contributed to the provision of poor relief.
→ **Resistance to Tudor rule:**
   The significance of popular resistance to demands for subsidies and taxes, the nature of the threat posed by popular risings from 1536–69, and the reasons for the decline of popular resistance from 1570–88.

TIMELINE

1348	Role of Justice of the Peace confirmed by Edward I's parliament
1439	Justices of the Peace had to own land worth at least £20 per annum
1472	Council in the North established by Edward IV
1473	Council in the Marches and Wales set up by Edward IV
1489	Council of the North re-established
1525	The Amicable Grant prompted tax revolt
1525	Council of the North re-established again by Henry VIII
1525	Thomas Cromwell altered the way the Council in the Marches and Wales worked
1530	Vagabonds Act
1534	Act of Supremacy
1534	Rowland Lee appointed Lord President of the Council in the Marches and Wales
1535	Laws in Wales Act passed
1536	Act to provide poor relief
1536–40	Dissolution of the monasteries
1536	Pilgrimage of Grace in Yorkshire and Lincolnshire
1537	Council of the North reorganised following the Pilgrimage of Grace
1543	All of Wales divided into 13 shires by this point
1546	Christ's Hospital donated to the City of London by Henry VIII
1549	The Prayer Book rebellions; Kett's rebellion; Edward VI gave the lieutenancy more functions so it could regain control
1552	Christ's Hospital admits its first orphans; Act established weekly collections for the poor
1553	Bridewell Palace donated to the City of London by Edward VI to become Bridewell Hospital
1555	Queen Mary introduced badges for licensed beggars to display
1560s	Post of Deputy Lieutenant created
1563	Poor Law passed, required contributions to parishes' poor boxes
1569	Rebellion of the northern earls
1572	Vagabonds Act passed, included licensing of beggars and harsh punishments for unlicensed beggars
1576	Parishes required to provide work for people without employment; houses of correction established to punish able-bodied beggars
1583	Throckmorton plot
1585	Elizabeth I made the position of Lord Lieutenants permanent
1586	Babington plot
1587	After this point Lord Lieutenants tended to be Privy Councillors
1598	Acts for the relief of the poor
1641	Council of the North abolished
1689	Council in the Marches and Wales abolished

3a: Tudor control of the country

Overview

Local government developed greatly under the Tudor monarchs. More burdens were placed on existing officers, such as Justices of the Peace, and other offices were created or made permanent, for example the Lord Lieutenants and Deputy Lieutenants. The regional councils, the Council of the North and the Council in the Marches and Wales, were re-established and strengthened with new powers. There was more reliance on a permanent bureaucracy and less on local noble elites. This was intended to prevent them building up local fiefdoms and causing military trouble for the central government when they did not get their way. The Tudor monarchs made active efforts to create uniformity. They aimed to regulate the economy, make provision for the poor, be militarily prepared for domestic and foreign threats, and ensure religious conformity in a period of great religious change.

Through local officeholders and nobles the government aimed to regulate and control the country. They made local government more uniform and easier to govern, tying the loyalties of the gentry to the state by giving them prestigious positions such as Justice of the Peace. Although this system was imperfect, it did mean that counties were run by those who knew them well and who were aware of events and developments that they needed to deal with. It also gave the government more representatives at a local level, and more information about reactions and events in the regions.

Officeholders at a regional level were often also members of the Privy Council from Elizabeth's reign onwards, enabling the commands of the Council to be relayed directly to (hopefully) trusted representatives in the counties of England and Wales.

This chapter examines Tudor control and government of the country through the following sections:

1 *The Council in the Marches and Wales and the Council of the North* explores the re-establishment or reinforcing of these two powerful regional councils, their function for the Crown and for the people of those regions, and their effect.

2 *The role of the nobility in maintaining order* discusses the part that the nobility could play in aiding the Crown. This includes using their authority to control their tenants or using their connections to influence the behaviour of important gentry families.

3 *The growing power of the Justices of the Peace* explores the development of this role in the sixteenth century. It looks at their expanded role and responsibilities, their increase in numbers and the reasons why the local gentry wanted to become Justices of the Peace.

4 *Lord Lieutenants under Elizabeth* looks at a role which was made permanent by Elizabeth I, in response to fears about potential Spanish invasions. It examines the demands of the role and the new role of Deputy Lieutenant which was created to extend the regional reach of the Lord Lieutenants.

Note it down

Use index cards (see page xi) to take notes on this section. For each role, council or office create an index card. On it, note important information such as: what the role was, why it was created or expanded, how it helped the Crown and how it helped the localities.

1 The Council in the Marches and Wales and the Council of the North

The Tudor monarchs aimed for uniformity of policy across their kingdom. This was easier said than done, however, as they ruled a country with a wide variety of regional and administrative traditions. Those regions of the country which were furthest from London experienced little in terms of direct attention from central government unless it was to punish a rebellion or enforce unpopular religious or economic policies. The north and the west of the Tudor kingdoms also maintained very different cultures and traditions from the south–east administrative centres. Although the Welsh felt to some degree bound by loyalty to a 'Welsh' **dynasty** (the Tudors had their family origins in Wales), they still had the remnants of different legal, administrative and social systems at the beginning of this period. Henry VIII's Acts of Union from 1536 to 1543 aimed to create more administrative uniformity and increase the sovereign power of the state over Wales. The north of England was dominated by powerful landowning nobles, who in the past had been allowed to maintain large private armies due to their role in governing the disorderly borderlands with Scotland. The need to maintain English control in the border counties meant that this power would continue longer than other areas. The two councils, the Council of **the Marches** and Wales and the Council of the North, were intended to reinforce royal control, execute royal policy and bring uniformity to these areas, which had in the past caused trouble for the monarchs of England.

Note it down

In order to make sure that you include enough detail in your index cards for this chapter, consider the following questions while you are making notes:

- When were the changes made to the Council in the Marches and Wales, and to the Council of the North?
- How did the councils extend royal authority in the borders, Wales and the north?
- How were the councils useful for the people who lived in these regions?

The Council in the Marches and Wales

The Council in the Marches and Wales was an established institution by the Tudor period. It was originally set up by Edward IV as a council for his son, the Prince of Wales, in 1473. The region's government had been extremely complex before that. There were powerful Marcher lords and landowners who had a great deal of power to rule as they liked, which made them a threat to the Crown on several occasions. Some parts of Wales were organised somewhat like English shires, while others were not. These areas were dominated by powerful office-holders, drawn from local families who often inherited offices and ran them as private fiefdoms. Disorder in Wales and the Marches often spread across the borders, causing complaints from Cheshire, Herefordshire and Gloucestershire.

Cromwell's reforms

Thomas Cromwell had made alterations to the way that the Council worked in 1525 but the continuing problems made him seek another solution. In 1534 he appointed his friend Rowland Lee as Lord President of the Council and Bishop of Coventry and Lichfield. Lee was a lawyer and had been involved in other administrative projects under Wolsey and

Cromwell, including the dissolution of the monasteries. Lee held the position of Lord President until his death in 1543. His aim was to bring law and order to the region. He did this by tirelessly prosecuting offenders, instituting harsh punishments even against powerful gentry families. Lee restored castles on the Marches to detain prisoners awaiting trial and instituted legislation to help prevent lawlessness.

Lee sought a more permanent solution to the disorder in the Marches and Wales, making suggestions to Cromwell. As a consequence Cromwell created legislation to divide all of Wales into shires like in England. The Laws in Wales Act of 1535, for example, abolished the Marcher lordships, created counties in the Welsh regions and absorbed some previously Welsh areas into English counties such as Shropshire and Herefordshire. The Welsh language survived in these areas well into the eighteenth century. By 1543 all of Wales was divided into 13 shires. This was part of larger reforms now generally known as the Act of Union. While Rowland Lee was extremely pessimistic about the ability of the Welsh gentry to operate as Justices of the Peace, he was proven wrong. His claim that the Welsh were too poor to be good Justices of the Peace was disproved as the change brought great improvements in law and order. It meant that more Welsh gentlemen and landowners had a stake in government and the state and the new positions gave them increased status locally. Although it didn't banish all crime and disorder in Wales, it did prove a more effective form of government.

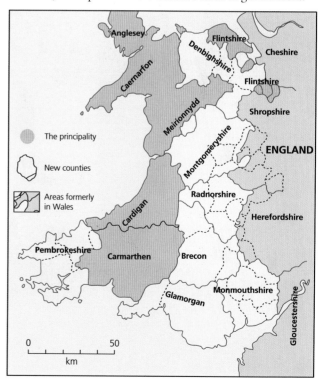

▲ Figure 1: Map of Wales after the Act of Union

Functions of the Council

The Council had two main functions – legal and administrative. It was a court that heard criminal and civil cases brought by people who did not wish to have their cases heard in London. This could be because of poverty, their inability to speak English, or the idea that they would achieve a more favourable result at Ludlow, where the Council was based. It also dealt with problems of misgovernment, such as influential nobility or gentlemen maintaining private armies. The Council in the Marches and Wales as a court was very busy. Its business increased greatly throughout the sixteenth century, as lawsuits became an increasingly popular way to settle feuds, family rows and business disputes.

The Council also aimed to maintain royal power in the borders and Wales. It administered the region and received commands from the Privy Council that it carried out. The Council had responsibility for economic and defence matters. The various threats to the Welsh coastline added to its importance in the sixteenth century. The possibility of invasion by Spain, incursions by pirates and other maritime threats made Wales more of a consideration for the English monarchs. It led to other measures that afforded Wales slightly different treatment to other Celtic regions, such as the translation of the Bible into Welsh (see page 58). J. Gwynfor Jones has argued that the Council of the North may have had its remit changed as a result of the developments to the Council in the Marches and Wales, becoming an administrator of the Crown's legal power rather than a personal council of the monarch in the north of England. This is possible, as the Council in the Marches and Wales had succeeded in a seemingly impossible mission of pacifying this difficult and complex region.

The Council in the Marches and Wales survived until the **Glorious Revolution** in 1689 after decades of complaints about its tyranny and a decline in business. Business had declined because the Council had been abolished in the Interregnum (1646–60) and the legal business of the Council was taken elsewhere in the meantime. It never recovered its former importance after the Restoration. Before this, it was generally thought to be a cheap, effective and successful way of governing Wales and

Ludlow Castle, Shropshire. Why do you think the Council was based in the Shropshire town of Ludlow rather than on the Welsh side of the Marches? What would Welsh people have to gain from pursuing justice in Ludlow rather than going to London?

Paper 1 England, 1509–1603: authority, nation and religion

the Marches. The positions as members of the Council were eagerly sought by Welsh gentlemen who saw the office as one of prestige. It wasn't uniformly effective – no government can solve all problems of law and order. Some gentlemen saw the Council as tyrannical, especially under Lee, who had little love for the Welsh. There were protests against heavy taxation and oppression, and there was some flagrant disobedience by powerful gentry families. In terms of its beginnings, however, the Council in the Marches and Wales was deemed to be very successful indeed in administering Wales.

The Council of the North

The Council of the North was established initially in 1472, again by Edward IV. It did not have the same level of continuity as the Council in the Marches and Wales, however, and was re-established in 1489 and again by Henry VIII in 1525.

Cromwell's reforms

As in Wales, the tendency of royal policy was to attempt to tie local noble and gentry families to the Tudor state by offering them positions as Justices of the Peace and councillors. The Council was re-established in 1525 in response to a tax revolt, but it would also come in useful when widespread northern resistance to the Reformation sprang up from late 1536 to early 1537 in the form of the Pilgrimage of Grace (see page 95). Before 1537 the Council had been governed by a powerful local noble like the Earl of Northumberland. After the Pilgrimage of Grace it was reorganised again, and put in the hands of a permanent bureaucratic council. The Council of the North was led by either a bishop or a peer, generally not from the north. The rest of the Council was composed of local gentlemen, lawyers and clergymen. It became the executive authority for all of the counties north of the River Trent.

Functions of the Council

Like the Council in the Marches and Wales, the Council of the North executed the orders of the Privy Council in the region. It had the following functions:

- It carried out **royal proclamations**.
- It sent orders to lesser officials like High **Sheriffs** and Justices of the Peace.
- It demanded taxes and subsidies when ordered.
- The Council also enforced religious policies, particularly after 1537.
- It was, to some extent, an effective way of making sure that local officials were carrying out their roles as the Crown wished. This would have been nearly impossible if monitored solely from London. It checked on Justices of the Peace and on the bishops.
- Like in Wales, it was also a court that heard cases from the region. As a court it dealt with similar issues to the Council in the Marches and Wales, like private armies, but also issues of **enclosures** (see pages 120–21) which weren't so prevalent in Wales at that point.

There were fewer problems for central government after the 1537 reorganisation of the Council, and in that way it could be seen as highly successful in increasing governmental control and implementing policies of uniformity. The rebellion of the northern earls in 1569 (see page 101) was the last great uprising of the northern nobility and was put down with relative ease. The Council of the North was abolished earlier than the Council in the Marches and Wales. It was suppressed in 1641 by the Long Parliament because it was seen by those MPs as a focus for royal tyranny and resistance to parliament rather than a beacon of law and order.

2 The role of the nobility in maintaining order

Historically, it was the powerful and wealthy landowning nobility who governed the regions on behalf of the Crown. In the medieval period such nobles had immense power and could pose a threat to the monarch if challenged or thwarted. By the sixteenth century their power had weakened slightly. Despite this, they still had great local influence over their tenants and local gentry. The nobility traditionally served the Crown in the localities and this continued in the sixteenth century. There were several ways in which the nobility could serve the Crown in the Tudor period – in war, regional government and hospitality to the monarch. These were honourable ways to behave, in an age when **chivalry** and honour were significant forces.

In regional government the noble families of England still retained significant power and influence. They were **patrons** of local gentry families, helping their sons to obtain positions and **patronage** with their families, other noble families and at court. They also had an impact on the appointment of local officers. During Henry VIII's reign the second and third Dukes of Norfolk were consulted over the appointments of sheriffs and arbitrated disputes among the local gentry. The nobility were also granted land by the Crown when there were particular areas that needed reliable control and government. There was no **standing army** in the sixteenth century, so the nobility were the frontline against popular uprisings and other kinds of disturbances. They used their influence with the gentry and their tenants to raise men to put down revolts quickly when they happened in the localities. Henry VIII granted land to his friend Charles Brandon, Duke of Suffolk, in East Anglia during the early years of his reign and in Lincolnshire after 1536 for this purpose. Henry VIII was particularly cautious about this, however, worrying that granting too much power to the nobles might make them too mighty in one region.

The nobility could use their local influence to maintain order (or to create revolts or disturbances). By managing their tenants and controlling their patronage they could insist that feuds or disorder end.

3 The growing power of the Justices of the Peace

In comparison to the other local government roles discussed in this chapter, that of Justices of the Peace was very long running. Justices of the Peace (or JPs) were confirmed as keepers of the peace by Edward I's parliament in 1348. After this their role grew rapidly. They had to be resident in their county and from 1439 they had to own land worth at least £20 per annum. This was so the office could be restricted to the wealthiest and most senior gentry in each county. There was a hierarchy among the JPs. One senior JP was appointed keeper of the records or *custos rotulorum*. This was a position of great honour and retained its prestige long into the seventeenth century. Those with legal training formed part of the *quorum*. This was an inner group of JPs. At least one of them had to be present in order for business to be done, and so they had an enhanced level of importance. The *quorum* was there to ensure that enough justices attended for the business to be carried out, and to guarantee that there was a justice present with legal knowledge and training.

How were JPs chosen?

JPs were chosen by the Privy Council on advice from courtiers, Privy Councillors and **assize judges**. They remained in office until their death, unless they were removed due to misdemeanours in a purge of the bench. These purges were rare in the Tudor period – they caused great resentment and social humiliation to those removed from an office of such prestige. Wolsey used his influence from 1513 to 1525 to choose JPs in the north who would support royal interests rather than local landed interests. Cardinal Wolsey, in particular, was determined that JPs would understand their duties and responsibilities.

He commanded new JPs to come to the Court of **Star Chamber** to be sworn in, and while there he read them a lecture on their duties and the relationship between the centre and the localities.

From 1348 to 1603 the numbers of JPs increased significantly (see Table 1). This reflected an increase in workload but also the social prestige of the office to the gentry.

Table 1: Numbers of JPs

	Numbers of JPs per county
1348	6 or more
1500	25–35
1570s	40–50
1603	40–90

The work of the JPs

There were two ways in which the JPs conducted their official business. The most important was at the quarter sessions. As the name suggests, they were held every three months of the year in important county towns. At the quarter sessions the JPs heard criminal cases and civil cases. They dealt with a huge range of offences as magistrates, from minor theft to murder. They also conducted administrative business. New felony offences were created under the Tudors, including those relating to rioting, property damage, witchcraft, **recusancy** and hunting. In Elizabeth's reign, JPs were expected to ensure the provisions of the Poor Law (see page 197) were carried out, that highways and bridges were maintained by parishes, alehouses correctly licensed and houses of correction managed properly. They supervised parish officers such as constables, churchwardens and overseers of the poor. This was a significant burden of work given that the office was voluntary and unpaid. The JPs also conducted business outside of court. They adjudicated local disputes and worked with local officials to carry out the orders of central government.

The reliance on Justices of the Peace could be problematic. They did not always co-operate with all of the government's demands. The JPs lived in the communities they served and had to maintain family and neighbourly relationships in those areas. This made it natural that they often prioritised local concerns over those of the central government that commanded them. One good example of this was the recusancy laws implemented under Elizabeth I. It was common for these not to be enforced uniformly, particularly in religiously conservative areas of the country.

4 Lord Lieutenants under Elizabeth

The title 'Lord Lieutenant' existed before the reign of Elizabeth. Before 1585, however, it was an occasional rather than a permanent role. Lord Lieutenants before this were appointed at times of crisis to take charge of the local militias. Edward VI gave the lieutenancy more functions after the Prayer Book rebellions in 1549 so that they could regain control in the affected regions. Sir John Russell, for example, was appointed Lord Lieutenant of Devon in 1552. Northumberland apparently thought about making the position permanent but did not carry this out. Mary appointed these officers infrequently, particularly after the threat of invasion by France fell away after 1558. It was Elizabeth I who made Lord Lieutenants permanent, in 1585. This was because of the long-running war with Spain and the need to have the militia permanently ready in case of invasion or attack. From 1585 Lord Lieutenants were appointed to nearly every county in England and Wales. After 1587 the positions were held in over half of the counties by Privy Councillors. This improved communications between the Privy Council and the localities. It was also a very prestigious position, and made the office-holder the leading authority in the county or region.

The role of the Lord Lieutenants

The Lord Lieutenants were responsible for the levying of forced loans, the detection of **recusants**, supervision of the JPs and the enforcement of economic regulations. Even if they were not members of the Privy Council they were responsible for communicating developments in their regions back to the Council. All other local officials were meant to obey Lord Lieutenants and their deputies. Commissions, documents that officially appointed officeholders, asked Lord Lieutenants to put their counties into a state of defence. This meant mustering all men who were eligible for military service, either abroad or locally in the militia. They had to arm and train the men. The Lord Lieutenants had deputies called Deputy Lieutenants who were responsible for most of the day-to-day work of the lieutenancy. The post had been created in the 1560s and was a prestigious office. It tended to be held by prominent landowners – either the less dominant peers or leading JPs. The Deputy Lieutenants had to be resident in the area in which they held office.

Although the Lord Lieutenants were made permanent to deal with a particular military situation, it was soon found that they were useful in a broader sense. They made the Privy Council much more aware of events in counties around the kingdom (or example rebellions or tax riots) and therefore made it easier for them to respond to those events if necessary. The office also gave useful responsibility to the resident nobility by allowing them to fulfil their traditions of defending the realm at a time of military need. It brought enhanced stability and consistency to the government at a key time. The role of Lord Lieutenant was not always without conflict, however, as the cost of training and equipping the militia was borne by each county. This caused friction between the shires and London, with the Lord Lieutenant in the middle of that conflict.

Conclusion

Government in the sixteenth century expanded greatly. It became more formalised and standardised across the country. From Henry VIII onwards the Tudor monarchs aimed to expand or maintain their authority, sometimes in the face of popular resistance to their policies. The amount of information available to Elizabeth I about events in the regions was much greater than that accessible to Henry VII. A reliance on local officeholders was not without problems – they frequently ignored orders, prevaricated or worked inefficiently. For many, status was their motivation and they were not especially active in return. Yet even the least active could be prompted into action by urgent national demands or direct commands from central government, and many were enthusiastic.

Recommended reading

Susan Brigden, *New Worlds, Lost Worlds: The Rule of the Tudors, 1485–1603* (Penguin, 2001).

Chapter 5, 'Bearing Rule', is a compelling summary of English government in the period.

Steven Gunn, *Early Tudor Government, 1485–1558* (Palgrave Macmillan, 1995).

This is a very clearly written and accessible book. The chapters on lordship and justice are particularly relevant to this section.

J. Gwynfor Jones, *Early Modern Wales, c.1525–1640* (Palgrave Macmillan, 1994).

This is especially relevant for the Council in the Marches and Wales, as well as the government in Wales in the sixteenth century.

John Lotherington, *The Tudor Years* (Hodder, 2003).

Chapter 8 on the rule of Elizabeth I includes a useful section on local government during her rule.

Question practice

1 To what extent were the governmental reforms of the sixteenth century motivated by a desire for control of the English population?
2 How far were the aims of those involved in popular rebellions in the years 1525–36 similar to those in 1549?
3 How far did attempts to deal with the problem of poverty change in the period 1530–72? **AS**
4 How far was religion the main motive for charity in the period 1509–53? **AS**

The Council in the Marches and Wales and the Council of the North

- Tudor monarchs aimed for uniformity
- They set up two councils to reinforce royal control, execute royal policy and bring uniformity
- The Council in the Marches and Wales was reformed by Cromwell in 1525
- Wales was divided into shires in 1513 and JPs established in all counties
- The Council heard legal cases and administered the borders and Wales in economic and defence matters. It checked officials were doing their jobs
- The Council of the North was re-established in 1525 in response to a tax revolt
- It had a similar function to the Council in the Marches and Wales

The Lord Lieutenants under Elizabeth

- Before 1585 this was an occasional not a permanent role due to the war with Spain
- They levied forced loans, supervised JPs and enforced economic commands
- They were responsible for mustering the militia
- They were seen as useful in keeping the Privy Council aware of events around the kingdom

TUDOR CONTROL OF THE COUNTRY

The growing power of the JPs

- This was a long-established role
- JPs had to own land worth at least £20 and be resident in their county
- They were chosen by the Privy Council on advice from courtiers, Privy Councillors and assize judges
- Unless they were removed for misdemeanours they often served for life
- They heard civil and criminal legal cases at the quarter sessions and executed demands of the government
- Their work grew as new felony offices were created and they had responsibility for poor relief
- They did not always obey every command

Role of the nobility in maintaining order

- The nobility had great influence over their tenants and the local gentry
- They aided with local and regional government, gave military support to the Crown and hospitality to the monarch
- They could influence local appointments of sheriffs
- They could also use that great influence to maintain order or create revolt

▲ Summary diagram: Tudor control of the country

3b: The state and the poor

Overview

Poverty was a significant problem for Tudor governments and a growing problem throughout the sixteenth century. Poverty was an economic and social problem because it caused tension and unrest, as well as being expensive for parishes and governments to deal with. It was also a moral problem, however, because poverty was seen as a symptom that society was not operating properly. It was also people's duty to take care of their poorer neighbours, and this was emphasised after the Reformation because the Church no longer had the responsibility for taking care of the poor as it had previously. During the sixteenth century successive governments tried to support those in poverty who they believed deserved help and to punish those who they felt were undeserving. Those punishments now seem harsh. Punishment was much more severe generally in the sixteenth century, however, and the penalties for offences like unlicensed begging reflected society's fear of vagrancy and beggars.

Charities were extremely important in providing aid for the poor. It was conventional for those with some money to leave an amount to the poor of the parish in their last will and testament. This could be given out by the Church, or could support a school or other institution. It was seen as a religious duty for both Catholics and Protestants to help

the poor, but this was not enough to prevent people from sinking into want or famine when there were bad harvests. Some towns and cities, like Norwich, had arrangements in place to help the poor, including apprenticeships and other employment schemes. There were significant factors that made poverty impossible to control, and others that were a result of the monarch's policies, such as the dissolution of the monasteries from 1536 to 1540.

This chapter examines Tudor control and government of the country through the following sections:

1 *Reasons for the growth of poverty in Tudor England* examines the extent to which poverty grew in the sixteenth century. It also explores the reasons why poverty grew in this period.

2 *Punishments for beggars and vagrants* discusses the perception of poverty in the Tudor period and the differing approaches taken to the 'deserving' and 'undeserving' poor. It looks at the punishments meted out to beggars and the legislation that supported those punishments.

3 *The importance of charities and local authorities in the provision of poor relief* looks at the way that charities could help to support the poor, and the varying schemes to either prevent or end poverty in some towns.

Note it down

Create a spider diagram (see page x) to take notes in this chapter. In the spider's 'body' write 'poverty.' Create 'legs' for the different subsections. Remember to pick out only the most significant points for the spider diagram. You can add to the diagram during revision with index cards, timelines and other note-taking tools.

1 Reasons for the growth of poverty in Tudor England

Socio-economic historian Paul Slack has studied the poor in early modern England. The records that Slack has examined suggest that a larger proportion of England's population was poor at the end of the sixteenth century than at its beginning. In towns, the poor were also more visible and existed in greater numbers. Susan Doran has estimated the percentage of poor who were permanently settled in towns as being between 15 and 30 per cent of the urban population. Young people, sick people and the elderly were particularly vulnerable as they were less able to earn a steady income.

There were numerous reasons for the increase of poverty during the Tudor period, but no single element was the ultimate cause of this problem. Instead, a number of interconnected factors combined to harm the kingdom's economic stability at roughly the same time. These included the closure of the monasteries and religious houses in the late 1530s, periods of illness or poor harvest, the depopulation of the countryside, rampant inflation during the middle of the century, the wars of the 1540s against France and the large increase in population during the period. Governments were afraid that **vagrancy** and poverty might cause disease, violence and unrest. Poverty featured in government legislation, pamphlet material and in people's wills. Price rises were mainly in foodstuffs, and wages were not rising at the same time. Rents rose, and enclosure meant that people were forced off the land. Unemployment was significant in causing poverty but each of these factors contributed to the growth of poverty in differing ways.

The dissolution of the monasteries

The closure of the monasteries and other religious houses, for example, contributed to more widespread poverty in a variety of ways. First, the religious people who had lived in the monasteries lost their way of life and were forced to find new ways of earning an income. When the religious houses were closed, these people also lost their homes, and were forced to search for new shelter. The closure of the religious houses hurt local communities by destroying sanctuaries for people who were ill or weak. They, too, were forced to seek new places to live and often had to resort to begging in order to gather enough money for food. The closure of the monasteries contributed to poverty by dismantling the monastic way of life and leaving the thousands of people who had lived in the monasteries without a means for supporting themselves. The unintended consequence of this was to destroy one of the most important systems for taking care of the sick and the poor. This, in turn, led to a greater number of people being forced to beg for their survival in the cities and towns.

The depopulation of the countryside

During the sixteenth century many people moved into the towns in search of a better life. This meant there were fewer people in the countryside, a process known as depopulation. Depopulation of the countryside contributed to poverty by depriving the country of people who could work in agriculture. This meant smaller harvests because farmers had less labour available to help them with tending and harvesting the crops. Instead, the young people went to urban centres in search of apprenticeships or other kinds of work. The problem was made even worse by the practice of enclosing land for grazing sheep. The sheep needed less care than growing crops, which left many people without jobs. The unemployed moved away rather than choosing to remain on the land (see pages 120–21). Furthermore, the sheep provided wool, a cash commodity, rather than a crop that could be eaten. This meant less food was produced. When combined with poor harvests, the depopulation of the countryside worsened poverty in the period, and led to hunger and price rises due to the scarcity of food (see page 193).

2 Punishments for beggars and vagrants

Poverty was a serious problem for the Tudor monarchs. On the one hand, the common belief was that if the kingdom was doing well and was a moral society, then the majority of its people would be prosperous. On the other hand, they believed in the biblical precept that the poor would always be around them, and that it was up to individual Christians to take care of their poorer neighbours. The question of the poor became even more crucial in the years after the Reformation. For centuries, the Church had been responsible for taking care of the poor. Monks and other religious people had collected and distributed alms for the poor. They had also provided shelter for the sick and homeless. But the Reformation had closed many religious institutions, so their personnel were therefore unable to carry out this charitable work (see page 89). The question of who should make provisions for beggars and vagrants in the community became a serious one, and governments began to consider this problem. Among the elites, humanism was another reason for taking care of the poor – an active citizenry should be able to look after the weaker in society.

The 'deserving' and 'undeserving' poor

One way that the Tudor monarchs dealt with the problem of poverty was by using parliamentary statutes to make provisions for the poor, and to punish those who were taking advantage of others. In his study of poverty in early modern England, historian Paul Slack argues that it is important to remember that there were different definitions of poverty during this period. For example, he notes that economic poverty was connected to morality. A person's moral status could have an effect on the way they were treated regarding their economic poverty. This difference is reflected in the way that the authorities distinguished between two different kinds of beggars. The first group were sometimes described as the 'deserving poor' or the 'respectable poor'. This group might include orphans, widows, elderly people who had no families to help support them, or people with physical disabilities. The respectable poor, as the label implies, had a positive moral reputation. Their poverty was not their own fault, as they were unable or less able to work.

The second group of beggars were known as 'sturdy beggars'. This group had a very poor moral reputation. Sturdy beggars were men and women who were well enough to work but did not. They were associated with thievery, idleness, treason and many other negative characteristics. In the eyes of the society in which they dwelled, this group was dangerous because they operated outside the expected social order. The social order was organised around the concept of the commonwealth, and according to this idea, individuals were responsible for putting the common good ahead of their own desires. This meant that everyone had to contribute to the common good in their own way. The perceived problem with sturdy beggars and vagrants was that they put their idleness first. They neglected their responsibilities to the commonwealth, and were instead parasites living off the hard work of others. Sturdy beggars and vagrants were punished by the authorities but the respectable poor were not. Instead, parliament used legislation in order to find ways to end their poverty and prevent its spread.

Government legislation

The Vagabonds Act of 1530 required the deserving poor to acquire licences in order to beg. This law was to ensure that only those who needed money from begging would be able to beg. This was a provision that enabled poor elderly people and those with physical disabilities to gain an income through begging because they were genuinely unable to work. Sturdy beggars and vagrants were to be excluded from getting these

Vagrants

Vagrants were seen as a serious problem that the Tudor monarchs sought to resolve. Vagrants were people who were typically homeless and had no work. They travelled from town to town aimlessly. Sometimes, they were looking for a new occupation or place to live. However, the government associated such people with lawlessness and disorder. As they had no masters and were not masters themselves, vagrants represented a threat to the social order – although the evidence of vagrant crime does not really support the perception. Vagrants were often considered sturdy beggars because they often begged in order to support themselves. Furthermore, there was a common recognition that sturdy beggars were able-bodied. In other words, this group of beggars were viewed as physically able to work, even though they did not. Vagrants could be classified in this category because they were well enough to travel between different towns.

licences. They would have to find work to support themselves. Individuals who broke these laws faced harsh punishments including whipping, branding and being locked in stocks in village squares.

The Act of 1536

Another parliamentary provision for the poor was the Act of 1536. One component of this Act was that every parish should take a voluntary monetary collection for the poor every week. Local officials were also told to record the needy poor, and to record the amounts of money that parishioners promised to give towards the relief of the poor. In 1572, parliament approved harsher penalties against vagrants and finally included a compulsory poor rate. This was essentially a set tax that people had to pay to their parishes for the maintenance of the poor. The law prescribed that vagrants should be whipped and bored through the ear the first time they were caught in vagrancy. For the second offence, they should be hanged. The only way out of these punishments was to find a master who was willing to employ the vagrant. These punishments were extremely harsh, and there is little evidence to show that they were carried out to their full extent. According to historian Steve Hindle, who has researched Elizabethan Essex, local vagrants may have been tolerated whereas those who came from further afield were severely punished. The nature of the justice system and the legislation meant that there was room for selective enforcement of these laws by the authorities.

Vagrants and employment

Legislation passed in the 1530s and repeated throughout the century made it a crime for individuals to be caught outside their home parishes without employment. The government's aim was to encourage vagrants to find work in the place where they came from. Many vagrants did find work, though it was often temporary in nature. Vagrants often found work on farms, helping to harvest crops during the late summer and autumn. They also found work mowing hay. Vagrants often found work in one area, completed it and then moved to another area in search of similar employment, and following their own usual routes. Vagrants sometimes had three or four different bases where they would seek employment during the spring and summer. In the winter, they would have a more difficult time finding employment, and would then perhaps move into towns or cities looking for work or other ways to support themselves.

▲ A vagrant being whipped as a punishment for begging. What does this woodcut say about Tudor reactions to the poor? Which different groups of people are portrayed here and how are they portrayed?

3 The importance of charities and local authorities in the provision of poor relief

Individual charity had always been an important way to support the poor, for example in wills. Local authorities in towns also provided aid for the poor and aimed to provide moral reformation and ways into work.

Note it down

There are some important dates in this section. In order to help you remember them, create an annotated timeline. Put the dates on one side of the timeline and the events on the other. Next to each event or policy, write brief details about it.

Individual charity

While Catholicism was still the dominant religion in England and Wales individual charity was embedded in the fabric of life and society. The Catholic doctrine of good works was one reason for this – Catholics believed that good works, for example giving money and other gifts to the poor, helped them to get to heaven more

quickly. Charity was also reciprocal for Catholics, as the poor prayed for their benefactors in return. This gave them a function and purpose. Money was given in life and after death in wills. At funerals a donation was made to the poor called 'doles', in exchange for which the poor would say prayers for the souls of the departed. Again, this was intended to get them into heaven quicker.

Protestants saw this approach as **superstitious**. They did not believe that good works helped people to get into heaven. They wanted people to give to charity without expectation of return. So while charity to the poor did continue, it did not have the same motivation for those who identified themselves as Protestants. It also meant that the function and purpose of the poor was removed, and they were not respected for a role that they played. Charity was less personal and more institutional, with personal gifts to the poor in wills (for example of bread and shelter) slowly declining. There were also conditions placed on this charity, for example that the poor had to behave in a godly way.

Obviously this was not the case for all. Some Protestant benefactors did retain a connection with the poor and tended to leave bequests to areas where they were born, lived or had family. They did leave money to the poor in wills. Catholicism did not die out either, although the widespread sense of the need for good works did. The change in attitudes to the poor was important; religious changes were not the only reason for it but did contribute.

Local authorities and poor relief

Henry VIII's Reformation changed the way the Church interacted with the people of England. In the past, the Church had been responsible for much of the charitable work that took place within the kingdom, but the Reformation meant that people no longer felt obligated to donate to the Church in the way that they had done previously. Furthermore, the Reformation led to the dissolution of the monasteries and other religious houses. These foundations had provided religious men and women a place in which to withdraw from the temptations of the secular world, but they also did a large amount of charitable work in the communities in which they dwelled. With these important religious institutions either destroyed or transformed, other groups sought to find solutions to the problem of helping the poor in their local communities. In smaller communities, parishes knew the individuals and families who were facing poverty, and were often able to provide for them accordingly. However, it was more difficult to manage the poor in towns and cities.

The London hospitals

The hospitals in London were one set of institutions that attempted to address the problem of poor relief. Edward VI donated Bridewell Palace to the City of London in 1553. It was to be refounded as Bridewell Hospital, a refuge for homeless or orphaned children and a house of correction. The children who were inmates in Bridewell were to be cared for, given a basic education, and trained in a trade. These steps would help the children to find employment when they were old enough to leave Bridewell. The second purpose of Bridewell was as a house of correction for vagrants, prostitutes and other 'undeserving' poor. They would have to work and pray for their moral reformation. The other hospitals in London – Christ's, St Thomas', St Bartholomew's, and Bethlehem – also provided places for the poor and vagrants. They did not focus so much on reform of the poor, however, but on health and education. St Bartholomew's and St Thomas' were intended to help the sick, while Bethlehem (established in the 1540s) was for the insane. Christ's Hospital was intended for orphans, was donated to the City of London by Henry VIII in 1546 and admitted its first orphans in 1552.

Case study: Norwich

Towns and cities established their own initiatives to help the poor in their communities, without direction from the Crown or parliament. Norwich is known in particular for the ways it attempted to address poverty, beginning in the 1570s. Norwich was one of the earliest cities to bring about reforms regarding the poor. The city took a census of the poor in 1556. Even earlier, in May 1549, the city government ordered a collection for the poor – independent from the efforts of central government. They initiated schemes designed to find employment and apprenticeships for poor children. They also appointed 'overseers' to ensure that the poor were living moral lives. Norwich's approach to poverty became well known, and was copied by other cities and towns at the end of the sixteenth century. Its example has even been credited as the inspiration for many of the legal reforms introduced to parliament during the same period.

Government legislation to tackle poverty

Poverty was viewed as a serious problem that harmed the stability of the social order. People believed that there was a link between poverty and crime, particularly theft. Vagabonds particularly were viewed with scepticism as they travelled through the country. Parliament began to address the problem of poverty through statutory legislation in the 1530s. This was because poverty was such a threat to the commonwealth and safety of the entire kingdom. The government considered a number of different poverty schemes throughout this period. Some of these were based on the successful initiatives that had been adopted in cities like Norwich, while other ideas were devised by reformers who were concerned about the welfare of the poor. For example, parliamentary drafts show that parliament considered special taxes and employment provided by the state as ways to help people who were searching for work. Parliament even considered setting the prices of goods in order to keep costs down so that the poor could afford necessities. The variety of different approaches to reducing poverty shows that the government realised that poverty was caused by a variety of factors. It also showed that people believed that poverty affected everyone, and that the best way to address it was through parliament.

The Vagabonds Acts of 1530 and 1536

The Vagabonds Acts (see page 87) established a form of licensing for beggars and punishing those who were unlicensed. These measures were largely punitive, tackling poverty by punishing those who the government felt were not making sufficient effort to get work or avoid begging. The Act of 1536 also made local civic leaders and churchwardens responsible for the provision of poor relief in their areas. They were to raise voluntary funds for supporting the poor people in their own communities. This Act was important because it established the parish as the link between the poor and the government's relief of poverty. Legislation addressing the problem of poverty would follow this model for centuries to come.

Parish collections from 1552

Other important measures were introduced later in the period. In 1552, an Act established weekly parish collections for the poor. Each parish was to appoint a person who would be responsible for collecting and distributing alms to the deserving poor. The law created registers for the poor so each parish would have records of the people there who were unable to work. Each parish was expected to take care of their own poor, and begging was completely outlawed. Vagrants were to be whipped out of the towns they visited. Queen Mary introduced badges for licensed beggars to display as part of her poor relief in 1555.

The Poor Laws of 1563 and 1572

Other innovative approaches to poor relief were attempted during Elizabeth's reign. The 1563 Poor Law required contributions to the parish's poor box. Individuals who refused to donate were brought before JPs for punishment. The 1572 Poor Law endorsed harsh punishments for beggars, like whipping or boring them through the ear on the first offence. It also introduced the poor rate to help support the impoverished people of local parishes. JPs were to determine how much money was required to support the poor of each parish. They then assessed a compulsory tax rate that individuals paid on their goods in order to provide for the parish poor. From 1576, parishes were required to provide work for people who could not find employment. This was enshrined in a law called the 'Act for Setting the Poor on Work'. They were given tasks like working with wool or iron so poor people would have a means to support themselves. JPs were required to buy raw materials to provide work for those who were able. The 1576 Act established houses of correction that punished able-bodied beggars. In these institutions, they would be forced to work in order to finance their maintenance. Poverty was therefore a problem that all the Tudor monarchs and their parliaments were concerned about and addressed.

Conclusion

Poverty was not a problem that was solved by 1588 – in fact it had got worse. While there were different ways to aid the poor there were simply too many causes of poverty. These were complex and very difficult to solve. Poor people who begged without a licence were severely punished, with a death sentence facing those who were caught twice. The government was afraid of the potential for landless and unoccupied people to create disorder and violence, as well as of poverty as a symptom of a society that was not working. The period up to 1588 saw the beginning of a shift from local charity to centrally administered poor relief.

Work together

Listen to parts 1–3 of the podcast: www.history.org.uk/resources/student_resource_4139,4143_108.html

In pairs, produce a handout that you could use to teach other students about this topic. Be careful to cover all of the different sections of the topic, and make your handout clear and interesting.

Recommended reading

Marjorie Keniston McIntosh, *Poor Relief in England, 1350–1600* (Cambridge University Press, 2014).

This interesting book covers medieval and early Tudor approaches to poverty in Chapters 2–4 and the impact of the Reformation on poverty in Chapter 5.

Paul Slack, *Poverty and Policy in Tudor and Stuart England* (Longman, 1988).

This is an academic book that provides a detailed analysis of early modern poverty, including the perceptions of poverty and the different classifications of the poor.

Paul Thomas, *Authority and Disorder in Tudor Times, 1485–1603* (Cambridge University Press, 1999).

Chapter 2 is an accessible summary of the law and justice in the Tudor period, while Chapter 10 explores the measures the government took to deal with the poor.

Reasons for the growth of poverty in Tudor England

- **Dissolution of the monasteries** – those employed in the monasteries lost their jobs and dissolution reduced the charity available to the poor
- **Urban migration** – this meant there were fewer people to work in the countryside, which led to smaller harvests
- **Bad harvests** – less grain meant higher food prices which poor people struggled to afford

THE STATE AND THE POOR

The importance of charities and local authorities in the provision of poor relief

- Individual charity declined or changed with the spread of Protestantism
- Local authorities became more responsible for charity
- The London hospitals were set up to help the sick and orphans. Bridewell was also a house of correction for the 'undeserving' poor
- Some towns set up their own schemes to relieve poverty, for example collections for the poor
- An Act in 1552 established weekly parish collections
- The Poor Laws of 1563 and 1571 were intended to support the poor, give them work and punish those who could yet weren't working

Punishments for beggars and vagrants

- Poverty was a serious economic and moral problem in the sixteenth century
- Some poor people were seen as 'deserving' poor – they would receive charity
- Some were labelled 'undeserving' and condemned and punished
- The Vagabonds Act of 1530 set up a licensing system for beggars. Unlicensed beggars would be whipped, branded and suffered other harsh punishments
- The Act of 1536 set up collections for the poor in each parish
- The Act of 1572 led to harsher penalties for vagrants and included a compulsory poor rate

▲ Summary diagram: The state and the poor

Essay technique: Argument

Essays that develop a good argument are more likely to reach the highest levels. As you know, your essays are judged on the extent to which they analyse. The mark scheme distinguishes between five different levels of analysis (this is a summary – the full mark scheme can be found on Edexcel's website):

Level 1 (LOW)	Simplistic or no analysis
Level 2	Limited analysis of key issues
Level 3	Some analysis of key issues
Level 4	Analysis of key issues
Level 5 (HIGH)	Sustained analysis of key issues

The key feature of the highest level is sustained analysis: analysis that unites the whole of the essay.

High level arguments

Typically, essays examine a series of factors. A good way of achieving sustained analysis is to consider which factor is most important.

Consider the following question:

> **How accurate is it to say that approaches to the problem of poverty changed significantly in the period 1536–76?**

The following introduction addresses the question, without developing an argument:

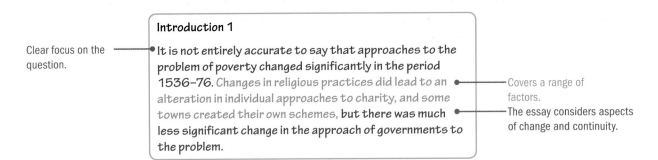

Clear focus on the question.

Introduction 1

It is not entirely accurate to say that approaches to the problem of poverty changed significantly in the period 1536–76. Changes in religious practices did lead to an alteration in individual approaches to charity, and some towns created their own schemes, but there was much less significant change in the approach of governments to the problem.

Covers a range of factors.

The essay considers aspects of change and continuity.

Introduction 1 could be improved by the inclusion of an argument. An argument is a type of explanation – a claim supported by a reason. A good way of beginning to develop an argument is to think about the meaning of the words in the question. For example, what is meant by 'approaches', and what is meant by 'significant'?

Here is an example of an introduction that begins an argument:

The argument begins with a claim: approaches did change, but not always significantly.

Introduction 2

Approaches to poverty in the years 1536–76 did change, but not always significantly. **The gradual move from traditional Catholicism to Protestantism affected the role and purpose of the poor and the kind of aid given. Some towns, like Norwich, established innovative approaches to supporting their poor.** These changes were significant because they had an effect on the type and volume of aid given. The government's approach to poverty, however, did not change as significantly, being based on punishment for those who were seen as undeserving. **The most significant area of change was the religious one, because it had a long-term effect on the image and treatment of the poor.**

The claim is supported by a reason, based on the meaning of the word 'significant'.

The introduction concludes with an argument about which aspect of change was the most significant.

Introduction 2 focuses on the question and sets out the key issues on which the essay will focus. However, it also sets out an argument that can then be developed throughout each paragraph and rounded off with an overall judgement in the conclusion. It also introduces an argument about which aspect of reform was most significant. Therefore, Introduction 2 is of a higher level than Introduction 1 (see page 92).

Activity: Developing an argument

Here is a plan in answer to the following question:

How accurate is it to say that approaches to the problem of poverty changed significantly in the period 1536–76?

Using your notes from the previous chapter:
1 Write a brief definition of 'approaches'.
2 List the approaches taken to poverty that changed in the period, and those that did not.

3 Write a paragraph that clearly answers the question.
   • Begin with a clear claim about the significance of the change.
   • Justify this with reasons based on your understanding of significance.
   • Make an argument about which approach involved the most significant change.

3c: Resistance to Tudor rule

Overview

Tudor governments had made immensely significant political and religious changes from the 1520s onwards. The period was also one of economic and social change, not all of which was formed by government policy. The changes also brought unrest among the people who felt the impact around the country. Those who suffered from rising prices and stagnating wage rates resented the additional financial demands made of them, leading to tax revolts. These revolts could prevent such demands from being carried out. There was also anger about the religious policies of Tudor monarchs, especially those of Henry VIII and Edward VI. The people who took part in these rebellions came from a wide cross-section of society and were deeply resentful of the alterations to their traditional worship, fearing the consequences for their souls. This resentment was made stronger because some policies that appeared religious, such as the dissolution of the monasteries, had severe economic consequences for local communities.

From 1570 onwards popular resistance declined. The stability of Elizabeth's government, government legislation, external threats and the clampdown on Catholics all affected popular resistance. This is not to say that it disappeared entirely. There were still plots (albeit on a small scale) and tensions within society at times of need, but the risk to government had declined greatly.

This chapter examines Tudor control and government of the country through the following sections:

1 *The significance of resistance to financial demands* explores the reaction of the population to changing financial demands made by Tudor governments, as well as the causes of that resistance.
2 *The nature of the threat posed by popular risings, 1536–69* examines the causes, events and nature of the threat that popular revolts posed.
3 *Reasons for the decline of popular resistance, 1570–88* looks at the reasons why such popular revolts declined in Elizabeth I's reign.

1 The significance of resistance to financial demands

There were massive changes to the government during the Tudor era. One of the key tenets that remained the same, however, was that the monarch needed permission from parliament to levy taxes on the people. In 1525, Henry VIII sought additional money to pay for a military expedition into France. Such warfare was unpopular at the time because Henry had made two previous unsuccessful military attempts in France, in 1522 and 1523. It was unlikely that parliament would support either war or a new tax. In response to this problem, Cardinal Wolsey devised a solution. This was called the 'Amicable Grant'. The Grant was to be a special, one-time tax on England's laity and clergy. Their goods were to be evaluated, and a tax would be levied based on the value of the goods. The clergy were expected to pay a greater tax on their property.

But the people had little money. They were still in the process of paying subsidies for the 1523 campaigns in France. They simply had no additional money to spend. The clergy wrote to Cromwell because they did not have the amount of money that was required by this grant. At Lavenham in Suffolk, around 10,000 men gathered, ready to rebel. The Amicable Grant was abandoned. The King and his ministers recognised that the people could not pay the Grant, and even pardoned the leaders of the failed rebellion. The Amicable Grant confirmed that the people would resist taxes that were not agreed in parliament. Furthermore, it showed that there were limits to the King's ability to enter warfare: if the people could not afford the endeavour, then it would simply have to be abandoned. As England could not afford war, Henry's attempts to invade France stopped until the early 1540s.

Note it down

Use the 1:2 method (see page x) to take notes on this chapter. Put the headings in the left-hand column and the main points in the right. Include causes, main events and consequences. Also begin to think about the detailed evidence that you need for your essays. You can either include this in your notes or highlight a photocopied section of the text.

▲ The King's procession to parliament in 1512. Why did the King not present his request to the parliament in 1525? What was the intention behind the Amicable Grant?

2 The nature of the threat posed by popular risings, 1536–69

The **popular rebellions** that happened in the period 1536–69 posed different kinds of threats to the Crown. There were loyal rebellions that aimed to bring problems to the attention of the monarch, and there were rebellions that wanted to overthrow the monarch. The popular rebellions posed varying degrees of threat and had different aims.

Note it down

It would be useful for you to understand what caused the rebellions and what the rebels wanted. You could also categorise the nature of each rebellion. As you read through the section make notes in a table like the one below:

Rebellion	Causes	Aims of the rebellion	Nature of the threat

The Pilgrimage of Grace

The most significant threat that any monarch may have faced in the sixteenth century was the Pilgrimage of Grace. This was a large rebellion that took place in the northern counties in the autumn of 1536.

Causes of the rebellion

Why did people participate in the Pilgrimage of Grace? There was a sense of great discontent among ordinary people around 1536. As with the Lincolnshire rebellion, people were afraid that their religion was under attack. Religious life was important to many people, and they valued their traditions. They genuinely believed that these traditions were under attack from Henry VIII's regime, and they simply could not tolerate compromising such an important element of their lives. Furthermore, many of the people believed that the religious houses were being treated unfairly by the regime. The Act of Supremacy of 1534 had caused the Church in England to leave the Roman Catholic Church. For the King, this meant that the religious houses would also have to change the way they practised religion. How could monks and nuns be considered his loyal subjects if they obeyed the rules established by religious orders in distant places? The religious houses raised money that was sent to Rome to support the Pope and the works of the Roman Catholic Church. In other words, they took money from the King's loyal subjects, and sent it to support the King's newest foreign enemy. For the King and his advisers, the religious houses needed to be investigated to determine their loyalty. Those that were corrupt would have to be closed.

Religion

The rebels in 1536–37 saw the investigations into the religious houses as a challenge to their way of life. Monasteries, abbeys and nunneries provided important services to the local communities in which they resided (see page 89). Many people rebelled because they believed the government was treating the religious houses unfairly. They understood recent parliamentary policies to be an attack on traditional religion. This was even expressed in the name of the rebellion, the Pilgrimage of Grace. Pilgrimages had been recently banned because the government saw them as superstitious. By choosing this name, the rebels expressed to the regime that they preferred traditional religious practices to the still undefined new religion. Religion was one factor that inspired people to rebel in 1536.

Economic factors

People were also prompted to participate in the Pilgrimage of Grace because of economic concerns. Economic difficulties were probably a lesser factor but they were still mentioned by the pilgrims in the documents they sent to the King. The 1535 harvest had been poor, which had led to an increase in food prices. Furthermore, people objected to the Statute of Uses. This statute made it easier for the monarch to tax sales of landed property. In the past, English **common law** had no way for feudal landowners to divide their land between beneficiaries through their will. Instead, landowners could only do this through a legal technicality called the 'use'. Uses allowed landowners to divide up land among a number of different people so that the landowner's original intent was maintained. A problem with uses was that they tended to create fraud and corruption, and the Statute of Uses was intended to prevent this from happening. But the Statute of Uses instead seemed to make fraud even worse. It was also seen as a burden on landowners, who were responsible for paying additional taxes on the land. Many people therefore objected to the financial implications of the Statute of Uses. One of the demands made by the rebels was that the Statutes of Uses be repealed.

Political reasons

A third factor that contributed to the Pilgrimage of Grace was the political climate of the 1530s. From 1529 to 1536, parliament had met. This became known as the Reformation Parliament because of the vast changes that occurred in these seven years. The Reformation Parliament is often associated with the religious reforms that it initiated (see page 17). However, the Reformation Parliament also brought about other major changes to the structure of English society. Many people believed that the ministers surrounding the King were responsible for the changes that they witnessed. They particularly despised Thomas Cromwell and Sir Richard Rich. They also believed that these ministers had caused the destruction of Catherine of Aragon, Henry VIII's first queen. Henry had finally secured an annulment from her in 1534, after breaking from the Roman Catholic Church. But Catherine of Aragon had been a popular queen and enjoyed wide support from the people. When they examined things like the royal marriage and unpopular policies, many people could only conclude that the King was listening to advisers who were not suited to perform this task.

Aims of the rebels

The articles issued by the pilgrims suggest that the rebels thought that the King would help them if he understood the problems that ordinary subjects faced, and the concerns they had. They believed that the King did not know about the extent of their poverty, and that he would do more to address their concerns if he could just hear about their troubles. They hoped that the harmful legislation that had been recently passed in parliament could be undone. They also believed that the parliament and the King's council were full of men who did not tell the King the truth. Since the work of parliament had harmed the people, the rebels requested the King to summon a new session of parliament. They wanted this parliament to meet at York rather than in London. They hoped that a parliament meeting in York would be able to prevent the men who had caused the harmful legislation from participating. The rebels thought that London had become corrupt. By moving the government out of London, it could once again be a political body that passed legislation for the good of all the people.

Events of the Pilgrimage of Grace

The Pilgrimage of Grace took place in three different phases. The first phase was known as the Lincolnshire rebellion. This rebellion took place from 2 to 12 October 1536. The second phase was the longest and included the largest number of participants, and took place predominantly in Yorkshire from 8 October until 8 December 1536. The final stage took place 16 January–10

February 1537, and involved a rising in Cumberland and Sir Francis Bigod's revolt in Yorkshire.

Stage 1: The Lincolnshire rebellion

The first stage of the rebellion occurred at a church on 2 October. The people were upset that a local religious house had been closed, and had heard rumours that Henry VIII was also planning to close local parish churches, or at least to take away their relics and valuable objects. The people simply would not tolerate this attack on local parishes. Beginning in Louth, in Lincolnshire, the rebellion spread to neighbouring villages and then throughout Lincolnshire. The rebels even occupied Lincoln Cathedral. News of the rebellion in Lincolnshire was passed through market networks and people travelling through the region. An estimated 20,000 common people rose against the King and his government in Lincolnshire. The rebellion was over by 12 October, when the Duke of Suffolk finally arrived with an army. The people dispersed, and the leaders of the rebellion were captured and executed for treason.

Stage 2: The Yorkshire rebellion

The Lincolnshire rebellion was unsuccessful but it prompted people to identify a sense of discontent with the government that many shared. A renewed rebellion started in Yorkshire on 13 October 1536. This rebellion spread throughout Yorkshire and parts of Cumbria, passed along by the same trading and news networks. This rebellion was led by Robert Aske, a barrister from Selby in Yorkshire. Aske led a group of about 9,000 rebels into York, and occupied the city. This rebellion was even larger than the rising that had gathered in Lincolnshire. An estimated 30,000 to 40,000 people took part in the Pilgrimage of Grace. They marched under the banner of the Five Wounds of Christ. The Five Wounds referred to the wounds that Christ received during the crucifixion, in his hands, feet, and side. The image was strongly associated with the traditions of the Catholic Church. The Five Wounds were also regarded as superstitious by some Protestants. By using this image, the rebels combined religious imagery with high politics. The Yorkshire rebellion was better organised than the rebellion in Lincolnshire. It also had better leadership. The rebels also called for specific demands from the King and his government.

Stage 3: Sir Francis Bigod's revolt

Sir Francis Bigod had unwillingly participated in the Pilgrimage of Grace. He was a Protestant, and had been captured by some of the Catholic pilgrims. However, he realised that he and the pilgrims shared some of the same goals regarding religion in England. Like the pilgrims, he believed that the monasteries should be reformed rather than dissolved. They also shared the belief that the Crown should not interfere in religious matters. Bigod became one of the leaders of the rebellion. He remained suspicious of Henry VIII's intentions and doubted that the King would keep his promises. He soon became disillusioned by the pace of the fulfilment of promises that the King had made to Robert Aske, the leader of the Pilgrimage of Grace. Bigod decided to take matters into his own hands on 16 January 1537. He sent out copies of the pilgrims' oath again, and attempted to reignite the rebellion by contacting former rebels. However, the rebels were not persuaded to rise against the King again.

Bigod attempted to launch a raid on Hull from Beverly but was raided before he could lead the assault. Sixty-two of his men were captured but Bigod escaped. Two loyal conspirators attempted to capture Hull and Scarborough but these attempts failed. Bigod was captured in Cumberland on 10 February 1537. He was held at Carlisle Castle before being executed on 2 June 1537. Bigod's revolt inspired a further attempt at rebellion in Cumberland. On 16 February 1537, Thomas Clifford unintentionally stirred up a revolt in Carlisle. Angry rebels marched on Carlisle but were quickly crushed by Clifford and Sir Christopher Dacre.

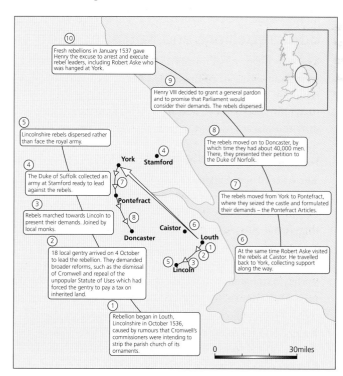

▲ Figure 1: Map of the Pilgrimage of Grace, 1536–37

The restoration of order

The Pilgrimage of Grace was the largest popular threat to any Tudor monarch. It was intended to be a loyal rebellion that brought the crucial concerns to the attention of the King. The Crown negotiated with the rebels for some time in exchange for their obedience. Henry VIII even invited Robert Aske to spend time with him in London over Christmas. The King promised to convene a parliament at York sometime in 1537, but he defended his prerogative to select his own advisers. Henry also refused to give in to the rebels' demand that he replace unpopular men like Thomas Cromwell and Sir Richard Rich. Peace returned to the north relatively quickly. The people promised to submit to the King. There were even rumours that the King would crown his new queen, Jane Seymour, at York Minster. However, these promises all faded by spring 1537. The rebel leaders were interrogated and punished. Robert Aske was executed, and his corpse hung from York's walls. In all, the Crown executed over 200 rebels. Sir Francis Bigod's revolt in the spring of 1537 found little support. He was also punished swiftly. The people had communicated their beliefs about problems in the kingdom through rebellion. Ultimately, however, the Crown was victorious, and order was restored.

The rebellions of 1549: The Prayer Book rebellions and Kett's rebellion

The two major rebellions of 1549 took place in the south-west and south-east of England. They were motivated by religious, economic and social concerns. There were also many minor rebellions as well. These happened in many different places around England.

Causes of the rebellions

The next major challenge to the Crown occurred in the tumultuous year of 1549. Edward VI's regime faced two major rebellions during this summer. Like the Pilgrimage of Grace, the rebellions combined ordinary men and women with more elite members of society. The grievances that the people expressed were similar to the 1536 rebellions, too. In 1549, the people cited the pace of religious reforms as a reason for rebellion. The rebels likewise believed that the King's advisers were the reason for the rapid pace of reform in 1549. There were also economic problems that contributed to the later rebellions. The economic situation was even bleaker during the 1540s. The kingdom had been bankrupted by wars in France and Scotland. The currency had been devalued, meaning that money was not worth as much as

it had been in recent years. This situation was reflected in the international market, and in the inflation that affected ordinary people at home. Furthermore, the practice of enclosing land harmed peasant farmers. It contributed to the depopulation of the countryside as labourers sought work in the towns and cities. In 1549, the rebels claimed that enclosure was one of the largest threats to their well-being, and they asked the government to address this significant problem.

Nature of the threat

The rebellions of 1549 were perhaps not as large or as organised as the Pilgrimage of Grace, but they were spread out through numerous counties in England. The rebellions in the west and in East Anglia were the largest during a particularly difficult summer. The 1549 rebellions were able to attract large numbers of supporters, although the numbers were not as large or concentrated as they had been during the Pilgrimage of Grace. Nevertheless, the government took their threat seriously. The people who participated in the rebellions were largely from the lower levels of the social order. These were the labourers who were most affected by the economic hardships of the 1540s. They were able to gain the support of small numbers of yeomen and local gentry but the rebellions were largely lower class. They rebelled in order to preserve the old ways, whether it was the old ways of the Church or the old system of reserving lands for public use.

The Prayer Book rebellion: Events

The first major rebellion that occurred in 1549 was the Prayer Book rebellion. This rebellion was largely confined to Cornwall and Devon. The primary catalyst for this rebellion was the First Prayer Book published in English (see page 55). It was introduced to parishes for Whitsunday. The people were used to celebrating the mass in Latin. The Prayer Book contained only simplified services in English. The clergy were also expected to follow new Protestant guidelines for church services. They were discouraged from wearing the **vestments** that they had worn in the past because these articles of clothing were viewed as being Roman Catholic. Altars had been seen for centuries as the most sacred places in churches, but these were replaced with communion tables in some churches.

The rebellion in this part of the kingdom had its origins in the unpopularity of William Body, the government's agent. Body was responsible for informing local parishes about changes to the kingdom's religious policies. Parish churches were ordered to remove their stained glass, altar candles and other materials because these were too closely associated with Catholic religious practices. It was Body's

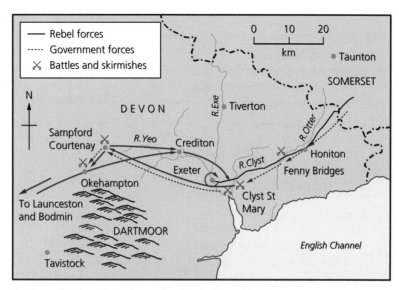

▲ Figure 2: Map of the Prayer Book rebellion, 1549

job to ensure that the churches in Cornwall had removed all their heretical images. On 6 April 1548, an angry mob killed him at Helston. As a result, the JPs investigated the murder, and hanged some of the mob's leaders.

Rebellion was reignited in 1549 when adoption of the new Prayer Book was made compulsory. The rebellion started in Bodmin, where the rebels gathered in a camp beginning on 6 June. They began an advancement into Devon and made plans to besiege Plymouth. Devon was already beginning its own independent rebellion. The villagers of Sampford Courtenay were furious that their priest had said the new service on Whitsunday. They persuaded him to return to the old Latin mass. The Devonshire JPs were unable to intervene. The rebels from Sampford Courtenay joined the Cornish rebels and a large number of others at Crediton. By July 1549, the rebellion grew to a force of 4,000–6,000 people. The rebels shared in common the idea that traditional religion should remain in place until Edward reached the age of majority.

On 2 July, the rebels advanced on Exeter and besieged the city. Somerset's government was slow to respond to the rebellion. This was in part due to the limited military resources he had at his disposal: the kingdom had no standing army, and the experienced military leaders were already trying to end disturbances in the Midlands. Nevertheless, the rebels were not able to seize Exeter. Lord Russell and an army of approximately 8,000 finally defeated the rebellion at Sampford Courtenay on 17 August.

Kett's rebellion: Events

The other major rebellion of 1549 is known as Kett's rebellion. The rebellion began after a religious feast in Wymondham on the weekend of 6 July 1549, after which

a group of people set off to destroy hedges and fences. These had been set up to enclose the land by powerful landowners. One of their first targets was Sir John Flowerdew. He was a local landowner and lawyer who had been involved in the demolition of Wymondham Abbey during the dissolution of the monasteries. Flowerdew bribed the rioters to attack Robert Kett's lands instead. Robert Kett was a yeoman farmer, a **tanner** and a significant figure in the local community. After listening to the rebels' grievances Kett became the leader of this rebellion. It was based in East Anglia, though it spread into nearby regions in July and August. Enclosures were the major complaint of the people who participated in this rebellion. A small number of rebels even attacked the fences and hedges that had been placed on enclosed land. Kett and his followers established a camp outside Norwich on Mousehold Heath for around six weeks. From his base there, under a tree known as 'Kett's Oak', Kett attempted to provide justice for the people who were hurt by the enclosures.

Enclosures were a major reason for the rebellion in East Anglia but the rebels were also unhappy about the religious changes. The Prayer Book was unpopular in this region of the kingdom among many people but there were evangelical Protestants involved with the leadership of the revolt. Religion was a secondary aim of the revolt and leaders like Kett encouraged Protestant ministers to preach to the rebels on Mousehold Heath. They encouraged the use of the Prayer Book and were frustrated with the slow progress of the Reformation in England. The rebels communicated with Protector Somerset about their unhappiness with economic and religious concerns. They wrote a list of 120 demands

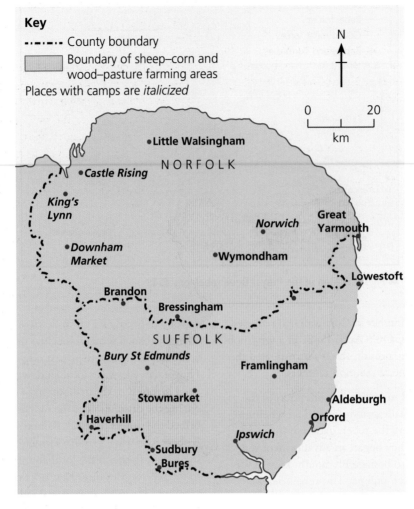

Key

- – · – · – County boundary
- ▨ Boundary of sheep–corn and wood–pasture farming areas

Places with camps are *italicized*

N

0   20
km

- •Little Walsingham

NORFOLK

- •Castle Rising

King's Lynn

Norwich
•

Great Yarmouth
•

- •*Downham Market*

- •Wymondham

- Lowestoft•

Brandon
•

Bressingham

SUFFOLK

Bury St Edmunds
•

Framlingham
•

Stowmarket
•

- •Aldeburgh

Haverhill

Orford•

Ipswich

•Sudbury
•Bures

▲ Figure 3: Map of Kett's rebellion, 1549

that they wished the government to address. These included concerns about enclosures (see pages 120–21), fishing rights, the measurement of crops and wardships. These were much more central than the religious demands described above. The rebels felt the impact of **dearth** and believed that widespread poverty could be stalled if the government restored Henry VII's policies regarding tenants and freeholders. The rebels communicated with Protector Somerset about their unhappiness with economic and religious concerns. The rebellion continued to grow over time. An estimated 15,000 people marched on Norwich. The rebels were defeated at Norwich by an army led by the Earl of Warwick with the aid of foreign mercenaries. Around 3,000 rebels were killed by Warwick's army, and another 300 were executed in Norwich. Kett was tried for treason and hanged on 26 November.

The lesser rebellions of 1549

The two major rebellions were not the only uprisings in 1549. All around England there were minor revolts over the summer of 1549. They happened in 23 counties, from a minor rising in May in Yorkshire against the chantry commissions to those in Oxfordshire and Buckinghamshire in July by conservative clergy. The local gentry were able to suppress some of the uprisings, for example those in Northamptonshire, Wiltshire, Hampshire, Berkshire, Surrey and Kent. The nobility were commanded to put down other rebellions. The Marquis of Dorset and the Earl of Huntington crushed an uprising in Leicestershire and Rutland in August and September 1549. The Earl of Shrewsbury contained the rebellion in Derbyshire, Shropshire and Nottinghamshire. Violent repression followed, including the execution of prominent rebels.

The revolt of the northern earls, 1569

The revolt of the northern earls, also known as the northern rising or rebellion, happened from November to December 1569. It was an unsuccessful attempt by Catholic nobles to remove the Protestant Elizabeth I and put Mary, Queen of Scots, on the throne.

Causes of the rebellion

The 1569 rebellion was largely about religious grievances. The rebels wanted to replace Queen Elizabeth with Mary, Queen of Scots, because Mary was a Roman Catholic. The Duke of Norfolk additionally conspired to marry Mary. This would make Norfolk the king of a Roman Catholic England.

In the rising in the north of 1569, the rebelling earls believed that Queen Elizabeth was a **heretic**. Furthermore, they believed that a heretic could not rule a kingdom. The rebel leaders convinced others to join their rebellion and used the promise of restored Catholic religion to gain support. The leaders of the rebellion were also furious that the Queen had removed them from important roles in the north. The Queen had placed predominantly Protestant men from the south into military and political offices that had been vacated in the north. This particularly made Thomas Percy, Earl of Northumberland, hostile to Elizabeth. He and the other northern earls saw Mary, Queen of Scots, as their best chance to restore traditional religion to the north, and to help them once again regain the prominence that Elizabeth had taken from them.

Nature of the threat

The threat posed by the powerful northern earls was very real. Many people in the northern regions of the kingdom still practised religion according to Roman Catholic traditions. The rebels gained some followers by using the same emblems as the Pilgrimage of Grace. However, the rebellion was not able to garner the support of a large number of ordinary men and women. The support that they did gain collapsed early on in the rebellion. The rebels were also unable to rescue Mary, Queen of Scots, from captivity. The attempt to place her on the English throne did not spring from a popular movement but instead had its origins in court politics. In all, the rebellion was small and unsuccessful because it was tied to high politics rather than also including the grievances of a wide spectrum of northern society.

Events of the rebellion

The final major popular challenge to the Crown occurred in 1569. Once again, this rebellion was based in Yorkshire, and is now known as the rising in the north, or the northern rebellion. As in 1536, the rebels

Thomas Howard, 4th Duke of Norfolk (1536–72)

Norfolk was the son of the poet Henry Howard (see page 135), the Earl of Surrey. He was brought up as a Protestant, tutored by John Foxe (see page 47), and was the second cousin of the Queen. He was the Earl Marshall of England and the Queen's Lieutenant in the north, as well as being commander of the English army in Scotland in 1560. Through his third wife he inherited lands in the north that had belonged to the Dacre family. Norfolk was sent as the head of the commission set up by Elizabeth I to enquire into Scottish political affairs after Mary, Queen of Scots' flight in 1568. He plotted to marry Mary, Queen of Scots, in 1569 and although he was released in 1570 it seems he also played a part in the Ridolfi plot in 1571, for which he was executed for treason in 1572. It appears that Norfolk planned to marry Mary in order to resolve the military and diplomatic difficulties between Scotland and England and had loyal intentions, yet did not ask Elizabeth for her permission. The Catholic earls became tired of waiting for this to happen, and rose up. Norfolk was arrested and imprisoned as part of the rising.

marched under the banner of the Five Wounds of Christ. However, other elements of this rebellion were different from 1536. Firstly, the northern rebellion was led by nobility. The Earls of Westmorland and Northumberland were helped by the Duke of Norfolk. Together, these three men were the rebellion's leaders. This is in sharp contrast to 1536, when the main leader was Robert Aske, a lawyer. A second difference between the two rebellions was their main objective. The 1536 rebellions included economic and religious grievances but the 1569 rebellions were based on personal dissatisfaction alongside religious complaints.

The rebellion was launched in November 1569 when the Earls of Westmorland and Northumberland captured Durham and celebrated a traditional Roman Catholic mass in Durham Cathedral. They planned to besiege the city of York but abandoned this and captured Barnard Castle instead. As they moved through the countryside, the rebels destroyed copies of the Book of Common Prayer when they found it in churches, and they took down the new communion tables that had been set up in place of traditional altars. They also offered the ordinary people money to support their cause. In all, the northern earls were able to convince only 4,600 people to join their cause in the rebellion. The Queen, however, sent her loyal nobles and an army numbering nearly 20,000 to stop the

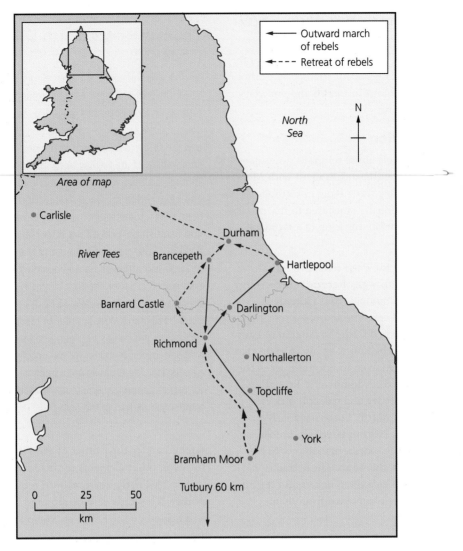

▲ Figure 4: Map of the northern rebellion, 1569

rising. The rebels were vastly outnumbered, and the earls were forced to retreat into Scotland in December 1569.

Ultimately, this rebellion was unsuccessful. The rebels failed to communicate a clear agenda, unlike the rebellions earlier in the sixteenth century. Hundreds of rebels from the lower orders of society lost their lives in the rebellion. They died because of loyalty to their rebelling lords rather than for a specific cause or agenda. The rebelling lords had misjudged the kind of support they would receive from other lords. They may have thought that the other lords and gentry felt the same way they did about religion, but instead of coming to their aid to get rid of Protestant religion, the other lords hurried to the north in order to support the Queen and stifle the rebellion. The impact on the great families of the north was devastating. The Percy family lost their lands in the north. The Nevilles fled, seeking assistance from Spain.

The Crown now held their lands and lordship over their tenants. This transformed the way the commons in the north interacted with the Crown. They had lost their familiar local leaders. In 1572, Elizabeth re-established the Council of the North. She chose her cousin, the third Earl of Huntingdon, to preside over it. He was another man with no ties to the north.

Threat posed by the rebellions of 1536–69

What was the nature of these popular rebellions? All of these rebellions shared similar grievances, primarily economic and religious. They also involved a large cross-section of the society in which they took place. Peasants, **the middling sort**, and elites all helped each other in order to communicate their grievances to the Crown. Rebellion was not good for anyone involved. The

Tudor monarchs were always able to find loyal soldiers to crush the rebellions. The rebel leaders were always punished, usually through execution. The rebels clearly believed that their causes were just or they would not have undertaken such a dangerous risk. The similarities between the rebellions also show that the people believed that rebellion was one way that they could draw attention to problems that they felt were not properly addressed through proper political channels. When economic problems arose, the people sometimes believed that the monarch's advisers were corrupt and failed to pass on important information. They sometimes thought that the monarch had lost control over the kingdom's religious situation. At other times, they believed that parliament had failed to pass laws that would benefit the common good. For many rebels, rebellion was the only way that they could communicate their concerns to the Crown.

3 Reasons for the decline of popular resistance, 1570–88

The rising in the north of 1569 was the last large-scale popular rebellion a Tudor monarch faced. However, this does not mean that the Crown was then free from challenges to its authority. The internal threats Elizabeth faced in the 1570s and 1580s were perpetrated by smaller groups of people. These are reflected in the Throckmorton plot of 1583 and the Babington plot of 1586. Like the rebellion of the northern earls, the objective of these plots was to replace the Protestant Elizabeth with the Roman Catholic Mary, Queen of Scots.

Historians have tried to determine reasons for the lack of large-scale popular resistance in the years between the rising in the north and the attempted invasion by the Spanish Armada in 1588. The period had better harvests and better economic conditions more generally. These factors may have contributed to a sense of stability that discouraged people from rebelling. The devastation of the northern lords may have served as a warning to those who considered rebelling against the Queen. The legislation against vagrants may also have had an impact on popular resistance. Harsher legislation directed against vagrants or those who were seditious may have discouraged people from attempting a rebellion. Another reason may be that the government monitored suspected Catholics more closely. They discovered small-scale plots and rather quickly prevented them from escalating. Elizabeth's government did face threats between the rising in the north and the attack of the Spanish Armada. However, the large-scale rebellions involving huge numbers of people died out as the century progressed.

One theory that was put forward by historians like Keith Wrightson, Andy Wood and Richard Hoyle from the early 2000s was that of 'incorporation' – where the wealthy **yeomanry** who used to lead popular protests aligned themselves with the concerns of the gentry instead of their poorer neighbours. This was because they were becoming richer and so aspired to be like the gentry instead of like their fellow yeomen. This has since been disputed but remains an influential idea. There is also the possibility that people found other ways to resolve their differences, for example in parliament and by lawsuits. There was certainly a rise in litigation in the sixteenth century, although not all of the economic and social problems that caused rebellions could be solved by litigation. Ultimately, nobody can be sure why popular resistance declined in the period 1570–88, and it may be that a combination of causes provides the answer.

Conclusion

Popular rebellion was the principal way in which large numbers of people could express their opposition and anger to the monarch and their policies. It was used by those with religious, economic, social and political grievances, often with the aim of changing those policies or bringing opposition to the attention of the monarch. The rebellions of the mid-sixteenth century show a popular awareness of the changes made and the impact on the customs and lives of the people. Their brutal repression demonstrated the monarchs' need to maintain authority at all costs. But the rebellions declined after 1569, as the changes were gradually accepted and legislation made an impact.

> ### Work together
>
> Work together to assess the seriousness of the threat posed by the rebellions in this section. Firstly, identify the causes of the rebellions. Then look at the aim of each rebellion. Next examine the events of the rebellions. Now for each rebellion consider how serious the threat was. You could think about the following questions:
>
> - Did the rebellion aim to threaten the monarch?
> - Was it a credible military or physical threat?
> - Did the rebellion force any concessions or changes?
> - If so, how long did they last?
> - What did the rebellion demonstrate in terms of the scale of opposition?
>
> After answering these questions, which do you think was the most serious threat?

The nature of the threat posed by popular rebellions

- The Pilgrimage of Grace, 1536
  - caused by religious discontent at policies in relation to the monasteries and traditional religion
  - also had economic causes in relation to food prices, poverty and land ownership
  - people blamed the King's ministers for these changes
  - it was a loyal rebellion to inform the King of their problems and concerns
  - it was a threat because of the size of the rebellion
- The Prayer Book rebellion, 1549
  - caused by loyal reactions to religious changes, especially the Prayer Book
  - they wanted a return to traditional religion
- Kett's rebellion, 1549
  - the main cause was economic in response to enclosures
  - there were also religious concerns
  - it attracted large numbers who wanted Henry VII's policies restored regarding tenants and freeholders
- Minor rebellions, 1549
  - widespread, if small in scale, and easily repressed
  - mostly about religion, in favour of a return to traditional religion
- The revolt of the northern earls, 1569
  - religious grievances caused the rebellion, which aimed to put Mary, Queen of Scots on the throne
  - it did not gain enough popular support
  - it was tied to high politics

The significance of resistance to financial demands

- The monarch needed to call parliament to levy taxes
- Henry VIII needed money to pay for his French wars in 1525 but knew parliament wouldn't grant it
- Wolsey devised the Amicable Grant – a tax
- People began to rebel and the tax was abandoned – the people couldn't afford it

RESISTANCE TO TUDOR RULE

Reasons for the decline of popular resistance

- Nobody can really be sure why popular resistance declined
- Possible economic causes, including better harvests and economic conditions
- Harsh punishments may have dissuaded people, plus there was the external threat from Spain
- A rise in litigation may mean people found different solutions to the problem
- The theory of incorporation proposes yeoman leaders became alienated from their poorer neighbours because they aspired to be like the gentry

▲ Summary diagram: Resistance to Tudor rule

Recommended reading

Anthony Fletcher and Diarmaid MacCulloch, *Tudor Rebellions* (Routledge, 2008).

This is an excellent and highly accessible study of the Tudor rebellions, with separate chapters on each of the popular rebellions of the sixteenth century.

Andy Wood, *Riot, Rebellion and Popular Politics in Early Modern England* (Palgrave Macmillan, 2001).

Chapter 2 is particularly useful for the Pilgrimage of Grace, Western rebellion and Kett's rebellion.

www.history.org.uk/resources/secondary_resource_4139,4146_123.html

This Historical Association podcast by Dr Steven Gunn is an insightful examination of the causes of the rebellions and the changes in the nature of the rebellions.

Essay technique: Counter-argument

Essays that develop a good argument are more likely to reach the highest levels, because argumentative essays are more likely to develop sustained analysis (see page 64).

You can set up an argument in your introduction but you should develop your argument throughout the essay. One way of doing this is to adopt an argument, counterargument structure. A counterargument is one that disagrees with the main argument of the essay. Setting up an argument and then challenging it with a counterargument is one way of weighing up or evaluating (see pages 140–1) the importance of the different factors that you discuss. Essays of this type will develop an argument in one paragraph and then set out an opposing argument in another paragraph.

Imagine you are answering the following question:

> **How far were the Tudor rebellions the result of religious discontent in the period 1536–88?**

You could write an essay in which the first two paragraphs set out the arguments as in the example in the table below. These two paragraphs could be developed into the beginning of a high level answer. However, you will need to resolve the tension between the argument and the counterargument (see pages 125–26) and write a conclusion that weighs up the different aspects of the essay in order to write a full essay.

Paragraph 1: Argument	Many of the rebellions in the Tudor period resulted mainly from religious discontent. From Henry VIII onwards the monarchs made significant changes to religious practice and policy, and these changes led to uncertainty and instability. It was an issue of profound importance for most people, and until Elizabeth's reign relatively few people supported a move towards Protestantism. This, therefore, led to religious plots and rebellions occurring in response to changes made by Henry VIII, Edward VI and Elizabeth I.
Paragraph 2: Counterargument	Not all rebellions were religiously motivated, however, and some of those that had religious motives also had economic and social causes. Even the Pilgrimage of Grace was caused by economic concerns about the dissolution of the monasteries as well as by the more important religious anxieties. It is fair to say, therefore, that Tudor rebellions were not always the result of religious discontent in the period 1536–88.

Activity: Relative importance

Imagine you are answering the following question:

To what extent were local government reforms the main way that the Tudor government extended its power in the years 1534–85?

Using your notes from the previous chapter:
1 Draw the following diagram:

2 Write the following factors on cards or sticky notes, and place them on the line according to their importance for the extension of royal power in the years 1534–85:
   • Local government reforms.
   • Religious policies.
   • Constitutional changes.

3 Now write a short argument justifying the relative importance of each factor.

   TIP: Remember, your argument must contain a statement and a reason.

4 Reverse the order of your first and second most important factors.
5 Write two sentences that explicitly argue that your second most important factor was actually the most important factor. This is your new counterargument.

   TIP: Remember, your new counterargument must contain a statement and a reason.

6 Use your original argument and counterargument as the basis for writing two paragraphs in answer to the question.

Theme 4 Economic, social and cultural change, 1509–88

The Big Picture

Tudor England and Wales experienced significant change in economic, social and cultural matters in the period 1509–88. This was partly due to the decisions made by English monarchs, and partly in response to trends and events elsewhere in Europe.

English trade revolved to a great extent around wool. Prices rose due to competition between wool exporters and those supplying textile manufacturers, meaning that the export of raw wool became unprofitable. This was significant for those merchant companies who had relied on this trade. They were also hit by the situation abroad. Even the cloth trade struggled in the earlier half of the sixteenth century, as English production methods resulted in cloth that was less attractive to foreign markets. This changed with the influx of Dutch refugees, who brought the 'new draperies'. This revitalised the English cloth trade. London itself became a centre of international trade, becoming a marketplace for foreign and English merchants to sell exotic goods from around the world, as well as ordinary commodities. Exploration and the changing trading opportunities that it brought added to England's economic strength. Although the English journeys of exploration were slow to get started, they became significant both in increasing trade and opening diplomatic relations, for example with Russia in 1553.

Internal trade grew significantly in the sixteenth century, partly to feed the greatly increased population and the growing metropolis of London. The population grew by over 80 per cent between 1500 and 1600, and this led to social and economic problems as well as opportunities for traders and merchants. Low wage rates and high prices meant that life for the poor was very precarious, and made them vulnerable to hunger and disease. This period also saw high levels of urban migration. The closure of the monasteries contributed to this, as it meant that important charitable provision for the poor was withdrawn, as was hospitality for strangers and educational opportunities. While the closure of the monasteries brought income to the Crown, it caused problems for many ordinary people. Enclosure was another trend that had a similar effect, forcing poor labourers and tenant farmers off the land and into vagrancy or the towns.

On the other hand, humanism meant that, for some, educational opportunities increased in the sixteenth century. Humanism's emphasis on literacy and literature meant that education became more valued. It also changed the kind of education offered by schools and universities and even influenced the design of buildings. Patronage became increasingly important in the rapidly developing cultural world of Tudor England, and patrons encouraged poets, musicians and playwrights to produce innovative and exciting material. The number of theatres and plays increased in the sixteenth century and became a very popular form of entertainment for all kinds of people. Music continued to be popular for all social groups, though the religious music of the medieval period was greatly threatened by the religious changes brought about by the Reformation.

The image of the monarch became more widely replicated, and became a focus for the nation to replace that of the Church. The sixteenth century was, therefore, an exciting, unstable and varied period in terms of society, economics and culture.

In this theme you will consider the following:

→ **Patterns of domestic and foreign trade:**
The significance of the textile industries, the development of the 'new draperies' from the 1560s, the migration of foreign textile workers, the role of London as a marketplace and the consequences of exploration for trade.

→ **The changing structure of society:**
The increase in the population, the impact of the dissolution of the monasteries, the spread of enclosures and its effect, the impact of growing urbanisation and the growth of the professional classes.

→ **Cultural change:**
The impact of the growth of grammar schools and universities, the effect of the printing press on culture, the impact of religious change, the significance of patronage, developments in drama, music, poetry and architecture, and the impact of the 'cult of Gloriana'.

TIMELINE

1476	First printing press in England set up by William Caxton
1485	Henry VII established the London-Antwerp trade route
1497	John Cabot's voyage discovered 'Newe Founde Land'
1505	Christ's College, Cambridge founded by Margaret Beaufort and John Fisher
1511	St John's College, Cambridge founded by Margaret Beaufort and John Fisher
1512	Polydore Vergil's *Anglica Historia* published
1517	'Evil May Day' riots in London
1517	Corpus Christi College, Oxford founded. First lectureship in Greek established
1529	First list of prohibited books issued
1535	Dissolution of the Lesser Monasteries Act passed
1536	Court of Augmentations set up; Pilgrimage of Grace
1538	Censorship extended to non-religious books
1538	Henry VIII began building work on Nonsuch Palace
1539	The Great Bible published, included frontispiece depicting Henry VIII
1540	Final monastery closed
1540	Henry VIII finished remodelling Hampton Court
1548	Enclosures commission set up
1549	Kett's rebellion and other East Anglia risings
1550	French and Dutch Protestant churches opened in London
1553	First English voyage to Guinea in Africa
1555	The Weavers Act protected artisan workers against new business practices
1555	The Company of Merchant Adventurers to New Lands changed its name to the Muscovy Company following the establishment of the trade route to Russia
1557	System of book censorship formalised, placed in the hands of the Stationers' Company
1557	Anthology of Surrey and Wyatt's poetry published by Richard Tottell
1557	The Woollen Cloth Act protected the traditional working practices of artisans and guilds
1557	The Merchants of the Staple lost their permanent home in Calais
1558	Customs rates were increased so that the government could benefit more from international trade
1559	Schoolmasters licensed to ensure religious conformity
1559	Elizabeth's proclamation on theatrical policy
1559	Elizabeth's injunctions confirm prioritisation of the written word over music in church services
1562	Sir John Hawkins became the first Englishman to profit from the Triangular Slave Trade
1563	John Foxe's *Acts and Monuments* published
1568	Elizabeth I offered refuge to Protestants fleeing the Dutch Revolt, including many textile workers
1575	Last performance of Chester mystery plays
1576	Martin Frobisher's voyage to the Arctic established English claims there
1576	First permanent theatre built by James Burbage in 1576
1580	Sir John Thynne finished rebuilding Longleat House, begun 1549
1587	Sir William Cecil finished building Burghley House, begun 1555
1581	The Turkey Company set up
1588	The African Company set up

4a: Patterns of domestic and foreign trade

Overview

Patterns of domestic and foreign trade reveal a surprising amount of continuity alongside the changes of the sixteenth century. Textiles continued to be a very important English trading commodity, even if the type of textiles produced changed and diversified. The northern European market was important throughout the period, but with the production of new fabrics England was able to sell her products in southern Europe as well. Foreign textile workers brought these new developments to England when they were offered religious and economic refuge from the violence existing on the Continent from the mid-sixteenth century onwards. London had long been an important centre for trade and commerce, and this only increased in the Tudor period. London's population and size expanded greatly, as did the range of products offered in its markets and shops. Exploration and international trade were to contribute greatly to this growth. Religion continued to be an important factor in economic developments, for example religious persecution on the Continent encouraged migration to England. Economic imperatives and the need to keep up with her European neighbours meant that England undertook an increasing number of voyages of trade and exploration. The eventual success of these voyages led to the development of new markets and colonies. This trading impulse would eventually grow into the British Empire.

This chapter will explore patterns of domestic and foreign trade through the following sections:

1 *The significance of the wool and cloth industries* looks at the importance of these industries to the English economy. It also examines the changes both domestically and in international markets that impacted on the English wool and cloth industries.

2 *The impact of the migration of foreign textile workers* discusses the effect of the migration of Dutch refugees and migrants from the mid-sixteenth century onwards into the textile-producing areas, particularly East Anglia and Essex. It explores the advantages that came with these highly skilled workers and the tensions that arose in times of difficulty.

3 *The role of London as a market for goods* examines the rapidly expanding metropolis of London from 1509 to 1588. It looks at London's increasing role within domestic markets and its development into an international centre of trade.

4 *The consequences of exploration for trade* explores the journeys of discovery made under the Tudor monarchs, and their significance for the economic development of England. It also examines the reasons for those journeys as well as the cargoes they brought back.

Note it down

Use a spider diagram (see page x) to make notes on this chapter. Subdivide your main sections of 'wool and cloth industries', 'migration of foreign textile workers', 'role of London' and 'exploration' in order to ensure your notes are properly and clearly organised. If you have been completing an annotated timeline and collections of index cards on personalities, there are several individuals and events you could add from this section, for example Sir Thomas Gresham and explorers like Sir John Hawkins.

1 The significance of the wool and cloth industries

The wool and cloth industries were vital to English trade. The textile industry was the only industry of note in England before 1550. Before the mid-1550s the most important English export commodity was woollen broadcloth, but this would shortly be overtaken by the lighter, cheaper and more colourful 'new draperies' from the 1560s onwards (see page 110). The cloth industries were crucial for customs revenue throughout the Tudor period and employed many people in town and rural areas. Foreign migrants, particularly the Dutch from the 1560s, brought new technology which made the English cloth industry more flexible. They were also the cause of tensions in textile areas as English workers feared the changes and blamed the migrants for economic problems that were actually largely caused by changing international markets and bad harvests. At the end of Elizabeth's reign the textile industries had changed and diversified but were still extremely important to the economic success of England and Wales, in terms of both foreign and domestic trade.

The English wool trade

Wool was important for both domestic and foreign trade. It was the backbone of the medieval English economy. Landowners began to enclose their land so that sheep could graze it and their wool could be sold (see page 120). Large areas of England were dedicated to the production of wool. Wool from these regions was sold by the landowners to either merchants or clothiers, businessmen who then organised for the raw wool to be turned into cloth (see Figure 1). Wool prices rose in the mid-sixteenth century as competition increased between the wool merchants who exported wool and those who bought wool to supply cloth manufacturers in England. This drove up costs for the wool merchants, until wool from Spain and other countries was cheaper to buy. It became less economic to sell English wool abroad.

English wool was traded abroad by a company of merchants, the Merchants of the Staple. They were based in London and Calais. Sales of English wool had been falling for a few years before Mary I's accession in 1553. The Merchants of the Staple in Calais had shrunk down to only 150 traders by 1540. When Calais (previously in English hands) fell to the French in 1557, the Staplers had to find other places to trade from, and tried Bergen, Bruges and Middleburg. But it was simply not profitable to trade English wool anymore, and the Merchants of the Staple folded.

The 'old draperies'

The staple of English trade, and particularly the English textile trade, before the mid-sixteenth century was woollen broadcloth. By 1550 approximately 130,000 cloths a year, roughly 75 per cent of all English exports, were exported to Antwerp. After the early 1560s this cloth became known as the 'old draperies'. This was heavy white undressed woollen cloth spun on looms. It was spun by skilled craftsmen, their **journeymen** and

apprentices in households. The main regions for textile production were the West Riding of Yorkshire, the West Country, and most importantly East Anglia, where 25 per cent of production was based. Thousands of people were employed this way, most of them part-time. The success of the textile industry attracted more people to these regions, which made the poorer workers vulnerable in periods of poor harvest and trade depression.

This traditional way of working was protected by successive governments. The Weavers Act of 1555, for example, prohibited clothiers from centralising looms in factories. This protected the jobs of the poor textile workers. There were similar Acts instituted by Edward VI in 1551 and again by Mary in 1557. The Woollen Cloth Act of 1557 placed heavy fines on factories built outside the traditional jurisdictions of urban guilds and craftsmen. The looms were leased to the craftsmen by the clothiers, who then bought the finished cloth off them. The cloth was then sold in Antwerp via a trade route established by Henry VII in 1485. The broadcloth was coarse and low quality cloth that had to be finished off in the Low Countries before it was up to the standard necessary to sell in European markets.

The Merchant Adventurers, a company of merchants based in London, owned the monopoly for the sale of woollen cloth. By the mid-sixteenth century sales of broadcloth were falling as new, more attractive textiles came on the market. Edward and Mary's governments attempted to react to this by banning foreign merchants from buying English cloth so that English merchants could profit from it instead. This was ineffective – new solutions needed to be found.

The importance of the 'new draperies'

The 'new draperies' were lighter, cheaper and more colourful textiles. The technology to create them was brought to England by Dutch immigrants in the 1560s. This was a new development in the cloth trade and was extremely successful. In order to make lighter fabrics the Dutch blended yarns, even including silk, with English wool. The Dutch imposed a strict system of quality control on these cloths before they were sold, which was essential for the reputation of the cloth. These 'new draperies' were popular in northern Europe but also in new markets in the Mediterranean. By 1600 they accounted for 20 per cent of total exports, whereas the number of 'old draperies' sold was the same as in 1540. The new draperies revived the English textile market and meant that it continued to be a mainstay of the English economy for many years.

2 The impact of the migration of foreign textile workers

There had been a population of 'aliens', or foreigners, in London for a long time, either as traders or immigrant craftsmen. They settled in particular areas and by 1550 French and Dutch churches were set up to cater for their religious needs. The French and Dutch inhabitants of London tended to be religious refugees – Protestants fleeing religious persecution by the French or Spanish government. The government of Edward VI was keen to offer protection to Protestant refugees and set up the churches in order to provide religious hospitality to them. Until 1568, however, the numbers were not large. After 1568 the population increased as the Dutch Revolt led to violence, looting and widespread disruption, as well as further discrimination by the Catholic Spanish government that ruled the Netherlands in that period. It is estimated that around 7,000 Dutch refugees arrived. They settled in London and in the textile areas of East Anglia and the south-east. The level of immigrants tailed off but did have an impact on the economy of England and on the perceptions of textile workers.

Elizabeth I offered a safe haven to the refugees in the 1560s. There were both religious and economic reasons behind this. Firstly, Elizabeth was ruling a Protestant country and, like Edward, wanted to offer help to fellow Protestants – especially as they were opposing the practices of Catholic Spain. Secondly, the new immigrants were skilled workers with access to new technology that could revive England's flagging textile trade. The trade in the 'old draperies' was struggling and the Dutch textile workers could introduce new ideas and products. This was an extremely successful idea. The Dutch immigrants brought the technology and skills to produce the 'new draperies', which sustained the English textile trade for a long time afterwards and opened it up to new markets (see page 112).

Yet the influx of Dutch textile workers was not entirely problem-free. The English textile workers were notoriously vulnerable to economic problems. In boom times large numbers of people moved to textile-producing areas to work, only to suffer when there were bad harvests or when there were trade problems. This was particularly true of the lowest-paid workers. When food prices rose or when they lost their part-time jobs they had little economic safety net. When foreign textile workers were encouraged to move to those areas they were blamed for the problems of the native English population. Artisans also worried about the impact that foreign skilled workers could have on their income. Occasionally this spilled over into xenophobic riots, such as 'Evil May Day' in London in 1517. A mob of over 1,000 people, many poor labourers, congregated on Cheapside and rioted through the streets of London. They looted and destroyed property that they thought belonged to foreigners. Most of the time, though, the native and foreign workers lived together peacefully. Many people recognised the positive impact on the textile trade, but it was seen as worrying and destabilising by others.

3 The role of London as a market for goods

London was the largest city in England and Wales in the sixteenth century, and in 1550 was the seventh or eighth largest city in Europe. The expansion of London as a trading centre and as a city is demonstrated by the fact that by 1650 it had become the second largest city in Europe. Its expansion was fuelled by prodigious levels of migration from rural areas that continued beyond the seventeenth century. London had long been a centre for trade. Alongside Newcastle, Hull, Southampton and Bristol its merchants traded with northern European ports and with each other in terms of internal trade.

Domestic trade

As London grew it consumed more and more products that came from different parts of the country. These were sold by their producers in the different regions of the country to London merchants, who would then sell them to consumers in the markets, businesses and shops of the city. At the port of London, for example, coal arrived from Newcastle. Coal was also mined in Yorkshire, Flintshire and in parts of Scotland. Coal consumption boomed in London from the sixteenth century onwards, to heat the mansions of the rich and fuel businesses and offices in the city. Rural Suffolk supplied the city's markets with cheese and butter, and Welsh drovers made money by driving cattle to London for sale in the markets there. Links between provincial merchants and the capital were reasonably close and their relationships profitable. As London grew it could not supply its own food needs and so depended on the various regions of the country to supply its food – to their profit. This could be problematic during times of shortage and meant that London prices could rise rapidly in those circumstances. This led to riots, like those in 1595 over the price of fish and butter. London was also used as a hub where products from one region would be sold to merchants from another, to be sold on to regional consumers.

▲ Map of London in the sixteenth century. What can this map tell us about London in the sixteenth century? What is central to the map? What do the labels tell us about the importance of particular buildings?

International trade

London was increasingly the centre of Britain's international trade. By 1540 nearly 90 per cent of the English export trade in textiles passed through London. From its many quays goods from across the world were bought and sold. Cargoes from the voyages of exploration (see pages 113–14) were sold in the markets of London, including spices, Russian furs and African ivory. The expansion of international trade led to a need for better facilities and even government action. Elizabeth I set up a commission in 1588 to choose quays that would specifically be used for foreign goods, all between London Bridge and the Tower. Merchant companies, such as the Merchant Adventurers, the Turkey Company and the Africa Company, reinforced the London merchant community. As the traditional cloth trade declined (see pages 108–10) the arrival of imports from distant lands became increasingly important. The boom in trade was viewed extremely positively by the government as they were able to levy taxes on imports and request loans from the city. In 1558 customs rates were adjusted so that 75 per cent more duty was paid on imported than domestic items. In return, the monarchy granted special privileges to the merchants.

London merchants also took advantage of events elsewhere in Europe to increase the city's standing as a centre of commerce. Antwerp had previously been the financial and commercial powerhouse of Europe but was badly affected by the Dutch Revolt from 1568. Antwerp's trade collapsed and London was only too keen to exploit that. The Royal Exchange was built in 1565 as a meeting place for merchants and brokers. This made it easier to conduct trade and it became a vital part of London's commercial enterprise. Elizabeth I's adviser Sir Thomas Gresham, himself a merchant, first proposed the Exchange and provided the land on which it was built. Gresham had lived and worked in Antwerp and had seen the benefits that such an exchange could bring. Foreign merchants also traded in London, especially the **Hanseatic League**, Italians and Flemish merchants. They chiefly concentrated on textile exports but also imported goods to sell. London's commercial position was well established by the end of the sixteenth century. The city had grown and its trade expanded. It was used by English and foreign merchants to trade goods from around the world. As a market, it was noisy, large and lucrative.

4 The consequences of exploration for trade

By the time that the English made their first tentative moves towards exploration, other European nations had been profiting from their voyages for over 100 years. Portugal was a pioneer in exploration, establishing trade routes down the western coast of Africa in the fifteenth century. They made huge profits from gold, slaves and ivory, before continuing around the Cape of Good Hope to discover India by 1500. There they opened up the spice trade with Southeast Asia, establishing a near monopoly on this extremely lucrative commodity. Spain, not wishing to be outdone by its neighbour, launched its own voyages of exploration in 1492 when Columbus travelled to the Americas. Many more journeys followed and enabled the Spanish to establish significant colonies in the Caribbean and South America. Hernando Cortes conquered Mexico in 1520, bringing almost unimaginable quantities of gold to the Spanish. The wealth and power of Portugal and Spain increased greatly as a result of their voyages of exploration. This was due to the trade routes, trading colonies and outposts set up following the voyages.

Early English voyages, 1497–1547

English monarchs were much more reluctant to support explorers. The voyages were costly and the priorities of the early to mid-sixteenth century were different in England, with its focus on religion and domestic government rather than international trade. Some tentative voyages did happen. John Cabot received support from Henry VII for his 1497 bid to find a western route to Asia. He failed to find such a route but did reach land, which he called 'Newe Founde Islande', now known as Newfoundland in Canada. He claimed this for the English Crown. Cabot's son Sebastian launched a bid to find a north-western

English merchant companies

Merchant companies developed in the later Middle Ages and had their origins in the medieval craft guilds that used to organise internal trade and production. While those guilds became largely irrelevant in the sixteenth century, merchant companies grew in importance. Originally they were loose associations or fellowships of merchants but they became more organised in the late 1500s. By the end of the sixteenth century most English merchants belonged to a company. They were founded by royal charter and often had a monopoly, either in a particular geographical region or in a product or commodity. The point of these companies was to license their members to trade and to regulate their conduct. They also established apprenticeships. The advantages for members were that they had collective representation in dealings with English and foreign governments, and they had a say in royal policies on foreign trade. For the monarchs, the companies could provide diplomatic services and insight into foreign affairs, as well as loaning them money.

Sir Francis Drake (c1540–96)

Drake was born in Devon, the son of a Protestant gentleman. His family moved to Kent following religious persecution during the 1549 Prayer Book rebellion, and this move was to lead to Drake's naval career. His father became a clergyman and ministered to the navy. Drake was apprenticed to his neighbour who was a ship's master. He was to make a career at sea as a sea captain, privateer, slaver and Vice Admiral. He made his first voyage to the Americas aged 23 and began his famed attacks on the Spanish treasure ships in 1572. Drake was the first Englishman to circumnavigate the earth following a three year voyage from 1577 to 1580. The Queen's share of treasure following that expedition was more than the rest of the Crown's income for that year. Drake was knighted in April 1581 and was the vice admiral in charge of the fleet sent to defeat the Spanish Armada. He continued to harry Spanish ships throughout his career. He died on a voyage in the Spanish Americas in 1596.

passage to Asia in 1508 but it was unsuccessful and the government doubted if he had ever been! Henry VIII sent Sebastian Cabot to explore the Caribbean and the coast of Brazil in 1516 to find out more about the Spanish colonies in that region, but Spanish military efforts forced them to withdraw. Fear of angering the Spanish would put a break on English exploration efforts until the break from Rome in the 1530s put the two countries on opposite sides of a religious divide. As a result, Sebastian Cabot was to leave England due to the lack of support for his efforts, working for the Spanish for 30 years before returning in 1547 to England. He worked for Edward VI, providing the navigational knowledge he had gathered while in the service of the Spanish to aid in exploration. Cabot became a director of the Company of Merchant Adventurers, founded in 1551, which sponsored many of the attempts to find a north-western passage to Asia.

Some trade was established with Brazil during the reign of Henry VIII. From 1530 to 1542 a number of merchants sent ships to South America and returned with valuable cargo. William Hawkins of Plymouth was perhaps the most well known of these. Hawkins' voyages in the years 1530 to 1532 included expeditions to Guinea and Brazil. On one of the journeys they appear to have captured an indigenous 'king' from Brazil, and presented him at court as an exotic novelty and evidence of their trip. In terms of more straightforward commercial cargo, these merchants bought ivory and brazilwood in Brazil and sold it in England at a huge profit. English traders also preyed upon Spanish and Portuguese shipping in this period. **Privateers** would attack Iberian trading vessels and steal their cargo to sell. This type of 'trade' was to flourish in Elizabeth's reign, with privateers such as Sir John Hawkins and Sir Francis Drake becoming particularly notorious.

Exploration diversifies: Africa, Asia and Russia

Edward's government also supported the first English voyage to Guinea in Africa. It left in 1553 after Edward's death but had been planned and prepared while he was still alive. The commander of this voyage was Thomas Wyndham, who was to die on the voyage of sickness contracted in Benin (now in Nigeria). The survivors of the voyage (only 40 of the original 140 crew) successfully brought home a profitable cargo and a second voyage set out in October 1554 as a result. Commanded by Thomas Lok, it traded successfully on the Gold Coast of Africa. The cargo of gold and elephant tusk that it brought home inspired many other ventures but it also angered the Portuguese who had dominated that coastline. Portuguese complaints temporarily halted such expeditions but only for a short while – in 1556 they began again and continued at a relatively low level and at irregular intervals into the 1560s.

Mary I's accession in 1553 and her subsequent marriage to Philip II of Spain in 1554 meant that, once again, the Crown was concerned to preserve good relations with Spain. This led exploration efforts in another direction – to discover a north-eastern sea route to Asia. The idea was that this would make trade with the East less dangerous and more direct, and so less expensive and more profitable. In 1553 the first voyage launched with this objective in mind. One of the ships, captained by Richard Chancellor, did reach the Russian coast. This was not the promised route to Asia and the Spice Islands but it did lead to highly profitable trade with Russia. Chancellor travelled overland, reaching Moscow and the court of the Tsar. In 1555 the Company of Merchant Adventurers to New Lands changed its name to the Muscovy Company as a result and from that point combined

Sir John Hawkins (1532–95)

Sir John Hawkins was born into a family of merchants and sea captains. His father, William Hawkins, was a sea captain and a friend of Henry VIII. Sir John Hawkins followed his father into the same trade and, although his early life is fairly obscure, he appears to have undertaken some diplomatic efforts in Spain. Hawkins established a syndicate of merchants to fund his first voyage to the Caribbean and realised the profit to be made from slavery, leading him to embark on two more such voyages. He was also a spy for the English government and played a part in revealing the Ridolfi plot in 1571, and as a reward became MP for Plymouth in the same year. He was appointed Treasurer of the Royal Navy in 1578 and undertook financial reforms of the navy, including a pay rise for sailors and improvements in ship construction. Hawkins was awarded a knighthood for his role in the Battle of Gravelines during the Spanish Armada crisis of 1588. Alongside his cousin Sir Francis Drake, Hawkins urged the Queen to begin seizing Spanish treasure ships to stop Spain rearming and attacking England once more. He carried out privateering voyages subsequent to this. In 1590 he and Drake founded a charity for the relief of sick and elderly mariners and, in 1592, a hospital. Drake and Hawkins both died of sickness on the same treasure-hunting voyage to the West Indies in 1595.

exploration of the north-east passage with trade across Russia. It was also in Mary's reign that British involvement in the slave trade began, with small-scale voyages by John Lok in 1555 and William Towerson in 1557.

Elizabethan exploration and trade

In Elizabeth's reign there was no need to please the powerful Spanish any longer. In fact, because of the long-running war between England and Spain that began in 1585, antagonising the Spanish was seen in a favourable light. Exploration received more support during Elizabeth's reign. More trading companies were set up, dedicated to long-distance trade. The Turkey Company was founded in 1581 and the Africa Company in 1588. All of these merchant companies aimed to discover new markets for trading English goods and exotic cargoes at a good price to import into Britain. British involvement in the slave trade would expand under Elizabeth. Sir John Hawkins, in 1562, became the first Englishman to take part in the triangular trade between West Africa, Caribbean or American colonies and Europe. Hawkins made three slaving voyages. He captured over 1,200 Africans and sold them as goods in the Spanish colonies in the Americas. It was the beginning of the British slave trade, which lasted until 1807 and in which British ships carried over 3.4 million Africans as slaves to the Americas. This was vastly profitable for the English captains and merchants who ran such voyages. For Hawkins his second voyage produced a 60 per cent return on the original investment. The brutal slave trade began in this period and was to bring increasing profits for the Crown. Sir John Hawkins introduced the potato to Ireland from the Spanish colonies and tobacco was also imported at this time.

Despite the profitability of slaving voyages, the desire to find a north-east passage to Asia remained strong in the 1560s and 1570s. Prominent figures who supported voyages to find such a route included the scientist and mystic John Dee, the merchant Michael Lok and the soldier and promoter of exploration Sir Humphrey Gilbert. The latter was the eldest half-brother of Sir Walter Raleigh and in 1583 became one of the founding fathers of the English settlement at Newfoundland. It was Martin Frobisher whose 1576 journey to the Arctic led to the English claims in the very north of North America. The voyage had originally aimed to reach the East but instead found the Arctic coast.

Conclusion

The wool and textile trades were essential to the English economy in the sixteenth century. They were vulnerable to changing market conditions, however, and needed to be able to make adaptations in order to maintain their success. This was achieved with the 'new draperies' introduced by the Dutch refugees and migrants, which preserved the trade for a long while afterwards. The 'new draperies' also boosted England's trade more generally, and opened up new markets with the Mediterranean. London expanded greatly in the sixteenth century, and in doing so created increased opportunities for internal trade in commodities such as butter, cheese and coal. It also became much more of an international marketplace. The Royal Exchange, built in 1565, provided a centre for that international trade and became a bustling marketplace for English and foreign merchants. Merchant companies flourished. Some merchant companies had been founded in the medieval period but in the sixteenth century they became more organised. Due to this they had more influence, helping to determine royal policy and providing diplomatic services to the Crown.

Exploration in the Tudor period began relatively late but towards the end of the sixteenth century was producing significant results for trade. Henry VIII did support some early journeys but it took until Elizabeth's reign for exploration to increase significantly. New exotic commodities, such as tobacco, were introduced into England and the increasing range of journeys meant that prices for some items (spices, for example) began to fall. Journeys to Africa and Russia led to a more diverse range of trade, and in the case of Russia to diplomatic relations being established. The first colonies were established and the colonial impulse would eventually lead to a large empire and trade between colonies. This increased under Elizabeth I because there was no longer a need to appease Spain, and so intervention in areas of the world where the Spanish previously had a near monopoly became much more common. The sixteenth century did not represent the peak of British international trade but it did establish many of the foundations for its development in the seventeenth and eighteenth centuries.

The consequences of exploration for trade

- English merchants were initially reluctant to support explorers due to the cost of voyages and their priorities
- Fear of angering the Spanish held back English exploration until the 1530s
- Some trade with Brazil was established in the 1530s
- Exploration diversified in Edward's and Mary's reigns, going to Africa, Asia and Russia
- British involvement in the slave trade began in the 1550s
- Exploration increased under Elizabeth
- More trading companies were set up to fund voyages and trade their cargoes
- These cargoes included slaves, gold and exotic spices and food
- State-sponsored piracy saw Spanish treasure and merchant ships attacked

The significance of the wool and cloth industries

- Wool and cloth were England's only industries of note before 1550, important for domestic and foreign trade
- Raw wool became unprofitable by the 1550s
- Woollen broadcloth was the main English export and the industry employed thousands
- Governments protected the traditional way of artisan production
- Sales of broadcloth fell by the mid-sixteenth century as new and more attractive textiles became available
- The 'new draperies' were lighter, more colourful and cheaper
- The technology was imported by Dutch migrants
- They revived sales of English cloth and opened up new markets

PATTERNS OF DOMESTIC AND FOREIGN TRADE

Role of London as a market for goods

- London expanded as a trading centre and city in the sixteenth century
- It was fuelled by huge levels of inward migration from rural areas
- As it grew it used more products from around the country
- This brought profit to regional merchants but also rapid price rises at times of shortage
- There was a huge expansion of international trade
- Elizabeth's government took measures to encourage this

Impact of migration of foreign textile workers

- Dutch Protestant refugees fleeing religious persecution were given refuge by the English government
- They brought new technology and skills that helped revive the textile trade
- The migration caused some problems and tensions because of the trade's vulnerability to economic problems and poverty

▲ Summary diagram: Patterns of domestic and foreign trade

Recommended reading

Susan Brigden, *New Worlds, Lost Worlds: The Rule of the Tudors, 1485–1603* (Penguin, 2000).

Chapter 9 examines the sea voyage to the New World and its impact on relations with Spain.

John Lotherington (editor), *The Tudor Years* (Hodder, 2003).

Chapter 13 on the economy and society of Tudor England includes a very useful summary on overseas and internal trade.

J. H. Parry, *The Age of Reconnaissance: Discovery, Exploration and Settlement, 1450–1650* (University of California Press, 1981).

This book explores the European voyages more generally but has much interesting information on the technology of the voyages, and on the different zones of exploration.

http://goldenhind.co.uk/education-centre.php

This is the website of the Golden Hind, a replica of Drake's ship. The website contains useful articles about Drake, his voyages, and Tudor exploration.

Question practice

1 How far was the dissolution of the monasteries responsible for an increase in poverty in the years 1536–72? **AS**
2 Were the improvements in education the main consequence of humanism in England from 1509–88? Explain your answer. **AS**
3 How far do you agree that English culture in the period 1509–34 was completely different to that under Elizabeth I?
4 How far do you agree that economic changes in Tudor England were primarily made in response to international considerations in the period 1550–88?

4b: The changing structure of society

Overview

Economic trends, religious policies and changing ideals of education all had their effect on English society in the sixteenth century. Some of these changes were the result of natural phenomena such as disease, while others like enclosure were manmade. Although for many people, particularly in the countryside, their way of life did not alter significantly in economic terms, a significant number moved into the growing towns in this period. This was in response to population increase and the resultant land shortage, as well as in some areas a response to the impact of Henry VIII's decision to dissolve the monasteries. The increasing tendency of landowners to enclose their lands led more people to head for urban areas, and made others feel angry and alienated. On the other hand, urbanisation led to great success for some individuals. It started to change patterns of settlement within as well as outside cities. There was an increase in those taking up professional jobs, particularly in the law. This was a function of the changes in the education system as well as of differing aspirations of gentry families.

This chapter examines the changing structure of society through the following sections:

1 *The increase in population* examines changes in the size of the population in Tudor England. It proposes some reasons for those changes and explores their impact.

2 *The impact of the closure of the monasteries* looks at the dissolution of the monasteries by Henry VIII and Thomas Cromwell that ended in 1540. It looks beyond its religious impact and considers the economic and social implications for the people who interacted with and depended on the monasteries.

3 *The spread and consequences of enclosure* explores the tendency of wealthy landowners to enclose their land in order to farm sheep (and thus reap the profits of the trade in wool). It examines the impact of this for those forced to move from their land.

4 *The impact of growing urbanisation* looks at the causes and impacts of the trend towards urbanisation in the sixteenth century. It traces the increase in the size of towns and explores the consequences.

5 *The growing professional classes* discusses the increase in those who could be described as members of the 'professions' – largely lawyers in this period.

Note it down

Use the 1:2 method (see page x) to take notes on this chapter. Note that there are some useful statistics in this section that you can use as specific evidence in your essays. When you have taken notes on the section you might like to highlight these numbers to remind you of them when revising.

1 The increase in population

One of the major tragedies of the Middle Ages was the Black Death. During the fourteenth century, Europe lost an estimated 30 to 60 per cent of its population. Historians still have not determined precisely how devastating this event was, but most do agree that the fourteenth century was a period of major turmoil and social upheaval. In England, population numbers did not recover until the early sixteenth century. There are no precise figures for population in Tudor England. Unlike today, there was no census, so historians have to estimate figures. Historian Euan Cameron has suggested that the population increased by 82.6 per cent between 1500 and 1600. He has calculated that in 1500 the population was approximately 2.3 million while by 1600 it had risen to 4.2 million (see Figure 1). The two periods that saw the most rapid population growth were probably between the 1520s and 1540s, and between 1561 and 1586. The most densely populated areas were Kent, Essex, East Anglia, Devon and Cornwall. The population rose at a rate of one per cent every year. This outstripped the food supply meaning that prices rose. It also meant that there was a greater amount of young labour but not enough jobs. This led to a situation where wage rates were low because people would accept lower rates of pay in order to have a job at all.

One of the most useful sources historians have for population history in this period is the register of births, marriages and deaths required by Thomas Cromwell from every parish from 1538 onwards. There are only a few examples of these that still survive but they do give us a rough picture. The average family size was between four and five people. As many as 40 per cent of the population was under 16 years old, and the average life expectancy was 35 years. Life expectancy rates in towns were lower. Problems like continued harvest failure had very severe consequences for the poor. If there were also periods of sickness (for example plague), the mortality rate could treble, as it did under Mary I. Fertility rates appear to have increased towards the beginning of the period. This suggests that there was better and more food available, and that perhaps the standard of living had also generally improved.

The increase in population contributed to a change in the structure of society. England was still largely an agricultural society during the sixteenth century. Nearly 90 per cent of the population lived in the countryside and in villages, rather than in towns. The only town of any significant size was London, although others such as Coventry, Norwich and Bristol did increase in size in the period. This meant that the majority of people laboured in agricultural work. But land was scarce, and this drove many people out of the country and into cities and towns. They sought employment and support from the work available there. These factors contributed to a population that was more mobile than it had been in the previous century.

▲ Figure 2: Population growth, England 1541–1601

2 The impact of the closure of the monasteries

Ordinary men and women were afraid that the closures of monasteries and other religious houses would harm the economies in the areas in which they lived. This prompted them to rebel in autumn 1536. The Pilgrimage of Grace was the largest armed resistance to any Tudor monarch (see page 95). One of the main causes of the Pilgrimage of Grace was tension over the fate of religious houses.

Monasteries were primarily religious places and the main focus of the community was a life of devotion to God. The second function of religious houses was to provide important services to the community:

- Monasteries distributed alms to the poor people who lived nearby.
- Monasteries were responsible for taking care of the sick.
- The houses provided hospitality to strangers travelling through remote regions.
- These houses also provided religious instruction and educational opportunities for local children.
- They were often considered centres of learning because of their large libraries and learned leaders.
- Their libraries were full of religious books but also texts about every topic, from science and medicine to poetry and sermons. In a period when there were only two universities in the entire kingdom, religious houses were important places for education and knowledge about the wider world.

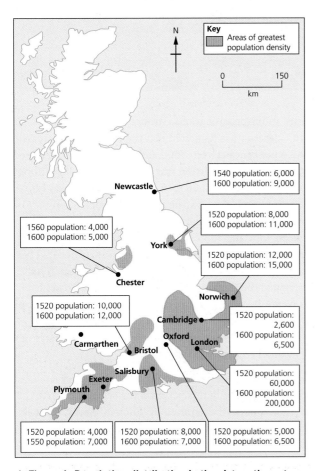

▲ Figure 1: Population distribution in the sixteenth century

The Dissolution of the Lesser Monasteries Act

In 1535, parliament enacted a bill known as the 'Dissolution of the Lesser Monasteries Act'. This Act authorised the Crown to close small religious houses. These were houses with an income of less than £200 each year. The monasteries and religious institutions were some of the largest landowners in sixteenth-century England. However, this **bill** demonstrates that they owned this much land collectively – the individual monasteries could be relatively small and seemingly unimportant. The people who lived in the small religious houses slated for closure were given the option to move to a larger nearby establishment so that they could continue to pursue their religious lives. However, all the land, buildings, and other property owned by these smaller dissolved religious houses became the property of the King.

The Court of Augmentations

In the first wave of monastic suppression, 243 religious houses were closed. The Court of Augmentations was established in 1536 in order to administer the closure of these religious houses. This court carried out important work like surveying the lands and determining the value of the Crown's new property. The Court of Augmentations also oversaw the conversion of some of the religious houses into parish churches and schools. After the first round of monasteries was closed, new legislation was passed. The Pilgrimage of Grace ultimately had a negative effect on the King's attitude towards the monasteries. Henry increasingly saw them as places of refuge for people who opposed the Crown and wished to commit treason. Eventually, further legislation was enacted that called for all the religious houses to surrender. Around 625 religious houses existed in England at the beginning of Henry VIII's reign. By the end of April 1540, the final monastery closed and religious houses were no longer a way of life in England.

Impact on the Crown

One clear impact of the closure of the monasteries was its effect on the Crown. The closure of the monasteries earned additional income for the Crown. The money

▲ Valle Crucis Abbey, Denbighshire, Wales. What can the ruins of the monasteries dissolved in this period tell us about the local communities that they were part of? How can such buildings be used as a source for historians?

raised from these new properties enabled the King to fund new coastal defences and build new warships in the 1540s. The monastic dissolution therefore helped the King prepare for a French invasion, a military threat that the kingdom genuinely feared in these years. Furthermore, the acquisition of these properties allowed the King to earn additional money by selling them to the rising elite. He also cultivated loyalty among the nobility by granting these properties to men who had proven their faithfulness to him during the years of reformation. The closure of religious houses therefore helped the Crown to create loyalty among the elite and generate income for the King's coffers.

Concerns about the impact on poverty

Other effects of the closure of the monasteries are harder to determine. The people who opposed the closure of monasteries and religious houses cited their fear that the people who were forced to leave the monasteries would fall into poverty. They were afraid that former monks and nuns would have no way to support themselves. As a result, they could fall into categories of people known as vagrants and sturdy beggars. These groups of people were feared because they had no stable source of income or place to live, and were therefore seen as disruptive to society. Furthermore, the religious houses had provided important support for the poor in their communities. In the absence of these institutions, others would have to find a way to take care of the kingdom's poor and weak. This was a significant worry in a society that was already concerned with poverty (see pages 85–90).

Impact on education

Some of the religious houses were refounded as grammar schools. The grammar schools provided an education for boys in a local community based on the new educational values arriving from Europe. The grammar schools also provided a place of employment for some of the former monks who had lived in religious houses. Six of the monasteries that were closed during this period became cathedrals, with completely new dioceses. These created new chapters and secular orders that religious men could join as alternatives to monastic life. At the same time, however, the closure of religious houses did result in the loss of knowledge. The books in the libraries were taken out; some of the books were destroyed. Others were taken into private collections. There was no tangible crisis as a result of the monastic dissolution, but the closure of the religious houses represented a significant social and cultural loss.

3 The spread and consequences of enclosure

Throughout the Tudor period, one economic problem recurs time and again. This is the problem of **enclosure**. Enclosure was indeed an increasingly common practice over the course of the sixteenth century. In the Middle Ages, most manors or villages retained fields for common use. Villagers could use these fields to grow the food they needed to feed their families or to graze cattle or other livestock. They were able to earn income by selling the surplus crops they grew. However, when this common land was enclosed, only the owner had access to the land. This meant that the tenants who had used this land to grow crops in the past had now lost one of the primary means for growing food to eat or additional crops to sell for money.

Enclosure as a political problem

As the rate of enclosures increased over the course of the sixteenth century, so did their importance as a political problem. Enclosures revealed tensions within the social order, largely between the poor rural people who relied on the land and the wealthier landowners. It also extinguished common rights over the land. These tensions were worsened due to the use that much of the land was put to: sheep grazing. In the early modern period, the English wool industry was growing rapidly (see page 108). Sheep were therefore viewed as a cash crop. The common perception was that the already wealthy landowners were simply trying to gain even more wealth by allowing sheep to graze the arable land. This activity was harmful to the poorer tenants. The tenants lost a serious source of income because they had often relied on the common lands for money, and the sheep also prevented the people from growing food on land that was perfectly suitable for raising crops. As a result, some of the commons were starving and poorer tenants lost their homes. The countryside also became subject to depopulation. People left their homes in the countryside and migrated to urban areas because they were unable to find farming work. In the national consciousness, the people lost their livelihood and had their ability to take care of themselves stolen by the rich in order to raise sheep.

Population increase and enclosure

Enclosures made another problem worse: the rising population. The structure of society was changing as a result of the population increase that occurred over the course of the sixteenth century (see page 118). It is important to remember that England's economy was still based largely on agriculture in this period. The vast majority of people still lived in the countryside and smaller villages instead of in the cities and towns. The devastating population loss in the fourteenth century due to the Black Death also led to enclosure. Fields had fallen fallow and farm buildings into disrepair. This led to them being enclosed by landowners, but the increasing population in the sixteenth century made these former fields seem attractive again (see Figure 3). When landowners refused to open these fields for the purpose of growing crops, the people became frustrated. For this reason, the increasing population during the period seemed worse because of the enclosures from the past.

▲ Figure 3: England enclosure in the sixteenth century

Enclosure commissions

The practice of enclosure, particularly for the purpose of grazing sheep, became an important political icon during the period. As early as 1516, Sir Thomas More pointed to the problem of greed and sheep in his *Utopia*. Enclosures were cited as the reason for rebellions during the mid-sixteenth century. Edward VI's government attempted to address the problem of enclosures in 1548 and 1549. During this time, enclosure commissions were established. These commissions travelled the countryside to hear the complaints of tenants who believed that they were wronged by the enclosing activities of landowners. The enclosure commissions were to investigate the claims made by the tenants,

and to ensure that people who were wronged by these actions received justice. The commissions became associated with social unrest in the late spring and summer of 1549. The problem of enclosure featured heavily in the demands made by the rebels who rose in East Anglia in July 1549 (see page 99). It was also a problem during Elizabeth I's reign. These problems are found in the numerous laws addressing the poor and vagrants during the late sixteenth century (see page 90).

4 The impact of growing urbanisation

People left the countryside in order to make their living in England's towns and cities during the sixteenth century. As a result England became increasingly urbanised during the reign of the Tudors. Urbanisation was due to a number of factors. First, the kingdom's population was rapidly increasing during this period. It was finally starting to reach the numbers it had been prior to the Black Death centuries earlier. A second reason for urbanisation was that the countryside was experiencing depopulation (see page 86). A third reason for urban growth was the increase in the kingdom's labourers who were landless. This group was more mobile than others. Without any specific attachment to lands, they were free to move to cities and towns. By the end of the sixteenth century approximately 22 per cent of England's population was living in towns, compared to 10–12 per cent at the beginning of it.

Just as the causes of urbanisation were numerous, so too were its effects on the kingdom's population and on the towns and cities themselves. As the kingdom's population grew, differences in living standards between rich and poor began to increase. The wealthy people living in towns and cities had better incomes and built larger homes, but the quality of life for the poor remained grim. Urban areas were unable to cope with the numbers of people moving into their workforces. This meant that workers who earned low wages were forced to live in squalid conditions. Cities and towns did not have the resources to aid new arrivals, who were sometimes forced to beg as they searched for employment and affordable housing. The influx of new people strained the resources available in urban centres. Beggars and **masterless men** seemed more common, and were increasingly viewed as a threat to the stability of the social order.

▲ Woodcut illustration showing a family forced to become vagrants in search of work. Are the poor depicted in a sympathetic way in this woodcut? Explain your answer with reference to specific aspects of the image.

5 The growing professional classes

Along with the increase in population experienced by English towns throughout the sixteenth century, the professional classes also experienced growth. The professional classes included such professions as law, the clergy, merchants, those who worked in the livery companies and those who were affiliated with corporations. The legal profession experienced particular growth during this period, as increasing numbers of people sought to conclude legal cases through the common-law courts. This is reflected in the number of barristers created in the period (see Table 1).

Table 1: The number of barristers created in the 1500s and 1600s

Decade	Number of lawyers called to the bar
1570s	184
1580s	383
1630s	515

Larger numbers of children were able to attend schools because of the increasing endowment of grammar schools in the wake of the Reformation (see page 129). Some of these children were able to attend university. Even a few years at university, without a degree, was enough to help young men find employment in the early modern period.

Some of them found work with the lawyers as clerks or secretaries, aided by their penmanship and knowledge of Latin. Those gentry sons who became lawyers or barristers used their rural connections to build up a list of clientele, thriving on the increased number of legal cases in all the different courts. Although this could sometimes tie them into working for free, it also brought in a lot of profitable work. These were just two reasons why it made sense for there to be a lawyer in every gentry family, and why younger sons were sent to train in the **Inns of Court** after their university education. Furthermore, people were pushed to move to the cities and towns when the rural areas had little or no work for them. Urban areas had more opportunities for employment offering goods and services than the countryside did at times. When opportunities became available, workers seized them.

Conclusion

In the 1500s the English population finally began to recover from the devastating impact of the Black Death. The population increased rapidly, which led to changes in the way that people lived and worked. It meant that wage rates were low, because there was so much young labour and competition for jobs that people would accept low pay just to be able to have a job. The dissolution of the monasteries also had a significant impact on the lives of English people in this period. It led to changes in the way that charity and education were provided, and meant that former monks and nuns were made homeless, having to find new places to live and work. Enclosure increased, and this added to problems of depopulation in the countryside. Although enclosure benefited wealthy sheep farmers, it thrust other people into poverty. This led to more migration into towns, and towns frequently did not have enough accommodation or services to cope well with the sudden influx of people from the countryside. English towns, trade and jobs become increasingly recognisable to modern eyes in the sixteenth century. London became an international thriving merchant city, other towns grew and developed new markets for their goods. There were more jobs for the newly educated younger sons of the gentry, in useful roles such as lawyers. They were able to aid their families and connections in the increasing number of legal cases. There were also economic problems, and some groups of people suffered disproportionately as a result. These were the landless labourers who were affected by enclosure, and the poor of the towns who had very little safety net in times of hardship.

Work together

Read this chapter carefully. In pairs, debate the impact of the economic changes that took place in this period. Each choose one change. Take it in turns to explain why the change you have chosen was the most significant to the lives of ordinary English people. Be prepared to defend your choice against that of your partner.

Recommended reading

Paul Slack, *The English Poor Law, 1531–1782* (Cambridge University Press, 1995).

This is a concise textbook that provides an overview of the development of the Poor Law. It dedicates a lot of space to explaining the development of the law during Henry VIII's reign, as well as the innovations that rulers including Edward VI and Elizabeth made.

Robert Tittler and Norman Jones (editors), *A Companion to Tudor Britain* (Wiley-Blackwell, 2004).

Chapters 18–20 look at the rural economy, urban society and London respectively. They are detailed and well-written accounts of these aspects of the period.

www.bbc.co.uk/programmes/b009jtq1

A downloadable radio discussion that covers the dissolution of monasteries, featuring contributions from historians Diarmaid MacCulloch, Diane Purkiss and George W. Bernard.

The impact of growing urbanisation

- The gap in living standards between rich and poor increased
- Quality of life for the urban poor was grim
- New migrants to towns lived in squalid conditions or had to beg
- The available resources in towns became stretched
- People worried more about beggars and their threat to social order

The increase in population

- Population increased by approximately 83 per cent between 1500 and 1600
- It outstripped food supply meaning prices rose
- Wage rates remained low because there was a surplus of labour
- This drove people to move to the towns and the cities

Impact of the closure of the monasteries

- Religious houses had both religious function and provided services to local communities
- Their closure prompted popular rebellions
- The Dissolution of the Lesser Monasteries Act of 1535 closed small religious houses – the property and goods went to the King
- The Court of Augmentations was set up in 1536 to administer the closures
- The Pilgrimage of Grace hardened Henry's attitude to monasteries and led to the closure of all monasteries
- It brought additional income to the Crown and land to use in patronages
- It removed a source of charity for the poor
- It had a severe impact on education, at least temporarily

THE CHANGING STRUCTURE OF SOCIETY

Growing professional classes

- Legal profession saw especially high rates of growth
- Increased interest in access to education – the Reformation helped to fuel this
- Law was a profitable and respectable area for younger sons of the gentry

Spread and consequences of enclosure

- Enclosure caused poverty for poorer people who relied on common land
- It became a political problem that revealed social tensions
- Poorer tenants lost their homes and others left for towns
- It seemed that the poor lost their livelihood to make the rich richer
- It made the problems of population increase worse as the amount of available farming land declined
- Commissions were set up in 1548 to investigate these claims and they became associated with popular unrest
- It continued to be a problem into Elizabeth's reign

▲ Summary diagram: The changing structure of society

Essay technique: Resolution

The highest marks in Sections A and B of the exam are available for sustained analysis. One way of achieving this is to write an essay that develops a clear argument (see pages 92–93) and counterargument (see pages 104–105).

Having set out an argument and a counterargument you should resolve the tension between the two. One way of concluding an essay is to resolve the debate that you have established between the argument and the counterargument.

Imagine you are answering the following question:

> **How accurate is it to say that enclosure hugely damaged and disrupted English society?**

Your essay plan could look like this:

Paragraph 1 Argument	Enclosure forced agricultural labourers and tenant farmers off the land in order that the landowners could graze sheep. This led to significant migration into towns and a change in population patterns.
Paragraph 2 Argument	Enclosure led to unemployment as many of those who were employed in agriculture lost their jobs if the lands were enclosed. It also led to a loss of common land. This led to increased poverty and social tensions.
Paragraph 3 Counterargument	Enclosure did lead to an increase in agricultural production, which was good for the economy in a broader sense. It was the start of a more scientific approach to agriculture, though it largely benefited the landowners who saw land values rise.
Paragraph 4	Enclosure did have some benefits but these were largely to landowners. It was much more negative for ordinary labourers and tenant farmers, who generally became poorer as a result.

This essay has two clear paragraphs arguing that enclosure was damaging to society, one paragraph countering this, and one that indicates the record was mixed.

The conclusion evaluates the argument and counterargument. It resolves the tension by identifying a problem with the counterargument, while also acknowledging that there is some truth in the counterargument. Even so, ultimately it returns to the main argument.

You can resolve the tension by weighing up the argument and counterargument in the conclusion. In so doing, you can reach a supported overall judgement. For example, your conclusion could look like this:

The conclusion begins with the main argument, which summarises paragraphs 1 and 2.

Identifies a problem with the counterargument.

Finally, the conclusion resolves the tension by evaluating the argument and counterargument, concluding that enclosure was damaging and disruptive.

> In conclusion, for the majority of English people enclosure had very negative effects, particularly in the short term. This was because it forced them off the land and made them poorer, reducing the common land that they could use to graze their livestock even if they did remain. The resulting migration caused tensions and shortages in towns. There were some benefits, however, in terms of an increase in food production and an increase in land values. Nonetheless, because these benefits generally were only available to landowners, it cannot be said that enclosure was helpful to society as a whole. So, although it did make landowners wealthier and boost some sectors of industry, it is easy to see why enclosure was so unpopular and was seen as damaging.

It continues by contrasting this with the counterargument from paragraph 3.

Acknowledges some truth in the counterargument.

TIP: The process of evaluating the argument and the counterargument is helped by the use of words like 'however' and 'nonetheless', which indicate that the paragraph is weighing up contrasting arguments.

Activity: Resolving tensions

Imagine you are dealing with the following Section A question:

How accurate is it to say that merchants were the only group to benefit from economic change in the years 1530–88?

Here is a possible plan:

Paragraph 1 Argument	In the years 1530–88 the merchants benefited greatly from economic change because exploration gave them new markets and new products, and could adversely affect their competitors.
Paragraph 2 Argument	The merchants benefited indirectly from the migration of the Dutch skilled textile workers who introduced the 'new draperies' because this product was more attractive and improved sales of English cloth.
Paragraph 3 Argument	They were some ways in which they suffered as well, however, because of changes to the international situation (e.g. the loss of Calais) and the decline in sales of raw wool.
Paragraph 4 Counterargument	Other groups also benefited from economic change, such as the nobles and gentry who owned large amounts of land. Land values increased and wages declined, meaning that even if they didn't enclose their land, they still could make more money from it if they chose.

1 Answer the following questions:
   a) Which is stronger, the argument or the counterargument? Why is it stronger?
   b) What are the flaws in the weaker argument?
   c) What strengths does the weaker argument have?
2 Having answered these questions, write a conclusion that weighs up the argument and the counterargument in order to reach an overall judgement.

   TIP: Use the words 'However', 'Nonetheless' and 'Therefore' to structure the paragraph.

4c: Cultural change

Overview

The numbers of grammar schools and those attending them increased greatly in the sixteenth century. Similarly the number of students at the universities increased, although there are no definitive figures of how many students achieved a degree. This reflected the increased status of education among the nobility and gentry, tied to the predominance of humanist ideals. For some gentry sons this resulted in academic, clerical or legal careers. For others, it was an experience that prompted a lifelong love of reading and learning, while for a large proportion it was a way to make connections and gain some social 'polish'. The printing press, and the increased availability of books, pamphlets and other printed materials, meant that it was easier to maintain an interest in intellectual pursuits, political news or scandal.

For those interested in the visual and creative arts, this was a very exciting period indeed in English history. There was an upsurge in theatre attendance among people of all social classes. People used manuals to learn how to play tunes on musical instruments like the virginal. Poetry was extremely popular, and so was cheap print. Patronage was crucial for those aiming for success in the arts, and noble patrons supported theatre companies, poets and writers while they produced their great (or not so great) works. In Elizabeth's reign the Queen's very image became a cultural icon, and featured in a range of forms from sermons to portraits, miniatures to stained glass. Elizabeth's image became closely associated with that of the nation. It is an image that lasts to this day.

This section examines cultural change from 1509 to 1588 through the following sections:

1 *The impact of the growth of grammar schools and universities* looks at the changes in education in the sixteenth century and assesses the impact they made.

2 *The impact of the printing press* examines the role of the printing press in leading to greater availability of books and printed material. It looks at the range of material available and the impact of that availability.

3 *The impact of religious changes on culture* explores the way that the religious policies of the monarchs affected visual culture, poetry and music. It also looks at the impact on history writing and on the depiction of the royal image.

4 *The importance of patronage* discusses the hugely important role played by noble and gentry patrons in supporting and developing artists' work. It examines the different ways in which patrons supported artists.

5 *Developments in drama, music, poetry and architecture* looks at the different ways in which culture changed over the sixteenth century. It examines the innovations made by a range of musicians, playwrights, poets and gentleman builders and assesses their significance.

6 *The impact of the 'cult of Gloriana'* examines the question of the frequently cited cult of the image of Elizabeth I, and evaluates its use. It looks at the ways that the Queen was portrayed and attempts an explanation of those portrayals.

Note it down

It would be useful to use the 1:2 method (see page x) again for this chapter. This is because it contains detailed explanations of trends alongside examples that you can use for evidence. As in the last section, highlight any books, statistics or other detailed examples that you can learn when revising. Remember that it can be useful to think about causes and consequences as well as the main events that are being discussed.

1 The impact of the growth of grammar schools and universities

It is very difficult to judge the impact of changing educational habits. Grammar schools and universities were largely (although not entirely) the preserve of the wealthy. It became a mark of social status for a gentleman's sons to attend school, university and then perhaps one of the **Inns of Court**. This was a world where social status was a vital determinant of so many aspects of one's life. It is important to remember that, although increasing numbers attended schools and universities, it did not necessarily lead to a highly literate and cultured population. Many gentlemen attending either Cambridge or Oxford saw it as an opportunity to enjoy themselves and make connections with other wealthy men rather than to gain deep learning. So while education and literacy were markers of elite culture and society, not everyone who attended a grammar school or a university participated fully in literate or literary culture.

There was a significant increase in literacy in the Tudor period, however, which enabled many more people to enjoy the new printed materials available from the printing presses of London (see pages 130–31). These were for ordinary people as well as members of the elite. Education in this period, both in school and university, was greatly influenced by the ideals of humanism. Humanism affected the quantity and type of educational institutions, the curriculum and reading habits beyond school and university.

Note it down

Consider the following questions and take notes on them while reading this section:

- What was humanism?
- What impact did it have on university education?
- How did education change over the period?
- What was education like for women in the Tudor age?

Humanism and education in the Tudor period

Humanism originally began in Italy as a desire to recover the original ancient Latin and Greek texts and translate them to understand afresh the ideas they contained. It became a political, educational and moral movement. **Humanists** believed that citizens should be educated and able to contribute actively to the civic lives of their communities – a good life was one actively lived in politics and community life. Education was necessary in order to contribute effectively and to achieve morally just outcomes. If more people were educated, the whole community would benefit. This was particularly, although not exclusively, important for elite groups who would be governing and leading their communities. Humanism inspired reformers to read and recover the meaning of biblical texts, leading to some of the impulses behind the Reformation. Many humanists in England were also religious reformers, but there were many Catholic humanists too, including Erasmus and Colet. Christian humanism was the most influential in England because of the influence of Erasmus on important English scholars like Colet and Thomas More.

Humanist education emphasised literacy, literature and rhetoric as skills to best fit men for participation in political life. A humanist education was also, particularly for Christian humanists, intended to improve religious life. The development of humanism and its adoption by the elite as a mark of status led to an increased interest in education, at universities and in schools. Founders of new schools and colleges believed that education would provide an answer to society's ills and would strengthen the bonds of social order.

University education

Humanist ideals began to have an effect on the type of education offered by the two universities in England, and the quality of that education. At the time there were only two universities in England – Oxford and Cambridge – and two in Scotland – at St Andrews and Glasgow. Of these Oxford is the eldest, with teaching existing in some form since 1096. Cambridge was founded in 1209, with St Andrews and Glasgow founded by papal bull in the fifteenth century. In Henry VIII's reign more colleges were founded at both Oxford and Cambridge. John Fisher, Bishop of Rochester and chaplain to Henry VIII's grandmother Lady Margaret Beaufort, worked with her to found a new college at Cambridge, St John's College, which was founded in 1511. Such colleges were founded specifically to promote humanist learning. There were also new colleges founded at Oxford, including Brasenose in 1509, Corpus Christi in 1517 and Christ Church which was refounded in 1546. The first lectureship in Greek was established at Corpus Christi in 1517. More such colleges were founded in Elizabeth's reign.

Humanism was not on the curriculum at every college in either university, however, and there were still strongly conservative elements who believed that the medieval curriculum should be retained. University courses did not operate the same as they do today. Students did not pick a subject or area to study for three or four years. The traditional medieval curriculum consisted of two levels. The first level was the trivium – grammar, logic and rhetoric. The more advanced level was the quadrivium – arithmetic, geometry, music and astronomy. Students could then go on and specialise, for example in law, **theology** or medicine. In Cambridge it took four years to complete a Bachelor of Arts degree, then a further three years for a Master of Arts.

At the same time the numbers of students **matriculating** every year increased greatly. Not all of these graduated with a bachelor's degree, but instead left after one or two years having had the experience of university life and education that they needed. The numbers appear to have more than doubled from Henry's reign (approximately 300) to Elizabeth's (700). For many of these students their education was intended to fit them for life as a gentleman, either as a landowner or (if a younger son) in a profession such as law. These men would often take on roles such as Justices of the Peace when back in their homes (see page 82). The growth of the universities meant that more country gentlemen, local office-holders and professionals had some degree of learning and education. They were keen to maintain their status and send their sons in the future, establishing an increasing tradition of elite education. Some would continue their education long after leaving the universities. They purchased, read and discussed the latest books and treatises.

Grammar schools

Grammar schools are seen as one of the glories of the Elizabethan **Renaissance**. They were not the only way that boys could gain an education, however. Many of the children of the rich continued to be tutored privately, and there were other kinds of schools which offered some Latin and some English tuition. Informal tuition was sometimes offered to promising students or gentry sons by the local vicar or a university graduate. The number of schools open to the laity increased hugely in the early modern period – from 30 in 1480 to over 400 by the mid-seventeenth century. This was actually a greater level of provision than existed even in Victorian times.

Grammar schools were frequently founded by wealthy people who left money in their wills for the school to be set up, built and a schoolmaster paid. These benefactors included courtiers, clergymen, lawyers, tradesmen and merchants. They left property and land that would bring in an income for the school to continue. The intention behind most of these foundations was religious, and the vast majority of founders were **evangelical reformers** who hoped that through this education the Gospel would spread. Most grammar schools, including Eton (founded 1441), Westminster (founded 1179) and Colfe's School (founded 1574), were meant to include at least some free education for poor boys, though as time went on they became dominated by the gentry. Few poor children went to these schools because of the cost, but also because their families needed their labour at home. This meant that most pupils at grammar schools were sons of the gentry.

The curriculum was founded on the study of Latin. Greek and Hebrew were also offered in some schools. There were long days made up of translating Latin texts into English and English texts into Latin. There were also Latin disputations or debates. This prepared the scholars for entrance to university at the end of their time at the grammar school. Schools aimed to promote social unity and the official religion of the state. The education they gained at school was intended to fit boys for their futures as servants of the state. As per humanist ideals, they would serve their community as active citizens. Schoolmasters were licensed from 1559 in order to ensure that they conformed religiously and were loyal to the state. Later on it became the bishops' responsibility to license schoolmasters, demonstrating how far education was linked to religion. The grammar schools increased the flow of students to the universities and enforced from a young age the importance of political loyalism and religious conformity. Thus the schools had a significant impact on the generations of gentry who would be educated at such establishments, and who went on to public life and professions.

Education for ordinary people

Education was available for ordinary people as well as the elites. There were 'petty' or 'alphabet' schools and charity schools that were open to the poor. These provided a very basic level of education. The petty schools concentrated on reading rather than writing, and were much more widely available in urban areas. The fact that schools for the poor concentrated on reading meant that for a long time it was presumed that the poor were not at all literate. Many could not sign their names but could read printed materials. This made such people a fertile market for cheap printed materials like ballads and tracts – songs, popular tales, political and religious material. At the beginning of Elizabeth's reign in 1558 it is estimated that around 20 per cent of men and 5 per cent of women were literate on the evidence that they could sign their names in church court depositions. In fact, because many more could read but not write these figures are likely to be an underestimate, particularly in London where there was more educational provision available for the poor. Demand for such schools certainly increased over the period, and girls were also allowed to attend such elementary schools.

There was much less education available to the rural poor in the Tudor period. Schools set up in the period did often allow for places for the children of the poor, but these were limited in number.

Literacy for Tudor women

It has long been known that girls and women received much less formal education than boys and men. Yet the increase in educational provision does seem to have had an effect on female literacy too. Evidence from women's letters suggests that more women were literate than has previously been estimated. James Daybell, who has written extensively about female letter-writers and literacy, argues that most elite women were literate to a greater or lesser degree. These women tended to be educated at home by tutors. Those who were very highly educated were often given this education as a deliberate decision of enlightened humanist fathers, like Sir Anthony Cooke and his five daughters in the 1530s and 1540s. His daughters were taught Latin and Greek. One daughter, Anne, published her own Latin and Italian translations. Another, Elizabeth, published a translation of a religious tract from Latin. Daughters were increasingly expected to have varied accomplishments which included literacy – although not in all cases. Although women were taught a different handwriting style to men, they did correspond on a great range of topics, from household and family matters to political and military events.

2 The impact of the printing press

The first printing press in England was set up in London in 1476 by William Caxton. He was a successful merchant and diplomat who had travelled widely in northern Europe. This included Cologne, now in Germany, where he saw the printing presses in action. Shortly afterwards he set up a printing press in Bruges, where he was responsible for the first book printed in English in 1473 – the *Recuyell of the Historyes of Troye* – which he had translated himself. When this was successful he sent up a press in Westminster, London. There were printed books in England before this, but these were in Latin or Greek, rather than English. Previously, books had been imported from the Continent. Caxton was a shrewd and successful businessman, so his move to England is likely to suggest that demand for English printed books had grown enough to be a viable business venture. Four-fifths of his books were printed in English. The press was a success, and was taken over in 1495 by Caxton's successor, Wynkyn de Worde. They printed mostly religious material and chivalric romances such as Thomas Malory's *Morte d'Arthur*.

The emergence of a new consumer market

The printing press led to gradual rather than immediate cultural change. It did, however, create a new consumer market for printed books. Noble and gentry book collectors bought the latest volumes and demand increased. There had been private libraries before the printing press, such as that of Duke Humphrey of Gloucester. He was

brother to Edward V and donated his collection of books to the University of Oxford on his death in 1447. Books had been too expensive for all but the richest men to afford before printing. They had to be individually copied by scribes, usually in monasteries. Printing made books much more accessible. After the invention of the printing press they could be mass produced. This took less time and was less expensive, which meant that books became cheaper. Although they were still to some extent a luxury item, books could be afforded by gentlemen from the fifteenth century onwards. Cheaper printed material was also produced. This was purchased by all classes of people but vitally extended the impact of the printing press to the man on the street. By 1510 at least 439 titles had been published. By the 1630s this had increased exponentially to 6,000. In Europe as a whole more than 150–200 million copies of books were produced in the sixteenth century, as opposed to only 20 million copies before 1500. This demonstrates the enthusiasm and profit to be made in print in this period.

Censorship

Printing also opened up new ideas beyond the clergy and the very richest courtiers. This meant that long-established ideas could be challenged as more people could read about and debate them. This became a problem for the government as unorthodox ideas began to challenge the messages of the state. As a result the government tried to control and censor the printing presses. Henry VIII's government issued the first list of prohibited books in 1529. These were largely religious books by evangelical

Cheap print

As literacy increased and printing became easier and cheaper, the variety of print expanded rapidly. Instead of being restricted to books people could now buy pamphlets, chapbooks, broadsides, libels and religious tracts. The prices varied greatly, as did the artefacts themselves. Some included woodcut images that made a political or satirical point. Cheap print was sold on the street by peddlers, customers being attracted by their pithy sales pitch or the topic of the publication. It was also sold at bookstalls in St Paul's Churchyard, London. From there it might be passed from person to person, or taken to the countryside to keep people outside London abreast of current affairs. Cheap print had a variety of purposes, for example to spread religious ideas or to attack a political or local opponent. These products also interacted with what was a vibrant oral culture, spreading rumours and ideas beyond their point of origin in alehouses and markets.

reformers. In 1538 censorship was extended to non-religious books. By 1557 the system was formalised and put in the hands of the new Stationers' Company. They policed printing for the government in exchange for a monopoly over London presses. This did not mean that banned books never reached an audience, but it was much more difficult for them to do so. Those disobeying these rules would be severely punished. The government was able to harness printing for its own benefit as well. It used the new technology to spread government propaganda and proclamations more easily to areas outside of London.

Printing and the Reformation

One important debate concerning printing is the extent to which it aided the Reformation. This is an impossible question to entirely resolve. The improved technology of printing did lead to more people learning to read. If people could read printed material, Reformation ideas were more accessible to them. But, on the other hand, Catholics used the printing presses as much as Protestants, setting up secret presses when they were forbidden to use licensed ones. As a result, it is more likely that printing simply coincided with reforming ideas about materials being available in the vernacular and the development of humanism which encouraged new publications and translations of new and ancient works. It did make the Reformation a lot easier than it would have been otherwise, with the clergy previously having control of the ideas and production of books.

John Foxe's *Acts and Monuments*

In writing his *Acts and Monuments*, otherwise known as Foxe's *Book of Martyrs*, the author aimed to create something completely new, using evidence that he believed could not be contradicted. He used accounts of those who suffered persecutions as well as copies of their writings and those of witnesses. Foxe wanted to create an indisputable account of the sufferings of Protestants. His account was almost immediately disputed. He tended to ignore material that did not suit his case, and edited other material to follow his argument. Yet his work was still an immense feat of scholarship and should be appreciated within the context of the time. He began writing the book in 1552 but when in exile collected more accounts from the Marian persecution happening at the time. He published the first edition of the book in 1563, a huge volume of over 1,800 pages. It was to be published in many further editions after its initial publication and is still being studied today.

3 The impact of religious changes on culture

The Reformation was a cultural as well as a religious turning point. It destroyed much of the medieval traditions in art, literature, music and theatre. The **iconoclasm** of the Reformation saw a visual tradition stripped away. Images and statues of saints were removed and destroyed, colourful and vivid wall paintings were whitewashed over. The crucifix, a symbol of suffering and redemption, was removed and replaced by the royal coat of arms. In some ways this is symbolic of the wider changes during the English Reformation. A different but vibrant culture grew up in its place, particularly at the heart of Elizabeth's court. Humanism and the broader **European Renaissance** were important in this. In some ways, words replaced images in terms of their centrality to culture. The word of God was much more important in reformed religion than images, which were seen as idolatrous and Catholic. New translations of the Bible, the Prayer Book and religious propaganda such as Foxe's *Acts and Monuments* were at the centre of the reformed faith. Cheap printed materials helped to fill some of the void in popular culture, combining striking woodcut images with memorable tunes and words in the case of ballads.

Humanism, history and political writing

Humanism did not just lead to religious and educational reform that formed part of the wider social and political culture of England and Wales. It also led to changes, for example in the way that history was written. Instead of the medieval chronicles which told stories of the supernatural and narratives of the actions of kings and heroes, history became a way to glorify the monarch while instructing the reader on the correct moral behaviour. Polydore Vergil's 1512 *Anglica Historia* (a history of England) is one example of this. He aimed to show how the Tudor **dynasty** had restored moral order to the country after years of corruption. Unsurprisingly, his work became a standard history for students to work from. Authors such as Edward Hall and Ralph Hollinshed produced histories of Britain that included sources and eyewitness accounts, weaving them into a narrative that glorified the Tudors as bringing a united Protestant nation. Humanist authors like Vergil also tried to be more critical when analysing evidence rather than accepting exactly what their sources said. They saw this as being closer to the practice of **classical** authors like Livy and

Tacitus rather than that of medieval chroniclers. John Foxe's *Acts and Monuments* was also a work of historical writing. Although it had a clear purpose in promoting Protestantism, Foxe did use a range of documentary in researching his book.

The Reformation also required writers to be more overt propagandists in the service of the state. Some humanists supported Henry VIII in his struggle to escape from his marriage to Catherine of Aragon. It was a humanist called Christopher St Germain who gave Henry VIII the legal theory that was to underpin the Act of Supremacy (see page 38). Scholars were also responsible for gathering together a collection of historical sources that supported the **Royal Supremacy**. The humanist writer Thomas Starkey was one of Thomas Cromwell's best propagandists, writing material in support of the Reformation and the religious changes implemented by Cromwell.

The Reformation and the royal image

The Reformation meant that the King was no longer merely a Christian prince but was a **patriarch** of a Church. This led to portrayals of Henry VIII as the biblical King Solomon – a wise and fair royal and religious figure – including that by Hans Holbein entitled *Solomon and the Queen of Sheba* from approximately 1534–35. The Great Bible, published in 1539, had a **frontispiece** which showed Henry ensuring that the word of God reached his people via the social and religious hierarchy. At the bottom the people chant 'God Save the King'. This united royal and divine images and reinforced the idea of the Royal Supremacy. The religiously inspired royal images of Henry VIII were surpassed only by those of Elizabeth I. Portraits of Elizabeth and images of her as the 'virgin queen' were full of symbolism of Elizabeth as the symbol of her country. It has been argued that the image of the 'virgin queen' was prompted by Puritan fears that she might marry the Catholic Duke of Anjou (see pages 13–14). They preferred the idea of the Queen remaining a symbol of her nation and an unmarried woman than marrying a Catholic and risking the return of that faith.

4 The importance of patronage

Patrons were absolutely vital for poets, musicians and playwrights in Tudor England. They allowed companies of actors to obtain a licence, provided financial support and could promote the work at court and to other wealthy people. In this way, patrons could either make or break an artist or writer. For patrons, **patronage** was a way of demonstrating their status and wealth. Artists were directly controlled by their patron. Writers and musicians were less so. As the success of the artist or writer depended on the success of the patron, artists had to be politically aware and adept in order to do well.

The importance of patrons to acting companies has been well studied. Part of the importance of patronage to actors was practical. As the sixteenth century progressed, laws were made that required acting companies to serve on licence under the patronage of patrons of increasingly higher rank. A patron, then, was important for them to be able to work legally. Under Henry VIII the patron could be a relatively lowly ranked esquire or justice of the peace. By the 1570s patrons needed to be barons or earls. This made noble patronage particularly vital in Elizabeth's reign. Indeed several nobles and noble families had strong records as patrons. These included Edward de Vere, Earl of Oxford; Ambrose Dudley, Earl of Warwick; Henry Stanley, Earl of Derby; Robert Devereux, Earl of Essex; and Katherine Willoughby, Duchess of Suffolk. The Queen herself became a patron in 1583 of a company called Queen Elizabeth's Men, poaching the best acting stars from different companies. William Shakespeare, perhaps the most well-known Tudor playwright, had different patrons over his career. They included Queen Elizabeth I and King James VI and I, as well as the Earl of Southampton and the Earl of Pembroke.

Patrons played a financial role in maintaining the fortunes of the acting companies they lent their names to. Royal **favourites** like Essex and the Earl of Leicester had a huge effect on the development of the arts and on introducing European trends to the country. This popularised such trends at court and, if a style or form was popular, then artists had to follow it to remain in work. These trends included the humanist classical emphasis. Royal patronage could set the pattern for developments in the arts. Henry VIII's love of music, for example, meant that amateur musicians sprang up at court and beyond. Composers who wrote popular songs for this market could have them printed and sell them to make a living. All of the Tudor monarchs encouraged **masques** and plays at court. Henry VIII frequently staged such diversions, but Edward and Mary did too. Under the Duke of Northumberland a huge temporary banqueting hall was set up for the visiting French ambassadors to be shown the best of English entertainments. Elizabeth is perhaps the Tudor monarch best known for her patronage and enjoyment of the arts. Many court masques were staged on her **royal progresses** around the country, meaning that new court trends had a wider audience.

5 Developments in drama, music, poetry and architecture

The Tudor period was a time of both change and continuity in culture. The English style in music and architecture in particular tended to blend continental European influences with traditional English ones. Although developments in poetry were perhaps influenced more by European Renaissance trends and ideals, this was not true across the entire British Isles, and the Celtic regions maintained and developed their own native traditions. The religious reformation was extremely influential on the music produced, and made its mark on architecture because of the dissolution of the monasteries.

Note it down

It is important to trace change and continuity in this section. Draw the following table and fill it in as you read the section.

	Change	Continuity
Drama		
Music		
Poetry		
Architecture		

Drama

The changes in drama in the sixteenth century were caused by commercial, religious and political developments as well as by literary innovations. Plays were written as polemics, religious and political propaganda, to give moral and political advice as well as to entertain. Once again, humanism was important here as it added to the body of material available to create plays – classical heroes, stories and other material. The classical allusions in these plays became more accessible as increasing numbers of people experienced a humanist classical education (see page 128).

Traditional performances

In the medieval period and for the early Tudor years most theatrical performances derived from holiday festivities. These were associated with important religious feasts such as Christmas, Corpus Christi (usually in June or very late May) and Whitsuntide (usually in May). Corpus Christi and Whitsun were both related to the Easter celebrations and were also times of popular festivity and celebration. Urban guilds held their cycles of mystery plays at these times of year – they were based upon biblical stories and

were enacted by members of the guilds. They were an act of worship and a performance to entertain the people. These were seen as 'popish' after the Reformation and were gradually banned. The last performance of the York mystery plays (until recent times) was in 1569, and the last performance at Chester was in 1575. Because such plays had already been suppressed at that point, the Mayor of Chester was tried in the Court of Star Chamber for allowing the mystery plays to go ahead. At the Inns of Court they elected a Christmas prince, who hosted festive proceedings including plays. There were court revels and lords of misrule in other institutions like universities. These traditions gradually either died out or were suppressed.

Polemical theatre

The theatre under Henry VIII and Edward VI was used for polemical and propaganda purposes. In the 1530s the radical reformer John Bale ran a company of eight players that produced religious, morality and nationalistic plays. He aimed to promote a reforming agenda and gain converts to evangelical Protestantism. This continued to some extent in the early months of Elizabeth's reign. The Twelfth Night festivities of 1559, for example, included an anti-Catholic court masque that represented cardinals as crows and abbots as wolves. This was to lead to the Queen's proclamation in May 1559, which set theatrical policy until 1571. It required local authorities to review all plays before they were put on, disallowing anything involving religion or government. This still allowed a lot of room for manoeuvre but aimed at preventing religious unrest.

Theatre buildings and theatre life

The first permanent theatre was built by James Burbage in 1576. It was called The Theatre and was in Shoreditch in London. This was an essential and hugely significant development for the performance of plays and for their audiences. There were professional acting troupes long before 1576 but they were not permanently based anywhere. The acting companies were very small – generally not more than five or six actors. They travelled the country and performed wherever they could (and wherever they could find an audience). The places where they performed included great houses, palaces, town halls, inns and churches. It was a difficult life, being both physically and financially risky. Although acting companies did continue to tour after theatres were built in London, it did mean that there was a more stable base for them in the meantime. Writing for the theatre was also a better way for poets and writers to earn money. Instead of relying on patrons who could stop funding you or who could fall from power, theatres were desperate for new material to keep their audiences interested. This gave financial stability to successful and popular writers and provided an increasing number of plays to be performed at the theatre. Additionally, it meant that acting companies could increase in size and their sets and costumes could become more elaborate given that they didn't have to move around.

Anxieties about the theatre: social disorder

The Elizabethan government increasingly began to worry about the theatre as a vehicle for social and moral disorder. There had always been worries about playgoing when it was not based in theatres, as people gathered together, often drank, and sometimes had fights. The existence of permanent theatres intensified these fears as they were based near other early modern 'leisure facilities' like bear pits, bowling alleys and brothels. The plays did not always uphold conventional morality either, for example Christopher Marlowe's *The Tragical History of the Life and Death of Doctor Faustus,* which considered the benefits as well as the horrors of its protagonist's pact with the Devil. The audiences were also incredibly diverse – a huge range of social groups attended the playhouses, all mixed together. Governments were concerned that with the topics that some plays explored, this could be an explosive mix. Mayors of London were particularly hostile, employing pamphleteers to attack the moral problems with playgoing. Puritans also loathed the theatre as they believed it incited people to commit sins like lechery and drunkenness. From 1575 the acting companies were forced out to the suburbs like Shoreditch unless (until 1594) companies could persuade inns to house their plays.

Music

Music was perhaps the most dramatically affected of the arts during the Reformation of the sixteenth century.

Sacred music and the Reformation

Sacred music was an absolutely central part of church services until the Henrician and Edwardian religious reforms. Complex and flamboyant melodies formed the basis of medieval music, known as **polyphonic** music. In this type of music the beauty of the melodies could obscure the religious texts used to form the words. Composers such as John Taverner, Thomas Tallis and Robert Jones were particularly known for polyphonic harmonies, and some of their work happily still survives. While Henry VIII did not have religious objections to sacred music, his dissolution of the monasteries did mean that their choirs, music libraries and composers were dispersed. There were no comparable institutions for them to move to, and a lot of this music and experience was lost. Edward's government did have

religious objections to sacred music. It was condemned by evangelical reformers as Catholic. In keeping with the rest of the reforms, those relating to music prioritised the words (seen as the word of God) over the music. Thomas Cranmer stressed this to Henry VIII in 1544. This was confirmed by Elizabeth I's 1559 injunctions.

Sacred music did continue in a few centres – cathedral schools, the colleges of the universities and royal establishments such as St Stephen's Chapel, Westminster. In fact, Elizabeth I's Chapel Royal offered a safe haven for several important composers of church music including Thomas Tallis and William Byrd. Tallis was appointed early in his career to Waltham Abbey but the abbey was dissolved in 1540 and the choir pensioned off. He moved to Canterbury Cathedral but shortly after was elected as a gentleman of the Chapel Royal, where he stayed and was protected for the rest of his life. The Chapel Royal was under Elizabeth's direct patronage and provides evidence for some of her more conservative religious tendencies. Byrd, for example, remained a Catholic but was allowed to make his living writing music for Anglican worship. Despite this, even under Elizabeth sacred music became more austere, simple and sober.

Increased popularity of secular music

One area of music that did expand in range and popularity in the Tudor period was secular music. Playing music for entertainment became more common. Henry VIII was fascinated by music and surrounded himself with musicians and composers. His household musicians included highly skilled Italian and Flemish minstrels. He also fancied himself as a composer and several of his compositions survive. He even educated all of his children to read and perform music. Elizabeth I certainly had a strong love of music. Music played a central part in her entertainments, feasts and pageants and the Queen had been taught how to compose and play music when she was young. Elizabeth was a skilful player of the **virginal**, a musical instrument like a harpsichord. This filtered down to the gentry and nobility. Musical accomplishment became a prized ability for men and women. Collections of music were published for amateurs to use, such as Nicholas Yonge's 1588 collection of Italian **madrigals** entitled *Musica Transalpina*. Several well-known church composers and musicians had a successful sideline in secular music, for example William Byrd and Thomas Morley. As well as music for its own sake, it was also composed and played to accompany dancing and other social situations. Most of this music has been lost – it was memorised by musicians and was never written down, except when incorporated into 'high culture' such as Byrd's work. This is also true of the songs and music of ordinary people.

▲ Queen Elizabeth I dancing with Robert Dudley, Earl of Leicester, c1580. What does this painting tell the historian about entertainment at the court? What does it tell us about the Queen's image?

Tudor music was distinctively English in style. English composers tended to honour traditional forms and techniques. They did not ignore foreign trends such as the madrigal but adapted them to English traditions and tastes. This was true of English church music as much as secular music. Only Englishmen could be choristers in chapel choirs and English music was used at services.

Poetry

The foundations of the courtly poetry of the Elizabethan period were laid by two important earlier poets – Henry Howard, Earl of Surrey, and Sir Thomas Wyatt. Surrey was executed by Henry VIII in 1547 due to Henry's probably unfounded fears that he was trying to usurp the throne. Wyatt had also been in grave danger due to his close friendship with Anne Boleyn in the mid-1530s. These two men were the first to introduce the sonnet to England that was later used to such effect by, among others, Shakespeare. As well as writing their own sonnets, together they translated the fourteenth-century Italian poet Petrarch's sonnets into English. Surrey was also the first English poet to publish blank verse. Both Surrey and Wyatt were included in an anthology printed in 1557 by Richard

Tottell, called *Songs and Sonnettes, written by the right honorable Lorde Henry Howard late Earle of Surrey, and other*. It was followed by other collections in Elizabeth's reign.

Poetry and the arts of the courtier

Poetry was formalised to a greater extent in the more stable political and social environment under Elizabeth. It became part of the arts of the courtier, one of the skills that an aspiring courtier needed to cultivate (along with music). This idea of the ideal courtier sprang from Italian humanist culture. Famous courtly poets of Elizabeth's reign include Philip Sidney and Edmund Spenser. Sidney's poetry was sophisticated and complex, and was an influence upon some of Shakespeare's comedies. His sonnets prompted the popularity of the form in the 1590s. They were really only surpassed by Shakespeare's varied, complex and dramatic sonnets which were published long after they were written, in 1609. Spenser perhaps represents the height of courtly poetry. In Spenser's *The Sheapheardes Calendar*, published in 1579, he introduced pastoral dialogue into English poetry. He was influenced by Greek Sicilian poets and used poetry as a way of discussing varied themes such as political controversy and religion. When Spenser's patron, the Earl of Leicester, fell in 1580 Spenser also fell from favour. He was sent to a post in Ireland and felt this to be a form of exile. This led him to produce sharp satires such as *Colin Clout's Come Home Again* of 1595, which concerned disillusionment with court life. Spenser's most well-known and ambitious poem was his *Fairie Queene* which he dedicated to Elizabeth and which incorporated myth, **chivalry** and England's Protestant heritage.

Welsh, Irish and Scottish poetry

Welsh poetry was resistant to the influences of European poetic forms like the sonnet. Bardic poets had produced lyrical and virtuoso poetry for centuries, which in Welsh poetry had evolved into demanding poetic forms like the *cywydd* and the *englyn*. It was governed by rigorous rules concerning alliteration, internal rhyme and strict numbers of syllables allowed in each form. Renaissance innovations, with their emphasis on classical poetry, held no interest or challenge for the Welsh bards. Humanists saw this as inflexible but this was a period in which some gifted Welsh poets operated and in which the art form flourished. Irish and Scottish traditions also persisted in this period in Gaelic. In the Celtic regions of the British Isles, continuity of form and style persisted instead of the influences of the Renaissance that were popular in England.

Architecture

In continental Europe developments in architecture formed a vital part of the Renaissance. In Florence in 1436, for example, the first octagonal dome in history was finished. This was the invention of Filippo Brunelleschi, who was inspired by classical ruins in Rome like other humanists were inspired by classical literature. The progress of architectural changes in England and Wales was much less smooth. In fact neo-classical buildings were not a consistent feature in the British Isles until the seventeenth century. There were many new and very grand buildings created in the sixteenth century, particularly after the dissolution of the monasteries in the late 1530s, but these were not particularly innovative.

The impact of Renaissance architecture

This is not to say that Renaissance architecture had no impact in England in the sixteenth century. A few wealthy nobles and gentlemen who had travelled around Europe brought ideas back and incorporated them into their houses. These included Sir William Sharrington at Lacock Abbey in Wiltshire. He had bought the abbey in 1539 during the dissolution of the monasteries and converted it into a private house. In around 1550 Sharrington added to the building and included Renaissance decoration

▲ Longleat House. What does the image tell the historian about Renaissance architecture?

when doing so. There was more consistent interest in Renaissance architecture in the late 1540s. Protector Somerset adopted Renaissance ideals and influenced others in his circle to do the same. Somerset remodelled Syon Abbey in the 1540s and from 1549 did the same in creating Somerset House. Another of Somerset's circle, Sir John Thynne, began rebuilding Longleat House on classical lines in 1549, finally finishing it in 1580.

Other notable buildings included Renaissance elements rather than being entirely neo-classical. Henry VIII showed his interest and enthusiasm for humanism when decorating his new palace. Work on Nonsuch Palace in Surrey began on 22 April 1538. The palace was not fully completed in Henry's reign but the decorative scheme was strongly influenced by the French King Francis I's palace at Fontainebleu. The decoration was inspired by humanist ideals, including images of the virtues and the Roman emperors. Henry's building work to extend Hampton Court, completed in 1540, also included Renaissance-inspired decorative elements. In Elizabeth's reign some newly built or renovated private houses also took a mixed approach to design, including older medieval tastes with new Renaissance elements. Sir William Cecil began building Burghley House in 1555, finally finishing it in 1587. Because Burghley House was built over such a long time it included different architectural fashions, including medieval, Italian Renaissance and French classical influences.

6 The impact of the 'cult of Gloriana'

The 'cult of Gloriana', it has been argued, showed a clever manipulation of the Queen's image in order to keep her subjects loyal and obedient. In 1977 Sir Roy Strong produced the most well-known account of this apparent phenomenon. He wrote that images of Elizabeth I took on a 'sacred' tone, with the cult of Gloriana buttressing social order and replacing pre-Reformation holy images of saints and the Virgin Mary. Celebrations of Elizabeth's birthday and Accession Day replaced the old festivities and centred public celebration around the person and image of the Queen. This has led to an intense concentration on portraits and other images, and a search to decode possible codes and symbols referring to the Queen, such as the roses present in the portrait 'Young Man Among Roses' painted c1587. There certainly seems to have been a myth of Elizabeth as a Virgin Queen, as Susan Doran and Thomas Freeman write, a 'solitary but glorious defender of the English Church and architect of England's greatness'.

Glorifying or criticising?

Since Strong wrote his book in 1977, his idea of a personality cult deliberately constructed by the state to mould an obedient populace has been moderated significantly. Since then historians investigating the topic of 'Gloriana' have found that there was a range of motives behind images glorifying the Queen. Not all of them were created by the Crown or its agents, and not all of them were positive. It does make the image of Elizabeth more interesting, however, because the meaning of it was not straightforward. It was contested and changed over time. Some images of Elizabeth, such as her portrayal in Foxe's *Acts and Monuments*, were covertly critical. While saying that God's providence saved the Queen, they implied that this meant she should go further in her religious reformation of the country. Outright criticism would clearly have led to punishment, so it was necessary to cloak it in flattery and inference. Elizabeth herself appears to have ignored such examples of criticism, adopting only the praise present in such material and turning it to her advantage.

Images were created by nobles and by comparatively ordinary people, and they had a mixture of messages. Some of them seem to contradict each other. Evidence from popular culture and arts shows Elizabeth as the great defender of England from her (Catholic) enemies. This includes sermons, parliamentary speeches, ballads, stained-glass windows, pictures and poems. Nobles, on the other hand, commissioned lavish portraits and written accounts. They variously depicted Elizabeth as a cool-headed and politically astute princess and as a hot-blooded warrior queen. This shows that there was no one image of 'Gloriana' and that people's picture of the Queen depended to some extent on their own reasons for creating those pictures.

Royal attempts at image control

Elizabeth certainly tried to control the visual images of herself as far as possible. She did not commission any of the large portraits of herself but her courtiers did. If they wanted to maintain their positions and not lose their position at court, they needed to make sure the depictions of the Queen were favourable to her. As the courtiers commissioned the portraits from the artists who painted them they were able to have close control over the end result. It was not possible for Elizabeth to control all images of herself, however, as the apparatus of government simply wasn't that efficient. There were written and visual negative images of Elizabeth I, created by Catholic propagandists such as Robert Persons (see pages 59–60) and Richard Verstegen. They portrayed her as a persecutor of English Catholics. Others portrayed her as sexually immoral. These images failed. The established, positive image is the one remembered today and portrayed in films, television programmes and books.

Conclusion

There were significant changes in education and culture in the sixteenth century. The number of schools increased, and the topics that were studied changed as the influence of humanist thought grew. More colleges were founded at Oxford and Cambridge, and it became increasingly fashionable for the sons of the gentry to attend university, even if it was not important that they were awarded a degree. The numbers of educated men and women increased in the Tudor period. This led to a parallel increase in the popularity of printed material (as enabled by the printing press) and to a range of significant developments in the visual arts, music and writing. New consumer markets for printed material emerged, for the poor as well as the rich. As literacy increased, so did the range of print available to Tudor people. This led to more censorship, as unorthodox ideas now became accessible to many more people. The royal image featured strongly in many of these developments, and others had the encouragement or support of monarchs and their consorts.

The Reformation had a significant cultural impact, making changes to the type of plays that people saw, and the way that people experienced music. Theatrical performances flourished, and the first permanent theatre was built. Although governments worried about the subject matters of plays, there was still plenty of opportunity for acting companies to put on a range of entertainment that appealed to a hugely diverse audience. Secular music became increasingly popular after the Reformation, as sacred music became confined to a few centres after the dissolution of the monasteries. People learned to play music at home, and a distinctive English tradition in music began to develop. Poetry became more formalised, influenced by humanist thought, and although architecture was not so quick to follow European styles there were Renaissance elements in the construction of new and splendid buildings. Although the sixteenth century saw the destruction or eclipse of many traditional English forms of culture, therefore, it did also lead to the development of new and exciting forms of music, theatre and poetry.

Work together

Work together to complete some further research on the image of Queen Elizabeth I. Read the section above and go online to find as many different images of the Queen as you can. Make sure (where possible) that these are from the sixteenth century. What kind of messages do you think your collection of images portrays? Does it vary? Do you think the Queen was successful in controlling her image?

Recommended reading

Susan Doran and Thomas Freeman (editors), *The Myth of Elizabeth* (Palgrave Macmillan, 2003).

This is a fascinating exploration of the myth of Gloriana and the depictions of the Queen.

Sir Roy Strong, *The Cult of Elizabeth: Elizabethan Portraiture and Pageantry* (Thames and Hudson, 1977).

This book pioneered the theory of the 'cult of Gloriana'. It is still a fascinating read in terms of the pageantry and portraiture of the time.

Greg Walker, 'The Renaissance in Britain' in Patrick Collinson, *The Sixteenth Century* (Oxford University Press, 2002), pp.145–87.

This useful chapter provides brief summaries of changes in theatre, music, literature and the arts.

http://ebba.english.ucsb.edu/

The online English Broadside Ballad Archive is a free resource that shows a huge range of examples of printed ballads and includes some that you can listen to being sung! An excellent insight into the range of cheap print in the early modern period. It also includes essays about ballads in their historical context.

Impact of the 'cult of Gloriana'

- Many images of Elizabeth were produced in her reign
- Historians argued that the 'cult of Gloriana' kept Queen Elizabeth's subjects loyal and obedient
- Since, there has been criticism of the idea because not all images were glorifying the Queen – some were critical
- The Queen tried unsuccessfully to control her portrayal in visual images

Impact of the growth of grammar schools and universities

- Encouraged by the popularity of humanism
- New colleges founded at Oxford and Cambridge throughout the period
- Number of students increased greatly
- Number of grammar schools hugely increased, set up by wealthy people in wills
- Made students eligible for university entry
- Mostly for sons of gentry
- Were schools for ordinary people too
- Literacy increased for men and women

Impact of the printing press

- Arrival of printing press led to gradual change and new consumer market for printed books
- Made books more accessible, if still a luxury item
- Was cheap print too that catered for a much wider market
- Censorship was introduced to combat the influx and spread of unorthodox ideas
- There is a debate about the extent to which printing aided the Reformation

CULTURAL CHANGE

The importance of patronage

- Patrons helped acting companies to gain a licence, provided financial support and promoted artists' work
- Theatre companies needed patrons to work legally
- Royal favourites did a lot to popularise particular theatrical forms
- The monarchs were also active patrons of theatre companies and composers

Developments in drama, music, poetry and architecture

- Traditional religious festive performances ended or were suppressed
- The theatre was used for polemical purpose under Henry VIII and Edward VI
- The first permanent theatres were built, bringing financial stability, successful writers and more plays
- There were anxieties about the theatre causing social and moral disorder
- Sacred music changed, becoming more austere and simple in response to the Reformation
- Secular music became more popular for people to play at home as well as to hear performed
- The sonnet was introduced to England and poetry became part of the art of the courtier
- There was not as much innovation in architecture but some neo-classical influences can be seen in the grand buildings of the day

Impact of religious change on culture

- Reformation was a cultural as well as a religious turning point
- Stripped away medieval artistic and theatrical tradition
- New cultures grew up, especially at court
- Histories were written that glorified England as a Protestant nation and promoted Protestantism
- The Royal Supremacy and the Reformation meant that royal and religious images became intertwined

▲ Summary diagram: Cultural change

Essay technique: Evaluation and relative significance

Reaching a supported overall judgement is an important part of doing well in Section A and B essays. One aspect of reaching the very highest level is to reach a supported overall judgement by evaluating the relative significance of different factors, in the light of a valid criteria. This section examines how to evaluate and how to establish valid criteria.

Evaluation

The purpose of evaluation is to weigh up arguments and reach a judgement. This means that evaluation needs to consider the importance of two or more different factors, weigh them up against each other, and then reach a judgement. Evaluation is a good skill to use at the end of an essay, because it helps to support your overall judgement.

For example, imagine you are answering the following Section B question:

> **How accurate is it to say that the Reformation transformed music more than any other cultural medium in the period 1529–88?**

You might want to weigh up the extent to which music was affected by the Reformation on one hand, and poetry and drama on the other. For example, your conclusion might read:

The first part of the paragraph focuses on the given factor, examining the way music was affected by the Reformation.

This part of the paragraph weighs up the given factor against other factors.

> In conclusion, clearly music was greatly affected by the Reformation from 1534 onwards. The monasteries and collegiate churches were the traditional strongholds of sacred music and these were dissolved from 1536 to 1540. Despite Mary I's best efforts and Elizabeth's protection of music, sacred music still changed greatly after 1534. Secular music became much more popular under Henry VIII and Elizabeth I and became distinctly English in style. Other types of culture were also affected, however, including drama and poetry. Traditional plays were built around religious themes, such as the mystery plays. These traditional and popular plays were seen as Catholic and died out, to be replaced by a more varied programme including the tragedies and comedies of Shakespeare. Poetry changed much less, being part of courtly life and culture, but it was altered by the influence of humanism which was to some extent linked to the religious changes. Despite this, music involved both a dying out of the traditional and the evolution of new and popular forms. It was more profoundly affected by the Reformation than the other forms discussed, which experienced more continuity than music in the period 1529–88.

The final part of the paragraph makes a judgement about the relative significance of the different factors.

In this example the evaluation is helped by using a series of words that help to weigh up the extent of change in music as opposed to poetry and drama. 'Clearly', 'However' and 'Therefore' are useful words as they can help contrast the importance of the different factors. This conclusion could be improved by explicitly weighing up the relative significance of the factors in the light of a valid criteria. An example of an improved conclusion can be found on page 141.

This section considers criteria of duration, impact and scope.

In conclusion, clearly music was greatly affected by the Reformation from 1534 onwards. Henry VIII's dissolution of the monasteries from 1536 to 1540 made a permanent impact on sacred music. Although Mary I attempted to revive sacred music and Elizabeth I supported it, the amount of sacred music declined and its style changed. It became more sober, austere and focused on words rather than harmony. On the other hand, secular music rapidly increased in popularity. Drama also changed significantly. Traditional theatre performance such as the mystery plays came to an end. Despite this, there was more continuity with theatre companies travelling the country. Theatre continued to be popular at court and enjoyed noble patronage. The programme of plays became more varied and permanent theatres were established. So drama did change significantly but experienced more continuity than music. Poetry changed much less than either music or drama. It became more popular at court, some new forms were introduced and it was altered to some extent by humanism. It was not catastrophically affected by the Reformation like music was, however, or even to the same extent as theatre in the period 1529–88. Therefore, music was transformed by the Reformation to a much greater extent than drama or poetry because it was permanently altered in form and content and sacred music suffered drastically.

This uses the same criteria to argue that theatre experienced less change.

This final sentence weighs up the factors and reaches an overall judgement.

Relative significance

Clearly, the Reformation brought changes in music, drama and poetry. However, the best essays will make a judgement about which changed the most based on a valid criteria.

It is up to you to come up with a valid criteria. Criteria can be very simple. The following criteria are often useful:

- **Duration:** Which factor was important for the longest amount of time?
- **Scope:** Which factor affected the most people?
- **Effectiveness:** Which factor achieved most?
- **Impact:** Which factor led to the most fundamental change?

For example, in this essay you could compare the factors in terms of their duration, impact and scope. For instance, you could argue that music was transformed to a greater extent because the scope, duration and impact of the change in this period was more significant than the transformation of drama or poetry.

This conclusion is an example of high level work because it reaches an overall judgement and supports through evaluating the relative significance of different factors in the light of valid criteria.

Activity: Weighing up the factors

Here is a plan in answer to the following question:

How accurate is it to say that there were significant changes in government in the period 1530–88?
- Royal control – very significant.
- Local government – significant.
- Parliament – some change.
- Ministers – not very significant.

Using your notes from the previous chapter:
1 Decide on the criteria that you are going to use to judge how accurate it is to say that there were significant changes in government in the period 1530–88.
2 Having established your criteria, write a sentence that summarises the extent to which government changed in the period 1530–88.
3 Support this by writing three or four sentences that weigh up at least three of the factors mentioned in your plan.

   TIP: Be explicit about the relative significance of the different factors in reaching your judgement.

   TIP: Use words such as 'however' and 'nonetheless' to weigh up contrasting points.
4 Write a final summary sentence that explicitly weighs up the different factors in terms of your criteria and reaches an overall judgement.

Historical interpretations: Was there a crisis of government in Elizabeth I's last years?

The Big Debate

Section C of the exam focuses on the period from 1589 to Elizabeth's death in 1603. Historians tend to agree that this period had a character of its own. Historian Patrick Collinson describes the period as the 'nasty nineties'. Others have described it as Elizabeth's 'twilight years'. Generally speaking the last years of Elizabeth's reign were dominated by a series of major problems. First, the defeat of the Spanish Armada in 1588 did not end the military threats to England's security. Between 1589 and 1603 there was a series of military issues. England was forced to fight a war on several fronts. English ships battled the Spanish navy off the shores of England and Spain, as well as in the waters of the New World. There were persistent fears of a Spanish invasion, as well as a rebellion in Ireland which led to years of bitter fighting. Secondly, there were problems in Elizabeth's court. Rivalry between Elizabeth's advisers led to tensions at the top of Elizabeth's government, which climaxed in a rebellion. There were also concerns over the succession. By 1589 Elizabeth was in her late 50s, she had no heir and there were controversies about who should replace her. Next, there were tensions between Elizabeth and her government on the one hand, and her parliament on the other. There were disputes about taxation and religion, among other topics, for most of Elizabeth's last years. Finally, the period 1589 to 1603 was a time of poor harvests, poverty, bread riots and rebellions. This social distress was heightened by the high taxes necessary to fight Spain and to deal with the Irish rebellion.

Clearly, there were many problems facing Elizabeth in her last years. Even so, Elizabeth's government survived, famine was avoided and her death did not lead to civil war or constitutional crisis. Therefore, there is considerable debate over how far there was a general crisis of government in Elizabeth's last years.

The exam focuses on four key aspects of Elizabeth's last years that could indicate the existence of a crisis.

Historians and historical debate

Section C of your exam focuses on interpretations of the past. Consequently, you will have to consider the work of historians. The nature of the 1590s has been debated for years, and many historians have put forward distinctive arguments about different aspects of Elizabeth's reign. While knowing which historian is associated with which view can be helpful it is not essential to doing well in the exam. Indeed, you can get full marks in the exam without knowing which views were put forward by which historian. The key thing is to be able to analyse interpretations of the past regardless of which historian they come from.

1 The significance of threats to national security from Spain and Ireland

Some historians argue that military conflict with Spain led to a crisis in Elizabeth's government. War with Spain and then in Ireland led to major military operations, unprecedented government spending and the constant threat of invasion. Moreover, while there were many battles between 1589 and 1603, there was no final victory. The endless war led to resentment over rising taxes and the continual conscription of troops. It also led to division within the government about how best to win the war.

2 The extent of faction at court and the succession issue

Faction fighting in Elizabeth's court and the related problem of the succession have also provoked discussion in the context of a 'crisis of the 1590s'. During the 1590s there was intense competition among Elizabeth's closest courtiers. Influence at court was key to influencing the direction of the war and the succession. The succession was also a major concern from the 1590s. Elizabeth had no direct heir. Moreover, in 1593 she turned 60. Clearly, she was nearing the end of her life, and yet she refused to resolve the issue of who would rule after her death. Uncertainty led to a destabilising discussion of the future of the monarchy, and Elizabeth's advisers feared it would lead to assassination plots or even a civil war as rivals fought to determine the succession.

3 The importance of growing conflicts with parliament and the session of 1601

Some historians also argue that events in parliament point to a growing crisis in Elizabeth's last years. Parliaments were increasingly concerned about poverty, crime and the cost of the war. Conflict between Elizabeth and parliament was particularly evident in 1601, due to Elizabeth's broken promises and perceived venality. Indeed, historian John Guy describes the problems in the parliament of 1601 as 'a minor constitutional crisis'.

4 The importance of harvest failures in the 1590s and the growth of social distress

Some historians point to the terrible poverty of the 1590s as another indication of crisis in Elizabeth's last years. Certainly, poor harvests between 1594 and 1597 caused a 'dearth': extreme shortages of food. Death rates, unemployment and food prices soared. Serious economic problems led to food riots, most notably in London as desperate people tried to get hold of the produce they could no longer afford to buy. Poor relief, whether from the government or charities, was never wholly adequate. The Queen's opponents claimed that the combination of bad harvests and continuing war was evidence that England was under a divine curse due to the sin of its people.

1 The significance of threats to national security from Spain and Ireland

Overview

England's rulers believed that war with Spain, and latterly in Ireland, was a profound threat to England's security in Elizabeth's last years. The war with Spain lasted from 1585 until 1604. Due to the size and influence of the Spanish Empire, the conflict took place on a number of different fronts. The main battlegrounds included: the English and Spanish coasts; the seas around the Azores, the Caribbean and Panama; the cities of Lisbon and Cadiz; and the Low Countries and France.

On several occasions in Elizabeth's last years there were invasion threats. In addition to the famous Armada of 1588, Spanish ships raided Penzance in 1595, and Philip II, the Spanish king, sent invasion fleets in 1596 and 1597.

The threat from Spain was only one of the dangers facing England. From 1594 rebellion in Ireland threatened to end English rule. Moreover, Elizabeth feared that an independent Ireland would ally with Spain and become a base from which Spain could attack England.

War led to further problems. It led to serious divisions within government and it led to higher taxes, which strained Elizabeth's relationship with her parliaments It also exacerbated the economic difficulties the country was facing and it led to a sense that England was under a curse.

However, in spite of the constant threat of invasion, the rebellion in Ireland and the economic strain of the war, England survived. England was never conquered by Spain and the rebellion in Ireland did not lead to an end of English rule. Elizabeth's defensive strategy did not lead to swift or decisive military victories, but it did protect England and in the long term it proved successful against her enemies in Ireland and in Spain. Therefore, there is considerable debate among historians over the extent to which war with Spain and in Ireland led to a crisis in Elizabeth's last years.

This section considers:
1 The Anglo-Spanish War
2 War in Europe
3 War in Ireland

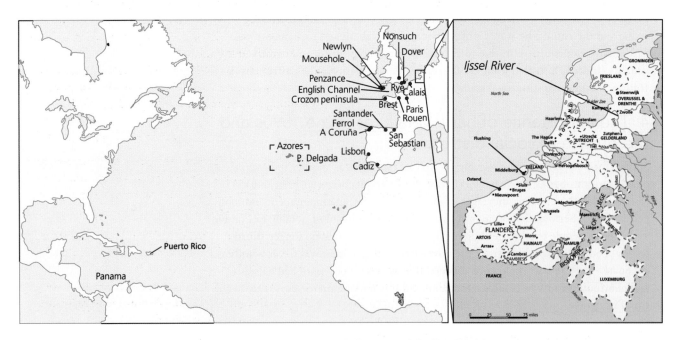

▲ Figure 1: A map to show important locations of Elizabeth's wars in Europe and the New World

1 The Anglo-Spanish War

Note it down

This chapter of the course is about the extent to which England faced a crisis in government in 1589-1603. Using a spider diagram, make notes on the following aspects of the potential crisis:

- Military crisis
- Financial crisis
- Political crisis

You could use different-coloured pens to note evidence that there was a crisis, and evidence that the government coped well with the different aspects of managing the war.

Causes

The Anglo-Spanish War (1585–1604) had several causes. First, there were religious differences. Spain was a Catholic nation. Elizabeth's England was Protestant, and fiercely hostile to **popery**. England supported an anti-Spanish rising in the Low Countries. In addition to religion, Philip II was outraged by English privateers who attacked Spanish ships. Raids by English privateers William Hawkins and Robert Reneger on Spanish treasure ships created a diplomatic crisis between England and Spain in 1545. In spite of Spanish protests, English privateers continued to capture Spanish treasure and as a result Anglo-Spanish relations deteriorated throughout the 1560s and 1570s.

Long-term religious disagreements, resentment about English interference in the Low Countries and privateering were all important causes of war. However, it was not until the 1580s that Philip II was in a position to attack England. In 1580 Philip had become King of Portugal. As a result he gained control of the Portuguese navy. The Portuguese galleons were powerful enough to strike at England. The immediate cause of the war was the Treaty of Nonsuch, signed in August 1585, which committed Elizabeth to send troops and money to aid the Dutch rebels who were trying to end Spanish rule in the Netherlands. Philip II responded with war.

Relations between England and Spain grew worse in 1587. The execution of Mary, Queen of Scots outraged Catholics, including Philip II, and the Pope gave Philip the authority to conquer England and replace Elizabeth with a Catholic ruler. Philip launched the Spanish Armada of 1588 in order to invade England and overthrow Elizabeth. However, his 130 ships were defeated by the English navy at the Battle of Gravelines before Spanish troops could

land. The defeat of the Armada enhanced Elizabeth's reputation among her subjects as a heroic queen.

Elizabeth's aims and strategy

Elizabeth's war aims were extremely pragmatic. In essence, she wanted to use military strength to force Spain to agree to a peace deal that protected her existing realm. Equally, she did not want to destroy Spain. She feared that total Spanish defeat would lead to the growth of French power. Therefore she wanted to maintain the balance of power between France and Spain, so that neither would be powerful enough to attempt war with England. Elizabeth's final goal was to keep the costs of war to a minimum.

Her strategy reflected her aims. She tended to wage war defensively, to protect England rather than to destroy Spain. Moreover, she preferred to send small forces overseas. Where offensive warfare was necessary she encouraged English privateers to take the lead.

War with Spain, 1589–96

The Anglo-Spanish War went through several phases after the defeat of the Armada:

- In the years 1589–91 England launched a series of naval attacks on Spain and the Spanish fleet to try and force an end to the war.
- The failure of these missions lead to a change in policy. Elizabeth's government backed no further offensive naval campaigns. Nonetheless, privateers continued to attack Spanish ships in order to acquire treasure.
- Between 1595 and 1597 the English navy continued the fight against Spain, and Spain launched two further armadas against England.
- Finally, between 1597 and 1603, England's focus was increasingly on war in Ireland. Sporadic indecisive fighting continued between England and Spain.

The Drake-Norris expedition, 1589

In the wake of the Spanish Armada's defeat Elizabeth had the opportunity to destroy the weakened Spanish fleet. Elizabeth agreed to a two-stage plan to achieve a quick attack but minimise cost:

- In the short term, a largely private fleet would attack the remnants of the Spanish navy that were in the waters off Lisbon.
- In the longer term, having defeated the Spanish navy, English ships could take the Azores and seize Spain's convoys from the New World.

This strategy would be largely funded by private investors. They would use the attack to invade Portugal and proclaim Don António king in return for lucrative trading rights.

Sir John Norris (1547–97)

Norris was one of the most celebrated soldiers of the Elizabethan period. He fought against Spain, and later against rebels in Ireland. He was also a lifelong friend of Elizabeth.

Sir Francis Drake (1540–96)

Drake was best known as a politician and seaman. He was celebrated for circumnavigating the globe in a three-year voyage from 1577 to 1580. He was also second-in-command of the English fleet that defeated the Spanish Armada in 1588.

Don António and the Portuguese throne

Don António claimed the right to the Portuguese throne, as he was grandson of King Manuel I of Portugal. He had been elected king in June 1580 by representatives of the Portuguese Church and people. However, he was forced to flee in August of the same year due to Philip II's successful invasion. Nonetheless, Don António continued to claim that he was the rightful king.

In late 1588 Sir John Norris and Sir Francis Drake led the campaign against Lisbon. Elizabeth invested £20,000 and sent six ships. A further £40,000 and 20 additional ships would be provided by private investors.

A failed expedition

The Drake-Norris expedition did not go as planned. First, in October 1588 English spies learned that the Spanish fleet had not returned to Lisbon. Nonetheless, Drake and Norris chose to continue with the invasion of Lisbon, as they hoped it would lead to profitable trade with the Portuguese East Indies. Consequently, there was no attack on the remnants of the Spanish navy, which had returned to the ports of Santander and San Sebastian (see figure 1 on page 144).

Second, recruiting and equipping the 17,500 people necessary was more difficult and expensive than anticipated. Consequently, Elizabeth was required to pay an extra £50,000 to finance the war effort.

Third, Drake and Norris made mistakes during the expedition:

- In May 1589 the expedition attacked and seized the port of A Coruña (see figure 1 on page 144), a town of no strategic value – simply to demonstrate the excellence of their troops.
- The siege alerted the Spanish to the English threat and they reinforced Lisbon.

- Drake and Norris overestimated support for Don António. The people of Lisbon were not prepared to fight for him, therefore English forces failed to take the city.

In summary, the Drake-Norris expedition was a complete failure. It failed to destroy the remaining Spanish ships, it failed to capture Lisbon, it failed to win the Portuguese throne for Don António and it failed to make a profit. Most significantly, from the point of view of Elizabeth's long-term goals, it failed to improve England's security.

The consequences of the expedition

The failure of the Drake-Norris expedition had serious consequences for England's national security. Spain's position was significantly strengthened:

- Philip was able to repair his ships.
- The failure to intercept wealth from the New World meant that Philip had the resources to build a new generation of warships. By the end of 1590, 12 new warships, the 'Twelve Apostles', twice the size of England's biggest ships, were being built in the port of Ragusa.
- The failure of an anti-Spanish uprising in Portugal strengthened Philip's position, as his rule in Portugal was clearly not in danger from an uprising in support of his rival.

The expedition weakened England's position:

- Spain's recovery after the Armada reawakened English fears of a Spanish invasion.
- Elizabeth lost faith in military schemes directed at Spanish territory. Therefore, naval budgets were kept small. Between 1588 and 1595 England was only able to build eight warships, all of which were smaller than the 'Twelve Apostles'.
- Government shipbuilding was suspended from 1597 to 1601.

Naval blockades, 1590–91

In 1590 Elizabeth approved a new strategy to promote England's security. In an attempt to strike at Spain before the 'Twelve Apostles' were complete, and in an attempt to seize treasure from the New World, Elizabeth backed a private venture to intercept Spanish convoys by blockading the Azores and the Spanish port of Ferrol (see figure 1 on page 144).

The 'double blockade' failed to intercept Spanish treasure for two reasons. First, attacks by English privateers in the Caribbean disrupted the Spanish convoy to such an extent that it did not sail during 1590. Secondly, silver was sent to Spain in two small fast frigates, which avoided the established convoy routes.

The English operation was a double failure. Not only did it fail to intercept Spanish treasure, the English squadron blockading Ferrol shifted location to the Azores in search of Spanish treasure ships. In so doing, Spanish ships were able to leave Ferrol and transport troops to Brittany, where they could be used against English forces in France (see page 150).

The blockade was renewed in 1591, as Elizabeth wanted to capture both the 1591 convoy and the convoy from 1590 that had been delayed. However, again English efforts failed, this time because they were outgunned and outnumbered.

The consequence of the failure of the blockades

The failure of the blockades of 1590–91 led to a change in British naval strategy. In order to safeguard England's security, Elizabeth backed no further attempts to intercept Spanish treasure until 1597. Moreover, due to the renewed strength of the Spanish fleet, the English navy was kept close to the English shore, in readiness to defend England against a new Armada.

Privateer action in the 1590s

In spite of these failures, English privateers continued to capture Spanish treasure. During the 1590s there were between 100 and 200 English ships in the Caribbean, the Azores and around Spain attacking Spanish ships. Privateer action was highly successful. Between 1588 and 1591 English privateers captured around £400,000 of Spanish goods in 300 raids. Significantly, this income was more than England had earned from trade with Spain before the war. Additionally, it was taxed and therefore helped improve government finances.

Elizabeth's authority as a war leader

Threats to national security from Spain had a particularly destabilising effect on Elizabeth's government, due to perceptions of her gender. A great deal of classical and Renaissance literature argued that women were not suited to warfare. For example, the fifteenth-century English lawyer John Fortescue argued that women should never govern as 'queens could not bear the sword'. For Fortescue, the essence of governing was the ability to protect a nation. As women were not, from his point of view, capable of leading an army, they could not ensure national security and therefore should not rule. According to the widely held medieval views, women were unfit to lead armies because they were generally naturally weak and submissive. Those women who did excel in battle, like the mythical tribe of Amazons, were believed to be unable to control their lust for bloodshed. The theologian John Knox described such women as 'monsters of nature'. Consequently, women were seen as either too weak or too bloodthirsty to lead a nation in battle.

Views about the proper role of women had a significant impact on Elizabeth's reign in the period 1589–1603. Crucially, Elizabeth did not enjoy the respect of her generals. This is clear from Drake and Norris' willingness to ignore Elizabeth's orders during their expedition. Robert Devereux, second Earl of Essex, the Queen's favourite and one of the most celebrated soldiers in England, was also concerned about Elizabeth's approach to war. He believed that he had to use his influence at court to overcome Elizabeth's 'feminine caution' and create a more 'aggressive and manly' military policy. Therefore, while war places a strain on any government, it created particular problems for Elizabeth because her generals did not respect her authority due to the fact that she was a woman.

The war at sea, 1595–96

Hawkins and Drake attack Panama

By 1595 invasion scares and Essex's continuing pressure to fight an aggressive war led to an extremely ambitious venture. Elizabeth sanctioned an attack on Spain's colonies in the New World by a fleet of over 30 vessels. The aim was to take Panama from the Spanish. Panama was of crucial strategic importance to the Spanish empire in the New World as it connected their colonies in South America with the Caribbean (see figure 1 on page 144).

The attack was a disaster. The English force was so large that it was impossible to keep secret, therefore Spain sent reinforcements to Puerto Rico. Hawkins and Drake both died on the mission, and after several changes of strategy the English fleet returned home in mid-1596, having failed to capture Spanish land or treasure.

The impact of failure in the New World

The failure of the attack on Panama had serious consequences for England's security and Elizabeth's government:

- The deaths of Drake and Hawkins were a terrible shock. Drake was widely respected as a hero due to his role in defeating the Armada of 1588. His death made Elizabeth's subjects feel more vulnerable, at the very point when Spanish forces were heading towards Calais, a French port at the narrowest point of the English Channel (see page 150).
- The failure of the mission also changed Elizabeth's policy towards war with Spain. She cancelled a planned attack on Spain that was being prepared by Essex and Lord Admiral Howard.

Threat from France

Elizabeth's response to the new threat was contradictory. Initially, she ordered Howard and Essex to divert their troops to defend Calais. However, at the end of March Elizabeth changed her mind, due to disagreements with Henry of Navarre, who claimed the French throne. When she finally authorised military action in mid-April it was too late, the Spanish had already conquered the port. Elizabeth's failure to act put further strain on her relationship with her military leaders. Essex was infuriated by Elizabeth's 'feminine' indecision. Subsequently, Essex was increasingly willing to ignore Elizabeth's orders and take the initiative.

Essex's attack on Cadiz, 1596

Essex's desire to guide Elizabeth's military policy was evident in his attack on Cadiz. He hoped that a successful expedition would lead Elizabeth to authorise further attacks on Spain and to a renewed commitment to supporting the war against Spain in France (see page 150).

Essex's force won an early naval victory, sinking two of the 'Twelve Apostles', and then captured Cadiz in less than two days with minimal English losses.

The victory certainly improved England's position in the war with Spain. The extent of the treasure that Philip lost forced him to renegotiate his debts. However, the victory left the bulk of Philip's fleet untouched, and therefore Spain still posed a significant threat to England's security.

Literature, pessimism and war

War with Spain did not merely lead to a military crisis, it also caused a crisis in confidence concerning England's future. This pessimistic atmosphere was reflected in some of the literature of the period. For example, the plays of the 1590s were dominated by kings such as Richard II and John, whose reigns were associated with humiliation and defeat in foreign wars. English culture was also increasingly dominated by what some historians describe as 'the new humanism'. Scholars, courtiers and playwrights studied the works of Tacitus, the historian who described the corruption and collapse of the Roman Empire. Indeed, Tacitus, who described corrupt men who pursued their own interests, began to eclipse Cicero, the historian and philosopher of virtue and the common good. Michel de Montaigne's *Essays* were also highly influential. The *Essays* were considered pessimistic about human nature because they attempted to describe people as they are rather than offering an ideal description of what they should be. All of these works indicated that the 1590s was a period of anxiety about the future rather than optimism.

Essex and Cadiz

Essex's victory also caused problems in government. Having captured Cadiz, Essex disobeyed Elizabeth's direct orders by temporarily turning the city into an English garrison. Elizabeth wanted Essex's troops to return home quickly, whereas Essex wanted to use the victory as the first step to further conquest of Spain. Essex also failed to ensure that Elizabeth benefited fully from Cadiz's treasure. First, he failed to stop the theft of large amounts of booty, second, he failed to capture £3.5 million of treasure contained in Spanish ships. Essex's behaviour enraged Elizabeth and gave him a reputation for disloyalty as he put his own military glory ahead of Elizabeth's financial needs. Nonetheless, Elizabeth was forced to work with Essex. He had proved himself a gifted military leader, and therefore played a crucial role in devising a defensive strategy against the anticipated Spanish attack.

War with Spain, 1596–97

Naval campaigns continued throughout the late 1590s, but neither side achieved a decisive victory.

- In July 1597 Essex launched a fleet of 15 ships and 5,000 men to destroy the Spanish fleet, seize the port of Cadiz and more Spanish treasure. The plan, which was designed to make England the dominant naval power and Elizabeth 'queen of the seas', failed due to high winds.
- In August 1597 Essex launched his 'Islands Voyage', a smaller fleet to intercept Spanish convoys and seize their treasure. The expedition lacked a clear strategy and failed to intercept the Spanish convoy.
- In October 1597 a Spanish fleet attempted to capture the English port of Falmouth. Essex had taken half of the fleet on his 'Islands Voyage' and therefore left the coast with little defence. Storms prevented the Spanish from landing and scattered the Spanish fleet.

Historians and historiography

Section C of the exam tests your ability to analyse interpretations of the past. You will be expected to analyse extracts from the work of historians. However, you are not expected to know the nature of the historiographical debate. This means you are not expected to know the opinions of specific historians.

Historical interpretations: crisis of confidence

Historians have considered the impact of war on English culture during the last years of Elizabeth's reign. David Armitage argues that the military and political troubles of the 1590s led to interest in more pessimistic political literature. Jim Sharpe, on the other hand, emphasises the religious impact of the ongoing war with Spain.

> **Extract 1** From David Armitage, *Shakespeare and Early Modern Political Thought*, published in 2009.
>
> At just the time in the 1590s when Shakespeare began his career, English political life was increasingly marked by growing religious tensions, war, impoverishment and mounting anxieties over the succession. This deterioration was accompanied by a growing pessimism and anxiety in political writing. Not surprisingly, European writers such as Montaigne now found an audience in England, marginalising the idealistic images of England presented by earlier writers. Similarly, the classical authors who had most deeply explored corruption, particularly Tacitus, were increasingly used to challenge the authority of Cicero.

> **Extract 2** From Jim Sharpe, 'Social strain and social dislocation, 1585–1603', in John Guyed., *The Reign of Elizabeth I: Court and Culture in the Last Decade,* published in 1995.
>
> A general mood of pessimism formed an important strand in the late-Elizabethan mentality. Traditional historiography has tended to portray the Elizabethan period as a self-confident and expansionary one. There is, however, another interpretation, which would rather present the contemporary image of England as that of the 'Beleaguered Isle', a small and worried nation on the fringe of Europe, nervously calculating the chances of its regime's survival in the face of internal and external enemies. Those Protestants who gave God the credit for the defeat of the Armada in 1588 were all too aware that this divine intervention might not be forthcoming a second time. The Almighty might either withdraw his support in the next time of crisis, or even send Philip II's forces to chasten an unworthy nation. Many thinking Protestants believed that they were living in the final phase of human history, the 'last days', a period of chaos which would precede the dissolution of human society and the **Second Coming**.

Having read Extracts 1 and 2:

1 Summarise the key argument of the two extracts.
2 Select three details from your own knowledge that support the argument of Extract 1. Write these down as a list under your summaries.

3 Swap your summaries and discuss your lists:
 ● Which summary best captures the argument of Extract 1?
 ● Which best captures the argument of Extract 2?
 ● Which details most precisely support the argument of Extract 1?

The last years of war

By the end of Elizabeth's life it was becoming increasingly clear that England could no longer afford to keep fighting. The new Spanish King Philip III, was in a similar position. England's strategy in the Low Countries had tied up Spanish forces and resources in the siege of Ostend (see page 151), and blocked Spanish aid reaching rebels in Ireland (see page 154).

Philip III of Spain (1578–1621)

Philip III of Spain inherited the throne to the Spanish Empire from his father in 1598. He was known for his religious **piety**, but also played a role in the decline of the empire. Like his father, he was unable to defeat England in war.

England's war effort was more successful, but no more decisive. In 1602, fearing a further attempt at direct invasion, English ships blockaded Spanish ports. The blockade proved ineffective.

Elizabeth never achieved peace with Spain, but her strategy drained Spain's resources and men. Sending troops to Ireland, sustaining the fight in the Low Countries, and intermittently with France (see page 150) had a dramatic effect on Spain's finances. Additionally, English privateers were continuing to harass Spanish ships in the Atlantic, off the coast of Spain and in the Caribbean. Therefore, Elizabeth's war effort played a major role in James I's peace deal with Spain, which was signed in 1604, the year after her death.

2 War in Europe

In addition to naval battles, English forces fought the Spanish in the Low Countries and France (for the location of hey sites, refer to figure 1 on page 144). These wars were important to England's security because they drained English and Spanish resources, and because they were potential bases from which to launch an attack on England.

> ## Note it down
> The war in Europe also created a series of difficulties for Elizabeth's government. Note these down using the 1:2 method (see page x). Under the main headings of the Low Countries and France you should again have subheadings dealing with the different aspects of the crisis.

War in France

English and Spanish forces also fought each other in France. The ostensible cause of the conflict was religion. Following the death of Henry III in August 1589, Henry of Navarre declared himself king of France. Henry was a Protestant, and therefore the **Catholic League** refused to recognise his right to rule. France descended into war, with Spain backing the Catholic League. Elizabeth feared that a Catholic government in France would aid Spanish efforts to invade England. Therefore, she sent troops and money to aid Henry. The war in France marked a major escalation of the conflict between England and Spain.

In October 1589 Elizabeth loaned Henry £15,000 and sent 3,600 troops conscripted from Kent. To limit the cost of the mission Henry promised to pay for the troops after the first month. However, Henry failed to provide sufficient shelter or food for the English troops. By the end of December, when the surviving troops returned to England, many were starving and suffering from all kinds of illness, including gangrene. The town of Rye in Kent had to pay for the care of the returning troops.

The siege of Paris

The focus of Henry's military strategy was to lay siege to Paris. However, his siege was thwarted by the arrival of new Spanish forces under the command of the Duke of Parma, the most celebrated Spanish commander of the period. Parma's forces, which had been transferred from the Low Countries, were extremely concerning for Elizabeth's government. Burghley particularly feared that they could be deployed against England. Nonetheless, while Parma's troops strengthened the Spanish position in France, their relocation weakened Spain's position in the Low Countries. Therefore, English and Dutch forces made important gains along Ijssel River in 1590 and in Steenwijk in 1591.

Spanish forces in France were further strengthened by the arrival of 3,000 troops in Brittany in November 1590. The troops were able to leave Spain due to the removal of the English naval blockade around Ferrol (see pages 146–47). Elizabeth was clearly worried by the events in Brittany. In November 1590 she sent 2,000 English troops from the Low Countries to France. Essex was sent to France to assist in the siege of Rouen. In spite of the new English troops and Essex's command, the siege of Rouen was a failure. The siege strained relations between Elizabeth and Essex. Elizabeth wanted the siege to succeed quickly and cheaply, Essex could not achieve this. Also Elizabeth was suspicious of Essex's closeness with Henry. She did not fully trust Henry due to his mistreatment of English troops under his command. Moreover, she suspected that Essex, like Henry, was more interested in military glory than in England's national security.

The end of the war in France, 1593–98

England's involvement in the war in France came to an end for a series of reasons. First, Henry converted to Catholicism in July 1593. This won him a great deal of support in France, but made relations with Elizabeth more difficult. Elizabeth withdrew troops from Normandy in 1593, although English troops stayed in Brittany to defend Brest from Spanish invasion.

The campaign against the Spanish went so well that by September 1594 English troops began fighting an offensive war against El León, the Spanish fort on Brittany's Crozon peninsula. English and French forces captured El León in early November. This victory ended the threat to England's security from the Spanish in Brittany, and English troops were withdrawn in February 1595. Henry was enraged by the withdrawal, but Elizabeth and Burghley believed that Ireland was a greater threat to England's security and therefore reassigned the troops.

Essex continued to put pressure on Elizabeth to send troops to aid Henry. The Spanish occupation of Calais in 1596 forced Elizabeth to send more troops due to the port's proximity to Dover. Elizabeth agreed to send 2,000 troops to aid the French King. However, this was far fewer than Henry wanted and, therefore, Henry opened peace negotiations with Spain. The war between France and Spain ended with the Peace of Vervins of May 1598. Elizabeth was infuriated that in spite of English help Henry had dropped out of the war.

War in the Low Countries

Historically, the Low Countries were part of the Spanish Empire. Elizabeth had sent troops to support a Protestant revolt against Spanish rule in the Low Countries in 1566. Subsequently, as a result of the **Treaty of Nonsuch**, the Low Countries became an English **protectorate**. By 1589 the English were maintaining a force of 6,400 troops and 1,000 cavalry in the Low Countries. This cost Elizabeth around £100,000 a year.

The siege of Ostend

The war in the Low Countries continued into the seventeenth century. In June 1601 Spanish forces laid siege to Ostend. This was of crucial significance to England's security as it was the only port on the northern coast that was under Anglo–Dutch control, and therefore was crucial for supplying England's troops. Therefore, Elizabeth sent 2,000 English troops to reinforce the garrison.

The significance of Ostend

Repelling the Spanish at Ostend was highly significant for England's security. First, in order to keep fighting, Philip III was forced to reinforce his troops with soldiers who had been preparing to invade England. In this sense defending Ostend stopped another Spanish invasion attempt. Secondly, the siege was part of a deliberate English strategy to force the Spanish army to use up huge resources that could otherwise have been sent to Ireland or used to attack England. Nonetheless, the siege did not end the war. Indeed, fighting continued until the truce of 1609, six years after Elizabeth's death.

Historical interpretations: military crisis

Historians disagree on the extent to which the European wars of the 1590s created a military crisis. Susan Doran argues that from 1594 Elizabeth had essentially achieved her objectives in Europe. Anna Whitelock, by contrast, argues that war weakened Elizabeth's position due to perceptions of her gender.

Extract 3 From Susan Doran, *Elizabeth I and Foreign Policy, 1558–1603*, published in 2001.

During 1594 the threat to England from continental Europe began to subside. In the Netherlands, the Dutch successfully captured Groningen, the last Spanish fortress in the north. In France, Henry won a series of victories after the death of Parma and his conversion to Catholicism in July 1593. At last in February 1594 he was crowned king, and the next month he entered Paris. In the autumn, the English captured the castle of Morlaix and the Spanish fort at Crozon.

By the end of 1594, therefore, Elizabeth was in a position to disengage from continental Europe. She had secured her main objectives: there was now little danger of Spain occupying the Channel ports or overrunning the northern Netherlands.

Extract 4 From Anna Whitelock, 'Woman, Warrior, Queen?' Rethinking Mary and Elizabeth in Alice Hunt, Anne Whitelook (eds.) *Tudor Queenship: The Reign of Mary and Elizabeth*, published in 2010.

The Portugal expedition of 1589 again illustrated Elizabeth's fundamental weakness as a wartime leader. The operation, under the command of Drake and Norris, was intended to destroy the remnants of the Armada that had made their way back to Spain; to seize Lisbon, thereby encouraging a **popular rebellion** against Spain; and finally to capture a base in the Azores from which to intercept Spanish treasure en route from the Americas. Elizabeth's instructions were ignored. The main fleet sailed direct to Corunna rather than first sailing to the ports to destroy the Spanish ships, and the mission turned out to be a disaster. By the time Norris' army arrived at Lisbon weeks later, the threat could be easily met. Drake's mission to the Azores ended in equal ignominy as his fleet was beaten back by adverse winds. The expedition had failed in all of its objectives.

Elizabeth's military leaders had little confidence in her ability to command and very often ignored her instructions and questioned her judgement.

Having read Extracts 3 and 4:

1 Write a paragraph stating how far you agree or disagree with Extract 3. Your paragraph should contain:
   ● a summary of the extract's argument
   ● evidence that either supports or challenges that argument
   ● a concluding sentence in which you analyse the extent to which the argument of the extract is valid.

2 Swap your paragraphs, read them and then write two suggestions about how the paragraph could be improved.

3 Finally, repeat the process for Extract 4. Make sure you incorporate the advice you have received about how to improve your paragraph.

3 War in Ireland

Trouble in Ireland also threatened England's national security. Losing Ireland posed a major threat to England's national security. An independent Catholic Ireland was a natural ally of Spain, and Elizabeth feared that Philip would use Ireland as a base from which to attack England. War in Ireland placed enormous burdens on Elizabeth's government. Indeed, the Nine Years' War (or Tyrone's rebellion as it is sometimes called) was the largest military undertaking of Elizabeth's reign.

Note it down

The war in Ireland caused Elizabeth's government problems:

● Skim read the section, looking at the subheadings and the key words. Make a list of the key aspects of the crisis and use these as main headings on a spider diagram.

● Read the section and make notes on the different aspects of the problems facing Elizabeth – remember you can use different colours to distinguish between evidence that there was a crisis and evidence that Elizabeth's government handled the situation well.

▲ Figure 2: A map of Ireland during the Nine Years' War

Origins of the Nine Years' War

The war in Ireland had several causes. Henry VIII had partially conquered Ireland, creating an English government in Dublin. However, supporters of England in Ireland had lost faith in English government due to high taxes and the limited benefits that England provided for Anglo-Irish nobles. Consequently, there was a growth in resistance to English rule, which included the rejection of Protestantism. In this sense, England's position in Ireland was similar to Spain's position in the Low Countries: in both cases an imperial power was trying to retain control against a local population who practised a different religion and wanted to end imperial rule. Moreover, just as England sent aid to anti-Spanish rebels in the Netherlands, so Spain sent aid to the Irish rebels. In that way, the Nine Years' War was part of the broader conflict between England and Spain.

The long-term causes of war in Ireland date back at least as far as 1155, when the Pope granted the English King the title Lord of Ireland. More recently, dominance in Ireland had been an important part of Henry VIII's policy. Henry viewed control of Ireland as crucial to England's national security. Specifically, Henry wanted to launch a war with France from a position of strength, and therefore wanted complete control of Ireland in order to prevent the French from using Ireland against him.

The spark that ignited war was a conflict between the English government and key Irish nobles. There was conflict in 1592 over County Donegal which spread to Ulster in 1593 (see Figure 2). The turning point came in 1595 when Hugh O'Neill, second Earl of Tyrone, joined the rebels. Tyrone was an extremely dangerous enemy. He was an English earl, and also a Gaelic chieftain, who was related to the rebel chieftains in Ulster. Tyrone's decision to join the rebels was a particular threat to Elizabeth's rule as it united formerly rival Irish houses against the English.

Conflict in Ireland and trouble in government

In addition to the national security threat, conflict in Ireland also caused problems in Elizabeth's government. In 1595 Elizabeth was faced with a choice: either to continue the fight against the Spanish in France or to focus her effort on Ireland. Elizabeth decided to focus on Ireland, and by April 1595 1,200 English troops under Norris' command were sent from France to Ireland.

This decision created huge controversy at court. Essex was convinced that the decision was wrong. He believed withdrawing troops from France was wrong because:

● it was a betrayal of Elizabeth's commitment to Henry
● it meant abandoning the fight against Spanish influence on the Continent

- Spain, rather than Ireland, was the real threat to England's national security.

By contrast, Elizabeth and Burghley wanted to withdraw from France as:

- they did not trust Henry
- they believed that continued war on the Continent would be extremely costly
- the costs of war needed to be limited in order to avoid rebellions against conscription and taxation in England
- defending England from the threat of Irish rebellion was more important for England's security than attacking Spain and her allies in France.

While Elizabeth got her way, Essex argued forcefully that France, rather than Ireland, should take priority. Essex's persistent opposition to Elizabeth and Burghley deepened divisions at court (see page 164). Essex's attacks on the Queen's policy were particularly damaging as they raised questions about her fitness to lead at a time of war. Elizabeth's authority was further eroded when Spanish ships attacked the Cornish villages of Mousehole, Newlyn and Penzance in July 1595. The attack seemed to prove that Spain was indeed the more dangerous enemy.

The Irish rebellion, 1595–98

In 1595 and 1597 Sir William Russell and Sir John Norris had tried to use their military might to force Tyrone to accept a peace deal. These attempts failed to achieve peace, but did lead to a series of truces. During these lulls in hostilities Tyrone attempted to win the support of the Spanish against their common enemy. Moreover, in 1596 the rebellion spread from Ulster to Connaught, and the leaders of the rebellion wrote to 'the gentlemen of Munster' encouraging Catholics in the south to join the fight against the Protestant English.

By January 1597 it was clear that Russell and Norris' strategy was not working. Consequently, Elizabeth appointed Thomas Burgh to command English troops in Ireland. In July, Burgh attempted to destroy Tyrone's forces by a co-ordinated attack on Ulster by land and sea but, with only 3,500 men he was unable to conquer Tyrone's stronghold.

The Battle of Yellow Ford, 1598

Following Burgh's death from typhus in October 1597, Sir Henry Bagenal took charge of the campaign in Ireland. Bagenal was responsible for one of the biggest military disasters of Elizabeth's reign. His troops were ambushed and he was shot during the Battle of Yellow Ford in August 1598. The battle led to the disintegration of Bagenal's army.

Bagenal's defeat was a sign of English weakness. Consequently, revolt spread across the whole of Ireland and threatened the end of English rule.

Disillusionment with Ireland

One aspect of the crisis in Ireland was the disillusionment with English colonisation. Elizabeth's goal was to create a Protestant Ireland, which was, in essence, an extension of her English kingdom. However, war and rebellion in Ireland persuaded some writers and politicians that this was not possible. The poet and sheriff of Cork Edmund Spenser, for example, wrote that establishing Protestant rule was almost impossible due to the 'savagery' and 'barbarism' of the 'wild Irish'. Therefore, Spenser argued that England must stamp out Irish traditions and assert English control through force.

Essex's campaign in Ireland, 1599

Elizabeth and her court certainly regarded the rebellion in Ireland as a crisis. Elizabeth and her advisers considered the loss of Ireland as the first step towards a successful Spanish invasion of England. Her response reflected the seriousness of the situation. To ensure England's security, Elizabeth's government committed unprecedented resources to the war in Ireland. The new phase of war that began in 1599 was on a bigger scale than any of the prior conflicts, and it caused enormous problems for Elizabeth's state.

Essex had been highly critical of the war in Ireland under Norris, Burgh and Bagenal. He also recognised that leading a victorious army in Ireland would strengthen his position within Elizabeth's court. Therefore, he campaigned for the command of the army in Ireland. Essex's 17,000 strong army was bigger than any other English force of Elizabeth's reign. Supporting an army of this size was also a huge financial burden on the government, the officers' pay alone was £290,000 annually.

Essex wanted to use the overpowering scale of his army to destroy Tyrone's rebellion swiftly. However, instead of launching an immediate attack on Ulster, he first restored English control in Leinster and much of southern Ireland. This was an important improvement in England's security situation because the Privy Council feared that Spanish forces were planning to land in southern Ireland. However, retaking southern Ireland weakened Essex's forces.

By July Essex realised that the Irish forces were too good to wipe out in a swift war. The only chance of success in Ireland was a long drawn-out war of attrition. Essex would have to stay in Ireland indefinitely, and therefore lose influence at court. Worse still, Elizabeth was displeased with Essex's slow progress against Tyrone.

Essex's military failure

Dwindling numbers of troops and difficulty attacking from the sea meant that Essex was in no position to win in Ulster. Facing an impossible situation in Ireland, and loss of influence at court, Essex began to plan moving his troops to Wales, and using his army to fight his enemies in Elizabeth's court.

Following Elizabeth's orders, Essex led an attack on Ulster in August. He was unable to win a military victory, but in September he agreed a new truce. Essex used the lull in the war to return to England in order to meet with the Queen. Essex felt compelled to return to save the Queen from enemies and plots that he imagined at court. However, his return was against Elizabeth's expressed orders and therefore he was arrested and imprisoned (see page 171). The war in Ireland entered a new stage.

Mountjoy's Irish campaign

Essex was replaced by Lord Mountjoy, who arrived in Ireland in February 1600. By the time he arrived, English forces had lost much of the territory in the south that Essex had previously regained.

Mountjoy recognised that the only way to beat Tyrone was to engage in a long drawn-out campaign. Starvation was central to Mountjoy's strategy. He planned to surround Ulster with a ring of forts, and cut Tyrone off from the rebels in the rest of Ireland. English soldiers would destroy Irish crops and live off supplies from England. In accordance with this plan, in May and June he burnt Irish harvests in order to create an artificial famine that would starve the Irish rebels into submission.

Moyry Pass

Mountjoy broke with military tradition by continuing hostilities throughout the winter of 1600–01. By May much of Munster was under English control. Mountjoy strengthened his position further in the summer of 1601 by establishing English garrisons at Moyry Pass and Armagh. At the same time, Mountjoy capitalised on rivalries between Irish lords by landing a force at Carrickfergus and then marching into eastern Ulster, territories controlled by Irish nobles who had lost faith in Tyrone.

Spanish aid

Even so, Tyrone was not beaten. Indeed, his position was strengthened by the arrival of 3,400 Spanish troops in September 1601. The Spanish landing caused panic in Elizabeth's court. In order to repel the Spanish invaders:

- 5,000 English troops were dispatched to Ireland in late September and early October

- 3,000 troops were conscripted from Ireland, at vast cost to Elizabeth
- the English fleet blockaded Irish ports to stop further Spanish landings.

Mountjoy won an important battle at Kinsale. This was significant for England's security as it forced Don Juan del Aguila, commander of the Spanish force in Ireland, to surrender. Peace with Aguila was signed in January 1602.

Equally significant was the English blockade of Irish ports, which was so successful that only 80 Spanish troops were able to land in Munster in December. Moreover, the blockade stopped new supplies from reaching Tyrone. With little help from overseas, Mountjoy's scorched earth policy, and the loss of his main ally, Tyrone's resources were close to exhaustion. From February 1602 he was no longer able to pay his troops. However, he refused to surrender.

The cost of the Irish war

The war in Ireland was the most expensive military conflict of Elizabeth's reign. Conservative estimates suggest that Elizabeth spent £342,000 in Ireland between 1595 and 1598. Essex's campaign in 1599 cost an additional £336,554. Finally, Mountjoy's campaign in 1600–02 cost £828,000. Higher estimates suggest that the whole campaign cost as much as £1.9 million. According to the same estimates, spending on the war in the Low Countries in the same period was only £534,000. Therefore, Elizabeth spent almost four times more on fighting in Ireland as she did on fighting in the Low Countries.

One of the reasons why Mountjoy's campaign was so expensive was his policy of creating famine. This meant that his soldiers could not live on Irish produce. Rather, the army had to import supplies from Britain. London merchants provided over ten million daily rations of meat, cheese, biscuits and butter to English troops in Ireland while Mountjoy commanded. This was possible due to the effectiveness of the 'Irish road', the supply chain established earlier in the war to deliver troops and materials to English commanders in Ireland.

Peace with Ireland

Peace with Ireland may have been essential for England's financial and military security, but it required Elizabeth to pardon Tyrone. Elizabeth, however, wanted to execute Tyrone as she blamed him for Essex's fate. Nonetheless, constant pressure from the Privy Council prevailed and in 1603 Elizabeth offered Tyrone a pardon, and most of his former land in return for his surrender. The Treaty of Mellifont, which ended Tyrone's rebellion, was signed at the end of March 1603, around a week after Elizabeth's death.

Historical interpretations: crisis in Ireland

The war in Ireland created new difficulties for Elizabeth. Paul E. J. Hammer concentrates on the reasons why Elizabeth spent so much attention on Ireland. Carole Levin focuses on the problems the war created, and the reaction in England.

> **Extract 5** From Paul E. J. Hammer, *Elizabeth's Wars. War, Government and Society in Tudor England, 1544–1604*, published in 2004.
>
> The prospect of utter disaster in Ireland forced Elizabeth and her government to treat the situation there with an urgency which had previously been reserved for invasion threats to England itself. Indeed, the Irish crisis was regarded as the first step towards invasion, for contemporary opinion held that Ireland had replaced Scotland as England's 'postern gate' – 'he who would England win, must with Ireland begin'. Elizabeth's own determination not to bow to 'rebel subjects' also ensured the new priority accorded to Ireland. As queen, she had spent her whole reign resisting the demands of domineering males and asserting her own royal primacy. Her refusal to bargain seriously with Tyrone in the early 1590s had in many ways driven him into oppositions, and the prospect that she might now face military defeat at his hands was as unpalatable to her as the idea that she might preside over a diminution of the royal inheritance which she had received from her father. The Elizabethan regime therefore poured men, money and supplies into Ireland on a scale far greater than any other enterprise of the reign, stretching the realm to its very limits.

> **Extract 6** From Carole Levin, *The Reign of Elizabeth I*, published in 2002.
>
> The situation in Ireland became even more difficult as Elizabeth's reign progressed. Insurrections or, as the English would term them, rebellions, led by the Irish to expel the English were not only expensive to suppress, but also extremely violent and bloody, leading to even more ill-will. Eventually, some English observers in Ireland, including Edmund Spenser, came to believe that reform was a miserable failure and it was impossible to ever achieve a rule of law in Ireland. William Palmer argues that, as a result, many in England believed the only solution was the immediate and complete forcible destruction of Irish culture.

1 Read Extracts 5 and 6 and make a list of ways in which the war in Ireland:
  - heightened existing problems
  - created new problems.

2 Swap your lists with a partner and discuss the extent to which you agree. Finally, write a paragraph answering the question:

How far did the war in Ireland create new problems for Elizabeth's government?

Historical interpretations: economic and social crisis

Prolonged warfare had an important social and economic impact on England. While most historians agree that the major economic problems of the 1590s were caused by other factors, John Guy argues that the economic strains of the war heightened these problems. Ian W. Archer focuses on the social problems caused by years of war.

Extract 7 From John Guy, *The Tudors*, published in 2010.

The strain of a war economy was cumulative. Conscription became a flashpoint as 105,800 men were impressed for military service in the Netherlands, France, Portugal and Ireland during the last 15 years of the reign. Conscription for Ireland after 1595 aroused the greatest resentment. In 1600 there was a near mutiny of Kentish cavalry at Chester as they travelled to Ulster. Pressure on the counties led to administrative breakdowns and opposition to central government's demands, while disruption of trade, outbreaks of plague (much of it imported by soldiers returning from abroad), ruined harvests in 1596 and 1597, and acute economic depression caused widespread distress.

Extract 8 From Ian W. Archer, *The Pursuit of Stability: Social Relations in Elizabethan London*, published in 2003.

People's fears in later Elizabethan England did have some grounding in reality, and the evidence that crime was committed by organised gangs was growing in the later 1580s and 1590s, because of the problem of disbanded soldiers. Their identification with crime was commonplace well before the continuous war of the closing years of the century. The habits of violence soldiers had acquired in the wars were compounded by the difficulties of reintegrating with civilian society, particularly in circumstances of rising unemployment and **dearth**. It was therefore often only by crime that the discharged soldier was able to support himself. The protests of the Privy Council against the gangs of highway robbers and burglars terrorising the city and its environs become a depressing theme of its correspondence in the 1590s, as waves of discharged soldiers repeatedly hit the south coast ports and headed for London.

Read Extracts 7 and 8 and make a list of the different social and economic problems caused by the war. Having done this, swap the lists and check that you both identified all of the different problems mentioned in the extracts.

Conclusion

Elizabeth's last years were a period of continual war. The threat of invasion and the possibility of losing Ireland spurred Elizabeth's government to fight a large-scale, but broadly sustainable, defensive war. The war had wide ranging implications for Elizabethan government and society. The implications for Elizabeth's court and society are explored more fully in the following chapters.

Extended reading

Historian Lucy Wooding examines the ways in which war with Spain and Ireland affected Elizabeth's rule in the years 1589–1603.

The defeat of the Spanish Armada in 1588 is one of the most iconic moments of Elizabeth's regime. It is easy to forget that 1588 was not the end of Elizabeth's problem with Spain, in fact, in many ways it was the beginning. For the rest of her reign Elizabeth would face hostility from Spain, who threatened England both by sea, and through involvement in Ireland, which had long been troublesome for the English Crown, and was raised to a new level of rebelliousness by the prospect of Spanish assistance. In many ways, then, the threats from Spain and Ireland were different sides of the same coin. These threats worked on three levels. There was the risk of invasion which, given the logistical challenge it posed to the enemy, was not a very realistic threat. There was the danger of involvement in a long drawn-out, exhausting and expensive campaign in Ireland, and this threat was realised. Finally, there was the threat of assassination by a Spanish agent at home but it could be argued that this had a beneficial effect upon Elizabeth's authority, by rallying public feeling in her support.

The Irish problem went back a long way. English kings had claimed lordship over Ireland since medieval times, but they had never managed to establish very firm control there, relying instead on alliances with the ruling Irish clans. Relations worsened when Henry VIII's break with Rome and dissolution of the Irish monasteries soured relations with the Catholic Irish. In 1541 Henry declared himself king of Ireland, but this grand gesture could not conceal the weakness of England's rule there. Elizabethan policy in Ireland was always hampered by the fact that her representatives were Protestants attempting to subdue a predominantly Catholic territory. This was the background to the 'Nine Years' War' of 1594–1603, when Hugh O'Neill, Earl of Tyrone, led a rebellion against English rule, aided by the Spanish. This challenge to Tudor rule in Ireland would not be defeated until after Elizabeth's death: the Irish finally surrendered to James VI and I in 1603.

The Spanish threat was a much newer one since Spain had for long years been England's traditional ally. At the start of Elizabeth's reign, Philip II had sought an alliance with England, and had even contemplated cementing that alliance by marrying Elizabeth, who had learned Spanish in order to be able to talk to him. Spain needed good relations with England to protect sea communications with the Netherlands, over which it was trying to maintain Spanish rule, while England needed to protect its trade with the Netherlands. Philip II also preferred Elizabeth as queen of England, despite her heretical tendencies, to Mary, Queen of Scots, whose mother was French, who had been raised at the French court, and who had briefly been queen of France. France was Philip II's arch-enemy, and he wanted England on his side, not that of the French.

The changing face of post-Reformation Europe brought about a shift in international relations, however. Protestant revolt in the Netherlands, slyly aided by Elizabeth, together with the 'Wars of Religion' in France, gradually eroded Philip II's network of alliances. By 1584 the reshuffle was complete: Philip II allied with the Catholic Guise party in France and the building of the Spanish Armada got underway. Elizabeth openly signed a treaty with the Dutch rebels and Mary, Queen of Scots, no longer any good as a deterrent to the Spanish, since Philip was now friendly to the Guises, was executed. The European map of international alliances had been redrawn under the pressure of religious conflict.

In the 1590s, then, England was repeatedly menaced by Spain, and Spanish hostility helped strengthen Irish opposition. Yet the threat posed here was more annoying than annihilating. The threat of assassination at home or invasion from overseas may actually have strengthened Elizabeth's position, as the political nation rallied around her. The lengthy campaigning in Ireland was a drain on money and also served to undermine her political credibility: her fury when the Earl of Essex signed a truce with O'Neill without her permission was symptomatic of Elizabeth's struggle to control her military commanders. Yet the English defeated the Spanish in Ireland at the Battle of Kinsale in 1601, in a victory which would prove decisive. The real significance of the combined Irish and Spanish threat was not to Elizabeth's authority so much as to her prosperity, but it also helped consolidate her role as the defender of her realm and religion.

Lucy Wooding is Senior Lecturer in Early Modern History at King's College London. Her research focuses on Catholic thought and identity in the English Reformation and religious culture in England between the fifteenth and seventeenth centuries. She published a biography of Henry VIII in 2009.

Activity

Having read the 'Extended reading' essay on page 157, answer the following questions.

Comprehension

1 Wooding argues that threats from Spain and France 'worked on three levels'. Which three aspects of the threat does she outline?
2 What does Wooding mean by the following phrases:
   - 'Henry VIII's break with Rome'
   - 'post-Reformation Europe'
   - 'By 1584 the reshuffle was complete'
   - 'political credibility'

Evidence

3 Make a list of the examples of problems facing Elizabeth's government mentioned in Wooding's essay.

Interpretation

4 Identify the passage in which Wooding gives her view on the extent of the threat facing England from Spain and Ireland in the period 1589–1603.
5 Summarise Wooding's interpretation in 25 words or fewer.

Evaluation

6 Using your own knowledge, write a paragraph explaining how far you agree with Wooding's interpretation of the extent of threat facing England from Spain and Ireland in the period 1589–1603.

Work together

Having completed the activity above, swap your notes with a partner. Consider the following questions:

1 Did you both spot the same evidence in Wooding's essay?
2 Has your partner missed anything?
3 Did you agree on which passage contained the interpretation? If not, who was right?
4 What was good about your partner's summary of Wooding's interpretation?
5 Can you learn anything about Wooding's interpretation from your partner's summary?
6 How far did you both agree with Wooding's interpretation?

Use these questions to feed back to each other and improve your analysis of the extracts.

Essay technique: Identifying the interpretation

Section C of the exam paper is different to Sections A and B (see introduction, page vi). Unlike Sections A and B, it contains two extracts from the work of historians. Significantly, Section C tests different skills.

In essence, Section C tests your ability to analyse different historical interpretations. Therefore, you must focus on the interpretations of the extracts.

The Section C question for AS level is different from that of A level, and some guidance about this is given on pages vii–viii. However, you will need to develop very similar skills for the AS exam, therefore the activities will help with the AS exams as well. There are also some AS-style questions in every chapter.

Interpretations and evidence

The extracts will contain a mixture of interpretations and evidence. The mark scheme rewards essays that focus on the interpretations offered by the extracts more highly than essays that focus on the information or evidence mentioned in the extracts. Therefore, it is important to identify the interpretations.

- Interpretations are a specific kind of argument. Like all arguments, they tend to make general claims such as 'War with Spain and Ireland created a crisis in England's security in Elizabeth's last years.'
- Information or evidence tends to comprise specific details. For example: 'War in the Low Countries cost Elizabeth around £100,000 a year.'

Imagine you are answering the following question using Extract 1 below and Extract 2 on page 160:

> **In the light of differing interpretations, how convincing do you find the view that 'late Elizabethan war policy was damaging from several viewpoints'** (Extract 1 line 1)?
>
> **To explain your answer, analyse and evaluate the material in both extracts, using your own knowledge of the issues.**

Extract 1 contains one key interpretation, supported by a great deal of information and evidence.

Interpretation ——

Evidence ——

Extract 1 From John Guy, *The Tudors*, published in 2010.

Late Elizabethan war policy was damaging from several viewpoints. The aims of Henri and his partners diverged, and when in July 1593 he converted to Catholicism to secure his throne as Henri IV, he soured hopes of a European Protestant coalition. Elizabeth, however, continued to support him, since a united France restored the balance of power in Europe, while his debts to the queen ensured continued collaboration in the short term. Next, the cost of the war was unprecedented in English history: even with parliamentary subsidies, it could only be met by borrowing and by sales of Crown lands. Lastly, the war, in effect, spread to Ireland. The Irish Reformation had not succeeded: Spanish invasions as dangerous as the Armada were attempted there. These, combined with serious internal revolt, obliged the Privy Council to think in terms of the full-scale conquest of Ireland logically induced by Henry VII's assumption of the kingship. Elizabeth hesitated – as well she might. At last her favourite, the dazzling but paranoid earl of Essex, was dispatched in 1599 with a large army.

Extract 2 From J. B. Black, *The Reign of Elizabeth 1558–1603*, published in 1959.

Seldom has the strategic situation in a great war been so manifestly favourable to England as in the aftermath of the battle of Gravelines. The command of the sea rested with the English fleet. However, England's war policy continued in the same old groove, fighting Spain on land in alliance with the Dutch, and the struggle on the sea went on spasmodically without any decisive victory. The result was that Spain was given time to recover and to become far stronger as a sea power in the later years of the century than at any previous period in her history.

This inconclusive and unsatisfactory state of affairs is reflected in the atmosphere of uncertainty that prevailed in England during the post-armada period and lasted unabated to the end of the reign. The confidence inspired by the triumph of 1588 was soon qualified by the presentiment that Spain would come again – as come she did. The general uneasiness was probably increased by the continuance of Jesuit propaganda and the publication of Persons' tract (1591), comparing England to the barren fig-tree of the gospels. Prevalent invasion scares kept the government continually on the alert throughout the 1590s.

Activity: Identifying the interpretation

1 Identify the following aspects of Extract 2:
  • The argument.
  • Information or evidence that supports the argument.
2 Having identified these, share your answer with a partner.
  • Did your partner correctly identify the interpretation?

  • Did you both spot the same information in the extract?
  • Has your partner missed anything?
  • Did you miss anything that you should note down?
  • What can you learn from your partner's approach?

Use these questions to feed back to each other and improve your analysis of the extract.

Activity: AS-style question

Study Extracts 1 (page 159) and 2.

Historians have different views about whether there was a general crisis of government in the last years of Elizabeth I's reign. Analyse and evaluate the extracts and use your knowledge of the issues to explain your answer to the following question:

How far do you agree with the view that Elizabeth's war policy undermined her government in the period 1589–1603?

2 The extent of faction at court and the succession issue

Overview

Debates regarding the extent to which there was a general crisis of government in the last years of Elizabeth's reign are often related to factionalism at court and the issue of succession. Dominating the court – the goal of factional activity – was the key to directing the war effort and influencing the succession. Moreover, some historians argue that factionalism was indicative of a crisis as it implied that Elizabeth was losing control of her government, at the very time when war with Spain, difficult relations with parliament and growing social distress required clear leadership.

The succession issue was also crucial during Elizabeth's last years. Elizabeth's impending death and her consistent refusal to name a successor led to debates, plots that undermined Elizabeth's authority, and the threat of civil war.

However, historians disagree over the extent to which factions and the issue of succession really did lead to a crisis in Elizabeth's government in her last years. There is considerable disagreement over the extent to which Elizabeth's government was dominated by faction fighting in the 1590s. Even the nature of factionalism is disputed. Finally, some historians stress the fact that the succession issue did not lead to the constitutional crisis or civil war that many of Elizabeth's contemporaries feared would erupt on her death.

This section considers:
1   The nature of factionalism in Elizabeth's court
2   Conflict and co-operation in Elizabeth's court
3   'Factional' activity, 1589–99
4   The issue of succession
5   Faction and succession, 1599–1603
6   The Queen's last years and the succession

1 The nature of factionalism in Elizabeth's court

Historians disagree over the nature of factionalism. Significantly, different definitions of factionalism lead to different assessments of how far factionalism was an issue within Elizabeth's court. In spite of these disagreements, there is no dispute that the 1590s was a time of great conflict within the court. Therefore, the absence of factionalism does not necessarily mean the absence of conflict or crisis at the top of government.

Note it down

This section deals with historical debate over the nature of factionalism. First, you should note down the various different definitions that historians have suggested. Therefore, draw two spider diagrams (see page x), one dealing with the definition of factionalism, one dealing with the number of factions at court. Use them to note down the different historical perspectives. Once you have read the whole chapter you should evaluate which definition is most persuasive.

What was factionalism?

Historians disagree over the exact definition of factionalism. At root, the issue of factionalism relates to conflict in Elizabeth's court between different groups of councillors. Conflict existed between men who, in some sense, supported either Robert Devereux, second Earl of Essex, or William Cecil, first Baron Burghley and his son Robert Cecil. Exactly how many groups there were, and the issue of what drove the conflict, is a matter of debate. It is important to realise that neither Essex, on the one hand, nor the Cecils, on the other, claimed to lead factions. Factions were rejected by all members of the court as a perversion of good government. There are at least three different accounts of the nature of Elizabethan factionalism.

Faction and patronage

Some historians link factions and **patronage**. Elizabeth had the final say on important appointments at court. Nonetheless, powerful members of the Privy Council could advise the Queen, and in reality had a significant influence over who was selected.

According to this view, a faction was made up of a series of **clients**, who sought the help of a central **patron** in an attempt to gain a job within the court. Clients were loyal to the patron because they wanted their patron to advance their careers. The patron supported his clients because he wanted his supporters in key positions within the government.

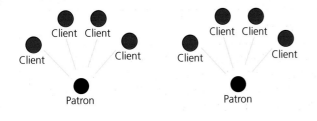

FACTION 1   FACTION 2

▲ Figure 1: Factions and patronage.

Factions and personal loyalty

Other historians argue that factions were groups of lesser courtiers, who felt considerable loyalty to a great courtier, and therefore opposed the influence of other great courtiers. According to this view, patronage was not necessarily central to a faction. Rather, factions were held together by personal loyalty.

Factions, policy and ideology

Some historians argue for another approach to factions. Conyers Read claims that factions represented different approaches to foreign policy. Natalie Mears makes a similar claim, arguing that factions were divided on ideological lines, reflecting different views of how best to serve the Queen. Both agree that factions were united by common values.

How many factions?

Historians also disagree over the number of factions in Elizabeth's court in the 1590s. There are two main views:

● John Neale argues that there were two factions in court in the 1590s: one based around the Cecils and one led by Essex.
● Historians Alexandra Gajda and Natalie Mears argue that there was essentially one faction: by 1598 Essex led a faction which opposed Cecil. However, Cecil was in a strong position in government and therefore had no need to organise a faction.

Patronage and faction

Patronage was an important part of Elizabeth's court. Nonetheless, the widespread use of patronage does not necessarily mean that factionalism was equally widespread.

Burghley's central position at court following 1588 gave him enormous powers as a patron. Indeed, historian Wallace MacCaffrey describes him as the 'patronage minister'. Burghley received between 60 and 100 letters a day asking for his support. Burghley considered this part of his role to be central to his service, as he wanted to ensure that educated and experienced people gained appointments in the court.

Rather than using his power to oppose Essex, in 1591 Burghley supported Essex's bid to gain military command of English forces in France. In this sense, Burghley was responsible for Essex gaining his first major military role.

Equally, Essex's use of patronage was not primarily designed to build a faction. Essex believed that nobles had a duty to promote the growth of the arts and sciences. Therefore, Essex attempted to advance the careers of scholars Anthony Bacon, Frances Bacon and Antonio Pérez. Certainly, he

believed that their advancement at court would benefit him, but not through the creation of a faction. He aided Pérez because he had once been Philip II's secretary and, therefore, hoped to get important insights into Philip's thinking. Francis Bacon helped Essex by writing books and letters that were published under Essex's name. Works such as Essex's letters of advice to the Earl of Rutland, which Bacon wrote on Essex's behalf in 1595 and 1596, gave Essex the status of a scholar as well as a warrior. Anthony Bacon helped Essex by establishing an intelligence network across Europe that would feed Essex with information about the activities of England's enemies.

Essex also acted as a patron to 'loyalist' Catholics, due to his belief in religious toleration. For example, in 1595 he gained a guarantee of religious freedom for Thomas Wright, a Catholic and former Jesuit priest.

In summary, Essex and Burghley used their power of patronage widely. However, this does not necessarily reflect the widespread presence of factionalism or conflict within Elizabeth's court.

Historical interpretations: the nature of factionalism

These three extracts contain different interpretations of factionalism in Elizabeth's court. Extract 1 claims that factions competed within the court for influence over patronage. Extract 2 directly contradicts this arguing that factions were held together by allegiances to competing great men. Finally, Extract 3 presents a different view, arguing that they were united by a common ideology and view of the nature of government.

Extract 1 John Neale, *The Elizabethan Political Scene*, published in 1949.

In Elizabethan England there were no political parties as we know them. True, from time to time there were differences among statesmen but since the Privy Council played a merely advisory role it did not foster the formation of parties. The place of party was taken by faction, and the rivalry of the factions was centred on what mattered supremely to everybody: influence over the queen, and, through that influence, control of patronage.

The competition at court was ceaseless. Success not only meant money: it meant power. On it depended the quality and size of a faction. A faction was an association of self-interest, a mutual-benefit society. Clients expected their patron to sponsor their interests at court.

Extract 2 Paul Hammer, 'Patronage at Court, faction and the Earl of Essex', in John Guy, *The Reign of Elizabeth I: Court and Culture in the Last Decade*, published in 1995.

. . . a courtly faction [was a group] consisting of a body of men who felt themselves personally bound to one particular great man and who saw themselves as necessarily opposed to other men who had a similar bond with a different leader. The identification of faction with patronage obscures, rather than illuminates, the nature of politics in the 1590s.

. . . Faction, in other words, involved a rigidity in personal relations which was contrary to the kinds of dutiful courtesies and horse-trading on which the normal pursuit of patronage depended. Faction was seen as the perversion of the patronage process, not its common manifestation.

Extract 3 Natalie Mears, 'Regum Cecilianum? A perspective of the Court', in John Guy, *The Reign of Elizabeth I: Court and Culture in the Last Decade*, published in 1995.

[The Cecils and Essex were] divided on ideological approaches to royal service. Burghley's letters exemplified the *noblesse de robe* that the Cecils, and other councillors, personified: though they sought personal advancement and profit this was always in respect of royal service within the circumference of a government based on civil and common law headed by the queen and one in which education was more of a prerequisite than blood. Essex, however, represented the French *noblesse d'epee* in which natural and martial law had precedence over civil and common law, and where natural social hierarchies were traditional and inflexible. As a nobleman perceiving himself as a natural councillor whom the queen had a duty to consult and reward . . . The *noblesse de robe* put Cecil firmly into the political establishment, providing an ideological or methodological sympathy with other councillors, whilst Essex effectively isolated himself by promoting a military stance, and one in which the element of personal allegiance could be dangerous.

Having read Extracts 1, 2 and 3, write short answers to the following questions:

1 What is meant by the following terms:
   Extract 1: 'statesman', 'an association of self-interest'
   Extract 2: 'horse-trading'
   Extract 3: *'noblesse de robe'*, *'noblesse d'epee'*
2 How does Extract 1 define a faction? How does it support its definition?
3 How does Extract 2 define a faction? Why does Extract 2 disagree with Extract 1?
4 How does Extract 3 define a faction? How does it support or challenge definitions in Extracts 1 and 3?

Having answered these questions, discuss them with a partner. How far do you agree? Where you disagree, how can you use the extracts and the information in this section to resolve your disagreements?

2 Conflict and co-operation in Elizabeth's court

Whatever the extent of factionalism, there were clear causes of conflict at court which could have led to a crisis in government. At the same time, there were also good reasons for co-operation between the Cecils and Essex.

Note it down

This section outlines the reasons for conflict and the reasons for co-operation at court.

- Draw a table, title one column 'conflict' and the other 'co-operation'. Use it to make notes on the different reasons for conflict and co-operation.
- Remember, there were several reasons for conflict and several more for co-operation, so make sure your notes distinguish between these different reasons.

Causes of conflict

The nature of government during Elizabeth's 'Second Reign'

Historian John Guy describes the last phase of Elizabeth's government as her 'Second Reign', due to its distinctive nature. One of the features of the 'Second Reign' are changes in the Privy Council, which made politics more oppositional. In essence, Guy argues that in the 1570s and 1580s, the Privy Council was a relatively large collegial body, in which decisions were made collectively. However, following 1588 this changed. Between 1588 and 1590 Robert Dudley, Earl of Leicester, Sir Walter Mildmay and Sir Francis Walsingham died. Consequently, whereas Burghley had once been one of many influential figures on the council, he now became its most senior figure. Additionally, during the 1590s, Guy argues, Elizabeth tended to avoid appointing new Privy Councillors. Therefore, the Privy Council shrank from around 20 in the 1560s to 13 in 1598. Guy's arguments are important in the context of factionalism and conflict because they explain the context in which conflict started to emerge. First, as the Council became smaller, the influence of each Privy Councillor became greater, therefore disagreements became more significant. Second, as Burghley grew older, competition grew among the younger councillors to replace him. Indeed, Burghley played an important role in this process by trying to gain an advantage for Cecil, his son. At the same time, Essex assumed that as the Queen's favourite and as England's greatest military leader he should succeed Burghley. Competition led to conflict within government, which had a destabilising impact on the government.

Policy over war with Spain

In terms of policy, the key area of disagreement between the Cecils and Essex was the war with Spain. Essex did not merely want to defeat Spain, he wanted England to replace Spain as the dominant power in Europe. Therefore, during the 1590s he used his influence to persuade Elizabeth to:

- invest large sums of government money in extravagant missions to capture Spanish territory
- play a large role in fighting on the Continent, rather than in Ireland. Essex viewed Ireland as a distraction and peripheral to England's real place in Europe.

The Cecils had very different military goals. Fundamentally, they wanted to protect English territory and minimise the costs of the war. Clearly, this view was much closer to Elizabeth's understanding of the English war effort, and her desire to fight a primarily defensive war.

This disagreement was part of a larger disagreement over the relationship between the military and the government. Essex believed in chivalric values, which, in this context, meant that military leaders should have complete freedom to determine their own strategy and lead their own campaigns. From this point of view the government should merely support the military. The Cecils, by contrast, believed that the government should set the military strategy and set limits on military action in accordance with what the government could afford.

Religion

A further difference that separated Essex from the Cecils was the issue of religion. While they were all Protestants, Essex was in favour of religious toleration for Catholics and Puritans, as long as they were loyal to Elizabeth. Burghley, on the other hand, believed that both groups were dangerous and therefore should not be tolerated.

The role of courtiers

Essex and the Cecils also had differing views on the role of courtiers. Essex's conduct was influenced by the doctrine of the 'mixed monarchy', and classical notions of virtue. According to the doctrine of the 'mixed monarchy', Elizabeth's power was only part of the whole constitution of England. As queen in a mixed monarchy, Elizabeth ruled with the advice of her senior nobles and with the consent of parliament. Essex also believed that noble men should live the *vita active*: the active life. This included the pursuit of military glory, the pursuit of knowledge, and the duty to offer wise advice to the monarch.

For Essex these two ideas complemented each other. He saw his role as a noble as being an adviser to Elizabeth in the context of a mixed monarchy. Moreover, he believed that as a man he had valuable insights into the nature of war that Elizabeth did not have because she was a woman (see page 147). Therefore, he believed it was central to his duty to play a leading role in the government. Essex also had a strong belief in **natural law**: he thought acting virtuously was more important than obeying English law, or even the Queen's commands.

Burghley approach to government was quite different. Whereas Essex was obsessed with military virtue, Burghley was a competent administrator who disliked soldiers. He believed that soldiering was an essentially unchristian activity, because wars were fundamentally unjust, and between wars soldiers served no purpose. Burghley passed this view on to his son. Burghley and Cecil were more concerned with money than with war or virtue.

Burghley believed that the true threat to Elizabeth's government was taxation – for the English people were naturally hostile to increased tax. Whereas Essex had a reputation for pursuing virtue, Burghley was believed to be sly, dishonest, ambitious and without conscience. Like Essex, he was keen to influence Elizabeth, and from time to time he believed that she had made serious mistakes. That said, Burghley did not overstep the bounds of his authority. Unlike Essex, he took the Queen's commands and English law seriously.

Relations with Elizabeth

Essex's relationship with Elizabeth had a profoundly destabilising effect on the court. Essex had become the Queen's favourite in the late 1580s due to his charm, grace, good looks and glamour. Elizabeth gave Essex titles, positions at court and a lucrative monopoly over the production of sweet wines. Crucially, Essex's pursuit of virtue was at odds with the culture of the Elizabethan court. He repeatedly disobeyed Elizabeth's direct commands, in order to prove his military virtue. For example, he secretly joined the Drake-Norris expedition in 1589, in spite of the fact that Elizabeth had forbidden him to leave her court.

What is more, Essex was domineering when advising the Queen. Essex's friend and adviser Francis Bacon warned him to hide his feelings and play the part of a humble courtier, but Essex was unable to do so. Therefore, he gained a reputation for being an 'over-mighty subject', someone who was arrogant and not sufficiently respectful of Elizabeth's authority. In spite of his disobedience, Essex was able to retain his position as favourite until 1599. He was less successful at retaining influence at court.

Burghley's relationship with Elizabeth was very different. While Essex was young and glamourous, Burghley was old and conventional. Elizabeth clearly trusted Burghley and spent a great deal of time with him, so much so that Theobalds Palace, his house in Hertfordshire, virtually became a royal residence.

Cecil was a stark contrast to Essex. Although he was around the same age, he was not considered handsome. He was short and had a deformed spine. Elizabeth nicknamed him 'her elf', due to his short stature. He tended to share his father's views on policy and the workings of government.

The reasons for co-operation at court

Setting aside the differences, there were also good reasons for collaboration and co-operation between Burghley, Essex and Cecil for much of the 1590s.

Mutual respect

Co-operation was possible because Essex and Burghley respected each other. Burghley had been Essex's childhood guardian and therefore there was a degree of trust between the two men. Additionally, Burghley seems to have believed that Essex had valuable military expertise that was useful to England's security. This respect was signalled by Burghley's repeated willingness to repair their relationship after disputes.

Mutual need

Natalie Mears argues that Essex had to work with the Cecils because he had few other friends at the higher levels of the court. The Cecils were well connected, reflecting Burghley's long-standing role in government. Therefore, Essex needed Burghley's help in order to achieve his objectives. Additionally, Mears argues that Burghley could not always count on getting his way and therefore he turned to Essex to use his influence with the Queen. Moreover, rather than using their access to the Queen simply to patronise their own clients, Essex and the Cecils would work together to seek positions for junior members of the court. For example, in 1593 Cecil helped Essex obtain military posts for Sir Christopher Blount and Captain St John. Even as late as May 1597, Essex and Cecil both supported William Cornwallis in his suit to obtain the post of **groom-porter**.

Cecil

A final reason for collaboration was that Essex did not consider Cecil as a serous rival until the mid-1590s. Until that point, they had a reasonably good working relationship because Essex did not view him as a threat.

3 'Factional' activity, 1589–99

Conflict at court was not constant. It went through different phases as a series of issues emerged over the course of the decade following the Spanish Armada.

Apparent unity, 1589–92

Initially, Burghley and Essex collaborated effectively. The common desire to capitalise on Spain's defeat led to a good working relationship between the two men. There was considerable agreement over the immediate necessity of destroying the Spanish fleet and seizing Spanish gold. However, the collaboration masked a deeper disagreement about the long-term goals of war with Spain.

Attorney general controversy, 1593

The appointment of a new **attorney general** led to disagreement between Essex and the Cecils. Essex petitioned Elizabeth to appoint Francis Bacon. Essex asked Burghley to support the appointment, assuming his willingness, as Burghley was Bacon's uncle. Initially, Burghley seemed to back Bacon. However, Burghley ultimately supported Sir Edward Coke, a more experienced lawyer. Cecil too backed Coke. Worse still, Burghley was critical of the way in which Essex had tried to bully Elizabeth into appointing Bacon.

Ultimately, Elizabeth appointed Coke. Her decision not to appoint Bacon had little to do with Essex. Rather, she recognised that Bacon was inexperienced and he had been disloyal to her in parliament over the triple subsidy (see page 183). However, Essex viewed this as a major defeat. Essex believed that Elizabeth had spurned him as a councillor, and that he had failed in his aristocratic duty to help his friend Bacon. Bacon complained to Essex that he had been persecuted by the Cecils. Finally, Cecil offered to support Bacon for the lesser role of a solicitorship, which Essex took as an insult.

War scare and Cadiz, 1594–96

Essex's greatest military triumph led to an even greater political failure, which gave the political advantage to the Cecils.

Conflict between Essex and the Cecils reached new heights following 1594. Scares of an imminent Spanish invasion gave Essex, Elizabeth's leading military strategist, new authority in the court. Burghley wanted to counter Essex's growing authority by securing Cecil's promotion to the positon of secretary of state – a role which would ensure regular access to the Queen. However, in 1595 Elizabeth was reluctant to give Cecil a larger role at court.

Therefore the Cecils sought other ways of undercutting Essex. In early 1596 they used their administrative power to delay deliveries of gunpowder to Essex, who was preparing for his assault on Cadiz (see page 148). Additionally, they deliberately withheld information from Essex by refusing to forward messages to him.

However, Essex's own behaviour was even more damaging. The nature of Essex's military triumph at Cadiz was extremely concerning to Elizabeth and her Privy Council:

- Rather than reflecting the glory of the victory on to Elizabeth, Essex took the credit for the military success, asking the Archbishop of Canterbury to proclaim a day of celebration at his victory.
- Essex failed to ensure that all of the Spanish treasure seized made it back to Elizabeth.
- Essex disobeyed Elizabeth's direct orders by temporarily turning Cadiz into an English garrison and, in so doing, opened the door to a bigger campaign than the one that Elizabeth had authorised.

Elizabeth responded by demanding an investigation into Essex's handling of the money. The investigation cleared Essex of any wrongdoing. But Essex's disloyalty led to Cecil gaining a central position in Elizabeth's government. Elizabeth appointed Cecil as secretary of state, breaking a promise that she had given to Essex before he had left that she would leave the position vacant until his return from Cadiz.

Essex was largely to blame for his political failure. Yet he and his advisers blamed the Cecils. The Bacons wrote to Essex claiming that the Cecils were plotting against Essex and had used his absence from court to turn the Queen against him. In sum, the consequence of Essex's victory in Cadiz was bitter conflict within the court.

Worsening relations, 1597–99

Relations between Essex and the Cecils worsened between 1597 and 1599 for three main reasons:

- Essex's reputation as a military genius was damaged by the failure of the Islands Voyage of 1597 (see page 148). Cecil capitalised on this by insisting on close government supervision of Essex's military missions.
- Burghley's death in August 1598 was a turning point. Essex had respected Burghley and while he was still alive there were attempts to co-operate. Moreover, his death left a vacuum in the court that Essex and Cecil both wanted to fill.
- The Bacons and Essex's other close friends encouraged him to see Cecil as his archenemy, nicknaming him Robert the Devil.

Conflict over Ireland

Existing tensions were exacerbated by Essex's mission to Ireland. Essex's claim to military expertise made him the obvious choice to lead the Queen's forces in Ireland. However, Essex viewed this as part of Cecil's plan to exclude him from court so that he could consolidate his position. Nonetheless, Essex felt he had a duty to comply with Elizabeth's order to command England's forces in Ireland. During preparations for the mission the relationship with Cecil worsened. Essex wanted more troops and equipment than Cecil was prepared to authorise. Cecil's main focus was keeping costs to a minimum.

Once the campaign began Essex was convinced that Cecil was using his influence to deny him supplies and re-enforcements. Moreover, in Essex's absence Cecil was able to influence a series of key appointments in court. Cecil's brother Thomas became president of the Council of the North, and Cecil himself was promoted to the lucrative position of master of the court wards.

Problems in Ireland and Essex's concerns over Cecil's plans for the succession led to Essex's final desperate attempts to replace Cecil as the power in Elizabeth's court and ensure a Protestant succession (see pages 171–72).

Historical interpretations: factionalism by 1598

Historians disagree on the extent to which Elizabeth's court was dominated by rival factions by 1598. Wallace T. MacCaffrey, for example, argues that both Essex and the Cecils were engaged in factional rivalry. However, Paul E. J. Hammer argues that there was still room for compromise between Essex and the Cecils as late as 1598.

Extract 4 From Wallace T. MacCaffrey, *Elizabeth I: War and Politics, 1588–1603*, published in 1992.

> The Cecils could only view with distaste the intrusion of a volatile, restless, and ambitious newcomer. In their eyes Essex was a political buccaneer, who would compete with them as a patronage broker and would be an ardent advocate of the strategy of all-out offensive warfare that Burghley had strongly opposed. They reacted with bland discretion. Far too shrewd to attempt to dislodge him from the royal affections, they played a careful hand, accepting him as a colleague.
>
> From the autumn of 1596 onwards Essex stood in open conflict with the Cecils and their allies on the Council. Reconciliations were patched together, but these were no more than truces in a continuing and open rivalry. The last of these, in the spring of 1598, endured as long as the English were seeking to keep the French from making peace with Spain.

Extract 5 From Paul E. J. Hammer, *The Polarisation of Elizabethan Politics*, published in 1995.

> Although rivalry between Essex and the Cecils was obvious even by 1593, no overt Cecil faction appeared. The professions of both Cecils about being first and foremost the queen's loyal servant were incompatible with open factionalism. Until 1597, or even later, the Cecils hoped that they could find a lasting compromise with Essex. Throughout these years of rivalry, they consistently sought to renew a *modus vivendi* with him. They believed that Essex would play a dominant role in English politics for long years to come and that building a relationship with him was critically important to the future both of the realm and of Cecil.

Read Extracts 4 and 5 and write a brief answer to the following questions:

1 What reasons do the extracts give for conflict and co-operation between Essex and the Cecils?
2 How far do the two extracts agree about the extent of conflict between Essex and the Cecils in the period 1590–97?
3 Extract 5 argues that 'rivalry between Essex and the Cecils was obvious even by 1593 … '. Which conflict of 1593 is Hammer referring to?

Having answered these questions share your answers with a partner. How far do you agree? Where you disagree, can you resolve your disagreements by referring to the interpretations of the extracts and the information in this chapter?

4 The issue of succession

Note it down

As you read this section, make notes on the following topics using the 1:2 method (see page x):

- The nature of the succession issue.
- The reasons why the unsettled succession caused problems for Elizabeth's government.
- The potential problems that the unsettled succession created for Elizabeth's reign.
- The key issues raised by the succession debate.
- How the issue of succession relates to the problems of the war and faction fighting.

TIP: Remember to make a note of the names, titles and dates of publication of the books that were published as part of the succession debate.

The succession issue presented Elizabeth's government with serious potential problems following 1589. The fundamental issue was that Elizabeth had no direct heir. Therefore at her death there were likely to be disputes over the succession. The problem became more worrying as the Queen aged. The issue became all the more important in the 1590s as the Queen was in her 60s and therefore clearly reaching the end of her life. The problems that Burghley foresaw included:

- uncertainty over whether the succession would lead to civil war due to a clash between the supporters of rival claimants
- the concern that Elizabeth's death would lead to the restoration of Catholicism and the widespread persecution of Protestants
- uncertainty over whether the succession would lead to attempts on Elizabeth's life as supporters of hopeful successors sort to gain an advantage in the battle for succession.

From the 1560s, Burghley and other members of the Privy Council wanted to minimise these problems by:

- legally determining Elizabeth's successor before she died
- executing Mary, Queen of Scots in order to prevent her, a Catholic, taking the throne.

Elizabeth agreed to execute Mary, Queen of Scots in 1587. However, she continually refused to agree to name her successor. Elizabeth argued:

- a successor would become the centre of plots to overthrow her, as she had been during Mary I's rule

- a named successor would diminish her authority. The new heir would be 'the rising sun', who would grow in authority as she, 'the setting sun', diminished in her final years
- naming a successor would split opinion in the country and in parliament – none of the possible successors had universal support and therefore naming a successor would lead to division
- naming a successor would commit her to someone irrevocably; she preferred to keep her options open.

The issue of succession before 1589

The succession had been an issue prior to 1589. Elizabeth's actions and the plans of her ministers in the early part of her reign influenced the later debate concerning how the succession was to be handled:

- In 1562 Elizabeth had small pox and was expected to die. The Privy Council insisted that she nominate a successor. Elizabeth eventually told her Privy Council that Sir Robert Dudley should rule. However, Elizabeth specified that he should not be king, but protector of the realm. In that sense Elizabeth's order failed to solve the issue.
- Threats to Elizabeth's life and the unresolved issue of succession prompted Burghley to propose the formation of a Grand Council that would have temporary authority to govern if the Queen died. The Grand Council would also be empowered to call parliament who would select the next monarch. Elizabeth rejected the plan, claiming that she alone had the authority to name her successor and call parliament.
- Continual plots against Elizabeth led to the execution of Mary, Queen of Scots in 1587.

Succession, factionalism and war in the 1590s

The issue of succession was clearly linked to issues of faction and war. Elizabeth's refusal to name a successor gave the leaders of her court considerable power to influence the succession, either by persuading Elizabeth to name a specific successor, or by choosing a successor on her death. Therefore, the struggle between the Cecils and Essex for influence at court was, in part, a struggle to guide the succession.

The unresolved issue of the succession was also linked to the war. First, it was widely assumed that Philip II's goal was to invade England and arrange the succession of his daughter, the Infanta Isabella Clara Eugenia. Secondly, the most obvious Protestant contender for the throne was James VI of Scotland. The war with Spain and in Ireland needed to be fought in such a way that did not alienate James. Moreover, there were rumours in 1595 that James might convert to Catholicism and invade England as an ally of Spain, if Spain gained the upper hand in the war.

Plots against the Queen

One way in which the unsettled succession caused problems for Elizabeth was through assassination attempts. Philip II was behind at least one attempt on Elizabeth's life in the 1590s.

William Hacket, God's messenger

In 1591 William Hacket, who believed himself to be a prophet, started a riot against Elizabeth in London. Accompanied by Puritans Edmund Copinger and Henry Arthington, Hacket proclaimed himself God's chosen messenger and king of England. The three were arrested and charged with trying to overthrow the Queen. Arthington was eventually released, Hacket was executed and Copinger starved himself to death in prison.

The Lopez Plot

In February 1594 Elizabeth's physician Dr Roderigo Lopez was found guilty of plotting with Philip II's cousin to poison the Queen. He was executed three months later. Historians disagree over his actual guilt. Historian Robert Lacey argues that Essex, who initially accused Lopez of treason, wanted to prove the effectiveness of his spy network and his dedication to the Queen's protection. Moreover, Essex knew that the Queen was considering peace with Spain, and he hoped that revealing the existence of a Spanish plot would end talk of negotiations. Lopez was an easy target, as he was Jewish and anti-Semitism was widespread at the time. Therefore, he had a good reason for wanting to accuse Lopez. Historian David Katz, on the other hand, argues that whatever Essex's motives, there is genuine evidence of a plot.

Edward Squire

Another attempt to assassinate Elizabeth involved the royal stablehand Edward Squire. Squire was allegedly converted by Jesuits after being captured by the Spanish during battle. Squire was then sent back to England in 1597, where he regained his old job working in the royal stables. Squire attempted to murder Elizabeth by rubbing poison on to Elizabeth's saddle. The attempt failed, as did his subsequent attempt to poison Essex. He was found guilty of treason in 1598 after the Spanish authorities, furious with Squire for taking their money but failing to assassinate the Queen, passed his name to the English government.

The succession debate

The unsettled succession made Elizabeth's government vulnerable as it provoked debate, not simply about who should succeed Elizabeth, but about the nature of the government. Senior members of the government clearly recognised the danger of this as, from the early 1580s, the **press censor** was given new powers to censor books dealing with the succession.

The next monarch?

Following the execution of Mary, Queen of Scots there were several candidates to succeed Elizabeth as English monarch:

- James VI had a strong claim to the throne in terms of **primogeniture**. He was also male and a Protestant – which were considered advantages by Elizabeth's court – and he had successfully distanced himself from the plots of his mother, Mary, Queen of Scots.
- The Infanta Isabella Clara Eugenia, daughter of Philip II, was descended from Henry III and Edward III and therefore had a claim to the throne.
- Philip II had a claim to the throne based on rumours that Mary, Queen of Scots had bequeathed the throne to him in her will. Spanish diplomats searched for the will following her execution.
- Arabella Stuart was another possible candidate to take the throne on Elizabeth's death. As James VI's cousin most Protestants regarded her as second in line to the throne. Moreover, Protestants who opposed the accession of James VI tended to support Arabella Stuart. Indeed, there was a significant minority of Protestants who did not want a Scottish king. Therefore in Elizabeth's last years there were various plans to try and ensure that Arabella, rather than James, took the throne.

Catholic succession literature

Catholic writers contested James' right to succeed to the throne. The most famous book arguing against James was *A Conference about the Next Succession to the Crown of England*, written by the Jesuit priest Robert Persons. The book argued in favour of an **elective monarchy**. Persons claimed:

- government was created by people and therefore monarchs do not have a divine right to rule
- citizens have a natural right to overthrow and kill **tyrants**
- citizens have a natural right to elect their ruler.

Persons' argument undermined James' claim to the throne as his claim was based on primogeniture rather than on the consent of the people. Moreover, Persons' argument had an effect on perceptions of Elizabeth's rule. Crucially, Persons argued that the people had the right to rule, and that the monarch's right to rule depended on the consent of the people. This undermined Elizabeth's authority as it meant that the people could withdraw their consent at any time.

The actions of the **Spanish Council** seemed to reflect Persons' argument. Up until 1602 they had backed the Infanta as the next English monarch. However, from

1602, they concluded that English Catholics should choose their own candidate to succeed Elizabeth. Moreover, they argued that the candidate should be English and that English Catholics should appeal to anti-Scottish feeling as part of their efforts to resist James' accession to the throne.

Protestant succession literature

The stress in Catholic literature on the election and consent clearly concerned Protestant writers. Books like Irenicus Phiodikaios' *A treatise declaring . . . the just title and righte of . . . Iames the sixt* (1599) argued that the divine right of kings was **hereditary** and therefore independent

---

Historical interpretations: the extent of the succession debate

The succession debate affected all levels of Elizabethan society. John Guy considers Burghley's plans, and therefore the view at the top of government. Susan Doran and Paulina Kewes consider the debate that went on outside government.

Extract 6 From John Guy, 'The 1590s: the second reign of Elizabeth I?' in John Guy ed., *The Reign of Elizabeth I: Court and Culture in the Last Decade*, published in 1995.

Burghley's contingency plans up to and including those of 1584-5 provided that, in the event of Elizabeth's death, the Privy Council and Parliament should not fail to act. His drafts for the succession variously envisaged a 'Council of State', 'Great Council' or 'Grand Council' which would form a provisional government in the absence of a ruler and which would adjudicate the claims of candidates for the succession in conjunction with Parliament. These plans became redundant after Mary's execution, since the succession of her son, the protestant James VI, became (at least theoretically) assured.

Extract 7 From Susan Doran and Paulina Kewes, 'The earlier Elizabethan succession question revisited', in Susan Duran and Paulina Kewes, *Doubtful and Dangerous: The Question of Succession in Late Elizabethan England*, published 2014.

Mary's execution not only failed to resolve the succession problem but in some ways threw it wide open. While in its wake the Catholics came off worse, being deprived of their sure-fire candidate, there was no unanimity among Protestants either. Whether the Stuart claim was vested in James meanwhile preoccupied the Spanish King and his English Catholic supporters. Back in 1586, Mary had indicated her willingness to cede to the Spanish King her title to the English crown. Spanish diplomats and agents went hunting after Mary's 'phantom will', while Persons and his allies spearheaded a print campaign designed to force the Catholic powers into action.

By the 1570s religion became the fundamental factor shaping attitudes towards the succession and the main stimulus for novel constitutional ideas. These ideas went well beyond the Cecilian interregnum schemes and included a variety of elective solutions. It was only when Persons appropriated election as a principle in the mid-1590s that Protestants drifted away from such experiments, and only after the Essex fiasco* that virtually everyone affected to subscribe to the hereditary succession and the Stuart title.

* see pages 171–72.

Having read Extracts 6 and 7 write a short answer to the following questions:

1 What impact did the execution of Mary, Queen of Scots have on the succession debate according to Extracts 6 and 7?

2 What is Extract 7 referring to when it mentions 'Cecilian interregnum schemes' and 'Persons appropriated election as a principle'?

Having answered these questions, swap your answers with a partner. How far do you agree? Whose answers analyse Extracts 6 and 7's claims about the impact of Mary's execution most clearly? What can you learn from each other's answers?

---

of consent. Other Protestant pamphlets, such as Peter Wentworth's *A Pithie Exhortation to her Majesty for establishing her Successor to the Crown*, urged Elizabeth to call a parliament and pass a law naming James as her successor.

Elizabeth continually refused to name a successor. Additionally, she was prepared to imprison those who, like Wentworth, persistently campaigned for her to do so. Nonetheless, Protestant writers were able to get around Elizabeth's censorship in two ways. First, pro-James books were published in Scotland. Secondly, a great deal of literature was published that contained covert discussion of the succession. One way of doing this was to publish books and plays about the biblical King David and the succession of David's throne to King Solomon. Many writers praised David's wisdom in nominating Solomon, with the support of his parliament, before his death. Edmund Bunny's *Coronation of David* (1589), Thomas Morton's *Salomon* (1596) and Mary Sidney Herbert's translation of the Psalms (1599) took this approach.

An English republic

The unsettled succession also encouraged discussion of republican ideas. Catholic critics of James (see page 169) argued that monarchy was not given by God. Republicans went further, arguing that there were forms of government better at protecting the liberty of the English. The 1592 **Aragonese revolt** against a tyrannical monarch led republican ideas to enter English political discussion. One of the leading writers who made the case against monarchy was Antonio Pérez, a scholar who was close to Essex. Pérez's *Relaçiones*, a manuscript in which he criticises monarchy, was never published, but it was circulated widely among nobles who were critical of Cecil and Elizabeth's government in the 1590s.

5 Faction and succession, 1599–1603

Note it down

As you read through this section note:
- key events of the period
- their significance for the factional conflict
- their significance for the succession.

You could use different-coloured pens to make notes on the significance of events for (i) the succession and (ii) factional conflict.

The Essex revolt

Faction and the issue of succession came together in the Essex revolt of 1601. The revolt, which threatened to transform Elizabeth's government and force the resolution of the issue of succession, took place in 1601, but its roots go back to the mid-1590s.

Essex and the succession

Essex believed that he had a duty to guide the succession. Consequently, with the help of Francis Bacon, he started corresponding with James VI in 1593. Essex wanted to ensure that James emerged as ruler following Elizabeth's death. Moreover, he hoped that James would reward him for his support with a central role in his new government. The correspondence was secret, as discussing James' succession could be considered treasonous.

Essex in Ireland

Essex's military failure in Ireland weakened his authority at court. Additionally, his absence from court strengthened Cecil's position. Worse still, Essex was convinced that Cecil was plotting treason. He believed that Cecil was working to ensure the succession of the Spanish Infanta. He believed that Cecil was an evil courtier who was poisoning Elizabeth's mind with talk of peace with Spain in order to make himself rich and powerful.

Essex's suspicions were so powerful that he considered calling a truce with Tyrone and using the English army to invade England and remove Cecil from government. He could then take his rightful place at the head of Elizabeth's government and ensure both victory against Spain and James' succession.

Essex decided against a full-scale invasion, but made a truce with Tyrone and returned to England in September 1599, to talk directly to the Queen. The truce and the return were against Elizabeth's direct orders and therefore Elizabeth ordered his arrest and imprisonment. In so doing, the Queen ended Essex's role at court, and the faction fighting with her government. Essex's fall left Cecil unopposed.

The 1601 rising

Essex's imprisonment did not end his desire to play an active role in government. Indeed, he believed that his fate was further evidence of Cecil's evil influence at court. Worse still, in May 1600 Essex learned that peace talks had started with Spain. Essex interpreted this as the first stage in Cecil's plan to ensure that the Spanish Infanta took the English throne. Towards the end of the year Essex began plotting a rebellion while under house arrest, to oust the majority of the Privy Council and end the influence of Cecil. He wrote to James outlining his plan. James agreed to send an ambassador to Essex to discuss the plot.

Essex's goal, having overthrown the government, was to persuade the Queen to appoint him as the great constable of England, a role that would allow him to rule England for a temporary period after her death and ensure the succession of James.

Essex's rising was too small to overthrow the government. In February 1601 Essex led 200 men into the city of London. Cecil had discovered enough of Essex's plan to prepare, therefore London was awash with government propaganda proclaiming Essex a traitor. As a result the popular uprising that Essex was depending on failed to occur. Essex was arrested and sent to the Tower of London accused of treason and was beheaded on 25 February 1601.

The consequences of the rising

The rising had a series of consequences:

- Essex was completely discredited. Therefore, Cecil was now in a position to guide the succession process. In April 1601, two months after Essex's execution, Cecil began secret negotiations with James, assuring him of

his loyalty and his intention to ensure that James took the throne on Elizabeth's death.
- The government used the plot to discredit English Catholics. Essex had conspired with Sir Christopher Blount, Sir John Davies and Sir Charles Danvers, who all confessed their Catholicism.
- James' knowledge of the plot was kept secret. James' decision to send an ambassador to Essex in the run up to the rising could have disqualified him from the succession. Keeping his relationship with Essex secret meant that he could still succeed to the throne.

6 The Queen's last years and the succession

Even in the last years of the Queen's life the succession remained unsettled. Cecil had assured James of his help in gaining the English throne on Elizabeth's death. However, even this was uncertain, as the Queen could still nominate another successor.

Elizabeth's health began to fail at the end of 1602. By March 1603 she was not eating or sleeping. Now 70, it was clear that the Queen's death was imminent. Her Privy Councillors asked her to nominate her successor. On her death she chose James. Cecil sent word to Edinburgh that James was the new king of England.

Conclusion

While there were tensions within government and intense rivalries between 1589 and 1598, there was generally an effective working relationship between the Cecils and Essex. However, the breakdown in the relationship that occurred in 1599 led to a rising against the Queen, which threatened to destroy Elizabeth's government at a time when England faced military threats from Spain and Ireland, as well as popular unrest due to high taxes and terrible poverty (see pages 193–95). Nonetheless, the rising was easily put down, and Essex's trial was turned to the Queen's advantage by demonising Catholics.

The succession issue also impacted the government. Certainly, it created anxiety about the consequences of the Queen's death. Even so, the absence of a clear successor following the execution of Mary, Queen of Scots meant that there were no serious plots to remove the Queen in the last decade of her life. Moreover, Cecil was able to ensure a peaceful transition of power to James.

Extended reading

Historian Natalie Mears considers the extent of factional conflict in the Elizabethan court of the 1590s, and its relationship to the issue of succession.

In the twentieth century, two of the most important Elizabethan historians, Sir John Neale and Conyers Read, argued that Elizabethan politics was factional. That is, Elizabethan politics was characterised by 'personal following[s] employed in direct opposition to another personal following' in disputes over policy or the exercise of patronage (Simon Adams). Most historians now agree that Elizabethan politics was not factional because Adams has demonstrated that many of the sources on which Neale and Read based their arguments were Catholic polemics that did not reflect the Elizabethan court accurately. The exception is the 1590s, when, it is argued, factions were led by Robert Devereux, second Earl of Essex, and Sir Robert Cecil, son of William Cecil, Lord Burghley. This essay will examine the evidence, arguing that the situation was more complex.

It is hard to argue that Elizabethan politics was factional in the first half of the 1590s. Though Essex did draw to him a group of men personally loyal to him, Cecil did not. Rather, the period can best be described as one of keen rivalry as the two young men sought to establish themselves as leading political figures at court. In 1593, they clashed over the appointment of the attorney-general and solicitor-general, positions that the earl wanted for his friend and client, Sir Francis Bacon, even though Bacon was out of favour with the Queen. 'Digest me no digestions', Essex told Cecil, 'for the attorneyship for Francis is what I must have ... and with tooth and nail defend and procure the same for him'. In 1594, Essex sought to exploit accusations that Elizabeth's physician, Dr Lopez, was plotting to kill her, partly because the Cecils did not believe them. There were also policy differences, though these were primarily between Essex and Burghley.

Things began to change in 1596 when Elizabeth appointed Cecil her principal secretary and, hence, the main channel of communication with her. This was a post that Essex had coveted for several years for William Davison. The appointment was a major blow to Essex's ambitions and his sense of honour. It also brought Cecil out of his father's shadow, increased his political stature beyond that of the Earl's and strengthened his position significantly on the Privy Council.

As a result, tension between Essex and the Cecils increased. The Earl opposed the appointment of Lord Cobham, Robert's brother-in-law, to the wardenship of the Cinque Ports, and his own uncle, Sir William Knollys, to the lord deputyship of Ireland. Policy disagreements intensified. In a Privy Council meeting in 1598, Burghley rounded on Essex's promotion of war, telling him 'he breathed forth nothing but War, Slaughter and Blood'. Pointing to his Psalter, he said, 'Men of Blood shall not live out half their days.'

However, this was a curiously lop sided factionalism. Essex continued to create a group of men exclusively loyal to him, to personalise politics and allow his political desires to override common sense. Lord Grey told Lord Cobham in 1598 that Essex 'forced mee to declare my self either his only frend to Mr Secretary [Cecil] and his enimy, protesting that ther could bee no neutrality.' In contrast, Cecil refused to create his own following, preferring to establish himself firmly among his colleagues on the Privy Council, and he continued to support obvious candidates for jobs.

Burghley's outburst in 1598 proved prophetic. Essex fell from favour, rebelled in February 1601 and was executed. Though Cecil did give a damning speech littered with false accusations against the Earl at his trial, Essex's demise was his own fault. He was ambitious, arrogant, impetuous and petulant. His actions at court and in Ireland led to him forfeiting the Queen's favour and her councillors and courtiers immediately followed suit. As the Elizabethan historian William Camden perceptively concluded, 'Fortune is seldome reconciled to her Foster-children whom she hath on[c]e forsaken; and Princes more seldome to those they before offended'.

How far was this so-called factionalism played out in the succession question? The answer is 'not much'. It is true that Essex was in contact with James VI of Scotland, Elizabeth's heir presumptive, from as early as 1589 and Cecil from 1600. Some historians also continue to accuse Cecil of 'plotting' to put James on the throne and to eliminate his rivals. However, there is absolutely no evidence for the latter and the former was prompted by deep and widely held fears that the realm would descend into chaos and be prey to foreign invasion if the transition to a new monarch was not smooth. Neither did either man's actions signal a diminution in Elizabeth's own power. Councillors had been attempting to settle the succession since 1558 and, if Elizabeth was 'losing her grip' in the 1590s, this was more to do with her age and her willingness to indulge younger men, like Essex, than their exploitation of her.

Natalie Mears is Senior Lecturer in Tudor History at the University of Durham. She has published widely on early modern politics, religion and the public sphere, especially on the reign of Elizabeth I. Recent books include _Queenship and Political Discourse in the Elizabethan Realms_, _Worship and the Parish Church in Early Modern Britain_ and _National Prayers: Special Worship Since the Reformation: Volume I_.

Activity

Having read the 'Extended reading' essay on page 173, answer the following questions.

Research

1 Using an internet search engine write a paragraph describing the life and career of:
- William Davison
- Sir William Knollys.

Evidence

2 Make a list of the evidence that Mears presents to show that factionalism was a minor part Elizabeth's court until 1596.

Interpretation

3 Identify the passage in which Mears evaluates the extent of factionalism in Elizabeth's last years.
4 Summarise Mears' interpretation in 25 words or fewer.

Evaluation

5 Using your own knowledge, write a paragraph explaining how far you agree with Mears' interpretation of the extent of factionalism in Elizabeth's court in the period 1589–1603.

Work together

Having completed the activity above, swap your notes with a partner. Consider:

1 Did you both spot the same evidence in Mears' essay?
2 Has your partner missed anything?
3 Did you agree on which passage contained the interpretation? If not, who was right?

4 What was good about your partner's summary of Mears' interpretation?
5 Can you learn anything about Mears' interpretation from your partner's summary?
6 How far did you both agree with Mears' interpretation?

Use these questions to feed back to each other and improve your analysis of the extracts.

Essay technique: Structuring your essay

In order to do well, your essay needs to focus on the interpretations of both extracts. Although there are only two extracts, your essay may have to deal with several interpretations, as each extract might contain an argument and a counterargument.

Your essay structure should allow you to:

- analyse all of the interpretations effectively
- deal with the different interpretations in turn
- deal with the different interpretations in a logical sequence.

Therefore, your essay should be structured around the key interpretations contained in the extracts.

Analysing the extracts

In order to deal with the different interpretations in a logical sequence, you should look for the ways in which they support and challenge each other.

Imagine you are answering the following question. Guidance on how to plan an essay in answer to this question is given on page 176.

In the light of differing interpretations, how convincing do you find the view that in the 1590s bitter factional discord 'tore at the very heart of Elizabeth's regime'? (Extract 1)

To explain your answer, analyse and evaluate the material in both extracts, using your own knowledge of the issues.

Extract 1 From Paul E. J. Hammer, *The Polarisation of Elizabethan Politics*, published in 1999.

The last decade or so of the sixteenth century has long been considered a distinct period in the reign of Elizabeth I. Compared to the glory days of the 1570s and early 1580s, the 1590s seem bleak and dark. These 'twilight years' of the reign are characterised by war and the heavy burdens which it imposed on the realm, the growing age of the queen and her councillors, and bitter factional discord which tore at the very heart of Elizabeth's regime.

Historians are equally agreed about the prime characteristic of high politics in the 1590s: faction strife between Robert Devereux, 2nd Earl of Essex, and a coalition of rivals led by Robert Cecil. This bitter rivalry turned the Elizabethan regime against itself and ultimately resulted in the destruction of the Earl of Essex.

Extract 2 From John Guy, 'The 1590s: the second reign of Elizabeth I?' in John Guy ed., *The Reign of Elizabeth I: Court and Culture in the Last Decade*, published in 1995.

The politics of the 1590s were driven by the ambition and spectacular misjudgements of Robert Devereux, the dazzling but paranoid second Earl of Essex. Essex's relationship with the Cecils soon became the motor of political strife. Yet the relationship was ambivalent until Burghley's death. Burghley had been one of Essex's guardians as a child and a mutual respect endured between them even when they came into conflict. It is likely that the feud was primarily between Essex and Sir Robert Cecil, who were roughly the same age.

In 1593 Essex was admitted to the Privy Council. But he made mistakes. By the end of 1596 the feud between Essex and Robert Cecil had escalated into a factional battle to dominate the Privy Council and control both royal policy and the succession to the throne. Moreover, this battle was as disruptive as anything since the death of Henry VIII, because Essex pursued ideology as well as patronage. He embellished his chivalric protestantism with demands that the war be run by generals and not civilians. He urged the switch to an aggressive strategy in Europe and the Atlantic. By contrast, the Cecils, like Elizabeth herself, saw England's goals as essentially defensive.

Planning your essay

In order to plan your answer to the question on page 175, you need to analyse the two extracts, that is to say, you need to break down the extracts into the different arguments, counterarguments and pieces of evidence they contain.

While you are doing this:

- look for contrasting arguments between the extracts – these can be the major sections of your essay
- look for aspects of the extracts that support each other, or aspects of the extracts that differ.

For example, your plan could look like this:

Extract 1		Extract 2
Argument: 1590s dark period due to faction fighting. Evidence: Rivalry between Essex and the Cecils. Ageing courtiers Essex's rebellion Essex's death	(1) [ARGUMENT] During the 1590s Essex's faction fighting did destabilise the government. (2) [COUNTERARGUMENT] However, while Burghley was alive there was some mutual respect between Burghley and Essex. Therefore, faction fighting did not destroy the heart of government. (3) [RESOLUTION] Faction fighting only genuinely threatened the government between Burghley's death in 1598 and the rebellion of 1601.	Argument: Politics driven by Essex's actions. (Privy Council battles of 1590s were most serious since death of Henry VIII.) Evidence: Intractable disagreements between Essex and Cecil about war and patronage. Counterargument: Burghley and Essex respected each other. Evidence: Factional battle only becomes a major issue after 1596.

Activity

Plan an answer to the following question using the extracts on page 177.

In the light of differing interpretations, how convincing do you find the view that the struggle for power of some of the younger men at court created serious problems in the last years of Elizabeth's reign? (Extract 3 line 2).

To explain your answer, analyse and evaluate the material in both extracts, using your own knowledge of the issues.
Follow the steps below:

1 Read both extracts.
2 Analyse them by looking for:
   - the main arguments
   - counterarguments
   - evidence.

3 Look for contrasting arguments between the extracts.
4 Look for aspects of the extracts that support each other.

TIPS:

- Your first main paragraph should analyse the interpretation set out in the question.
- Your second paragraph should analyse the interpretation that contrasts most strongly with the interpretation in the main paragraph.
- Other paragraphs should deal with other arguments that the extracts put forward.
- Try and use both extracts in each paragraph.
- Overall, you can try and achieve an argument – counterargument – resolution structure.

Extract 3 From Carole Levin, *The Reign of Elizabeth I*, published in 2002.

In a number of ways, the final 15 years of Elizabeth's reign after the defeat of the Armada were difficult. A serious problem was the struggle for power of some of the younger men at court for Elizabeth's favour, and the factions, with clear ideological components, hardened in a way that was detrimental to Elizabeth's ability to rule. Her relationship with her last favourite, Robert Devereux, Earl of Essex was especially difficult, and he perceived himself as the enemy of William Cecil's son Robert, and of Sir Walter Raleigh. While Cecil saw England's position as more one of defence, Essex believed his country's natural role was the champion of Europe against Spain at whatever cost. Alternately Essex cajoled and threatened Elizabeth in an effort to gain power and get his way on policy and for rewards for his followers. Essex led a disastrous campaign in Ireland to subdue rebels. The disgrace he faced when he returned to England without leave eventually led him to stage a rebellion against the Queen in 1601.

Extract 4 From Janet Dickinson, *Court Politics and the Earl of Essex*, published in 2012.

One of the chief truisms of early modern political history is that court politics were shaped by the mechanisms of 'factions'. This picture does not supply us with a satisfactory account of politics in the 1590s. The emphasis on crisis and conflict obscures our understanding of how the regime survived and operated during a period of intense strain. On many counts, one could argue that late Elizabethan government was remarkably successful. For the ageing Elizabeth to have survived the continuing war with Spain, the open question of succession and the economic crisis, the regime might be said to have been operating at an unprecedented level of effectiveness. We need to look more carefully at the evidence of cooperation in government ... there is substantial evidence of cross-court patronage, of applicants appealing to both Essex and the Cecils throughout the decade.

In fact, contemporary evidence reveals the court not to have been factionally divided at all. The politics of the 1590s were not about attacks and counter attacks of two defined factional groupings, but about the process by which Essex and a group of friends and followers became convinced they were being denied power and influence by their 'enemies' at court.

Work together

Having completed the activity on page 176 consider the following questions with a partner:

1 Did you both identify the same arguments and counterarguments in the extracts?
2 Did you agree about which aspect of the extracts was the biggest contrast to the main argument of Extract 3?
3 How was your partner's plan different to your own?
4 Did you miss anything that you should note down?
5 What can you learn from your partner's approach?
6 Which plan better answers the question and why?

Use these questions to feed back to each other and improve your analysis of the extracts.

Activity: AS-style question

Study Extracts 3 and 4.

Historians have different views about whether there was a general crisis of government in the last years of Elizabeth I's reign. Analyse and evaluate the extracts and use your knowledge of the issues to explain your answer to the following question:

How far do you agree with the view that, during the last 10 years of Elizabeth's reign, factionalism at court created serious problems in English government?

3 The importance of growing conflicts with parliament and the session of 1601

Overview

The extent to which there was a general crisis of government 1589–1603 is related to debates over Elizabeth's relationship with her parliaments. Some historians argue that there were continual tensions between Elizabeth and her parliaments over religion, tax, the succession, the rights of parliament and monopolies. According to this view these tensions were part of a more general crisis that came to a head in the English Civil War, in the generation after Elizabeth's death. More recent historians have focused much more on co-operation between the Queen and her parliaments. Clearly, there were contentious issues, as well as MPs who were prepared to oppose the Queen. Nonetheless, recent historians have argued that, more often than not, the Queen was able to work with her parliaments by picking her battles carefully, compromising where necessary, using the power at her disposal and appealing to the general anti-Catholic feeling.

This section considers:

1 Elizabeth's relationship with parliament
2 Sources of conflict
3 Elizabeth's parliamentary management
4 The extent of conflict between the Queen and parliament

Note it down

Make notes in the form of a spider diagram (see page x) showing the powers of Elizabeth and of her parliament. You will need two main headings:

- Elizabeth's powers
- Parliament's powers

Use arrows to show the way in which the different powers conflicted or complemented each other.

Finally, make sure you note down a bullet-point list of the technical vocabulary that explains the relationship.

1 Elizabeth's relationship with parliament

Parliament was an extremely important part of Tudor government. Parliament was made up of two houses: the Lords and the Commons. The Lords was also known as the Upper House, and the Commons the Lower House, but in reality the Commons was the more powerful chamber as the Commons alone had the right to initiate tax legislation. Parliament had a series of important functions:

- **Tax:** Parliament alone could authorise taxation to support the government.
- **Law making:** Parliament was England and Wales' supreme law-making body. Statute law (law that was passed by the Commons, the Lords and the Queen) was considered superior to common law and **royal proclamations**.
- **Representation:** Together, the House of Lords and the House of Commons claimed to represent the interests of the whole of England and Wales. Therefore, they believed they had a duty to pass laws to address the problems of the nation.
- **Counsel:** MPs and lords believed that, as representatives of the whole of the kingdom, they had a duty to advise the Queen on the government of the country.

In spite of parliament's importance, it met rarely. In Elizabeth's 44 years on the throne she called only ten parliaments, and the average duration of parliament was less than ten weeks. During that time, 433 **bills** became law, over 900 others failed to become law either because they failed to pass both houses or because they ran out of **parliamentary time**.

Between 1589 and 1603 parliament met on four occasions: 1589, 1593, 1597 and 1601.

Elizabeth's dependence on parliament

Parliament's right to authorise taxation was undisputed. This meant that the Queen had to call parliament whenever the government needed more money. However, calling a parliament placed Elizabeth under an obligation to listen to the advice and grievances of her MPs. Parliamentarians took their advisory and representative roles seriously. Therefore, they used each parliamentary session to comment on the Queen's government, and argue for change. This made the Queen vulnerable as parliament had the potential to become a forum for opposition to the Queen.

Elizabeth was particularly vulnerable in the years 1589 to 1603 because she was repeatedly forced to summon parliaments due to the financial strains of war.

Constitutional relationship

The Queen's relationship with parliament was complex. The nature of the constitutional relationship between Elizabeth and her parliaments was disputed. Parliament clearly had rights, and Elizabeth had **prerogative powers** as queen, but the extent of these rights and prerogatives was a subject of hot debate.

Certainly, parliament alone had the right to authorise taxation. The Queen could not force parliament to agree to taxes. Equally, parliament could make laws, although the Queen argued that it could not make laws on every issue. Speaking on the Queen's behalf in 1571, Nicholas Bacon, **Lord Keeper**, argued that parliament had the right to make laws for the good of the commonwealth, but parliament should not interfere in matters of state. For Bacon, the good of the commonwealth meant the good of the people, and therefore included matters such as relief of the poor, and the welfare of towns and cities. Matters of state, which Elizabeth alone had the right to deal with, included the kingdom's relationship with other countries, war and peace and religion. Bacon's 1571 speech set out Elizabeth's understanding of her relationship with parliaments until the end of her rule. Even so, this distinction was not respected by all MPs.

The Queen had the right to veto bills, even when they had been passed by the Commons and the Lords. Moreover, Elizabeth was prepared to use this power: she vetoed 72 bills during her reign.

2 Sources of conflict

There were several sources of potential conflict between Elizabeth and her parliaments:

- **Parliament's role:** The Queen and parliament both had certain rights. There was disagreement between the Queen and her advisers and MPs over the extent of the royal prerogative and parliament's right to interfere in the Queen's business.
- **Taxation:** The Queen routinely needed more money. However, some MPs argued that increased taxes were putting a significant burden on the poor.
- **Religion:** Some MPs wanted England to become more clearly Protestant. The Queen argued that the government of the Church was part of her prerogative and therefore parliament should not interfere.
- **Monopolies:** The Queen had the right to grant exclusive licences for the production of goods. Parliament objected to monopolies because they forced the price of goods up and made life more expensive for the Queen's subjects.

3 Elizabeth's parliamentary management

While the role of parliament, taxation, religion and monopolies all proved sources of conflict, the Queen used a variety of methods to manage parliament and therefore minimise clashes. The Queen could not directly control parliament, but she could manage it indirectly through her speeches in parliament, through her parliamentary supporters and through ceremony and patronage.

> ### Note it down
> The Queen had a variety of ways in which she could manage parliament. Make notes in any form you choose on:
> - the methods the Queen used to manage parliament.
> - specific examples.

Elizabeth's parliamentary speeches

The Queen did not attend parliament, but she was present at the opening and closing of each parliament. On these occasions she could set out her agenda and appeal to the loyalty and common interest of her subjects. In 1589, for example, she appealed to anti-Catholic and anti-Spanish feeling when asking for money to cover the costs of the victory against the Armada. In addition to her official speeches at parliament, Elizabeth could speak to groups of

MPs while parliament was in session. Her famous 'golden speech' of 1601 was given to 141 MPs and effectively diffused tensions over the royal monopolies (see page 185).

The Privy Council

One way in which Elizabeth could influence parliamentary debate was through her supporters in the Commons and the Lords. Members of the Privy Council sat in parliament and acted and spoke on the Queen's behalf. First, privy councillors worked with lawyers prior to the parliamentary session to draft key legislation. This process allowed members of the Privy Council to think through important bills before parliament met and create bills that were likely to receive the support of the majority of the Commons. Secondly, members of the Privy Council could put Elizabeth's case to parliament. In so doing, they could win over opposition. For example, in 1589 Elizabeth's Lord Chancellor Sir Christopher Hatton made a crucial speech arguing that new money was needed to allow England to stand against the Pope, who Hatton described as 'that wolfish blood sucker'. Similarly, in 1593, Burghley explained to the Lords why Elizabeth's wars were so expensive. In so doing, he justified the need for a triple subsidy rather than the double subsidy that had been offered by the Commons (see page 183). Thirdly, Archbishop Whitgift was able to use his position as England's most senior bishop to remove Puritan dissidents from parliament. In so doing, Whitgift was able to quietly remove supporters of Peter Wentworth's succession bill from the Commons (see page 183). Clearly, Elizabeth's close advisers were able to minimise opposition in parliament by drafting legislation that was likely to receive support, by arguing the Queen's case in parliament and by removing the most outspoken sources of opposition.

The speaker

The Queen could also influence the Commons through the speaker. Although the Commons had the right to elect the speaker, in practice the Queen nominated the speaker and the Commons approved the nomination. This helped Elizabeth control parliament because the speaker could help manage the Commons. The speaker gave priority to bills proposed by privy councillors. Therefore, the speaker made sure that parliament's main role was always to ensure that government business was dealt with. Moreover, the speaker could influence which of the bills that were initiated by the MPs got debated by the Commons. Elizabeth put pressure on the speaker to ensure that some bills were never debated. For example in 1601 she instructed the speaker to 'have a special eye and regard not to make new and idle laws'.

Ceremony

Ceremony also emphasised the Queen's power and prerogatives. In so doing, it created an incentive for MPs to support the Queen and therefore helped to minimise dispute. The opening of parliament was an important occasion as it established the Queen's authority in the eyes of her MPs. It began with a procession from the Palace of Whitehall to the Palace of Westminster, where parliament met. The Queen emphasised her authority during the procession by wearing a crown and red parliamentary robes. Her superior status was also highlighted by her entourage. During the procession, the Queen was surrounding by royal bodyguards and knights. On the first day of parliament, the Queen sat on a throne that dominated the chamber where the Lords and Commons met. The throne was embroidered with gold and pearls to emphasise the majesty of the Queen. These informal techniques emphasised the Queen's power and right and, in so doing, helped to remind the MPs that they were in parliament to serve the Queen rather than to oppose her.

Patronage

Patronage also helped the Queen to manage parliament. Simply put, she could reward MPs who supported her and refuse to help those who opposed her. In so doing, she could influence the way in which parliament voted. For example, in 1593, the Queen refused to appoint Francis Bacon to the position of attorney general following his criticism of the triple subsidy in parliament (see page 183).

4 The extent of conflict between the Queen and parliament

Although the Queen had a series of techniques that she could use to ensure she got her own way, there was still conflict between the Queen and her parliaments. Historians have disagreed over the extent of this conflict.

The following section examines the extent of conflict over the role of parliament, taxation, religion, and monopolies, considering the views of different historians.

Note it down

In order to understand the extent of conflict between Elizabeth and parliament, it is necessary to understand parliament's role and the different issues that caused conflict.

Using the 1:2 method (see page x), make notes using the subheadings as a guide. At the end of each major section write a paragraph evaluating the extent of conflict.

Parliament's role

One source of conflict was the correct relationship between the Queen and parliament. This relationship was disputed partly because of constitutional issues. Although Nicholas Bacon had sought to define parliament's role in 1571, MPs continued to try and pass laws on matters that the Queen believed were part of her prerogative. In 1593 Peter Wentworth, a Puritan leader and long-standing MP, proposed a bill requiring the Queen to call a parliament to settle the matter of the succession. He also used parliament to defend the rights of MPs, arguing that there should be complete freedom of speech in parliament (see page 184). Elizabeth argued that the succession was part of the royal prerogative and therefore that parliament had no right to discuss or legislate on the issue. Wentworth was arrested and imprisoned in the Tower of London until his death in 1596. Significantly, parliament did not protest against Wentworth's punishment.

Parliament's role was also disputed because parliament itself had changed during the Tudor period. First, as Elizabeth was a woman, MPs tended to take their advisory role more seriously than if the monarch had been a man. It was traditionally assumed that women lacked certain virtues, particularly relating to warfare (see page 147). Therefore MPs, who were exclusively male, sought to supply the male wisdom that they felt the Queen lacked. Secondly, parliament had traditionally been viewed as a forum in which problems could be presented to the monarch. However, under Elizabeth, parliament became more assertive. Elizabeth's parliaments did not merely raise issues, they also began to propose solutions. In this sense, parliament began asserting its own authority and acting independently of the Queen. Third, parliament had changed because MPs themselves had changed. In 1563 only one third of MPs had attended university or the Inns of Court. By 1593 this had increased to over a half. Consequently, by the end of Elizabeth's reign more MPs were educated and therefore were better able to draft and review legislation, as well as having greater confidence to debate and propose laws.

Tax

Taxation was also a source of conflict between parliament and the Queen.

Historical interpretations: Elizabeth's parliament

Several historians have linked the changing nature of parliament to increased tension between parliament and the Crown. For Neale, this greater education of MPs led to a greater willingness to challenge the Queen and therefore to greater conflict. MacCaffrey argues that the changing nature of the Commons strained the relationship between the Queen and parliament.

Extract 1 From John Neale, *Elizabeth I and her Parliaments, 1581–1601*, published in 1953.

> Birth and education, expert knowledge, practical experience, and corporate solidarity – all were present in abundant measure in the Elizabethan House of Commons. And so was character ... The House of Commons reached maturity in Elizabeth's reign. The instrument was tempered with which the crown was to be resisted and conquered.

Extract 2 From Wallace MacCaffrey, *Elizabeth I: War and Politics, 1588–1603*, published in 1992.

> In encounters between crown and Commons, Parliament was being imperceptibly transformed from its traditional function of presenting and remedying grievances and smoothing frictions, into a forum in which the political classes were airing their views on large issues of state and, on their own, advancing schemes of action. These novel aspirations of the Commons aroused royal anger. The queen resented intrusions into her prerogative. These changes put Elizabeth into a novel and difficult role.

Having read Extracts 1 and 2:

1 Summarise the argument of Extract 2 in one sentence.

2 Write a paragraph arguing either for or against the argument in Extract 2. Use your own knowledge and Extract 1 to justify your claim.

3 Swap paragraphs with a partner. Now write a counterargument to your partner's argument.

Established taxes

According to **parliamentary convention** the first parliament of each reign voted to allow the monarch to collect import and export taxes for the whole of their reign. In addition to this the Queen claimed the following:

- **The 15th and 10th taxes:** These taxed the **movable wealth** in each parish.
- **The lay subsidy:** This taxed the income of **lay persons**.

However, the wealth and income taxes were problematic. They had to be assessed locally without government supervision. Therefore, people tended to underrate their wealth and income in order to pay less tax. Moreover, as people became accustomed to the way the system worked they found it easier to dodge taxes. This meant tax revenues dropped from £140,000 in 1588 to £80,000 in 1603. Elizabeth's government was aware of the decline. In 1593, Chancellor of the Exchequer Sir John Fortescue told parliament that Elizabeth was raising only half of the tax that Henry VIII had done.

The lack of revenue was particularly worrying in the context of Elizabeth's expensive wars. Warfare and declining income from established taxes led Elizabeth to request tax increases from her parliaments.

The triple subsidy, 1593 and 1597

One of the most contentious taxes was the triple subsidy of 1593. Indeed, historian Michael Graves argues that the

---

Historical interpretations: dispute over tax

Historians have interpreted disputes regarding tax very differently. David Dean argues that parliament essentially supported the Queen's desire to raise revenue, whereas T. A. Morris argues that war and the increasing demands for money turned English subjects against their queen.

Extract 3 From David Dean, *Law Making in Late Elizabethan England*, published in 1996.

> As we have seen, MPs certainly voiced concerns over the burden placed on the localities and on the poorer sort. However, whatever their worries, no Elizabethan MP ever suggested that the request for subsidies be refused or even seriously questioned. No subsidy was ever jeopardised by their concerns and although this was in part due to careful management – 1593 aside – it was primarily because there was simply no opposition. No later Elizabethan MP ever objected to granting a subsidy and none suggested that the grant should be made conditionally.

Extract 4 From T. A. Morris, *Europe and England in the Sixteenth Century*, published in 2002.

> In the two crisis periods of 1590–1 and 1599–1601, Elizabeth was obliged to sell crown lands to the value of £645,000 ... the war contributed to tensions resurfacing. The measures to which Elizabeth had to resort for money caused bitterness and resentment. In 1593 the extraordinary request for three subsidies led to three weeks of heated debate before the crown narrowly got its way. The conduct of the war also provoked increasing criticism, especially as it came to be associated with financial and other burdens for the citizen. R. B. Wernham strikes a fair balance in his conclusion that 'the Elizabethan war with Spain and the long-drawn-out burdens that it imposed, did play a considerable part in changing sixteenth–century England from a king-worshiping nation into a king-criticising nation'.

1 Having read Extracts 3 and 4 write a paragraph which:

- identifies the main difference between Extract 3 and Extract 4
- explains why Extract 3 and Extract 4 appear to be arguing different things
- evaluates the extent of the difference between the two extracts.

2 Working in pairs, swap and read each other's paragraphs. Discuss which most clearly identifies and explains the difference. Which paragraph contains the most effective evaluation?

triple subsidy led to 'the most serious confrontation of the reign'. Parliament had agreed to double the lay subsidy in 1589, to pay for England's defeat of the Spanish Armada. In order to support the war against Spain in France, the Commons proposed a double subsidy again in 1593. However, Burghley argued that the government needed a triple subsidy, which was larger than anything ever requested before. Francis Bacon led opposition to the triple subsidy in the House of Commons, arguing that it placed too much of a burden on poor people. However, Bacon was outvoted and the triple subsidy became law.

Significantly, conflict between Elizabeth and parliament did not merely focus on the level of the subsidy. Members of the Commons were also concerned about the way in which the government approached the subsidy. The Commons alone had the right to initiate legislation concerning tax. However, the government proposed that the subsidy should be discussed by a joint meeting of the Lords and the Commons. MPs were outraged by this infringement of the traditional rights of the Commons, and rejected the proposal for a joint meeting by 217 votes to 128.

Even so, there was still room for compromise. Members of the Commons met with Burghley in private, so that Burghley could make his case. As a result, members of the Commons initiated new legislation to grant the triple subsidy. Burghley wanted the full payment in three years but the Commons would only agree to payment over four. The compromise that emerged was that the Commons proposed a triple subsidy to be paid over four years. The new tax was passed by the Commons in spite of Bacon's opposition. Broadly speaking the compromise pleased the Commons and the government: the government got the subsidy it requested and the Commons retained its right to initiate taxation legislation.

The Commons initiated a similar tax in 1597 to sustain the war effort. On this occasion agreement was reached much more quickly. The Commons offered a triple subsidy, payable over three years. Bacon, who had opposed the triple subsidy in 1593, was one of the MPs who proposed the 1597 tax bill. The 1597 triple subsidy passed with little controversy.

Subsidies in the parliament of 1601

The issue of taxation also caused conflict during the parliament of 1601. The ongoing war with Spain and the campaign in Ireland had led to a huge **government deficit**. Consequently, the Queen needed to raise more money. Cecil reported to parliament that the government had a debt of £140,000 and would need an additional £300,000 in order to keep fighting. To raise this money

he asked for an unprecedented four subsidies, or quadruple subsidy. Many in the Commons were horrified. Poverty was widespread in the late 1590s (see pages 192–94) and monopolies had increased the price of many necessities (see page 185). Even so, MPs had to balance their concerns about the high levels of tax required against the news that Spanish troops had recently landed in Ireland. As a result, parliament passed a new tax law agreeing to the four new subsidies.

During the 1590s England was taxed more highly than at any other time under the Tudors. The government tax take rose from around £33,000 a year in the 1570s to around £90,000 a year in the 1590s. Moreover, much of the 1590s, unlike the 1570s, was a time of poverty. Significantly, the new higher taxes were supported by the House of Commons.

Religion

Religion was a concern for many of Elizabeth's parliaments. Earlier parliaments had put forward radical Puritan bills, demanding the abolition of the liturgy and the government of the Church by bishops. However, the Queen had consistently asserted that she alone, as 'Supreme Governor of the Church', could govern the Church and that parliament had no right to pass laws on religion.

Elizabeth's last parliaments tended to be dominated by issues to do with financing wars or dealing with poverty, and therefore religion ceased to be a major cause of conflict between the Queen and parliament in her last years.

The major exceptions to this were debates over the succession and the free speech of MPs. These debates were not explicitly about religion. Nonetheless, parliament's attempts to legislate for the succession were related to earlier religious debates, as parliament was attempting to ensure Elizabeth was replaced by a Protestant king. Equally, the concern for free speech had emerged in the 1570s in response to Elizabeth's practice of locking up MPs who sought to use parliament to reform the Church.

Peter Wentworth played a key role in both debates in the years 1589 and 1593. In 1589 Wentworth raised the issue of the succession. His strategy was to ask Essex to present his pamphlet *A Pithie Exhortation* (see page 170) to the Queen, and then to seek support in parliament. However, before he could initiate his plan he was imprisoned and the manuscript for his pamphlet was confiscated.

Wentworth returned to the succession issue in 1593. On this occasion he linked it with free speech. Wentworth, who had first been sent to the Tower for making a speech in parliament in 1576, had advocated the free speech of MPs for over a decade by 1593. He planned to continue his campaign in the 1593 parliament. Elizabeth resisted these demands, fearing that free speech would be used to criticise and therefore undermine her government. Elizabeth argued that MPs were free to discuss matters related to the commonwealth, but not matters of the state, which was controlled by prerogative power and therefore for the Queen alone.

Wentworth's campaign for free speech in parliament consisted of drawing up a draft bill guaranteeing free speech, submitting a petition to the Queen, and meeting with other MPs before parliament opened to discuss tactics. Elizabeth responded by imprisoning Wentworth in the Tower before parliament began. As he refused to admit his error he stayed there until his death in 1596. Wentworth's fate did not arouse protest from MPs.

His imprisonment did not stop demands for free speech in the Commons. The issue was raised in 1597 and 1601. Crucially, very few MPs argued for total freedom of speech. Most wanted freedom to discuss specific issues, such as monopolies, rather than the general freedom of speech that Wentworth demanded. In 1597 the Queen continued to oppose their demands, using her power to imprison seven MPs. By 1601, however, the Queen had modified her position. In response to the demand for freedom of speech within parliament the Queen merely asked MPs not to waste their time arguing about things that were not their concern.

Historical interpretations: parliamentary independence

Historians disagree over the significance of parliamentary pressure for free speech. Wallace MacCaffrey argues that the Queen was unable to resolve the issue of parliamentary independence. Christopher Haigh, on the other hand, views Elizabeth's management of parliament as largely successful.

> **Extract 5** From Wallace MacCaffrey, *Elizabeth I: War and Politics, 1588–1603*, published in 1992.
>
> Elizabeth stayed the tides of Parliamentary pressure, but it was a holding operation not a victory ... There was an emerging sense that the house was a forum in which they [MPs] were free to set their own agenda, free from royal restrictions. Further they were free on the floor of the house to speak their minds. This was an unresolved conflict that Elizabeth bequeathed to her successors.

> **Extract 6** From Christopher Haigh, *Elizabeth I*, published in 2014.
>
> Freedom of speech was permitted, but only if it was exercised with discretion. Those who, like Peter Wentworth, went too far were punished by the Commons.
>
> The queen did not always, or even usually, manage to confine Parliamentary debate to 'safe' issues. In 1601, when MPs were determined to secure some reform of monopolies, there were long debates on how to proceed on a matter that closely touched Elizabeth's sovereign authority. We should not imagine that Parliament sought deliberately to challenge the powers of the monarchy. Rather, by invoking her prerogative in novel ways, Elizabeth could limit discussion and avoid confrontation. By tactical manoeuvre, skilful oratory, and occasional concessions, Elizabeth usually prevented her Parliament from passing objectionable Bills. And if her techniques failed, she could always veto them. But it is a measure of Elizabeth's success that she rarely exercised the veto on major issues: she did not need to.

1 Having read the extracts:

   a) summarise the key argument of Extract 5 and of Extract 6

   b) select three details from your own knowledge that support the argument of Extract 5. Write these down as a list under your summaries.

2 Working in pairs, swap your summaries and discuss the lists.

   a) Which summary best captures the argument of Extract 5?

   b) Which summary best captures the argument of Extract 6?

   c) Which details most precisely support the argument of Extract 5?

Monopolies

A final cause of conflict was the issue of monopolies. Indeed, it was outrage over monopolies that caused conflict in the parliament of 1601. The Queen had the power to grant individuals the exclusive right to produce certain commodities. These lucrative monopolies could be sold to the highest bidder, or given out as signs of royal favour. Sir Walter Raleigh, for example, had monopolies over the production of tin and playing cards, and Essex had a monopoly over the production of sweet wine. While the Queen had a right to grant monopolies, these led to price rises as sole producers could demand whatever price they liked. The price of steel doubled due to the production monopoly, and the price of starch tripled. This was particularly problematic for monopolies of basic necessities like salt. Elizabeth's subjects had no means of challenging the high prices charged by monopolists because monopolies were based on royal prerogative and therefore law courts, which could only enforce laws passed by parliament, could do nothing.

Some MPs argued that the problem should be solved by parliamentary legislation. However, this would be a radical move because it would directly interfere in the Queen's prerogative powers. Nonetheless, some MPs argued that monopolies clearly affected the commonwealth and therefore, even according to Nicholas Bacon's understanding of the rights of parliament, MPs had a right to consider the issue.

The 1597 Parliament

Monopolies were a major source of tension in the parliaments of 1597 and 1601. The 1597 Parliament, which was called in the context of disastrous harvests and widespread poverty, was dominated by discussion of poor relief. Monopolies were discussed, in part, because the high prices they caused exacerbated poverty. However, the Commons were reassured by the Queen's promise to investigate monopolies and allow her subjects to challenge unjust monopolies in courts of law. These promises meant that the Commons did not pass any legislation to deal with the issue. In this sense the Queen's promises avoided a constitutional crisis because they persuaded the Commons not to initiate legislation which would have interfered with the Queen's prerogative.

The 1601 Parliament

Several historians argue that the 1601 Parliament was Elizabeth's most difficult. According to Neale, the storm over monopolies that had blown up in the 1597 Parliament 'raged' in the parliament of 1601. John Guy concurs, describing the 1601 Parliament as 'the most fractious of the reign'. Monopolies were at the heart of the trouble. In spite of her promise, from 1597 to 1601 the Queen did little to stop the growth of monopolies. Indeed, between 1597 and 1601 Elizabeth granted many new monopolies, including monopolies of currants, iron, cloth, vinegar and pilchards. Consequently, the 1601 Parliament demanded action. MP Robert Wingfield reminded the Commons of the Queen's broken promises, and called on MPs to make a law restricting monopolies – this would have been clear interference with a royal prerogative. Robert Cecil, the most influential man on the Privy Council following Essex's fall, was responsible for the management of parliament. However, he was repeatedly unable to control MPs. Moreover, on one occasion the parliamentary lobby was taken over by a large crowd demonstrating against monopolies. Cecil, clearly alarmed by the demonstration, stated that these actions could have been the first step to overthrowing the Queen and establishing parliamentary rule. Yet, in spite of its strong desire to end the worst of the monopolies, the Commons was not united on how to deal with the issue. Francis Bacon made a speech saying that the issue could only be dealt with by the Queen. Some demanded a bill to end monopolies, others a new petition asking the Queen to act.

Rather than producing deadlock or a major constitutional crisis, strong feeling in parliament led Elizabeth to compromise. First, she sent a message to the parliament recognising that action was needed. Secondly, she invited 141 MPs to a private meeting at which she gave what became known as her 'golden speech'. In the speech she praised the wisdom of her MPs, acknowledged that their concerns were just, stated her desire to defend English people from every kind of tyranny, and announced an immediate royal proclamation to end the worst monopolies. Within three days a proclamation was published ending 12 of the monopolies that MPs had complained about, suspending several more, and restating the right of all subjects to take unjust monopolies to court. In so doing, she won back the loyalty of parliament and preserved her prerogative.

Crisis of patronage

One reason why monopolies became a controversial issue in the 1590s was the crisis of patronage that emerged in Elizabeth's last years. Traditionally, monarchs had exercised patronage by granting titles, with a royal pension. However, due to the war with Spain, Elizabeth could not afford to exercise patronage in this traditional way. Therefore, Burghley advised that the Queen grant monopolies as an alternative to titles. Monopolies did not cost the Queen money, and yet they were a good way of demonstrating royal favour. Consequently, in the later part of her reign Elizabeth increasingly awarded monopolies.

Historical interpretations: the parliament of 1601

Historians tend to agree that the parliament of 1601 was difficult, but that Elizabeth's compromise was a triumph. However, there is a range of views regarding the seriousness of the conflict in 1601:

Extract 7 From Michael A. R. Graves, *Elizabethan Parliaments*, published in 1996.

In the 1590s the financial pressure of war compelled Elizabeth to reduce direct material rewards ... so monopolies rapidly multiplied. Thus far she could hardly be blamed, but when, in 1597, the Commons grumbled about the proliferation of monopolies, she promised reform and did nothing. In 1601 the pent up anger of the governing class exploded in the Lower House. At last Elizabeth was obliged to act. She promised the immediate cancellation of some monopolies, the suspension of others, and that the rest would be examinable before the law courts. This Parliamentary episode must be seen in the right perspective. Parliaments were occasions for the monarch to take counsel. Elizabeth had not heeded such counsel in 1597 and was paying the price for it in 1601. But this was no more than the normal give and take of Parliamentary process.

Extract 9 From Carole Levin, *The Reign of Elizabeth I*, published in 2001.

It was monopolies that caused the crisis with Elizabeth's last Parliament in 1601. Members of Parliament brought up the abuses of monopolies in the House of Commons in 1597 and Elizabeth promised she would end the abuses. Nothing was done to reform the situation, however, and indeed in the next four years the abuses and grievances became much more intense. When Parliament met again in October 1601, members of the House of Commons were furious not only over the abuses, but also over Elizabeth's Privy Council's failure to do anything about these destructive practices.

Elizabeth, at the last moment, took control of the situation. She promised to cancel those monopolies that caused the most harm. In three days a royal proclamation cancelled the worst of the monopolies and promised punishment to those who had abused the system. The proclamation also, however, asserted the queen's right to issue patents if she so desired.

Extract 8 From John Guy, 'Elizabeth's second reign', in John Guy ed., *The Reign of Elizabeth I: Court and Culture in the Last Decade*, published in 1995.

The monopolies debates of 1597–98 and 1601 produced the ugliest parliamentary scenes before the revival of many of the economic privileges and abuses promoted by courtiers and privy councillors solely for their private gain ... Shortly before the 1601 Parliament assembled, Lord Treasurer Buckhurst and Cecil attempted a last minute survey of monopolies in an effort to prune the worst of them before it was too late. But the task was not completed, and when the 1601 Parliament assembled, the outcome was a minor constitutional crisis.

1 Having read the three extracts:

   a) draw a table, with columns labelled Extract 7, Extract 8 and Extract 9
   b) in the first row list all of the causes for conflict during the 1601 Parliament
   c) in the next row comment on how significant the issue of monopolies was as a source of conflict, according to each extract
   d) in the final row summarise the extent of Elizabeth's success according to each extract.

2 Now swap tables with a partner. How far do you agree on the extracts' interpretations of the 1601 Parliament?

Assessing the 1601 Parliament

Historians disagree over the extent of conflict during the 1601 Parliament. On the one hand, there was outrage concerning the Queen's inaction over monopolies and indignation over the request for four subsidies. Yet, on the other hand, the Commons eventually accepted the tax increase and the issue of monopolies was settled without a constitutional crisis.

The 1601 Parliament was also responsible for the extension of the Poor Laws, which were designed to remedy the extreme poverty that England had experienced since the mid-1590s (see page 197). The effectiveness of the Poor Laws is discussed in the next chapter, but crucially the passing of the Poor Laws did not produce controversy. The 1601 laws drew together previous poverty legislation and built on it, creating a more extensive system of poor relief. Significantly, the Commons were acting within their constitutionally defined rights by addressing issues of commonwealth, and the Queen supported their initiative, as she was concerned for the well-being of her people. Moreover, the 1601 Poor Laws were created by co-operation by the Commons, the Privy Council and the Queen.

Conclusion

Elizabeth's final parliaments were not easy. There were disputes over taxation, the extent of parliament's powers, religion and monopolies. However, there was also co-operation, often over the same issues and most notably over the Poor Laws. Crucially, while parliament challenged Elizabeth's government, the constitutional relationship between queen and parliament remained intact. The Queen retained her prerogative powers over monopolies, and parliament was able to represent the nation and seek solutions to the problems of the poor. Consequently, through skilful manipulation and artful compromise, the Queen was able to ensure the tax revenues and the support from parliament that she needed.

Extended reading

Historian Stephen K. Roberts considers the nature and significance of Elizabeth's relationship with her last parliaments.

The parliament that sat between 27 October and 19 December 1601 was the tenth and last of Elizabeth I's reign. Altogether, the Queen had built up long experience of handling the Commons and Lords. It is surprising then that the last one was marked by so much bad temper. It is true that half the members of the Commons in 1601 were new to parliament, but there were still 157 MPs who had sat previously. The government's business was in the hands of Sir Robert Cecil, who was a second-generation manager, following his father, Lord Burghley. The problems of 1601 cannot therefore be attributed to lack of experience by MPs or the Queen's advisers. The Queen's reason for summoning the parliament was entirely financial. Faced with an active military threat from Spain, there was a need for revenue from taxation, and a grant by MPs of the main direct tax, the subsidy, became what someone at the time called 'the alpha and omega of this parliament'.

It used to be thought that Elizabethan parliaments were marked by a growing spirit of independence, which made them harder for monarchs to govern. In this view, embodied in classic works on Elizabethan parliaments by Sir John Neale, this waywardness arose from the increased self-confidence of prosperous gentry, merchants and lawyers, which was given a sharp edge by the rise of a 'puritan choir' in the parliaments of the 1560s and 1570s. Much of this interpretation is no longer accepted by historians, in particular the idea of a steady deterioration in relations between queen and parliament. Both the monarch and the parliaments she called needed each other. The Queen needed consent by the House of Commons to tax the propertied, and the members of both houses of parliament wanted these assemblies to continue, so that the problems of the country, known as 'grievances', could be met. Grants of taxes and discussion of 'grievances' were normal parliamentary business, and historians have tended in recent decades to focus on these normal features, rather than on conflicts.

Even though we need to see the conflicts in these parliaments as structural tensions rather than as a prelude to a breakdown in the state, certain significant changes in how parliaments operated can be seen over the whole history of Tudor parliaments. Membership of the House of Commons was expanding, from 310 MPs in 1529 to 493 in 1604. Also there were procedural developments. For example, from the 1590s, there were 'general committees' of MPs, in which the rules of debate were relaxed, allowing members to make more than one speech on the same topic. It used to be thought that this was a device created by opposition groups to allow themselves freedom to speak without fear of government control, but it is now accepted that the queen's ministers

Activity

Having read the essay, answer the following questions.

Comprehension

1 What is meant by the following words and phrases:
- 'the subsidy, became what someone at the time called "the alpha and omega of this parliament".'
- '"puritan choir"'
- '"grievances"'
- 'monopolists'

Research

2 Using an internet search engine, write a definition of the 'court of exchequer'.

Interpretation

3 Summarise Roberts' criticisms of Sir John Neale's interpretation of the relationship between Elizabeth and her last parliaments.
4 Summarise Roberts' interpretation of the causes of conflict between Elizabeth and the 1601 Parliament.
5 Summarise Roberts' interpretation of Elizabeth's relationship with her last parliaments.

Evaluation

6 Using your own knowledge, write a paragraph explaining how far you agree with Roberts' interpretation of the relationship between Elizabeth and her parliament in her last years.

welcomed the development as a means of getting more business more speedily through the House.

The main issue that soured the atmosphere of the 1601 Parliament was that of monopolies. These were grants to individuals, by which they enjoyed the sole right to produce particular goods or services. There was a very large range of monopolies or 'patents', as they were called: salt and playing-cards were examples. Monopolies were actually very useful devices for the Queen, because in exchange for a patent, the monopolist would have to pay a large sum of money to the cash-starved government. Elizabeth had exploited this means of raising revenue ruthlessly, and had not responded to the growing calls for redress. The monopolists were hated – 'bloodsuckers of the commonwealth', one MP called them – and some sat in parliament. By 1601 calls for their abolition had become a clamour, but their presence in the Commons did nothing to cool the over-heated atmosphere. When the list of patents was read out in the Commons, William Hakewill asked sarcastically whether bread was on the list, implying that even that staple commodity would soon be monopolised. The ensuing argument in the Commons on whether to bring in a bill or to petition the Queen again, which became dangerous when a London crowd invaded the lobby and stairs of the parliament building, was defused when ministers announced that a proclamation by the Queen would outlaw many monopolies. The Queen herself intervened on 30 November, with a majestic address later called the 'golden speech'.

A number of bills that were introduced into the Commons, notably on reforming the Court of Exchequer and on exporting cannons, failed to make any progress in this parliament, but probably the most significant bill to fail was the bill on pluralities, which would have placed restrictions on the right of a clergyman to hold more than one church living. It was the kind of bill that Puritans would wholeheartedly support, but in this parliament it was unsuccessful, and the debates brought out the negative, anticlerical temper of the MPs, rather than any Puritan zeal. Neale interpreted this failure as reflecting the muted quality of Puritanism in this parliament, but we should note the recent destruction of the faction around the Earl of Essex, leaving the Cecil family unchallenged. It may be that we need to see the most vocal expressions of Puritanism in Elizabethan parliaments not as forerunners of civil war conflicts, but as symptoms of faction-fighting in Elizabethan Privy Councils.

Stephen K. Roberts is a historian based at the History of Parliament Trust. He is currently working on the history of MPs and constituencies of Devon. His publications include *Recovery and Restoration in an English County*: Devon Local Administration.

Work together

Having completed the activity, swap your notes with a partner. Consider:

1 Did you both spot the same criticisms of Sir John Neale?
2 Did your partner miss anything?
3 Did you identify the same causes of conflict in Roberts' essay?
4 Did you agree with your partner's summary of Roberts' interpretation of Elizabeth's relationship with her last parliaments?

5 What was good about your partner's summary of Roberts' interpretation?
6 Can you learn anything about Roberts' interpretation from your partner's summary?
7 How far did you both agree with Roberts' interpretation?

Use these questions to feed back to each other and improve your analysis of the extracts.

Essay technique: Integrating your own knowledge

Section C of the exam requires you to evaluate the interpretations offered by the two extracts. You will need to consider the interpretations in the light of your own knowledge of the debate. Therefore, once you have identified the interpretations (see page 159), and worked out the structure of your essay (see page 175), you will need to integrate your own knowledge into your essay.

Imagine you are answering the following question:

> **In the light of differing interpretations, how convincing do you find the view that in the last years of Elizabeth's reign there were 'collisions between rulers and ruled' (Extract 1)?**
>
> **To explain your answer, analyse and evaluate the material in both extracts, using your own knowledge of the issues.**

You should integrate your own knowledge to support and challenge different aspects of the extract. You can plan this quickly in the exam by annotating the extract; you could use different-coloured pens to indicate support and challenge.

As you go through the extract consider the strengths and the weaknesses of the interpretation. It is a good idea to make a brief note of your overall judgement at the bottom of the extract.

An example has been done for Extract 1:

Support: Neale argues that Elizabeth's parliaments were a forum of conflict.

> **Extract 1** From G. R. Elton, *Studies in Tudor and Stuart Politics and Government*, published in 1981.
>
> Historians have traditionally concentrated on conflict between the queen and parliament. John Neale, to take a very relevant case, found an accumulation of unremitting political differences. The impression he leaves is that meetings of the Elizabethan Parliament were notable mainly because they set the stage for collisions between rulers and ruled and gave dissent an opportunity to disrupt government. It could be argued that parliamentary conflict only demonstrated the existence of disagreements, which parliamentary debate helped to solve. Parliament might be regarded as a safety valve in the engine of government. However, there is really no sign that in the sixteenth century disputes in either House helped to ally conflict. From the 1590s the history of parliament is one of increasing criticism, increasing exasperation, increasing failure to restore stability.

Challenge: Parliament helped deal with problems.

Support: From 1590s parliament was increasingly unable to restore stability.

Extract 2 From Paul Johnson, *Elizabeth I*, published in 1976.

Elizabeth was not to know that her 'Golden Speech' was to be printed and reprinted, in the next two generations, as a testament to her political virtue, and an admonition to her successors, so that James I and his hapless son were to come to regard her as possessing some mystical ownership of the affections of the English people. Among other things the 1601 Parliament summarised and codified the social legislation on poverty and employment, which had been one of Elizabeth's abiding interests.

Elizabeth's last Parliament was critical, active and vigorous in viewing the shortcomings of society. But it still had a strong sense of partnership with the monarchy, and gratitude to the remarkable woman who had made this possible.

Activity: Using own knowledge

Using the question on page 190 complete the following activity:

1 Read both extracts and analyse them by looking for:
   • the main arguments
   • counterarguments
   • evidence
   • contrasting arguments between the extracts
   • aspects of the extracts that support each other.
2 Make notes on Extract 2 to show how you can support or challenge different aspects of the extract using your own knowledge.
3 Make a brief note of your overall judgement on Extract 2.
4 Make a full essay plan, showing how you will structure your essay, and where you will use the different aspects of both extracts and where you will bring in your own knowledge.

TIP: Own knowledge should be used to support or challenge the interpretations contained in the extracts; it should not dominate the essay.

Work together

Having completed the activity 'Using own knowledge', consider the following questions with a partner:

1 Did you both identify the same arguments and counterarguments in the extracts?
2 Did you agree about which aspect of Extract 2 was the biggest contrast to the main argument of Extract 1?
3 How did your partner's use of own knowledge differ from your own?
   • Did they use it to support the same things?
   • Did they use it to challenge the same things?
4 Did you miss anything that you should note down?
5 What can you learn from your partner's approach?
6 Whose use of own knowledge best analysed the interpretations contained in the extracts?

Use these questions to feed back to each other and improve your essay planning.

Activity: AS-style question

Study Extracts 1 and 2.

Historians have different views about whether there was a general crisis of government in the last years of Elizabeth I's reign. Analyse and evaluate the extracts and use your own knowledge of the issues to explain your answer to the following question:

How far do you agree with the view that the last 10 years of Elizabeth's reign was a period of constant conflict between the Queen and her parliament?

4 The importance of harvest failures in the 1590s and the growth of social distress

Overview

The 1590s was characterised by poverty and social distress. Repeated bad harvests, population growth, inflation, and declining wages led to a decline in living standards for most and starvation for some. Elizabeth's subjects coped with the dearth in a variety of ways. Some sought charity, others were helped by government poor relief, some turned to crime or resorted to prostitution, others rebelled or discussed the possibility of a new and better government.

According to some historians these economic problems threatened to destabilise Elizabeth's government. According to this view, social distress was exacerbated by continual warfare which led to high taxes, further impoverishing communities. Many returning solders, unable to find work or to readjust to the rhythms of civilian life, turned to crime or rebellion. Some historians link poverty and social distress to problems at the top of government. According to this view, Burghley and Cecil feared that popular unrest would lead to a nationwide rebellion. Therefore, they were concerned by the growing popularity of Essex, fearing he might become the leader of a popular rebellion. Cecil, particularly, was concerned with the political consequences of the dearth in the context of Elizabeth's imminent death. He feared that rabble rousers would capitalise on the political instability caused by her death and widespread poverty to create a revolution. Therefore, he made every effort to ensure a smooth and clear succession in 1603. Bad harvests also lead to religious agitation. After all, it was widely assumed that poor harvests were a sign of God's displeasure with England and some even believed that it reflected God's rejection of Elizabeth's rule.

Other historians have focused on the ways in which Elizabeth's government sought to solve these problems. A combination of state welfare, harsh punishments, compromise made at a local level, and the support of the gentry and the yeomanry prevented a mass rebellion. Neither Essex's rebellion in 1601 nor Elizabeth's death in 1603 led to the civil war that Burghley and Cecil had feared.

This chapter considers:
1 The causes of harvest failure and social distress
2 The extent of social distress
3 Social distress and political crisis
4 Sources of Elizabethan social stability

1 The causes of harvest failure and social distress

The major cause of poverty and social distress was long-term population growth. The English economy was simply unable to provide sufficient work and food for the growing population. Bad harvests did not cause the fundamental problem but they did make poverty worse, particularly in the period of dearth from 1596 to 1598. The war also exacerbated the problem, particularly in areas where troops were stationed on their way to Ireland or the Continent.

Population growth

Population growth was the primary cause of poverty. Although figures for the population of England in the sixteenth century are imprecise, the best estimates suggest that England's population grew from around 2.3 million in 1524 to around 4.1 million in 1603. In Elizabeth's reign alone the population grew by approximately 35 per cent.

Social distress

Social distress is a phrase used to refer to a variety of problems experienced as a result of economic hardship. Poverty is one of the most obvious aspects of social distress. However, it also refers to the loss of status that accompanies unemployment or loss of income. It may also refer to profound hopelessness, caused by economic problems.

Population growth had a series of social and economic consequences:

- **Growing inequality:** The gap between the rich and the poor widened under the Tudors.
- **Food shortages:** As the population grew, English and Welsh farms struggled to feed the population.
- **Unemployment:** There were too few jobs for the growing population.
- **Price rises:** Shortages of food led to rising prices.
- **Fall in wage rates:** Competition for jobs forced wage rates down.

Overall, rising population led to widespread poverty.

Harvest failures

Poverty and social distress were primarily the result of long-term trends in population growth. Nonetheless, poor harvests led to short-term problems that accentuated the long-term issues. Good harvests would make the life of the poor a little easier, whereas poor harvests would make poverty worse.

England and Wales experienced regular harvest failures during the Tudor period, due to bad weather and the simple farming methods of the period. Elizabeth's later reign was no exception to this. Prior to the 1590s, there had been bad harvests in the years 1586 and 1587. These impacted the early 1590s as the consequences of bad harvests were felt for many years afterwards. It was not until the abundant harvest of 1592 that the impact of these poor harvests lessened. The worst harvests of the period occurred in 1596 and 1597. Again, their impact was felt beyond these years, into the late 1590s.

Harvest failure led to a higher mortality rate among the poor. Indeed, at the peak of the dearth from 1596 to 1598, mortality rates were 26 per cent higher than they were in the 1580s. While death from starvation was rare, long-term malnutrition led to a greater susceptibility to disease. Additionally, more people died from eating rotten food. Parish registers for years of dearth show increased mortality rates in Essex, Kent and Suffolk, but the worst affected areas were in the north of England.

Historical interpretations: the importance of harvest failures

Historians have different perspectives on the impact of harvest failures on late Elizabethan England. John Guy argues that even in the 1590s famine did not lead to mass starvation. On the other hand, Roger Lockyer argues that the dearths caused a nationwide problem and a much higher death rate.

Extract 1 From John Guy, *The Tudors*, published in 2010.

The greatest triumph of Tudor England was its ability to feed itself. A major national subsistence crisis was avoided ... Poor harvests resulted in localised starvation and higher mortality, the most serious crop failures being in 1555–6 and 1596–7. In fact, as the effect of a bad harvest in any particular year lasted until the next good or average crop was gathered, the severest dearths lasted from 1555 to 1557, and from 1596 to 1598. Yet devastating as dearth and disease proved for the affected areas, especially for the towns of the 1590s, famine did not lead to mass mortality on a national scale.

Extract 2 From Roger Lockyer, *Tudor and Stuart Britain: 1485–1714*, published in 1964.

For the greater part of Elizabeth's reign harvests were reasonably good, with occasional years of abundance. But 1594–7 saw four successive years of crop failure which produced such an acute shortage of grain that there were food riots in many counties. The north east was harder hit than the south with reports that some of the poorer inhabitants were 'starving and dying in our streets for lack of bread.' But even in the southern town of Reading, the number of deaths increased fourfold. Over the country as a whole the death rate in 1596–8 may have been as high as six percent.

1 Having read Extracts 1 and 2:

   a) summarise the key argument of the two extracts
   b) select three details from your own knowledge that support the argument of Extract 1. Write these down as a list under your summaries.

2 Swap your summaries and discuss your lists:

   a) Which summary best captures the argument of Extract 1?
   b) Which summary best captures the argument of Extract 2?
   c) Which details most precisely support the argument of Extract 1?

Warfare

Elizabeth's military campaigns also had an impact on poverty. Estimates suggest that during the period 1585 to 1603 the government spent:

- £161,000 defeating the Armada
- £424,000 on the war in France
- £575,000 on naval warfare
- £1,420,000 on war in the Low Countries.

Added to this, in the period 1593 to 1603 the government spent £1,924,000 on war in Ireland. The majority of this money was raised by taxation (see page 183). High taxation added to financial pressure on Elizabeth's subjects.

In addition to the general pressure of high taxation, the military placed burdens on specific regions. Kent was particularly hard hit. Taxes on Kent from 1589 to 1603 totalled £107,000, more than other regions due to the need to sustain coastal defences. What is more, soldiers were garrisoned in Kent on their way to war in France and the Low Countries, and many soldiers were **demobilised** in Kent on their return. This added to food shortages in the county as the soldiers needed to be fed. It also added to problems of crime and **vagrancy** when the soldiers returned.

2 The extent of social distress

The extent of social distress changed over time, and differed from region to region. Nonetheless, there is clear evidence that social distress was widespread during the 1590s.

Note it down

Skim read this section and note down the different categories of social distress discussed. Use these as the headings in a note-making style of your choice. Finally, make detailed notes on the extent of social distress across the country in the 1590s.

The scale of poverty

Elizabethan records show high levels of poverty across the country:

- Figures from London indicate that at least 16 per cent of the capital's population lived in poverty during the mid-1590s.
- The Ipswich census of 1597 indicates that 13 per cent of the population lived in poverty.
- There was no official definition of poverty in the 1590s. Rather, these figures reflect the proportion of people receiving regular relief.

Poverty was clearly much worse in the 1590s than it had been earlier in the century. For example, estimates suggest that in 1517 there were only around 1,000 poor people living in London. This grew to around 12,000 in 1594, and 16,000 in 1596 – one of the worst years of the dearth. The population of London doubled in that period; rates of poverty increased sixteenfold.

Prices, pay and charity

Growing hardship was evident in rising prices, falling pay and diminishing charity.

In terms of food, the price of grain doubled in the mid-1590s. Londoners were particularly hard hit. Food prices were at least 25 per cent higher in the capital than in the regions. For example, in London the price of grain rose from 17 shillings in 1592 to 47 shillings in 1596. Grain was not the only commodity affected. Price increases affected all types of food. Indeed, it is estimated that a diet of bread, beer, cheese and butter which cost 1 ¼ pennies a day in 1585 would have cost 2 pennies in 1595, an increase of 75 per cent.

While prices rose, earning and charity declined. By 1600 **real wages** were between 30 and 50 per cent lower than they had been in 1500. Additionally, while total charitable giving increased, the amount available had fallen in **real terms**. In London, for example, it is estimated that the value of charitable donations to the poor fell by around 9 per cent from 1570 to 1597.

3 Social distress and political crisis

Social distress led to various forms of popular discontent. These included riots, uprisings and petitions. Social distress also led to rising criminality, military mutinies and talk of **sedition**. Finally, bad harvests and social distress led to concern that God had abandoned England.

Popular discontent

Grain riots were one of the most extreme reactions to food shortages. They were also one of the reactions most feared by the Privy Council. In Kent alone, there were eight riots between 1594 and 1603. The rebellion of 1595 in Wye, a village in the east of Kent, was started by 20 women stealing corn. Similarly, a major riot occurred in St Dunstan's in 1596 when locals stopped a grain cart from leaving the village. Riots were a feature of life in London too. In March 1595 there were riots in Southwark due to the lack of availability of fish. There were further riots at Tower Hill in October concerning starch, a product made from grain. On top of this there were disturbances, if not riots, almost weekly in the capital through the period of dearth due to food shortages.

One of the most worrying events, from the government's point of view, was the Oxfordshire rising of 1596. The dearth led poor people of Oxfordshire to send a petition to their Lord Lieutenant. The petition threatened violence against the rich and their property if grain prices were not lowered. When the Lord Lieutenant failed to act, four men attempted to start a rebellion on Enslow Hill. However, the four conspirators were unable to provoke a rising, and were quickly arrested. Two were **hanged, drawn and quartered** for their part in the scheme.

While the Oxfordshire rising came to nothing, plots and riots filled the Privy Council with dread. They believed that they had the potential to turn into widespread rebellion.

Rising criminality

Dearth also led to a variety of criminal behaviour. Criminal behaviour increased following the end of a period of good harvests in 1592. From 1593 to 1598 the number of crimes prosecuted in common law courts rose every year. For example, in the south-east of England in 1592 there were around 160 criminal cases taken to court. This figure rose to over 350 in 1598. The rise in criminality was linked to the rising grain price. As the price of grain rose due to successive years of poor harvest, criminality increased. Criminality peaked from 1596 to 1598, the worst years of the dearth. The rise in crime was predominantly related to property crime, such as theft and burglary. Again, this indicates that poor harvests were the cause of rising crime rates in the mid- and later 1590s.

Criminality was a particular problem in the cities. Unable to find work in the country, people flocked to the towns. London's population grew rapidly, doubling in the sixteenth century. The growth was particularly fast due to the dearths of the 1580s and 1590s. The population of Whitechapel, for example, grew from about 7,000 in 1570 to about 21,000 in 1600. However, work was scarce in London too. Therefore, people turned to crime, including begging, vagrancy and theft. Prostitution was also a major issue during this period. It is estimated that there were over a hundred brothels in London during the 1590s. The mid-1590s also saw a growth in crimes committed by gangs of former soldiers, who, unable to find work following their demobilisation, resorted to crime.

Military mutiny

Military mutiny was another expression of popular discontent. Mutinies had various causes, but economic factors played a significant role. Soldier's pay was routinely held back to help spread the costs of the war. Rather than getting their full pay, soldiers were given weekly 'imprests' or 'lendings'. Full pay was given only at the end of the campaign. Weekly payments were kept to an absolute minimum and therefore soldiers had to live on extremely limited rations.

Serious mutinies took place in London in 1589 and 1598. The first was in a period of relative poor harvest, the second in a period of dearth. Chester also experienced mutinies. The town was an important base for troops on their way to Ireland. Mutinies erupted there in 1594, 1595 and 1596. Chester experienced a near mutiny of the Kentish cavalry in 1600. Soldiers in Ireland threatened mutiny in 1599 due to their poverty.

Soldiers were not the only people who were provoked to rebel due to Elizabeth's war economy. Tradesmen responsible for supplying the army with food, or horses or people involved with army recruitment, were often forced to wait for months for their pay. This led to unrest in Bristol and Chester in 1602.

Sedition and succession

Sedition was also a concern for Elizabeth's government. Elizabeth's advisers were so concerned about rebellion that sedition laws were made more severe. People guilty of seditious speech were forced to pay a £200 fine, or have their ears cut off. Magistrates also had the power to sentence those guilty of sedition to death. Speculation about a change of government following the Queen's death was also criminalised. Failure to report seditious speech was also criminalised, and local justices of the peace were authorised to report any seditious speech directly to the Secretary of State.

In spite of these harsh penalties, prosecutions for seditious speech continued throughout the 1590s. There were a number of common complaints about the Queen in the 1590s. People accused of claiming that the Queen was a 'bastard' or a 'whore' or that she had many **illegitimate** children appeared regularly before magistrates. The Queen was not the only target of popular discontent. Sir John Spencer, the Lord Mayor of London, was extremely unpopular. In 1595 reports that Spencer was working with **'aliens'** to deprive Londoners of food spread around the capital. Gallows were set up outside his house, symbolising the hatred with which he was viewed. Again in 1597 rumours spread that the Lord Mayor was deliberately creating the famine for his own gain.

While there are no exact figures for the numbers accused of sedition, or punished for speculating about the succession, the fact that the law was strengthened indicates the concern felt by law makers. William Lambarde, Elizabeth's **Keeper of the Rolls** in the 1590s, expressed the concern of the whole government when he argued that seditious speech could destroy 'the bands and sinews of all government …'

Historical interpretations: how far did social distress lead to popular protest?

Historians have disagreed over the extent to which poverty in the 1590s provoked popular unrest. Peter Clark argues that the dearth lead to widespread protests in Kent. Jim Sharpe, by contrast, argues that the failure of the Oxfordshire rising showed that the dearth, on its own, was not enough to cause popular revolt. Finally, Ian W. Archer argues that riots did not pose a genuine threat to England's social order. Rather, they reflected values that were shared by the poor and the elite.

Extract 3 From Peter Clark, *Popular Protest and Disturbance in Kent, 1558–1640*, published in 1976.

The last years of the reign saw severe economic difficulty. After good harvests in the early 1590s there were four bad or poor years in 1594–7. In 1594 it was said that 'all sorts of corn and grain and especially wheat became for the most part both smutty and withered'. In addition the county suffered from trade disruption and recurrent military levies as a result of the Anglo-Spanish war. There was almost an epidemic of peasant abuse against the regime.

Extract 5 From Ian W. Archer, *The Pursuit of Stability: Social Relations in Elizabethan London*, published in 2003.

Disillusionment with the elite does not appear to have been generalised. One of the libels of 1595 owed a lot to Spencer's peculiarly unpleasant personality. Moreover, the disorders, when examined individually, do not seem particularly threatening. The 300 apprentices who assembled in Southwark on 13 June took upon themselves the office of clerk of the market, selling butter at 3d. per pound whereas the owners demanded 5d. They also issued a proclamation demanding that butter be brought to the markets and not sold in inns or private houses. The other food riot occurred when apprentices sent to purchase mackerel at Billingsgate found that the stocks had been bought up by fishwives. A crowd of between sixty and eighty apprentices pursued the fishwives and took their fish, paying for it at the rates appointed by the Lord Mayor. But this account makes it clear how disciplined these crowds were. It was a familiar pattern: disciplined crowds operating according to values which were shared to some extent by the elite in actions designed to remind the magistrates of their duties. The magistrates took seriously the warnings from the crowd that they were failing to discharge their duties properly, for the repression of rioters was accompanied by measures to tighten the machinery of market regulation.

Extract 4 From Jim Sharpe, 'Social strain and social dislocation, 1585–1603', in John Guy ed., *The Reign of Elizabeth I: Court and Culture in the Last Decade,* published in 1995.

In the south at least, there existed a substantial body of poor people who faced hunger and the worsening of their already precarious way of life when the harvest failed. Not all of these people faced escalating bread prices with fatalism.

The limited potential for successful large-scale risings, their capacity to create official fears, and the poor's capacity for pointed comment about their betters were all demonstrated by an abortive rebellion, the Oxfordshire rising of 1596. Without doubt, the background to this rising was bad harvests: dearth. The men at the centre of the conspiracy came together on Enslow Hill on 17 November 1596 in expectation of initiating a popular uprising. Nobody joined them. They were arrested a few hours later, and two of them were hanged, drawn and quartered eight months later at the place where they had hoped to start their rising. The misery and suffering caused by dearth were evidently insufficient, in the absence of other factors, to create a mass revolt.

1 Having read Extracts 3, 4 and 5:
   ● write a paragraph stating how far you agree or disagree with Extract 5.

   Your paragraph should contain:
   ● a summary of the extract's argument
   ● evidence that either supports or challenges that argument
   ● a concluding sentence in which you analyse the extent to which the argument of the extract is valid.

2 Working in pairs, swap your paragraphs, read them and then write two suggestions about how the paragraph could be improved.

God's judgement

The dearth also caused political problems because of its religious implications. It was commonly assumed that bad harvests were a sign of God's judgement. Puritan preachers argued that the sin of the English and the Welsh had caused God to blight the country. They pointed to rising crime, and particularly riots, as evidence that the English people deserved God's wrath rather than his blessing. Moreover, they argued that Spanish forces were being sent, by God, as further punishment for the nation's sin. Some Puritans believed that the dearth and the war, and the plague that struck London in 1593, was evidence that the world was going through the Great Tribulation, the period of suffering described in the Bible as the prelude to the Second Coming of Jesus and the end of the world. Again, they associated this with God's judgement.

Sermons pointing to the sin of the world were not considered seditious, as they blamed the troubles of England on the poor rather than on the Queen. However, they did undermine Elizabeth by indicating that she was queen of a cursed nation, and by suggesting that the Queen's reign would soon be over due to the Second Coming.

4 Sources of Elizabethan social stability

In spite of widespread poverty and fears of rebellion, there was a variety of sources that kept Elizabethan society stable in the 1590s. Sources of social stability indicate that, although there were serious problems of social distress in the period, Elizabethan society had resources that prevented a collapse or overthrow of Elizabethan government. Sources of social stability included the Poor Laws that provided welfare, discipline and punishment to the poor, astute political compromises, and the growing support for the regime from the gentry and **yeomanry,** who benefited from Elizabeth's rule.

Note it down

Using a note-making style of your choice, make notes on the sources of social stability in late Elizabethan England. Using the subheadings as a guide, make sure that your notes:
- explain the reason why these different factors led to social stability
- give details of the different aspects of these sources of stability.

Having made notes on this section, write a paragraph explaining which source of social stability was the most significant.

Poor Laws

The Poor Laws of 1598 and 1601 were an important source of social stability in the 1590s. They reflected the religious views of the day in three ways:

- First, the Poor Laws provided economic relief for the poor, reflecting the Protestant view that the rich had a responsibility to provide for the poor.
- Secondly, the economic relief was minimal. This reflected the view that God had created a world in which there was a natural hierarchy. According to the New Testament, the Church (which in the 1590s was believed to be the same as the nation) was a body, which like the human body, was made up of many parts. The rich were like the nation's stomach which received lots of good things and then circulated them to the rest of the body. Workers were like the hands, who would never grow rich but performed the equally important function of manual labour. Based on this view of the nation, the Poor Laws did not attempt to create social or economic equality.
- Finally, the Poor Laws contained measures to punish and discipline the poor. This reflected the Protestant belief that poverty was the result of sin, particularly the sins of idleness and drunkenness. Therefore, the poor needed to be punished for their sin and disciplined in order to live more righteous and prosperous lives.

The origins of the Poor Laws

The Poor Laws passed by the Parliaments of 1598 and 1601 were passed primarily in response to the dearth of 1596–98, which made poverty an important issue for Elizabeth's last two parliaments. MPs realised that consequences of the dearth of the 1590s were more severe where there was no provision for the poor. Therefore, late Elizabethan poverty legislation built on measures passed by earlier parliaments, particularly those of 1563, 1572 and 1576, to create a national system.

Moreover, the new laws extended the Poor Laws to cover a new group. Existing laws divided the poor into two groups: 'the impotent poor' and the 'vagrant poor'. The former were people who could not work due to old age or disability and therefore qualified for economic support. The latter were considered criminal and therefore subjected to various forms of corporal punishment, including whippings or being pilloried or put in the stocks. By the late 1590s it was recognised that there was a third group: the 'labouring poor', people who worked but were poor due to falling wages, rising prices and occasional unemployment, who also required discipline and help.

Welfare and discipline

The late Elizabethan Poor Laws continued to offer welfare to the 'impotent poor'. The Poor Laws worked through local parishes. The 1598 Act gave overseers the authority to collect a 'Poor Rate', a compulsory contribution from everyone in the parish. The Poor Law also established a mechanism for transferring money from rich parishes to poor parishes. Poor Law overseers were also required to pay a pension to the parish's 'impotent poor'. The usual rate was sixpence a week, but more was available at times of extreme hardship, and there are accounts of more being available at Christmas. As working people spent between 10 and 15 pence a week on food in the 1590s, these rates were not enough to live on, but they were a valuable supplement to the money that the 'impotent poor' made from activities such as

collecting and selling firewood, **gleaning** and from charity. By 1603, across London around eight per cent of households received weekly Poor Law pensions. However, records show that another seven per cent of households were in need of occasional support.

The late Elizabethan laws also covered 'the labouring poor'. This group was problematic because they did not fit into the existing Elizabethan assumption that most poverty was a result of sinful idleness. Nonetheless, law makers recognised that an increasing number of working people were poor. Specifically, they were concerned that working people were being drawn away from godly work towards ungodly crime by their poverty. Therefore, the late Elizabethan Poor Laws attempted to help the 'labouring poor' in two ways:

Historical interpretations: the significance of the Poor Laws

The Poor Laws helped promote social stability in a variety of ways. Steve Hindle considers the extent of economic help that they provided, whereas Ian Archer focuses on the Poor Laws as a method of social control.

Extract 6 From Steve Hindle, *Poverty and the Poor Laws* in Susan Doran and Norman Jones (eds.) *The Elizabethan World*, published in 2014.

The Elizabethan poor laws constituted a tremendous political achievement and were revolutionary by European standards. No other European nation had the political ambition, let alone the infrastructural reach, to co-ordinate a national system of parish–based taxation to fund payments to its poorer subjects. The targeted system of payments of cash sums recorded in overseers' accounts, supplemented as they were by occasional gifts of food, fuel and clothing, are entirely characteristic of a system that could be remarkably sensitive to local need. But the system could also be grudging, never contributing enough to the household budgets of the poor to allow them to subsist entirely 'on the Parish'.

... Poor relief was, furthermore, a privilege only ever enjoyed by a tiny minority, for the poor on relief were a relatively small core surrounded by a periphery of people, who were still making shift * even when the poor laws were being enforced.

*making shift: trying to survive by doing odd jobs and making the most of the small amount they had.

Extract 7 From Ian W. Archer, *The Pursuit of Stability: Social Relations in Elizabethan London*, published in 2003.

The operation of the poor law in the later sixteenth century served to emphasise the dependence of the poorer members of the community on the wealthy, who therefore also enjoyed greater opportunities to mould the behaviour of the poor. Proclamations, statutes and sermons pushed ever more vociferously the binary classification of the poor into the categories of the deserving and undeserving. Such a system of classification offered a means of defining the boundaries of acceptable behaviour among the poor, fitting well with the ambitions of the godly to reform popular manners.

Having read Extracts 6 and 7:

1 List the different ways in which the Poor Laws supported social stability.
2 Write a paragraph explaining which aspect of the Poor Laws was the most effective at creating social stability.
3 Swap lists and paragraphs with a partner. Discuss which list is the most comprehensive, and which paragraph puts forward the most convincing argument.

- First, funds were allocated to buy hemp or wool for the 'labouring poor' to turn into yarn or cloth in order to supplement their incomes. Law makers believed that the extra work would provide an alternative to crime and that the hard work would help discipline the 'labouring poor' and, in so doing, save them from a life of sinful idleness.
- Secondly, the Poor Laws forced the children of the poor into apprenticeships. This ensured that parents would not have the burden for providing for their children. Moreover, the children would be disciplined by the apprenticeship. Consequently, the parents would be saved from poverty and the children from a life of idleness.

Punishment

In addition to providing welfare for the 'impotent poor' and discipline for the 'labouring poor' the Poor Laws helped generate social stability by authorising the punishment of the 'vagrant poor'. The 'vagrant poor' or 'sturdy beggars' were believed to be poor due to their own ungodliness. The Poor Laws authorised parish constables to round up rogues and vagabonds, people who were guilty of theft or begging, and either force them to work or whip them and order them to leave the town or village. Vagrants could also be enslaved or branded with a 'V' for 'vagrant' or 'R' for 'rogue' as a warning of their moral character.

The 1601 Act criminalised a new range of activities, thus extending the opportunities to punish the 'vagrant poor'. Drunkenness, swearing, spending more than one hour in an alehouse, foul language, **bastard-bearing**, working on the **Sabbath** and gleaning were all criminalised. Rogues who engaged in these activities were subject to public punishments, which were examples to the rest of the community. Public punishment was designed to discipline rogues but also remind the rest of the community of the Protestant values of hard work, civility and **chastity**. In this way, the Poor Laws helped to promote civil order by enforcing moral standards across the community. The ultimate punishment, used against the most persistent rogues, was execution. As crime rates rose during the 1590s so did the number of executions. A variety of crimes carried the death penalty. These included murder, rape, sodomy (a term that covered a variety of sexual 'crimes'), arson, robbery, theft of anything worth more than 12 pennies, and witchcraft. Due to the harshness of the punishment some juries refused to convict people for the lesser crimes as they believed the punishment was unfair. Minor crimes, including small acts of theft, were punished by whipping,

branding, cutting off either a hand or an ear, or being publically locked in stocks or a pillory. Imprisonment was rarely used, except for people who owed money.

Table 1: Number of people sentenced to death in the south-east of England, 1595 to 1598

1595	50
1596	64
1597	80
1598	124

Welfare and civility

Welfare was also used to keep order. Not only did it give people an alternative to a life of crime, it also obliged them to behave well. People who received a parish pension were expected to demonstrate their gratitude by living exemplary lives. They were expected to show gratitude to rich members of the community. Crucially, any sign of resentment, such as criticising the rich, complaining at the price of grain or complaining about Elizabeth, was an indication of sinfulness and, therefore, could lead to withdrawal of their pension. In this sense, the Poor Laws were not merely a means of controlling the 'vagrant poor', they also kept the 'impotent poor' in order.

Compromise with the poor

In addition to discipline and punishment, social order was maintained in times of dearth through compromise. Indeed, although rioting was common, petitions were often the first response of working people to economic hardship. Petitions set out the demands of the poor, and gave mayors and other local leaders an opportunity to address their concerns. Petitions often demanded a fixed price for certain food, and an end to either starch making (which used grain) or to grain exports. Often compromises were reached.

In reality the grain riots were less of a threat than the Privy Council believed. The riots in the Kentish villages of Wye and St Dunstan's (see page 194) actually involved fewer than a hundred people. Moreover, they merely wanted a reduction in the price of grain, there was no desire to overthrow the government. For example in 1596 there were proclamations in Chester, a town that had witnessed a great deal of disorder (see page 195), outlawing the manufacture of starch. In London authorities stockpiled wheat and bread which they sold at below the market price regularly during the 1590s. Similarly, in Coventry the government supplied between 600 and 700 people a week with relatively cheap grain in 1597 and 1598. Finally, systems of credit became available which provided short-term loans in order to allow people who faced periodic unemployment to keep buying food.

Compromises of this sort were effective because often the demands of those who rioted were very limited. Rioters did not want to overthrow the government, they merely wanted cheap bread, and with planning this could be delivered. Moreover, the number of people who took part in riots was actually quite small. In Kent, where there were many riots in the 1590s (see page 194), crowds were reasonably small, never more than 100. Even the 1595 riot in Southwark attracted fewer than 300 people, from a city of 200,000. Notably, women played a leading role in these riots. This was partly because of the sexism of local constables. Peasants learned quickly that constables were more likely to punish men than women for violent crimes. Additionally, women rioting may have been a result of the difficulties they experienced in feeding their families. This is one of the reasons why so few of those who rioted in Kent were punished. Magistrates were also prepared to recognise that some grievances were genuine, again indicating a willingness to compromise on the part of the authorities.

Compromise helped to defuse social tension by meeting enough of the demands of the poor enough of the time to avoid widespread rebellion.

Religion, charity and racism

Religion did a great deal to promote social stability, although from 1599 this was at the expense of black people living in England. First, religion promoted charity and hospitality. The campaign to encourage fasting and alms giving began in London in August 1596. On Christmas Day 1596 the Archbishop of Canterbury devoted his sermon to the need of the rich to repent, at which point it became a national campaign. The Archbishop argued that the famine was partly caused by the sin of **gluttony**. Rich people had been eating too much and allowing the poor to go hungry. He recommended that the rich should repent by fasting, living frugally and sharing food with the poor. The Privy Council joined the campaign by asking rich people to fast one day every week and to give the food that they did not eat to the poor.

The campaign helped to preserve social stability in a number of ways. First, the campaign encouraged voluntary charity at the height of the dearth, and in response to the riots of 1595 and 1596. In this sense it attempted to address the concerns of the poor. Second, it recognised the inadequacies of the Poor Law prior to the 1598 reforms. It did this by addressing the issue of the 'labouring poor', who were not covered by the pre-1598 legislation. Remarkably, the campaign did not appeal to the traditional distinction between the 'impotent' and 'vagrant' poor. In this sense, all of the poor, whatever their moral character, were supposed to benefit from the charity of the rich. Therefore, the 'labouring poor' were encouraged to expect charity from the local aristocrat, the local gentry and the yeomanry. Third, the campaign was tied closely to Elizabeth. Statements and sermons that promoted the campaign stressed Elizabeth's desire to help the poor, due to 'her gracious and tender affection' for her subjects. In this way it presented the Queen and the government as the benefactors of the poor rather than their enemies. Finally, the campaign led to some impressive acts of charity that genuinely aided the poor. For example, in Worcester the rich fed 200 poor citizens every week throughout 1597. Additionally, in Sussex, Lord Buckhurst spent £154 on grain that fed the poor in six villages from January to March 1597.

However, the concern about sin had a more sinister side. Elizabeth was concerned that black people were responsible for the hardship of the 'natural subjects'. Black people were often brought to England as slaves. Slavery was justified on the grounds that Africans were naturally 'savage' and naturally suited to menial work. In this sense the white English people believed themselves naturally superior to the black Africans who they enslaved. Whatever white people thought, many black people had, on arriving in England, made their own way, working in Elizabeth's court as entertainers, starting families and working in rich households. Others were forced to continue as slaves or work as prostitutes. Elizabeth linked black people to England's economic problems in two ways. First, some, she claimed, received Poor Law pensions, thus, she implied, depriving white people of money. Second, she was concerned that they were 'infidels, having no understanding of Christ or his Gospel', and were therefore ungodly. Consequently, Elizabeth issued two edicts in 1599 and 1601 ordering the deportation of black people from England. This action reflected hatred of 'aliens' in England at the time. In 1595 a pamphlet was circulated in London accusing 'aliens' of plotting with the Lord Mayor to starve London. Also, hatred of immigrants had been a theme in the riots that took place in London that year. During the 1590s immigrants were often scapegoats for England's economic difficulties. In that sense, Elizabeth's racist edicts helped generate social stability by showing that the government was doing something to remove people who were regarded as racially, morally and economically harmful during the dearth.

Social change in Elizabethan England

A final reason for social stability is the changing nature of Elizabethan society. In essence, Tudor England saw the 'the rise of **the middling sort**': the growth of the gentry and the yeomanry, a new class of property owners. These classes benefited from the sale of Church lands under Henry VIII, and to some extent from the sale of Crown lands to finance the war. The gentry, who had considerable estates, and the yeomanry, who owned smaller estates, became rich during the late sixteenth century through farming. Indeed, as grain prices rose, their profits rose too. Elizabeth's Poor Laws, dating back to the 1560s, protected land owners from the poor. In this sense, the new property owners were protected by Elizabeth's government, and were therefore loyal. Indeed, during the 1590s, these classes identified with the interests of the government rather than the poor. As they became richer they became better educated. They used their education in service of the government. Increasingly it was the local yeomanry who became constables and overseers, using their authority to discipline the poor. Therefore, this new class was an important reason for social stability as they sided with the government and used their position in the community to keep the poor from rebelling.

Black people in Tudor England

Black people have made England their home since Roman times. However, there was a significant rise in the number of black people who lived in England in Elizabeth's last years. This was due, in part, to exploration and England's involvement in the slave trade. English merchants became involved in the Atlantic slave trade in the early 1560s. Sir John Hawkins was the first English trader to transport enslaved people from Africa to Spanish colonies in the Caribbean.

It is estimated that around 1,800 black people lived in England in 1600, approximately half of whom lived in London. Records indicate that there were also relatively large numbers of black people in the port towns of the south-west. Some of England's black population were enslaved. However, enslaved Africans did not work in plantations in England. Rather they tended to work as household servants. Enslaved Africans were also forced to work on some English ships. Indeed, reports from Spanish officials in Peru indicate that Francis Drake employed black people on board his ship. Apparently the enslaved Africans on Drake's ship acted as messengers and spies because they spoke both English and Spanish.

Some black people were employed as entertainers. Indeed, a painting by Marcus Gheeraerts from 1575 shows Elizabeth I surrounded by courtiers including black musicians and dancers. Other nobles followed Elizabeth's lead and employed black entertainers.

Some black people grew rich. Indeed, there are reports from 1597 of black people who owned property and built their own houses in London. Parish records show black people being baptised, married and buried in English churches. Indeed, some of the marriages were between black people and white people, although these appear to be quite rare.

Historical interpretations: causes of social stability

Historians have considered a variety of different sources of social stability. Peter Clark, writing primarily about Kent, argues that there was a variety of causes, not least the provision for the poor and the absence of widespread starvation. Jim Sharpe, on the other hand, emphasises the importance of the yeomanry.

> **Extract 8** From Jim Sharpe, 'Social strain and social dislocation, 1585–1603', in John Guy ed., *The Reign of Elizabeth I: Court and Culture in the Last Decade,* published in 1995.
>
> The emergence of a more affluent and more self-confident gentry has long been a familiar theme of Tudor and Stuart historiography, but more recently attention has focused on the stratum immediately below the gentry, the yeomanry and other lesser property owners. The process was very regionalised, and perhaps at its most marked in the south-east, but recent research is demonstrating how, at least in many arable areas, this group was becoming richer, more market oriented, and more literate and outward looking ... The implications of this process were massively important. It was such men, the natural leaders of village society, whose support and leadership were vital if a large-scale rebellion were to get off the ground. But if they were increasingly regarding themselves as having a stake in the status quo, and if they were increasingly willing to differentiate themselves culturally from the poor, such support and leadership was less likely to be forthcoming. Moreover, the smooth running of local administration, one of the ultimate tests of governmental efficiency, depended upon men from this social level.

> **Extract 9** From Peter Clark, *Popular Protest and Disturbance in Kent, 1558–1640,* published in 1976.
>
> How do we explain the limited scale of popular disturbance in the period 1558–1640? One factor may have been the absence of widespread starvation and famine such as recurred in France during this period. In Kent there are few signs of starvation during the difficult 1590s and the same is probably true of most of the lowland zone. Also influential was the related development of a credit mechanism allowing even poorer folk to secure basic necessities to tide them over the worst years of difficulty.
>
> Another economic factor influencing the size of English disturbances was the increasing levels of poor relief. Finally, the scale of English popular disturbance was also probably affected by political variables, including the growing effectiveness of town and county administration under the late Tudor regime and the attitude of the landed gentry, who increasingly dominated county government.

Read Extracts 8 and 9:

1 List the different sources of social stability.
2 Summarise the argument of Extract 8 in one or two sentences.
3 Write a paragraph that develops a counterargument to Extract 8.
4 Swap your summaries and paragraphs with a partner. Discuss which summary most accurately reflects the interpretation offered by Extract 8. Which paragraph develops the most effective counterargument?

Conclusion

The 1590s was undoubtedly a time of economic crisis. Population growth led to widespread poverty, which was at its worst due to bad harvests during the dearth of 1596–98. Poverty was worse in the 1590s than at any other part of the century, leading to high mortality, rising crime and misery. However, charity, compromise and official poor provision prevented widespread starvation. Riots and seditious speech horrified privy councillors, who believed they were signs of impending rebellion. Religion played a complex role in partly supporting the hierarchy in implying that the poor deserved their misery, partly moving the rich to provide for the poor, and partly undermining faith in the government by implying that England was a land that God had cursed. Nonetheless, English society had many sources of stability which stopped the economic crisis from becoming a political rebellion. The loyalty of the gentry and the yeomanry, church campaigns promoting fasting and alms giving, punishments and social pressure all helped to stabilise England during the troubled 1590s.

Extended reading

Historian Stuart Minson considers the extent to which harvest failures and social distress led to a crisis in Elizabeth's last years.

During the final decade of Elizabeth's reign, back-to-back harvest failures and a period of price inflation across Europe saw the wages of workers reach their lowest value relative to the price of goods at any time between the Black Death and the present day. Yet weather conditions and the course of the European economy were not really in the government's control. It was perhaps the structural inequalities of early modern English society which actually made harvest failures and price increases problematic, but it is neither a surprise nor an aspect of crisis that Elizabethan governors should have failed to address this. In fact, the government's responses to these problems was better co-ordinated and more effective than elsewhere in Europe. If the severity of the dearth is measured in terms of actual mortality, it appears that northern France and the Rhineland fared worse than England, while for the English themselves the 1590s were not as bad as the 1550s or 1630s. Moreover, deaths far above the norm were limited to the terrible year of 1597–98, and only in particular areas, such as Cumberland or Newcastle, did many people actually perish. In some regions like Kent people rioted repeatedly over grain supplies, but these episodes were small in scale and limited in aim. London experienced only one serious riot, in 1595, and the city's government did much to alleviate famine and build solidarity. The Poor Laws of 1598 and 1601 were not new ideas, but they turned the strategies of poor relief, pioneered in towns and national legislation since the early 1500s, into a form that could be systematically implemented. In themselves they had little effect in the 1590s, but they reflect the extensive apparatus of poor relief which was already in operation at this time.

Certainly there was an acute 'sense' of crisis among the elite, as seen in the terrified reports of the Somerset JP Edward Hext on the breakdown of law and order or the dangerous over-reaction by the Privy Council to a failed attempt at a popular march in Oxfordshire in 1596. There was also a sense of desperation among the wider population. Analysis has shown that peaks in prosecution for theft coincided with times of greatest dearth. However, it must be noted that capital convictions, while significantly increasing in 1598, only did so after a third harvest failure followed the previous two. Indeed, the fear and desperation which people experienced was not just a product of conditions during Elizabeth's final years. They were also part of a longer-term process of social polarisation which was dividing families of middling wealth and status down the centre, some being pushed into poverty while others enlarged their property and began to identify with the values of the social elite. Importantly, while the latter were terrified of the possibility of popular rebellion, this also spurred action. A combination of preventative measures, attempts to mitigate the worst suffering, and severe repression of those caught in agitation served to contain unrest. For instance, in London, the provision of subsidised grain stocks and the central organisation of poor relief was combined with the execution of rioters and the appointment of new officials like the provost marshal to co-ordinate policing across the wider metropolitan area.

It must be understood that an actual crisis involves either a breakdown or transformation as a result of problems. In some respects, the harvest failures and unrest of the 1590s did contribute to change. The management of the agricultural economy became more co-ordinated and strategies for insulating communities against problems like famine, plague and disorder were improved. But again, these were part of a longer process, and if the stresses of the 1590s affected this, they were neither a necessary or sufficient cause. Ultimately, the government continued to function, the strategies employed were traditional in themselves, and the structures of government were not drastically transformed. The poor faced crisis on a daily basis, and many lost their lives, but society as a whole did not; the broadening of the elite turned those who might previously have led a popular uprising into loyal supporters of the status quo. The government saw itself as facing crisis conditions, but that is not the same as a 'crisis of government'. Of course, that is not to say that Elizabethan government was just or successful. As J. A. Sharpe has pointed out, although Elizabethan England survived, it did so at the unjustifiable expense of society's most vulnerable and disadvantaged.

Stuart Minson completed his undergraduate studies at the University of Melbourne, and his doctoral work at the University of Oxford. His research focuses on political culture and urban space in Tudor London. He teaches the history of early modern Britain and Europe, in the Department of International History at the London School of Economics, and at the Centre for Medieval and Renaissance Studies, Oxford. He has recently published a piece entitled 'Public Punishment and Urban Space in Early Tudor London.'

Activity

Having read the essay on page 203 answer the following questions.

Comprehension

1 What does Minson mean by the following phrases:
   - 'price inflation'
   - 'there was an acute "sense" of crisis among the elite'
   - 'social polarisation'
   - 'preventative measures'

Evidence

2 Make a list of the examples that indicate that the dearths of the 1590s did not threaten the stability of Elizabethan England.

Interpretation

3 Identify the passage in which Minson defines the term 'crisis'. Paraphrase his definition.

4 Summarise Minson's interpretation of how far harvest failures in the 1590s and social distress created a crisis of government in three sentences or less.

Evaluation

5 Using your own knowledge, write a paragraph explaining how far you agree with Minson's interpretation of the impact of harvest failures and social distress on Elizabethan government.

Work together

Having completed the activity above, swap your notes with a partner. Consider:

1 Did you both spot the same evidence in Minson's essay?
2 Has your partner missed anything?
3 Did you agree on which passage contained the definition of 'crisis'? If not, who was right?

4 Discuss the definition – how good is it, can you think of alternative definitions that might be better?

5 How far did you both agree with Minson's interpretation?

Use these questions to feed back to each other and improve your analysis of the extracts.

Extended reading

Historian Jonathan Healey considers different aspects of the crisis of Elizabeth's last years, evaluating how far the government faced a crisis in the years 1589–1603.

Early in the morning of Sunday 8th February, 300 people assembled outside Essex House on the Strand, the townhouse of Robert Devereux, 2nd earl of Essex. Taking the Crown's emissaries hostage, Essex's band marched into the city of London. Here, they found the Sheriff unwilling to join them, and that barricades had been raised against them. Repulsed on Ludgate, his men slipped back to Essex House by boat, where they prepared for a siege. But once the Crown's forces had brought a cannon from the Tower, Essex knew the game was up. The rebels surrendered in exchange for a fair trial, which did them little good. The traitorous Essex was executed just a fortnight later on the 25th.

It was, all in all, a terrible mess, but the fact that the government was faced with such turmoil, in the capital, and led by someone who had been at the heart of the government just a few years ago, certainly gives a clear appearance of a serious governmental crisis. Nor was this all. Despite the failure of the first Armada, war continued with Spain. This hit trade hard, and meant that the roads of southern England thronged with poor disbanded (and often disabled) soldiers. There were further invasion scares in 1596, 1597, and 1599: on each occasion it was probably only the weather that saved England from oblivion. And there was the looming issue of the succession. Elizabeth studiously avoided naming her successor, as she did not want an opposition party to form around him. James VI of Scotland was the obvious candidate, but would others contest it? If they did, this would mean civil war.

Most severe of all was the social crisis of the 1590s. A series of bad harvests, unusual even by the standards of the time, meant that prices rose drastically. In fact, this was one of the greatest 'cost-of-living' crises in English history. Apprentices rioted in London, and there was dark talk of a mass killing of gentlemen in Oxfordshire.

And yet, in many ways the government was more stable than it had been for years. Though the succession remained a thorny issue, the fact there was a viable Protestant candidate (now Mary, Queen of Scots was out of the way and her claim had passed to her son James VI) meant it was less likely to bring war. This was because England was more comprehensively protestant – the Anglican Church was relatively settled, and the challenges from Catholics and Puritans had not been as threatening as many had feared. The last of the great popular religious revolts had been defeated as long ago as 1570. The last religious revolution, in 1563, was now a generation in the past, and the political nation was made up of people who had grown up under Anglicanism.

Nor did economic conflict have much chance of boiling over into serious upheaval. Arguments over monopolies in parliament were bitter, to be sure, but hardly the stuff of social revolution. When, in 1596, a group of poor farmers from Oxfordshire did hatch a plot to kill local gentlemen, virtually no-one joined in – though the government was concerned enough. Essex's rebellion turned out to be little more than an aggravated street brawl. It would have taken a very unlikely turn of events for this to bring down the government, or even do much more than mildly irritate it.

Indeed, perhaps the biggest lesson is that government functioned quite adequately despite the stresses it faced. Nowhere was this more the case than in local government. Crimes were prosecuted, and taxes were collected. The militia, whose efficiency has perhaps been underestimated, became a useful bedrock in the defence of the realm. The latest research suggests that many local communities, particularly in the south and east, were effectively organising relief for the poor by the end of the reign, giving some succour to those hardest hit by the economic crisis of the 1590s.

So the idea of a crisis is too strong. What is still the case, however, is that there were long-term structural problems that the late Elizabethan state proved incapable of or unwilling to deal with. Puritanism and Catholicism were still there, and discontent from these groups would be seriously destabilising in the seventeenth century. Most serious of all was the failure of Elizabeth's governments to reform state finances. Pandering to the taxpaying classes, who did not want to increase their contributions to the state, meant that in a reign of quite serious inflation, the amount of tax collected actually fell. In real terms, of course, this equated to quite a catastrophic drop. The lack of a viable tax settlement would be a constant thorn in the side of Elizabeth's successor James; and it would be a major reason behind the collapse of Charles I's government in 1639–40, a crisis which did lead to civil war and revolution.

Jonathan Healey is a historian who specialises in early-modern British social and economic history. He is a Fellow of Kellogg College and University Lecturer in English Local and Social History at the Oxford University Department of Continuing Education. He has written articles on the development of poor relief in England and agrarian society 1574–1830.

Activity

Having read the essay on page 205 answer the following questions.

Comprehension

1 What does Healey mean by the following words:
- 'traitorous'
- 'studiously avoided'

2 What does Healey mean by the following phrases:
- 'long-term structural problems'
- 'state finances'
- 'The lack of a viable tax settlement'

3 Who was:
- Robert Devereux, 2nd Earl of Essex

Evidence

4 Make a list of the examples of problems facing Elizabeth's government listed in Healey's essay.

Interpretation

5 Identify the passage in which Healey gives his view on how far there was a general crisis of government in Elizabeth's last years.

6 Summarise Healey's interpretation in 25 words or fewer.

Evaluation

7 Using your own knowledge, write a paragraph explaining how far you agree with Healey's interpretation of the extent of a general crisis of government, 1589–1603.

Work together

Having completed the activity above, swap your notes with a partner. Consider:

1 Did you both spot the same evidence in Healey's essay?
2 Has your partner missed anything?
3 Did you agree on which passage contained the interpretation? If not, who was right?

4 What was good about your partner's summary of Healey's interpretation?
5 Can you learn anything about Healey's interpretation from your partner's summary?
6 How far did you both agree with Healey's interpretation?

Use these questions to feed back to each other and improve your analysis of the extracts.

Essay technique: Overall judgement

Reaching a supported overall judgement is an important part of doing well in Section C. The judgement that you should reach in Section C is similar to the judgement that you should reach in the other sections of the exam (see pages 74–75). However, in Section C, your judgement should be based on an evaluation of the interpretations offered by the extracts, as well as reflecting the overall argument of your essay.

Imagine you are answering the following question:

> **In the light of differing interpretations, how convincing do you find the view that in the 1590s Elizabeth's government was fragile in time of distress (Extract 1)?**
>
> **To explain your answer, analyse and evaluate the material in both extracts, using your own knowledge of the issues.**

Extract 1 From David Dean, 'Elizabethan Government and Politics', in Robert Tittler and Norman Jones eds., *A Companion to Tudor Britain,* published in 2008.

On 21 November 1596 Bartholomew Steer, a carpenter living in the village of Hampton Gay, Oxfordshire went up to Enslow Hill. Only a few men joined him and after two houses they gave up and returned home. Arrested, charged and found guilty under the treason laws, two of the conspirators were executed, others died in prison, possibly as the result of torture. The severity of the government's response to this aborted rising, occasionally described by historians as the 'rebellion of 1596', indicates the fragility of Elizabethan government at a time of distress. Yet, it also demonstrates the stability of the Elizabethan regime. Despite severe economic hardship, few among the poorer and middling sort were willing to join the conspiracy. This 'rebellion', like every other during Elizabeth's long reign was a failure.

In the autumn of 1596 England was in the grip of the worst subsistence crisis of the century. The Privy Council itself noted that the poorer sort had suffered 'great misery and extremity'. Yet when local authorities wanted to prevent grain leaving Oxfordshire the government refused, worried that depriving London markets of grain would provoke food riots like those led by apprentices in 1595. Meanwhile, between forty and sixty men visited Henry, Lord Norris at Rycote, who as lord lieutenant was responsible for law and order in the county. They asked him to help the poor, but warned if he did nothing 'they would seek remedy themselves, and cast down hedges and ditches, and knock down gentlemen'.

Extract 2 From Joseph P. Ward, *Metropolitan London* in Robert Tittler and Norman Jones (eds.), *A Companion to Tudor Britain*, published in 2008.

The mid-1590s, and particularly 1595, was an especially tense period in London. Although some historians have interpreted urban protests as a release-mechanism that ultimately helped to keep society on an even keel, riots over the high prices of fish and butter on 12 and 13 June 1595 apparently served only as a prelude to the marching of a crowd of one thousand apprentices in the direction of Tower Hill two weeks later, with the rumoured intention of looting gunshops and then overturning the City government. In the event, order was restored, although at the cost of placing the City under martial law for the remainder of the summer. The fact that 1595 marked the high point of disturbances in Tudor London even though the economic crisis inflicting the City would not run its course for another two years suggests that London's governors understood their responsibility to respond – or at the very least to appear to respond – to the hardships faced by their subjects. In this way, riots such as those in June 1595 can best be understood as a form of communication among London's social groups.

Planning your essay

Your essay plan might look like this:

Paragraph	
Main argument 1	**Extract 1:** Government's reaction to the 'rebellion of 1596' reflects the fragility of the government. (**Extract 2:** London placed under martial law in 1595.)
Main argument 2	**Extract 1:** Uprisings and protest were a key feature of social life in the 1590s: e.g. Oxfordshire, Rycote and London. **Extract 2:** Government was unpopular and therefore fragile.
Counterargument 1	**Extract 1:** Yet, the government was stable, because rebellions were small scale. Indeed the government had the support of the 'middling sort'. **Extract 2:** Rebellions in London declined during the worst years of the dearth – again indicating stability of the regime.
Counterargument 2	**Extract 1:** National government was stable because the Privy Council was also aware of the 'great misery and extremity' of the people and took steps to ensure grain supplies to London. **Extract 2:** London government was stable because it took its responsibilities seriously and responded to hardship.

The focus of your judgement

Your judgement should focus on the specific interpretation raised in the question. In this case, you need to focus on the extent to which the dearths of the 1590s led to fragility in the government.

Judgements that focus on the specific issue raised by the question are likely to do better than judgements that focus on the general issue of social distress in the 1590s.

Therefore, you could begin your conclusion like this:

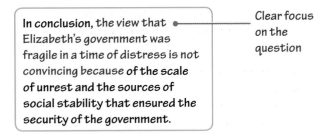

In conclusion, the view that Elizabeth's government was fragile in a time of distress is not convincing because of the scale of unrest and the sources of social stability that ensured the security of the government.

Clear focus on the question

This is a good beginning as it focuses on the key interpretation, and therefore focuses precisely on the question. However, the judgement is not supported and therefore cannot be awarded marks in the highest levels. An improved introduction is given on page 209.

Supporting your overall judgement

As in Sections A and B it is important to support your overall judgement. This can be achieved by evaluating the given interpretation. Specifically, you should weigh up the given interpretation against the other interpretations you have examined in the essay.

For example, the overall judgement you have just read on page 208 could be improved by adding the following evaluation of the different interpretations:

Direct focus on the question.

In conclusion, the view that Elizabeth's government was fragile in a time of distress is not convincing because of the scale of unrest and the sources of social stability that ensured the security of the government. Certainly, Extracts 1 and 2 indicate that the Privy Council monitored unrest closely indicating that they felt Elizabeth's reign was fragile. Mutinies, grain riots, risings particularly in London in 1595, all worried Elizabeth and her councillors, particularly in the context of an ongoing war and uncertainties over the succession. However, in reality, as Extract 1 argues, risings were of a very small scale, and never gained the support of many among the poor, let alone those of the 'middling sort' who were doing relatively well in the 1590s. Moreover, Extracts 1 and 2 both indicate that the government took its duty to provide welfare seriously. Extract 2 argues that this was true of government in London and the parliaments of 1598 and 1601 which passed nationwide poor laws, indicating that at a national level too there was a desire to help those who were worst affected by the dearths. Therefore, although the Privy Council was continually concerned about the threat of rebellion, state welfare, state discipline, effective government action and the support of the new class of gentry and yeomanry meant that Elizabeth's government was far from fragile even in a time of social distress.

Main argument from Extracts 1 and 2 is supported with own knowledge.

Counter arguments from Extracts 1 and 2 are weighed against the main argument.

The final judgement is supported by a summary of the overall argument, and linked back to the question.

This conclusion is an example of high level work because it reaches an overall judgement and supports it by evaluating the interpretations offered by the extracts.

Activity

Plan and then write a conclusion for the question on page 210.

Follow these steps to make a plan:
1 Identify the interpretations offered by the two extracts – remember there may be more than two.
2 Look for contrasting arguments between the extracts, and look for aspects of the extracts that support each other.
3 Make notes on the extracts in order to add your own knowledge.
4 Note down a brief overall judgement.

Follow these steps to write a conclusion:
1 Start by giving a judgement that focuses on the given interpretation.
2 Support your judgement by weighing up the different interpretations contained in the extracts.

TIPS:
- Make sure you refer to both extracts in the conclusion.
- Make sure you use some details from your own knowledge to help weigh up the interpretations from the extracts.
- Use the words 'However', 'Nonetheless' and 'Therefore' to structure the paragraph.

In the light of differing interpretations, how convincing do you find the view that the last years of Elizabeth's reign were marked by a decline and decay in government (Extract 1)?

To explain your answer, analyse and evaluate the material in both extracts, using your own knowledge of the issues.

Extract 1 From John Guy, The Tudors, published in 2000.

The most obvious area of decline in Elizabeth's last years was that of government. Did Elizabethan institutions succumb to decay during the war with Spain? Criticism centres on the inadequacy of taxation, local government and military recruitment; the rise of corruption in central administration; the abuse of royal prerogative to grant lucrative 'monopolies' or licences in favour of courtiers and their clients, who might also enforce certain statutes for profit; and the claim that the benefits of the Poor Laws were negligible in relation to the rise in population and scale of economic distress in the 1590s.

Elizabeth allowed the taxation system to decline despite soaring levels of government expenditure. The strain of a war economy was cumulative. Conscription became a flashpoint. 35,105,800 men were impressed for military service in the Netherlands, France, Portugal and Ireland during the last 15 years of the reign. Conscription for Ireland after 1595 aroused the greatest resentment. In 1600 there was a near mutiny of Kentish cavalry at Chester as they travelled to Ulster. Pressure on the counties led to administrative breakdowns and opposition to central government's demands, while disruption of trade, outbreaks of plague (much of it imported by soldiers returning from abroad), ruined harvests in 1596 and 1597, and acute economic depression caused widespread distress.

Extract 2 From Jim Sharpe, 'Social strain and social dislocation, 1585–1603', in John Guy ed., *The Reign of Elizabeth I: Court and Culture in the Last Decade*, published in 1995.

The 1590s also witnessed increases in the levels of crime, notably in 1596–8, years of recurrent bad harvests. The link between high grain prices and high levels of indicted crime was uncertain before 1591, but became much closer over the later 1590s. Figures demonstrate clearly that the surge in indicted crime in the 1590s was accounted for largely by a rise in property offences: larceny, burglary, robbery.

The notion of the threat from below was part of a more general mood of pessimism which formed an important strand in the late-Elizabethan mentality. The law enforcing activities of the more godly justices of the peace were given an additional edge by their conviction that if the sinful nature of the English were not curbed, the Almighty might either withdraw his support in the next time of crisis, or even send Philip II's troops to chasten an unworthy nation. Many thinking protestants believed that they were living in the final phase of human history, the 'last days', a period of chaos which would precede the dissolution of human society and the Second Coming.

Work together

Having written your conclusion, swap it with a partner. Consider:

1 Does your partner's conclusion begin by focusing clearly on the given interpretation?
2 Does your partner's conclusion mention both of the extracts?
3 Does your partner's conclusion use their own knowledge to help evaluate the validity of the interpretations offered by the extracts?
4 Was your partner's overall judgement properly supported by an evaluation of the different interpretations offered by the extracts?
5 Does your partner's conclusion contain anything that you missed?
6 What can you learn from your partner's approach?
7 Whose conclusion better reached an overall judgement?

Use these questions to feed back to each other and improve your writing.

Activity: AS-style question

Study Extracts 1 and 2.

Historians have different views about whether there was a general crisis of government in the last years of Elizabeth I's reign. Analyse and evaluate the extracts and use your own knowledge of the issues to explain your answer to the following question:

How far do you agree with the view that dearth and poverty weakened Elizabeth's government during the years 1589 to 1603?

Paper 2 Luther and the German Reformation, c1515–55

The Big Picture

The Holy Roman Empire changed enormously during the sixteenth century. At the beginning of the century religion was determined by the Catholic Church, governed by the Pope in Rome. Yet by the end of the century the Church was divided. A new form of worship, later called 'Protestantism', had been created and hundreds of thousands of people chose to adopt it.

The Holy Roman Empire in the sixteenth century

There were many other changes making an impact at the beginning of the sixteenth century. Politically, the princes were consistently attempting to increase their territorial power through conflict, by gaining land and exploiting economic changes. This made for a less harmonious Empire. The Holy Roman Emperor, Charles V, found it increasingly difficult to dominate the princes and to rule effectively. Economically, towns increased in number and size, new industries were established and grew and many people moved from the countryside into urban areas. There were also changes to the Church in Germany. Those at the top of the Church hierarchy became increasingly involved in politics outside of the Church. Some of them paid much less attention to their dioceses, focusing on affairs of state rather than the religious welfare of the people. At the beginning of the century most people did not protest about this but, as new ideas began to challenge different aspects of Church behaviour, that soon changed.

Luther's early challenge to the Catholic Church

Luther did not begin by challenging the mighty Catholic Church. His *Ninety-Five Theses*, written and published in 1517, protested about a cause that many had spoken about before – the fundraising indulgence campaigns. Luther argued that the campaign to refurbish St Peter's Basilica in Rome was being conducted immorally. He condemned a particular group of preachers operating in Germany and attempted to start an academic debate. A letter to his archbishop, and the fact that Luther's ideas were printed and circulated without his permission, meant that the Pope was forced to respond to Luther and make him an example to others. A series of debates with representatives of the Church only provoked Luther and made his ideas more radical. The Pope excommunicated Luther in 1520. This placed Luther outside of the Church but only pushed him further into condemning the Pope and coming up with even more radical ideas.

The development of Lutheranism, 1521–46

The Diet of Worms was arranged in 1521. Luther was tried there for his religious ideas. Despite Luther's arguments he was declared an outlaw by the Emperor. Frederick the Wise, ruler of Electoral Saxony, protected him by faking a kidnap and sheltering him in his castle at Wartburg until May 1522. During Luther's absence radical preachers took the Reformation in directions Luther would not have dreamed of. Andreas Carlstadt encouraged iconoclasm (the removal and destruction of religious images) and Thomas Muntzer called for religious violence. Radical preachers played a part in the Peasants' Wars of 1525 and it was only Luther's complete denunciation of the peasants that meant that the princes supported his cause after 1525. In the meantime, Luther had been working on a German translation of the Bible, a German mass and catechisms – books by which the new faith could be taught to adults and children. It was important to Luther that people should have access to the biblical scriptures in their own language. As Lutheranism grew, spread and developed it could not remain the work of one man. Aside from the radicals, there were other reformers who worked with Luther. Individuals like Philip Melanchthon represented Luther at diets, organised his ideas, and wrote some of the key texts that were to determine the future of Lutheranism.

The spread and survival of Lutheranism, 1521–55

The period 1521–55 was marked by attempts to unite the Catholic and Protestant faiths. These attempts were made by the Emperor and involved Catholic and Protestant representatives debating the doctrines of the Church. Charles was desperate for these attempts to work – he saw his role as ruling over Christian Europe. Despite these efforts the divide grew wider. The German princes played a role in the division and in the continuation of Lutheranism. Princes who converted to Lutheranism allowed their subjects to do the same. This made Lutheranism virtually impossible to defeat once powerful individuals like Albrecht of Hohenzollern and Philip of Hesse had converted. Lutheran princes also set up military associations like the Schmalkaldic League in order to defend Lutheran lands militarily. This led to war with the Emperor from 1546–47. Even the Catholic princes did not support Charles consistently or strongly. They were afraid that his power would grow and that he would be able to threaten their independence. So while religion was at the heart of the sixteenth-century upheavals, it was strongly intertwined with politics. Charles V was overburdened with concerns. He was King of Spain as well as Holy Roman Emperor and had to defend his lands against attacks by the Ottoman Turks and the kings of France. This made it very difficult for Charles to systematically attack Lutheranism, which in turn helped it survive.

Key Topic 1 Conditions in early-sixteenth century Germany

Overview

The Reformation happened as a result of long-term changes as well as catalysts like Martin Luther. These long-term changes were vital in creating the conditions for Luther's ideas to make such an impact. The government of the Holy Roman Empire had been reformed over the centuries of its existence. By 1519 when Charles V was elected Emperor it was not the strong central government that might be expected. The princes' power had grown as they acquired more and more territory and this created the conditions for further princely expansion of power. The Catholic Church had resisted movements by those who attempted to change its doctrines and practices. It had termed these 'heretical' and punished their followers severely. Yet calls for reform began with the growth of humanism and this time the Church could not repress them. These calls for reform had been prompted by a closer relationship between the Church and politics. Some bishops were also mighty landowners and held political positions for princes. The economy of Germany was also changing. More people moved to towns while conditions worsened in the countryside. New industries were created and grew rapidly – including the printing industry. More people became literate and were able to read the new printed materials. None of this change happened overnight, but it is important in explaining the events of 1517 onwards.

This chapter will focus on the situation in Germany before the Reformation began. It will examine changes that were taking place in the Holy Roman Empire, the Catholic Church and the economy of Germany. It will look at the religious, social, political and economic conditions that existed before Martin Luther began the debate that was to lead to the Reformation. This will help you to understand the environment from which Luther came. It should also make you begin to think about why the Reformation happened when it did.

This chapter examines these issues through the following sections:

1   *The Holy Roman Empire* explains how the Holy Roman Empire was governed, including the role of the Emperor, imperial estates and the imperial diet. It also covers the 1519 imperial election in which Charles V was elected to the role that he would hold until 1555.
2   *The state of the German economy* covers the rapid growth of towns before the Reformation, as well as the changes in trade and communications between German states. It looks at how these changes affected the German people in the years before 1517.
3   *The German Catholic Church* examines the hierarchy of the Catholic Church and the powers of the bishops. It looks at popular religion and views on the Catholic Church before the Reformation. This section also examines the effect of humanism on religious developments.

TIMELINE

1494	The Fugger family established their first public company, a mining company
1420	The papal court moved back to Rome from Avignon
1450	The movable type printing press invented by Gutenberg in Mainz
1512	At the Diet of Cologne the Holy Roman Empire's name was changed to the Holy Roman Empire of the German Nation
1513 March	Giovanni di Lorenzo de' Medici became Pope Leo X
1517	Johann Tetzel appointed commissioner for indulgences for all Germany
1517 October	Luther's *Ninety-Five Theses* published
1519 January	Holy Roman Emperor Maximilian I died
1519 June	The imperial election – Charles V elected Holy Roman Emperor

1 The Holy Roman Empire

The Holy Roman Empire developed from the **Middle Ages**. It was a complex of territories in Central Europe. Within the Empire there were different states ruled by a range of rulers, different languages and different ethnicities. In theory it was the largest territory in the world and the Emperor had supreme power over all of the territories. In reality, however, it was not so simple. The structure of the Empire was complicated and unique. In this period there was one imperial election, in 1519, and it was to be crucial in determining the response to the religious changes from 1517 onwards.

Note it down

Use the 1:2 method here (see page x). There are different sub-topics to break down and explain, and the 1:2 method gives you the space to do this. Write the sub-topic heading in the left-hand column (for example, 'What was the Holy Roman Empire?') and in the right-hand column write the points that you need to summarise or define.

The structure of the Holy Roman Empire

The Holy Roman Empire was already 500 years old by the time of the Reformation. There were two main forces within the government of the Holy Roman Empire: the Emperor and the imperial estates. The Emperor had very few powers of his own and his rule depended on his authority as a prince of his own state. If an Emperor was a powerful territorial ruler, he was, theoretically, more likely to be a strong Emperor. The Emperor was elected. The imperial estates were the group of rulers of states and imperial cities who voted for the Emperor. The members of the imperial estates were the greatest, wealthiest and most powerful princes of the Holy Roman Empire.

The Holy Roman Empire had existed in different forms since AD800. It was an attempt to revive the Roman Empire in the west, and began with the crowning of Charlemagne (a hugely powerful ruler who extended his kingdom and forcibly converted many areas of Europe to Christianity) by **Pope** Leo III on Christmas Day AD800. Over time the Empire became a loose federation of states, the majority of which are in what is now Germany. Indeed after 1512 the name of the Empire reflected that – at the Diet of Cologne the name was changed to the Holy Roman Empire of the German Nation. This included large states such as Bavaria and individual cities known as 'imperial cities'.

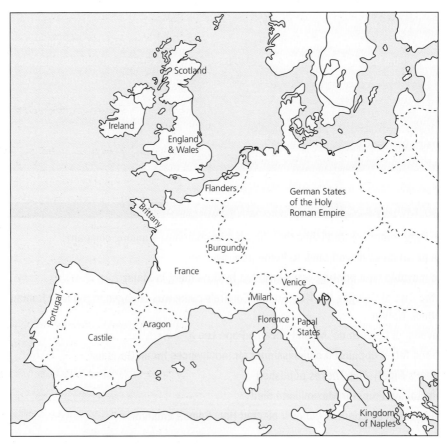

▲ Figure 1: Europe and the Holy Roman Empire, c1530

The Holy Roman Emperor

The Emperor was supreme head of the Empire. This meant that he was at the head of the hierarchy of the Empire and (in theory) of **Christendom**. Few elections were contested – but one of those was the election of Charles V, who ruled the Empire when Luther began his fight against the Catholic Church. As the title of Emperor did not come with many powers of its own, it followed that the Emperor had to come from a ruling family that wielded a lot of power in its own right. This is why the Habsburg family dominated the Empire from the late fifteenth century until the dissolution of the Empire in 1806. They had vast lands that spread across Europe, including immense territories in the Empire, but also in Spain and Italy. Their power and influence meant that as Emperors they could rule effectively over the German lands. This weak imperial authority did cause problems for the Emperor, no matter how strong a ruler he was in his own state, as it meant that the individual princes and rulers also exercised strong authority in their own lands. This was to prove a significant problem for Charles V when trying to deal with Martin Luther.

The Emperor was also supreme feudal overlord. This meant that he ruled over the other princes of the Empire. In theory the Emperor could dispossess a prince of his lands for certain actions, for example, not aiding the Emperor militarily. In practice, this rarely happened because of the potential for conflict and the local power of the princes. As supreme feudal overlord the Emperor also had powers relating to the Catholic Church. He could approve or reject the pronouncements of the Pope and could appoint commissioners who could take part in elections of German archbishops, bishops and abbots. This clearly had great potential to set the Emperor at odds with the Pope.

The office of Holy Roman Emperor was not meant to be hereditary. An Emperor's reign ended with death, deposition or abdication. Following that, the new Emperor would be elected. The Emperor was elected by a majority vote of the prince-electors.

The electors and their powers

There were, at this point in the Empire's history, seven electors. There were three spiritual or **ecclesiastical** electors:

- The Archbishop of Mainz.
- The Archbishop of Trier.
- The Archbishop of Cologne.

There were four temporal or lay electors:

- The King of Bohemia.
- The Count Palatine of the Rhine.
- The Elector of Saxony.
- The **Margrave** of Brandenburg.

They formed the Council of Electors in the imperial diet and were presided over by the Archbishop of Mainz. He had precedence over the other electors and thus was in a very powerful position. The electors chose the new Emperor by voting for their preferred candidate. Candidates put themselves forward and the electors chose between them. Elections were rarely contested but when they were the electors could be paid substantial sums of money by candidates to secure their votes.

The imperial diet

The imperial diet was a form of parliament. It was the law-making body of the Empire and the court of final appeal for people in the Empire. Representatives of all the lords of the Empire sat in the diet. The 52 imperial cities also sent representatives. Technically, the imperial diet could make laws that overruled those of the territories within the Empire. However, this was very hard to achieve because the member states also had certain powers to make their own law and the voting procedures were extremely complex. Meetings of the imperial diet were central to the events of the Reformation, for example the Diet of Worms of 1521. This commenced on 28 January 1521 and during 16 to 18 April saw Martin Luther defending his religious views in front of the Emperor. It was an opportunity for Luther to present his views to the representatives of the Empire and led to the **Edict** of Worms made by Charles V. Other important decisions were made at the diets because they were the main forum for discussions to take place that involved all the different states of the Holy Roman Empire.

> **Source A** An account by Quirini, ambassador of Venice, in 1509.
>
> The king, or Emperor, has full authority, as soon as the diet has dissolved, to order every one to obey its decisions. If, nevertheless, some one ventures to disobey, the whole Empire, in order not to see its commands disregarded, always turns upon the offender, as happened in recent years in the case of the count palatine, who, for his refusal to accede to what was determined upon at the diet of Augsburg, which was especially concerned with the heritage of Duke George of Bavaria, roused the anger of the king and the whole Empire against him, and in a brief space of time was destroyed. For this reason all the princes and free towns are careful to follow the decisions of the diets, nor do they venture to contravene in any way what has been established. Decisions of the diet cannot be changed except by another diet similar to that which first ratified them.
>
> What does Source A tell us about the power of the diets? Why did the princes and towns support the decisions of the diets?

The imperial election of 1519

Maximilian I was Holy Roman Emperor in his own right since 1508 but ruled with his father from 1483. He died on 12 January 1519 after being instrumental in imperial reforms in his lifetime. His death triggered an imperial election. Maximilian had been trying to secure the succession for a member of his house since 1517 in order to keep the imperial title within the Habsburg family and to prevent Francis I of France from gaining the throne. To do this he had to persuade the electors to elect his grandson Charles as King of the Romans. If elected to this position, Charles would have been able to avoid an imperial election.

Maximilian secured a loan of 1 million **gulden** from the Fugger banking family to secure the votes of electors through bribery. Before his death he had succeeded in gaining the votes of Mainz, Cologne, Brandenburg and Bohemia for his chosen candidate, his grandson Charles. Maximilian's death in 1519 halted this progress temporarily and the electors considered the situation afresh. Maximilian is generally considered to have failed in his aim to have secured the imperial Crown for his family – although Charles did become Emperor it was largely through Charles' own campaign.

Charles was the ruler of vast tracts of Europe. This included Castile and Aragon, the Netherlands, Naples, Spanish possessions in the New World and large parts of central and eastern Europe. This worried the imperial electors. For them, there was the potential for Charles to use his huge territorial power alongside his imperial authority, forming a stronger state and reducing their **autonomy**. This was extremely unattractive – it had taken a long time for the princes to build up their power in their own states and they did not want to lose it. Pope Leo X was also worried about the potential for Charles to threaten him and his secular power in Italy. The princes also worried that Charles' international empire might drag the German states into expensive European wars and conflicts.

The only other plausible candidate was Francis I, the King of France. He wanted, like the electors, to prevent Charles building an enormous empire close to his borders and was afraid that Charles would threaten his power. The other, less plausible, contender was Henry VIII of England. He stood very little chance of success principally because he was less influential in European affairs. Both Charles and Francis tempted the electors with huge bribes and promises. Both men were seen as bringing foreign influence – Charles with his Spanish possessions and title and Francis born in France and ruling as King of France. One consequence of their rivalry were the lengthy Habsburg-Valois Wars (1494–59) during Charles' and his son Philip's reigns – so even after the election the resulting rivalry continued. Charles was a member of the Habsburg family who had held the imperial Crown for generations. His family was rooted in the Holy Roman Empire and Charles was viewed as a German candidate as opposed to Francis who was King of France.

Eventually Charles succeeded in winning the election through the use of enormous bribes to the electors, funded (like Maximilian's fighting fund) by the Fugger family. The Habsburg family paid 850,000 gulden during the imperial election. Half of this was paid in outright bribery to electors, councillors and servants. It was not a success without limitations, however, as before the electors would agree to Charles' election he had to agree to a 36 point 'electoral capitulation' where he promised to uphold certain powers of the estates. Charles believed wholeheartedly in the role and power of the Holy Roman Emperor. He believed that the secular head of the Holy Roman Empire should co-ordinate strongly with the spiritual head – the Pope. This helps to explain why Charles intervened repeatedly in the religious changes of the Reformation despite his many other conflicting priorities including his rule in Spain and his wars with France and the Ottomans.

Conclusion: The Holy Roman Empire

The Holy Roman Empire was not a powerful centralised state. While the title 'Holy Roman Emperor' sounded grand it did not mean that the Emperor had great power or could automatically dominate the other princes. Charles V won the 1519 imperial election and had the largest territorial reach of any European ruler. Including the New World territories that he held as King of Spain, his lands reached from South America right up to the border with the Ottoman Empire. Yet in practice this meant that his time was divided and he had to rely on the princes to help him rule Germany, giving them more influence in the process. The electoral capitulation that Charles was forced to sign meant his actions were constrained. This would be important when the Emperor was trying to fight against Lutheranism from the 1520s onwards.

Work together

Take it in turns to use each other's notes you have made (page 214) to explain the terms and topics in this section. If you think a definition is unclear or needs further information, discuss what needs to be added.

2 The state of the Germany economy

The sixteenth century was a time of immense change for the states of the Holy Roman Empire. Towns and cities grew in number and size. Working and living conditions in the countryside were changing too, and people increasingly left to try and secure a better life in the town. For many people in the sixteenth century life changed profoundly. Trade increased, communications improved and consequently news of developments in religion and politics also reached different areas more quickly. New industries developed, like banking and large-scale mining, and resulted in new types of jobs. It was not just a time of progress and improvement, however, as there were significant economic problems as well. An increase in population meant that land was scarcer in the countryside and that more people moved to the towns. Towns were hostile to poor migrants and developed rules to prevent them staying in the urban areas. These developments were extremely significant for the religious Reformation and are an important part of the context to it.

Note it down

Use a spider diagram (see page x) to take notes for this section. With a central circle entitled 'German economy', make 'legs' for the different sections: growth of towns and cities; development of the printing press; the German economy; economic problems. Read the different sections very carefully, highlighting important points if you are able. Then add the key points for each section to your spider diagram.

The growth of towns and cities

Across Europe in the Middle Ages cities and towns had grown, and had become centres of trade, administration (of the Church as well as secular administration) and of military defence. Most were protected by town walls and defended gates in case of attack. They had enormous cathedrals, town halls and market halls. They became increasingly independent, with their own rules and governments. Most European towns by the end of the Middle Ages were ruled by an **oligarchy**. The composition of these governments varied a lot. Some, like Hamburg, did not allow knights to live in the cities because they saw them as a threat to their independence. This was because powerful and wealthy knights and noblemen could use their influence to try and dominate and change the governments of such towns and cities. Others, like Lubeck, were run by landowners or like Frankfurt, by a small number of families.

By the sixteenth century, increasing numbers of people were moving from the country to the towns. They wanted a better life with more opportunities, and it seemed like the towns offered that. Some who moved to the towns became very successful, and ended their lives wealthy and respected. But many more did not, and so there was a lot of poverty in early modern towns. When a town had very high levels of poverty tensions increased, leading to riots and rebellions.

Some towns and cities were more independent from their sovereign ruler than others. As we have seen in the last section, the princes of the Holy Roman Empire in the sixteenth century were able to rule with a high degree of autonomy. There was a similar situation for the towns from the thirteenth century onwards. German towns were especially independent because the central government (the Emperor and imperial government) was weak. This meant that there was more urbanisation in German larger towns, and these towns were very protective of their rights and independence. While they did have more autonomy, the towns of the Holy Roman Empire were regularly forced to defend this against the territorial ambitions of neighbouring princes. Over the years some cities were absorbed into principalities while others kept their independence. If they remained independent, their economic success and specialisation often played a part – they remained too wealthy and strong for the princes to be able to take them over.

Towns and cities in the Holy Roman Empire varied greatly in size. Cologne was the largest town in the late fifteenth century. It had 30,000 inhabitants. Other large cities included Lubeck, Danzig and Hamburg. The smallest cities had around 5,000 inhabitants, for example, Dinkelsbuhl in Franconia. Some towns had only a few hundred inhabitants. While these populations seem small in comparison to the cities and towns of today, they seemed enormous at the time.

The numbers and concentration of people in the cities and towns meant that new ideas quickly spread. The towns also housed cathedrals and universities, where many new ideas were first conceived. The towns were the first places to popularise the new ideas about religion and the Church that became known as the Reformation. The ideas were discussed by lecturers or preachers, teachers or humanist writers. These ideas were also probably more popular because the first confrontations between secular authorities and the Church hierarchy had started in towns.

Trade and communications between states

Trade and communications between German states varied greatly depending on their location within the Empire. There were considerable regional variations. Along the northern coast the **Hanseatic League** controlled trade. To the west of the Empire, Westphalia and the lower Rhine were closely connected with the Netherlands, for example.

Trade

There was considerable trade between states, generally in the well-established markets and towns around the Empire. One problem was that there was no central economic policy for the whole Holy Roman Empire. This meant that each German state had its own different policies. They had different weights, measures and coinage. There were many different tolls at the borders of states, on roads and waterways, making it expensive and difficult to trade between states. There were attempts to abolish these tolls but they were limited because they provided income for the governments of the different states. Goods were also traded beyond the Empire. The states traded with many different countries, including England, Spain, Scandinavian countries and the east. They imported goods from other regions such as cattle, salt and textiles.

Internal trade using the waterways was improved in the sixteenth century. Improvements to canal construction made it easier to trade inland via the rivers and canals of Germany. By 1578, for example, Berlin was connected with the North Sea and the Baltic Sea. This meant that it was easier to trade beyond its borders. Much trade was done using the rivers. The rivers Oder, Elbe and Weser were exceptionally useful for trade. Merchants were able to sell local goods and buy imports. Via the Weser and road links from Westphalia, for example, wood and grain were sold to Hamburg. The Rhine was another significant river for trade. Going upstream the trade consisted of fish, textiles and consumer goods. Going downstream there was wine, timber and grain.

Urban fairs were also crucial. Most towns had a fair or market. Having the right to hold such events was very important because it meant that trade would increase and more people would visit the town. Merchants and craftsmen would bring their goods to sell at the fairs, and people would come from far around for a large and varied market. Frankfurt fairs were well known in the Hesse region, and in the south there were important fairs at Worms and Strasbourg. In Saxony, Leipzig held a very successful fair. Fairs were also meeting places where deals could be done, rumour and gossip spread, and a lot of money changed hands.

Communications

People could communicate more easily and quickly than we might suspect in this period, but it was obviously much slower and more limited than now. Goods and letters could be sent via the merchant ships plying the rivers. Postal services were set up, and improved greatly under the Hapsburg Emperors. Under Emperors Maximilian and Charles V monopolies were agreed to run postal services between Germany and other countries such as Spain and France. However, war (such as the Turkish and Habsburg-Valois Wars) disrupted postal services and instead, governments, courts and merchants used news services. These were provided by merchants like the Fugger family who traded all around Europe and could carry news and information alongside their normal business.

The development of the printing press

The printing press was invented in the mid-fifteenth century in Mainz in the Rhine Valley. Before that point all books were handwritten – copied by monks in monasteries or in cities to satisfy the demand for books. This meant that they were very expensive and that few copies were made of each book. Literacy was the preserve of the rich, and new ideas spread relatively slowly. Ordinary people would not have access to copies of religious texts apart from in their parish church, and then those were in the hands of the priests and were in Latin rather than German. This meant that the ability to produce many copies of books, as well as new cheap media like pamphlets – with old and new ideas, in different languages and of different sizes and shapes – brought huge change to Europe.

The new invention spread rapidly. The growth around the same time of humanism (see page 226), literacy, the universities and the need for copies of standard school books, meant that there was a massive demand for the new printed books. Only 20 years after its invention in 1450 there were already printing presses in 30 cities. By 1490 there were innovations in fonts, decorative letters and **woodcut** images. More people became involved in the book industry and jobs associated with it, like bookbinders and booksellers. All of this made books less expensive and, therefore, available to more people. As well as books other, cheaper, printed material was produced. Pamphlets, ballads and other cheap mass-produced material used images to attract the illiterate and to spread news to wider audiences. This meant that new ideas, like those of Martin Luther, spread much more quickly than ever before.

Printing originated in Germany and remained extremely popular in the towns, cities and principalities of the Holy Roman Empire. The first commercially-viable centres of printing were Nuremberg, Augsburg, Basle and Strasbourg, but the main base for printing in Germany was Nuremberg. The boom in printing was aided by book fairs at Leipzig and Frankfurt-am-Main. The development in graphics meant that travel booklets, guides, itineraries and maps became popular. These early maps and itineraries showed how to travel between main towns. One example is a travel map of central Europe published by Erhard Etzlaub in 1501. It placed Nuremberg at the centre of the map and showed all of the major routes radiating out. Other printed material was also very popular. Between 1500 and 1530 over 10,000 pamphlets were published in Germany. The German Bible sold in extremely large numbers (see page 271). To demonstrate how much debate Martin Luther's writings caused, over three-quarters of these were published between 1520 and 1526. Religious and political controversy was particularly popular.

The German economy in the sixteenth century

As with trade, there was great variation in the German economy in the sixteenth century. There was variation between the towns and the country, between the elites and the ordinary people and in different regions or areas of Germany. There were changes that brought great

Case study 1: Banking and investment

The sixteenth century saw an explosion in credit and credit instruments. It led to the establishment of investment and banking companies that became highly influential in politics and religion as well as in business. Many cities in southern Germany that had previously specialised in manufacturing became financial centres in this period. It was investment from German trading and finance companies that led to the establishment of mines, foundries and other early industrial ventures in central and eastern Europe. This included the Slovakian copper and silver mines that the Fuggers invested in. This generated huge profits for the Fuggers – yearly profits that were three times their original investment. Other Augsburg bankers became involved in Austrian mines, for example the Baumgartners and Höchstetters. The profits from these mines were then used to fund further financial investments and loans. Firms like the Fuggers of Augsburg became international bankers to emperors and kings. Their company spread across most of Europe. Based in Augsburg in Germany, the Fuggers spread north and east into Poland, and into other German cities like Cologne, Leipzig and Frankfurt. They had branches or representatives in some of the greatest cities in sixteenth-century Europe, including the great trading hub of Antwerp, Rome, Lisbon and Seville.

The success of the banking firms and the rise of credit were not universally popular. Ordinary people thought that many of the new financial products were wrong. Loans, for example, needed to be paid back with interest – a fixed percentage or sum on top of the original sum borrowed. This acted almost like a fee for borrowing, and meant that the banking company would make a profit from the loan.

To many people in the sixteenth century this was usury. Usury was a sin – the sin of lending money at exorbitant interest rates. Monopolies were also very unpopular, among tradesmen who also wished to sell or produce a product but also among the masses. This led to complaints to the diet of the Holy Roman Empire. The world was changing, but not without resistance from those who believed that the changes were wrong and counter to many central ideas of religion and morals. This is one reason why the 1519 election of Charles V was controversial. It also made Albert, Archbishop of Mainz' actions when seeking the post of Mainz even more questionable in the eyes of many. He also used Fugger loans to bribe those making the appointment, then used the profits from indulgences to pay the loans off. This blend of high politics, corruption and religion provides important context to the Reformation and its popularity.

Case study 2: Mining

Mining was a very important part of the economy in some parts of the Holy Roman Empire. In the Upper Palatinate, for example, 20 per cent of people were employed in the iron business. The area initially produced more iron than the whole of France. Mining was very risky. Entrepreneurs needed a lot of money to start a mine, to invest in surveys for minerals, for equipment, wages and materials. The mining industry was also notorious for being vulnerable to changes in demand. The German silver mining industry was one example of this. Germany was the major source of silver in Europe until the Habsburgs began importing substantial amounts of silver from their colonies in South America. Whole towns and secondary industries grew up around mines and mining.

prosperity to some places. They led to the establishment of new towns and meant that new commodities were available for people to buy. There were also severe economic problems, however, and some groups of people were particularly disadvantaged. Rural labourers were one such group. These problems led to rising tensions, some of which were to explode during the Reformation. The economy was important in determining the culture and prosperity of a place, and with prosperity tended to come a desire for more independence or autonomy. These trends became intertwined with religious changes in the sixteenth century.

The princes

Most of the princes relied on the revenues of taxes and loans. They did have other streams of income. Some, like the Electors of Mainz, Cologne and the Palatinate, made money from river tolls. Others had income from mining rights, for example, for minerals (the Elector of Saxony) or salt (the kings of Bavaria). In this period the **secular rulers** and administrators aimed to have more control over Church finances. They wanted to tax the clergy, have access to some of the money from tithes and indulgences (see page 238) and to use that revenue to pay for infrastructure like roads. They became increasingly hostile to taxes raised by bishops and by the Pope. All of these pressures provide some partial explanation for the success of Protestantism after the Reformation. These varying revenues paid for military expenses, imperial taxes, and maintaining or establishing administrations.

The economy of the towns

Many have argued that there was a strong link between the extent of urbanisation and the performance of the economy. Historians believed that states with higher proportions of people living in towns as opposed to those living in the country would perform better economically. This was because towns were centres of manufacturing and consumption. This was not necessarily the case, however, and it is now argued by historians such as Tom Scott, that there was actually a fairly weak correlation between urbanisation and good economic performance. As you shall see below, towns had extreme poverty as well as incredible individual success stories.

The rural economy

Agriculture and forestry dominated the rural economy in terms of employment, and as sources of revenue for the government, the Church and the nobility. They were sources of capital and of food, fuel, building materials and commodities for manufacturing. Germany produced very large amounts of corn and other food crops. Most

ordinary people in the countryside were employed as agricultural labourers. In this period the way that an agricultural labourer was paid began to change. Traditionally labourers had not been paid in cash. They would receive accommodation and food, and would be able to farm small plots of their own land to make a small amount of money. This protected them when food prices rose. Yet in the fifteenth century more and more peasants started to be paid in money because it made leases less complex and payments less difficult to track. This meant that when populations and food prices rose, they were more vulnerable to poverty and other problems. Landowners would make their money by selling the crops farmed by the peasants. The size of estates varied greatly with some being extremely large.

One relatively new development was the brewing industry. Brewers required the large-scale growing of hops in order to make their beer. There were three main advantages for farmers to producing hops:

- It was an industrial crop.
- It improved with storage.
- It could be exported regionally.

This led to a profitable brewing industry in Franconia and Lower Saxony, for example, in Nuremberg.

The rural economy was not just confined to agriculture. The German countryside was also home to the manufacturing of textiles like linen, fustian and wool. Production had moved to the countryside during the late fourteenth century after business owners sought to avoid the restrictions imposed by urban guilds and by the civic administration of the towns. In Saxony, Chemnitz was the base of the linen industry in the mid-fifteenth century. This was a cottage industry where the textiles were produced in the homes of the workers. The countryside of north-western Germany produced another non-food crop used in the textile industry. In Thuringia in western Saxony woad was produced and harvested. It was a dye that was then used by the woollen industries in Hesse and Lusatia.

Economic problems

In sixteenth-century Europe, prices of commodities, especially food, increased significantly. Germany suffered comparatively less than other places but the cost of grain still increased by 250 per cent. This was better than France, where the prices rose by six and a half times, but is still a significant increase. This would not have been such a big problem had wages risen at the same rate. Unfortunately they did not. In Austria wages actually fell, while in northern Europe more generally the wages rose by 50 per cent at best. This sounds like a lot, but if essential commodity prices were rising by two and a half times, the ordinary person's wages would buy an awful lot less of the items that they needed. The reasons for price rises are complicated but include:

- **rise in population after 1500** – meaning there was more labour available. More people were competing to work on the same amount of land, so employers had more power to set the wages low and traditional leases were negotiated on worse terms for the peasant tenant.
- **political intervention** – in some towns, magistrates could set maximum wage rates in order to maintain the support of craftsmen who used hired labour.

In rural areas people who held traditional leases could be sheltered from the worst of these price increases by being paid in kind. This meant that their 'wages' might include principally free accommodation and food in the farmer's household. Despite this, peasants around the Holy Roman Empire felt under pressure.

Towns were also experiencing tensions in this period. As more people from rural areas were driven into towns their populations increased, sometimes rapidly. Newcomers were not granted citizenship so had no ability to influence events in towns, and this created a large body of people without a voice or stable employment. Thus, when the economy declined, these people were the first to be affected. Bringing poverty and dissatisfaction, migration created a potentially troublesome situation. Also in periods of recession towns stopped immigration, adding to discontent in rural areas. These tensions were added to by the widening gulf between the rich, who were getting richer, and the poor, who were increasingly vulnerable. The availability of new luxury consumer goods and the conspicuous consumption of them by the newly rich made this even worse, and led to resentment and envy.

Conclusion: The German economy

Both town and countryside in the Holy Roman Empire saw huge changes in the sixteenth century. Towns grew up around new industries such as mining. They were boosted by others, such as printing. The number and size of towns grew and so the population distribution of Germany changed. More people moved into towns, centres of trade between different states and countries, and where new ideas and rumours spread quickly. Changes in the countryside made migration to the towns increase, as conditions became harder for peasants and farmers. While these were times of great success for some, they were also difficult for others. Problems of poverty perhaps became more obvious and the increase in migration to towns caused tension and fear. This was not a period of stability but one where many different factors combined to create a changing and unstable economic situation for many people.

Source B A new Poor Law for Augsburg, 1547, from B. Ann Tlusty, *Augsburg During the Reformation Era: An Anthology of Sources*, published in 2012.

> Although an Honorable Council of this laudable city of Augsburg is most desirous and inclined to offer their benevolent generosity and alms not only to their poor, needy fellow citizens and residents but also to afflicted outsiders and foreigners who come to this city and its environs in great numbers every day, they nonetheless find that God's commandment holds them more accountable to come to the aid of those who have sworn allegiance to them, and who are found within these city walls. For [the local poor] have also reached such numbers that it is nearly impossible to continue to help them as we have up to now, even without tolerating outsiders coming in to collect alms and taking the bread out of the mouths of locals ...

What was the attitude of Augsburg's city council to poor outsiders migrating to the city in Source B? Why did they decide to support the local poor rather than the outsiders?

Work together

Working with a partner, one of you look at the urban economy and the other at the agricultural economy. Produce a table as follows:

	Urban economy or agricultural economy
Features (for example, expanding, shrinking)	
Products	
Geographical areas/ examples	
Economic problems	

Fill in your respective tables and then compare them. If there is any extra detail you feel you need, use the recommended reading at the end of the chapter (page 228) to find it.

3 The German Catholic Church

In the early sixteenth century many long-term religious, political and economic changes were happening. One notable trend was the changing way in which people viewed authority. Authority was fragmenting. This happened with the Holy Roman Empire but it is also visible within the Church. Traditional authority figures like bishops saw their role becoming even more political. This led them away from the **dioceses** that they governed. The **papacy** was criticised from within Germany which damaged its authority to some degree. Reformers questioned the authority of priests to dictate the beliefs of the people. They used stereotypical representations of scandalous priests to make their arguments carry more weight.

Nationalism is a modern concept but this period did see the beginning of the emergence of national characteristics, for example national churches with their own characters. This development tied in to the demands of the princes and other secular rulers for more independence from, and power over, the Church. It began to cause difficulties for the papacy as objections to Rome became more frequent. The papacy was slow to act against these demands because it was preoccupied with problems in Rome and with its own power in other areas. As we will see with Luther's works, the idea of a German people became more developed in this period.

There was also a lot of continuity. That should not be overlooked in the rush to see Luther's rise to prominence as inevitable. The German Catholic Church had governed over the seasons and lives of Germans for centuries and for most people this continued. Popular beliefs in **purgatory** led to a continued enthusiasm for saints' cults, relics and indulgences that were not entirely the work of the Catholic Church itself. The Catholic Church in this period should also be seen, therefore, against a pattern of loyalty and sincere belief by most ordinary people.

Note it down

Use the 1:2 method of note taking (see page x) in this chapter. This means writing the big points in the left-hand section and the supporting points in the right-hand section. For example: 'Complaints about the papacy' in the left-hand section and a bullet-point list of the complaints in the right-hand section.

You could also begin your collection of index cards here (see page xi). Write a term that you need to define on the front of an index card (for example 'purgatory') and the definition on the back.

A united Church?

The early sixteenth-century Church was a diverse institution in which there was considerable variety of religious custom and style of worship. Nonetheless, there was a degree of unity. This was founded on the authority of the papacy and the definitions of the faith. Both of these aspects were relatively uniformly accepted. The majority of ordinary people continued to be fervent supporters of the Church and did not reject its theology or practices. Despite this, there were criticisms of the Catholic Church across Europe about all different levels of the Church hierarchy for a range of reasons. These formed challenges to the Church in this period.

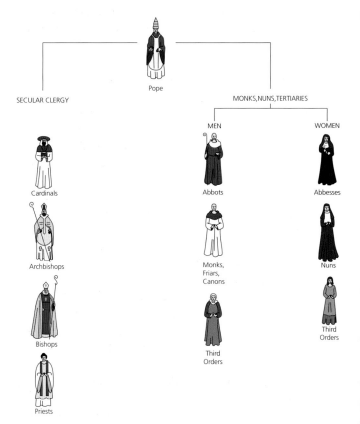

▲ Figure 2: The Church hierarchy

The papacy

The Pope was the head of the Roman Catholic Church. The papacy was based in Rome. In this period papal government became increasingly dominated by Italians. After the 1400s **cardinals** were no longer required to be resident in Rome. This led to fewer non-Italians living in Rome and the city became a focus for in-fighting and **factions**. At the same time, it also meant that non-resident cardinals became more influential in their local churches. Consequently, national churches began to emerge. These had a distinct character of their own. Additionally, power moved slowly to the regions. Some of this power was now held by princes and other secular rulers, who wanted to build up their own local authority. They began to challenge the pope's right to make local appointments and to resist paying papal taxes. The development of stronger national churches led to regional competition for power, money and influence – all forces that made change in the Reformation more likely, alongside new ideas about religion.

Resentment of the papacy in Rome united all different parts of the German Church. As long ago as 1451 one German priest had written to the cardinal of his country to complain about the abuses of the papacy. Here are some of the specific German complaints about the Pope:

- He awarded valuable Church livings to those who paid the most, despite their level of education or fitness to be a priest.
- He gave these livings to non-Germans.
- Many of these priests did not live in the places they were appointed to – and appointed **curates** to do their work who were poorly paid and ill-educated. This meant the spiritual care of Germans was being neglected.
- Some Church offices in Germany were sold while the people who held those positions were still alive – people paid to 'reserve' the job.
- The Pope took the first year's income of those who secured high office in the German Church. These payments were called '**annates**'. The Archbishop of Mainz, for example, paid between 20,000 and 25,000 gulden to the Pope. This was then recovered from the local churchgoers.
- If a German clergyman died while in Rome, the Pope would take his benefice, his position that granted property and income in exchange for his services, and grant them to a person of his choice. This person may well not be German.
- The Pope granted absolution for great sins if enough gold was paid.
- The threat of **excommunication** was used to extract payments from poor Germans, like buying masses (see page 226).

> **Source C** Girolamo Aleander on the anti-papal sentiment in Germany, 8 February 1521.
>
> At present, all Germany is in commotion: nine out of every ten cry 'Luther', and the tenth, if he do not care for what Luther says, at least cries, 'Death to the Court of Rome!' ... And those who ought to do most for us, yea for themselves, some out of timidity, some for spite, others, each for his own interest.
>
> What does Source C tell the historian about the reasons for the 'commotion'? Why does the writer argue that people don't stand up for the Church?

Many of these complaints were true and were the subject of calls for reform from within the Church. Others were exaggerated, such as the level of education and commitment of the clergy. It is important to remember that despite all these complaints about the papacy the majority of people still supported the Church. Others wanted reform but not wide changes. Those who wanted complete change were in a very tiny minority.

The power of the bishops

Bishops were the most powerful figures, spiritually and politically, in the local church. They were responsible for a group of churches and for the priests who ministered in them. Their area of operation was known as a diocese. The extent of their power and their relationship with the local church changed dramatically in the sixteenth century.

In the **late medieval period** bishops became increasingly remote from their **flocks**. The local bishop was the person who represented the power and authority of the Church to the ordinary people – both spiritually and politically. Many increasingly powerful bishops ceased to have meaningful relationships with their dioceses. Some bishops governed several large **dioceses** far away from each other. As a result, they did not have to live in their dioceses. This made them the focus for criticism and calls for reform before the Reformation.

> ### Key debate
> #### The state of the Roman Catholic Church
> Traditionally, historians like Geoffrey Elton described the late medieval Catholic Church as a decaying and corrupt institution. More recently others, such as Diarmaid MacCulloch and Euan Cameron, have disagreed. They argue that the Church was actually popular in many parts of Europe. In fact, in much of Europe people were giving more time and money to the Church. The critics in most places were in a minority and most people were deeply loyal to the Church as well as being fervent believers.
>
> Significantly, the state of the Church before the Reformation varied greatly from region to region. Criticisms of the German Catholic Church did not necessarily apply elsewhere in Europe and even in Germany contained exaggerations and simplifications of the religious situation.

Bishops were also administrators or politicians in this period. Many were nobles, and were related to princes and other rulers. Archbishop Albert of Mainz, for example, was brother to the Elector of Brandenburg and himself Margrave of Brandenburg. Their family ruled this German state and, as electors, had a say in determining who the next Holy Roman

Emperor would be. Some noble families saw the office as bishop as their right. There were some outrageous abuses such as the nomination of minors for bishoprics, for example, the seven-year-old son of the Duke of Mecklenburg was nominated as Bishop of Schwerin in 1516. For others their political authority was built into their position as bishop. Indeed, several bishops were 'prince-bishops' – territorial rulers as well as spiritual ones. This meant that they spent less time on their spiritual duties than people expected. While it was a consequence of political developments as much as corruption, this was viewed negatively. As their power increased and their relationships with their **flocks** became less intimate, bishops were increasingly viewed as remote figures who were more interested in power than in **piety**.

The bishops were also blamed, alongside the Pope, for the financial burden on the people of Germany. The German Church was extremely wealthy. It owned a lot of property and valuable items such as jewelled vestments and silver chalices to use at **communion**. These objects were donated and generally not resented but the Church as a landlord did cause concern. At the end of the fifteenth century it owned one third of the land in Germany and received a lot of income from rents. Money also had to be raised for annates payable to the Pope. Annates were the payment of the first year's income for a new bishop. This money could come from rents, church taxes and the sale of indulgences. This came from the people of Germany and was resented, especially by secular rulers who thought that they should have more power and control over their regions.

Monastic houses

Monastic houses were places where those who wanted to live an entirely religious life outside of secular society went to devote their lives to God. They lived by certain rules, such as those of **St Benedictine**. Some were completely secluded and took vows of silence, while others were integrated into the community and performed important roles of hospitality and medicine. Examples of monasteries where the rules were strictly observed included those at Erfurt and Mecklenburg. Initially they were meant to surrender all private property and their former lives outside of the monastery or nunnery.

Source D 'Allegory of monasticism', a woodcut by Hans Sebald Beham, 1521.

Look carefully at Source D. What kind of corruption or scandal does the artist accuse the monks of? What can you infer from this source about attitudes of reformers to the Catholic Church?

Yet monastic houses also became very wealthy because of donations of property, land and money. This made abbots, the heads of monastic houses, powerful figures locally. Consequently, abbots could challenge the authority of local secular rulers. An abbot's behaviour tended to affect the popularity of his abbey. Local people were prepared to criticise unpopular abbots. One example of this is the Abbot of Kempten. In 1492 his tenants gathered together to write down their grievances against him, including raising rents despite the terms of the abbey charter, seizing the estate of dead tenants so their partners could not inherit, and going against his promise to confirm ancient customs on issues like land ownership and marriage. Moreover, local rulers were also prepared to criticise abbots in order to defend their own power.

Monks were also in competition with priests for their control over the congregations in local areas. This led to arguments between those representing the monastic orders and parish priests. Both sides argued that the other was corrupt and self-serving. This argument led to a lasting impression in the historical record which has meant that priests have been seen as ignorant and monks as scandalous.

The stereotype of monks and nuns in this period owes a lot to the pamphlets of reformers and later critics of the Church. Their alleged scandalous financial and sexual behaviour is, of course, sensational and interesting nowadays as it was when the pamphlets were published. It does not represent an accurate portrayal of all abbeys, convents and other monastic houses. While there were certainly institutions that were scandalous, that is not true of all.

The parish clergy

The parish clergy were the lowest level in the Church hierarchy. They were responsible for church services, religious guidance and ceremonies such as christenings in local parish churches. This meant that they were the representatives of the wider Church that the ordinary people would see on a regular basis. As the Pope, the cardinals and the bishops had become increasingly remote, it was even more important for the health of the Church that the parish clergy be perceived well. Historians such as Geoffrey Elton claimed the Church was suffering from a crisis of confidence in the period just before the Reformation. They described a situation in which:

- top positions in the Church were monopolised by a corrupt and greedy aristocracy
- monastic orders had become wealthy and **worldly**

- peasants were ministered to by uneducated, poor and greedy parish clergy
- priests were greedy landlords, criminals and committed sexual improprieties with local women.

A traditional view on the Catholic Church

According to Elton, the Catholic Church was in a state where:

... its reputation for corruption, envy of its Wealth, hatred of its spiritual claims so little accompanied by a spiritual life [meant that] the Church was suspect; the clergy, and especially the religious orders, had become more worldly and uninspiring ... the problem was particularly developed in Germany where the Church stood in an even worse case and earned more deserved resentment than in other countries. Its high places were monopolised by the aristocracy, with the usual abuses of simony and nepotism rampant ... the lower clergy were poor and grasping, and often ignorant ... in Germany they were also quite exceptionally numerous.

G. Elton, *Reformation Europe 1517–1559* (Fontana Press, 1963), pages 27–28

There is no doubt that there were individual priests, abbeys or areas that fitted this pattern. Yet more recently historians have reassessed the quality of parish clergy. According to Diarmaid MacCulloch, between a third and a half of clergy in Germany had some experience of university education – an improvement from earlier times. By the later fifteenth century, the clergy were better educated and more committed to their parishes than ever before. They had more resources to learn how to preach to their congregations effectively even though many of them had a comparatively small income. Two possible reasons for the critical view of parish priests are:

- criticisms have survived mainly because they were recorded. Historian Larissa Taylor has commented that many villagers were content with their priest and that was seldom communicated to bishops or to the courts
- the pamphlets of reformers which aim to show parish priests in the most negative light. In the past, some historians have tended to take their criticisms at face value because the evidence against them was difficult to find and interpret.

One reason for the bad reputation of the parish clergy was that they were locked in a battle for the hearts, minds and money of their congregations with the monks. A lot of the **anticlerical** rhetoric which created the impression of a corrupt clergy came initially from their rivals, the monks and friars of the monastic orders.

Purgatory

Purgatory is believed to be a state of suffering where souls go to make amends for their sins before being allowed into heaven. The late medieval Church recognised a variety of methods to reduce the time spent in purgatory:

Endowment of masses – people paid money or other donations to the Church to provide for priests to sing masses for their souls.

Chantries – wealthy people built chantry chapels, either inside a parish church or as separate buildings on private land, especially dedicated to saying masses for the souls of the donator.

Good works – included people giving charity to the poor and donating to the Church.

Indulgences – issued by the Church to reduce the time spent in purgatory. Since Pope Sixtus IV's papal bull *Salvator noster* (1476), indulgences had been allowed to be sold in order to raise money for the Church.

Late medieval spirituality

Late medieval Catholicism was a highly theatrical, festive and celebratory culture, structuring the calendar year with popular festivals linked to the saints and biblical events. It clearly had some serious problems but was not entirely the corrupt and despised institution that it was portrayed as by the reformers. Many of the aspects of Catholicism that Martin Luther opposed were key features of spirituality in Europe in the sixteenth century.

These included the idea of purgatory and practices such as chantries, indulgences, and the endowment of masses.

These practices were popular because they made it possible to do something about the time you spent in purgatory through your actions on earth. They were not uniformly popular across Europe. For example, the endowment of masses was much more common in Germany than it was in Spain and Italy. The fact that this practice was more common in Germany possibly helps to explain why Luther's message against the endowment of masses had much more impact in the north than the south of Europe.

Challenges to Catholicism

While the Church was generally popular in the period, there were clearly criticisms of the behaviour of particular churchmen and of the Church hierarchy. There were criticisms of abuses like simony, nepotism, sexual misconduct, the abuse of the indulgence system and financial mismanagement. Aside from criticisms of the activities of churchmen in Germany in this period, there were also broader challenges that the Church had to face. Some of these challenges came from movements that proposed new ways of thinking or behaving, such as humanism. Others came from 'heretics' or religious groups that differed from Church doctrine. Finally some calls for reform came from within the Church, from people who believed that the Church would lose support if it did not change the way that it operated.

Humanism

Humanism was an intellectual movement that spread across Europe from the mid-fifteenth century onwards. It had a huge influence on politics, religion and education. Over time, the humanist movement influenced a diverse range of people including Catholics and Protestants, philosophers and schoolboys. Even for ordinary people who had not received a humanist education it was important. This was because many of those who ruled them and made decisions on their behalf had been influenced by humanism in different ways.

Humanism could be defined as the study of the language and literature of the **classical world**. It promoted the relevance of classical study to the contemporary world. For example it taught rhetoric, appropriate behaviour for gentlemen and politicians, promoted active involvement in politics and civic life and aimed to recreate positive aspects of the classical world of the Greeks and Romans. It advocated a return to the study of original Latin and Greek documents and, for historians, a more rigorous analysis of their sources.

Humanism developed further because of:

- the discovery of classical manuscripts from the east
- the discovery of similar manuscripts in the monastic houses of Europe
- the technological advances of the printing press which meant that the knowledge found in the manuscripts could spread and be studied widely amongst educated people.

Humanism proved a challenge for the Catholic Church in two main ways:

1 It led to a questioning of elements of the Church and its behaviour that had not previously been challenged to the same degree, for example, Martin Luther published a German translation of the Italian scholar Lorenzo Valla's work. His work exposed a medieval document as a forgery – it had supported the power of the Pope in the western Mediterranean, and the wider aspirations of the papacy towards universal power in Europe. Humanism was very important in influencing the new ideas of the reformers.

2 Humanism was not just for the religious reformers who became known later as 'Protestants'. Catholics were also humanists, and that included a questioning and interrogation of existing approaches and ideas. Catholic humanism is said to have led to a religious indecisiveness that meant that reformers were left unchallenged for political reasons. This was linked to humanism's advocacy for involvement in politics and civic life. So some bishops were reluctant to condemn Martin Luther and his ideas because they were worried about strengthening the power of the Emperor, who was also opposed to Luther.

Heretics and heretical movements

The Catholic Church had been challenged before by people who did not agree with its doctrine since the very early days of Christianity. Since the fourteenth century individuals such as John Wycliffe and Jan Hus, and movements like the Lollards, had new ideas that opposed some of the teachings of the Church. Although they were not based in Germany, their ideas became known to educated men across Europe and they formed the basis for later reformers' ideas. They were branded 'heretics' – people who dissented from the official dogma of the Catholic Church and held controversial opinions. They were opposed to the hierarchical structure of the Church. They proposed that there would be poor itinerant priests instead who would rely on donations and so be closer to the ideal of a holy man. The translation of the Bible from Latin into English (or other vulgar tongues) was also an important feature of their beliefs. The Church had to strike against the ideas to maintain its hierarchy, wealth and authority. Although their followers were a very small minority, decisive action was taken against these groups because the threat they posed was so great. The early Czech reformer Jan Hus had criticised the power of the Pope and indulgences. He argued that the Bible should be translated from Latin so more people could access it and also condemned the immorality of priests. Hus was tried for heresy at the Council of Constance in 1415 and put to

John Wycliffe (c1330–87)

John Wycliffe was an English philosopher, reformer and theologian at Oxford. He was an opponent of papal power, called for the translation of the Bible into English, and believed that it was important for every individual to be able to interpret scriptures. He died in 1384.

Jan Hus (c1369–1415)

Jan Hus was a Czech priest and reformer whose calls for moral reform of the clergy, views on the mass and condemnation of indulgences led to his excommunication and execution in 1415. He was greatly influenced by the ideas of John Wycliffe.

death at the stake on 6 July 1415 in order to prevent his ideas spreading. This did not have the intended effect as it led to the **Hussite Wars** but does demonstrate the fear of such movements and the action taken against them by the Church.

Calls for reform

Some challenges to the Church came from those, unlike the Hussites, who did not wish for wholesale change but who wanted to improve certain aspects of the Church to retain support or to return the Church to a more holy state. Such calls for reform did not start with Luther. They began a long time before Luther began publishing his new ideas and came from the following groups:

- **Members of the Church hierarchy** – different people had called for change at meetings of the Church for 150 years before the Reformation itself, for example, at Konstanz in 1417 and Basel from 1431 to 1449. The problem was that they thought that change should happen only to others, not themselves. So popes thought that secular rulers should change the way they behaved, bishops believed that the parish clergy and the papacy should be reformed and so on. This meant that some sensible changes did not happen.

- **The princes** – they wanted more territorial power and resented the power of the Church. Despite their deep involvement with some of the abuses of the Church that were so criticised by reformers, they wanted changes that would lead to them having more say in how the Church was run. See page 220 for examples of the challenges that the princes posed to the Church.

Conclusion: The German Catholic Church

The German Church faced challenges and calls for reform in 1500. These were financial, ideological and political. Yet they were not new. Critics had been calling for change for over a hundred years before Luther's *Ninety-Five Theses* were written in 1517 (see page 238). These challenges were an important long-term cause of the Reformation but are only a partial explanation. The Catholic Church was also not unpopular in this period. It was supported and beloved of many who made it the centre of their daily existence. Church rituals marked the passing of the seasons and celebrated important milestones in people's lives, for example, birth, marriage and death. It is clear that many different groups of people were unhappy about some of the tendencies within the Church but equally so that a majority were distinctly less critical.

Recommended reading

E. Cameron (ed.), *The Sixteenth Century* (Oxford University Press, 2006).

Chapter 1 provides an excellent overview of the European economy in the sixteenth century. The 'Town and cities' section of Chapter 5 is also useful. Chapter 5 includes a good summary of the religious situation before the Reformation.

M. Hughes, *Early Modern Germany, 1477–1806* (Macmillan, 1992).

Chapter 2 covers Germany on the eve of the Reformation. An excellent analysis of the political situation in the Holy Roman Empire before the Reformation.

H. Kellenbenz, *The Rise of the European Economy: An Economic History of Continental Europe from the Fifteenth to the Eighteenth Century* (Holmes & Meier, 1976).

There are several useful sections of this book that provide a detailed account of the changing industries and agricultural situation in Europe in the sixteenth century.

D. MacCulloch, *Reformation: Europe's House Divided 1490–1700* (Penguin, 2004).

This is an essential text – Chapters 1 and 2 on the Church before the Reformation are particularly useful for this topic.

Work together

Firstly, compare the notes that you have made on this section with a partner. Add anything that you have missed and check anything that you have disagreed on. Next, divide your paper into two. One of you should identify positive aspects of the German Catholic Church before the Reformation. The other should note the negative aspects. After you have finished, combine your findings. Overall, how would you describe the German Catholic Church at the beginning of the sixteenth century?

Chapter summary

- The Holy Roman Emperor had weak authority over the princes and other rulers over whom he was overlord.
- The power of the princes was growing because of this. They wanted more influence and control over their territory in both secular and religious matters.
- The papacy was worried about the power of the Emperor and the competition for power that it represented to the Church. This meant that the Pope sometimes opposed the Emperor rather than supported him at critical times.
- New industries and services like banking developed greatly. This changed the way that people viewed loans and money-lending and made credit available to rulers such as Charles V.
- Wages did not rise at the same pace as prices for essential commodities like food. Poverty increased, therefore, particularly in towns.
- There were rising social and political tensions caused by increased migration to towns and cities. As political participation was limited by town governments, dissatisfaction was amplified.
- The printing press meant that new ideas could spread quickly throughout the educated men of Europe, but visual and spoken forms of communication remained crucial because literacy rates were comparatively low.
- Although the German Catholic Church was popular among most ordinary people, it faced intellectual, social and religious challenges even before Martin Luther spoke out against it.
- Humanism led to the questioning of many assumptions, including religious ones, and laid great importance on education and the reading of texts. This created the background to later opposition to some of the ideas of the Church.
- As well as outspoken opponents of the Church, people called for change from inside the Church.

Conditions in early-sixteenth century Germany

The Holy Roman Empire

- Structure – loose federation of states
- Headed by the Holy Roman Emperor
- Imperial diet
  - form of parliament
  - law-making body of Empire
  - meetings central to events of Reformation, e.g. Diet of Worms
- 1519 imperial election – Charles V elected emperor by a vote of prince-electors

The state of the Germany economy

The growth of towns and cities
- Increase in migration from country to towns
- Some towns and cities more independent from sovereign rulers than others
- Large towns including Lubeck, Danz and Hamburg
- Ideas were conceived and spread quickly in towns and cities

Trade and communication
- Each German state had its own trade policies
- Trade was done via rivers and canals
- Postal services and news services were ways of communication
- Merchants helped spread news and information
- Invention of printing press – huge increase in books and cheap pamphlets spread information to wider audiences

Economy
- Emergence of new industries such as mining
- Economic problems
  - rural labourers disadvantaged
  - increase in prices of commodities
  - tensions due to population increase and migration

The German Catholic Church

A united Church?
- Unity but criticisms over hierarchy
- Emergence of national churches
- Resentment of papacy in Rome
- Bishops
  - increase in power
  - less intimate with their fleet
- Pope and bishops blamed for financial burden of Germany
- Conflict between monastic orders and parish priests
- Parish clergy – level of correction debated

Challenges to Catholicism
- Humanism – led to a questioning of existing approaches and ideas
- Previous challenges
  - Lollards
  - Hussites
- Calls for reform before Luther inside and outside the Church

▲ Summary diagram: Conditions in early-sixteenth century Germany

Section A: Essay technique

Focus on the question and understanding the sources

The A level Section A question requires you to deploy a variety of skills. The most important are source analysis and evaluation. In essence, the question asks how much a historian could learn about a specific issue from the two sources. This is a complex task, and requires a range of skills which will be covered in this section and at the end of Key Topics 2–4. These include the ability to:

- understand the focus of the question and the sources (this section)
- structure an essay and write good introductions (Key Topic 2, pages 250–52)
- select information and make inferences from the sources (Key Topic 2, pages 254–55)
- place the sources in their historical context (Key Topic 3, pages 279–81)
- evaluate and weigh up the evidence of the sources (Key Topic 4, pages 302–04)
- reach and support a final judgement (Key Topic 4, pages 305–07).

The Section A question for AS level is different from the Section A question for A level, and some guidance about this is given on page viii. However, you will need to develop very similar skills for the AS exam, therefore the activities will help with the AS exams as well. There are also some AS-style questions in every chapter.

The focus of the question

In order to answer the question successfully you must understand how the question works. Here is a typical Section A question. The question is written precisely in order to make sure that you understand the task. Each part of the question has a specific meaning:

'How far' indicates that you must evaluate the extent of something, rather than giving a simple 'yes' or 'no' answer.

They key word here is **together**. You must examine the sources as a pair and make a judgement about both sources, rather than separate judgements about each source.

> **Study Sources 1 and 2 before you answer this question.**
>
> **How far could the historian make use of Sources 1 and 2 together to investigate powers of the Holy Roman Emperor in the early sixteenth century?**
>
> **Explain your answer, using both sources, the information given about them and your own knowledge of the historical context.**

This is the essence of the task: you must focus on what a historian could legitimately conclude from studying these sources.

The final part of the question focuses on a specific topic that a historian might investigate. In this case: 'the Holy Roman Emperor in the early sixteenth century'.

This instruction lists the resources you should use: the sources; the information given about the sources; your own knowledge of historical context that you have learnt during the course.

Overall, all Section A questions ask you to make a judgement about how far two sources are useful to the historian. However, the second half of the question specifies what a historian is focusing on.

So, the first part of the question sets up the **general task**, which is true of all Section A questions:

'How far could the historian make use of Sources 1 and 2 together to investigate …'

And the second part of the question establishes the **specific focus**, for example:

'… powers of the Holy Roman Emperor in the early sixteenth century?'

As you write your essay, you need to focus on both aspects.

How to focus in a source question

Source questions are different from questions that only require you to use your own knowledge. There are a variety of ways to ensure you maintain your focus on the question that are appropriate to this type of question:

- Use the phrases 'Source 1' and 'Source 2', when dealing with the sources so that it is clear which sources you are focusing on.
- Use words such as 'useful' or 'utility' to ensure that you are explicitly addressing the general task.
- Use comparative words and phrases such as 'Sources 1 and 2 disagree' to show that you are using the sources together.

Section B: Essay technique

Focus and structure

Section B essays, like all of your examined essays, will be judged on how far they focus on the question, and the quality of their structure. You may have already considered advice on how to write a focused introduction, and how to structure your essays in Paper 1 (see pages 22–23).

Different types of question

Section B questions, like Sections A and B questions in Paper 1, can focus on a variety of concepts. These include cause, consequence, change/continuity, similarity/ difference and significance. These different concepts require slightly different approaches. Here are some examples of these concepts in questions.

These questions require you to explain the **causes** of opposition.

1 'Luther published the *Ninety-Five Theses* solely because of the indulgence crisis.' How far do you agree with this statement?

2 'The indulgence crisis was the main reason for Luther's publication of the *Ninety-Five Theses*.' How far do you agree with this statement? AS

3 'Between 1519 and 1555, the most significant consequence of the spread of Luther's teaching within Germany was a decline in the authority of the Roman Catholic Church.' How far do you agree with this statement?

4 'Between 1519 and 1555, the main consequence of the spread of Luther's teaching within Germany was a decline in the authority of the Roman Catholic Church.' How far do you agree with this statement? AS

These questions ask you to evaluate the **consequences** of Luther's teachings within the Holy Roman Empire.

These questions require you to evaluate the extent of **change/continuity** in the development of Lutheranism caused by the publication of the *Loci Communes*.

5 How far was the publication of the *Loci Communes* the main turning point in the development of Lutheranism in the years 1521–46?

6 How far was the publication of the *Loci Communes* the main development in Lutheranism in the years 1521–46? AS

7 'Popes Leo X and Paul III used radically different methods to oppose the spread of Lutheranism in Germany.' How far do you agree with this statement?

8 'Popes Leo X and Paul III used different methods to oppose the spread of Lutheranism in Germany.' How far do you agree with this statement? AS

These questions require you to evaluate the **similarity/difference** of the approaches of Pope Leo X and Paul III to opposing the spread of Lutheranism in Germany.

These questions require you to evaluate the **significance** of the publication of the *Loci Communes* for the development of Lutheranism in the years 1521–46.

9 How significant was the publication of the *Loci Communes* in the development of Lutheranism in the years 1521–46?

10 How far was the printing press responsible for the spread of Luther's ideas in the years 1517–20? AS

Structuring your essay

As in Paper 1, your essay should be made up of three or four paragraphs, each addressing a different factor (see page 22).

However, essays that focus on different concepts will need a slightly different structure:

- **Cause essays** require you to explain why something happened. Therefore, each paragraph should deal with a different possible cause.
- **Evaluative essays** require you to weigh up the extent of something. Most essays will require you to evaluate at some point, as weighing up is essential to reaching a conclusion. In essays that focus on evaluation each paragraph should weigh up a different factor. For example, if you were dealing with the question, 'How widespread was opposition to Luther's teachings within the Holy Roman Empire in the years 1517–26?' each paragraph could weigh up the support or opposition to Luther in a different part of the Holy Roman Empire. For example, one paragraph could deal with support or opposition from the German princes, another with the extent of opposition from the Church and finally, one paragraph could deal with support and opposition among the common people.
- **Success or failure essays** require you to evaluate the extent to which something succeeded. Therefore you will need to start by considering the aims in order to establish the criteria for success. You should go on to consider aspects that succeeded and weigh them up against aspects that failed in order to reach a conclusion.
- **Continuity and change essays** require you to evaluate the extent of change. Therefore your essay will have to weigh up what changed and what stayed the same.
- **Consequence essays** require you to evaluate which of a range of consequences was most important.

It is crucial to be able to distinguish between the different types of question. Confusing a cause essay with a consequence essay could seriously affect your grade.

Activity: Question types

1 Below are five different Section B questions. Work out what types of question they are.

a) To what extent was Luther's inability to travel the main cause of the decline of his influence on the German Reformation in the years 1530–46?

b) How far did Luther achieve his aims of religious reform in the period by 1555?

c) How effective was Charles V opposition to Lutheranism in the years 1521–55? AS

d) Why did Luther's influence on the German Reformation decline in the years 1530–46? AS

e) How far was increased princely support the main consequence of Luther's denunciation of the Peasants' War?

2 Having worked out what types of question you are dealing with you should now write plans for each question. You can plan either as spider diagrams or a bullet-point list. Make sure your plan reflects the kind of essay that you are dealing with. For example, if you are dealing with a success or failure essay, you should highlight which parts of the plan deal with success and which deal with failure. Complete one plan at a time, and after each discuss it with a partner.

Work together

Having completed a plan in activity 2 above, swap it with a partner. Consider:

1 Did you agree on what type of question you were dealing with? If not, discuss it and work out who was right.

2 Whose plan most clearly focused on the specific type of question?

3 Did your partner's plan miss anything?

4 Did you miss anything that you should add to your plan?

5 What can you learn from your partner's approach?

Use these questions to feedback to each other and improve your question spotting and planning.

Key Topic 2 Luther's early challenge to the Catholic Church, 1517–20

Overview

This chapter will focus on Luther's early challenge to the Church. It begins by discussing the early life and education of Luther. This is important because it helps to explain some of the reasons for his actions later on. The events of 1517–20 were set against the backdrop described in the previous chapter. Humanist tendencies in education and its emphasis on a return to the study of scripture were influential in Luther's life. Medieval Catholic fears about sin and hell featured strongly in Luther's early life, and concerns about the hierarchy of the Church were crucial in prompting his initial explosive work. Even before he entered the monastery in July 1505, Luther was worried about his soul and sought ways to ensure his salvation. It was partly this search for freedom from sin and guilt that was to push him into new approaches from 1517 onwards.

The chapter then examines Luther's writing and publication of the *Ninety-Five Theses* in 1517, the reaction of the Church to this publication and the Pope's response. Luther was very concerned with the way that the indulgence campaign for the restoration of St Peter's was being conducted in Germany. He hated the way that particular preachers manipulated the poor. His initial aim appears to have been to raise a debate about the problem and to bring it to the attention of the authorities. The chapter investigates how the response of the Pope to Luther's call for an end to indulgence campaigns prompted Luther to become more radical in his ideas, and looks at the consequences of Luther's works, debates and ideas. It

explains some of the key ideas in Luther's books and pamphlets, and also why those ideas spread so far in the early days of his challenge to the Church.

The chapter examines these issues through the following sections:

1 *Luther's early life and influences on him* explores Luther's upbringing and education. It looks at the career path that Luther was meant to take and the events that led to him changing course. It then goes on to examine Luther's life as a monk and his subsequent academic career.

2 *The* Ninety-Five Theses, *1517*, begins by examining the background to Luther's famous protest against indulgences. It looks at his previous complaints on the issue, the reasons why this particular indulgence campaign angered him so much, and how he went about publishing his ideas.

3 *The shaping of Luther's beliefs* discusses the ways in which Luther's ideas were moulded following the publication of the *Ninety-Five Theses*. It examines the debates that he had with representatives of the Church, and the materials that he wrote as a result. These materials demonstrate an increasing shift in Luther's ideas.

4 *Luther's excommunication, 1520*, explains Luther's excommunication by the Pope in 1520 and his reaction to that. This includes his writings following the excommunication and the burning of the bull of excommunication in Wittenberg.

TIMELINE

1483	Luther born in Eisleben, Saxony	1513	Luther became professor of theology
1501	Luther entered the University of Erfurt	1515	Pope Leo X issued the papal bull *Sacrosanctis*
1505	Luther underwent a conversion experience and entered a monastery in Erfurt	1516	Luther first preached against indulgences
		1517	Luther published his *Ninety-Five Theses*
1507	Luther took priestly orders	1518	Meeting of the Augustinians at Heidelberg
1508	Luther moved to a monastery at Wittenberg to begin teaching theology	1518	Luther summoned to Rome
		1518	Luther met with Cajetan at the Diet of Augsburg
1510	Luther was chosen as a representative of his monastery to go to Rome	1519	Debate with Johann Eck at Leipzig
		1520	Luther was excommunicated
1512	Luther was awarded his doctorate in theology	1520	Luther burned the papal bull

1 Luther's early life and influences on him

There were no early signs that Luther would be such a significant figure in the history of religion, Germany or Europe. He had a relatively normal upbringing and education for a man of his class and period. He was destined for a career in the law but an incident on his journey back from home to university apparently changed the course of his life. This section will cover influences in Luther's early life. His journey towards a religious life, his experiences in the monastery and in Rome all had an impact on the course that Luther took from 1517 onwards.

Note it down

In this section try using a spider diagram to take notes (see page x). Draw a circle in the middle of your page with the heading 'Luther's early challenge to the Church' inside it. Draw four lines coming out of the central circle that lead to the section headings of this chapter – Luther's early life and influences, the *Ninety-Five Theses*, shaping of Luther's beliefs and Luther's excommunication. Write important points on lines coming out from the section headings and write small points coming out from them.

Luther's upbringing and education

Luther began his adult life destined for a very different career to the one he finally took. His upbringing, education and conversion to a religious life were all important in making him the man, and the thinker, that he became.

Birth and family background

Martin Luther was born on 10 November 1483 in the town of Eisleben, Saxony. His father Hans came from a prosperous farming family but had moved into the mining industry, becoming an independent shareholder in a small copper smelting company. His wife Margarete Lindemann was from an urban merchant family of a higher social status and of greater education. Her family had produced lawyers, doctors and academics and were able to help Luther gain a higher level of education that he may have otherwise had. They were also very pious, which no doubt had some impact on Luther as he grew up.

Education

Luther's father wished for him to be a lawyer, paying for his education at the University of Erfurt. He entered the university in 1501 to study secular law (the law of the Holy Roman Empire). This was a rational choice on the part of Luther's father – it was a respected profession that represented an elevation in social status and a stable income. While at university Luther studied humanism (see page 226) as well as his legal studies. Although it is not clear that Luther himself was a humanist, it seems to have had a long-term effect on his teaching methodology and biblical study. This is because humanist thought led to a new interrogation of texts and an emphasis on study and education which we see at work in Luther's career and education. Humanists had also formed part of the challenge to the doctrines of the Church on issues like indulgences. The sense of enquiry which made humanists return to classical texts also meant an increased interest in, and study of, scripture. He graduated with his bachelor's degree in 1502 and master's degree in the arts in January 1505 and enrolled in law school the same year.

It was at university that Luther learned the skill of argument. Students were required to attend and take part in disputations, or debates. Students were given a set of arguments or 'theses' that they had to defend using logic. Luther's *Ninety-Five Theses* followed this form of disputation, demonstrating that his education had some impact on his later style of writing and argument.

Crisis and change of course

For reasons which remain unclear, Luther took a vacation from his legal studies halfway through term in 1505. He entered an Augustinian monastery in Erfurt in July 1505. There are different reasons given for this change:

1 **Luther's dramatic conversion experience**
   Luther later wrote that it was a terrifying experience that made him devote himself to a religious life. According to Luther, he was on a journey back to university from his family's home at Mansfeld on 2 July 1505 when he was caught in a terrifying thunderstorm. Luther said that following his near escape from a lightning strike he vowed to St Anne (the patron saint of miners) that he would become a monk.

2 **A long-term religious and philosophical crisis**
   Historians have traced the roots of Luther's change in course to a longer-term dissatisfaction with his life.

Luther appears to have had a certain amount of anxiety before entering the monastery. Elsewhere, Luther wrote that he entered the monastery because he despaired of himself, and there are other indications that he had been searching his soul because of spiritual worries. This mentality makes the later success of Lutheranism perhaps even more remarkable, given that rejecting the doctrines of the Church and behaving in a 'heretical' manner put your soul at risk of eternal damnation.

We have no idea whether it was either or both of these possibilities that drove Luther to make such an apparently sudden decision to enter the monastery in July 1505. It is clear, however, that this was the beginning rather than the end of his religious journey.

> **Source A** A letter from Martin Luther to his father Hans, from the dedication of *On Monastic Vows* (1521) about his decision to become a monk and his father's response to that.
>
>> It is now sixteen years since I became a monk, having taken the vow without your knowledge and against your will. You were anxious and fearful about my weakness, because I was a young blood of twenty-two, that is, to use St Augustine's words, it was still hot youth with me, and you had learned from numerous examples that monkery [for example, the monastic life] made many unblessed and so were determined to marry me honourably and tie me down. This fear, this anxiety, this non-consent of yours were for a time simply irreconcilable ...
>
> How useful is Source A as evidence of the differing priorities of Luther and his father? What can it tell us about perceptions of monastic life in this period?

Luther's monastic and academic career

Luther entered the monastery in 1505 intending to devote himself to God. He did this to the point of obsession, affecting his health in the process. Luther's talent for theology and biblical argument was recognised and he eventually became professor of theology at the University of Wittenberg in Electoral Saxony. It was against this background that he made his first moves into religious controversy.

Luther's monastic life

Luther entered a monastery where a spiritual life was pursued thoroughly. It was certainly not one of those monasteries that fitted the stereotype of luxurious life and material greed. There were six religious services a day, beginning at 2 a.m. Between the services the monks prayed, and completed spiritual exercises and meditations. Luther threw himself into this routine, and soon exceeded it. He was extremely anxious about whether he would go to hell, and tormented himself over the question of pleasing God. He fasted, prayed and completed long vigils in a quest to satisfy God. Luther later regretted the time he spent in this quest. The theology and sermons at the monastery reinforced what was taught in most of Europe at the time – that **salvation** was a matter of God's grace and that only God could grant salvation. To gain God's grace people had to do their part and act well. As nobody alive could know if they had acted well enough and tried hard enough there was a widespread preoccupation with avoiding hell. Luther was more anxious than many people in this regard and tortured himself thinking about it. He formally became a priest in 1507.

In 1508 Luther left the monastery in Erfurt for one in Wittenberg. This was to be an important move for his theological and academic development. Here he was aided by a superior in the Augustinian order who he originally met in Erfurt – Johann von Staupitz. Von Staupitz called for Luther to teach theology in Wittenberg. He was an important mentor for Luther and insisted that he take his doctorate. From 1508 Luther taught theology at the brand-new University of Wittenberg where von Staupitz was the professor of biblical theology.

Visit to Rome

In 1510 Luther was chosen as a delegate for a consortium of Augustinian monasteries in Saxony. He was to represent these monasteries in Rome to plead for strict reform of the order and an end to divisions and arguments within it. He left Germany in autumn 1510 and spent four weeks in Rome. He then returned to Wittenberg in spring 1511. As the journey was made on foot it took many months travelling. Like many other aspects of Luther's early life we rely on his later recollections for our knowledge of this period. He later described the corruption that he had seen in Rome, his disappointment at the ignorance of the priests and the light-hearted attitude of its inhabitants. Historian Patrick Collinson has described Rome in the sixteenth century as 'the Las Vegas of its day' and both he and Diarmaid MacCulloch see Luther's visit as an experience of 'culture shock'. Luther had high expectations of Rome. While Luther was to focus in hindsight on the negative aspects of corruption and decadence, it seems like his spiritual experience was actually relatively satisfactory in the short term. During his time in Rome, Luther said mass at several holy sites and visited several important churches and relics as a pilgrim.

Academic career

Luther had been teaching in the faculty of arts at Wittenberg since he arrived in the town in 1508, only interrupted by the journey to Rome. He was awarded a doctorate in theology in 1512 and succeeded von Staupitz as professor of theology. He started lecturing in this job in winter 1513–14. This was very important for Luther's ideas. Teaching others and having to explain texts to them made Luther himself study even harder. His personal religious quest continued throughout this. In fact, Luther held this job for the next 30 years, lecturing to different generations of students while the turmoil of the Reformation went on. His early lectures on the Book of Psalms and St Paul's Letter to the Romans, from 1514 to 1516, provided a foretaste of his future thought, which his own search for salvation had influenced. Here is a summary of Luther's ideas:

- People are hopelessly sinful.
- They should approach God with self-condemnation and humility.
- Their hope for salvation was through God's mercy, not through their own actions.

This was the basis of Luther's later, revolutionary, thinking. It was the beginning of a big change from the idea that people could affect their own destiny through good works.

The post of professor at Wittenberg was important to Luther for another reason. He was supported in achieving the post in 1513 by the Prince of Saxony Frederick III.

Known as Frederick the Wise, he was devoted to the university that he had founded. The university was Frederick's pride and joy. Luther's lectures drew many students to the university, particularly after his ideas became publicised. When Frederick was later so protective of Luther he was protecting one of the most prized professors at his university as well as fostering the development of new ideas.

Views on corruption within the Catholic Church

It is difficult to determine exactly what Luther's views were at the time about corruption within the Catholic Church. As a representative to Rome calling for strict reform, it is apparent that he valued a unified and pious religious life. He was also uncomfortable with the material aspects of life in Rome. Yet it is hard at this stage in his career to see evidence of the hatred for corruption that Luther described later. An important point of development was the indulgence crisis of 1516 and the actions of Johann Tetzel.

Conclusion

Luther had a conventional upbringing and education but was prompted, by religious anxiety over the possibility that his soul would linger in purgatory, to change his career path from the law to the Church. In his early days in the monastery Luther sought to become a better and more truly religious person in order to avoid damnation, starving himself and praying constantly. It was his mentor von Staupitz who steered him into a more academic pathway. Luther's subsequent teaching and study was to change his ideas on the basis of faith and salvation, as well as prompting him to address what he saw as significant problems within the Church.

2 The *Ninety-Five Theses*, 1517

The *Ninety-Five Theses* was Luther's first move in his battle with the Catholic Church. There is still significant debate about his intentions in publishing them, although there are no indications that Luther meant to set in motion such seismic changes. Luther's *Ninety-Five Theses* attacked abuses in the Church and asked that changes be made in order to reform the Church. They spread widely due to the unauthorised involvement of printers – and soon became a serious problem for the Catholic Church.

Note it down

In this section use index cards (see page xi) to note ideas and debates. Read the section carefully and highlight or indicate in the margin of your notes where an idea or theory is explained. Examples in this section include the justification for indulgences, ideas that criticised indulgences and the argument that Luther was starting a debate. For each idea put the name or a title on one side of the card and an explanation of the main points of that idea on the other side. Bullet point your explanation and use abbreviations if it will help you fit all your notes on one topic onto one card. You can then use these for revision or you can use the cards to test yourself with a partner.

Luther's rejection of indulgences

Luther was far from the only person to attack indulgences. Although they were not universally unpopular, several theologians and writers had already spoken out about their use. Luther began his attack on indulgences in 1516 in response to the activities of Johann Tetzel. He continued with the *Ninety-Five Theses* and his arguments soon became widely discussed.

Luther's early attacks on indulgences, 1516

Indulgences were a common feature of Catholic religious practice in order to avoid purgatory (see page 226). The Church had put a monetary value on blessings or pardons offered for personal sins. An indulgence (certified with a piece of paper) was given in return for a payment or donation towards the Church. This payment counted as a good work. Luther's emerging theology was clearly on a collision course with this practice, as he had begun to argue that good works would not help people to receive God's mercy. He preached against indulgences three times in 1516, even before the indulgence crisis would bring him to prominence.

Actually Luther was mostly opposed to the abuse of indulgences and the consequences of over-confidence in them rather than all indulgences per se. His criticism was brave both religiously and politically because:

Archbishop Albert of Magdeburg and Mainz (1490–1545)

Archbishop Albert was a member of the powerful Hohenzollern family. They were Imperial Electors of Brandenburg and wanted to expand their influence over the Church. Albert became Archbishop of Magdeburg in 1513. The following year Mainz fell vacant and Albert was determined to secure it for himself. The man who held this position was in charge of the Catholic Church in Germany. He would also be Imperial Chancellor and an Imperial Elector as part of the role of Archbishop of Magdeburg. If Albert was awarded this job, he would gain immense amounts of power for himself and his family. Bishops were not usually allowed to hold more than one **diocese** at once, however, and to achieve it large fees had to be paid for 'dispensations' from Rome.

- indulgences were a good source of money for religious authorities
- they were also good for secular authorities, who received a cut of the money raised
- attacking indulgences could look like an attack on both of those authorities
- specifically, Luther's first attacks on indulgences were on those funding the university he worked for and a church in Wittenberg – so he was attacking those that provided his job and income.

Luther was not the first theologian who had opposed indulgences. In the fifteenth century the Dutch theologians John of Wesel and Wessel Gansfort had spoken out against the abuse of the practice. Thomas Wittenbach of Basel University had also done so.

Luther and the crisis over indulgences

The 1517 indulgence crisis was both political and religious in origin. It formed part of a long-term change whereby aristocratic churchmen were influenced by secular political motives as well as religious ones. The specific issue that was to lead to the publication of the *Ninety-Five Theses* began in St Peter's Basilica in Rome. St Peter's Basilica was one of the holiest Catholic sites. It was reputed to be the burial site of Saint Peter, one of the apostles and, according to Catholic tradition, the first **Pope** and Bishop of Rome. It had been under renovation for at least 70 years and was still nowhere near the point of completion. Pope Leo X wanted to finish the renovation for God's glory and for his. This was, however, very expensive. Leo X turned to indulgences to achieve his aim, issuing the papal bull *Sacrosanctis* in 1515.

A campaign of indulgences was launched. This meant that preachers would travel around the different dominions of the Church across Europe, selling indulgences. The money raised would then be donated to the restoration of St Peter's. This campaign would need money to get started, however, as the Pope needed to pay the initial expenses of preachers and the secular authorities who were allowing them in to preach. To finance the indulgence campaign in Germany the Pope approached the powerful Fugger banking family (see page 216). The Fuggers agreed to help on the condition that another Fugger customer would also benefit from the deal.

The Pope, the Fuggers and Albert came to an understanding. Albert would promote the campaign of indulgences for St Peter's Basilica in Germany. The Fuggers would work out a financial deal. The Pope would get the money he wanted for the renovation (10,000 ducats coming from Albert) and Albert would become archbishop of Mainz. From the campaign of indulgences half of the money would go to the rebuilding of St Peter's Basilica, half towards repaying the Fuggers for their loan to Albert. All of the money from the campaign was raised from ordinary German people. It was an enormous amount of money – in comparison, Martin Luther himself never earned more than 400 ducats a year. This is one reason why the campaign was opposed.

There were objections to the campaign from different directions. It angered Frederick the Wise because it favoured his political opponents the Hohenzollerns. It also meant that other indulgences could not operate at the same time – which in turn affected the campaign to raise money for relics in Wittenberg. Frederick banned the campaign from his area.

Johann Tetzel

Others, humanist academics and pious Germans, objected to the way the campaign was run in Germany by Johann

Johann Tetzel (1465–1519)

Johann Tetzel was born in 1465 at Pirna in Meissen. He studied theology and philosophy at the University of Leipzig, in Ducal Saxony and graduated in 1487. He entered a Dominican monastery in 1489. He moved to a monastery in Glogau, in the province of Poland, and while there was appointed inquisitor for Poland by Cardinal Cajetan in 1509. Teztel subsequently returned to Leipzig and was appointed inquisitor of the Saxon province. He first became known as a preacher of indulgences in 1503. From 1503 to 1510, Teztel was responsible for the preaching of indulgence campaigns in different parts of Germany. In 1503, for example, he was in northern Germany in Magdeburg, Bremen and Riga. In 1509 he was at Strasbourg and in 1510 he was in Nuremberg, Wurtzberg and Bamberg. Tetzel reappeared in 1516, aiding the preaching of the indulgence campaign for St Peter's Basilica in Rome and it is that which gained him the notoriety that he still enjoys today. He was banned from preaching in Electoral Saxony by Frederick the Wise. It was his preaching that led to Luther writing the *Ninety-Five Theses*. A response was published under Tetzel's name (but written by the theologian Konrad Wimpina). Tetzel was heavily criticised for his views on the power of indulgences to release the souls of the dead from purgatory. He became the archetypal indulgence preacher, a figure satirised and mocked in reforming propaganda. Tetzel hid in a Dominican monastery in Leipzig in fear of popular violence springing from the outcry at his preaching. He died there on 4 July 1519.

Tetzel. Tetzel, a Dominican monk and the man put in charge of preaching this campaign in Germany, was not allowed to do so in Luther's parish because of Frederick's ban. He did come fairly close, however, so some of his parishioners did hear Tetzel preach and buy an indulgence. Tetzel would enter towns with a fanfare of trumpets and drums and a great procession. He would give an alarming sermon and then offer indulgences for sale on a sliding scale depending on an individual's income. Luther's parishioners returned to him saying that they no longer needed **confession**, **penance** or mass because the indulgence meant they were going to heaven. One of Tetzel's popular slogans was: 'As soon as your money clinks in the bowl, out of purgatory jumps the soul.' Luther saw Tetzel's promises of salvation as wrong and his campaigning style as an abuse of the system of indulgences. This apparently angered him so much on behalf of his parishioners that he wrote the *Ninety-Five Theses* and published them by pinning them to the door of the Castle Church.

Source B From Johann Tetzel's *Sample Sermon for Priests Selling Indulgences*, c1517. This was a sermon given as a sample for other indulgence preachers to use, designed to attract the highest possible donations.

Listen! Every mortal sin requires seven years of penance even after confession and **contrition**. The debt must be paid in this life or the next. How many mortal sins do you commit each day? How many every week? Per month? Yearly? Throughout your life? The total is infinite and infinite is the penance which must be suffered ... Won't you part with even a farthing to buy this letter? It won't bring you money but rather a divine and immortal soul, whole and secure in the Kingdom of Heaven.

Read Source B. Why do you think some people objected to Tetzel's style of campaigning?

The publication of the *Ninety-Five Theses* and their impact

Over the centuries historians and writers have held varied opinions about Luther's aims in publishing the *Ninety-Five Theses*. It is hard to argue about their impact, however, which was far greater than Luther himself could ever have envisaged. The theses themselves were a list of 95 objections against the sale of indulgences and other clerical abuses like **simony**. These objections were each one sentence long, and summarised Luther's calls for reform.

Luther's aims in publishing the *Ninety-Five Theses*

Luther apparently pinned his *Ninety-Five Theses* to the door of the Castle Church in Wittenberg on 31 October

1517. Later Lutheran reformers pictured this as a dramatic gesture of defiance, a young man railing heroically against a corrupt and powerful Catholic Church. It is much more likely that Luther was, to start with, actually trying to start an academic rather than a popular debate, for the following reasons:

- The form of the *Theses* was a conventional way of expressing a debate in German universities (see page 235).
- They were written in Latin, not German, so were in the language of academic debate.
- The door of the Castle Church was not chosen to make a point against the Catholic Church but rather a convenient public place to announce a debate.
- Luther's points were not revolutionary – others had said the same thing before, and Luther himself had on three occasions.
- Luther's arguments were not against fundamental points of theology, for example good works or purgatory.
- Luther did not immediately publicise or print the *Ninety-Five Theses* in any other way.

The importance of the printing press

The significance of Luther's work was not that his ideas were very new or revolutionary. Rather, it was significant because it was printed, circulated widely and discussed across Germany. It was not printed with Luther's permission. Developments within the printing industry and the initiative taken by printers in their quest for new and bestselling material partially help to explain the popularity of Luther's ideas. This relatively new industry sold materials at a range of costs and production quality. They needed a constant stream of new material to keep their educated readers interested. Enterprising printers in Germany's relatively new printing industry decided to publish the *Ninety-Five Theses* as a **broadside**. They printed versions in Latin and in German.

This prompted a pamphlet war between German theologians. Dominican writers, opponents of Luther's Augustinian monastic order, rushed into print to defend Johann Tetzel against Luther's criticisms. This was because Tetzel was a Dominican and Luther was an Augustinian. These two monastic orders were rivals in Germany. The debate reflected this rivalry as much as a difference in ideas, but did even more to publicise Luther's *Ninety-Five Theses*.

Luther's 1520 pamphlets also reached a wider audience and so the demand for Luther's works continued and grew. Cartoons, such as the one produced by Cranach before Luther's debate with Eck, were satirical and political. They required much visual literacy and an understanding of the doctrines at the heart of the joke. Again, these sold widely and to arrange audiences.

The impact of the *Ninety-Five Theses*

It seems that Luther's work prompted an increase in printing in Germany. There was a six-fold increase in printed material in the years 1518–24. A large proportion of this material was by Luther – 30 titles and approximately 300,000 copies. This was still a period where most people relied on oral culture rather than printed material, however, and the spoken word was also important in spreading Luther's ideas. They reached ordinary people in Germany because of preachers, many former students of Luther in Wittenberg, who preached sermons about the issue to their congregations.

The *Ninety-Five Theses* reached a large audience and sparked a debate about the abuse of indulgences. It was an audience both of educated literate people and the illiterate masses. They also drew attention to the actions of Tetzel and the conduct of the indulgence campaign in Germany. The Church could not control the response to the *Ninety-Five Theses* or the level of interest. It placed the Church under huge pressure to discipline Luther in order to suppress debates about such a vital aspect of Church practice.

Conclusion

Luther's objections to indulgences and his broader desire for changes to the Church were brought together in the *Ninety-Five Theses*. This long list of complaints about the indulgence campaign and other abuses within the Church were a call for a debate about how to renew the Church. Their printing and publication was to widely publicise Luther's views. It did indeed start a debate, but a much wider and more public one than Luther had expected or desired. Although this led to Luther's protest being taken seriously, it also meant that the Church had to take a strong line in response in order to keep discipline.

> ### Work together
>
> Working together in pairs, create a diagram or flowchart that expresses Luther's journey from traditional orthodox Catholicism to his early challenge in 1517. Some factors or events will overlap and you must take that into account when designing your diagram. After you have finished, discuss which elements of this journey were most important in prompting the change in Luther's ideas. You could assign colours to the different levels of importance. Be prepared to explain or justify why you think some factors are more important than others.

3 The shaping of Luther's beliefs

Luther's beliefs evolved greatly from the publication of the *Ninety-Five Theses* onwards. They were moulded by the response of the Pope and the Church hierarchy. This response was ill-thought out and provoked Luther into a more extreme rejection of the Pope and the Catholic Church.

> ### Note it down
>
> In this section you will be reading about some complex ideas and responses to those ideas. In this situation, the spider diagram is probably not the best way to make notes because it would be difficult to fit your explanations onto the page so it's best to use the 1:2 method (see page x). Divide your page in two. On the left you will put the big points. The first subheading, for example, might be 'Luther's written protest to Albert of Mainz'. On the right you will put the small points that explain or develop this subheading. Again looking at the first subheading, on the right-hand side you might write something like 'Luther naïve, believed Albert unaware of Tetzel's actions'. It would be best to bullet point the small points.

The protest to Albert of Mainz

As well as pinning his *Ninety-Five Theses* to the door of the Castle Church, Luther sent a politely worded protest to his local archbishop. This included the *Theses*. This was naïve as the local archbishop was none other than Albert of Mainz. Luther perhaps believed that Albert did not know what Tetzel was doing and that his appointee was abusing the authority of the Church in order to raise money. The *Ninety-Five Theses* questioned Albert's actions and the indulgence campaign. It was because of this that Albert sent the *Theses* to Rome. This, in turn, meant that the papacy was forced to respond as the *Theses* were perceived as an attack on papal authority. This response of the papacy was muted at best. Albert of Mainz did not respond to Luther's letter because the issue was so serious that only the papacy could deal with it. This lack of response drove Luther to spread his ideas more widely and it also meant that the Pope sent a series of **envoys** to demonstrate that Luther was wrong.

Response of Pope Leo X to Luther's early challenge

There were three main aspects to the Pope's response to Luther's early challenge:

- The Pope's preoccupation with Italian politics.

- The rivalry between the Dominicans and the Augustinian orders of monks.
- The desire of the Church to defend religious practice even if discredited.

Italian politics

Pope Leo X was Italian. Before becoming Pope in 1489 he was known as Giovanni di Lorenzo de' Medici, second son of Lorenzo de' Medici, who ruled Florence until his death in 1492. In 1517 Leo X was preoccupied with Italian politics and the politics of his family, for example the capture of Urbino in a dynastic war. He was also trying to thwart his enemies among his **cardinals**. After a plot to poison him, he executed one cardinal and made radical changes within the College of Cardinals. Leo X was also anxious about the threat posed by the Turks who were threatening **Christendom** from the east. He saw the Luther affair initially as a petty fight between the Augustinians and the Dominicans, so ordered the Augustinian authorities in Germany to find a solution at their meeting in Heidelberg in April 1518.

Dominican and Augustine rivalry

The Dominicans and the Augustinians were rivals for monastic power and influence. The Dominicans had for the previous 50 years seen themselves as the guardians of religious doctrine and champions of the pope's authority. The **papal curia** at this time included a number of Dominicans. They saw Luther's attack on Tetzel, indulgences and the Pope's power to grant salvation through indulgences as an attack on papal authority. They campaigned relentlessly for Luther to be punished. A Dominican theologian, Silvestro Mazzolini of Prierio (known as 'Prierias') was instructed by the papacy to write a report about the *Theses* and Luther's conduct. Their persistence led eventually to an order being sent to Luther summoning him to Rome within 60 days of him receiving it. It arrived, with the attack by Prierias, on 7 August 1518.

The Augustinians met in Heidelberg on 26 April 1518 to discuss Luther's ideas. Luther had called for a debate, and von Staupitz (the head of the Augustinian order in Germany and Luther's mentor) ordered that this debate should happen at the regular meeting of the order at Heidelberg. At the disputation Luther put forward his ideas and a debate took place. No decision was made about the validity of Luther's protest. It was as a result of the inconclusive debate that Johann Eck (a Dominican) proposed a debate between himself and a representative of Luther's ideas.

Failure of the papal response

Finally, the papal response was badly mishandled in a way that was likely to gain Luther more supporters. It

meant that the Church aligned itself to protect some of the aspects of religious practice that had attracted the most criticism from a range of groups and individuals. This denial of the need for reform and the attack on Luther led to Luther's further disillusionment and determination to address the problem. This was made worse when the various representatives sent by the Pope would not answer Luther's arguments. This drove Luther further away from the Church and also meant that his ideas attracted more supporters and more attention.

Debate with Cajetan, 1518

Luther was initially summoned to Rome to answer charges about his conduct. There was a clear threat that he would not return and because of that Luther wrote to Frederick the Wise to request that he intervene with the Pope. As Frederick was highly protective of his university (see page 237) and the professors who taught at it, Luther was successful. Luther requested a hearing in Germany before an impartial judge or group of theologians. Frederick knew that he had a good chance of success in achieving this because the Pope wanted the support of the German princes for his planned crusade against the Turks. Once again, it was political events which helped Luther to survive and escalated the issues he was drawing attention to. The result of this negotiation was a meeting with Thomas de Vio, Cardinal Cajetan, at the imperial diet in Augsburg in autumn 1518.

Cajetan was one of the greatest Dominican theologians of the age. He was the leader of the Dominicans and was attending the imperial diet as **papal legate**. The original purpose of his attendance was to attract support for the Pope's crusade against the Turkish threat. It was convenient, therefore, that he interrogate Luther after Frederick's request was granted. Cajetan was a distinguished theologian and in other circumstances may have been an ideal person to debate with about indulgences. At Augsburg, however, he was representing the authority of the Pope and did not feel that a debate was suitable. He was angry when Luther seemed determined to have a debate with him. Cajetan and Luther met four times, all unproductive. Cajetan told Luther in the first meeting that he needed to do three things:

- Repent and revoke his errors.
- Promise not to teach again.
- Refrain from future disruption.

Luther did not promise to do these but insisted instead on a debate. By the final interview Cajetan was completely exasperated. He cut the interview short and told Luther that he should not return unless it was to recant. Meanwhile rumours spread in Augsburg that Luther was to be arrested and taken to Rome. His friends and supporters in Wittenberg panicked. They hustled Luther back to Wittenberg. It turned out that they escaped just in time. Cajetan complained to Frederick that Luther's insistence on debate was insolent, while Luther responded that Cajetan had broken a promise to discuss the issue of indulgences. As with the rest of the papal response to Luther's criticisms, this made Luther question his position even more.

Debate with Eck, 1519

The next significant event in the development of Luther's ideas and position was the debate with doctor Johann Eck at Leipzig in July 1519. It was an attempt by the Dominican Eck to shut down the debate that Luther had started, to defeat Luther and discredit his ideas. It was significant because it was the first time that Luther's ideas were so publically interrogated. In the debate, Eck provoked Luther into sounding much more radical than he had before, refusing to condemn condemned heretics like Jan Hus (see page 227).

Rather than challenge Luther directly, Eck challenged a colleague of Luther's at the University of Wittenberg. Andreas Rudolf von Bodenstein, otherwise known as Andreas Carlstadt, was a theologian and academic who, as Luther later said of his own experience, had his beliefs challenged during a stay in Rome from 1515 to 1516. He wrote his own series of theses in 1516 that attacked what he saw as corruption in the Catholic Church. Even the negotiations to set up the debate were lengthy and resulted in a small pamphlet war. Carlstadt commissioned his friend Lucas Cranach to draw a cartoon criticising his opponents'

beliefs. This became very popular before the debate and made their Dominican opponents extremely angry.

The debate was presided over by the other Saxon prince, Duke George, and the topic was the authority in the Church. Luther was not meant to feature in the debate but it was clear that he, rather than Carlstadt, was the main target. Sure enough Luther did debate with Eck at Leipzig. While Carlstadt was meant to be the participant, Eck drew Luther into the argument quickly, demanding that he respond to questions about his views. Eck was a highly skilled debater. He managed skilfully to steer the debate away from areas that Luther wanted to discuss (such as the relationship with the churches of the east who were not obedient to the Pope) and into some highly dangerous areas. These included the authority of the Pope and the degree to which Luther agreed with Jan Hus, executed leader of the Hussite movement. Luther was drawn to admit that he did not reject Hus entirely and believed that some of the ideas the Hussites were condemned for were 'truly Christian'. Luther also admitted that he favoured the sole authority of scripture rather than believing in the authority of the Pope. This was both crucial and dangerous for the following reasons:

- Hus had been condemned as a heretic and executed for his ideas. The Church would be seen as inconsistent or weak if it did not act similarly towards Luther.
- The pope's authority was a matter of great debate in this period and **secular rulers** were trying to increase their own powers. This meant that the Pope was on the defensive in this matter and, again, would be forced to act severely against Luther.

Johann Eck (1486–1543)

Johann Eck was central Europe's leading theologian. He was a professor of theology at the Bavarian University of Ingolstadt. Eck was of a very similar age to Luther but his thinking developed in the direction of traditional rather radical ideas. Although he initially corresponded in a friendly manner with Luther, he subsequently turned into one of his most effective enemies. He was a strong defender of obedience to papal authority and so believed that Luther was completely wrong in regards to indulgences, the indulgence campaign and justification by faith (see page 244). He went on to pursue Luther's excommunication after the debate at Leipzig.

The debate was seen as a success for Eck. After the debate he drew up a formal indictment of Luther for heresy and sent it to Rome. Eck went to Rome to help prepare Luther's condemnation. This was to come on 15 June 1520 in the form of the papal bull *Exsurge Domine*.

Conclusion

Luther's ideas were shaped by the responses of others as well as by his own thought and study. When the Church rejected his criticisms and supported a series of hostile debates against him Luther became increasingly angry and alienated. He started to see deeper problems with the papacy and Church teachings than he had previously. Luther's writings reflected this, and his debate with Eck showed how far he had travelled theologically since 1517.

Work together

Here you will attempt to summarise the arguments between the various Church representatives and theologians that Luther was faced with from 1517 to 1520. Work in pairs. One of you will represent the Church. You need to explain the point of view of the papacy. This might include the reasons not to get involved in debate with Luther, as well as arguments for why Luther was a heretic. The other person in the pair will represent Luther. You will explain Luther's reasons for wanting a debate, and his ideas about faith and papal authority. When you have finished come together and re-read your notes. If there are any sections that you found difficult to explain, then add more detail to your notes or work together on a better explanation.

---

4 Luther's excommunication, 1520

Luther's thinking had changed greatly from his initial objections to indulgences in 1517. It had moved further away from the traditional teachings of the Church. Between 1519 and 1520 Luther developed his idea of 'justification by faith alone'. He also wrote pamphlets addressed to different audiences, in order to explain and spread his ideas further. These pamphlets were extremely popular and sold many copies. Luther was also excommunicated by the Pope in 1520. Although this had extremely serious consequences in traditional Catholic doctrine, Luther's new ideas about the corruption of the Pope meant that he did not perceive the excommunication with as much fear or anxiety as he might have done.

Note it down

You could use either the 1:2 method here or further add to your collection of index cards (see page xi). The important thing with this section is that you note down the idea, for example, justification by faith alone, and an explanation of that idea. There are four main concepts that you will need to understand and explain here in order to use them effectively in essays and source exercises. No matter which of the two suggested methods you choose, remember to bullet point the different aspects of the idea and explain them clearly in a manner that you will understand and remember.

Luther's tower experience

Between Luther's publication of the *Ninety-Five Theses* and his excommunication in 1520 Luther had been thinking hard about the implications of his ideas. At some point in those three years Luther had what became known as his 'tower experience'. This apparently happened in 1519 and was called the tower experience because it was said to have happened in his study in the tower of the monastery where he lived. Luther himself described this as a conversion experience. He said that it was this experience, not the publication of the *Theses*, which formed his breakthrough. The breakthrough came after Luther had been reading a chapter of the Bible, meditating hard on its implications for days and nights. From this experience came one of Luther's most well-known ideas, 'justification by faith alone'.

Justification by faith alone (*sola fide*)

Luther had begun to believe that the only authority he would accept for a religious practice or belief was the Bible. As a result he rejected the idea that the Pope was God's appointed representative on earth. This was because that claim was not in the Bible. Following on from that, for Luther, the whole structure of the Church hierarchy was invalid. It also meant that the Pope could not judge Luther or his ideas, and so could not condemn him.

Luther was reading Romans 1:17. In this part of the Bible it is written that 'in the gospel the righteousness of God is revealed – a righteousness that is by faith from first to last, just as it is written: "the righteous will live by faith"'. From reading this closely and studying it over many hours, day and night, Luther constructed the idea of justification by faith. The literal translation from Latin of the word justification is the making of someone to be righteous. So, justification by faith means that a person can only be saved by faith in God. This was revolutionary because it rejected the importance of good works and practices like indulgences (see page 226) in preventing people from going to hell. This was central to the practice of the Catholic Church and so set Luther on a collision course with it.

1520 pamphlets addressed to the clergy, nobility and German people

Following the debates and upheavals of 1517–19 Luther produced a series of pamphlets that clarified his ideas and explained them to people he saw as key audiences. These helped to form the basis of Lutheran theology. They also represented a complete break from Rome and the culmination of three years of hard work and thinking on the part of Luther.

The *Address to the Christian Nobility of the German Nation*

This pamphlet was extremely popular. The initial print run of 4,000 copies sold out in only five days. It went on to be published in a further 16 editions. The *Address* was directed to the secular rulers of Germany, the princes and the Emperor, and it asked them to undertake a full programme of reform of the abuses within the Church. Again, the theology that the appeal was based on was new. It said that the distinction between those in the Church hierarchy as 'religious' and the princes, knights, craftsmen and peasants as 'secular' was false. Luther argued that there was no difference between the two groups except the work they did. He said that the organisation of the clergy was a betrayal of the Church, a selfish interest group that only benefited those within it. This became known as Luther's doctrine of 'the priesthood of all believers', where all believers had a role in spreading God's word rather than just the priests. This was revolutionary because it denied that there was anything special about the officials of the Catholic Church. It was dangerous for the Church because if it spread widely, obedience to the Church would decline at all levels of society. It was also contrary to religious teachings. From this idea key features of Protestantism would emerge. These included married ministers, the use of the word 'ministry' rather than 'priesthood' and the involvement of governments in religious affairs.

Another reason for the popularity of this pamphlet was that it used anti-papal language and arguments. These were not new and had been used in arguments between secular rulers and the papacy over previous centuries. The argument was that the Pope was not God's chosen representative on earth but an impostor who had been put there by the devil. The Pope, therefore, was the Antichrist. If the pope was the Antichrist it meant that he was a threat to the government of the Holy Roman Empire. In the *Address* Luther argued that as well as dealing with papal corruption, the secular rulers had a God-given duty to overthrow the Pope as Antichrist.

The pamphlet was addressed to the newly elected Emperor, Charles V, and the princes and nobles of the Holy Roman Empire. It was not aimed at the masses in Germany. The 'Nation' in the title meant the Holy Roman Empire, not the whole nation of Germany. So while this pamphlet is sometimes called nationalistic this is not what Luther intended.

The Babylonian Captivity of the Church

Another pamphlet published in October 1520, *The Babylonian Captivity of the Church,* developed this theme for a different audience. This time Luther was writing to the clergy. Here Luther rejected the belief that the clergy were special, with duties that only they could execute. He argued that every true Christian was a priest and that you did not need a special group of people to help you make contact with God. This became one of Luther's most well-known ideas. Luther redefined the sacraments and the mass. He believed that good works or human merit had little value in God's eyes. The clergy were just the servants of the Church. If you return to look at Luther's original theses, it is clear that the conflict he had experienced with the Catholic Church had prompted him to think

> **Source C** From Luther's cover letter to the Holy Roman Emperor and the nobility of the German nation, enclosing his *Address to the Nobility of the German Nation*, 1520.
>
> It is not out of sheer forwardness or rashness that I, a single, poor man, have undertaken to address your worships. The distress and oppression which weigh down all of Christendom, especially of Germany, and which move not me alone, but everyone to cry out time and again, and to pray for help ... I now intend, by the help of God, to throw some light upon the wiles and wickedness of these men, to the end that when they are known, they may not henceforth be so hurtful and so great a hindrance ... it came to pass of old that the good Emperors Frederick I and II and many other German Emperors were shamefully oppressed and trodden under foot by the popes, although all the world feared them. That it may not so fare with us and our noble young Emperor Charles, we must be sure that in this matter we are dealing not with men, but with the princes of hell, who can fill the world with war and bloodshed, but whom war and bloodshed do not overcome ... The popes and the Romans have hitherto been able, by the devil's help, to set kings at odds with one another, and they may well be able to do it again, if we proceed by our own might and cunning, without God's help.
>
> What does Luther say that the popes have done in Source C? How does Luther approach Charles V in this letter and how does he try to appeal to him?

new thoughts in directions far away from the Church's teachings.

Burning of the bull of excommunication in 1520

In June 1520 Luther was excommunicated by the Pope. The bull of excommunication, sent directly by the Pope in Rome, had severe consequences. It meant that Luther was an outcast from the Catholic Church. All obedient Christians would refuse to have any dealings with him. His soul would burn in hell for eternity. This was publicised by reading the document from the pulpit of every church. This first bull was called *Exsurge Domine*, from the first line which meant 'Lord, cast out'. Bonfires were made of Luther's writings around Germany.

On 10 December Luther and his colleagues at the University of Wittenberg organised a counter-demonstration. A bonfire was lit and books by Eck as well as volumes of **canon law** were thrown onto the flames. Finally Luther himself came forward. He threw the bull of excommunication into the fire. This was a public demonstration of Luther's contempt for the Pope and the Church. Luther was very aware of the significance of his actions and spoke about it while teaching at the university. The faculty returned to the university but the students continued to demonstrate against the Pope until two days afterwards when the town authorities finally ended the demonstration. Shortly afterwards Luther produced a pamphlet whose title *Against the Bull of the Antichrist* claimed that the Pope was the devil. There was no way back from this point for Luther. The final bull of excommunication, *Decet Romanum Pontificem* appeared in January 1521.

Source D An early portrait of Martin Luther that appeared on the title page *Babylonian Captivity of the Church*, 1520. Like many of the Luther images in circulation at the time, this **woodcut** is based on a portrait by Lucas Cranach the Elder.

AETHERNA IPSE SVAE MENTIS SIMVLACHRA LVTHERVS
EXPRIMIT·AT VVLTVS CERA LVCAE OCCIDVOS
·M·D·X·X·

What impression does Source D give of Martin Luther? Why do you think it aims to give this impression?

Conclusion

1520 was a year of breakthroughs for Luther. His theological breakthrough, the idea of 'justification by faith alone' was to form the backbone of Lutheran doctrine. It was a substantial move away from traditional Catholic teaching. Other central features of Lutheranism were to emerge from the pamphlets published in 1520. These included clerical marriage and the involvement of governments in religious life. This came from Luther's denial in those pamphlets that the clergy were a special group who were needed to act as intermediaries between the people and God. The anti-papal content of Luther's works increased due to his excommunication. The point of no return was reached with *Against the Bull of the Antichrist*. From this point forward it would have been very difficult to reunite the Church.

Work together

In your pairs re-read pages 222–26 on the medieval Catholic Church. On a piece of paper, each of you draw two overlapping circles. A CD is the perfect size for this exercise. You will each be constructing what is called a Venn diagram. The point of this diagram is to highlight areas of similarity and difference. Label the left-hand circle 'ideas and practices of traditional Catholicism' and label the right-hand circle 'Luther's ideas'. Use all the material in this chapter and that on pages 222–26. One of you should fill in the left-hand side and the other the right-hand side. Inside the part of the circle that does not overlap right the ideas or practices specific to the group you have been assigned. When you have noted the different aspects of either idea, come together and explain your side of the diagram to your partner. Together you should look at the middle section. This will contain the similarities between the two sides. At this stage, until 1521, there were still some ideas that both sides had in common. Use both of your notes to highlight these and put them in the diagram.

Chapter summary

- Luther originally intended to become a lawyer but had a conversion experience at some point. This led him to become a monk and then theologian instead.
- Luther was extremely anxious about his spiritual salvation and how to achieve it. He studied the Bible intently to find solutions.
- He visited Rome and found the experience shocking, if satisfactory in spiritual terms.
- Luther's role as professor of theology led him to develop his own ideas about salvation. They were also influenced by his own search for salvation.
- Luther attacked the practice of indulgences in lectures and in the *Ninety-Five Theses* in 1516 and 1517. This was due to the campaign to renovate St Peter's Basilica and the way it was operated in Germany by Johann Tetzel.
- It is probable that Luther did not intend the *Ninety-Five Theses* to be a gesture of defiance but instead to start an academic debate.
- Printers, looking for material to print and sell in Germany, printed and publicised Luther's work without his permission.
- The Church could not control the response and so was forced to try and control Luther.
- The papal response was mishandled, and protected discredited practices while refusing to engage with Luther's objections. This meant that Luther's response escalated further.
- Luther's 'tower experience' of 1519 apparently led to a breakthrough and the formulation of one of his most important ideas – justification by faith alone.
- A series of pamphlets in 1520 directed to different groups explained Luther's ideas and formed the basis of Lutheran theology. They represented a complete break from Rome.

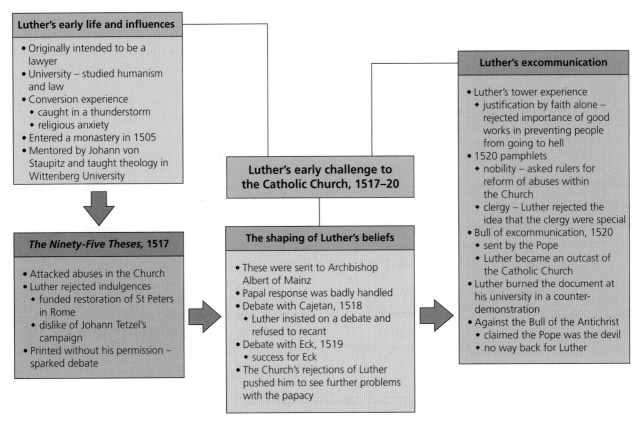

Luther's early life and influences

- Originally intended to be a lawyer
- University – studied humanism and law
- Conversion experience
  - caught in a thunderstorm
  - religious anxiety
- Entered a monastery in 1505
- Mentored by Johann von Staupitz and taught theology in Wittenberg University

Luther's early challenge to the Catholic Church, 1517–20

Luther's excommunication

- Luther's tower experience
  - justification by faith alone – rejected importance of good works in preventing people from going to hell
- 1520 pamphlets
  - nobility – asked rulers for reform of abuses within the Church
  - clergy – Luther rejected the idea that the clergy were special
- Bull of excommunication, 1520
  - sent by the Pope
  - Luther became an outcast of the Catholic Church
- Luther burned the document at his university in a counter-demonstration
- Against the Bull of the Antichrist
  - claimed the Pope was the devil
  - no way back for Luther

The Ninety-Five Theses, 1517

- Attacked abuses in the Church
- Luther rejected indulgences
  - funded restoration of St Peters in Rome
  - dislike of Johann Tetzel's campaign
- Printed without his permission – sparked debate

The shaping of Luther's beliefs

- These were sent to Archbishop Albert of Mainz
- Papal response was badly handled
- Debate with Cajetan, 1518
  - Luther insisted on a debate and refused to recant
- Debate with Eck, 1519
  - success for Eck
- The Church's rejections of Luther pushed him to see further problems with the papacy

▲ Summary diagram: Luther's early challenge to the Church, 1517–20

Recommended reading

Patrick Collinson, *The Reformation* (Weidenfeld & Nicolson, 2003).

Chapter 4 provides a good summary of Luther's early challenge to the Church and Chapter 5 is particularly useful regarding the radical reformation.

Diarmaid MacCulloch, *Reformation: Europe's House Divided* (Penguin, 2004).

An essential text for this topic.

Steven Ozment, *Protestants: The Birth of a Revolution* (Doubleday, 1993).

An interesting account of the birth of Protestantism that includes primary sources. It includes the origins as well as the progress of the Reformation among ordinary people.

Russell Tarr and Keith Randall, *Access to History: Luther and the German Reformation 1517–55* (Hodder, 2008).

A good basic account of Luther's Reformation. Chapter 2, on Luther's ideas from 1517–21, is particularly relevant to this section.

Section A: Essay technique

Understanding the sources

Understanding the sources is crucial to doing well in Section A questions. The most important aid in this understanding is a detailed knowledge of the period. There are also techniques to aid understanding. Here are a few tips to get you started:

- Read the source word for word – if it helps, read it out loud when you are doing practice questions. This makes it much less likely that you will miss anything in the source.
- Think about the question as you are reading. You will then look out for relevant information within the source.
- Make index cards before your exam of the specific vocabulary for the topic you are studying, for example, purgatory, souls, indulgences, pardons.
- Look up terms and definitions that you don't recognise in practice questions.
- Make index cards of the people who might be quoted in the sources, and the documents that might be used as sources on the examination paper such as Albert of Mainz, Johann Eck and Cardinal Cajetan. Make notes on who they are and their attitudes to the key issues you have studied.

Comprehension

Comprehension is the most basic source skill. It simply means understanding the source's meaning and you can demonstrate this in the following ways:

- **Copying**: writing out the words of the source in your essay.
  TIP: Avoid copying any more than a sentence at any point in your essay.
- **Paraphrasing:** putting part of a source in your own words.
  TIP: Avoid simply rewriting more than a sentence from the sources in your own words, before using a higher level skill.
- **Summarising:** summing up the meaning of the entire source, or a large part of the source, in a single sentence.
  TIP: Summarising can be useful in introductions and conclusions.

These are low level source skills. Therefore, they should not dominate your essay. However, small quotes, short paraphrases and occasional summaries can be useful to support higher level skills.

Higher level skills

Higher level skills include:

- using the sources together (see pages 230–31)
- making inferences (see pages 254–55)
- analysing sources in their historical context (see pages 279–81)
- evaluating the evidence presented in the sources (see pages 302–04)
- reaching an overall judgement regarding the usefulness of the sources (see pages 305–07).

Source 1 From Martin Luther's letter to the Archbishop of Mainz, 1517. The letter protested the Archbishop's sale of indulgences. The Archbishop was entitled to sell indulgencies according to cannon law, and part of the money raised went to the papacy.

Papal indulgences for the building of St Peter's are circulating under your most distinguished name, and as regards them, I do not bring accusations against the outcries of the preachers, which I have not heard, so much as I grieve over the wholly false impressions which the ordinary people have conceived from them. The unhappy souls believe that if they have purchased letters of indulgence they are sure of their salvation – that as soon as they cast their contributions into the money-box, souls fly out of purgatory ... How great is the horror, how great the peril of a bishop, if he permits the Gospel to be kept quiet, and nothing but the noise of indulgences to be spread among his people! ... But what can I do except pray your Most Reverend Fatherhood by the Lord Jesus Christ that you would deign to look on this matter with the eye of fatherly care, and do away entirely with that treatise and impose upon the preachers of pardons another form of preaching; in case one may arise, who will publish writings in which he will disprove both them and that treatise, to the shame of your Highness.

Having read Source 1 on page 249:

1 a) Make a list of words and phrases that you don't understand.
   b) Look them up in the glossary of this book or online. You should repeat this activity regularly with the sources that you encounter. This will help with many of the sources you will examine as you study Luther and the Reformation, as sources from the same period, referring to the same topic, will tend to use a similar vocabulary.
2 a) **Copy** the sentence that best expresses Luther's view of indulgences. Make sure you put the quote in 'quotation marks'.
   b) **Paraphrase** one of Luther's reasons why the Archbishop of Mainz should impose 'another form of preaching' on preachers.
   c) **Summarise** Luther's message in Source 1 in no more than 25 words.

3 Source 1 is a letter. Letters are often written to individuals or groups. They tend to refer to the writer, the recipient and other people as well. In order to understand the letter it is important to understand who the letter is referring to.
The following words and phrases refer to specific individuals, copy them down and then write next to them who they are:
   – 'your most distinguished name' (line 2)
   – 'the preachers' (line 4)
   – 'ordinary people' (line 6)
   – 'The unhappy souls' (lines 6–7)
   – 'your Most Reverend Fatherhood by the Lord Jesus Christ' (lines 14–15)
   – 'the preachers of pardons' (line 17)
   – 'your Highness.' (line 20)

Work together

Having completed activities 1–3, swap your answers with a partner. Consider:

1 Did you both identify the same words that needed to be defined?
2 Were your partner's definitions clear and accurate?
3 Did you both agree on who the letter was referring to in the who's who activity?
4 Did you both copy the same bit of the source? If not, which quote better summarises Luther's message in Source 1?
5 Is your partner's paraphrase clear? Does it accurately reflect one of Luther's reasons why the Archbishop of Mainz should impose 'another form of preaching' on preachers?
6 What can you learn from the approach of your partner to Source 1?

Use these questions to feedback to each other and improve your analysis of the source.

Structuring an essay and writing introductions

Well-structured essays are likely to receive higher marks than essays in which the structure is unclear. The structure of your essay should reflect the nature of the task that you are performing. Therefore, it should help you evaluate how far the two sources together are useful to a historian who is investigating a specific topic.

Macro structure

The overall structure of your essay should include:

- an introduction, which focuses on the question and sets out the essence of your answer
- a conclusion that summarises your essay in order to weigh up the extent to which the evidence of the sources is useful, and reaches an overall judgement
- the main body which presents a detailed evaluation of the evidence of the sources.

TIP: Remember, the question asks you to consider the sources *together*. Therefore, a structure which analyses Source 1 and then moves on to Source 2 is unlikely to do well. It would be better to structure your essay in a way that allows you to deal with the sources together.

Micro structure

Each paragraph should set out an analysis of the usefulness of the evidence of the two sources. Therefore, you need to discuss both sources in every paragraph.

TIP: One way of doing this is to make sure that you discuss both sources in almost every sentence.

For example, imagine you are answering the following question:

> How far could the historian make use of Sources 2 and 3 together to investigate the relationship between the papacy and Germany in early sixteenth-century Germany?

Source 2 From Martin Luther's *Address to the Christian Nobility of the German Nation*, published in 1520.

The Romanists have, with great cunning, drawn walls round themselves, with which they have hitherto themselves, so that no one could reform them, whereby all Christendom has fallen terribly.

First, if pressed by the temporal power, the Romanists have affirmed and maintained that the temporal power has no jurisdiction over them, but, on the contrary, that the spiritual power is above the temporal.

Let us, in the first place, attack the first wall.

It has been devised that the Pope, bishops, priests, and monks are called the spiritual estate; princes, lords, artificers, and peasants, are the temporal estate. This is an artful lie and hypocritical device, but let no one be made afraid by it, and that for this reason: that all Christians are truly of the spiritual estate, and there is no difference among them, save of office alone. A priest should be nothing in Christendom but a functionary; as long as he holds his office, he has precedence of others; if he is deprived of it, he is a peasant or a citizen like the rest.

Source 3 From a letter from Berardo Navagiero to the Doge and Senate of Venice. Navagiero was the Venetian ambassador to the Court of Charles V for almost three years. The letter was written following his return to Venice in July 1546.

I will next speak of the Emperor's disposition towards the Pope. The potentate is to be regarded in two lights. First, as the head of our Religion. Secondly, as a temporal Price. In his spiritual capacity, he has always been treated by the Emperor with due respect. The Pope and Emperor appear perfectly united on the subject of the Lutheran heresy. But I know for certain that little affection exists between them. And that the Imperial Court does not trust the promises of the Pontiff.

Activity: AS-style questions

1 Why is Source 3 valuable to the historian for an enquiry into Pope Paul III's relationship with Charles V?
2 How much weight do you give the evidence of Source 3 for an enquiry into Catholic response to Luther's challenge?

Here are three examples of introductions that could answer this question. Read them and carry out the activity on page 252.

Answer 1

> Source 2 says that 'The Romanists have, with great cunning, drawn walls round themselves'. This means that the Catholic Church are defending themselves. It also says that they are doing this so they do not have to reform. It goes on to say that this wall is not right. It was written by Martin Luther who was a monk who started the Reformation. Source 3 is a letter from Berardo Navagiero who was the Venetian ambassador to the Court of Charles V for almost three years. It says that Charles V respected the Pope. It also says he did not like the Pope and did not trust his promises. The letter (Source 3) was written following his return to Venice in July 1546.

Answer 2

> Source 2 is useful to a historian because it sets out Martin Luther's view of the relationship between the papacy and Germany. Source 3, is also useful because it gives an eyewitness account of the opinion of Charles V of the Pope and their relationship.

Answer 3

> Both Sources 2 and 3 are useful to a historian investigating the relationship between the papacy and Germany in early sixteenth century Germany. Both indicate that the relationship was understood as a temporal and spiritual relationship and both indicate that the relationship was difficult. However, neither source is wholly useful. Source 2 presents Luther's view of what the relationship should be like, rather than what it was, while Source 3 considers the personal relationship between the Pope and the Emperor rather than the relationship between the papacy and Germany.

Selecting information

Another skill vital for success in Section A is that of selecting the right information from the sources. So what is the 'right' information?

- Information that is relevant to the question.
- Information that illustrates the main point of the source.
- Information that illustrates the points that you want to make.

In addition to the source material, the exam paper also contains a short description of the source's provenance printed immediately above the source. Selecting the important material from the provenance will also help you do well. You could select information that helps you to evaluate the evidence:

- Information that would help to explain the motives of the writer.
- Information that helps to explain the purpose of the document.
- Information that helps to contextualise the source (see pages 279–80).

TIP: Don't just copy information from the provenance, make sure you use the information to help weigh the evidence that the source presents.

Imagine you are answering the following question:

> **How far could the historian make use of Sources 4 and 5 to investigate Luther's reasons for publishing his objections in the *Ninety-Five Theses*?**

You need to think about the focus of the question – here the question is asking you about what these two sources can tell us, as historians, about the reasons why Luther publically exhibited his ideas in the way he did.

Remember the historical context: Luther wrote the *Theses*, but his work was circulated by printers seeking to make a profit from a sensational pamphlet. Therefore, the question is not saying that Luther *published* his ideas in the way that we would mean now.

Source 4 A letter from Martin Luther to his friend Christoph Scheurl, 5 March, 1518.

> You wonder I did not tell you of them. But I did not wish to have them widely circulated. I only intended submitting them to a few learned men for examination, and if they disapproved of them, to suppress them; or make them known through their publications, in the event of their meeting with your approval. But now they are being spread abroad and translated everywhere, which I never could have credited, so that I regret having given birth to them ... this way of instructing the people is of little avail.
>
> From the rapid spread of the theses I gather what the greater part of the nation think of this kind of Indulgence.

Source 5 Martin Luther to Pope Leo X, 30 May, 1518.

> Some time ago the preaching of indulgences was begin, and soon made such headway that these preachers thought they could say what they wished, under your Holiness's name, alarming the people at such malicious, heretical lies ... They use your Holiness's name to allay the uproar they cause, and threaten them with fire and sword. Complaints are universal as to the greed of the priests, while the power of the Pope is being spoken of evilly in Germany. And when I heard of such things I burned with zeal for the honour of Christ; and yet I felt it was not my place to do anything in the matter except draw the attention of some prelates to the abuses. Some acted upon the hint, but others derided it ... I thought it best not to be harsh, but oppose them by throwing doubts upon their doctrines, preparatory to a debate. So I threw down the gauntlet to the learned by issuing my theses.

Activity: Selecting from the sources

Read the question and then the sources.

1 Make a bullet-point list of the information that you would select from Sources 4 and 5 to answer the question.

2 Now have a look at an example of the information that you could have selected for Source 5 on page 415.

3 Check your notes – did you select the same kind of information for Source 5? Look back at the criteria for the successful selection of information. The selected information should all be relevant to the question, not merely giving facts of an event or date, and information that would help a historian investigating this issue.

4 Now read over your own notes again. Add anything into your notes on Source 5 that you might have missed, and check that your examination of Source 4 was as thorough. Add any new information you find to your notes.

5 Having read Source 4, and selected pieces of information to use in your answer, consider the following questions with your partner:

a) Did you both select the same information for the source? If not, whose selections were:
   i) most relevant to the question?
   ii) most characteristic of the whole source?

b) Did either of you select any information from the provenance?

c) Did you both select the same information from the provenance? If not, whose selections were:
   i) most relevant to the question?
   ii) most helpful to a historian evaluating the information contained in the source?

d) Did you miss anything?

e) What can you learn from this task?

Having discussed these questions make a bullet-point list of three things that you can do to make sure you answer Section A questions effectively. Review the list with your partner.

Activity: AS-style questions

1 Why is Source 4 valuable to the historian for an enquiry into Luther's intentions for issuing the *Ninety-Five Theses*?

2 How much weight do you give the evidence of Source 5 for an enquiry into Luther's justification for issuing the *Ninety-Five Theses*?

Making inferences

Making inferences from sources is one way to demonstrate your understanding of the source and of the period. An inference is a deduction or conclusion that comes from reading between the lines of a source – it's not about what lies on the surface but what's hinted at below. It isn't wild speculation but a conclusion that is drawn from reasoning or evidence. A detailed knowledge of the period is vital to making inferences.

Imagine you are answering the following question:

> How far could the historian make use of Sources 6 and 7 to investigate religious divisions in Germany in 1519?

There is a lot of information in Source 6 which is purely on the surface. But beyond that, you can use your own knowledge, to draw out more complex and insightful conclusions as the annotations below show.

The reference to Leipzig, and the date of the letter indicate that Eck is describing an aspect of the Leipzig Disputes, formal debates between Eck, Luther and Carlstadt which took place in June 1519. It is clear from the letter that he is describing Luther's arrival for the Disputes and the negotiations that went on before the disputation took place.

Carlstadt was a colleague of Luther who had attacked corruption in the Catholic Church. Eck challenged Carlstadt to the debate, even though his main target was Luther.

Source 6 From a letter by Johann Eck written to his colleagues at Ingolstadt University on 1 July 1519.

He came in great state to Leipzig with two hundred students of Wittenberg, four doctors, several masters, and a great number of his partisans: some schismatics from Prague, and some Hussites, who glorify Martin as a stupendous apostle of truth, as equal even to their own Jan Hus.

I have done Luther a good mischief, of which I will tell you orally. At his arrival I heard that he did not want to debate, and I moved everything to get him to. We met in the presence of the ducal commissioners and of representatives of the university. They wanted Luther to debate on the same conditions as Carlstadt. But Luther said much about the instructions of his prince.

The people of Wittenberg are full of gall, rage and poison against me. People still put their hopes on Luther, but none whatever on Carlstadt.

The Hussites were branded heretics by the Catholic Church and their leader Jan Hus was burnt at the stake. Hus criticised the power of the Pope. By equating Luther with the Hussites he implies that Luther is a heretic for undermining papal power.

Ducal commissioners worked for Duke George. The reference to them is a reminder that the Duke hosted the Dispute and preceded over the debate.

This is a reference to Fredrick the Wise, who had founded Wittenberg University, where Luther was based.

Source 7 An eyewitness account of the Leipzig Dispute, written by Petrus Mosellanus in July 1519. Mosellanus was a German humanist scholar and professor at Leipzig University. He gave the opening speech in the Leipzig Dispute.

Martin is of middle height, emaciated from care and study, so that you can almost count his bones through his skin. He is manly and vigorous, and has a clear, penetrating voice. He is learned and has the Scripture as his fingertips. He knows Greek and Hebrew sufficiently to judge of the interpretations. A perfect forest of words and ideas stands at his command. He is affable and friendly, in no sense dour or arrogant. He is equal to anything. In company, he is witty, lively, always cheerful and full of joy no matter how hard his adversaries press him.

Everyone chides him for the fault of being a little too insolent in his reproaches and more caustic than is prudent for an innovator in religion or becoming to a theologian. Much the same can be said of Carlstadt, though in a lesser degree. He is smaller than Luther, with a complexion of smoked herring. His voice is thick and unpleasant. He is slower in memory and quicker in anger.

Eck is a heavy, square set fellow with a full German voice supported by a hefty chest. He would make an actor or town crier, but his voice is rather rough than clear, his eyes and mouth and his whole face remind one more of a butcher than a theologian.

Below is an example of how you could develop the inferences annotated around Source 6 into a paragraph in answer to the question:

Both sources are useful to a historian investigating religious divisions in Germany in 1519 because they show that there was already considerable polarisation between the reformers and the traditionalists. Both sources are written in the context of the Leipzig Dispute of 1519. For example, in Source 6 Eck links Luther to 'some schismatics from Prague, and some Hussites' and 'Jan Hus'. In the context of the time, he is linking Luther with people already regarded as dangerous heretics. Similarly, there is a big difference between the description of Luther and Eck in Source 7, which again implies polarisation. Whereas Source 6 implies that Luther is a heretic, Source 7 describes him as 'learned' and having 'the Scripture as his fingertips', indicating that he truly understands the message of the Bible. Source 6 gives a very different account of Luther stressing his dependence on 'the instructions of his prince'. Therefore whereas Source 7 implies that Luther is a Godly man doing God's work, Source 6 implies that he is a heretic who is acting on behalf of a secular prince. By contrast, Source 7 implies that Luther is Godly, by emphasising his moral goodness. The source describes him as 'friendly, in no sense dour or arrogant'. Source 7 is much less sympathetic to Eck. Whereas Luther is learned and good, Source 7 describes Eck as being like 'an actor or town crier' implying that he is loud and good at playing a part rather than being a good theologian. Finally, both sources imply that there is no willingness to find common ground or compromise. Source 6 states that Luther's supporters are 'full of gall, rage and poison' towards Eck, and in Source 7 Eck acknowledges that he 'done Luther a good mischief'. Clearly, the two sources are useful for studying religious divisions in Germany in 1519 because they point to the bitterness of the division between Eck and his supporters on the one hand and Luther and his followers on the other.

Activity: Inferences

Having read the question on page 254 and example opposite you can now practice making inferences from Source 7. Remember.

- your inferences should help you to answer the question
- inferences should be informed by your contextual knowledge of the period.

Answer the following questions:

1 Source 7 describes the Leipzig Dispute. From your own knowledge:
   - what issues were debated?
   - what led to the debate?
2 Source 7 mentions Carlstadt. What role did Carlstadt play in the German Reformation to 1519?
3 Compare Sources 6 and 7. Together, what do they imply about religious divisions in Germany in 1519?

Work together

Having completed the activity, consider the following questions with your partner.

1 Did you both make the same inferences from Source 7?
2 If you differed, look at the source again, discuss your points of view and try and work out which inference is more likely to be correct.
3 How can the inferences that you have made help you to answer the question?

Having discussed these questions make a bullet-point list of three things that you can do to make sure you use inferences effectively in Section A questions. Review the list with your partner.

Activity: AS-style questions

1 Why is Source 6 valuable to the historian for an enquiry into the Catholic Church's attitude to Luther in 1519?
2 How much weight do you give the evidence of Source 7 for an enquiry into Luther's reputation in Germany in 1519?

Section B: Essay technique

Detail and analysis

Paper 2 Section B questions, like Paper 1 Sections A and B questions, need to be detailed and analytical. You may have already read the advice on how to write detailed and analytical essays for Paper 1 (see pages 32 and 64). Now is a chance to practise these skills in the context of Luther and the Reformation.

Activity: Detail and analysis

Imagine you are answering the following question:

How significant was Luther's debate with Eck in the development of his religious ideas in the early 1520s?

1 Identify the kind of question (see pages 232–33).
2 Make an appropriate plan: write down the main points of your three or four paragraphs.
3 Next to each of the points add three supporting details – you could use a different colour if you have one.
4 Write one analytical sentence to conclude each paragraph.

Work together

Having finished the activity on detail and analysis swap your work with a partner. Consider the following questions:

1 Did you agree on what type of question you were dealing with? If not, discuss it and work out who was right.
2 Whose plan most clearly focused on the specific type of question?
3 Were the details that your partner selected the most appropriate to support their points?
4 Could either of you have used detail that better supports the points that you wanted to make?
5 Were all of your partner's sentences truly analytical?
6 What can you learn from your partner's approach?

Use these questions to feedback to each other and improve your use of detail and analysis.

Question practice

1 'Luther's tower experience was the most significant event in the development of his theology.' How far do you agree with this statement?
2 How accurate is it to say that the Catholic Church responded poorly to Luther's challenge in the years 1517–20? [AS]
3 How accurate is it to say that the Catholic Church was unpopular and corrupt in the years before the German Reformation?
4 How successful was Luther in the debate with Eck in 1519? [AS]
5 How significant were the actions of Albert of Mainz in shaping Luther's challenge towards the Catholic Church in the period 1517–20? [AS]

Key Topic 3 The development of Lutheranism, 1521–46

Overview

Luther's trial at the Diet of Worms was an important and dramatic event, but it was only the beginning of the story of Lutheranism. The central ideas and beliefs of Lutheranism developed greatly in the period 1521–46. Philip Melanchthon, a follower and friend of Luther, was responsible for the writing of several key documents that laid out the beliefs and practices that had begun as a patchwork of ideas. These include the *Loci Communes* and the Augsburg Confession. Following the Peasants' War of 1524–25 Lutheranism moved away from any sense of support for radical political and social change. Luther himself wrote an angry pamphlet *Against the Murderous, Robbing Hordes of Peasants* that condemned the violence of the Peasants' War – unfortunately published at the same time as the princes were brutally repressing the revolts. While this meant that Lutheranism lost support from the poorest people, it also meant that it was no longer a dangerous option for those within the social and political elite. Finally, Luther's declining influence within Lutheranism and the reform movement more generally is explored. Luther's participation in events was limited by his inability to travel beyond Saxony. His responses were also increasingly intemperate and the moderate and conciliatory Melanchthon was sought out as a representative of the movement. This period from the Diet of Worms in 1521 up to the defeat of the Lutheran princes' Schmalkaldic League in 1546 was a crucial time in the survival, spread and development of Lutheranism.

This chapter focuses on the development of Lutheranism from 1521 to 1546. It looks at the impact of Luther's trial at the Diet of Worms in 1521. It critically examines Luther's attitude to the radicalism that his ideas had unwittingly sparked, both religiously and politically. After considering Lutheran beliefs in this period the chapter explores the way that Luther's place in the Lutheran movement changed.

The chapter examines these issues through the following sections:

1 *The Diet of Worms and its aftermath* explains how Luther came to be on trial at Worms, and the part that Frederick the Wise and Charles V played in that trial. It looks at the events of the trial and the consequences of Luther's condemnation.

2 *Luther's attitude to political and religious radicalism* explores the ideas of different radical reformers, for example Andreas Carlstadt and Thomas Muntzer. It also looks at Luther's reaction to these religious radicals. This section also explains the causes, events and consequences of the Peasants' Wars and Luther's reaction to them.

3 *Lutheran beliefs and their influence* discusses Luther's key ideas that were formulated in this period. It explores the German Mass and Luther's translation of the Bible into German, as well as important concepts like justification by faith alone. This section looks at the material that Luther wrote to explain Lutheran beliefs to different audiences and for teachers to educate their children.

4 *Luther's declining influence, 1530–46* looks at Luther's changing role within Lutheranism. It explores Melanchthon's contribution in terms of creating a coherent doctrine out of Luther's ideas. It examines negotiations between Catholics and reformers in this period and Luther's minimal but important part in them. Finally, the section covers the Philip of Hesse affair and its impact on the reputation of reforming leaders.

TIMELINE

1519	Luther's debate with Eck at Leipzig
1519	Charles V elected Holy Roman Emperor
1520	Coronation of Charles V as Holy Roman Emperor
1521	*Loci Communes* first published by Melanchthon
1521	Diet of Worms
1522	Carlstadt's reforms in Wittenberg

1521	Luther stays at Wartburg Castle
1524	The Peasants' War
1525	Luther's *An Admonition to Peace* published
1525	*Against the Robbing and Murdering Hordes of Peasants* published
1529	The *Large Catechism* published

1 The Diet of Worms and its aftermath

Luther had been condemned by the **Pope** and excommunicated from the Catholic Church. He had challenged the authority of the Pope, some important Catholic doctrines and had advocated new and radical ideas. Yet he still had the opportunity to appeal to the Holy Roman Emperor as a way to avoid the severe consequences of his **excommunication**. Given the treatment of previously condemned heretics, such as Jan Hus, this was a sensible move. Luther's trial at Worms illuminates some of the key issues within Germany at this time, such as the desire of the German princes for more independence from the Church and Empire; the potential for conflict between princes, Emperor and Pope; and the growing support for Luther in the face of the opposition of the Catholic Church.

Note it down

Practise using the 1:2 method in this section (see page x). Remember to put the big points or headings in the left-hand column and the smaller or supporting points in the right-hand column. If you are revising or you are organising your notes thematically, you could colour code the different points as to whether they are political or religious. This may help you later when trying to answer questions about reasons for the events that you are studying.

Luther's condemnation as a heretic and outlaw

Luther had been excommunicated by Pope Leo X following his debate with Eck in June 1519. Frederick the Wise continued to support Luther following the excommunication. He appealed to the Holy Roman Emperor, Charles V, on Luther's behalf.

Why did Frederick the Wise intervene?

- Frederick claimed it was not because he approved of Luther's theology.
- He said he just wanted Luther to have a fair trial.
- Frederick previously supported Luther because he wanted to protect the university he founded (see page 237) and one of its most well-known professors.

The constitution of the Holy Roman Empire

Charles V, Holy Roman Emperor, signed a constitution at his coronation in 1519. This constitution committed him to many things. The significant articles for Luther's situation, however, were those that declared that no German would be tried outside of his own country and that no German would be condemned without a fair trial. If Charles had denied Luther this opportunity, he would lose face in the struggle for political power with Rome. So Luther was again aided in his programme for reform by long-term political factors. It was due to these clauses, as well as much discussion and negotiation between Frederick, Charles V and the Pope, that Luther was sent for by the Emperor to stand trial at the Diet of Worms in April 1521. Frederick had achieved his aim, as well as safe passage for Luther to and from the diet. Despite this, Luther's decision to attend the diet was dangerous – Jan Hus, also excommunicated, was burned at the stake in 1415 despite the same promise of safe passage.

Luther's appearance at the Diet of Worms, 1521

The meeting of the imperial diet (see page 215) where Luther was to be tried was held at Worms, a town in the south of Germany. His journey was accompanied by supporters in the form of cheering crowds and when he preached at towns along the route he attracted large audiences. Luther arrived at the diet on 16 April 1521 and the trial began the next day. Luther faced the Holy Roman Emperor, the princes, the papal **envoys** and any lords who were present. He hoped for a hearing and a chance to explain his ideas, but once again it became clear that what was sought was a recantation without a debate. The Emperor asked Luther to consider 'the great danger, discord, unrest, insurrection and bloodshed that your **doctrine** has let loose upon the world, but which could be stopped by the suppression of your books'. Luther was examined by Johann Eck, the chancellor of Trier (not to be confused with the Eck he had debated with at Leipzig). He showed Luther a pile of books and asked firstly whether they were his work. Secondly, he was asked if he wanted to defend any or all of them. Luther answered that they were his books and asked for more time for the second question. The assembly was adjourned until the next day for Luther to think about his answer. The next day Luther returned with his answers. He answered positively again to the first question. To the second, Luther answered that there were three categories that his books fitted into:

1 Those that set forth the faith so simply that his enemies had to acknowledge their worth.
2 Those that lamented the ungodly state of **Christendom.**
3 Those that attacked individuals.

Luther said that within the third category he had not always been as moderate as he could have been. He was pressed further by Eck, at which point Luther famously said, 'Here I stand, I can do no other'. He made antipapal arguments, arguing that the **papacy** was tyrannical and godless, and declared that he would only recant if convinced by scripture or reason. In this way Luther declared his faith at the Diet of Worms.

The argument of the Catholic Church was the same as it always had been. This was that the Catholic Church had settled the ideas that Luther was discussing and that they could not be changed at his whim. Luther was convinced that his ideas were better than the Catholic Church. However, the Church viewed this as pure arrogance. They also argued that his resistance to Church authority promoted chaos and instability in religious and political matters because it encouraged people to come up with radical ideas of their own with little fear of punishment. Without discipline there would be no united Church.

> **Source A** From a report of Luther's statement of beliefs during his trial at the Diet of Worms, 1521.
>
> Unless I am proved wrong by the testimony of Scriptures or by evident reason I am bound in conscience and held fast to the Word of God ... therefore I cannot and will not retract anything, for it is neither safe nor salutary to act against one's conscience. God help me. Amen.
>
> Which of Luther's key ideas is he expressing in Source A? What does he mean when he says it is not safe to 'act against one's conscience'?

Luther's condemnation as a heretic

Following Luther's testimony the electors who would decide his fate were summoned by the Emperor. Charles V had an **edict** drawn up which declared Luther a heretic and placed him under the imperial ban. The consequences of this were as follows:

● Luther was an outlaw.
● So was anyone who gave him support.

● His writings were condemned as heretical and ordered to be burned.
● The subjects of the Holy Roman Empire were forbidden to communicate with Luther or help him, on pain of arrest and confiscation of their property.

All seven electors said they supported this move, but only four signed. This was enough support for Charles, who went ahead with the edict. This became known as the Edict of Worms. Luckily for Luther, one of those who did not sign the edict was his employer and protector, Frederick the Wise.

Attitude of Charles V

Charles V had only recently been elected Holy Roman Emperor after a bitter and contested election (see page 216). Charles was very young, only 19 years old. He was serious and pious, however, and Luther's ideas offended him. Charles had a great sense of destiny as the leader of Christendom. His vast territory, spanning Europe, was no doubt a factor in this. Charles, as a sincere Catholic, was worried about the moral and institutional state of the Church but also had big plans for consolidating his power in Germany. He wanted to strengthen the power and authority of the Emperor. The Reformation, and its unintended consequences regarding the territorial power of the princes, worked against his plans. Luther's ideas were opposed to Charles' on two grounds – firstly in challenging the doctrine of the orthodox established Church, and secondly with their implications for the unity of his new Empire. The Emperor traditionally acted as a secular vicar over the Church in Germany, almost like an overseer. This governing and protective role was greatly threatened by Luther's ideas and actions. Charles wanted to act firmly to secure Luther's recantation and to do God's will. These desires saw him fight against Luther and Lutheranism for most of the rest of his life, until his abdication in 1555. This was because, unlike other problems within the Empire, the religious issues of the sixteenth century clearly needed decisive action.

Protection of Frederick the Wise

On his return journey to Wittenberg Luther was 'kidnapped' and taken to Wartburg Castle. Wartburg belonged to Frederick the Wise in Electoral Saxony, and is yet another example of that prince protecting Luther in his journey from orthodox monk to religious radical. The kidnapping was done at the orders of Frederick and with Luther's knowledge. Luther was disguised as a knight and was hidden by Frederick the Wise in Wartburg Castle for nearly a year, from early May 1521 to early March 1522, where he completed his translation of the New Testament into German. Luther completed other works during this time such as a commentary on Psalm 68 (May 1521), and his ideas on monastic vows (October 1521) and the sacrament (April 1522). Luther's sudden disappearance made his ideas and story yet more of a talking point.

Frederick's protection was clearly important in allowing Luther to continue developing his ideas. There were limits to Frederick's influence, however, and his ability to shield Luther from the effects of papal excommunication and the imperial ban did not extend beyond his territory of Electoral Saxony. As a consequence Luther remained in Electoral Saxony for the rest of his life. His participation in the ongoing Reformation was, by necessity, limited to his writings, his correspondence with other reformers and to his representatives who were free to travel. At home in Wittenberg, Luther continued to teach at the university, write and think, and preach.

Conclusion

Luther made a bold declaration of his faith at Worms, despite being given the opportunity to recant and save himself from further difficulty. This was a great turning point for Lutheranism, as it led Luther to complete his break from Catholicism and, in Wartburg, devote time to developing and publishing his ideas. The Diet of

Worms made Charles V a lifelong enemy of Lutheranism, but did not lead to Frederick the Wise withdrawing his support for his famous academic. Luther was protected by Frederick and allowed to continue working in Wittenburg, preserving the Reformation.

Work together

Listen to the BBC 'In Our Time' podcast on 'The Diet of Worms'. You can download this from the following site for free: www.bbc.co.uk/programmes/p0038x8z

You can listen to this together or on your own. Then come together to discuss the programme. What did you learn from it?

2 Luther's attitude to religious and political radicalism

While Luther was in Wartburg Castle, the Reformation did not stand still. It carried on without him. Although some aspects pleased Luther (such as the introduction of clerical marriage), others went far beyond what he had aimed for and envisaged. The 'Radical Reformation' became a source of consternation for Luther and he felt

Frederick the Wise (1463–1525)

Frederick the Wise succeeded his father as elector of Saxony in 1486. He was one of the most powerful territorial rulers in the Holy Roman Empire. He was very interested in education and learning, and founded the University of Wittenberg in 1502. While he protected Luther, Frederick was not a reformer himself. He had a large collection of holy relics, did not promote the Reformation in his territories and died within the Catholic faith. This may make his protection of Luther seem even more remarkable. Frederick was also a patron of the arts, employing the artists Albrecht Durer and Lucas Cranach the Elder. He was friend and patron to the humanist Georg Spalatin, who was a correspondent of Luther for many years. Frederick supported the election of Charles V as Holy Roman Emperor in 1519 despite being the Pope's candidate for the role. He died unmarried in 1525, and was succeeded by his brother Duke John of Saxony.

that he had to pronounce against what he saw as dangerous developments. These included the preaching of Andreas Carlstadt and Thomas Muntzer, as well as the Peasants' War of 1524–25. Luther had been unable to foresee that, in encouraging the reading of the scripture, others would see it differently to him. He was astounded and also defensive when radical ideas took root within 'his' Reformation.

Note it down

As this section covers two different topics you could use different note taking techniques for each. For the first section, on Luther's views on the radical Reformation, use a spider diagram: Draw three legs, one for Carlstadt, one for Muntzer and the other for Luther's reaction to the two. For the second section, on the Peasants' War, use the 1:2 method. Put the big points or headings on the left, and the supporting points on the right. See page x if you need to remind yourself of the different methods.

Luther's views on the radical Reformation

Even while Luther was still in Wartburg Castle the Reformation continued to develop in both 'Lutheran' and more radical directions. Luther returned from his period in Wartburg Castle to realise that even in Wittenberg reformers had instituted changes beyond what he himself had called for. There were many different reformers in different parts of Germany. They preached a great range of new ideas, some moderate others very radical. We will look at case studies of two of the more radical preachers, Carlstadt and Muntzer and Luther's reaction to them.

The Zwickau prophets

While Luther was busy translating the Bible into German, Wittenberg had become a beacon for others with reforming ideas. Some of these saw themselves as prophets and wanted to push Luther's reforms even further. They did not claim to have found their ideas in the Bible like

Luther had. They believed that they were delivering a message directly from God. As a number of them were from the Saxon town of Zwickau they became known as the Zwickau prophets. One of their most prominent ideas was that the bread and wine used during mass were symbols that recalled the sacrifice of Christ, rather than physically the body and blood of God. This was very different from both the Catholic Church and Lutheran ideas. The Catholic Church teaches that the bread and wine of **communion** are changed into the body and blood of Christ. Luther believed that the bread and wine were changed but they were still present, co-existing with the body and blood of Christ. The Zwickau prophets also rejected infant baptism because they believed that one must choose to be a believer before being baptised – and children could not make that conscious choice. In the Catholic Church, on the other hand, children were baptised as close to their birth as possible so that they were received into the Church and would not risk damnation if they died soon after. Their ideas were influential for radicals who became more notable, such as Carlstadt.

Andreas Carlstadt

Andreas Rudolf von Bodenstein, otherwise known as Andreas Carlstadt, had been an early disciple of Luther's. It was he who was meant to debate with Eck at Leipzig (see page 243) in 1519. Carlstadt has been described as a volatile and fiery tempered man who had stormy relationships with colleagues and an inferiority complex about his own status. Luther, equally, was far from calm and secure. These two colleagues were thrown into opposition by the Reformation and Carlstadt's adoption of more radical ideas. Carlstadt viewed himself as the guardian of Luther's ideas while he was in Wartburg Castle. In Wittenberg he preached in a simple black gown rather than the ornate vestments of the Catholic Church. He preached using an abbreviated **liturgy** after the liturgy made a declaration that faith alone was all that was needed to celebrate mass. He preached in favour of clerical marriage, and married a 15-year-old girl in order to demonstrate the sincerity of his beliefs. These ideas were

---

The changing definition of radicalism

'Radical' is a word that is used frequently in this book and in any that examines the German Reformation. It is applied at some points in the period to Luther and at others who were very much less conservative, including Thomas Muntzer and later Anabaptists. The reason that this is possible is that the definition of 'radical' changed over the period. Luther's ideas were very radical in 1517 as compared to the traditional

doctrines of the Catholic Church. By 1522, however, the Reformation had developed rapidly, and Luther was conservative in relation to those who advocated religious violence and only baptising believers. 'Radical' was not a stable and unchanging term, but rather one that altered according to the context and the times.

not too far from Luther's ideas concerning the importance of faith in gaining God's grace and clerical marriage. But Carlstadt took his reforms further. In January 1522 he provoked an attack on the use of art and images in worship. Carlstadt had preached that sacred images were devilish conceit and should be destroyed. For the Elector Frederick of Saxony this was too much. It meant turmoil in his beloved Wittenberg and risked the destruction of some of the large collection of relics that Frederick himself had built up over the years. He sent for Luther to come and address the problem.

When Luther returned he quickly reversed the changes. Rather than bringing Carlstadt back into line, however, it only drove him into more radical measures. Perhaps driven by a need to compete with Luther, Carlstadt rejected the real presence of Christ's body during mass and infant baptism. He decided to reject his academic status and achievements. He began dressing in the costume or clothing of a peasant and asked to be called 'brother Andy'. He is said to have tried farming. Carlstadt's theological ideas were also in conflict with Luther's. He believed that individuals had to overcome self-will and suffer physically in order to achieve inner renewal.

Carlstadt left Wittenberg and became the parish pastor of a small town not far away. He started to put his programme of reform, interrupted in Wittenberg, into place. His colleagues at Wittenberg were worried about the implications of Carlstadt being allowed to practise in this way. They began legal moves to evict him. Eventually Carlstadt was banned from the entire Electoral Saxony because of fears about the possible impact of his radical ideas. Peasant unrest was spreading throughout the region, and was associated with the radical preachers. Carlstadt travelled through south-west Germany, had contact with Anabaptist radicals and tried to get his tracts against infant baptism published. He had contact with Muntzer along his journey. He did not have a permanent position though. Ultimately Carlstadt became a wandering preacher who eventually died in 1541 of the plague in Basel, Switzerland.

Thomas Muntzer

Thomas Muntzer was apparently influenced by Luther's *Ninety-Five Theses* to become a reformer. By 1520 he was minister of Zwickau and it was there that he first rejected infant baptism. He was ejected in April 1521 because of his extreme beliefs, and after a short spell in Prague wandered in Germany until 1523. At this point Muntzer became minister of Allstedt in Electoral Saxony. He married a former nun in June 1523, was interrogated about his ideas by the elector, Frederick the Wise, in November of that year and produced the first completely German liturgy in December 1523. Previously the liturgy had only been

Anabaptist radicals

The Anabaptists emerged from the Reformation movement in Switzerland. Their beliefs began to form from 1524 when the Swiss movement started to split into the more conservative reformers under Ulrich Zwingli and the radicals led by Conrad Grebel and Georg Blaurock. The radicals gradually developed a belief that infant baptism was wrong. They came to argue that a pure Church only included those who had chosen to be baptised, and that children could not rationally do that. Their strong belief in the importance of free will was linked to that. Anabaptists had a practice of re-baptising converts, claiming that their first baptism was void and that the re-baptism was in fact their first true baptism. They thought that the Second Coming of Christ was near and they refused to swear oaths to civil authorities, meaning that they were not bound to obey them. After its beginnings in Switzerland, Anabaptism spread across into Germany and the Low Countries. The Anabaptist radicals were persecuted as they were seen as too radical and dangerous both in religious and political terms.

conducted in Latin. Reformers such as Muntzer believed that in order to truly participate in the service the liturgy had to be in the language of the congregation. This contradicted the Church. In July 1524 Muntzer delivered his famous *Sermon to the Princes* in which he preached that he could interpret the dreams of princes and argued that the kingdom of God would consume all the kingdoms. This was clearly inflammatory and Muntzer was called before the Duke of Saxony. He fled soon after. Luther's *Letter to the Princes of Saxony on the Rebellious Spirit*, also of July 1524, is probably another reason why Muntzer was called to the hearing with the Duke of Saxony. In this pamphlet Luther warned the elector (Frederick the Wise) and Duke George of Saxony about the activities of Muntzer and Carlstadt.

Muntzer's theology was certainly very radical. He was a charismatic preacher who rejected the authority of the written word. This included the Bible. He emphasised that God's spirit should directly lead the faithful. Like Carlstadt, Muntzer encouraged his followers to take part in iconoclasm. He also encouraged them to refuse the payment of tithes. He called for a form of social justice and redistribution of goods from the rich to the poor. Perhaps the most controversial aspect of Muntzer's theology was that he saw Church activity as a form of holy war. He thought that those outside of the true Church were only worthy of death and that it was the responsibility of the Church to slaughter the ungodly in order to create God's kingdom on earth. This preaching of holy violence was clearly seen as threatening to the peace and order of Germany. Muntzer saw Luther as far too conservative. Although he initially followed Luther's doctrines, he soon took them far beyond Luther's original intentions. He believed that Luther was a sell-out who had given in to the princes and betrayed the Reformation. Muntzer thought that far greater change was needed than that which Luther was prepared to accept.

Luther's reaction to Carlstadt and Muntzer

Luther believed that Carlstadt had gone too far – a fact that he explained in reference to Carlstadt's ambition rather than religious fervour. This is why he reversed the changes at Wittenberg. Luther saw Carlstadt's belief as heresy, much as the Catholic Church saw Luther's own beliefs. Luther believed that Carlstadt's chosen image as a man of the people was ridiculous and played a prominent part in Carlstadt's ejection from Electoral Saxony. He had become convinced that Carlstadt was a supporter of Muntzer who, as we have seen, preached religious violence. Luther, in many ways, was fairly conservative. He had called for limited changes to the practice and the beliefs preached by the Catholic Church. He was horrified by the events that had unfolded partly at his instigation. This may explain the strength of Luther's reaction to radicals like Carlstadt and Muntzer.

Unlike the Zwickau prophets, Carlstadt, and Muntzer, Luther was absolutely certain that infants should be baptised. This was because he supported the principle that all members of society should also be members of the Christian Church. Baptism was the way that this membership was proven. Most mainstream reformers upheld this idea. Luther was more conservative because he carried on defending the presence of the body and blood of Christ during the mass. Furthermore, Luther did not support iconoclasm. He saw a use for sacred images as evidence of the beauty of God's creation and thought that efforts to destroy sacred art gave it more importance than it should have.

The violence advocated by Muntzer was complete anathema to Luther. He had no desire to disrupt society in the way that Muntzer appeared to. Luther completely disagreed with holy violence as a way of cleansing the Earth. Although Luther's ideas have proven to be the catalyst for the Reformation, he was a social conservative and, supported by Frederick the Wise, gave no support for a movement that intended to cause chaos or violence.

It has also been suggested that Luther had less noble motives for rejecting Muntzer and those like him. He believed that people like Muntzer had not earned the right to attempt such changes. In Luther's eyes he had put his life on the line when defending his ideas against the papacy and the Holy Roman Empire. So some have explained the strength of his reaction to Muntzer as a form of jealousy at the following Muntzer was gaining. Luther did react this way to other reformers, and so this is far from implausible, yet it is likely that he opposed Muntzer because of the far-reaching and chaotic implications of his ideas as much as jealousy.

The revolt of the Imperial Knights, 1522–23

This revolt is seen as a precursor to the Peasants' War of 1524–25. It had a range of causes but did claim Lutheran ideas as a motivating force. The choice of the Archbishop of Trier as a target and the call for greater freedoms made it appear in part a religious revolt.

Causes of the revolt

The Imperial Knights were a group in decline. They were free nobles of the Holy Roman Empire whose overlord was not a territorial prince but the Emperor himself. They were, in theory, equal in status to the territorial rulers of the Empire, including the princes and archbishops. In the sixteenth century the knights saw their influence being eroded by the increase of princely power. Military developments like gunpowder had led to the knights being sidelined in favour of cannon and infantry regiments. The trend towards urban development and the decline in importance of agriculture had decreased their income. A law passed by the Diet of Worms in 1521 outlawing private noble feuds was the final straw. This was the main source of income for the financially distressed Imperial Knights, who had

> ## Key debate
> ### Muntzer's role in the Peasants' War
> Muntzer was to meet a violent end in the Peasants' War of 1524-25. He was captured and beheaded along with many of his small band of followers during the brutal repression of that uprising. Historians have argued about the degree of influence that Muntzer had during the Peasants' War. Geoffrey Elton and others have argued that Muntzer had a prominent role in events, stoking the rebellion and leading his followers onto the battlefield. More recently, historians such as MacCulloch have disagreed with this. According to MacCulloch, Muntzer has been given a prominent role in these events that he does not deserve, contributing little except leading his followers to a wretched death.

Franz von Sickingen (1481–1523)

Franz von Sickingen was a wealthy Imperial Knight. One way for Imperial Knights to earn money was to work for princes and rulers as mercenary commanders. Von Sickingen achieved great success in this role. He fought for the Emperor Maximilian I against Venice in 1508. He led campaigns against Worms in 1513 for a private citizen and Metz in 1518 to intervene in a civil conflict between the citizens and the town government. In 1518 he led the army of the Swabian League against Duke Ulrich I of Wurttemberg when he disobeyed instructions of the diet. Von Sickingen was also a humanist and a reformer, becoming friends with Ulrich von Hutten around 1517. He was interested in science and learning. He sheltered other reformers in his castles, offering Luther a retreat in this period. He became one of the leaders of the Imperial Knights when they rose in rebellion in 1522. When the siege of Trier failed, von Sickingen lost much of his support and he was declared an outlaw. His remaining forces in his castles fell one by one and finally he was besieged at Landstuhl. He was wounded in the siege, capitulated and died the next day.

Ulrich von Hutten (1488–1523)

Ulrich von Hutten was also an Imperial Knight. Unlike von Sickingen, however, von Hutten was not a mercenary soldier for most of his life. He was originally intended by his father to be a monk but ran away from the monastery in 1505. He studied at Frankfurt in 1506 and Greifswald in 1509. He wandered around Germany making contact with humanists and scholars, moving on to study law at Pavia in Italy in 1512. Von Hutten served as a soldier in the Emperor Maximilian's army around 1512 but then returned to Germany. Gradually he became a religious reformer, perhaps initially prompted by his feud with Duke Ulrich of Wurttemberg over Duke Ulrich's murder of one of von Hutten's relatives. He was a writer, a humanist and a supporter of Luther. He wrote pamphlets in favour of Luther in the 1520s but even before that produced satires against the princes and the Church. He joined von Sickingen in the revolt of the Imperial Knights in 1522. He fled to Zurich in Switzerland after the failure of the Knights' War, where he was given a refuge by Zwingli. He died there penniless soon after of syphilis contracted while fighting for the Emperor.

fought for the princes in these private wars and been paid handsomely for it.

Events of the revolt

The revolt was led by the evangelical mercenary captain, Franz von Sickingen and supported by Ulrich von Hutten, a humanist and poet. Von Hutten had long been a critic of the Catholic Church. He had been a monk, a soldier and had developed a jaundiced sense of secular and Church government. He was an early convert to Lutheranism, but thought that it was acceptable to force the pace of change through military action. In August 1522, 600 Imperial Knights met at Landau on Lake Constance in the south of Germany. They formed an association to defend their rights, as well as the Lutheran faith. So this revolt (like the subsequent Peasants' War) did not have one cause – it was inspired by social, economic, political and military concerns. It did also have a religious element. Von Hutten saw Luther's calls for an end to abuses in the Catholic Church as being part of their cause. His call for reform struck a chord for the Imperial Knights, who partly blamed the princes of the Church for displacing them from their position of power. Spurred on by Luther's position against the secular power of the Church hierarchy, they attacked the powerful Archbishop of Trier. The Archbishop was a staunch opponent of Luther and an important landowner and political force. It was an attempt

to attack the rise of powerful churchmen to secular positions. The knights' declaration of war encouraged the population of Trier to rise up and overthrow their archbishop. This did not happen, and the siege of Trier failed after one week. Monasteries and churches were plundered in the meantime. This was seen as an intolerable challenge by the princes, who raised an army under Philip of Hesse to end the revolt in 1523 with a siege of von Sickingen's castle. Those who had strongly supported the revolt had their lands and castles confiscated.

Luther and the Peasants' War, 1524–25

Peasant unrest had been a feature of European life for the last century. Long-term social and economic changes were resisted by the peasants and other inhabitants of rural regions. In 1524 there began a wave of peasant uprisings and unrest across Germany. This was linked to the activities of religious reformers at the time and angered and frightened Luther. He responded to the events in two pamphlets, *An Admonition to Peace* and *Against the Robbing and Murdering Hordes of Peasants*. His response was controversial even for those who agreed with him that the radicals had gone too far. It had consequences for the future of the Reformation and for Luther's position within the Reformation. Historian Peter Marshall has described the Peasants' War thus: 'Luther had sown the wind; now he would reap the whirlwind.'

Origins and causes of the Peasants' War

There was no single cause of the wave of unrest that became known as the Peasants' War. Many of the causes were long term and rooted in changes to society and to the rural economy. Lists of peasant grievances included economic, legal, political, governmental and social issues. These problems had been unresolved for more than two centuries. They can be broadly categorised as follows:

- **Economic strategies by landlords** – after the agricultural crisis of the late medieval period landlords aimed to secure their income by increasing rents, changing the terms of leases, enclosing common land and increasing grain tithes.
- **Competition and tension between urban and rural areas** – increasing urban poverty and migration from the countryside (see page 221) led to town councils making laws to try and stem the influx of poor people from the countryside. Peasants also competed with town dwellers at markets to sell their produce.
- **Long-term attempts by princes and territorial rulers to extend control** – peasants often lost out in battles between different territorial rulers who were aiming to extend their control of land at the expense of others. The desire of nobles for uniform territorial control frequently meant negative changes in the legal and economic conditions of peasants.
- **Anticlericalism** – landlords were both secular and ecclesiastical. Monastic houses and bishops were landlords as well as having religious responsibilities. When they attempted to tax or change conditions of their tenants this led to anticlericalism caused by economic change as well as dissatisfaction with some aspects of religious practice.
- **The dissatisfaction of towns** – towns as well as rural regions took part in these revolts. Some welcomed the revolts because they were also fighting against noble and ecclesiastical privilege. Towns wanted greater political participation and some groups within towns wanted more influence in town government.

So where does the Reformation fit into this pattern of causes? The Reformation added further instability into an ongoing and difficult conflict. Particularly for the peasants and other rural dissidents, it added extra justification for their grievances and gave them an explanation for their resistance. That some of the landlords represented the wealthy and allegedly corrupt Church made the Reformation a very useful weapon. This does not mean that the Reformation was just an excuse for the peasants. We should not assume that their beliefs, when they were expressed, were insincere. It is true, however, that the new ideas of the Reformation were adapted and fitted to the long-held grievances of rural Germany. Some historians have argued that the masses misunderstood Luther's ideas. It is more likely that they selected those of Luther's ideas that made sense to them, and, in particular, resolved their grievances. Printed material like simplistic woodcuts tended to support the peasants' interpretation of Luther's ideas.

Events of the Peasants' War

There are two important caveats to discuss before examining the events of the Peasants' War. Firstly, the Peasants' War did not just involve peasants. It involved people at different levels of rural society who had grievances against their social superiors. Secondly, the nature of the war varied greatly in the different regions of Germany.

Reasons for revolt

The grievances varied, for example, in parts of Saxony grazing rights were an issue. Landlords had begun raising large flocks of sheep which threatened the livelihoods of small farmers. Mining areas also had specific grievances as did regions that produced textiles. In some regions anti-Semitic attacks took place because the Jews were seen as allies of the nobles, protected by them and causing economic distress. The Peasants' War was not co-ordinated, was localised and was not always motivated or maintained by the same causes.

The breakdown of order

The initial stages of revolts across Germany were frequently peaceful, involved negotiations, and only later turned into armed revolts. There is debate about exactly when the Peasants' War began. There had been a wave of disturbances since 1521 and some of these were linked to radical religious movements. On 30 May 1524 there was a rebellion against the Abbey of St Blasien in the Black Forest, but contemporary writers saw the revolt of the peasants of Lupfen and Stuhlingen on 24 June 1524 as the real beginning of the Peasants' War. The peasants initially organised public demonstration and then agreed to negotiations. They chose a skilled negotiator as a spokesman and raised a banner to which they could rally. This banner was for the colours of Austria, and was a sign perhaps that the peasants were aiming for protection from Austria. The breakdown of negotiations and the stubborn attitude of the local ruler, Count Sigismund, meant that the revolt escalated and the peasants left their territory on a march to recruit others. From this point the rebellions spread rapidly and widely. The peasants sought allies with the towns, including those that were centres of radicalism,

The Peasants' War has long been the subject of intense debate among historians. It has been used to support arguments in contemporary politics as well as for its own sake. The Nazis depicted it as a nationalist revolt and named a SS division after one of the leaders of the Peasants' War. In communist East Germany in the 1960s and 1970s the Peasants' War was depicted by Marxist historians as the first step towards the bourgeois revolution and the fight against the feudal lords. This fitted their theory of an inevitable journey towards communism. Other historians in the 1960s, such as Peter Blickle, concentrated on one area of Germany (Upper Swabia) rather than examining southern Germany more widely. Their view of the intense antagonism between the economically weakened peasantry and their landlords has been criticised by Tom Scott for this reason. Historians have also argued whether the revolt was caused by religious factors (such as the rise of Lutheranism) or political and economic ones. By the late 1970s most historians, including Peter Blickle and Tom Scott, agreed that the Reformation fuelled the uprisings in 1524-25 – but as only part of the story, not as the main or only cause. More recently, historians see the Peasants' War as a series of revolts that had a wide range of causes, objectives and individuals involved. The increase in local studies has helped form this impression.

for example Waltshut. A radical preacher called Balthazar Hubmaier operated a form of **evangelical** radicalism in the town. Muntzer was possibly also in contact with Hubmaier. The evangelical Swiss city of Zurich provided volunteers and by 1525 some groups of rebels justified their actions through an appeal to the 'word of God'. There was a short-lived Christian Union of Upper Swabia in March 1525. There was also a Christian Union of the Black Forest rebels. The negotiator from Lupfen and Stuhlingen, Hans Muller, was at the head of their campaign, which besieged the towns of Freiburg and Breisach in May 1525. The different bands of rebels pulled down noble castles, sacked monasteries and besieged towns in the name of the gospel and with demands that serfdom be ended.

They swore allegiance to the reform programme known as the Twelve Articles formulated in south-west Germany. This acted as a manifesto of the revolt. The revolt in

Thuringia has been seen as the high point of the Peasants' War. Historians have concentrated on the urban revolt in the imperial city of Mulhausen where the preaching of the radical reformer Heinrich Pfeiffer and long-standing grievances against the ruling **oligarchy** led eventually to the election of a new government called the Eternal Council. Muntzer was involved with Pfeiffer in the establishment of this council, although he soon believed it did not go far enough. Muntzer rallied his followers under the banner of the Eternal League of God. He intended to spread rebellion throughout the region of Thuringia. Revolt also spread across much of the region. It led to rulers having to accept the demands of peasants and the institution of new councils of religious radicals. By the end of April 1525 the Muhlhausen rebels had gathered an army of 10,000 peasants. Muntzer also tried to establish alliances with other towns and bands of peasants. This success was short lived. The nobles were able to gather their strength, unite, and on 15 May 1525 the army of the princes under Philip of Hesse crushed the rebels at the Battle of Frankenhausen. Muntzer himself was captured, forced to apologise for his actions and then beheaded.

The Peasants' War and religion

The precise relationship of the peasant uprisings to the Reformation is unclear. In some areas of Germany the connection is more obvious than others. The events at Muhlhausen is one example of this. Muntzer declared that he was beginning the Apocalypse and that they would witness the Second Coming of Christ. Marxist historians, however, have depicted this as a period in which the peasants used the language of religion to achieve their economic aims because this was the most effective way to achieve it. However, the Marxist view is difficult to credit in many of the patchwork of rebellions that took place in 1524–25.

The repression of the Peasants' War

Like the revolts themselves the response to the events of 1524–25 was varied. The peasants of Swabia disbursed after talks while those of Thuringia were slaughtered on the battlefield or subsequently tortured to death. It has been estimated that over 100,000 people were executed following the suppression of the Peasants' War. The brutal response of the princes was intended as a deterrent both for religious radicals and those with economic grievances. Social order had to be maintained and this was seen as the most effective way to achieve that. Yet it was not uniformly popular even amongst those who disagreed with the rebels because of its brutality.

The Twelve Articles of the Swabian peasants

The demands of the Twelve Articles are summarised below.

1 The freedom to elect (and depose, if necessary) their own pastor.

2 That the current system of tithes was unfair – the collection of the tithes should be fairer and should be managed by the churchwarden of each parish. They were opposed to laymen buying the right to collect tithes, believing that the tithes should be for each community to pay their pastor and help the poor.

3 That the Bible said that they are free, not serfs owned by the landowners.

4 That game, wildfowl and fish should not be kept by landowners privately because it was selfish and 'unbrotherly'. They should be shared by the community.

5 That wood should also not be kept for the use of the landowner only but shared by the community.

6 Landlords should not increase their workload unreasonably but should refer back to how their ancestors were treated.

7 In future landlords would have to make agreements with peasants regarding work and services, rather than forcing them to do extra work without pay.

8 Rents should be fair, not increased so that peasant farmers could not afford them.

9 Punishments for crimes should be impartial, not affected by ill will.

10 Some had taken common land into private ownership and the peasants wanted this returned to common ownership.

11 Feudal dues such as the **heriot** should be abolished.

12 These articles would be abandoned if they were found to be against the word of God. They would add to them if further articles were to be found in scripture and to be a burden to their neighbours.

Source B From Count Philipp von Solm's report to his son Reinhard of the aftermath of the Battle of Frankenhausen, 16 May 1525.

We began to storm the town at once and conquered it speedily, and killed everyone caught there. Many of them were found in the drainage canal of the salt works or else in the houses, and goodly numbers were not captured by the soldiers and horseman until the evening, last night, and this morning, and their lives were spared. The pastor of Allstedt, called Muntzer, was also captured. He had been the band's preacher and leader and threatened Count Ernst, my son-in-law, and has always been rebellious. He was turned over to Count Ernst by our gracious lords, the princes, to deal with him at his pleasure. He had him sent to Heldrungen within the hour and he would have received his just deserts there. Over 5000 peasants were slain and left for dead, others were captured as mentioned above, some are still in hiding and others have escaped, but not many ...

What can Source B tell us about the princely response to the battle? Is this a reliable source? Explain your answer.

Luther's response to the Peasants' War

In April 1525 Luther wrote a pamphlet entitled *An Admonition to Peace* directed at both peasants and rulers.

He aimed to prevent the misinterpretation of the Bible to justify violence, to rebut the Twelve Articles and prevent further peasant violence. He also admonished the rulers, however, and encouraged them to be more considerate in order to prevent further outbreaks. He bemoaned their combination of luxurious lifestyle and harsh treatment of the peasants. Luther reproached both the peasants and the rulers for their unchristian behaviour, warning of the divine punishments that could follow. Subsequently, Luther embarked on a tour of Thuringia where he witnessed some of the violent events there. It was after this that he wrote *Against the Robbing and Murdering Hordes of Peasants* (see Source C on page 268). In this pamphlet Luther justified the actions of the princes against the peasants by explaining that if a subject had become faithless, disobedient and rebellious, then the ruler had the right to punish them. He glorified those who fought against the peasants as martyrs and encouraged the rulers to crush the rebellions. Luther used biblical authority to justify his response, quoting Romans 13:1–7 which states that all authorities are divinely appointed and so should not be resisted. In fact, Luther had originally addressed this tract to the 'other' peasants – the first pamphlet was addressed to the 'good' peasants. The printers, however, had removed this from the title, looking like Luther was calling all peasants robbers and murderers. This was not known at the time, so the response to Luther can only be judged on the information available to those who criticised him.

There are several possible reasons why Luther responded the way he did in the second pamphlet:

- Luther was aware that it was his ideas that had catalysed the Reformation and was disappointed at the course that it had subsequently taken.
- His enemies in the Catholic Church had argued from the very beginning that Luther's ideas would lead to anarchy and rebellion and so it was important that Luther disassociate himself from the Peasants' War and the violence associated with it.
- Luther wanted to separate himself from radicals like Muntzer – in his second pamphlet he described Muntzer as the 'archdevil who rules at Muhlhausen'.
- Luther aimed for **liberty of conscience** from certain aspects of the Catholic Church, and no more than that.
- In order to preserve 'his' Reformation, he portrayed radicals as alien to the true spirit of the Reformation and its mainstream leaders.
- Luther was afraid of the public unrest and disorder.
- He believed that Satan was using the peasants to disrupt the spread of the gospel.
- While on his tour of Thuringia, Luther saw some of the violence, and had a poor reception by some of the peasants there.

The consequences of Luther's response

Luther's response looked insensitive and inhumane because it was published, coincidentally, right at the time when the peasants were being brutally repressed, for example, on the battlefield at Frankenhausen. His Catholic opponents claimed that he had backed the peasants, only to turn traitor and reject them when they were not successful. While this was clearly untrue, it does give a sense of Luther's declining reputation following the Peasants' War. His response to the war lost Luther support among the poorest people who previously saw him as a symbol of liberation from oppression, particularly through his idea of a 'priesthood of all believers' (see page 245). Some respectable people who had been inclined towards Luther's ideas were also turned off by his response to the brutal repression of the Peasants' War.

On the other hand, it did reassure some of the rulers who were inclined to reform that Luther was not hostile to the princes and their powers. In fact the way he described the princes in his 1525 tracts demonstrated that Luther was a conservative who was not aiming, as Muntzer had been, for violent social upheaval.

The effect of Luther's conservatism on the German princes

The Peasants' War was important in determining the attitudes of the German nobility to the Reformation after 1525. Before this most of the princes had been able to ignore the religious changes happening from 1519 onwards. The events of 1524–25 showed that this was no longer possible. The princes from this point forward took a more active part in the Reformation, aiming to either fight against it or ensure that it happened in a controlled way.

Luther's response had reassured them that this was possible. The mainstream leaders of the Reformation would work with the princes not against them. Luther himself wanted to maintain public order as well as the support of the princes. To some extent, Lutheranism was appealing to **secular rulers** because if they declared themselves Lutherans, they would be free from obligation to the papacy. This would lessen the financial burden on them and would give them more power over the Church in their territory. It is unlikely, however, that this was the only reason that rulers converted to Lutheranism. It is an oversimplification and we must beware of failing to credit the princes with legitimate beliefs as we have done with the peasants before them.

Conclusion

While Luther's ideas represented a radical change from the traditional doctrines of the Catholic Church, they were moderate compared to the beliefs of Carlstadt, the Zwickau prophets and Muntzer. Luther did not support iconoclasm, or religious violence. His Reformation was peaceful and restrained, producing a renewed faith that still identified with many of the practices of Catholicism. He was appalled at the violence of the Peasants' War and his response

reflected his horror at that and the social implications if the peasants had been successful. His ill-timed response lost him support amongst certain groups but it simultaneously made Lutheranism more respectable for rulers and princes. This was important in the next stage of Lutheranism's development.

3 Lutheran beliefs and their influence

As Lutheranism began to spread it demanded a more concrete system of beliefs than in the very earliest days. From 1521 to 1529 many of Lutheranism's main ideas, liturgies and texts were created. Their influence was enormous.

Importance of justification

The concept of 'justification' was central to Lutheran theology. It grew out of Luther's outrage at the abuse of indulgences by the Catholic Church. 'Justification' refers to the way in which an individual is made righteous by God (see page 244). According to Luther, a person could only be saved by God rather than by their own free will in choosing to commit good works, such as helping the poor or donating to the Church. This did not mean that good works have no place within Lutheranism, just that this was not the way for people to achieve **salvation**. In Lutheran

Luther and nationalism

As with Luther's appeal to the German nation, this was not necessarily evident that Luther himself was a German nationalist. Rather, he wanted to open up the understanding of religion to the ordinary people rather than limiting the understanding of the scriptures to the priests as in the Catholic Church. It is true that Luther, like many others within Germany, opposed the degree of control that the Italian papacy had in his land. But it was one thing to want a more independent Church within Germany and yet another to call for German **nationalism**.

theology people would commit good works anyway if they were chosen by God, whereas those who did not were sinners and, therefore, damned to go to hell. It is important to understand this doctrine because it is one of the main things that divide Protestantism and Catholicism to this day.

The German Mass

Luther published the German Mass in 1526. He had published an earlier Latin Mass, *Formula Missae* in 1523. According to Luther the point of the Mass was for the word of God to be heard. The Mass was chanted rather than spoken, apart from the sermon. The sermon was extremely important because it was the point at which the congregation learnt about the scriptures. Luther was clear in the preface to the German Mass that it was a suggestion, not compulsory, and that it was a matter of liberty of conscience. He also explained the reasons for the German Mass:

- To create an acceptable mass rather than 'the different kinds of new masses, that every one makes his own, some with a good intention and others out of conceit to introduce something new themselves and to make a good show among others'. Here he is probably referring to religious radicals.
- To have a suitable mass in the German language so that 'the simple laymen' and the young would hear the word of God. He described the situation before this as 'just as if we held Divine Service in an open square or field amongst Turks or heathen'. Luther wanted to draw people sincerely to Christianity rather than them listening without understanding.

Doctrine of the Real Presence

Traditional Catholics held that the bread and wine used in the mass was changed into the body and blood of Christ. This process is termed 'transubstantiation'. Luther was rare among reformers in that he maintained the belief that Jesus Christ really was present in the bread and wine that is used during mass (see page 261). He believed that (slightly differently to the Catholic Church) the bread and wine were still present at the same time as the body and blood of Christ. This is termed 'consubstantiation'. Others rejected this and saw this presence as merely symbolic not physical. Luther saw anyone who rejected this belief as heretical. It is a particularly conservative aspect of Luther's theology, but was one that became enshrined in Lutheran doctrine.

Luther's translation of the Bible

Since the earliest days of his career Luther had believed that understanding the scriptures was absolutely central to Christian worship. He believed that every person could make direct contact with God with the priest assisting, rather than acting as an intermediary. This made it much more important that the Bible was translated. Luther's original case for reform was based around the notion that the Catholic Church was wrong and had, over the years, strayed from Christ's teaching and the Bible. Again, this made it imperative that Lutherans had access to a Bible in their own language so that they could understand the true teachings of the scriptures. Luther's translation of the Bible into German was not the first attempt at this task. It was, however, the most popular. Luther's first attempt at translating a section of the Bible took place in 1517, before he rose to prominence with the *Ninety-Five Theses*. He carried on translating sections of the Bible into German from 1517–19 and was encouraged by friends such as Philip

Melanchthon to translate the whole Bible. Luther was deeply absorbed in his translation of the New Testament while in Wartburg Castle from May 1521 to March 1522. This was finished before he left the castle to return to Wittenberg. It was published in September 1522 and an improved edition followed in December of that year. Following this Luther proceeded to translate the Old Testament, publishing it in sections as they were finished. The whole Bible was finally finished in 1534 and printed with 114 different woodcut illustrations. In the meantime his New Testament had appeared in over 16 editions and over 50 reprints. This did not mean that Luther's translating efforts came to an end. In fact, the final edition of the Bible that Luther published was only a year before his death, in 1545.

Luther's German Bible was greeted with great enthusiasm. Between 1534 and 1574 the printer Hans Lufft of Wittenberg printed and sold about 100,000 copies (not including reprints). This was an absolutely huge number for that period. It was read by millions because copies were shared, kept in churches and passed down within families.

The German Bible has been said to have been greatly influential in the spread of Lutheranism:

- More people could read and understand the Bible than could read Latin. They wanted to read the scriptures in their own language.
- The woodcuts within Luther's German Bible would aid understanding for those whose literacy was less strong.
- Scholars were interested in the translation and the language used to translate the Bible.
- Luther was well known by this point and both his followers and his enemies wanted to see his translation.

Luther's translation was influential for other reasons. It aided in the creation of a standard form of German. There were many different German dialects and Luther's translation helped to popularise the Saxon form of German as the literary language. Historian Patrick Collinson has described Luther's translation as 'the first work of art in German prose'. It became part of German national heritage and made a significant impact on education within Germany. Education became more important once it became possible to read the Bible in one's own language. Luther also inspired others in different countries to undertake the same task, spreading reformed Christianity around Europe.

Source E Woodcut from the title page of volume 2 of Luther's German Bible.

What does the woodcut in Source E say about Luther's intentions for the German Bible? How did he envisage it being used?

The *Large Catechism* and the *Small Catechism*

Luther's writings of the *Large Catechism* and the *Small Catechism* was prompted partly by his visitation to Saxony. In 1527, the Elector John of Saxony sent Luther and other reforming clergy to visit the parishes of the territory in order to make sure that they were worshipping correctly (see page 287). What Luther found appalled him. He realised that very few common people knew anything of Christian doctrine. Consequently, Luther felt that the Church needed to promote its message in a more systematic way, via teaching. Luther also believed in a 'priesthood of all believers' (see page 245). People did not need the intervention of a priest because they had all been given access to God through the intervention of Christ. This did not mean, however, that he was naïve about the need of ordinary people to have help when approaching the scriptures. It was one thing reading the words and yet another thing understanding them and the message behind them. With a clear and understandable statement of the central beliefs of Lutheranism people without an educated reformed priest would be able to teach themselves and their children. Both catechisms took the form of questions and answers and were intended to be read regularly so that believers would have a deep understanding of the faith. It also meant that, for example, fathers could test their children and that teachers could test their pupils on the contents of the catechism.

The catechisms included the Ten Commandments, **the creed**, and the Lord's Prayer. They also included explanations of baptism, the Lord's Supper, instruction for **confession**, morning and evening prayers and grace to be said before meals. Luther's approach in these catechisms was replicated many times over the centuries by both Catholics and Protestants who were trying to educate people about their faith.

The *Large Catechism*

The *Large Catechism* was aimed at adults, specifically those who were trying to teach others. It was published in April 1529 and was addressed by Luther to clergyman. The intention was to help them teach their congregations about the central principles of Lutheranism. Luther hoped that it could also be used by teachers, either in the classroom or at home. To his disappointment, due to the limited number of schools in Germany, this did not quickly become a reality.

The *Small Catechism*

The *Small Catechism* was aimed at children and ordinary people. It aimed to make the basic elements of the Christian faith applicable for everyday life. It included a wall chart and a booklet. It reinforced Luther's idea that God calls people to serve him by loving others and reinforced social structure and hierarchy.

The growing popularity of Lutheranism within Germany, 1521–29

From its beginnings in Wittenberg in 1519, Lutheranism grew and spread across Germany. By 1529 Luther's ideas and beliefs had been adopted in towns and villages across the Holy Roman Empire. It was spread by preaching, printed materials and groups of individuals. Much emphasis has been placed on the impact of the printing press. The printing press was certainly influential, and enabled Luther's message to be spread to literate people on a large scale. Scholars and educated men learned about Luther's ideas by reading his works. After reading Luther's ideas they then chose either to reject or accept Luther's ideas. Either way they spread word of the new theology either by passing pamphlets on or by alerting other scholars to their existence.

Woodcuts within Luther's books, pamphlets and printed sermons did help to explain his message to ordinary illiterate people. But the principal way that ordinary people who could not read or write found out about Lutheranism was by hearing a sermon or being taught the new ideas by their parish priest. Luther's students had been preaching his message since the very beginning and as his reputation grew so did his disciples. While there were some who became radical reformers, many did not and stuck to the moderate beliefs of Lutheranism. It was from the parish pulpit, then, that the Reformation was given to the ordinary people. Luther himself never stopped preaching or ceased his teaching career at Wittenberg. His sermons were heard by many and were also published. Sometimes, and in some places, the Reformation happened with the agreement of local rulers and in other areas it happened in the face of great resistance.

Once Lutheran ideas had been accepted by a majority of people within a parish they took action to change religious practice. This often meant that sacred images were removed, monasteries were closed, clergy got married and the German Mass was used in services.

Conclusion

The period 1521–29 was one of great productivity for Luther. He made great progress in translating the Bible, finishing the New Testament before he left Wartburg Castle in 1522 and the entire Bible by 1534. This was important as Luther believed that everyone should have access to the scriptures because they had a personal relationship with God, not one that needed priestly intermediaries. This made reading the Bible in their own language particularly important. Luther produced tools for teaching people how to understand the messages that he saw in the scriptures, The *Large Catechism* and the *Small Catechism*. Through published printed material, sermons and woodcuts knowledge of Lutheranism spread and support for it increased.

Work together

Read this section again carefully. Working in pairs, divide the content into two. One of you should take the first half, the other takes the second. Each of you needs to read the section for a third time. After you have read it put your notes and this book away and explain your 'half' to the other person. Note down any areas that you struggled to explain or where the explanation was unclear. These will serve as reminders to revise this section further.

4 Luther's declining influence, 1530–46

Luther's ideas were the catalyst for the German Reformation and for reform movements across Europe. Yet it was impossible for such a large and varied religious movement to revolve around one man. Luther was also hampered by his inability to travel beyond Saxony due to the imperial ban of 1521. This meant that others had to take on and develop his ideas, as well as acting as representatives for Luther and Lutheranism in important meetings of the diet (such as the Augsburg Diet in 1530) in Germany and beyond. Circumstances also conspired to discredit Luther in this period, for example, his advice to Philip of Hesse in 1540. While this period saw the spread of Lutheranism and some of Luther's ideas more widely around Europe it also saw the beginning of the eclipse of Luther the man within the movement itself.

Note it down

This is another opportunity to add to your themed collection of index cards (see page xi). In this section there are theological works and political/religious events. Follow the pattern of providing a definition, notes on the reason for it and the consequences or impact. Then fit these cards into your two themed collections – one on theological works and ideas, the other a timeline of religious and political events. Read through your other cards, and add any detail that you now understand because of your additional progress through the book.

Philip Melancthon's codification of Luther's ideas

Philip Melanchthon was an early supporter of Luther. It was Melanchthon who was to formally set down and explain the principal ideas and doctrines of Lutheranism. This was important because, rather than a patchwork of different ideas arrived at over years, it gave the impression to those interested or opposed to Lutheranism that it was a permanent and coherent system of belief.

Loci Communes of 1521

In 1521 Melanchthon wrote *Loci Communes rerum theologicarum seu hypotyposes theologicae,* since known as *Loci Communes.* It was a highly influential theological textbook. In this book Melanchthon discussed the 'leading thoughts' of the **Epistle to the Romans** and presented the ideas of Luther in the light of that discussion. This was meant to guide the reader to a proper understanding of the Bible. It also functioned as an explanation of Lutheran ideas and it has been said that the existence of this book explains why Luther never wrote a systematic theology of his own. It was the first book to systematically explain Lutheranism in this way. The *Loci Communes* proved extremely popular and went through three editions before the end of the year 1521, reaching 18 editions by 1525. Melanchthon produced modified editions of the book in 1535, 1543 and 1559. From 1535 Melanchthon began to revise the notion of **predestination** that had appeared in earlier volumes. From this point onwards he preferred

Philip Melanchthon (1497–1560)

Philipp Melanchthon.

Philip Melanchthon was born Philipp Schwartzerdt in Bretten, south-west Germany in 1497. His uncle was the great humanist scholar Johann Reuchlin (1455–1522), who was a great influence on Melanchthon in his earliest days – in fact it was probably Reuchlin who suggested that he changed his name to 'Melanchthon', a translation of Melanchthon's original surname into Greek. This was a trend amongst humanists of the time. He studied at the universities of Heidelberg and Tubingen before accepting a position from Martin Luther at the University of Wittenberg in 1518 when Melanchthon was still only 21 years old. He became professor of Greek and on his arrival set forth a humanistic programme. Melanchthon became one of Luther's strongest and most loyal supporters, present at the Leipzig disputation in 1519 and representing Luther at Augsburg in 1531 and on various other occasions. He was a moderate and cautious man whose temperament was a counterweight to Luther's more outspoken approach. He did not produce many original theological ideas but was very good at organising and explaining those of others like Luther. Melanchthon has been described as 'Luther's quiet craftsman'. He died in 1560 and was buried next to Luther in Wittenberg.

to say that God called the saved to heaven and that the Divine Mercy allowed the human will to receive grace. He excluded discussion of predestination from the Augsburg Confession. This shows a movement away from Luther's original ideas and could be used to demonstrate Luther's increasing irrelevance to the movement.

The Augsburg Confession of 1530

The Augsburg Confession was produced as the Lutheran contribution to the negotiations between Catholics and Protestants in 1530. The basis of it came from Luther's contribution to the Marburg Colloquy. It was edited and amended for the Augsburg Diet and became one of the foundational documents of Lutheranism.

The Marburg Colloquy, October 1529

The protestation signed by four evangelical states and 14 free imperial cities and submitted at the Diet of Speyer in April 1529 concerning the maintenance of the 1526 religious agreement (see page 285), led Philip of Hesse to organise a meeting between the Lutherans and the followers of Zwingli. The edict that resulted from the

Diet of Speyer in 1526 had instituted a temporary religious toleration in Germany, and this was revoked in 1529. This decision was the cause of the 'protestation' by five princes who had converted to reformed religion. It was also signed by representatives of several imperial towns that had converted. The protestation was a petition that the decision be reconsidered, but it was unsuccessful. Because that protestation was signed by both Lutherans and Zwinglians, Philip was hopeful that it might be possible to create a united Protestant front against the Emperor and for the good of the Reformation. He arranged for the two sides to meet at his castle at Marburg in October 1529. This was an unsuccessful venture. The participants did manage to draw up a list of articles that touched on all of the important points of doctrine discussed, but they did not agree on the central disagreement about whether Christ was really present in the bread and wine at mass. Luther refused to agree with Zwingli about the doctrine of the Real Presence (see page 270) and there was no compromise made. There was one long-standing impact of the meeting at Marburg. Philip Melanchthon was to use the 14 articles drawn up by Luther at Marburg to form the

Ulrich Zwingli (1484–1531)

Zwingli was born in 1484 in Switzerland. He studied at the University of Vienna in 1498 and Basel in 1502. He graduated from Basel in 1504 and became a priest. He served as an army chaplain and accompanied the soldiers to fight in the Habsburg-Valois Wars and began to question

the main ideas of Catholicism from 1516. Zwingli claimed that he had never read any of Luther's ideas until 1518 when he moved to Zurich. Indeed his ideas did not become radically different to the Catholic Church until his illness in 1519 and his brother's death in 1520. Zwingli converted the Council of Zurich to his point of view and this was followed by Basle and Berne. Zwingli's 'Sixty-Seven Articles' emphasised preaching, the removal of images, allowed clerical marriage, dissolved monasteries and encouraged the wealth of the monasteries to be spent on the poor. He strongly emphasised the importance of scripture. From 1525 radicals within the Swiss Reformation movement began to split away from Zwingli's more moderate stance. He resisted this in disputations and pamphlets but radical ideas spread nonetheless. Zwingli disagreed with Luther, who wrote disparagingly of the Swiss reformer as being just like Muntzer and the other radicals. They specifically disagreed about the mass, as Zwingli and his followers rejected consubstantiation (see page 270) and believed that the bread and wine were symbols of Christ's sacrifice rather than physically transforming into his body and blood. Zwingli was killed at the Battle of Keppel in 1531 while acting once again as services chaplain. His ideas were carried on by his son-in-law Heinrich Bullinger and other Swiss reformers.

basis of the Augsburg Confession. This was to become one of the canonical documents of Lutheranism.

The Augsburg Confession, June 1530

Charles V had been a persistent and committed opponent of Lutheranism. His commitment to the Catholic faith was unwavering. Yet by 1530 Charles was facing threats on many different fronts. At this point he was particularly anxious about the potential for Turkish invasions due to the fall of Hungary in 1526. This made it particularly important for Charles to try and resolve other long-standing issues such as the split in the Catholic faith following the Diet of Worms in 1521. There were also other, spiritual, rewards to be gained from possibly reuniting Christendom. Surely any ruler who healed this division would be rewarded by God in heaven. The imperial diet at Augsburg provided an opportunity to unite all Christians. Representatives of the Catholic Church and of the Lutherans attended. Philip Melanchthon was there to represent Luther. Luther was unable to attend because he was still under the imperial ban which made him an outlaw within the Holy Roman Empire. In many ways Melanchthon was an ideal representative, as he was conciliatory in nature and, although he was a strident defender of Lutheranism, he did see the value in a possible compromise.

Melanchthon produced a draft document which he hoped could form the basis for discussions. He used the articles that Luther had drawn up at Marburg as the basis for this. Once again, Melanchthon was responsible for one of the fundamentally important statements of Lutheran beliefs. The document, known as the Augsburg Confession, was presented to Charles V on 25 June 1530. It laid out the fundamental beliefs of Lutheranism on matters including justification by faith, the role of the priesthood, good works, the divine presence, mass and monastic vows. The Augsburg Confession became one of the foundations of Lutheranism and was the starting point for other declarations of faith. It introduced into Lutheranism principles of order and uniformity.

Although there was some possibility of a settlement between Catholics and Lutherans at Augsburg, it was not to happen. Charles was defined too strongly by his sense of divine destiny about his role as defender of the Church. He listened to the representative of the Pope rather than his own moderate advisers. Following the rejection of the Augsburg Confession by Charles V, Melanchthon produced the *Apology of the Augsburg Confession* in 1531 which was an eloquent and knowledgeable work of theology intended to refute the Catholics' response to the Lutheran Augsburg Confession. This was also to form part of the Lutheran *Book of Concord*, published in 1580. The *Book of Concord* contained all the major statements of Lutheran faith.

Source F A letter from Martin Luther to Philip Melanchthon on 29 June 1530. Melanchthon was at the Augsburg Diet where the Emperor seemed increasingly inclined to agree with the Catholic representatives and condemn Lutheranism. Luther commented on the events there.

> I have read the beautiful speech in which you apologise for your silence, and meanwhile I have sent two letters satisfactorily explaining my not writing. Today your letter came, full of unmerited reproaches, as if by my silence I had increased your work, danger, and tears. Do you really imagine I am sitting in a garden of roses and not sharing your cares? ... I have received your *Apology*, and wonder at your asking how far one may yield to the Papists. For my part I think too much has been conceded. If they do not accept it, what more can we do? ... I am as ready as ever to grant them everything if they only leave us a free gospel, but I cannot give up the gospel.

What does Source F tell us about Luther's involvement in the negotiations at Augsburg? Did Luther agree with Melanchthon's approach? If not, why?

Luther and the Philip of Hesse affair, 1540

Philip of Hesse had been one of the early princely converts to Lutheranism at the young age of 21. He was also to be one of Lutheranism's most constant supporters. After Frederick the Wise died in 1525, he became the leading defender of Lutheranism. Philip was a complex character, however, and was prone to mood swings. The heightened religiosity of the age he lived in also no doubt afflicted him.

Philip of Hesse's marital problems

While still very young Philip was forced by his family to marry Christine of Saxony. The marriage was arranged as a political alliance between the states of Hesse and Saxony. It was certainly not a marriage of love. He did not find her attractive and she appears to have been sickly. Whatever the reason for the failure of the marriage Philip, from the very beginning, was adulterous with a string of mistresses. This apparently caused Philip great anxiety and intense religious guilt because of the sins he was committing. He was sincerely religious and wanted to find a solution to his problem. Philip's chosen solution was **bigamy**, since the marriage was clearly legitimate and there was no way out for him.

Philip had been thinking about potential courses of action for a long time before the point at which he finally asked for advice in 1540. He approached Luther, Melanchthon, and Martin Bucer to ask their advice on the matter of bigamy. Bucer was a Lutheran supporter who led the

Reformation in the German city of Strasbourg. Eventually, all three reluctantly gave Philip permission to go ahead with a bigamous marriage to one of his sisters' ladies-in-waiting, on the condition that all parties were agreeable. Luther based his judgement, typically, on extracts from the Old Testament. There was also the logic that bigamy was better than constant adultery. Philip easily obtained the agreement of his wife and the marriage went ahead. The problems for the reformers began when the news of the bigamous marriage leaked out.

Consequences for Luther and the reformers

Luther's permission for the bigamous marriage was a gift to the Catholic opponents of Luther and the other reformers, particularly the Holy Roman Emperor Charles V, as it discredited the reformers and the princely opponent of Catholicism. Luther had claimed to be a protector of conservative family values and yet was involved in an apparent conspiracy to agree a bigamous and unlawful marriage. It also undermined the political position of Protestantism. It revealed the political naïvety of the reformers in that they failed to understand the impact that it would have on the reputation of reform. The Catholics were able to utter howls of moral outrage (albeit gleeful ones) at the lack of respect that the reformers showed to the sacrament of marriage. The situation also gave Charles V a real political advantage. Philip was forced to give in to Charles on several issues after these revelations, including promising to stand with Charles against all his enemies but the Schmalkaldic League and offering to further Charles' territorial aims in relation to France. In 1532 the imperial law code had been changed to introduce the death penalty for bigamy. Charles had the ability to grant an imperial pardon in Philip's case and chose to do so. This meant that Philip was in his debt and that Charles had a certain amount of leverage over Philip from this point.

Conclusion

Luther's place within the movement for Reformation was assured by his pioneering moves and the use of his ideas for the foundation of Lutheran beliefs. Yet he could not remain the only force within Lutheranism, and this period saw other names come to the fore. This was partly because they had skills that Luther did not (or was not interested in) such as Melanchthon's ability to construct an organised doctrine out of Luther's ideas. It was also because the Edict of Worms had placed strict limitations on Luther's movements – he could not go beyond the territorial boundaries of Electoral Saxony (where he was protected initially by Frederick the Wise) or he risked arrest, imprisonment and death. This led to others representing Lutheranism at meetings with the Catholics at the Diet of Augsburg and the Zwinglians at Marburg. His reputation (alongside that of the other Lutheran leaders) was damaged by the Philip of Hesse bigamy affair, but overall Luther's status as a prophet of the Lutheran movement was assured for the long term.

Work together

Look back over the rest of the unit. Working together, draw up a timeline of Luther's involvement in the Reformation. Include his works, his ideas, his response to various events and his presence at important points. Then consider at what point Luther began to be less important in the development of the Reformation. Note the reasons for this. Research detailed biographies of those who took over from Luther, and add them to your own collection of index cards (see page xi).

Chapter summary

- Luther had been excommunicated by Pope Leo X following the debate with Eck in June 1519.
- Frederick the Wise intervened to secure a trial for Luther in front of the Emperor rather than him being taken to Rome.
- Luther declared his faith at the Diet of Worms, 1521, refusing to recant his works.
- The Emperor, Charles V, condemned Luther as a heretic, outlawed him and placed him under the imperial ban.
- Luther was 'kidnapped' on the way back from Worms and taken to Wartburg Castle, where he stayed for a year from May 1521 to March 1522, protected by Frederick the Wise.
- While Luther was in Wartburg Castle more radical reformers seized the initiative in Wittenberg. The Zwickau prophets inspired Carlstadt to introduce radical changes including iconoclasm.
- Thomas Muntzer was another radical who preached the rejection of the written word, holy violence and the destruction of those who were not members of the 'true Church'.
- Luther preached against the radical ideas of Carlstadt and Muntzer and reversed Carlstadt's changes.

- The German Peasants' War of 1524–25 was actually a wave of unrest with a list of economic, political, legal and social grievances expressed by peasants against their landlords and princes.
- The peasants were brutally defeated by the princes and Luther defended the princes' actions. This lost him support from some moderate as well as radical reformers.
- Luther's response to the Peasants' War did attract princes to the reformed cause, as it seemed his reforms were not as radical as they feared.
- Luther refined his ideas in the 1520s, publishing the German Mass, *Large Catechism* and *Small Catechism* in order to provide for the reformed congregations and educate them.
- Philip Melanchthon codified Luther's ideas and published the *Loci Communes* in 1521. The Augsburg Confession was another of Melanchthon's works which became a foundation of Lutheranism.
- The Philip of Hesse affair damaged the reputation of leading Lutherans and led to a political weakness in favour of Charles V.

Recommended reading

Patrick Collinson, *The Reformation* (Weidenfeld & Nicolson, 2003).

For this section Chapters 3, 'Words, books and languages' and 6, 'Alternative patterns of Reformation' are an excellent summary.

Philip Melanchthon, Humanist and Reformer www.melanchthon.de/e/

A good website that includes useful biographical information on Melanchthon's background, studies, and his impact on the Reformation.

Tom Scott and Robert W. Scribner, *The German Peasants' War: a history in documents* (Amherst, 1991).

The introduction to this exceptionally useful collection of documents provides insightful analysis into the topic of the Peasants' War.

Lutheran beliefs and their influence

- Luther's beliefs centred on
  - justification
  - the German Mass
  - the doctrine of the Real Presence
- His translation of the Bible helped spread Lutheranism
- His catechisms spread teachings to teachers and children
- Printed materials, sermons and woodcuts helped spread support for Lutheranism

Luther's declining influence, 1530–46

- Philip Melanchthon
  - supporter of Luther
  - set down the doctrine of Lutheranism
  - *Loci Communes*
- Augsburg Confession
  - produced by Melanchthon
  - one of the foundations of Lutheranism
- Charles V failed to unite all Christians at the Augsburg Imperial Diet
- Luther's allowance of Philip of Hesse's bigamous marriage damaged his reputation

The Diet of Worms and its aftermath

- Meeting of the imperial diet, April 1521
  - Holy Roman Emperor
  - princes
  - papal envoys
- Luther declared a heretic and placed under the imperial ban
- Luther protected by Frederick the Wise and hidden at Wartburg Castle

The development of Lutheranism, 1521–46

Luther's views on the radical Reformation

The radicals

Revolt of the Imperial Knights, 1522–23

- Inspired by social, economic, political and religious elements
- Led by Franz von Sickingen and Ulrich von Hutten
- A failed attempt to attack the rise of powerful churchmen to secular positions

The Zwickau prophets

- Wanted to push reforms further
- Rejected infant baptism
- Argued bread and wine used in mass were just symbols and not the physical body and blood of Christ

Andreas Carlstadt

- Took Luther's reforms further
- Clashed with Luther over religious changes
- Banned from Electoral Saxony due to fear of his radical ideas

Thomas Muntzer

- Radical in Electoral Saxony
- Rejected the authority of the Bible
- Preached holy violence

Luther and the Peasants' War, 1524–25

- Peasants adapted Luther's ideas that resolved their long-held grievances in rural Germany
- Waves of disturbances with different causes and grievances
- Uprisings were brutally repressed by princes
- Luther's *Against the Robbing and Murdering Hordes* supported the princes' actions
- Luther's conservation helped rulers convert to Lutheranism

▲ Summary diagram: The development of Lutheranism, 1521–46

Section A: Essay technique

Contextualising the sources

In order to understand the sources properly, you need to place them in the context in which they were written. Specifically, you need to consider the background or environment in which the source was produced. This may sound obvious, but sixteenth-century sources were produced by sixteenth-century people, and therefore reflect their experiences, beliefs and prejudices. This means that sources are never standalone documents – they should be understood within the context of the values and assumptions of the society that produced them.

In essence, your task when contextualising the sources is to try and understand the world in the same way as the writers of the sources. In short, you should try and see things their way.

Understanding the context is an important part of evaluating the evidence that the sources contain.

Imagine you are answering the following question (the sources are on pages 280–1):

> **How far could the historian make use of Sources 1 and 2 together to investigate the religious beliefs of German peasants in the mid-1520s?**

You have read about the Peasants' War in this Key Topic. If you wish to remind yourself of the events of 1524–25 re-read the chapter or your notes. This is important before embarking on an exercise about context.

One way to contextualise the sources is to begin by asking the question: what debate is this source contributing to? The reason for this is that sources are written to contribute to ongoing discussions. For example, around 1525 there were a series of discussions going on in Germany about:

- whether the clergy should marry
- what happened to the bread and wine during mass
- whether reformed theology lead to political and social disorder
- whether the Pope was the Antichrist
- what should be done to improve the life of the peasants?

Many of the documents written at the time would have contributed to one or more of these debates. Working out which debate the source is contributing to, and which side of the debate the source is on can help you evaluate the evidence the source contains.

Here is an example of an attempt to put Source 1 in context:

The immediate context is the Peasants' War. The most significant revolts in early 1525 took place in upper Swabia and involved thousands of peasants.

The Twelve Articles were written in the early stages of the Peasants' War. In the early stages of the rebellions, local groups of peasants had produced documents setting out their grievances and demands for change. The Twelve Articles were compiled from some of these documents produced in upper Swabia. Therefore, they represent views from across the region.

Likely to have been Christoph Schappeler, a Protestant preacher who had been banned from preaching due to his use of Lutheran theology to defend the rights of the poor.

The writings of Roman Catholic figures such as Johann Eck who opposed reform and the goals of the Swabian peasants.

The writer of the introduction clearly claims that the Twelve Articles are a response to Roman Catholic criticisms of reformation theology.

Source 1 From the introduction to the **Twelve Articles of the Swabian Peasants,** 27 February–1 March 1525. These were a series of demands made by the peasants. The introduction was drafted by a preacher and the articles included demands for an end to serfdom and tithes.

There are many evil writings recently which take the chance, because of the assembling of the peasants, to cast scorn upon the gospel, saying 'Is this the fruit of the new teaching, that no one should obey but that all should everywhere rise in revolt, and rush together to reform, or perhaps destroy altogether, the authorities, both ecclesiastic and lay?'. The articles below shall answer these godless and criminal fault-finders, and serve, in the first place, to remove the reproach from the word of God and, in the second place, to give a Christian excuse for the disobedience or even the revolt of the entire peasantry.

The purpose of the document was to set out the grievances and demand of the peasants. These were used to attempt to negotiate with princes, bishops and city authorities to achieve change. The Twelve Articles were also printed and circulated among the German peasantry. In this way, they were used to form larger peasant leagues across Franconia.

In context 'new teaching' refers not only to the Lutheran teaching, but also the teaching of radical reformers.

This is a reference to the arguments of writers who opposed reformed theology, claiming that it would lead to chaos and anarchy.

It is crucial to relate your analysis of context to the question.

The context for Source 1 helps answer the question in the following ways:
- The Twelve Articles were based on documents written by peasants across Upper Swabia who were involved in a revolt against the local princes and bishops. Therefore, they are likely to reflect the views of many of the peasants involved in revolt across Upper Swabia.
- However, the introduction was written by a single preacher – Christoph Schappeler. Therefore, his theological views may not reflect the views of the entire Upper Swabian peasantry.
- Nonetheless, the Twelve Articles were widely read and helped bring peasants together across the whole of Franconia. This suggests that many peasants across the whole of Franconia were broadly sympathetic to the theology contained in the Twelve Articles.

Therefore, Source 1 is useful to the historian studying the religious beliefs of German peasants in the mid-1520 because it indicates there was widespread sympathy for reformed theology among the peasants engaged in revolt in Upper Swabia and Franconia. However, there are limits to the source's usefulness because it is difficult to tell how far the peasantry of Swabia or Franconia, let alone the whole of Germany, felt about the author's specific religious views.

Source 2 From a letter from the peasant army of the Black Forest to representatives of the city of Villingen on 8 May 1525. The letter accompanied a copy of a proposed constitution of a Christian association. The army of the Black Forest proposed that the city of Villingen join a Christian association of German towns and villages.

> Honourable, wise and favourable lords, friend and dear neighbours. In the recent past heavy burdens, much against God and all justice, have been imposed on the poor common man in the cities and in the countryside by spiritual and **worldly** lords and authorities. These burdens and grievances can no longer be borne or tolerated, unless the common man is willing to condemn himself to a life of begging.
>
> It is our friendly request, expectation and brotherly petition that you join us willingly, and submit as friends to this Christian association so that the common Christian good and brotherly love are again established and increased. If you do, the will of God will be realized, as you fulfil the commandment about brotherly love.
>
> But if you reject this petition, we will place you under the worldly ban [excommunication]: we will have absolutely nothing to do with you, we will neither eat, drink, bathe, grind grain, bake, work the fields, nor harvest them for you.

Activity: AS-style questions

1 Why is Source 1 valuable to the historian for an enquiry into the Peasants' War in Swabia?
2 How much weight do you give the evidence of Source 2 for an enquiry into the causes of peasant rebellion in 1525?

Activity: Seeing things their way

Now try contextualising Source 2.

Re-read the question – remind yourself of the specific task you are focusing on.

1 Ask yourself the following questions and annotate a copy of the source with the answers:
   a) Are there any events in May 1525 that might have influenced the writing of Source 2?
   b) Which debate is Source 2 likely to be contributing to?
   c) The source may reflect the views of specific groups of peasants – which peasants?
   d) Does the source reflect the views of peasants across the whole of Germany?
   e) Who wrote the source?
   f) Why was the source written?
2 Next, write a series of bullet points outlining:
   a) The aspects of the source that are useful for answering the question.
   b) The aspects of the source that are less useful.
   c) A summary of the extent to which the source provides useful evidence concerning the religious beliefs of German peasants in the mid-1520s.

Work together

Having read Source 2 and completed the activity above, discuss the following questions with a partner:

1 Did you both agree on:
   a) the reasons why the author wrote Source 2?
   b) the debate that Source 2 is addressing?
   c) the extent to which Source 2 might reflect the religious views of peasants across the whole of Germany?
2 Did you both agree on:
   a) the aspects of the source that were useful for answering the question?
   b) the aspects of the source that were less useful?
   c) the overall extent to which the source was useful to the historian investigating the religious beliefs of German peasants in the mid-1520s?
   If you disagreed on the answers to any of these questions, try and work out whose answer was better and why.
3 What else would it be useful to know about the source in order to answer the question?

Use your discussion to make a three point list of the ways in which you can use contextual knowledge to improve your essay writing.

Section B: Essay technique

Overall judgement

An overall judgement is as important to a Paper 2 Section B essay as it is to essays in Paper 1. You may have already read advice about the characteristics of a good overall judgement (see pages 74–75). Remember, good judgements are supported, and the best judgements consider the relative significance of the key factors you have discussed in your essay.

Now you can practise writing an overall judgement to an essay concerning Luther and the Reformation.

> ### Activity: Detail and analysis
> Imagine you are answering the following Section B question:
>
> > **How far was the support of the German princes responsible for the survival and spread of Lutheranism in the years 1521–55?**
>
> 1 Read the question and work out what type of question it is.
> 2 Make a plan that is appropriate to the specific question. Remember it should consist of three or four main points.
> 3 Add three pieces of detail to support each of your main points. Remember, use the detail that best supports the points you want to make.
> 4 Write an analytical sentence to conclude each of your main points.
> 5 Now write a conclusion to the essay.
>   ● Start by asserting an overall judgement.
>   ● Support this by weighing the different main points in your plan.
>   ● Summarise your overall judgement in the final sentence.

> ### Work together
> Having completed a plan in the activity, swap it with a partner's. Consider:
>
> 1 Did you agree on what type of question you were dealing with? If not, discuss it and work out who was right.
> 2 Whose plan most clearly focused on the specific type of question?
> 3 Did you both begin your conclusion with a clear judgement?
> 4 Did you both weigh up the different key points to support your judgement?
> 5 Whose overall judgement was better and why?
> 6 What can you learn from each other's work?
>
> Use these questions to feedback to each other and improve your essay technique.

> ### Question practice
> 1 How far do you agree that the Diet of Worms of 1521 was the main turning point in the development of the German Reformation in the period 1519–46?
> 2 How accurate is it to say that Luther's reaction to the Peasants' War was the main reason for the support of the German princes for Lutheranism from 1525? AS
> 3 How significant was Philip Melanchthon's codification of Luther's beliefs for the development of Lutheranism in the period 1521–46?
> 4 How accurate is it to say that Luther's translation of the Bible was primarily responsible for the growing popularity of Lutheranism within Germany in the years 1521–46? AS
> 5 'The imperial ban of 1521 was the most significant for Luther's declining influence within the Lutheran movement in the period 1521–46.' How far do you agree with this statement?

(282) **Paper 2 Luther and the German Reformation, c1515–55**

Key Topic 4 The spread and survival of Lutheranism, 1521–55

Overview

The fortunes for Lutheranism and for the religious reform movement in general fluctuated greatly in the period 1521–55 with many political and religious twists and turns. The series of negotiations between Lutheran and Catholic representatives led to an acknowledgement of the division between the two faiths rather than the unity desired by the Pope and Emperor. The 1530s saw the development and consolidation of a group of powerful, wealthy and influential Protestant princes who were prepared to fight for their beliefs against the might of the Holy Roman Emperor. The creation of the Schmalkaldic League in 1531 meant that reformed Protestants now had military support and were less threatened by imperial military might. The League was inspired by religious zeal but made Lutheranism attractive to princes with more material economic and political motives. It was, however, a threat to the Emperor, who was compelled to act. Charles V's core religious beliefs did not change. He stayed loyal to the Catholic Church and through military means and negotiation attempted to reunify the Church. Over this period, however, the Emperor became slowly more conciliatory. He was worn down by three decades of fighting in Germany and elsewhere in his empire. Our period ends with the Peace of Augsburg of 1555. This treaty ended the fighting and enshrined in law the division between Catholic and Protestant.

This chapter focuses on the role played by the elites at this stage of the Reformation. It looks at the actions of Reformation and Catholic leaders in the negotiations, the role of the princes in spreading Lutheranism, the response of Charles V and the actions of the popes. The chapter examines these issues through the following sections:

1 *The failure of the Lutheran-Catholic negotiations* examines the series of meetings between Catholics and Protestants, intended to reunite the Church but instead formalising its division.
2 *The role of the German princes* looks at the actions of the princes after the Diet of Worms. It explores the impact of the support of Frederick the Wise and the conversion of the princes from 1525. It examines the consequences of princely support for the Reformation.
3 *Charles V and Lutheranism* examines the actions of the Emperor in response to the Reformation. It looks at his religious beliefs, reasons for opposing Luther, and the obstacles he faced in doing so effectively. It also explores Charles' changing approach to Lutheran opposition.
4 *The papacy and Lutheranism* discusses the Pope's response to the challenge of Lutheranism. It examines the actions of successive popes and their attempts to suppress Lutheranism. It looks at their differing approaches and the reasons why they failed. It also considers the reforming attempts of Paul III and the opening of the Council of Trent.

TIMELINE

1526 August	The Diet of Speyer's temporary resolution	1545 March	The papal bull *Laetare Hierusalem* convened the Council of Trent
1529 March–April	The Diet of Speyer and the 'protestation'	1546 July–1547 May	The Schmalkaldic War
1530 June	The Diet of Augsburg and the Augsburg Confession	1548 May	The Augsburg Interim was implemented
1531 February	The formation of the Schmalkaldic League	1552 January	Treaty of Chambord: Princes agreed an alliance with Henry II of France
1537 March	The report of the *Consilium* was presented to Pope Paul III	1552 August	The Peace of Passau
		1555 September	The Peace of Augsburg
1541 April–June	The Diet of Regensburg	1556 January	Charles V abdicated from the throne of Spain and retired to a monastery

1 The failure of the Lutheran-Catholic negotiations

The period 1529–41 saw a series of negotiations between representatives of the Catholic and Protestant faiths. These were brokered by the Emperor, Charles V, who aimed to reunite Christianity with himself as secular head. The first two events in this period, the Diets of Speyer of 1526 and 1529, were edicts or declarations rather than negotiations. They both in different ways represented a failure of Charles and his attempts to bring the Lutherans back into line. Subsequently, the Emperor seems to have realised that a measure of negotiation was necessary. This led to events such as the Diets of Augsburg and Regensburg where genuine negotiation, albeit unsuccessful, took place.

Note it down

You will now be familiar with the three main methods of note taking (see pages ix–xi). We will now look at using these methods in a thematic way. This can help to organise your notes and can even be used to plan essays. Using index cards as before, write the date on the front and the name of the event at the top of the card on the other side. Make very brief notes on the event itself and slightly longer ones on the causes and consequences of the event. Make themed cards and colour code the fronts (or backs). Here you could have a theme of religious/political negotiations. When you use these cards at the end to make a timeline, it will be clear how a particular theme runs across the period.

Growing divergence between Catholic and Lutheran beliefs

It was only a few years since Luther had published the *Ninety-Five Theses* yet significant differences had already grown between Catholic and Lutheran beliefs. This was partly because of the need to codify Lutheran beliefs. Once Lutheran beliefs were codified it became much harder to negotiate on them. It also clarified differences between Lutheranism and Catholicism. These differences became greater as the period progressed. Catholics also felt the need to codify and explain exactly what made them different and this gradually widened the gap between the two beliefs. The division had caused a certain amount of bitterness between those who had opted for the reformed beliefs and others who had chosen to remain loyal to traditional Catholicism.

The Diets of Speyer, 1526 and 1529

The Diets of Speyer of 1526 and 1529 were two meetings of the imperial diet (see page 215) that took very different approaches to the growth and development of Lutheranism. They formed part of a broader struggle within the Holy Roman Empire. The Emperor wanted to reunite Christianity but he did not want to compromise with Luther and the other reformers like Melanchthon and Bucer. To a certain extent, he was hampered by his own conflicting priorities and his desire for unity both of Christianity and the Empire.

The Diet of Speyer, 1526

The Diet of Speyer of 1526 was intended by Charles V to be a final settlement of the matter of religion in Germany. He had hoped to be there to produce this settlement. However, Charles was overburdened with responsibilities. His extremely large empire caused him severe problems in terms of prioritisation, especially because there were so many military and dynastic challenges facing him, such as war with France and the Ottoman Turks. This meant that Charles, despite his hopes, was absent from the 1526 Diet of Speyer. This left the imperial estates, made up of the princes and the imperial cities, to make their own settlement. They agreed a temporary resolution on 27 August 1526.

Every ruler and imperial city was recommended to follow their own conscience in the matter of religion until the General Council of the Church be convened. For Luther it effectively meant that the Edict of Worms was suspended. This was a political solution but it had a real effect on religious affairs. Once the freedom to determine religious practice was granted it was extremely difficult to take it back. Charles V was horrified and absolutely determined to rescind this decree. His first effort to do this can be seen at the 1529 Diet of Speyer.

The Diet of Speyer, 1529

The Edict of Worms was reinstated by Archduke Ferdinand (Charles V's younger brother), on behalf of the Emperor, at the Diet of Speyer in 1529. Although Charles sent a message to Ferdinand to pursue a line of conciliation, Ferdinand did not receive the message in time for the start of the diet. Religious innovations were banned, no more church lands were to be secularised and the enforcement of the 1521 edict was made compulsory. Charles hoped before the diet to reverse the concessions of 1526. This would always have been difficult because the estates had been allowed to determine their own religious practices for a whole three years. In this time, a powerful and organised party of reformed princes and cities had emerged. This made it even more difficult to reverse the concessions made at the 1526 Diet of Speyer. A coalition of six princes and 14 imperial cities signed a 'protestatio' or protestation on 25 April 1529 against the move to reinstate the Edict of Worms (see Source A). It is from this document that we gained the word 'Protestant'. Because the signatories held a spectrum of reformed beliefs this term does not just refer to Lutherans. The Emperor ignored the protestation and maintained the edict but the protest had made it clear that Luther and the other reformers had built up a body of powerful and influential support.

The protestation further cemented differences between the Catholic and reformed princes. There were now two opposing religious parties with clear divisions between them. Slowly it became less plausible for territorial rulers and cities to sit on the fence.

Source A The protestation, 1529.

Therefore, in consideration of this previously settled, written and sealed decree [the Diet of Speyer, 1526], as well as for the following well-founded reasons *we cannot and may not consent to the annulment of the aforesaid articles, to which we unanimously agreed and which we are pledged to uphold, nor even to the supposed or intended moderation of the same,* which yet is nothing of the sort.

For the first of our well-founded reasons, we therefore think it beyond question that his imperial Majesty—as an honourable, upright and Christian Emperor, our most gracious Lord—and the majority also of you, the other princes, having once agreed in mind and will, pledged, written and sealed, would no less than we hold [the decree] to the letter as perpetual, fixed and inviolable, execute it and not scruple at anything therein, neither be nor act against it. *Therein we desire and seek honor, praise, forbearance and justice, not only our own but first of all his imperial Majesty's, and for all of us.*

As to others, we do not know in what way to answer such with a good conscience toward Almighty God as the sole Lord, Ruler and Upholder of our holy Christian saving faith, as well as toward his imperial Majesty as a Christian Emperor.

Look at Source A. What is the main objection made in the protestation?

The Diet of Augsburg and the Augsburg Confession, 1531

We have already seen on pages 274–75 how the Augsburg Confession developed from the Diet of Augsburg and became one of the foundational documents of Lutheranism. It is also important, however, to discuss it briefly from the point of view of its implications for Catholic and Lutheran negotiations. The Diet of Augsburg marked the first occasion that Charles V was prepared to negotiate and possibly compromise with the reformers. Charles convened the diet on 8 April 1530 in order for both sides to discuss important questions of religious **doctrine**. He invited participants on 21 January 1530 and expressed the hope that they would restore the unity of the German nation and Catholic Church.

The Elector of Saxony asked the Wittenberg reformers to draw up a document that outlined Lutheran beliefs as soon as he received the invitation to the diet. Melanchthon was the principal author of the document, adapting material from Luther's Marburg Articles of October 1529 (see page 274). When the Augsburg Confession was read to Charles on 25 June 1530 he did not respond immediately. Charles met with his advisers and representatives of the **Pope**. The Catholic response, entitled the *Confutatio Augustana* (the Confutation of Augsburg), refuted the statements of the Augsburg Confession and called for a return to Catholic doctrine. This response had taken several revisions before it reached an acceptable form, but was presented to the Lutherans on 3 August. The Emperor gave the Lutherans until 15 April 1531 to respond to the *Confutatio* and the result was to be known as the Apology of the Augsburg Confession. Written by Melanchthon, it was a defence of the Confession and was signed as a confession of faith by many Lutheran rulers and clergy.

Although it failed as an attempt to reunify the Church, the Diet of Augsburg was significant in signalling that Charles was aware that Lutheranism was a force to be reckoned with. It was also yet another sign of how important Charles believed the unity of the Church was for himself and for the people of his empire. The Diet of Augsburg was the first attempt at an open theological debate between Catholics and reformers. The Apology also formed the basis of the later negotiations at the Diet of Regensburg.

The Diet of Regensburg, 1541

The Diet of Regensburg produced what was later known as the Colloquy of Regensburg. It was the culmination of a series of attempts to reunify Christianity within the Holy Roman Empire. The Emperor was particularly keen to settle the situation in Germany because of the threat of war with the Ottoman Turks. He was also preoccupied with the actions of the French king who was negotiating with the Protestants in his country.

The diet opened on 5 April 1541. The Catholic delegation was led by Cardinal Contarini (see page 296) as the **papal legate** and the Protestant delegation included

Melanchthon, Bucer and the German minister Johannes Pistorius. The intention of the meeting was to negotiate common ground and aim to come to a compromise on issues of difference. Secret negotiations before the conference had achieved some agreement, for example on original sin, and offered the potential for agreement on the matter of justification. The conference itself did not produce an agreement. Contarini could not give up on the doctrine of transubstantiation in relation to the question of the divine presence in the mass while the Protestants would not agree that **confession** with a priest was necessary. Messages from the Pope in Rome and from Luther in Saxony also indicated that the limited agreement they had come to about justification would not be accepted by either. So while initially the meeting at Regensburg looked optimistic, it ended in failure. It was left to later attempts to either reunite or settle the division of the Christian Church.

Conclusion

The assumption of the Emperor that Lutheranism could be quashed was proven wrong in the period 1526–41. Attempts to forbid religious toleration at the Diet of Speyer were counter-productive, resulting in the closer alliance of religious reformers rather than a return to traditional Catholicism. The protestation coined the word 'Protestant' and signified a more united approach by religious reformers to the question of their survival and legitimacy. In the 1530s Charles V's strategy regarding Church unity changed, moving towards negotiation and compromise. Although the Diets of Augsburg and Regensburg saw discussion of the differences between Catholics and Protestants, the two sides had moved too far apart to come to an agreement.

2 The role of the German princes

We have already seen the impact and importance of Luther's protection by the German prince Frederick the Wise – he secured for him the opportunity to face the Emperor at Worms in 1521, protected him in Wartburg Castle from 1521 to 1522 and defied the imperial ban intended to ostracise and arrest him (see pages 258–60). Frederick allowed for Lutheran preaching in his lands and let the Wittenberg reformers publish their ideas. It must be stressed, however, that he did not legitimate the Lutheran movement or take steps to establish a new Church. In fact Frederick, with his large collection of relics and sacred objects, remained Catholic and did not convert to Lutheranism. So while the role that Frederick played was an extremely important one at the very early stages of Lutheranism, it needed more and more organised support to protect and develop Lutheranism after this point. Other princes and rulers were to play this role.

It is important to remember that not all princes supported Lutheranism. Some of them viewed Luther as a heretic and opposed even the early stages of the Reformation. They were traditional Catholics and feared the impact of Lutheranism on religion and social order in their territories. William of Bavaria and George of Saxony are two examples of such princes. They both tried to prevent the spread of Lutheranism into their territories and to stamp it out once it had arrived. In order to do this they arrested and ejected Lutherans. Other princes, such as Philip of Baden and Joachim of Brandenburg, were unsure of Lutheranism's impact. While not supporters of the movement, they merely restricted it rather than banned it.

Work together

This activity involves further reading and research. Doing independent reading and research is very important for achieving the highest grades. It gives you access to more detailed evidence but it also develops your independent thinking and research skills, which are useful for your coursework and then for university. First divide up the terms, events and documents discussed in this section. This could include the Augsburg Confession, the Diet at Regensburg and the *Confutatio*. Using the recommended reading in this book, your class notes, online research and other independent reading of your own, try and find out more about each of the diets and documents explored here. Share the notes that you have made with a partner and make sure that you read them together, explaining any terminology or external events that you have found out about.

Note it down

Draw a spider diagram (see page x). Label four 'legs' of the spider as follows: Frederick of Saxony, Albert of Hohenzollern, Philip of Hesse, John of Saxony. At the end of the legs note the following:
1 Biographical information about the four princes.
2 Their actions in the period.
3 Their impact on the spread of Lutheranism.

Read this section carefully and fill in your diagram. You may need to refer to other parts of the book as appropriate.
For extra biographical information, consult the glossary or search online for extra information.

The conversion of Albert of Hohenzollern, Philip of Hesse and John of Saxony

Once Luther began to explain and publicise his ideas from 1521 onwards, Lutheranism spread further and gained more followers. Luther could not control who those followers were, and this meant that anyone from the poorest peasant radical to respectable town governors supported his call for religious reform. One group that had been reluctant to support Luther was the princes of Germany. They were afraid that he was an extreme radical (which he was, compared to the Catholic Church, although not in comparison to Muntzer and the Zwickau prophets). Luther's response to the Peasants' War set their minds at ease and afterwards several important and powerful princes converted to Lutheranism.

The impact of the Peasants' War

Luther responded angrily to the Peasants' War of 1525. His conservative response to peasant violence and his encouragement of the rulers' brutal repression of the revolts meant that Lutheranism became disassociated from social radicalism. Lutheranism's new reputation as a religiously reformed but conservative faith that supported the existing social hierarchy made it much more attractive to the princes. Again, not all princes reacted in the same way to Luther and the Peasants' War. Casimir of Brandenburg-Ansbach-Kulmbach believed that Lutheran preaching had led to the unrest and that it was the duty of **secular rulers** to impose order. Although before this point he had been undecided on the question of reformed religion, this meant that he imposed a return to traditional worship in his territory.

Early princely converts to Lutheranism

The first major territorial ruler to convert to Lutheranism was Albert of Hohenzollern (1490–1568). He was formerly the grand master of the Teutonic Knights. They were a crusading order originally set up in the Middle East by German crusaders which then moved to the Baltic region to Christianise the pagan peoples there. Albert was a priest who converted in 1525 to Lutheranism. He secularised the lands of the Teutonic Knights. He married a Danish princess, Dorothea of Denmark, in 1526. This was significant because only in Lutheranism and other reformed faiths could priests marry. Most importantly, in 1525 Albert retitled himself the Duke of Prussia. This converted a religious state into a secular one. Albert was to build a powerful and successful state and became very active in imperial politics.

Philip of Hesse converted to Lutheranism at around the same time. He joined Luther after a personal meeting with Philip Melanchthon in 1524, although he had been interested in Luther's ideas since seeing him at the Diet of Worms in 1521. Philip's conversion was extremely important. He acted as a leader of the Lutheran princes for the rest of his life. He was instrumental in organising coalitions of Lutheran states and in resisting the Emperor, Charles V. After the Diet of Speyer in 1526 Philip decided to call together all of his clergy to draw up a plan for reforming religion in Hesse. Luther rejected the resulting ideas and Philip would turn to Luther for advice from that point forward. John, Elector of Saxony, inherited the title from his brother Frederick the Wise in 1525 following Frederick's death. He was also known as 'John the Steadfast' for his continual support of Lutheranism in the same manner as his brother. Unlike Frederick, however, John was a Lutheran. John put in place a system of measures to firmly establish a Lutheran Church in Saxony. He made sure the Wittenberg reforms were instituted, but most importantly he organised a system of visitations. The visitations were meant to ensure that Lutheranism was being preached in every parish. Visitors, important clergymen like Luther himself, were sent to each parish to check that they were worshipping in the right way. New clergymen were appointed, Catholic priests were dismissed and church services were standardised using the **liturgy** devised by Luther. Philip of Hesse also copied this model.

The impact of princely conversions

These princely conversions were vital for Lutheranism at its early stages. Lutheranism was still growing and spreading rapidly but it was vulnerable to political and religious attacks by the Emperor and the Pope. While neither of these figures could prevent people from believing in Luther's ideas, they could make sure that they were persecuted and that followers of Luther were harassed, arrested, and executed. If all of the princes persecuted Lutherans, it would restrict the movement's support and make it difficult to worship openly. People who were attracted to Luther's ideas would be put off converting to Lutheranism if the movement appeared too radical, as they did not want to lose status and risk their safety if branded heretics. Princely support, alongside the weakness of the imperial authority, meant that in particular territories Lutheranism was effectively protected. It also meant that there were representatives arguing for Lutheranism at imperial diets and at the highest level of society. Later conversions, for example Duke Ulrich of Wurttemberg in 1534 and Duke Henry of Saxony in 1539, were also helpful in shoring up Lutheran support by adding to Lutheran

The princes' motivation in converting to Lutheranism

Historians have argued about the motives of the princes for converting to Lutheranism. It is possible to argue cynically that they converted largely for territorial or political reasons. Lutheranism allowed them more control over their territories because it gave them authority over religion as well as giving them motives to form coalitions and resist the Emperor. H. G. Koenigsberger, G. Q. Bowler and George L. Mosse argued in 1989 that political ambition and a desire for greater power also entailed a religious commitment on the part of such princes. Geoffrey Elton agreed that religion, power and authority came together in motivating the princes. Lutheranism did provide political advantages. However, there were also many princes who chose not to convert and who repressed Lutheranism in their territories. This, and the determination with which Lutheran princes instituted the reforms in their territories, means that it is difficult to argue that secular motives were the most important. Historians like C. Scott Dixon have argued that religion was the central reason for the reforming programmes undertaken by the Lutheran princes.

'territory', protecting worshippers there and increasing the number of territorial rulers who would speak up for Lutheranism at an imperial level.

Formation of the Schmalkaldic League, 1531

In 1531 the first significant and successful military and political alliance of Lutheran princes was founded. There had been previous attempts. In 1526 Protestant princes, including Philip of Hesse and John of Saxony, set up the League of Torgau to oppose the Edict of Worms. Other original members of the Torgau League included Brunswick, Anhalt and the cities of Magdeburg, Mansfeld, Bremen, Strassburg and Ulm. This had not been successful because it had limited military power. The Schmalkaldic League was set up by Philip of Hesse and John of Saxony. It was agreed in the Thuringian town of Schmalkalden on 27 February 1531. The League was set up at this point because there was a fear that the Holy Roman Empire, under Charles V, was going to launch a military strike against the Protestant powers – in particular Hesse and Electoral Saxony due to their behaviour at the Diet of Speyer in 1529. The members of the League agreed to defend each other should they be attacked by the Emperor. They agreed to provide in total 10,000 infantry and 2,000 cavalry split between the members. John of Saxony also insisted that in order to become a member of the League each ruler or city had to agree to the Augsburg Confession (see page 275). Other rulers and imperial cities joined the Schmalkaldic League. These included Wurttemberg, Augsburg and Frankfurt. It became a territorial political movement as well as a religious one. It was obvious to some who joined that the movement offered economic advantages because of the release it offered from financial obligations to the Catholic Church. Again, this does not necessarily mean that they did not also have some sincere religious convictions. It also offered the opportunity to fight against the Holy Roman Emperor who had aimed to increase his authority over the princes and the imperial estates.

Luther was asked by Elector John Frederick of Saxony to produce the Articles of the Schmalkaldic League in 1537 for the League's meeting that year. John wanted a summary of Lutheran doctrine that could be adopted by the League before a proposed Council of the Church (see Source B). The potential Council would include Catholics and Protestants. The League did not adopt Luther's Articles in 1537. Melanchthon played a part in influencing them not to do so, because he believed Luther's Articles would divide Protestants rather than uniting them. The Articles of the Schmalkaldic League did live on as another statement of Lutheran beliefs, however, and Elector John Frederick incorporated them into his will to show his devotion to the faith.

For Charles, the formation of the Schmalkaldic League was also a military threat within the Empire. This was bad news for Charles, who was also battling the French and the Turks. Indeed Francis I, King of France, joined the League in 1535 specifically to fight against Charles, although he later withdrew because of French domestic problems. The Ottoman Sultan, Suleiman the Magnificent, encouraged the League to ally with Francis against Charles for his own military reasons. The Schmalkaldic League made military alliances with other Protestant states, for example Denmark in 1538. They confiscated Church lands, expelled Catholic bishops and aided in the spread of Lutheranism in Germany. Charles was unable to fight the League until 1544 when he had made peace with Francis. This gave the League time to grow and consolidate its influence, although not enough to succeed in the war against Charles in 1547.

I verily desire to see a truly Christian Council, in order that many matters and persons might be helped. Not that we need it, for our churches are now, through God's grace, so unenlightened and equipped with the pure Word ... But we see in the bishoprics everywhere so many parishes vacant and desolate that one's heart would break, and neither the bishops nor canons care how the poor people live or die ... Besides such necessary **ecclesiastical** affairs, there would also be in the political estate innumerable matters of importance to improve. There is the disagreement between the princes and the states; usury and avarice have burst in like a flood ... wantoness, lewdness, extravagance in dress, gluttony, gambling, idle display, with all kinds of bad habits and wickedness ...

How useful is Source B in telling us Luther's ideas on the links between religious and political problems? What does Luther think is the solution?

The League's significance for the spread of Lutheranism

The Schmalkaldic League was significant for the spread of Lutheranism for several reasons:

- **The League was inspired by religious zeal**. According to historian Diarmaid MacCulloch the Schmalkaldic League 'was only in existence to do God's work: it was not merely a diplomatic association of convenience'. Given the success of the League in attracting members and in enforcing Lutheranism in their territories, this is an extremely significant reason.
- **It was a significant military force.** This meant that Protestant states were able to resist Catholic pressure with the confidence that they had military support behind them.
- **It was attractive to rulers and states who were not necessarily motivated by religion but by economics and self-interest.** These rulers and states were made to sign up to the Augsburg Confession before joining. Consequently, Lutheranism was spread even when it was not the rulers' main aim in joining the League.
- **Because the Lutheran states were united in the League they had more political leverage.** This was true internationally as well as domestically. The League were seen as a potential ally by others who had an interest in defeating Charles V, including the Ottomans and the French.

Conclusion

After 1525 Lutheranism gained princely converts. This brought several key advantages. The princes could protect Lutherans and allow them to worship freely in their areas. They could speak up for Lutheranism to other princes and the Emperor in the diets. They could offer military and financial support. It also made Lutheranism seem more respectable and less radical now that some princes were prepared to support it. The Schmalkaldic League was set up to provide defensive military support for Lutheran states but also brought political advantages to Lutheranism.

Work together

Consider the following motives for states to join the Schmalkaldic League: religious, economic, political. Working in a small group of three, prepare for a debate. Each of you takes one motive. On your own, prepare a case that your motive was the most important. Look at the Articles of the Schmalkaldic League and find out more about the rulers of the member states and their behaviour before and after the League was founded. Meet together as a group again and deliver your justifications. Afterwards, discuss the following:

- Whose case was the strongest?
- Which motives worked well together in explaining why states joined the League?

3 Charles V and Lutheranism

Charles V saw himself as the 'protector of all **Christendom**' in his role as Holy Roman Emperor. For all of his life he fought to maintain the unity of Christianity in Europe. He fought against invasions of Christian lands by the Muslim Ottoman Turks and against the Lutherans in Germany. Yet Charles abdicated from the thrones of Sicily and Naples in 1554, from the Netherlands in October 1555 and from the Spanish throne in January 1556. He retired, exhausted from his efforts to defend his lands and the Catholic faith, to a monastery in Spain. Charles died only three years later with his empire split between his brother Ferdinand and his son Philip II. There was never again to be an empire of the size of the one that Charles attempted to manage between 1519 and 1554. Charles' dedication to the Catholic faith was sincere and consistent, but he was hampered in his attempts to maintain its unity by two main factors – his conflicting priorities and the limited support given to him in Germany by the Catholic princes. The approach of the **papacy**, political instability, the desire for expansion and changing social and economic conditions also prevented Charles from achieving his aims.

Note it down

For this section you can try an adaptation of the spider-diagram technique (see page x). Print out a blank map of Europe. If you search online for 'blank map of Europe sixteenth century', this should find a number of maps that you can download and print out. Read the section below and label the map with the relevant areas, including Spain, France, Naples, Milan, Hungary and the Holy Roman Empire. When you have done this, draw lines out from these areas and make notes from this section about the events that took place in, or involved, these countries, cities and regions.

Charles' conflicting priorities in Spain, France and against the Ottomans

Charles had an enormous empire. It covered parts of central, western and southern Europe including Spain, France, Austria, Italy, as well as the Spanish colonies in the New World. Charles saw his role as protecting the unity of his empire and defending his dynastic lands. It may seem like governing such large areas of Europe would be

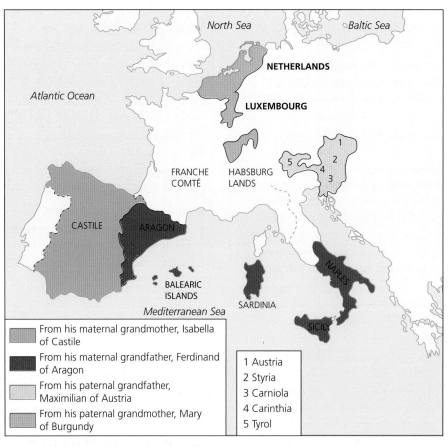

From his maternal grandmother, Isabella of Castile

From his maternal grandfather, Ferdinand of Aragon

From his paternal grandfather, Maximilian of Austria

From his paternal grandmother, Mary of Burgundy

1 Austria
2 Styria
3 Carniola
4 Carinthia
5 Tyrol

▲ Figure 1: Charles' inheritance

advantageous, but throughout Charles' reign it brought him constant trouble in the form of military conflict and financial strain.

Wars against France and the Ottoman Empire

Aside from the lands in the New World, Charles had gained his empire through inheritance rather than conquest. The main problem facing Charles was that his inheritance included lands that other powers either wanted or already saw as their own. His main rivalry throughout his reign was with France. The French monarchy aimed to expand into northern Italy, especially into Milan. The French kings also attacked Naples, Luxembourg, Savoy and Artois. Their justification for these repeated attacks was Valois family dynastic rights. Francis I believed that he had the right to claim these lands because they had formed part of his mother's or father's ancestral territories. These claims were not always well supported, but it was important for reasons of honour to make them, rather than waging wars of open conquest. The Habsburg-Valois Wars between the two families began in 1494 and did not end until Charles' son Philip II signed the Treaty of Cateau-Cambresis in 1558. These wars were largely defensive on Charles' part – the French attacked Charles' territories on many occasions. These included Luxembourg in 1521, Savoy and Piedmont in 1536, Artois, Luxembourg, Brabant and Navarre in 1542 and Lorraine, Luxembourg and Artois again in 1552. Charles did attack Milan, pursuing his dynastic rights in 1521 and Tournai in the same year. He also conquered Friesland in 1522 and Guelders in 1543.

Charles was obliged to defend his dynastic and imperial lands – it was a matter of honour and reputation for his title and his Habsburg lineage. The wars were, however, hugely expensive and disruptive to Charles' ability to rule his other lands effectively. Francis could raise extremely large armies – his campaigns in Italy saw him bring armies of 10,000–25,000 to the field. Charles had to at least match this in order to defeat or defend against Francis. Francis was also prepared to ally with other enemies of Charles in order to win. He requested help from the Ottomans in 1526, leading to the invasion of Hungary and the defeat of the Hungarian king. The resulting partitioning of Hungary led to the Habsburgs being involved in wars with and for that country for the next 70 years. Francis allied with Sultan Suleiman the Magnificent in 1536 against Charles, threatening the Holy Roman Emperor with a war on two fronts. Suleiman was not just a threat when allied with France. He threatened Charles' eastern European territories consistently and also attacked his Mediterranean lands. In retaliation Charles conquered the Ottoman city of Tunis in 1535 with a 'Holy League' of 60,000 men. Only three years later the same Holy League was defeated by the Ottoman Empire in the Battle of Preveza, the Turks capturing key Greek island Christian outposts.

Charles I, King of Spain

A second problem was that Charles was also King of Spain. He became King of Spain in 1516 but the Spaniards were very uneasy with having a potential Emperor as king – they (rightly) feared that Spain would become one possession among many and that it would have to support other territories while having an absentee monarch. Charles had to appease the Castilian **Cortes** by promising to appoint Spanish advisers, learning the Spanish language and marrying an **Iberian** princess. Spain was to provide military and financial resources for the rest of Charles' reign – it was principally Spain and her New World territories that funded the incessant wars with France and the Ottomans. As a result, Spain became bankrupt under Charles' son Philip II.

All of these distractions – each one of them a threat to Charles' territories and government, and all persistent throughout his reign – meant that it was nigh on impossible for him to devote all of his attention to the Lutheran threat in Germany. Indeed, Charles was away from Germany for ten years after the Diet of Worms dealing with other problems. Maintaining Christian unity and then reuniting the Church was one of Charles' highest priorities but it had to take second place to territorial threats. This meant that Charles was distracted at key moments (like the Diets of Speyer in 1526 and 1529) and unable to be present to reinforce his commands. He could not concentrate on the problem and strike ruthlessly against the Lutherans or enforce obedience among the princes. This was worsened because Charles frequently needed to request help or resources from the German princes in his battles against his other enemies. Effectively, Charles' distractions meant that Lutheranism was allowed to grow unsupervised in Germany with only sporadic efforts from Charles to repress it.

Limited support for Charles from the Catholic princes

Charles clearly faced a challenge from the Protestant princes. Another, perhaps more unexpected, problem, was that the Catholic princes were not very supportive either. This stemmed from fears about Charles' intention to increase his authority over the territories of the Empire, and his determination to rule as one secular authority. At the beginning of his reign Charles had been determined to strengthen the authority of the imperial title and consolidate his power within the Empire. The Catholic princes were worried that Charles wanted to increase his authority at the expense of theirs. So when Charles challenged the Lutheran princes the Catholic princes were reluctant to intervene on his behalf – on the principal that German princes should have the authority to act as they wished in their own territories. Even though they shared a faith with Charles, they believed that the result of any effort to bring the Lutheran princes back into line would also ultimately affect them.

This situation was temporarily altered by the rise of the Schmalkaldic League because the Catholic princes feared that the military might of the League could be used against their Catholic territories. This motivated them to support Charles in the Schmalkaldic War. However, their support did not last. Following the Emperor's victory in the war, the Catholic princes were still unprepared to agree to a change in the imperial constitution that would give the Emperor more authority within the Empire. Ultimately, this atmosphere of suspicion meant that Charles did not have access to the Catholic princes as military or political allies against the Lutherans as might be expected.

Significance of the Schmalkaldic War, 1546–47

In 1546 Charles finally had the chance to take military action against the Schmalkaldic League. This marked a change in the Emperor's approach. Charles had decided that since negotiation had not worked (for example at Regensburg, see pages 285–86), that perhaps war would persuade the Protestant princes to see sense. A war would not involve religious concessions and might help him achieve his objective of unity through force rather than toleration. At that point he was at peace with both the Ottomans and the French, a rare window in which action against the Protestant princes of Germany was possible. His situation was improved because one of the more powerful princes, Duke Maurice of Albertine Saxony, had left the League in 1542 and defected to the Emperor's side. This was because he felt that the integrity of the Holy Roman Empire was more important than religion. The war itself was very short compared to others of Charles' experience. It lasted from 10 July 1546 to 23 May 1547 and ended in victory for the Emperor.

Events of the Schmalkaldic War

Charles V won the war partly due to military strength at the Battle of Muhlberg on 24 April 1547, but also because

there was disagreement, indecision and disunity on the part of the Protestant leaders. They could not decide if, when and where to attack the imperial army and were taken by surprise by imperial allies such as Duke Maurice invading their lands. The imperial cities, sensing failure, submitted to the Emperor. Therefore, Lutherans that had been expected to rise in support of the League failed to do so. At the final Battle of Muhlberg the leaders of the Schmalkaldic League were indecisive again. This gave Charles and his commander the Duke of Alba the chance to attack their defences. The Protestants were taken by surprise by this action. The battle was a disaster for the Schmalkaldic League. Over 7,000 men were killed in the fighting and over 1,000 taken prisoner. The League's leaders, Philip of Hesse and John of Saxony, were also imprisoned after the defeat. John of Saxony was forced to resign most of his lands to his cousin Maurice of Albertine Saxony (who had benefited greatly from his change of allegiance) and the Schmalkaldic League was dissolved.

Consequences of the Schmalkaldic War

The consequences of the Schmalkaldic War were, unhappily for Charles, not especially long lasting or severe for the Protestant territories. Although the main Protestant leaders, John of Saxony and Philip of Hesse, were imprisoned, the forces that Charles had drawn together to defeat the League were soon disassembled. The Pope's army retreated to Rome. The Protestant territories defeated in the war refused to return to Catholicism and the Emperor's alliances with Protestant princes such as Maurice fell apart. The Emperor's triumph was temporary and a new Protestant league was formed as early as 1551 under his former ally Maurice. One consequence that had more influence was the Augsburg Interim of 1548.

The Augsburg Interim

The Augsburg Interim was an attempt by Charles to implement a temporary edict that would deal with the religious situation while being more conciliatory than previous edicts. Charles wanted to make this settlement acceptable to as many moderates on both the Catholic and Protestant sides. The Augsburg Interim was drafted on 15 May 1548 at the Diet of Augsburg and became imperial law on 30 June of that year. The Interim rejected the key Lutheran doctrine of justification by faith. It also reinforced the authority of the pope over the Church. It ordered Protestants in the defeated territories to re-adopt traditional Catholic practices. This, and other articles that rejected Lutheran beliefs including those about the divine presence in mass, made it unacceptable to many Protestant leaders. The Interim was significant, however, because it did also attempt to make significant concessions:

- It allowed Protestant clergymen to marry – a stipulation upheld by the Pope.
- It allowed the laity to take **communion** as well as priests.

In this it was a first step towards the fuller compromises of Passau in 1552 and Augsburg in 1555 (see page 294). Historian Diarmaid MacCulloch has described this process of change from Augsburg to Passau as a journey towards the political and religious legitimisation of Protestantism. At the time, however, it was unacceptable to Catholic princes as well as most Lutherans.

The Augsburg Interim divided Protestants between those who were inclined to accept it or work towards a moderated version because they wanted an end to the conflict (including Melanchthon) and those who rejected it outright. Because of the defeat at Muhlberg the Interim was to be implemented across Charles' territories. This resulted in the exile of some German Protestant theologians, including Martin Bucer. Others were imprisoned and some executed.

However, Charles' triumph was a temporary one. He once again became preoccupied by conflicts elsewhere in his empire against the Ottoman Empire and the French (see page 290) and Protestant anger at the result of the Schmalkaldic War was enough to form another coalition like the Schmalkaldic League as early as 1552.

The Peace of Passau, 1552

The Treaty of Chambord was an alliance between Henry II of France and Protestant princes led by Maurice of Saxony. Formed in January 1552, it stipulated that the French would provide funding and assistance to the Protestants. In return for this assistance Henry II would gain lands in western Germany at the expense of Charles V. These included the bishoprics of Metz, Toul and Verdun, and the fortresses situated in these **dioceses**. While this was part of the long-running conflict between Charles and the French kings it was also an important boost to the fortunes of the German Protestant princes. They successfully chased Charles out of the Tyrol,

Source C Portrait of Emperor Charles V. This was painted during the imperial diet of Augsburg in 1548.

What impression of Charles V is portrayed in Source C?

hereditary Habsburg lands, into Italy and Henry captured the fortresses of Metz, Verdun and Toul. Charles was to launch a further campaign to regain these after concluding the Peace of Passau.

The peace negotiations after this campaign were held in Passau, in the south-east of Germany, in the summer of 1552. All parties were desperate for peace at this point. The military conflict had lasted sporadically since 1546 and the political conflict since the 1520s. Even the Catholic princes were prepared to agree terms in order to secure a lasting peace. The result was that in August 1552 Charles agreed terms that meant that Lutheran religious freedoms were guaranteed. The much disputed Augsburg Interim was cancelled and the princely prisoners taken after the Battle of Muhlberg were released. Even this, however, was a temporary peace. It was granted by Charles V until an imperial diet could be called to negotiate further. It did make it clear, however, that Charles' lifelong effort to secure the unity of the Church and an end to the 'heresy' of Lutheranism had failed.

The Peace of Augsburg, 1555

The Peace of Augsburg was the final nail in the coffin of European religious unity. Charles V was not present at the diet and authorised his brother Ferdinand to act for him. The diet opened on 5 August 1555 and the treaty concluded on 25 September 1555. The Treaty made the following stipulations:

- Princes within the Empire were free to choose to either keep Catholicism or adopt the Augsburg Confession and so choose Lutheranism. This is usually summed up by the Latin phrase, '*cuius regio, eius religio*' or 'Whose religion, his religion.'
- The inhabitants of each princely territory had to adopt the religion that their prince chose, or move to another territory.
- Only Catholicism and Lutheranism were recognised in the Peace of Augsburg – no other reformed faiths.
- Cities were allowed to choose Lutheranism as long as they also allowed Catholic worship to take place.

The implications of the Peace of Augsburg were obviously far-reaching. There was no longer one official religion in the Empire and warfare concerning religion was banned. The Reformation had not been suppressed or defeated.

Conclusion

The sheer size of Charles' empire caused him many problems. It would have been very hard to administer such a large empire in times of peace but the various wars and conflicts of the period made it nearly impossible. The wars with the Ottoman Turks and with France diverted Charles' attention from Germany. His commitments in Spain also distracted him from the Lutheran threat in the Empire. This meant that Charles found it even more difficult to prevent the spread of Lutheranism than he would have done otherwise. It also led to him making treaties and compromises because he needed to deal with issues urgently elsewhere. Charles was very committed to his role as defender of Catholicism and his abdication in 1555 was partly due to his failure in this matter. Suppressing Lutheranism would have been highly problematic for any ruler but for Charles it was one challenge too far.

Work together

This is the final section that explains the different laws, edicts, treaties and negotiations through which Charles V aimed to deal with the problem of Lutheranism. If you have carried on making 'date and definition' index cards, you should now have a complete set that you can colour code on the theme of 'religious/political negotiations' as in the previous 'work together' activity on page 284. Working in pairs, use both of your sets of index cards on this theme. Place the cards in chronological order to begin with. In your pairs, you will now move them around and re-order them differently in the light of these questions:

- Which of these events was the biggest turning point in the survival of Lutheranism?
- Which of them represents the greatest change of approach from Charles V?
- Which one was the least effective in Charles V's fight against Lutheranism from 1519 to 1548?
- Which one was the most effective in Charles V's fight against Lutheranism from 1519 to 1548?

You can think up other questions yourselves in order to test your understanding of the events and their significance for the growth, survival and development of Lutheranism in this period.

4 The papacy and Lutheranism

The medieval popes were the undisputed spiritual rulers of Christendom. They had political conflicts with territorial princes over power and authority but few disputes about doctrine or theology that they were unable to quash effectively. Luther's actions in 1517 and the Reformation that resulted from them brought this to an end and instituted an age of division, instability and insecurity for the papacy. It led to ineffective edicts and **excommunications**, religious war and theological debate. At the end of the period the papacy emerged with its authority intact and with a strengthened sense of Catholic doctrine and identity but this was by no means inevitable.

Failure to respond to Luther effectively

The papacy had never before faced a threat like Lutheranism that could not be defeated by excommunication, execution and persecution. The response, when it came, was poorly judged and reactionary – although the novelty of the threat was one reason for that. It was not until the 1540s that efforts were made to address the issues raised by Luther and by this point the movement was well established in Germany.

The response under Leo X

We have already seen in Chapter 2 how the papacy's response to Luther's early challenge from 1518–20 was too late and inadequate. It provoked Luther to take a more radical line and to move further away from traditional Catholic worship. The theological debate with Eck and the meeting with Cajetan demonstrated to Luther that the Catholic Church was not prepared to listen to his grievances and those of many other Catholics. Luther did not react to their intransigence by backing down but instead carried on developing new ideas by his constant study and interpretation of the Bible. Pope Leo X's excommunication of Luther was ultimately ineffective in persuading him and others to change their ways, and in fact led to more publicity and support for Luther. The bull of excommunication, *Exsurge Domine*, appeared in June 1520 and was publically burned by Luther and his followers in Wittenberg five months later. This was seen as an outrage by traditional Catholics and as a demonstration of Luther's contempt for the Pope. His pamphlet *Against the Bull of the Antichrist*, which depicted the Pope as Satan, went even further. Luther's interpretation of the Pope's response to his ideas was that it was the Pope who was actually the source of all the problems within the Catholic Church. The Pope

had good reason not to listen to Luther – after all, if the divine representative of God were to listen to every theologian who disagreed with the Church's ideas, there would be little stability in Catholic doctrine. However, his political mismanagement of the response to Luther's protest provoked a storm that the Pope could not then control. Pope Leo X issued the final papal bull of excommunication, *Decet Romanum Pontificem*, in January 1521.

Adrian VI and reform

In December 1521 Leo X died of a sudden infection. He was succeeded by **Pope** Adrian VI (1459–1523). Adrian VI was only Pope for two years before his death. Before he became Pope in 1521 he had been Charles V's tutor, co-regent of Spain and, since 1516, a cardinal. Adrian VI was opposed to corruption and was unpopular in Rome due to his refusal to spend freely on expensive entourages. Adrian refused to employ more people than he needed, so some people who were relying on the patronage of the papacy were left out of work. He should have been an ideal pope to address the issues that Luther had raised about the corruption of the Church. Yet Adrian also wanted to re-unite Christendom and had, while in Spain, been leader of the inquisition that tried to enforce religious uniformity in that country. This made him opposed to the Lutheran 'heresy' and he called on the princes to unite against it. Unlike Leo X, Adrian recognised that the Lutheran movement needed to be taken seriously. However, he was unable to act successfully against it. He died after only two years as pope and was succeeded by another **Medici** pope – Clement VII. The Medici family were known for their extensive use of patronage, love of luxury and interest in the arts. Even the churchmen of the family were deeply involved in secular politics and in many ways were excellent examples of the problems Luther fought against.

Note it down

Here we will use the 1:2 method (see page x) with a slight alteration. As usual, note down the 'big points', or headings, in the first column. In the second column write the supporting points in note form. This time add a third column. Here, note down any concepts, terms, documents or historical figures that you would like to research further. This could include Pope Leo X, the League of Cognac or the *Consilium*. When you have completed this section you can then research these points and add the information into this column.

Clement VII and Lutheranism

Clement VII was the cousin of Leo X. Like his cousin, he was more preoccupied by Italian politics than by the Protestant Reformation. Politically, Clement could not decide who to support in the battle between Charles V and Francis I of France. Initially he supported Charles until 1524–25 when he changed sides and joined Italian princes in allying with France. Clement swapped sides again when Francis I was defeated at the Battle of Pavia in 1525. In 1526 Clement changed his mind once again and joined Francis in founding the League of Cognac. This was an alliance opposing Charles. Charles grew tired of Clement's constant indecision and changing alliances. Charles also needed to act against the League of Cognac. The Emperor allowed his troops to sack Rome in May 1527 and imprisoned the Pope. Unfortunately, Charles released Clement before he could secure a promise from him that a general Council of the Church would be called to address the problem of the Lutheran Reformation. Clement was afraid of offending the French in this matter and, even after he and Charles had reconciled, never acted firmly against the Protestants of Germany. Clement was preoccupied with politics and underestimated the threat that the Reformation posed to the integrity of the Catholic Church. As a result, the Reformation could spread during Clement's papacy relatively unrestrained by papal repression. Charles, too, was preoccupied with military affairs outside Germany. Instead of military intervention and edicts, the Emperor opted for negotiation.

Paul III and attempts at reform

Pope Paul III became Pope on the death of Clement VII on 13 October 1534. Unlike his three immediate predecessors, Paul was aware that the Reformation could prove catastrophic for the Catholic Church. Paul initially attempted to organise a General Council of the Church. However, the Lutherans objected to the meeting taking place in Italy. He also appointed the Venetian Gasparo Contarini cardinal in May 1535. Contarini was a humanist who wanted to reform the Catholic Church, and became one of the Pope's closest advisers. It was Contarini who proposed the reform commission that was to produce the report known as the *Consilium*. Paul supported this and organised a committee of churchmen and laity to act as a commission for improving the Church. Paul III officially recognised the Jesuit order in 1540 which was to prove so instrumental in taking strict action, or persecution, against the Protestants of Europe. On the other hand, he sent negotiators to the Diet of Regensburg (see page 285) to attempt a settlement with the Protestants in 1541. Paul also called the Council of Trent which produced some of the more far-reaching reforms of the Catholic Church in this period. Paul was praised for his reforming zeal and recognition that the Church needed

Table 1: Popes during the German Reformation

Pope	Biographical summary
Pope Leo X (1475–1521)	• Born Giovanni di Lorenzo de' Medici • Became pope in 1513 • Began the indulgence campaign to pay for St Peter's Basilica • A great patron of the arts • The first pope to attempt to respond to Luther's challenge
Pope Adrian VI (1459–1523)	• Born Adriaan Florensz • Had a career as an academic, tutor to Charles V before being made Cardinal in 1517 • Elected pope in 1522 • Attempted reform but was prevented from doing much by his cardinals • Strongly opposed to Lutheranism
Pope Clement VII (1478–1534)	• Born Guilio di Giuliano de' Medici • Became pope in 1523 • Made cardinal by his cousin, Pope Leo X • Was a patron of the arts • Imprisoned by Charles V in 1525 • Had to decide on the issue of King Henry VIII of England's marriage
Pope Paul III (1468–1549)	• Born Alexander Farnese • Became pope in 1534 • Came to be pope at a time of great instability • Convened the Council of Trent and began the move towards Catholic reform

to reform itself. He has been credited for beginning the Catholic Reformation or Counter-Reformation that saw the Catholic Church renew itself. Although Paul did not achieve all he aimed to during his papacy and the Church remained divided, he did at least recognise that the Reformation was a serious problem and attempted to act decisively to ameliorate the problem.

The *Consilium*, 1537

The reform commission that met in Mantua in 1537 produced a report for the Pope entitled the *Consilium de emendenda ecclesia*, later known as the *Consilium* (see Source D). Even though Paul was clearly aware that reform was necessary, the report went further than expected. It contained a clear declaration of papal authority but also condemned previous popes as the cause of much ruination of the Catholic Church. It also outlined serious abuses within the hierarchy of the Church.

Source D From the *Consilium*, 1537.

[T]he origin of these evils was due to the fact that some popes, your predecessors, in the words of the Apostle Paul 'having itching ears heaped up to themselves teachers according to their own lusts' (II Timothy 4:3), not that they might learn from them what they should do, but that they might find through the application and cleverness of these teachers a justification for what it pleased them to do. Then it came about, besides the fact that flattery follows all dominion as the shadow does the body and that truth's access to the ears of princes has all been most difficult, that teachers at once appeared who taught that the Pope is Lord of all benefices and therefore, since a lord may sell by right what is his own, it necessarily follows that the Pope cannot be guilty of simony. Thus the will of the Pope, of whatever kind it may be, is the rule governing his activities and deeds; whence it may be shown without doubt that whatever is pleasing is also permitted.

Read Source D carefully and answer the following questions:

- What does the report blame previous popes for?

- What particular abuse does it accuse Paul's predecessors of committing?

- How would this please reformers and give them ammunition against the papacy?

What did the *Consilium* say?

The commission's report listed abuses within the Church. This included abuses that Luther and the reformers had highlighted in the 1520s, such as the abuse of Church offices, clerical misbehaviour, **simony** and pluralism. Their solution to the problems of the Church was very different to that of Luther and the other Protestants. The Lutherans believed that the Church needed to be fundamentally reformed in terms of the role of the priests and of scripture. The Catholic commission saw the problem as existing in the Church hierarchy. They thought that the hierarchy of the Church needed to be reformed in order to make the Church flourish again. They proposed a radical programme of reform with Contarini at its head.

The response to, and consequences of, the *Consilium*

It is perhaps predictable, given that senior members of the Church hierarchy had a vested interest in keeping the hierarchy the same, that the majority of the hierarchy of the Church were opposed to the reforms. They wanted to keep the situation the same and worked hard to make sure the reform programme was not implemented. Although the reformers within the Catholic Church were powerful, they were in the minority.

Although the Pope was powerful, he was not powerful enough to force the reforms through. The conservative cardinals were not entirely motivated by self-interest. They also thought that the reforming Pope was making the Church look weak. It would enable the Lutherans to make political and religious mileage out of the Church and its weakness. The Catholic hierarchy knew how the Lutheran propagandists would depict reform coming from within the Church. They were correct. Martin Luther translated the *Consilium* for a Lutheran audience. Rather than portraying it as positive progress within the Catholic Church, he explained it as an attempt by the Catholic hierarchy to fool the ordinary people of Europe with reforms that were not genuine.

Yet this was not the end to Paul III's attempts to reform the Church. Although the Catholic reformers lost a certain amount of credit after the *Consilium*, the situation was not entirely irredeemable. The conservatives gained the upper hand after 1541 but could not stop the summoning of the Council of Trent.

The Counter-Reformation

The Counter-Reformation was the response of the Catholic Church to the Protestant Reformation begun by Luther. Writers like Erasmus had been calling for reform from within the Catholic Church even before Luther's actions in 1517. Before the Council of Trent in 1545, reform within the Church took the form of clerical discipline and attempts at creating a more spiritual form of religion. From 1498 Cardinal Ximenes introduced reforms in Spain that aimed to improve the education of the clergy and enforce discipline amongst the clergy. Catholic reform of this early period also focused on **asceticism**. The Theatine order were founded in the 1524 as a much more ascetic and severe monastic order. They lived according to strict monastic rules and observed a rule of poverty. One of the founders of the order was Giovanni Pietro Carafa, later Pope Paul IV. Other monastic orders and groups were founded along the same lines, like the Capuchins and the Jesuits. Pope Paul III was the first pope to consider ideas of internal renewal in the Catholic Church. The Council of Trent began a movement to reform the discipline of the clergy while preaching against Lutheranism. It attacked corruption within the clergy and established the Roman Inquisition to investigate heresy. The Counter-Reformation also emphasised missionary efforts to convert new territories to Catholicism (such as the New World and Asia) as well as re-converting areas that had formerly been Catholic.

Summoning of the Council of Trent, 1545

Pope Paul III summoned the Council of Trent in the papal bull *Laetare Hierusalem* issued on 19 November 1544 and it eventually convened in 1545. It was held in the town of Trent in north Italy, although it later moved to Bologna. The Pope had made previous attempts at reform but this time he was also encouraged by the Emperor Charles V. Charles had been pressing for a Council of the Church for a long time. The aims of the Council were to reform the Church hierarchy, to clarify the doctrine of the Church and oppose the ideas of the Lutherans. It was part of a long process to revitalise Catholicism after the impact of the Protestant Reformation. According to historian Peter Marshall, the Council of Trent was part of the process of Catholicism remaking itself after the shock of the Protestant Reformation.

The reforms of the Council of Trent

The Council of Trent took place over a period of two decades. It was not continuous, took place in two different cities and involved different people over the course of its existence. There were two main purposes of the Council – to formulate a distinctively Catholic doctrine and to reform the hierarchy and institutions of the Catholic Church.

The earlier sessions, which ran from 1545 to 1547, dealt with doctrine. They created a unified Roman Catholic Church with a clear doctrine rather than the looser definitions of the late medieval Church. The later sessions, which ran from 1562 to 1563, looked at institutional reform. The reforms included orders for bishops to live in their dioceses and not act as aristocrats or politicians and the setting up of **seminaries** to properly train and educate the clergy.

The end result was a much more authoritarian and disciplined Church by 1563. The divisions between Protestants and Catholics had been solidified and made permanent, and the fact that both had then consolidated their doctrine meant that there was very little room for return.

Conclusion

The papacy faced a very different situation in 1555 to that in 1517. The Pope no longer presided over *the* Church but over *a* Church. Christendom was divided and treaties in Germany had effectively sanctioned Lutheran worship in the Holy Roman Empire. The papacy was slow to respond to the Reformation. Its early response was poorly judged and counter-productive, provoking Luther into more radical ideas. It was not until Paul III became pope that concerted efforts were made to address the abuses within the Church or to significantly reform the Church as an institution. When these efforts were made it was within the context of a permanently divided Church.

Work together

In this final 'Work together' activity you will check each other's notes to make sure they are complete. Together, go through the specification and all four key topic chapters. Create a table. In the first column put the section heading, for example, 'The role of the German princes'. In the second column put the subsections, for example, 'The formation of the Schmalkaldic League'. Head the third column 'Notes' and the final column 'Revision'. Now swap folders and complete the following tasks for your partner:

- Put your partner's notes in order.
- In the 'Notes' column, tick if your partner has a good set of notes on a subtopic. Leave it blank if they do not. You can also use this column to record the type of notes, for example class notes, index cards, independent reading.
- Leave the 'Revision' column blank. As your partner revises they can then use this column to tick off the subtopics as they go.

Now swap your folders again. This should highlight any areas of strength and weakness in your folders. You can fill in the gaps with further notes, diversify your notes by doing more index cards, more reading or different types of note taking. Then you can move on to revision!

Chapter summary

- Significant differences had grown up between Catholic and Lutheran beliefs from 1517 to 1529. Negotiations took place from 1529 to 1541 to try to reunite the two.
- The Diet of Speyer, 1526, temporarily allowed every ruler to follow their conscience and the Edict of Worms was suspended. Charles V was horrified at this.
- Three years later, the Diet of Speyer of 1529 reinstated the Edict of Worms. A coalition of princes and imperial cities signed a protestation on 25 April 1529 against this move.
- The Augsburg Diet of 1531 was the first time that Charles V would negotiate with the reformers in an attempt to unite the Church.
- The Diet of Regensburg of 1541 was the end of a series of attempts to reunite the Church. It ended in failure despite looking optimistic to begin with.
- In the 1520s several important princes converted to Lutheranism and provided vital support for it in its early stages.
- The Schmalkaldic League was formed in 1531 as a military and political alliance of Lutheran princes. It led to the spread of Lutheranism.
- Charles V was opposed to Luther's ideas on principle and saw himself as the defender of the Catholic Church.
- Charles had vastly conflicting priorities in France, the Ottoman Empire, Spain and Italy.
- Charles lacked support from Catholic princes because they feared that he might gain more authority over them and their territories.
- The Schmalkaldic War was a victory for Charles but did not last long – the alliance that secured him victory soon fell apart and a new Protestant alliance formed.
- The Augsburg Interim of 1548 had more long-lasting significance, as a first step towards religious compromise.
- The Peace of Passau of 1552 and the Peace of Augsburg in 1555 meant that princes were free to choose to keep Catholicism or choose Lutheranism instead. There was no longer one official religion in the territories of the Holy Roman Empire.

The spread and survival of Lutheranism, 1521–55

The failure of Lutheran-Catholic negotiations

- Charles V wanted to reunite Catholics and Lutherans
- Diet of Speyer, 1526
  - a temporary settlement
  - every ruler and imperial city was to follow their own conscience in matters of religion
- Diet of Speyer, 1529
  - Charles V wanted to reverse concessions of 1526
  - the Edict of Worms was reinforced
  - the protestation cemented differences between the Catholic and reformed princes
- Diet of Augsburg, 1531
  - Charles V prepared to negotiate with reformers
  - failed attempt to reunify the Church
- Diet of Regensburg, 1541
  - an attempt to reach a compromise
  - failed to settle the division of the Church

The role of the German princes

- Lutheranism became an attractive option after the Peasants' War
- Albert of Hohenzollern and Philip of Hesse's conversions to Lutheranism were important
- The Schmalkaldic League, 1531
  - military and political alliance of Lutheran princes
  - aided the spread of Lutheranism
- Princes who converted could protect Lutherans and allow free worship in their areas
- Princes had varying motives for converting to Lutheranism
- Not all princes supported Lutheranism. Traditional Catholic princes tried to prevent its spread

Charles V and Lutheranism

- Charles was distracted in other areas of his empire, especially with wars against France and the Ottoman Empire
- Reuniting the Church was a high priority but took second place to territorial threats
- Charles had limited support from Catholic princes
- The Schmalkaldic War ended in victory for the Emperor, but its consequences were not long lasting
- The Augsburg Interim ordered Protestants in defeated territories to re-adopt Catholic practices
- In 1552 Charles agreed to terms that guaranteed Lutheran religious practices
- The Peace of Augsburg allowed princes to choose either Catholicism or Lutheranism

The papacy and Lutheranism

The Pope's responses

- Leo X – the Pope's responses to Luther provoked Luther into further reforms
- Adrian VI – recognised the importance of the Lutheran movement
- Clement VII – more preoccupied by Italian politics – switched allegiance between Charles V and Francis I of France
- Paul II – supported reform of the Catholic Church

The Consilium, 1537

- Outlined abuses within the hierarchy of the Church
- The commission's report proposed a radical programme of reform
- Reforms were opposed by conservative cardinals

The Council of Trent, 1545

- Summoned by Pope Paul III
- 1545–47 sessions focused on creating a clear doctrine
- 1562–63 looked at institutional reform
- Resulted in a more authoritarian and disciplined Church

▲ Summary diagram: The spread and survival of Lutheranism, 1521–55

Recommended reading

Peter Marshall, *The Reformation: A Very Short Introduction* (Oxford University Press, 2009).

This is an excellent short introduction for the whole topic of Luther and the Reformation. Sections on the princely reformation and the Catholic responses in Chapter 2 would be particularly useful in relation to this chapter.

C. Scott Dixon, 'The Princely Reformation' in Andrew Pettegree (ed.), *The Reformation World* (Routledge, 2000), pages 146–65.

This is a good summary of princely responses to the Reformation and the changes wrought in Germany as a result.

Bruce Gordon, 'Italy' in Andrew Pettegree (ed.), *The Reformation World* (Routledge, 2000).

This contains very useful information regarding Catholic attempts at reform.

Wim Blockmans, *Emperor Charles V, 1500–1558* (Bloomsbury, 2002).

A biography of Charles V – with helpful detail and analysis in Chapter 3, 'Honour, rights and land' and Chapter 4, 'The Protector of the Catholic Church'.

H. G. Koenigsberger, G. L. Mosse and G. Q. Bowler, *Europe in the Sixteenth Century* (Routledge, 1999).

This book provides a good and clear overview of the sixteenth century in Europe. Chapter 9, 'The Catholic Reformation' and Chapter 10, 'Empires' are particularly relevant to this chapter.

Section A: Essay technique

Evaluating the sources

Evaluating the sources is essential to doing well in the exam. It means working out how far the sources contain evidence that is useful to a historian doing a specific task.

There are different levels of evaluation, which are rewarded to different extents.

Firstly, your source evaluation must be relevant to the question:

- Source evaluation that is not clearly linked to the question will be awarded marks in the lower levels.
- Source evaluation which is clearly relevant to the question will be awarded marks in the higher levels.

Secondly, there is the issue of the criteria you use to evaluate the sources (see table below).

Level 1	**No criteria** – evaluation is extremely superficial, it does not relate to any criteria.
Level 2	**Questionable criteria** – evaluation is based on a criteria, but the criteria is invalid, simplistic or poorly understood.
Level 3	**Formulaic criteria** – evaluation is based on a discussion of the **nature, origin and purpose** (NOP) of the source.
Level 4/5	**Valid criteria** – at this level responses will use criteria that reflect the kind of source and the kind of specific task that the question focuses on. In this sense the evaluation will be tailored to the question. At Level 4 the criteria will not be applied rigorously. At Level 5 the criteria will be applied rigorously.

Evaluating the sources: The criteria

Imagine you are answering the following question:

> **How far could the historian make use of Sources 1 and 2 to investigate attitudes of reformers in Wittenberg to the use of sacred imagery in churches in the early 1520s?**

Source 1 From Andreas Carlstadt's *On the Removal of Images*, published in 1522. Carlstadt was a theologian who was excommunicated by Pope Leo X in 1521 due to his reformation theology. Carlstadt preached reformed theology and encouraged reformed religious worship in Wittenberg following the Diet of Worms in 1521. He encouraged the removal and destruction of images and statues from churches in January 1522.

> i. That we have images in churches and houses of God is wrong and contrary to the first commandment. Thou shalt not have other Gods.

> ii. That to have carved and painted idols set up on the altars is even more injurious and diabolical.

> iii. Therefore it is good, necessary, praiseworthy and pious that we remove them and give scripture its due.

God's houses are buildings in which God alone should be glorified, invoked and adored. ... God hates and is jealous of pictures, and considers them an abomination, and proclaims that all men in his eyes are like the things they love. Pictures are loathsome. It follows that we become loathsome when we love them.

The images bring death to those who worship or venerate them. Therefore, our temples might be rightly called murderers' caves, because in them our spirit is slain. May the Devil reward popes who thus bring death and destruction upon us. It would be a thousand times better if images were set up in hell or the fiery furnace than in the houses of God.

Source 2 From Luther's Invocavit Sermons, preached at Wittenberg on 12 March, 1522. Luther had returned from Wartburg Castle to Wittenberg due to Fredrick the Wise's horror at the destruction of images and statues that had been taking place. On his return, Luther preached a series of eight sermons, this passage comes from the fourth.

Dear Friends,

We have heard the things which are necessary, as for instance, that the mass is regarded as a sacrifice. Then we considered the things which are left to our liberty, such as marriage, the monastic life and the abolition of images. On the subject of images we saw that they ought to be abolished only if they are going to be worshiped, otherwise not. Although I wish they were abolished everywhere because they are abused. But this is not sufficient reason to abolish and burn all the images – and why? Because we must admit that there are still people to whom they may be useful. Although they are few, we cannot and should not abolish anything which is still useful to the devotions of any man. We should teach that images are nothing ... that we would do better to give a poor man a gold-piece than to give God a golden image. If people heard this teaching, images would cease without any uproar or tumult.

Simplistic source analysis

Having read the sources it is clear that Luther disagrees with Carlstadt's policy of destroying sacred images. Therefore, you could say that: 'Luther is biased against Carlstadt.' However, this would be a low level response, because it is not clear why you consider Source 2 biased. Additionally, it is not clear how this statement answers the question.

You could say that: 'Source 2 is unreliable because Luther was not in Wittenberg when Carlstadt started destroying images.' However, this is based on questionable criteria: it assumes that only eyewitnesses are useful to historians, which is not true. Additionally, Luther is not claiming to be an eyewitness – so the criteria are not appropriate to the source.

Based on this, here are two basic tips:
- Avoid simply saying 'Source 1 is biased'. Statements like this are very simplistic and are therefore unlikely to get you a good mark.
- Avoid assuming that the only useful sources are eyewitness accounts.

Nature, origin and purpose

One way of evaluating the sources is to ask questions about the nature, origin and purpose of the sources:

- **Nature:** what type of source is this?
- **Origin:** when and where does the source come from?
- **Purpose:** why did the author write the source?

This approach is a good place to start. It is also better than making simplistic statements about sources. However, it can lead to formulaic responses, which are unlikely to gain top marks.

Evaluating sources in their own terms

The best way of evaluating sources is to try and understand them in their own terms. Reading the sources in the context of the time is a good way of evaluating their usefulness. By situating the sources in their context, we can argue the following:

- First, Source 1 argues in favour of abolishing images. It was published in 1522 at a time when Carlstadt was encouraging the destruction of images. By contrast, Source 2 argues that destroying images is wrong. It is from a sermon preached in March 1522, at a time when Luther had returned to Wittenberg to challenge the destruction of images that Carlstadt had initiated. Therefore, both sources are useful in the sense that they reflect the positions of two preachers who we know from historical context were influential in Wittenberg during this period of the reformation.

- Second, we know that Fredrick the Wise wanted Luther returned to Wittenberg to challenge Carlstadt's destruction of images. Therefore, it could be argued that Luther only argued against the abolition of images to please his protector. However, this would be simplistic, as Luther had theological reasons for opposing the destruction of images that had nothing to do with Fredrick's protection.

- Even so, Fredrick is still important to the question. Indeed, the sources are useful because they show that there was significant common ground between the reformer Luther and the Catholic Fredrick the Wise. In this sense the two sources are useful to a historian studying attitudes of reformers to the use of sacred imagery in the Church in the early 1520s because they demonstrate that there were significant theological differences between radical and moderate reformers over the role of images in this period.

TIPs:
- Use what you have already learned to help you understand the sources.
- The dates of the sources are often significant. Use what you already know to explore the possible significance of the dates, places and people mentioned in the sources.
- Remember that sources are contributing to a debate, use your knowledge to situate the sources in the wider debate.

Having read the advice on evaluating the sources on pages 302–03, try to evaluate the sources in order to formulate an answer to the question below:

> How far could the historian make use of Sources 3 and 4 together to investigate the influence of Lutheranism on religious practice in Nuremberg in the mid-1520s?

Source 3 From Cardinal Lorenzo Campeggio's description of the attitude of the people of Nuremberg in March 1524. Campeggio was papal legate to the 1524 Diet of Nuremberg, he was describing life in Nuremberg to the Pope.

In this city the sincere faith in Christ is utterly abolished. No respect is paid either to the Virgin Mary or to the saints. They ridicule the papal rites and call the relics of the saint's bones of men who have been hanged. In Lent they eat meat openly. Confession is neglected, as they say it should be made only to God. They take communion in both forms. They make a laughing stock of the Pope and Cardinals by circulating drawings and caricatures. In short they consider Martin Luther their enlightener, and think that until now they have lived in darkness.

Source 4 From an account of the religious practices issued by the Diet of Nuremberg. The account was sent to Frederick the Wise and the Bishop of Meissen due to the influence of Duke George of Saxony.

We have heard that priests celebrate mass in lay habit, omitting essential portions. They consecrate the holy sacrament in German, rather than Latin. The recipients are not required to have made prior confession. They take the elements into their own hands and in both kinds. The blood of our Lord is served not in a chalice but in a mug. The sacrament is given to children. Priests are ragged from the altars by force. Priests and monks marry, and the common people are incited to frivolity and offense.

Work together

Having completed activities 1–3, swap them with a partner. Consider:

1 How far did you agree on the context of the sources?
2 How far did you agree on the usefulness of the sources?
3 If you disagreed on the context or the usefulness, what was helpful in each other's approach?
4 Whose summary of the usefulness of the sources was better and why?

Use this discussion to make a note of three ways that you can improve your Section A technique.

Activity: Evaluating the sources

1 Having read Sources 3 and 4 above, try and put them in context by answering the following questions:
   a) What events were taking place in Nuremberg at the time the sources were written?
   b) What debate are the sources contributing to?
   c) What is the theology of the writers of the sources?
2 Now try and evaluate the usefulness of the sources by answering the following questions:
   a) What do the sources argue about the religious practices taking place in Nuremberg?
   b) How similar are their arguments?
   c) How far do the sources reflect the full range of debate over the religious practices taking place in Nuremberg in the early 1520s?
3 Summarise the extent to which the sources are useful to the historian studying the influence of Lutheranism on religious practice in Nuremberg in the mid-1520s. Make sure you deal with the ways in which they are useful and the limits of their usefulness.

Activity: AS-style questions

1 Why is Source 3 valuable to the historian for an enquiry into Catholic views of Lutheran religious practices?
2 How much weight do you give the evidence of Source 4 for an enquiry into changing religious practices in Germany in the 1520s?

Reaching an overall judgement

Having understood, contextualised and evaluated the sources, you should finish your essay with an overall judgement. Reaching a supported overall judgement is an important part of doing well in Section A. Your judgement in Section A is similar to the judgement that you should reach in the other sections of the exam (see page 74). However, in Section A, your judgement should be based on an evaluation of the evidence offered by the sources.

Your judgement should:

● clearly answer the question
● be supported by weighing up the evidence of the sources.

In addition to this, the very best essays will distinguish between the levels of certainty of the different aspects of the conclusion.

Imagine you are answering the question on page 304.

Having already read the sources and evaluated them in their context as you did in the activity on page 304, it is possible to reach the following overall conclusion. This is a high level conclusion as it focuses on the question, reaches a supported judgement and discusses the different levels of certainty of the different claims it makes.

The sources are used explicitly and together.

The sources' limitations are acknowledged.

The extent to which the sources are useful as a description of Luther's influence is weighed.

> Together, Sources 3 and 4 are of some use to a historian investigating the influence of Lutheranism on religious practice in Nuremberg in the mid-1520s. They clearly show that reformed practices such as changes to the mass (Sources 3 and 4), neglect of the saints (Source 3) and the marriage of priests (Source 4) are taking place in Nuremberg. While the authors of both sources might have reason to exaggerate this, and to underplay the piety of Protestants in Nuremberg there is no reason to doubt that reformed practices were taking place in the city. However, neither Source 3 or 4 provides clear evidence that the influence is that of Luther. Changes in the mass could reflect the influence of Carlstadt who had written and preached on the reform of the mass and had pioneered a new approach to the mass in Wittenberg in 1522. Nonetheless, there is some evidence that the people of Nuremberg attribute their new faith to Martin Luther, as Source 3 states that the local people 'consider Martin Luther their enlightener'. Finally, although both sources are useful to some extent in describing the influence of reform in Nuremberg, together the sources reflect a similar perspective. In that sense their use is limited not only as they potentially down play Protestant piety, referring to reform in general rather than Luther's influence specifically, they are also limited as neither presents the view of a witness who was sympathetic to the Reformation. Even so, the sources are still of some use particularly due to their description of the influence of reformed practice.

This focuses directly on the question.

Contextual knowledge is used to explore the limits of the sources' usefulness.

The limits of the sources are summarised.

The uses are also summarised, and a conclusion reached which is supported by the rest of the paragraph.

Conclusions are made up of a series of claims. A claim is a statement, in this case about the usefulness of the sources for investigating the influence of Lutheranism on religious practice in Nuremberg in the mid-1520s.

1 Count the number of claims made in the conclusion on page 305.
2 Do you agree on the number of claims – if not discuss your different views and try and resolve the disagreement.

3 The different claims deal with a series of issues that are not all certain. List the words and phrases that are used to describe the different degrees of certainty.
4 Did you both spot the same words and phrases?

Use the list and your discussion to make a note of how you could improve your writing.

Imagine you are answering the following question:

> **How far could the historian make use of Sources 5 and 6 to investigate Luther's changing attitude to the papacy from 1517–20?**

Source 5 Luther to the Pope, 3 March 1519.

It is those [who demanded his recantation], O holy father, who have done the greatest injury to the Church in Germany, and whom I have striven to oppose – those who, by their foolish preaching and their insatiable greed, have brought your name into bad odour, sullying the sanctity of the papal throne ... I declare before God that I have never had the slightest wish to attack the power of the Church or your Holiness in any way, or even to injure it through cunning. Yes, I declare openly, that there is nothing in heaven or earth which can come before the power of this Church, except Jesus Christ alone – Lord over all ... I also gladly promise to let the question of Indulgences drop if my opponents restrain their boastful, empty talk.

Source 6 Luther, *Babylonian Captivity of the Church*, October 1520.

I say that no Pope or bishop or anyone else has the right to impose one letter of law on a Christian man without his consent. If this is done it is tyranny ... To be subject to their rules and dictatorial laws is to be made a slave of men. This ungodly and desperate tyranny springs from the Pope's followers who trot out and misuse Christ's words. The Pope's traditions bind no one. No one needs to listen to the Pope except when he teaches the Gospel and Christ ... It is blindness, pure blindness which rules the Pope.

Activity: Write your own conclusion

1 Read the question, the sources and the information about the sources.
2 Put the sources in context:
   a) What is the significance of the dates of the sources?
   b) What debate or debates are the sources contributing to?
   c) How far do the sources agree on the role of the Pope?
   d) Why did Luther write the two sources?
3 Read the question again.
   a) Next, write a series of bullet points outlining:
      ● the aspects of the sources that are useful for answering the question
      ● the aspects of the sources that are less useful
      ● a summary of the extent to which the sources provide useful evidence concerning Luther's changing attitude to the Pope.
   b) Now write the conclusion, remember:
      ● you need to weigh up the evidence, and therefore you should use words that help you to do that such as: 'clearly', 'however' and 'nonetheless'.
      ● you should weigh up the sources *together*, rather than separately. Make sure you use words and phrases that make it clear that this is what you are doing.
      ● you should try and specify how certain you are about your various concluding claims. Look at the example of a conclusion you have just read and try and use similar words and phrases to show which of your concluding claims are certain and which are less definite.

Work together

Having completed your conclusion in the activity on page 306, swap it with a partner. Consider the following questions:

1. How far did you agree on the context of the sources?
2. How far did you agree on the usefulness of the sources?
3. Which conclusion most effectively weighed up the evidence of the sources? How was this achieved?
4. Did both conclusions really consider the sources *together*? How could you improve this aspect of your writing?

5. Which conclusion most effectively expressed the different degrees of certainty? How was this achieved?
6. Which conclusion most effectively focused on the question?

Use this discussion to make notes on how you can improve your Section A technique.

Activity: AS-style questions

1. Why is Source 5 (page 306) valuable to the historian for an enquiry into Luther's attitudes to the Pope in 1519?
2. How much weight do you give the evidence of Source 6 (page 306) for an enquiry into Luther's teachings concerning the Catholic hierarchy?

Section B: Essay technique

Argument, counterargument and resolution

The highest marks in Section B of the exam are available for sustained analysis. One way of achieving this is to write an essay that develops a clear argument, counterargument, and then reaches a resolution. This approach is outlined in the activities that support Paper 1 (see page 125). This kind of structure is equally applicable to Paper 2 Section B.

Activity: Detail and analysis

Imagine you are answering the following Section B question:

'Lutheran negotiation failed primary because of Catholic failure to recognise the popularity of Lutheranism.' How far do you agree with this statement?

1 Read the question and work out what type of question it is.
2 Make a plan that is appropriate to the specific question. Rather than simply picking four relevant factors, develop an argument, a counterargument and a resolution to the argument.
3 Add three pieces of detail to support each aspect of your essay. Remember, use the detail that best supports the argument you are creating.
4 Write an introduction that sets out the essential aspects of your argument, counterargument and resolution.
5 Now write a conclusion to the essay.
   - Start by asserting an overall judgement.
   - Support this by writing an evaluative summary of your argument, counter argument and resolution.
   - Summarise your overall judgement in the final sentence.

Work together

Having written your introduction and conclusion, swap them with a friend. Consider:

1 Did you agree on what type of question you were dealing with? If not, discuss it and work out who was right.
2 Whose plan set out the most compelling overall argument?
3 Which introduction most clearly set out the key claims of your essay?
4 Which conclusion best summarised and evaluated the argument, counterargument and resolution?
5 What can you learn from each other's work?

Use these questions to feedback to each other and improve your essay technique.

Question practice

1 'Charles V was primarily responsible for the failure to contain Lutheranism during the period 1521–55.' How far do you agree with this statement?
2 How successful were Pope Paul III's attempts at reform of the Church from 1534? **AS**
3 How far did Lutheranism change in the years 1520 to 1555?
4 How far were political motives the main reason for the princes' conversion to Lutheranism? **AS**
5 How far were Charles V's conflicting political and military priorities the main reason he failed to prevent the spread of Lutheranism from 1521–55?

Paper 2 The Dutch Revolt, c1563–1609

The Big Picture

The Dutch Revolt was a revolution in favour of traditional rights that ended in a complete political change for the people of the Netherlands and the King of Spain. In 1563 the Netherlands were part of the Spanish Empire. The king of Spain, Philip II, ruled the region through a regent who lived in the Netherlands. The different states within the Netherlands were ruled by local nobles who also played some role in advising or aiding the regent. The nobles, feeling frustrated and alienated from Spain, led the revolt from 1567 onwards which saw the Netherlands experience war, violence, sieges and economic hardship in the battle to free themselves from Spanish rule. The causes of the Dutch Revolt, however, were not simple – a complex mix of social, economic, religious and political factors all combined to create the revolt.

Origins of the Dutch Revolt, c1563–67

The Dutch Revolt had its origins in several long-standing situations. The Dutch nobles had generally played a significant part in ruling the Netherlands alongside the King of Spain. They saw themselves as having traditional rights and roles which should be respected by Philip II. When this did not happen, their frustration and anger boiled over into opposition and, finally, revolt. Philip's style of rule did not help, nor did his delayed response to calls for aid from the regent, Margaret of Parma. Philip's attempts to introduce a Spanish-style religious regime were disastrous and created a climate of mistrust and violence. As the revolt began, the more authoritarian Duke of Alva was sent to the Netherlands and Margaret of Parma resigned.

Alva and Orange, 1567–73

The Duke of Alva was determined to resolve the situation by force and authoritarian rule rather than negotiation. After military success against the rebels in July 1568 he executed two of the leaders of the revolt, the counts of Egmont and Hoorn, which proved extremely unpopular. The two men were important members of the Dutch nobility and Alva's action again trampled traditional rights and expectations. Alva also tried to impose religious uniformity via the Council of Troubles. During these attempts over 1,000 people were executed and many fled abroad to countries such as England. It was soon seen as another sign that Philip was a tyrant. Alva's attempts to impose harsh taxes further provoked the Netherlands.

This period also saw the rise to prominence of William of Orange who soon became one of the leaders of the revolt. From 1568 Orange argued that the infringement of traditional rights and liberties by Philip II meant that it was legitimate and just to overthrow him. Orange launched invasions into the Netherlands in that year and, although initial successes were followed by defeat at Jemmingen in July 1568, Orange remained committed to the fight. More provinces rose to support Orange in the subsequent years and in 1572 Orange led another invasion supported by the Sea Beggars. This was much more successful, although it did not permanently defeat Alva and the Spanish. The sustained revolt did mean that Alva was forced to resign, and in the meantime the Dutch continued their legal and political justifications of the rebellion.

Spain and the reconquest, 1573–84

The period 1573–84 was one of great instability in the Netherlands. There was a succession of different Spanish regents and more violence in the provinces. Alva's replacement was Don Luis de Requesens, but he died only two years after assuming the role and this left the Netherlands with no regent for a time. Don John became regent just as the 'Spanish Fury' happened in Antwerp, where Spanish troops mutinied and rampaged around the city. This shocking violence prompted the Pacification of Ghent, an anti-Spanish document that cemented a temporary alliance between the rebelling provinces and those that still supported Spanish rule. Archduke Matthias of Vienna became Governor-General in 1577 but was inexperienced and unable to solve the many problems and tensions that had arisen. Increasingly, alliances began to form that either supported the King or the rebels. The Union of Arras in 1579 split the provinces into two divided groups, a harbinger of what was to come.

Securing the independence of the United Provinces, 1584–1609

From 1584 onwards, despite Spanish military successes of the Duke of Parma, the power of the rebel United Provinces grew while that of Spain declined. Maurice of Nassau became stadtholder after the assassination of his father, William of Orange. Maurice proved to be an extremely able organiser and military tactician. Supported politically by Johan van Oldenbarnevelt, Maurice achieved notable military success, which further strengthened the United Provinces. Trade increased and the United Provinces became financially as well as politically viable. Support from the English Queen, Elizabeth I, in the form of money and troops also added to the momentum of the revolt and diverted Philip's attention from the Netherlands to a war against the English. Spain was suffering financially and the military defeat against England was a major dent in morale. The Truce of Antwerp signed in 1609 brought a form of independence to the United Provinces and ended the war for the next 12 years.

Key Topic 1 The origins of the Dutch Revolt, c1563–67

Overview

The sixteenth century was a dynamic period for the 17 provinces that made up the Low Countries. The 17 provinces enjoyed a tradition of political autonomy even though they were part of Charles V's vast Holy Roman Empire. Some of Charles' policies granted the region a degree of political independence. This was to cause difficulty when Charles' son, Philip II, attempted a more authoritarian form of rule that did not take account of the traditional rights of the Dutch nobility. The role of the regent or Governor-General was also problematic under Philip II. Traditionally the Governor-General handled the day-to-day government of the Netherlands, but Philip's micromanagement was to make that difficult even for able Governor-Generals. This change in approach was to provoke friction and tensions in the Netherlands, not least among the Dutch grandees. Philip's determination to introduce religious uniformity meant that the relatively recent spread of Calvinism was to cause immense difficulty.

This chapter examines these themes through the following sections:

1 *The Habsburg Netherlands* looks at the Netherlands before the Dutch Revolt began. It explains the governmental structure of the Netherlands and the traditional role and rights of the Dutch nobility.
2 *The situation, c1563* examines the situation in the Netherlands on the brink of the revolt. It looks at the policies of Philip II in relation to the region, the regency of Margaret of Parma and the role that Cardinal Granvelle played in this crucial period.
3 *The opposition of the Dutch grandees* explores the ways in which the Dutch nobles began to make alliances to resist Philip's religious and political policies. It looks at their initial strategies and the government's response to them.
4 *The impact of Calvinism* examines the role that this form of Protestantism played in provoking the revolt. It looks at the origins of Calvinism in the Netherlands, events involving Calvinists and the consequences of Calvinist involvement in this early period of the Dutch Revolt.

TIMELINE

1500 February	The future Emperor Charles V was born in Ghent
1506 September	Philip I died suddenly; Charles became Lord of the Netherlands
1519	Charles was elected Emperor Charles V of the Holy Roman Empire
1548	Treaty of Augsburg
1549	The Pragmatic Sanction
1555 October	Charles V abdicated his Dutch titles in an elaborate ceremony at Brussels
1558 September	Death of Charles V
1559 October	Philip II left the Netherlands for Spain; Margaret of Parma became regent
1559	Philip established 14 new bishoprics in the Netherlands under Bishop Granvelle
1561 July	Egmont, Hoorn and Orange banded together and sent letters to Philip
1566 5 April	The Dutch nobility presented Margaret of Parma with their 'Compromise'
1566 August	The Iconoclastic Fury attacked traditional religious houses in retaliation against the hated heresy placards
1567 August	Philip sent the Duke of Alva to the Netherlands with 10,000 soldiers; Margaret of Parma resigned as regent

1 The Habsburg Netherlands

The Habsburg Netherlands were a collection of separate states. These states were governed by local nobles, whose overlord was the King of Spain. The King was represented by a Governor-General, supported by the **States General**. The traditional rights and contributions made by the nobles had long been respected by the ruler of the Netherlands, and they presumed that this would continue to be the case.

Note it down

Use a spider diagram to take notes on this section (see page x). In the 'body' of the spider, write the title of the section ('The Habsburg Netherlands') and on the legs, the subheadings (the 17 provinces, the extent of local autonomy, the traditional rights of Dutch grandees). On the end of the 'legs' break down the information from each subsection.

The 17 provinces

The Netherlands were geographically and politically distinct in the sixteenth century. Part of the lands of the **Habsburg** kings of Spain, they depended on the co-operation of the regionally powerful nobles with the agents of the Spanish Crown in the Netherlands.

The geography of the Netherlands

In the period 1563–1609 the Netherlands were much larger than they are today. The Netherlands, a region known as the Low Countries because of their relatively flat terrain and nearness to sea level, have been described by historian Paul Arblaster as the collection of **principalities** and smaller states located between France and Germany. They have often served as a buffer zone between France and Germany. In the early modern period, this region encompassed today's Netherlands, the whole of the country we would today recognise as Belgium, the **duchies** of Artois and Luxembourg, the region still known as Friesland, and a collection of other principalities. The territory even included regions of modern-day France, and stretched south-east toward Switzerland. In all, a total of 17 separate provinces made up the Habsburg Netherlands. The provinces were diverse in their landscape, with hills, marshes, and farmlands but this was also the most urban area in all of Europe at the time. Many of Europe's largest cities were located in these provinces with a variety of languages and dialects still spoken in the region today. Some of the provinces had a coastline, whilst others had large rivers flowing through them. The 14 northern provinces spoke Dutch dialects while the three southern ones spoke **Walloon**. Many of the nobles also spoke French and Latin.

The Dutch grandees

The sixteenth-century Netherlands were ruled by a collection of local dukes and **grandees** who held a variety of different titles. All of these nobles ruled at least one province, although some, such as William of Orange, ruled more than one. These nobles owed their political allegiance to the Habsburgs, one of the largest and most powerful families of Europe. Their most prominent family member, the Emperor Charles V, ruled the Holy Roman Empire (roughly modern-day Germany but also a number of principalities and lands across Europe) from 1519 until 1555. Over the course of his reign, Charles V consolidated power over all of the provinces that formed the Low Countries. He won some territories, like Tournai, through battle, but he inherited others from princes and dukes who identified him as their heir in their wills. For example, Charles inherited the area around the important city of Utrecht because a nobleman **bequeathed** his titles and lands to Charles. The question of inheritance was serious when Europe's nobility considered Charles' vast empire. He had assembled a territory larger than any other ruler in European history through the lands he inherited or won on the battlefield.

The Emperor and the Pragmatic Sanction of 1549

An Emperor was elected for life by the nobility, so a candidate from virtually anywhere across Europe could rule after Charles' death. Indeed, even Charles' great rivals, Francis I of France and Henry VIII of England, had put their names forward as candidates for the **imperial election** he won in 1519. The title of 'Emperor' was held only by the noble who was elected, but it was possible for the Emperor to grant his territories to a successor of his choice through **decree** or bequeath land or titles in his last will and testament. This meant that the lands he ruled could be inherited by one person, or they could be broken up into numerous different lands and titles. In 1549, the Pragmatic Sanction was approved by the States General. This document confirmed that all Charles' territories in the Low Countries could be inherited as a single, cohesive group by one person. The provincial state assemblies promised to recognise Charles' successor as their prince. All of the titles and lands connected to the Low Countries would therefore be inherited in one unified piece rather than 17 different parts. When Charles abdicated and retired to a monastery in 1555, he divided his immense empire between his brother, Ferdinand, and his son,

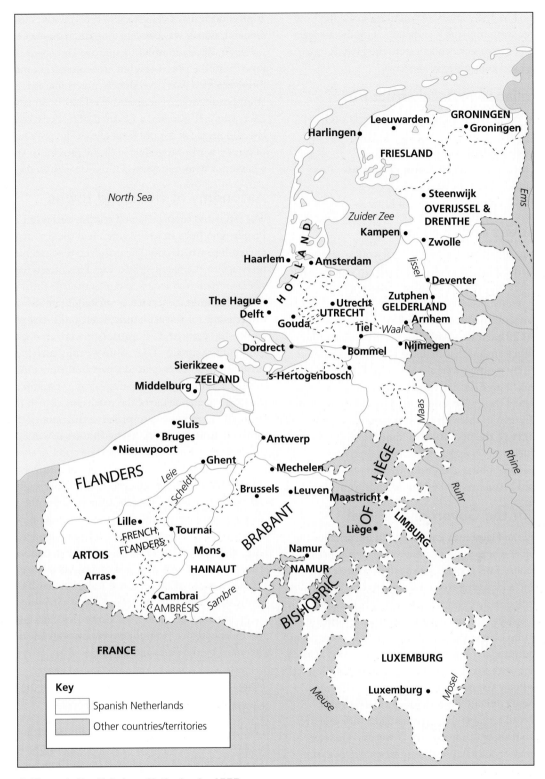

▲ Figure 1: The Habsburg Netherlands, 1555

Philip II. Ferdinand inherited Charles' lands in the Holy Roman Empire, in Austria, and in central and eastern Europe. Philip's lands were more spread out geographically. He inherited Charles' territories in Spain, the New World, Italy, and the Netherlands.

The extent of local autonomy

Philip II was a distant ruler, and chose to rule his geographically vast realm from his base in Madrid. Charles V had ensured that there would be no conflict between Ferdinand and Philip when it came to administering justice in the region. The 1548 Treaty of Augsburg made the Low Countries free from imperial jurisdiction. This meant that the 17 provinces were independent from the Holy Roman Empire's legal and administrative systems.

Philip's reliance on local structures

In ruling the Netherlands, Philip relied heavily on local structures such as:

- the grandees and their courts
- the Governor-General and **Council of State**, Privy Council and Council of Finance
- the States General and Councils of Justice.

The grandees and their courts

Underpinning the social order was a network of grandees and their courts. These nobles were rivals, in competition with each other for political prestige, patronage and power. They enjoyed staging celebrations and events like formal entrances into cities. Despite this, the grandees were also less affluent than they had been in preceding centuries, which meant that their political support could be purchased by more powerful rulers like Charles V and Philip II in exchange for titles and money. All of these strategies helped the grandees ensure that they remained prominent figures in their local communities and among the community of the nobility. Meetings of the States General, which were composed of representatives from the provincial assemblies and cities, were another way that Philip exerted influence in the Netherlands from afar.

The role of the Governor–General

Another way the Habsburgs ensured good governance in their absence was to appoint a Governor-General for the Netherlands. This person was usually a relative of the sovereign, and a close and trusted delegate. The Governor-General handled daily political matters while the sovereign retained the power to handle more important political issues, including convening the States General and making political appointments. The Governor-General was assisted in governance with the help of three councils: the Council of State, the Privy Council and the Council of Finance. Together, these councils were made up of nobles and professional civil servants. Each group had a different area of expertise but they all advised the Governor-General on specific matters of state, such as military defence, the implementation of legislation and taxation.

The role of the States General and Councils of Justice

A third way good governance and justice were ensured in the 17 provinces was through the **provincial states** assemblies and the States General. Each province was governed by its own representative political body, known as provincial states. These sent representatives to the States General, which was convened by the King or Governor-General, usually in order to approve and co-ordinate raising taxes from the provinces, but also to sanction major changes to governance. We have already noted that this body had an important role in adopting the 1549 Pragmatic Sanction. Each province also had a Council of Justice to administer law and justice at a more local level. The provincial Council of Justice worked together with the provincial **stadtholder**, a governor who represented the sovereign in the province.

Autonomy of cities and towns

The cities and towns enjoyed relative autonomy as well. People who lived in towns often had the privilege of citizenship, which could be achieved through birth, marriage or the payment of a fee. The citizen had to swear an oath to the city, and promised to fulfil civic duties like military service or serving in public office, in exchange for the economic, legal and social privileges citizenship granted. City patricians were an important group of townsmen. They were wealthy merchants and financiers who often played a part in the government of towns. Philip's government placed a restraint on the political independence of the patricians, which they greatly resented. They wanted to preserve their political leadership rather than having it eroded by Philip's new mode of government. Towns were the major point of social and political identification for average Dutch citizens. The cities also had a tradition of rebelling against sovereigns who attempted to exert too much influence over them. The civic magistrates, patricians who formed the government of towns, were often ambitious. They made decisions about issues such as local government, trade and commerce. They also often dreamed of securing a city-state status similar to those of Renaissance Italy. Participation in local political communities was therefore of vital importance to the inhabitants of the Low Countries. Self-governance and independence from the sovereign were ideals that were cherished by the cities and provinces alike.

The traditional rights of the Dutch grandees

The Dutch nobility were highly competitive and enjoyed displays of political power. They were ultimately loyal to Charles V while he was Holy Roman Emperor, and had promised to be loyal to his son, Philip II. They served on the Council of State, and as local stadtholders. The nobles were at the top of the social and political structures in their local areas. They advised on political matters, and were often responsible for implementing the changes that came about as a result of advice. The nobles were also influential when it came to determining who could serve in local office in their provinces. They wielded a relatively large amount of power in their areas, a power that brought them into direct conflict with Philip II.

Their traditional privileges varied from province to province. Broadly speaking, they fell into the following categories:

- **Religion** – right of patronage, a role for their younger sons within the Church, ability to tolerate other religious faiths should this benefit them, for example, for trade.
- **Taxation** – the right to determine taxation.
- **Trade and commerce** – the right to determine trade relations and treaties with other provinces and states.

These privileges had given the Dutch nobles a lot of power. Under Charles V they were consulted on a wide range of matters, and their advice generally accepted. They were, therefore, very angry when Philip showed a marked lack of regard for their traditions and privileges. The fact that Philip, in a tour of the provinces in 1549, had confirmed the list of privileges called the 'Joyous Entry', a list of constitutions and privileges dating back (in one case) to 1356, made this even more frustrating.

> **Source A** From *A short exposition of the rights exercised by the knights, nobles and towns of Holland and West Friesland from time immemorial for the maintenance of the freedoms, rights, privileges and laudable customs of the country, 1587.* This was a pamphlet that argued that the historical rights of the Netherlands was central to the causes of the Dutch Revolt against Spain.
>
> > It is well-known that for 800 years the countries of Holland, West Friesland and Zeeland have been governed by counts and countesses to whom the rule and sovereignty over these countries was legally entrusted and granted by the knights, nobles and towns, representing the estates of the country [the States General]. They displayed such great discretion and moderation in their government, that they never decided to declare war or make peace, levy taxes or contributions on the countries, or take any other measures concerning the state of the country ... without hearing the opinion and obtaining the consent of the nobles and towns of the country who were on all such occasions convoked and assembled for that purpose. But apart from asking for advice themselves, they were always prepared to listen to the nobles and towns of the country, to grant them complete faith and to pass wise resolutions on all suggestions concerning the state and welfare of the country which the states had put forward.
>
> How could the historian use Source A as evidence of opinions on the King of Spain's rule? What is the value of this source as evidence?

Conclusion: The Habsburg Netherlands

Government and stability in the Netherlands relied on a precarious system of co-operation between the King, the Governor-General, the States General and the nobles. The roles and responsibilities of these different people or groups were not especially well defined. Self-governance and autonomy were central to the Dutch image of themselves and ideals for governance. This is one reason for the outbreak of revolt – Philip II of Spain challenged this and imposed his own ideas from afar.

> **Work together**
>
> To check that you have understood everything in this section work with a partner to test each other. Put your notes and your book away after reading them carefully. Write the subheadings on a piece of paper and take it in turns to explain the content of each to your partner. Note down any that either or both of you struggle with. When you have finished, revisit these and read over them again.

2 The situation, c1563

When Philip II inherited the Netherlands from his father in 1555, he began to rule over provinces that had their own unique political system. The people of the Netherlands prized local influence and autonomy. They had sworn to be loyal to Philip, and they believed that it was Philip's duty to protect their traditional privileges. However, the things that sixteenth-century inhabitants of the Netherlands valued the most were the very things that their new ruler sought to change. This section will examine Philip's main policies towards the Netherlands in the early years of his reign. It will also introduce two key figures, Margaret of Parma and Antoine Perrenot de Granvelle.

> **Note it down**
>
> Use index cards (see page xi) in this section to make notes on the significant people you read about. On the front of the card write the name of the person and the dates they lived. On the back, note down points on their actions and significance. Over the course of the book you will build up a biographical dictionary of significant people. You should also use the 1:2 method (see page x) in this section to note key events and developments. In the left-hand column write the headings, and note down the most important points of content in the right-hand column.

Philip II's policy towards the Netherlands

Charles V formally transferred his power over the Netherlands to Philip II in an elaborate ceremony before the States General in Brussels on 25 October 1555. Philip stayed in the Netherlands for four years. During this time, he used the Netherlands as his base as he waged the Italian War of 1551–59, which pitted Henry II of France against Charles V and Philip II. Although Philip returned to Spain when the war ended, he still wanted to exert a great deal of control over the Netherlands and his policy towards it was affected by several factors:

- His responsibilities in his other territories.
- His lack of regard for established traditions.
- His religious beliefs.
- His style of rule in terms of personal appointments.

He believed he could exert this control through his religious policy and political appointments.

Philip's religious policy and the new bishoprics

One of the ways Philip believed he could control the Netherlands was by creating new Roman Catholic **bishoprics** in the region (see Figure 2 on page 317). In the 1550s, the 17 provinces of the Netherlands had only three bishoprics. In 1559, Philip obtained **papal bulls** that established 14 new bishoprics and three **archbishoprics** in the Low Countries. The new **primate** of the Netherlands would be the Archbishop of Mechelen. Philip selected his trustworthy adviser, Antoine Perrenot de Granvelle, to serve as the first archbishop of Mechelen in 1561. This was not a popular appointment as Granvelle was another outsider chosen for his loyalty to the King. The appointment became even less popular after Granvelle reorganised the bishoprics.

Philip, and the Pope, hoped that the new bishops would encourage religious unity in the Low Countries. Philip was a faithful Roman Catholic, and he wanted all of the realms he ruled to be just as faithful in their Roman Catholicism. He thought that he could prevent the spread of **Protestantism** in the Netherlands by adding more bishops who would be responsible for teaching the Catholic faith and for quashing any **heretical beliefs** before they became popular. Philip also wanted the new bishops to have inquisitorial powers, just like the Spanish **Inquisition**. This meant that the bishops could appoint officials to question people about their religious beliefs. Men and women who were deemed to be heretics could be imprisoned, or could be sentenced to death.

The new bishoprics also challenged the traditional privileges of the Dutch nobles. Granvelle's reorganisation meant that there were fewer Church appointments open to the Dutch nobles – they normally had extensive rights of patronage to such positions and could grant them to family members or important associates. A career in the Catholic Church was the main avenue for younger sons

Philip II of Spain (1527–98)

From an early age Philip received memoranda from his father giving him advice about his duties and how to rule. This was advice that he attempted to follow all of his life. From the age of 16, Philip was regent of Spain when his father was abroad, giving him an early experience of ruling a country. Philip travelled through the Habsburg lands from 1548 to 1551, visiting Germany, Italy and the Netherlands. Despite his attempts to get to know the Netherlands that he would one day inherit, Philip was unpopular due to his aloof attitude and inability to speak any language but Castilian Spanish. From 1559 to the end of his life Philip never again left Spain, ruling instead through appointees that he personally chose. He worked extremely hard, following his father's advice about the duties of monarchy. Philip received written reports, advice and memoranda from his minister and his regents. He then worked through this material, making personal decisions on all matters. This made government extremely slow, and inflexible in reacting to change. Philip was also distrustful of his advisers, another stipulation of his father. This led to the downfall of several regents of the Netherlands as well as others elsewhere in his lands. Philip worked hard and saw his role of monarch as God-given and of vital importance. This explains partly why he was unable to respond flexibly to the concerns of the nobles in the Netherlands or to respect their traditional liberties.

Cardinal Antoine Perrenot de Granvelle (1517–86)

Granvelle was born in Burgundy, an area within the Holy Roman Empire that is now largely divided between France and Belgium. His father was an important politician who became chancellor to Emperor Charles V. Granvelle studied law and divinity and became a clergyman. He was quickly promoted, becoming a bishop aged only 23 years old. Granvelle's success in various diplomatic missions led to him playing an increasing role as an adviser to Charles V. He became chancellor of the Empire in 1550 and on Charles' abdication he was sent to work for Philip in the Netherlands.

He was appointed chief counsellor to Margaret of Parma, the regent of the Netherlands, in 1560. Granvelle became a **cardinal** in 1561. As might be expected from his career, he was a strong monarchist and supporter of Philip II. This provoked opposition in the Netherlands where he attempted to enforce Philip's policies against the wishes of Dutch nobles like Orange, Egmont and Hoorn. He was extremely unpopular and was forced to withdraw from the Netherlands in 1564. He later worked for Philip in Italy and Spain, dying in 1586.

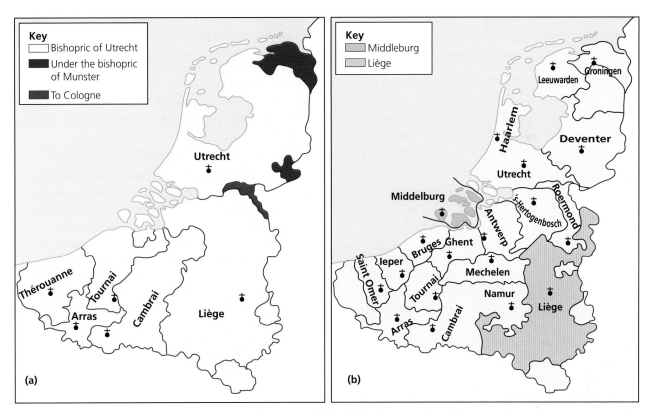

▲ Figure 2: The bishoprics of the Netherlands, before (a) and after (b) the introduction of the new bishoprics in the years 1559–70

of the nobility who would not inherit titles or lands, as it could still bring status and wealth. This reorganisation challenged the nobility's traditional dominance of the Church hierarchy. This is because instead of choosing sons of the nobility as bishops, they were chosen for their efficiency, zeal and loyalty.

Philip's political appointments

Another way Philip exerted influence over the Netherlands was through his political appointments. The Dutch nobles had often served as advisers to the regent as members of the **Council of State**. With Philip's

reign, however, some of the Dutch nobles were replaced with Spanish **favourites**. Margaret of Parma's personal secretary was a Spanish man called Tomás de Armenteros, who was the cousin of Philip's secretary of state. The King also placed two Spanish members of his household, Alonso del Canto and Cristóbal de Castellanos, in Antwerp. They were charged with the tasks of handling the royal monies and monitoring **heresy** in the city. The addition of Spanish councillors angered many of the Dutch nobles; they viewed it as a sign that their opinions would not be heard, and that their influence had declined at court.

Key Topic 1 The origins of the Dutch Revolt, c1563–67 (317)

Philip also needed to appoint another regent to rule on his behalf in the Netherlands. When Charles V abdicated, his regent in the Netherlands, Mary of Hungary, also resigned. Between 1555 and 1559, the 17 provinces had no regent. Instead, the day-to-day business of administering the realm was handled by a Governor-General. The man Philip selected for this task was Emmanuel Philibert, Duke of Savoy. Savoy was young and inexperienced but he proved to be a valiant military commander. He was also personally trusted by Philip. He led his soldiers to victory in the important Battle of St. Quentin in 1557. When the war ended, Emmanuel Philibert left the Netherlands to rule personally over his duchy of Savoy. Philip decided to replace him with his half-sister, Margaret of Parma.

Philip's policy towards the Netherlands, then, could be characterised as one of change. He brought peace to the region with the conclusion of the Italian War, but he also introduced numerous changes. The addition of new bishoprics meant that he could choose men he trusted to exercise greater control over religion in the Netherlands. Philip gave important political roles to individuals he brought into the Netherlands from elsewhere in his vast realms. These actions led to resentment and suspicion on the part of the Dutch nobles.

The Italian War, 1551–59

The Italian War started between Henry II of France and Charles V. The war received its name because Henry II's primary objective was seizing Charles' territories in Italy. In the early years of the war, Henry believed that capturing the Empire's Italian lands would keep Charles' powers in check. This would neutralise the threat the Empire posed to the French. The war finally ended with the 1559 Treaty of Cateau-Cambrésis. According to the terms of the Treaty, Henry II returned the territories of Piedmont and Savoy to the Duke of Savoy. Peace between the two regions was confirmed in two marriages: the Duke of Savoy married Henry's sister, Margaret, the Duchess of Berry, and Philip II married Henry's daughter, Elisabeth of France. Ultimately, Henry II's strategy backfired. Although the Treaty weakened the Habsburg family's position in Europe, Spain's power increased. The Spanish became the only dominant power within Italy, and the war showcased their military might.

Philip's lack of regard for local traditions

The Dutch were fiercely protective of their local customs and privileges. The local people had enjoyed these traditions and rights for centuries, and they were older than the Dutch provincial system itself. Each town and city, therefore, sought to protect those unique customs and rights that helped shape their identity. Philip's major disregard for local traditions and privileges came in the form of the immense power that he gave to Granvelle, the Spanish garrisons he built for the Spanish soldiers that remained in the Netherlands, the new bishoprics he established, the inquisition he established to interrogate suspected heretics, and the imposition of a Tenth Penny Tax on all sales (see page 340). All of these actions showed that Philip did not care about Dutch rights and privileges, and showed that he did not understand how much the Dutch prized their local customs. Philip's measures failed to take into account the vast pride the Dutch grandees had when they imparted advice to their rulers. Instead, these actions showed that the Spanish had little understanding for the ways the Dutch provinces worked.

The regency of Margaret of Parma

The role of regent had been undertaken successfully by female appointees before. Charles V had appointed his sister, Queen Mary of Hungary, as his regent in the Netherlands during his reign. The 17 provinces flourished during Mary's regency. The cities grew as the merchant economy developed. The Dutch nobles were often allowed to make local political decisions themselves. Charles was consulted in matters of extreme importance such as taxation and trade agreements, but Mary handled most political affairs herself. She also relied on the advice that the Dutch nobles offered her through the Council of State. Her regency contributed to the sense of autonomy that the Dutch nobles valued. Philip appointed Margaret of Parma as Governor-General in 1559 with the expectation that she would be similarly successful. Circumstances had changed, however, which made the early stages of Margaret's regency difficult. She often had to mediate between Philip and the Dutch, and the Dutch were unhappy with many of Philip's policies.

The younger Dutch nobles were especially proud of the autonomy their region enjoyed and resisted any changes to local privileges. Philip, on the other hand, wanted to exert greater control over policies and events in the Netherlands. This meant that Margaret often had to wait for Philip's

Margaret of Parma (1522–86)

Margaret of Parma was the illegitimate daughter of Charles V and a Dutch woman, Johanna Maria van der Ghenyst. She was brought up by two of Charles' powerful female relatives – her great-aunt the Archduchess Margaret of Austria and her aunt Mary of Austria. Margaret of Parma was multilingual and intelligent. She was forced, for political reasons, to marry the Duke of Parma in 1538. At 15 years old, this was her second marriage. The child that resulted from this unhappy marriage was brought up by the Habsburgs in exchange for more power for the family of the Duke of Parma. In 1555 Margaret left for the Netherlands to be with her half-brother Philip. When he left for Spain in 1559 she was appointed Governor-General of the Netherlands. Despite her lack of experience she had been trained to rule by her aunt and great-aunt, and did have the advantage of being born in the Netherlands to a Dutch mother. During this period, however, she had to cope with rising dissatisfaction and tensions, a difficult relationship with Philip's adviser Granvelle, and the need to have every action approved by Philip. In other circumstances Margaret could perhaps have been a successful ruler, but was faced with a succession of complex problems which would have been difficult for anyone to solve.

decisions about important disputes rather than making them herself. Spanish experts were placed in important positions around her and were in charge of financial and Church matters. Margaret's secretary, one of the most important roles in an early modern court, was a Spaniard. Philip also instructed Margaret to listen to the advice of the Dutch nobles but to follow the opinions expressed by the men he had selected to serve on her Council of State. In time, the Dutch realised that Philip preferred to take the advice of his Spanish councillors, even in matters relating to the 17 provinces. This meant that tensions between the Dutch and Spanish escalated in Margaret's regency as Sources B and C illustrate.

> **Source B** A letter from Philip II to Margaret of Parma, 17 October 1565. This is an extract from one of the 'Segovia Woods' letters, where Philip issues detailed commands to Margaret and responds to her requests for advice.
>
> You say that I did not make it clear in the afore-mentioned instruction that it was not my intention to ask you or the seigniors of the state council [the Council of State] in the Netherlands for more advice in this matter but in fact you were made to understand my definitive intention. As to whether I would wish to ask the advice of the private and great councils and of the governors and provincial councils, this would be a considerable waste of time since my mind is made up. I have not asked others at all but followed the advice of the above-mentioned assembly as much as possible and as seemed fitting.
>
> What does Source B tell us about Philip II's approach to government? What was his attitude to Margaret and the Council of State?

> **Source C** Petition of 5 April 1566, drafted by John Marnix of Tholouse and Louis of Nassau, and presented to Margaret of Parma in the name of the nobles on 5 April 1566.
>
> We are not in doubt, Madame, that whatever His Majesty formerly ordained and now again ordains regarding the inquisition and the strict observance of the edicts concerning religion has some foundation and just title and is intended to continue all that the later Emperor, Charles ... decreed with the best of intentions. Considering however that different times call for different policies, and that for several years past these edicts, even though not very rigorously executed, have caused most serious difficulties, His Majesty's recent refusal to mitigate the edicts in any way, and his strict orders to maintain the inquisition ... makes us fear that the present difficulties will undoubtedly increase. But in fact the situation is worse. There are clear indications everywhere that the people are so exasperated that the final result, we fear, will be an open revolt and a universal rebellion bringing ruin to all the provinces and plunging them into utter misery.
>
> How much weight can Source C bear as evidence of attitudes to Philip's religious policies? What is valuable about it? Are there any problems with it? Explain your answer.

Spanish soldiers in the Netherlands

Philip had left a regiment of 3,000 Spanish soldiers in the Netherlands when he returned to Spain. The presence of these soldiers became a source of major conflict between the Dutch and Philip. From the King's perspective, a regiment of soldiers positioned in the Netherlands was a smart defensive move. If France or England attacked, the regiment could respond quickly. However, the Dutch nobles regarded the presence of these soldiers with suspicion. They thought that the regiment remained in the Netherlands in order to control them and the Spanish soldiers were a visible reminder to the Dutch that their ruler was the King of Spain. The States General began to use the presence of the soldiers as a bargaining chip and refused to keep their promise of funding the soldiers' garrisons. Margaret begged Philip to remove the Spanish soldiers and, in January 1561, he finally agreed to send them to one of his Mediterranean bases. The tension over the presence of the soldiers was a major testing point in the relationship between Philip and the Dutch nobles. Just as the Dutch were suspicious of the soldiers' presence, Philip became wary of the nobles, and began to question their loyalty to him.

Taxes

The role of the Spanish soldiers caused other long-term problems in the early years of Margaret's regency. Although the soldiers left the Netherlands in 1561, there still remained the question of paying for them. Neither the King nor the States General had upheld their promises in contributing to the expense of housing, feeding or paying the soldiers. Furthermore, the Netherlands had amassed enormous debts over the course of the long Italian War. The taxes that the States General raised were not enough to keep Dutch soldiers paid, or to keep the government operating.

Margaret was left with no choice but to ask individual provinces for additional taxes, but this strategy led to confusion: were these new taxes, or were they part of an earlier agreement? The answer to this question was important to the Dutch people. The autonomy that they valued so much was bound to privileges like the right to decide on policies like rates and frequency of taxation. The provinces and their governors began to see matters of military defence as a problem that should be handled only by the States General, but the King and Margaret disagreed with this perspective. They were unable to reach a compromise with either the Dutch nobles or the States General about the power to tax.

Complicating these matters of debt and defence was the first French civil war, which broke out early in the summer of 1562. Although Philip wanted to join the fight against Protestantism in France, Margaret and all her councillors wanted to keep the Netherlands out of another war. But, ultimately, Margaret was weak and inexperienced in politics. Her inexperience paved the way for one of Philip's favourites, Antoine Perrenot de Granvelle, to step into the fray, and gain enormous power.

The influence of Granvelle

Granvelle was one of Philip II's most trusted advisers in the Netherlands. Granvelle supported the idea that the

King was the source of authority in the realms he ruled. In practice, this meant that Granvelle believed that assemblies like the provincial states and the States General simply delayed the implementation of policy. He even thought that such assemblies harmed the King's authority. Like the Spanish soldiers who inhabited the Netherlands in the wake of the Italian War, Granvelle became a visible reminder that the King was distant and foreign.

Granvelle received his instructions from the King but he also reported on Dutch events back to Philip in Spain. He wrote to the King about the way that the nobles used their power to offer patronage to less wealthy nobles and civic clients. Granvelle explained that he believed that the nobility were too ambitious in their patronage and in their opposition to some of the King's policies and were therefore a threat to Philip's authority. He feared that these nobles could persuade their clients within the States General or the provincial assemblies to support or oppose policies as they chose. In order to ensure Dutch loyalty, Granvelle suggested that the King bestow Spanish lands and titles on some of the Dutch nobility. He thought this would inspire loyalty among those who hoped to be granted such titles. Philip, however, disagreed with this idea and tensions between Granvelle and the nobles continued to increase.

Conclusion: The situation, c1563

The early years of Philip's reign over the Netherlands witnessed a change in the relationship between the King and the inhabitants of the 17 provinces. The Dutch were accustomed to handling local political matters themselves. The presence of Spanish soldiers and Spanish councillors served as an unwelcome reminder that the King was an outsider who resided far away from the 17 provinces he ruled. The Dutch fiercely guarded their local privileges, and they believed that rulers like Philip II were responsible for safeguarding these privileges. In contrast, Philip believed in personally making political decisions in his realms, even if he was based far away or knew little about the details involved. He placed trusted Spanish councillors into prominent positions in the Netherlands. As a result, tensions between the Dutch and the Spanish began to intensify over the course of the 1550s and 1560s.

Work together

Work in pairs to create a timeline of events relating to this section. Divide the section in two, and each highlight important dates. Then come together and create your own annotated timeline. Note the date and event, as well as any key consequences of the event. Add to this timeline either as you go along, or during your revision.

3 The opposition of the Dutch grandees

The most influential Dutch people in the 17 provinces during this period were the nobles who began to oppose Philip and Margaret's rule in the Netherlands. Three nobles were of particular importance: William of Orange, Philip de Montmorency, Count of Hoorn, and Lamoral, Count of Egmont. These men were the first to react significantly to the changes that Philip initiated during Margaret's regency. Philip's religious policies were particularly provocative and led to further noble and popular opposition. It was in response to these changes that the Compromise was presented in 1566 and the Confederacy of Nobles was formed.

Note it down

Use the 1:2 method to take notes on this section (see page x). Write the subheadings in the left-hand column and the main points in the right-hand column. Remember to note down key points, for example the causes, main events and consequences of events.

The alliance of Orange, Hoorn and Egmont

In July 1561, William of Orange and Lamoral, Count of Egmont, wrote to Philip II complaining about Granvelle's activities. They thought that Granvelle was largely responsible for the harsh treatment of non-Roman Catholics. On a personal level, they believed that they were excluded from the decision-making process at Margaret of Parma's court. They were also frustrated that Granvelle, who they believed was inexperienced and unfit for such an important office in the Netherlands, wielded so much power in the realm.

Orange, Egmont and Philip de Montmorency, Count of Hoorn, became the most important figures of the Dutch Revolt. These three men had many things in common:

- They were all respected by the Dutch and the Spanish alike.
- They served on Margaret of Parma's Council of State. Each was a stadtholder.
- They were proven military leaders, and were all knights of the **Order of the Golden Fleece**.

They saw many of Philip's actions as a threat to their privileges, and finally decided they would no longer allow a distant Spanish king to compromise their traditional rights. The issue that brought the three of them into a political alliance was their intense opposition to Granvelle, particularly because of his appointment as Archbishop of Mechelen, the richest diocese in the Netherlands. His position as Archbishop after the reorganisation (see pages 316–17) gave him significant power and a rich living.

Between 1561 and 1564 Orange, Hoorn and Egmont wrote a series of letters and petitions addressed to Philip II. They wanted the King to change his policies, particularly his religious policies, in the Netherlands. They also believed that Granvelle simply wielded too much authority within the Netherlands. The trio of nobles urged the King to remember his position as the person who upheld Dutch privileges. Philip did not answer their petitions, and finally the three men decided that they needed to take drastic measures in order to make their frustration known. They decided that they would all withdraw from Margaret's Council of State in protest at the way their advice was ignored.

Margaret and Philip took notice when Orange, Hoorn and Egmont withdrew from the Council of State. Orange was perhaps the wealthiest and most influential Dutch noble of the time: his actions would be known throughout the realm and could instigate trouble for the King. Philip finally decided to recall Granvelle from the Netherlands in March 1564. This may have been a temporary solution to the problem at first, but Granvelle never returned to the Low Countries.

Resistance to the reform of the bishoprics

Philip encouraged the addition of 14 new bishoprics in the Netherlands in 1559 (see page 316), a complete restructuring of the religious hierarchy in the 17 provinces. The Dutch nobles became increasingly unhappy with the situation when circulating rumours suggested that Spanish nobles were to take the important roles of bishops. Furthermore, the nobles were upset that they had not been consulted in such an important matter. For them, this was confirmation that the decisions that affected their realm were being made in Spain, rather than in the Netherlands. This was a political reality that was completely opposite of their own political ideal of autonomy and self-government.

Tensions between Granvelle and the Dutch nobles were already present in the early 1560s and the reform of the bishoprics made relations between them even worse. Granvelle accused the nobles of wanting to block such reforms so they could continue to influence members of the provincial states. On their part, the nobles argued that the new bishoprics would be funded from the wealth of local monasteries. This would drastically reduce the incomes of the **prelates** who served in the monasteries.

William of Orange (1533–84)

William of Orange was the eldest son of William, Count of Nassau. His was one of the more powerful noble families in the Netherlands. William inherited the estates and title of his cousin, the Prince of Orange, in 1544, founding the house of Orange-Nassau that was to be so significant in the Dutch Revolt and beyond. He was educated by the Emperor Charles V under the supervision of Mary of Hungary. He gained more lands and titles upon his marriage to Anna van Egmond en Buren, including the titles of lord of Egmond and Count of Buren. Charles V favoured him and he was rapidly promoted, commanding an imperial army aged only 22. Orange was a member of the Council of State and was appointed stadtholder of the provinces of Holland, Zeeland and Utrecht in 1559. With these positions, titles, lands and experience, William was one of the most powerful politicians in the Netherlands. He married again in 1561 to Anna of Saxony, gaining influence in this key German state and leading him to hope for German support when the Dutch Revolt began. His move into opposition was gradual. He had been extremely loyal to Charles V, but disapproved of the direction of Philip's policies. Orange was one of the young nobles who diligently guarded traditional Dutch privileges. He was powerful and wealthy, and had been an effective military leader during the Italian War. But he was also seen as a voice of wisdom and compromise. He was to be one of the most dangerous rebel leaders of the Dutch Revolt because of his political and military abilities. Having been declared an outlaw by Philip II, Orange was assassinated in 1584 by a Catholic Frenchman and supporter of Philip II.

Philip of Montmorency, Count of Hoorn (c1518–68)

Philip of Montmorency inherited his step-father's lands and title in 1540. He was a chamberlain at Emperor Charles V's court, and became stadtholder of Gelderland and Zutphen in 1555. He commanded imperial troops in the **Schmalkaldic War** (1546–47) for Charles V and was an admiral of Flanders. Hoorn was the commander of the fleet which carried Philip II back from the Netherlands to Spain in 1559 and remained at the Spanish court in 1563. When he returned to the Netherlands, Hoorn was a member of Margaret of Parma's Council of State.

It was upon his return that he moved into opposition to Granvelle and Philip's religious policies. Although his alliance with Orange and Egmont was instrumental in catalysing opposition to Philip, he refused to support Orange's plan for armed resistance. He returned to his home where he remained until 1567. Invited by the Duke of Alva to discuss a reconciliation, he was imprisoned, convicted of treason and heresy by the Council of Troubles and was executed alongside Egmont on 5 June 1568 (see page 339).

Lamoraal, Count of Egmont (1522–68)

Lamoral became Count of Egmont upon the death of his father in 1541. He had received a military education in Spain and was married to the sister of the Elector Palatine, one of the most powerful princes of the Holy Roman Empire. Like Orange and Hoorn, Egmont was trusted by Charles V, becoming one of his closest advisers. He was a military commander who achieved victories against the French for Philip II. In 1559 Egmont became stadtholder of Flanders and Artois. He was also a member of Margaret of Parma's Council of State. Like Hoorn, Egmont opposed Granvelle's religious and political policies, his opposition leading to the removal of Granvelle. He also refused to engage in armed opposition to Philip II and remained loyal to the Spanish King. Egmont retired to his estates in Flanders and suppressed **Calvinist** uprisings there. Again, like Hoorn, Egmont was arrested when meeting Alva in Brussels (see page 339). There were pleas from across Europe that Egmont be saved, including from the Holy Roman Emperor Maximilian II, but they were ineffective. He was executed on 5 June 1568, causing widespread outrage.

These prelates were often the younger sons or brothers of the wealthier lords. As younger children, they would not inherit their fathers' wealth. The monasteries provided a means for these sons to accumulate wealth and power independent from their families.

Inquisition

More important than the question of who should be appointed bishop, was the policy of inquisition that dominated these religious reforms. Philip, like his father Charles V, was a faithful Roman Catholic and believed that, as King, he should decide religious policy in his territories. For the nobles and civic leaders of the Netherlands, however, religion was not a matter that should be determined in far-away Spain. They saw religion as a concern that should be handled in the local areas, by people who understood the implications of religious policies. The cities and towns within the 17 provinces had prospered because they had not restricted themselves to trading with others of one religious belief over another. The civic leaders were also afraid of the persecution that could follow if the Roman Catholic officials gained too much power in the realm and, therefore, believed it was better to tolerate a wide spectrum of religious beliefs. This opinion, shared by the civic leaders and Dutch nobles alike, was bolstered by events in neighbouring France. France broke into a civil war in 1562 over religion. The Roman Catholic leaders in France wanted to expel the **Huguenots**, French Protestants, and therefore persecuted this religious minority. The Dutch were tired of war, thanks to their experience fighting the Italian War (see page 318). They wanted to avoid new wars on their lands at all costs. For these reasons, they were sceptical of the harsh inquisitions that accompanied the reform of the bishoprics.

The removal of Granvelle

After years of tension between the Dutch and Granvelle, Philip realised that the enmity between the two parties was dangerous. Granvelle would have to leave the Netherlands if Philip was going to achieve stability and support from the Dutch people. Granvelle represented everything about the Spanish that the Dutch hated, and the King could simply no longer afford to have him occupy such powerful political offices. There were outbreaks of unrest and violence in the spring and summer of 1563. The nobles were also actively mounting campaigns (of petitions, see page 321) to have him removed. Philip feared that these would only worsen, and that the only way to prevent further violence was to dismiss Granvelle. In December 1563, Philip was forced to dismiss Granvelle and upon the King's suggestion Granvelle retired to France

Margaret and the heresy laws

The least popular policy in the Netherlands was the use of **heresy laws**. These laws, sometimes called the heresy **placards**, were another way that Philip encouraged Roman Catholicism in the realm. These were encouraged by Granvelle, and were one reason why he was so unpopular with the Dutch people. The numbers of those prosecuted for heresy in the Dutch provinces grew considerably in the 1560s. There were over 600 prosecutions in the province of Flanders in 1562 (see Figure 3). According to the laws, anyone who was not a Roman Catholic was considered a heretic. Suspected heretics were examined before the inquisition and, if found guilty, the punishment was death by burning at the stake. Less serious laws could also be issued. Some of these included the banning of songs or plays that mocked priests in any way. The nobility and urban elites were both critical of these and thought that capital punishment was excessive in matters of religion. The Netherlands shared borders with territories that already had large Protestant populations. These included parts of France and Switzerland, and some of the German-speaking regions belonging to the Holy Roman Empire. The civic elite feared that the laws could harm trade and commerce with their Protestant counterparts.

Margaret witnessed the hostility displayed in response to the heresy laws and knew that they were wildly unpopular among the majority of Dutch people. When a priest favourable to Philip's ideas was **consecrated** Bishop of Roermond by Granvelle without the consent of the States General, Margaret was worried. Although he had been consecrated, she refused to allow him to take his office because she was afraid that there would be trouble from the people. She was willing to make compromises regarding the heresy laws with the nobles and even promised to halt all burnings of heretics, a move that was forced to come to an end thanks to Philip's Segovia Woods letters.

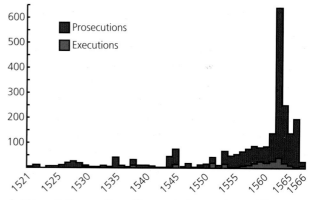

▲ Figure 3: Persecution of heresy in the province of Flanders, 1521–66

In the spring of 1565, Egmont personally travelled to Spain to negotiate with Philip about the role of the nobles in Dutch political life, and to convince the King to ease the laws against heresy. Unfortunately, Egmont misunderstood Philip, and he wrongly believed that Philip had promised to ease the heresy placards. This was more likely to have been due to Philip's courteous reception of Egmont than any assurances Philip gave him. The Dutch nobles received letters from Philip written from his palace in the Segovia Woods dated 17 and 20 October 1565, turning Egmont's victory into a shattering defeat.

Key debate

The Segovia Woods letters

Historians of the Dutch Revolt have long taken interest in the Segovia Woods letters. Many historians, including Jonathan Israel and James Tracy, believe that Philip had simply lied to Egmont when they met in Spain earlier in 1565. They think that the King simply told Egmont what he wanted to hear so that he would return to the Netherlands with good news, and that Philip never intended to fulfil the promises he made to the Dutch grandees. Others, however, like Geoffrey Parker, think that Philip may have been open to compromise. Parker suggests that these letters may reflect the influence of the Duke of Alva. Did Philip always intend to direct such harsh policies against the Netherlands? Or was he nudged in the direction of tyranny by the influential advisers around him?

The Confederacy of Noblemen

Although Granvelle had left the Netherlands, persecution of non-Catholics continued. The provincial states began to demand a meeting of the States General to finally resolve the religious question and end the inquisitions. Around 400 Dutch nobles banded together and asked Philip to find a solution. This band of nobles became known as the Confederacy of Noblemen. The leaders of the Confederacy were minor nobles such as the Count of Brederode and the Count of Nassau. Their goal was to protect their local privileges and customs. They did not want a war to break out in the 17 provinces, but Philip was relentless in his position: he argued that the only way to prevent violence was through stern treatment of those who were not Catholic.

The Compromise of 1566

On 5 April 1566, around 200 members of the Confederacy of Noblemen marched to Margaret's palace in Brussels. They presented a petition to the regent, called the Compromise, demanding the abolition of the heresy laws and a meeting of the States General. They had given Philip numerous opportunities to resolve the problem, but he simply continued to attack those whom he deemed heretics. The nobles were determined that it was the responsibility of the States General to finally make a clear decision about the position of religion in the Low Countries.

The Compromise sought to make the States General the most important centre of political power in the Netherlands, just as they had once been. It was written by two Calvinists, John Marnix, Lord of Tholouse, and Nicholas de Hames, **herald-at-arms** of the Order of the Golden Fleece. It was then approved by Brederode and Nassau. The Confederacy recognised that the nobles and the King were too much in competition with each other for political work to be achieved in an effective way. They hoped that restoring the prominence of the States General would mean that the Netherlands would once again prosper without religious persecution. Another important aspect of the Compromise was that it was a petition that both Roman Catholics and Protestants could support because of their desire to maintain trade with Calvinist merchants. Furthermore, the Compromise was a traditionally Dutch document: those who supported it believed that it was a way for them to defend their privileges from attack.

Margaret was frightened by the large numbers of nobles who presented the Compromise to her and acted quickly in response to their demands. She agreed to lessen the severity of the heresy placards, and informed the provincial states of her movement towards moderation. Outside the cities, Protestant preachers could now preach freely without interference from royal authorities. But Philip still refused to give his assent to easing the heresy placards completely.

The 'Beggars'

One of the most important political icons to emerge from the Compromise was the adoption of the name 'Beggars'. One of Margaret's ministers had referred to the Confederacy of Noblemen as 'mere beggars'. This name, as well as the visual symbols of a beggar's wooden bowl and a double-pouched sack, became the emblematic features of the Compromise. These were powerful symbols that could be adopted by those who wished to support the movement. What had started as a put-down in order to dismiss the members of the Compromise as unimportant, became a potent symbol of change. Even after the immediate crisis had finished, the Beggars' symbols were used in printed propaganda as a reminder of their actions. The image of the rebellious nobility as beggars would be used for the rest of the sixteenth century.

Conclusion: Opposition of the Dutch grandees

The opposition of the Dutch grandees was powerful and became increasingly organised, presenting a threat to the King and the Governor-General because they relied on the grandees to help them rule. The adoption of the 'Beggars' image provided a focus for others who wished to support the cause. Although Margaret of Parma saw that it was important to deal with the concerns of the nobles, Philip's stubbornness meant that it was not possible to entirely appease them.

> ### Work together
> Work with a partner to produce a flow diagram that illustrates the changing alliances from July 1561 to April 1566. At each stage of the diagram include the following: the name of the group or alliance, the people involved, and the aim of the alliance.

4 The impact of Calvinism

One key factor to consider when assessing the causes of the Dutch Revolt is religion. As already discussed, clashes erupted over the treatment of individuals who did not adhere to the Catholic faith. The matter was complex: it was not simply a question of Dutch Protestants revolting against Spanish Roman Catholics. Instead, religion was connected to local privileges. It was also tied to Dutch merchants and their desire to conduct business with foreign merchants regardless of religious affiliation. This section will examine the impact of one particular Protestant group, Calvinists, on politics in the Netherlands. First, the Huguenot migration from France will be explored. Next, the impact of Calvinistic hedge preaching on the Iconoclastic Fury of 1566 will be considered. Finally, this section will examine how order was restored to the Netherlands as well as an assessment of Calvinism in the early modern Netherlands.

> ### Note it down
> Use two methods of note taking in this section. Use the 1:2 method (see page x) to note the main points about these important events. Use index cards (see page xi) to note information about important individuals and groups who played a part in the events.

The Huguenot migration from France

Protestant beliefs were not unfamiliar in the early modern Netherlands. The Low Countries were exposed to a large number of different faiths because of their successful merchants who traded with people of many different religious backgrounds. The cities and towns welcomed strangers from all over Europe in order to conduct business. The merchants traded goods with many different Protestant groups from across Europe, including Huguenots from France, and Calvinists, and wanted to continue their profitable trade with these different groups. They could not afford to tolerate the persecution of their business partners over religious beliefs.

> ### John Calvin and Calvinism
> Calvinism is a major branch of Protestant Christianity. Sometimes called 'Reformed Protestantism', it was founded by the French theologian and pastor, John Calvin (1509-64). Some of the main teachings of Calvinism include:
>
> - salvation is through grace alone, not works
> - baptism and the Lord's Supper are signs of God's grace
> - the Lord's Supper is a representation of Christ's body
> - the idea of the 'elect' those individuals predestined for salvation
> - churches should be governed by local congregations
> - hostility towards images, which are seen as idolatrous.

The arrival of Calvinism in the Netherlands

Calvinism arrived in the Netherlands in the 1540s and rapidly became the most popular variety of Protestantism in the Low Countries. One of the key ways that the faith came to the Netherlands was through the French territories. Huguenots spread their beliefs from France into the neighbouring Dutch regions. Furthermore, John Calvin sent his student, Pierre Brully, into the Netherlands with the specific purpose of spreading Calvinist Protestantism in the realm. Civic leaders tolerated Calvinism because its adherents were quiet about their affiliation.

Persecution of the French Protestants

In France, some Protestants were given the nickname 'Huguenots'. The origins of this nickname are obscure, but the name was used to refer to Protestants who followed the beliefs of John Calvin in particular. Tensions between Roman Catholics and Protestants in France led to a vicious civil war that broke out in 1562 at Vassy (see page 320). On 1 March 1562, the French Duke of Guise encountered a group of French Huguenots practising their religion in a barn on his way to mass. Fierce words were exchanged when his soldiers attempted to gain access to the barn. The two groups began to throw rocks at one another. The situation rapidly escalated, with the Duke's men setting the barn on fire. In the end, 62 unarmed Huguenots were killed and over 100 others were injured in the massacre. Fearing for their lives, a large number of Huguenots fled France. As many as one million French Protestants eventually left their homes in search of a place where they could safely practise their religion. Many of them ended up in the nearby Low Countries. This greatly added to the number of Calvinists in the Netherlands.

Hedge preaching

Another key way that Calvinism spread in the Netherlands was through the use of preachers, particularly through the practice of 'hedge preaching'. The heresy placards meant that Calvinists could not meet for worship in usual places, like churches or in homes within urban areas. It was the duty of the civic authorities to arrest people they knew were practicing a religion other than Catholicism in the areas under their jurisdiction. Hedge preaching took people who wanted to meet to worship following Calvinist practices out of the towns and cities and into the countryside. There, they would be safe from breaking the laws of the towns and cities. Adherents of Calvinism often met in fields to accommodate the large size of the groups who wanted to hear the preachers. Huge congregations would gather together to sing psalms and listen to the preachers as they taught the tenets of the Calvinist faith. Historian Peter Arnade reports that one group who gathered to listen to hedge preaching in Ghent in 1566 numbered perhaps 9,000 people.

Many Dutch people were interested in the messages spread by the hedge preachers. They may have offered a new perspective on recent political and economic events in the Netherlands. In the mid-1500s, the message that these preachers spread resonated with many Dutch people. They had experienced years of hardship and taxation caused by the Italian War. The merchants were losing money thanks to cheap wool imported from England and, on top of these problems, there were harsh winters and poor harvests in the late 1550s. People began to face financial difficulties and starvation and many eagerly listened to the messages these new preachers brought.

Calvinism, however, appealed to members of every economic and social group. It was not a movement that was restricted to the poor or lowly. The different social classes mixed as one group when they met to hear hedge preachers. The movement was widespread: though it originated near France, hedge preaching had spread as far north as Amsterdam within just a few years.

Responses to hedge preaching

Margaret of Parma recognised the danger that hedge preaching could represent. The proponents of Calvinism saw hedge preaching as a means to create public awareness of their religious movement. The royal government understood that hedge preaching could be a visible threat to their authority. It was already illegal according to the terms of Philip's heresy placards. In July 1561, 78 of 98 known attendees of a hedge sermon were arrested and charged with heresy. Twelve of these were sentenced to death. On 1 May 1563, hedge preaching was made a capital offence. The Calvinists continued with their hedge preaching despite this: hedge preaching grew in popularity, and Calvinism continued to spread throughout the 17 provinces despite the persecution they faced from the King and his regent.

The Iconoclastic Fury of 1566

By 1566, popular unrest about the way Protestants were treated in the Netherlands continued to increase. Philip continued to push for harsher policies towards those who were not Roman Catholic. In response, Calvinism grew, and religious protests became more common. Finally, in 1566, **iconoclasm** broke out across the Netherlands. The greatest round of iconoclasm erupted at Steenvoorde. A Calvinist preacher named Sebastian Matte preached before huge crowds in the north. On 10 August, he preached a sermon outside the monastery at St Laurence near Steenvoorde. His words inspired some of the people who heard it to break into the monastery and smash the statues and images inside. The next day, around 100 members of Matte's audience repeated the actions following his sermon at Poperinghe. Other preachers followed Matte's lead. Inspired by these hedge preachers, protestors entered churches and monasteries in August of 1566.

Known as the *Beeldenstrom* in Dutch, the Iconoclastic Fury swept across the Netherlands. Beginning in Flanders, groups of iconoclasts broke into religious buildings. The plunderers moved south and destroyed religious artwork in the houses of worship on their way. They shattered stained-glass windows, smashed statues, and desecrated decorations that offended their Calvinistic religious sensibilities. They stole the precious gold objects that were housed in the churches and burned the vestments worn by the priests who served the churches. Within two weeks, these actions were copied and spread throughout the rest of the Netherlands. The angry mob finally arrived in Antwerp on 21 August. They attacked every church in the city, all 40 of them. These were acts of vandalism, though local authorities did little to stop their actions. Historians are uncertain why this fury started but they think that people were simply tired of religious repression and moved by zeal for the preachers.

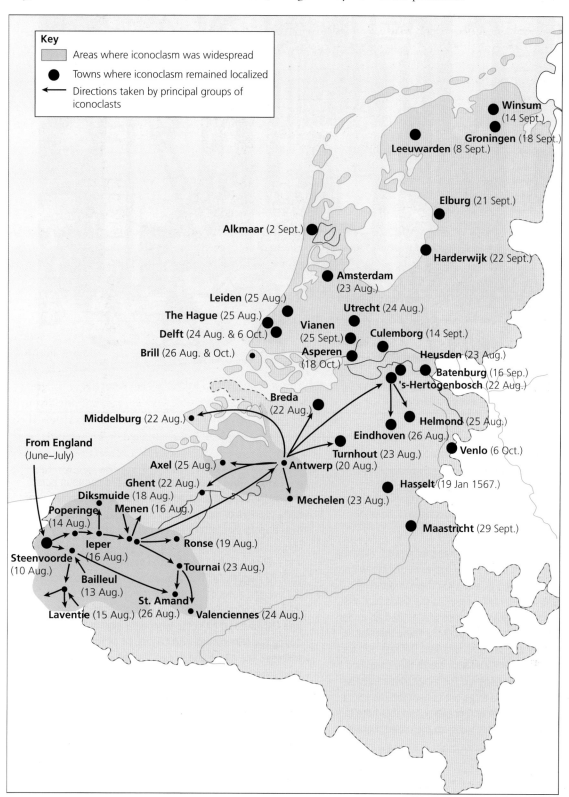

Key

▨ Areas where iconoclasm was widespread

● Towns where iconoclasm remained localized

← Directions taken by principal groups of iconoclasts

Winsum (14 Sept.)
Groningen (18 Sept.)
Leeuwarden (8 Sept.)
Elburg (21 Sept.)
Alkmaar (2 Sept.)
Harderwijk (22 Sept.)
Amsterdam (23 Aug.)
Leiden (25 Aug.)
Utrecht (24 Aug.)
The Hague (25 Aug.)
Vianen (25 Sept.)
Culemborg (14 Sept.)
Delft (24 Aug. & 6 Oct.)
Brill (26 Aug. & Oct.)
Asperen (18 Oct.)
Heusden (23 Aug.)
Batenburg (16 Sep.)
's-Hertogenbosch (22 Aug.)
Breda (22 Aug.)
Middelburg (22 Aug.)
Helmond (25 Aug.)
Eindhoven (26 Aug.)
Turnhout (23 Aug.)
Venlo (6 Oct.)
From England (June–July)
Axel (25 Aug.)
Antwerp (20 Aug.)
Hasselt (19 Jan 1567.)
Ghent (22 Aug.)
Diksmuide (18 Aug.)
Menen (16 Aug.)
Mechelen (23 Aug.)
Poperinge (14 Aug.)
Maastricht (29 Sept.)
Ieper (16 Aug.)
Ronse (19 Aug.)
Steenvoorde (10 Aug.)
Tournai (23 Aug.)
Bailleul (13 Aug.)
St. Amand (26 Aug.)
Laventie (15 Aug.)
Valenciennes (24 Aug.)

▲ Figure 4: The Iconoclastic Fury in the Low Countries, 1566

Source D The destruction of images by Calvinists in 1566.

What can Source D tell historians about the Iconoclastic Fury? How useful is it as evidence? What are the problems with such images as evidence?

Source E From an anonymous account of a nun in s'-Hergotenbosch, Friday 23 January 1566. This Catholic nun wrote in horror of the image-breaking and violence that happened during the 'Iconoclastic Fury'.

So it happened on 21 July that a preacher arrived, claiming that he had been sent by one with higher authority, as he told the people from Den Bosch and other surrounding parts, who came to hear him preach in the fields as Christ had done. He was not exactly fearless for he had an armed escort for his protection, unlike Christ ... There then came a second preacher whose name was Jan. The first one was called Cornelis [Walraven] and henceforth they preached in competition with one another. The magistrates forbade anyone in the King's name to go out to hear the preaching on pain of forfeiting his life and property. But the more this was forbidden, the more they went, so the crowd thereafter grew larger. They [the Calvinists] set up a common purse and distributors of alms and they contributed sometimes thirty guilders or more, some indeed gave the rings from their fingers. And after they had preached here, they entered the town in great strength with armed men, guns and halberds ... He continued to preach outside in this way until 22 August. On Thursday about five or six o'clock in the evening news came that all the churches, chapels and monastic churches at Antwerp had been destroyed. They [the Calvinists] then set to work here also in St. Janskerk during the benediction and continued all night and they smashed the altars and gilded statues. They relieved themselves in the priests' chests and tore up the books.

What does Source E tell us about the actions of the Calvinists in 1566? What impact could the source's authorship have on the account within it?

Dutch responses to the Iconoclastic Fury

Margaret wrote to Philip, claiming that half the country's population were heretics. She began to gather resources and soldiers for an army. When various provincial states met that autumn, they were worried about the effects of the Iconoclastic Fury. They demanded that the States General were summoned so that the matter of religion could finally be settled. But the Fury had a negative impact on the way Calvinism was perceived by many Dutch. The majority of the nobles, including William of Orange and Egmont, were opposed to the destruction the iconoclasts had wrought. Despite their support for religious **toleration**, the nobles could not support the widespread destruction and revolutionary activities of these Calvinists. Preaching and Calvinist forms of worship were halted in the Netherlands by the spring of 1567 as a result of the Fury. The heresy placards remained in effect, and the States General still were not summoned.

Philip's response to the Iconoclastic Fury

Once again, Philip took his time in responding to the Fury. He and his Spanish councillors in Madrid were afraid that the situation in the Netherlands could escalate to a full-blown civil war if they failed to act. The King initially decided to send the Duke of Alva, a well-known military hero, into the Netherlands with a large force. He would then arrest some of the ringleaders of the Fury alongside known supporters of Calvinism. This tactic would overawe much of the population. After Alva had accomplished this work, Philip would himself travel to the Netherlands from Spain. But due to Philip's need to deal firmly with his eldest son Prince carlos it became

clear that he could not leave Spain. Margaret wrote to Philip in the spring of 1567, observing that the climate had changed greatly in the Netherlands. Calvinism had lost its allure for many of the Dutch, and the realm was peaceful once again. She believed that it was unnecessary for the King to send Alva and a large group of soldiers. Margaret feared that a military force would only create unnecessary tensions. The council in Spain considered the matter once again and Philip sent a military force of 10,000 men under the Duke of Alva into Brussels in August 1567.

The effects of Calvinism on the Netherlands

In some ways, Calvinism was the catalyst that encouraged the Dutch to rebel against their king. The Iconoclastic Fury in 1566 was clear evidence that the people and government were hopelessly divided on the question of religion. Religion became the major battleground over questions of power between the Dutch and the Spanish. The Dutch believed that religion should be a matter under the control of the local civil governors, but Philip thought religion was related to his own authority. He would not tolerate any subjects who followed a religion that was different from his own. The question of religious persecution was the main subject of numerous letters and petitions that the nobles sent to the King and the regent. Their distaste for religious persecution brought Orange, Hoorn and Egmont together as leaders. The unsettled question of religion, brought into the open with the Iconoclastic Fury, finally forced the King and the nobles to act. While tolerating Calvinism did mean that the Dutch could trade with them, the violence and instability that this produced meant that it was of questionable value in the long term.

Conclusion: The impact of Calvinism

Calvinism was a crucial factor in provoking the revolt. Although Calvinists were less numerous in the Netherlands than Catholics, they were an outspoken group and valued the *de facto* toleration that had grown up in the Netherlands. The outbreaks of religious violence in 1566 showed the impact they could have if threatened. This clashed sharply with Philip's views on religious uniformity. As Philip's religious policies did not take account of Dutch traditions regarding religious freedom, they became an issue of government as well as religion.

Work together

Use the index cards that you have created, along with any other similar cards that you have produced on the events or people in this chapter. Work in pairs. Test each other on the contents of the cards - either the people or the events. Note where you find anything particularly difficult and revisit it at the end.

Chapter summary

- The early modern Netherlands emcompassed a larger territory than today's Netherlands, and included parts of Belgium, France and Germany.
- Under Emperor Charles V, the Netherlands flourished and enjoyed a degree of autonomy.
- Philip II became a distant ruler, living in the Netherlands in the early part of his reign but then completely relocating his court back to Spain.
- Philip tried to encourage Catholicism (and prevent Protestantism) through the creation of new bishoprics and the use of unpopular heresy placards.
- The continued presence of Spanish soldiers in the early 1560s was a source of disagreement between the Dutch people and their Spanish rulers.
- The Compromise of 1566 was an important movement towards reform in the Netherlands.
- The French Wars of Religion were significant for the Dutch because they drove Protestants out of France and into the Netherlands. The fleeing people brought their Calvinist faith with them.
- The Dutch nobles saw religious tolerance as one of the traditional Dutch rights.
- The Iconoclastic Fury of 1566 was a turning-point in relations between Roman Catholics and Calvinists, and between the Dutch and the Spanish.
- Philip was slow to respond to Margaret's request for aid. When he finally did respond, he sent General Alva to the Netherlands.

Recommended reading

Paul Arblaster, *A History of the Low Countries* (Palgrave, 2012).

Chapter 3 is particularly useful for this section, explaining the complex political situation of the Low Countries in the period leading up to the revolt. Arblaster also provides a good introduction to the wider political culture of the period.

Peter Limm, *The Dutch Revolt 1559–1648* (Routledge, 1989), Chapters 1 and 2.

These two chapters provide an excellent summary of the immediate political context of the Dutch Revolt, explaining how the Habsburg family fitted into Dutch governmental structures and focusing on the political situation after Philip returned to Spain.

Andrew Pettegree, *Europe in the Sixteenth Century* (Wiley-Blackwell, 2002), Chapter 9.

Pettegree's book is a great introduction to Europe in this period, and helps to place the Low Countries into a wider European context.

The Habsburg Netherlands

- Consisted of 17 provinces, independent from the Holy Roman Empire's legal and administrative systems
- Ruled by nobles who owed their allegiance to the Habsburgs
- Philip II inherited Charles V's territories in Spain, Italy and the Netherlands in 1555
- Philip II relied on local structures such as the grandees, the Governor-General and Councils of Justice
- Traditional privileges had given nobles a lot of power but Philip II showed a lack of regard for these
- Self-governance and autonomy were central to Dutch identity

The situation, c1563

- Tensions between the Dutch and Spanish intensified in the 1550s and 1560s
- Philip II controlled the Netherlands by creating new Catholic bishoprics
- New bishops challenged the Dutch nobles' traditional privileges
- Margaret of Parma was appointed regent in 1559
- Granvelle was an unpopular figure amongst Dutch nobles
- The presence of Spanish soldiers in the Netherlands and taxes were sources of conflict

THE ORIGINS OF THE DUTCH REVOLT

The opposition of the Dutch grandees

- Orange, Hoorn and Egmont disliked Granvelle's activities and saw Philip II's actions as a threat to their privileges
- Granvelle was recalled from the Netherlands in 1564
- Nobles and civic leaders viewed religion as a local issue and not one to be dictated by Spain. They were strongly against the use of heresy laws
- Non-Catholics were persecuted
- The Confederacy of the Nobles wanted to protect local privileges and customs
- The Compromise of 1566 was an attempt by the nobles to suspend the Inquisition and the enforcements of heresy placards

The impact of Calvinism

- Religious toleration was important for trade
- The persecution of French Protestants increased the number of Calvinists in the Netherlands
- Calvinism spread through hedge preaching
- Iconoclasm broke out in 1566
- The Iconoclastic Fury prompted Philip II to send the Duke of Alva and a military force to the Netherlands

▲ Summary diagram: The origins of the Dutch Revolt, c1563–67

Section A: Essay technique

Focus on the question and understanding the sources

The A level Section A question requires you to deploy a variety of skills. The most important are source analysis and evaluation. In essence, the question asks how much a historian could learn about a specific issue from the two sources. This is a complex task, and requires a range of skills which will be covered in this section and at the end of Key Topics 2–4. These include the ability to:

- understand the focus of the question and the sources (this section)
- structure an essay and write good introductions (Key Topic 2, pages 353–54)
- select information and make inferences from the sources (Key Topic 2, pages 355–58)
- place the sources in their historical context (Key Topic 3, pages 376–78)

- evaluate and weigh up the evidence of the sources (Key Topic 4, pages 398–400)
- reach and support a final judgement (Key Topic 4, pages 401–03).

The Section A question for AS level is different from the Section A question for A level, and some guidance about this is given on page viii. However, you will need to develop very similar skills for the AS exam, therefore the activities will help with the AS exams as well. There are also some AS-style questions in every chapter.

The focus of the question

In order to answer the question successfully you must understand how the question works. Here is a typical Section A question. The question is written precisely in order to make sure that you understand the task. Each part of the question has a specific meaning:

'How far' indicates that you must evaluate the extent of something, rather than giving a simple 'yes' or 'no' answer.

They key word here is **together**. You must examine the sources as a pair and make a judgement about both sources, rather than separate judgements about each source.

> **Study Sources 1 and 2 before you answer this question.**
>
> **How far could the historian make use of Sources 1 and 2 together to investigate the causes of the Dutch Revolt in 1566?**
>
> **Explain your answer,** using both sources, the information given about them and your own knowledge of the historical context.

This is the essence of the task: you must focus on what a historian could legitimately conclude from studying these sources.

The final part of the question focuses on a specific topic that a historian might investigate. In this case: 'the causes of the Dutch Revolt in 1566'.

This instruction lists the resources you should use: the sources; the information given about the sources; your own knowledge of historical context that you have learned during the course.

Source 1 This is a letter from Philip II to his half-sister and regent, Margaret of Parma, on 17 October 1565. Philip writes to command Margaret to enforce the inquisition despite the protests of the Dutch.

Madame my dear sister ... [M]y orders are designed for the welfare of religion and of my provinces and are worth nothing if they are not obeyed. In this way you can keep my provinces in justice, peace, and tranquillity. Now that you know the importance of this, I pray you again to take steps to bring this state of affairs into being. Thus I shall be most satisfied with you and with the seigniors [on the Council of State] who are with you. You must pass on my wishes to them. I trust they won't fail to do what I want as they know what satisfaction this will give me. Thus they will do their duty according to their rank and to the obligation they have to serve God and me, and to further the common welfare of the provinces in the Netherlands.

Source 2 This is an excerpt from the Compromise of 1566, produced by representatives of the Confederacy of Nobles and presented to Margaret of Parma. It was written by two Calvinists before being approved by the leaders of the Confederacy of Nobles.

> [W]e, the undersigned, have been duly and sufficiently warned and informed that there is a great crowd of foreigners [Philip's foreign advisors including Granvelle] – men without any concern for the safety and prosperity of the provinces in the Netherlands, with no care for God's glory and honour or for the commonweal, driven only by private avarice and ambition, even to the disadvantage of the king and all his subjects – who pretend to be zealous for the maintenance of the Catholic religion and the union of the people and have managed to persuade His Majesty by their well-turned remonstrances and false information to violate his oath [of 1549] and to disappoint the expectations he has always let us cherish, by not only failing to mitigate the edicts already in force, but by reinforcing them and even by introducing the inquisition in all its strength. Not only is this inquisition iniquitous and against all divine and human laws, surpassing the worst barbarism ever practised by tyrants, it will also most certainly lead to the dishonouring of God's name and to the utter ruin and desolation of the Netherlands.

All Section A questions ask you to make a judgement about how far two sources are useful to the historian. However, the second half of the question specifies what a historian is focusing on.

So, the first part of the question sets up the **general task**, which is true of all Section A questions:

'How far could the historian make use of Sources 1 and 2 together to investigate …'

And the second part of the question establishes the **specific focus**, for example:

'… the causes of the Dutch Revolt in 1566?'

As you write your essay, you need to focus on both aspects.

How to focus in a source question

Source questions are different from questions that only require you to use your own knowledge. There are a variety of ways to ensure you maintain your focus on the question that are appropriate to this type of question:

- Use the phrases 'Source 1' and 'Source 2', when dealing with the sources so that it is clear which sources you are focusing on.
- Use words such as 'useful' or 'utility' to ensure that you are explicitly addressing the general task.
- Use comparative words and phrases such as 'Sources 1 and 2 disagree' to show that you are using the sources together.

Activity: A focused introduction

1 Write a short introduction which provides a focused answer to the question on page 332. See page 353 for advice on writing introductions. Also remember that this is a question about two sources.
2 Having written an introduction, swap it with a partner. Consider:
   a) Which introduction best focuses on the question? Remember, your introduction needs to focus on the **general task** and the **specific focus**.
   b) Which introduction best deals with the sources *together*?
   c) Which introduction gives the clearest answer to the question?
   d) What can you learn from each other's approach to the question?

Use these questions to feedback to each other and improve your instructions.

Activity: AS-style questions

1 Why is Source 1 valuable to the historian for an enquiry into Philip II's style of rule?
2 How much weight do you give the evidence of Source 2 for an enquiry into the causes of the Dutch Revolt?

Understanding the sources

Understanding the sources is crucial to doing well in Section A questions. The most important aid in this understanding is a detailed knowledge of the period. There are also techniques to aid understanding. Here are a few tips to get you started:

- Read the source word for word – if it helps, read it out loud when you are doing practice questions. This makes it much less likely that you will miss anything in the source.
- Think about the question as you are reading. You will then look out for relevant information within the source.
- Make index cards before your exam of the specific vocabulary for the topic you are studying, for example, States General, stadtholder, regent, hedge preaching.
- Look up terms and definitions that you don't recognise in practice questions.

- Make index cards about the people who might be quoted in the sources, and the documents that might be used as sources on the examination paper such as Philip II of Spain, William of Orange or Johann Oldenbarnevelt. Make notes on who they are and their attitudes to the key issues you have studied.

Comprehension

Comprehension is the most basic source skill. It simply means understanding the source's meaning and you can demonstrate this by:

- **copying**: writing out the words of the source in your essay
  TIP: Avoid copying any more than a sentence at any point in your essay.
- **paraphrasing:** putting part of a source in your own words
  TIP: Avoid simply rewriting more than a sentence from the sources in your own words, before using a higher level skill.

- **summarising:** summing up the meaning of the entire source, or a large part of the source, in a single sentence.
  TIP: Summarising can be useful in introductions and conclusions.

These are low level source skills. Therefore, they should not dominate your essay. However, small quotes, short paraphrases and occasional summaries can be useful to support higher level skills.

Higher level skills

Higher level skills include:

- using the sources together (see pages 355–56)
- making inferences (see pages 356–58)
- analysing sources in their historical context (see pages 376–78)
- evaluating the evidence presented in the sources (see pages 398–400)
- reaching an overall judgement regarding the usefulness of the sources (see pages 401–03).

Activity: Test your understanding

Having read Source 2 on page 333.
1 **a)** Make a list of words and phrases that you don't understand.
   b) Look them up in the glossary of this book or online.
   You should repeat this activity regularly with the sources that you encounter. This will help with many of the sources you will examine as you study the Dutch Revolt, as sources from the same period, referring to the same topic, will tend to use a similar vocabulary.
2 **a)** **Copy** the sentence that best expresses the nobles' view on Philip's foreign advisers. Make sure you put the quote in 'quotation marks'.
   b) **Paraphrase** one of the reasons why the nobles were angry at Philip II in relation to the religious edicts.

   c) **Summarise** the nobles' message to Margaret of Parma in no more than 25 words.
3 Source 1 is a letter. Letters are often written to individuals or groups. They tend to refer to the writer, the recipient and other people as well. In order to understand the letter it is important to understand who the letter is referring to.
   The following words and phrases refer to specific individuals, copy them down and then write next to them who they are:
   - 'Madame my dear sister' (line 1)
   - 'My orders' (line 1)
   - 'my provinces' (line 2)
   - 'the seigniors' (line 7)

Work together

Having completed activities 1 and 2, swap your answers with a partner. Consider:

1 Did you both identify the same words that needed to be defined?
2 Were your partner's definitions clear and accurate?
3 Did you both agree on who the letter was referring to in the who's who activity?
4 Did you both copy the same bit of the source? If not, which quote better summarises the nobles' view of Philip's foreign advisers?

5 Is your partner's paraphrase clear? Does it accurately reflect one of the reasons why the nobles were angry at Philip in relation to the religious edicts?
6 Whose summary more precisely expressed the nobles' message in Source 2?
7 What can you learn from the approach of your partner to Source 2?

Use these questions to feedback to each other and improve your analysis of the source.

Section B: Essay technique

Focus and structure

Section B essays, like all of your examined essays, will be judged on how far they focus on the question, and the quality of their structure. You may have already considered advice on how to write a focused introduction, and how to structure your essays in Paper 1 (see pages 22–23).

Different types of question

Section B questions, like Sections A and B questions in Paper 1, can focus on a variety of concepts. These include cause, consequence, change/continuity, similarity/difference and significance. These different concepts require slightly different approaches. Here are some examples of these concepts in questions.

These questions require you to explain the **causes** of opposition to Philip's religious policies.

> **1** Why was there such widespread opposition to Philip's religious policies from 1559 to 1567?
>
> **2** How far was Philip's disregard for Dutch traditions the main reason for opposition to his religious policies from 1559 to 1567? [AS]
>
> **3** 'Between 1563 and 1584 the main consequence of Philip's style of rule was a decline in relations with the Dutch nobles.' How far do you agree with this statement?
>
> **4** Was the deteriorating relationship with the Dutch nobles the main consequence of Philip's style of rule? Explain your answer. [AS]
>
> **5** How far was William of Orange's 1572 invasion the main turning point in the escalation of the Dutch Revolt from 1566–84?
>
> **6** How far was William of Orange's 1572 invasion the main turning point in the Dutch Revolt from 1566–84? [AS]
>
> **7** 'The Duke of Alba and the Duke of Parma used radically different approaches in their attempts to defeat the Dutch rebels.' How far do you agree with this statement?
>
> **8** How accurate is it to say that the Duke of Alba and the Duke of Parma used different approaches in their attempts to defeat the Dutch rebels? [AS]
>
> **9** How significant was the challenge posed by foreign intervention to Spanish containment of the Dutch revolt in the years 1566–88?
>
> **10** How significant was foreign intervention in the development of the Dutch Revolt from 1566–88? [AS]

These questions ask you to evaluate the **consequences** of Philip's style of rule.

These questions require you to evaluate the extent of **change/continuity** in the escalation of the Dutch Revolt.

These questions require you to evaluate the **similarity/difference** of the approaches of the Duke of Alva and the Duke of Parma in their attempts to defeat the Dutch rebels.

These questions require you to evaluate the **significance** of foreign intervention in the development of the Dutch Revolt from 1566–88.

Structuring your essay

As in Paper 1, your essay should be made up of three or four paragraphs, each addressing a different factor (see page 22).

However, essays that focus on different concepts will need a slightly different structure:

- **Cause essays** require you to explain why something happened. Therefore, each paragraph should deal with a different possible cause.
- **Evaluative essays** require you to weigh up the extent of something. Most essays will require you to evaluate at some point, as weighing up is essential to reaching a conclusion. In essays that focus on evaluation each paragraph should weigh up a different factor. For example, if you were dealing with the question: 'How far was the opposition to Philip's religious policies from 1559 to 1567 due to religious belief?' each paragraph could weigh up the different reasons for opposition to Philip's religious policies. For example, one paragraph could deal with opposition from nobles who felt their privileges were being eroded, another could look at opposition from Calvinists and other Protestant groups, and another could examine opposition due to the loss of money in trade.
- **Success or failure essays** require you to evaluate the extent to which something succeeded. Therefore, you will need to start by considering the aims in order to establish the criteria for success. You should go on to consider aspects that succeeded and weigh them, against aspects that failed in order to reach a conclusion.
- **Continuity and change essays** require you to evaluate the extent of change. Therefore, your essay will have to weigh up what changed and what stayed the same.
- **Consequence essays** require you to evaluate which of a range of consequences was most important.

It is crucial to be able to distinguish between the different types of question. Confusing a cause essay with a consequence essay could seriously affect your grade.

Activity: Question types

1 Below are three different Section B questions. Work out what types of question they are.

   a) How significant was the spread of Calvinism to the outbreak of the Dutch Revolt in 1566? AS

   b) How accurate is it to say that Maurice of Nassau's military leadership was a success in the period 1587–1609? AS

   c) How far was the founding of the Dutch East India Company the main turning-point in the success of the United Provinces?

2 Having worked out what types of question you are dealing with you should now write plans for each question. You can plan either as spider diagrams or a bullet-point list. Make sure your plan reflects the kind of essay that you are dealing with. For example, if you are dealing with a success or failure essay, you should highlight which parts of the plan deal with success and which deal with failure. Complete one plan at a time, and after each discuss it with a partner.

Work together

Having completed a plan, swap them with a partner. Consider:

1 Did you agree on what type of question you were dealing with? If not, discuss it and work out who was right.
2 Whose plan most clearly focused on the specific type of question?
3 Did your partner's plan miss anything?
4 Did you miss anything that you should add to your plan?
5 What can you learn from your partner's approach?

Use these questions to feedback to each other and improve your question spotting and planning.

Key Topic 2 Alva and Orange, 1567–73

Overview

In response to the Iconoclastic Fury of 1566, Philip sent the Duke of Alva into the Netherlands in an attempt to restore order. However, Alva's repressive stance provoked further opposition and only made the revolt more entrenched. William of Orange was the main opposition leader. He resisted Philip's policy of uniformity and argued for the right for the Dutch to rule themselves and for the toleration of a variety of religious beliefs. He used the rebel naval forces, the Sea Beggars, to fight against Spanish control and provide another military tool to combat Alva's army. Yet the rebel leaders, for example Orange, were not cowed by Alva's repressive approach and returned with some success in 1573. Battles between Orange and Alva represented the differences between the Spanish and the Dutch view of politics.

This chapter considers the aftermath of the first major revolt in the Netherlands and examines these issues through the following sections:

1 *Alva's rule* looks at the replacement of Margaret of Parma and the changes instituted by Alva. It explores the Council of Troubles and reactions to it, as well as the executions of Egmont and Hoorn. This section also discusses the impact of the new taxes introduced by Alva in order to help Spain's dire financial situation.

2 *Orange's failure* examines William of Orange's invasion of 1568, the initial success of the rebels and their defeat at Jemmingen in July 1568 at the hands of Alva.

3 *The role of the Sea Beggars* explores the impact of the Sea Beggars on Orange's success. It looks at who the Sea Beggars were and what role they played in the revolt. This includes their capture of the towns of Brill and Flushing.

4 *Orange's triumph* discusses the invasions of 1572 and Orange's establishment of control over Holland and Zeeland. It includes a discussion of the meeting of Dordrecht and Alva's failure to retain control over the provinces.

TIMELINE

1567 August	Alva arrived in Brussels
1567 September	Margaret of Parma resigned
1567 December	Alva became Governor-General
1568 May	Rebels won the Battle of Heiligerlee
1568 June	Egmont and Hoorn executed for treason
1568 July	Rebels defeated at Jemmingen
1569	Alva summoned States General; attempted to level taxes
1572 April	Sea Beggars landed in Holland and Zeeland
1573 November	Alva resigned as Governor-General

Note it down

Use the 1:2 method (see page x) to take notes on this section. Put the headings in the left – hand column and make notes on the main points in the – right hand column. Remember you can also add these events to your annotated timeline from Key Topic 1. You should also think about adding any new figures or terms to your collection of index cards.

1 Alva's rule

The Duke of Alva arrived to provide military support for Margaret of Parma but was soon appointed as her replacement. Philip intended Alva to be a strong governor who would put down the rebellion and restore order. Alva used **authoritarian** methods to enforce Philip's religious and political policies. He trampled on the traditional rights and roles of the Dutch nobility and used Egmont and Hoorn's executions as exemplary punishments to show the Dutch that their actions would be harshly punished. Alva established a Council of Troubles to deal with the '**heresy**' of **Protestantism** within the Netherlands, and punished many using imprisonment and execution. Many fled and formed opposition groups overseas.

The replacement of Margaret of Parma

The Duke of Alva arrived in Brussels in August 1567 with a large army (see page 329). Margaret had observed first hand the events in the Netherlands. She wrote to Philip to argue that the presence of a large army led by Alva was an unnecessary precaution so many months after the destructive events of the Fury. She was not successful in persuading Philip that the army was unnecessary. Margaret of Parma urged Alva to be lenient when dealing with the majority of the population. She wanted the main leaders of the revolt to be punished but also realised that the Spanish could win popular support if they granted numerous **pardons**. Traditionally, the **Governor-General** granted the populace pardons after a rebellion. This helped to restore the usual order quickly after a period of strife. Margaret resigned from her position and left the Netherlands on 30 December and Alva became the Governor-General in her place. He had not expected to take political power at this point, and was ill prepared to take over from Margaret.

Changes under Alva

Philip sent Alva to the Netherlands with an army of 10,000 men despite the objections of Margaret of Parma (see page 329). The King granted Alva full military powers so that he could restore order. Alva used his military powers to establish an emergency council called the Council of Troubles and to relentlessly pursue the heretics and rebels who had become Philip's primary enemies.

Alva enforced the heresy **placards** and reasserted Roman Catholicism as the only acceptable religion in the region. He sent soldiers to cities that were known for violence or Calvinism and built a new fortress in Antwerp, the centre of government.

Alva soon arrested influential nobles, including prominent members of the **Order of the Golden Fleece,** of which Alva was also a member. No matter how locally important these men were, Alva was determined to punish them for the opposition to the King of Spain. These activities threatened to transform the way that traditional political life operated in the Netherlands.

Alva wanted to demonstrate Spanish power over the provinces and his harsh methods prompted many to flee the Netherlands.

The Council of Troubles and the attacks on heresy

Alva established the Council of Troubles shortly after arriving in the Low Countries in August 1567. The Council was based in Brussels but was assisted by 170 investigators who operated throughout the 17 provinces. The Council of Troubles encouraged ordinary men and women to spy on their neighbours, and to report heretical or rebellious activities to the authorities. Individuals who were found guilty before the Council lost their property. Thousands were executed. This Council had the reputation for extreme brutality. It became known among the Dutch people as the 'Council of Blood' for its harshness. The Council aimed to restore the link between Roman Catholicism and loyalty to the King. It tried to

Fernando Alvarez de Toledo, 3rd Duke of Alva (1507–82)

The Duke of Alva was a general, politician and diplomat who worked and fought for Charles V and Philip II of Spain. He was multilingual, speaking French, German, English and Latin. He had a **humanist education** and was a pious Catholic. He became Duke of Alva on the death of his grandfather in 1531, and served the kings of Spain throughout his life. Alva was a military commander against the Ottoman Turks and the French from 1532 to 1542, and led elite Spanish troops in the Schmalkaldic War from 1546 to 1547. He was commander-in-chief of Charles V's forces in Italy from 1555 to 1559, leading the Emperor's invasion of Rome and imprisonment of the Pope in 1557. It was his military skill, loyalty, Catholicism and forceful approach that led Philip II to send Alva to the Netherlands in 1567. Alva's authoritarian and ruthless approach was provocative rather than successful in restoring order. He was hugely unpopular due to his repressive measures, including the Council of Troubles (also known as the Council of Blood) and its execution of Egmont and Hoorn. Alva was replaced in the Netherlands in 1573, and returned to Spain. He continued to play an important role at the Spanish court, leading an army to invade Portugal in 1580 and being rewarded with titles of viceroy of Portugal and constable of Portugal by Philip II on his success.

complete the reform of the **bishoprics** that Granvelle had started. The Council censored books and regulated schools. Alva used whatever means he could to restore the King's order. He stopped at nothing to achieve this objective. This even included suspending the civic and provincial rights that the nobles had tried so hard to defend.

Alva and the Council of Troubles were especially interested in the people who gathered to listen to the hedge sermons. Alva wanted to find out information about the hedge sermons because he believed that it would bring him to the leaders of Calvinism in the Netherlands. He also thought this knowledge could help him find and punish those who had been involved in the Iconoclastic Fury. The Council of Troubles operated for nine years. Historian Geoffrey Parker has estimated that 60,000 people fled the Netherlands to escape punishment from the Council of Troubles. Over the course of the same period, 8,568 people were tried for heresy, treason or both. Of these, 20 people were banished while 1,083 were executed. Most of these executions took place within the first two years of the Council's establishment. Those imprisoned included prominent men like Jacob van den Eynde, the advocate of the states of Holland, who was imprisoned by Alva in Brussels and died shortly after. The brunt was born by the upper-middle class below the level of local officials and governors, however, including wealthy citizens. The Dutch saw the Council as a way for Alva to punish people without using the traditional avenues of justice. They abhorred the way it operated and soon came to see it as one of the symbols of Philip's growing tyranny.

The executions of Egmont and Hoorn

Egmont and Hoorn met with Alva a few days after he arrived from Spain. They saw themselves as loyal Spanish subjects, having taken no part in any violence against Philip's plans. Together, they reviewed Alva's plans to build **citadels** in select Dutch cities which were intended to house the Spanish soldiers that Alva had brought with him. The meeting has been portrayed as a ploy intended to lure Egmont and Hoorn to Brussels. After dining with Alva, Egmont and Hoorn were arrested on 9 September 1567. Egmont resisted at first, refusing to surrender his sword to anyone but Philip, but was overcome and imprisoned. In January 1568 the Council of Troubles charged Egmont with 82 crimes and Hoorn with 63. They remained imprisoned in Ghent until the following June. On 1 June, 18 noblemen who had participated in the Compromise of 1566 (see page 324) were beheaded in Brussels. Egmont and Hoorn were taken out of Ghent on 3 June and ordinary people lined the streets to pay their respects to these two men as they were removed from the city. Egmont and Hoorn were taken back to Brussels.

There, on the night of 4 June, the Council of Troubles pronounced death sentences for both men.

As part of the Dutch nobility and as members of the Order of the Golden Fleece, Egmont and Hoorn were entitled to a trial by a jury of their peers. However, this was ignored and on 5 June 1568 Egmont and Hoorn were beheaded. Their heads were stuck on spikes and left on the scaffold in the main square in Brussels for two hours.

Reasons for Egmont and Hoorn's execution

Alva knew that Egmont and Hoorn, along with Orange, had been instrumental in preparing the petitions representing the Compromise in 1566. He therefore saw them as the most dangerous figures in opposition to Philip's royal authority. Their executions were intended to send a clear signal to the rest of the population and served as examples of what could happen to anyone who disobeyed the King. If great nobles could be executed, anyone who opposed the King's policies could face the same consequences.

Alva considered this a policy of exemplary punishment. He reasoned that executing many members of the lower classes could lead to a bloodbath, something that Philip wished to avoid. But by executing members of the noble elite, knights of the Golden Fleece, Alva created a shock within the Dutch political community. Ordinary people, too, were upset by the executions. The crowd that had gathered to witness the executions dipped their handkerchiefs into the dead men's blood. In doing this they took away a 'souvenir', or something to remember the executed person. It was a mark of great respect and made the men martyrs for their cause. People lined the streets as coffins carried their bodies to their final resting places and both men became the subjects of popular ballads and visual prints. These depicted Egmont and Hoorn as loyal and faithful subjects. The villains of each piece were clear: Philip and Alva were the tyrants.

Reasons for the introduction of the Tenth Penny Tax

Alva's main tasks were to restore order and to find and punish heretics and rebels. A secondary task Philip gave him was to raise taxes so that the 17 provinces paid for their own government. Alva had expected to pay his massive army with silver sent from Spain, but this was delayed because Philip had severe financial troubles and simply could not afford to pay for Alva's army. Philip also had to deal with the Ottoman Turks who threatened to dominate the Mediterranean with their naval fleet and attempts to seize Spanish territory. This was extremely expensive, and meant that Alva had to come up with another way to pay his army.

In March 1569 Alva devised three different taxes in order to do this:

- The Hundredth Penny Tax: a tax of one per cent on land. It was to be levied one time, and then never again.
- The Twentieth Penny Tax: a permanent tax on **immovable goods**.
- The Tenth Penny Tax: a permanent ten per cent sales tax on **movable goods** sold in the Netherlands.

The **States General** agreed to the Hundredth Penny Tax but Alva met resistance to Twentieth and Tenth Penny Tax. The amount of money raised by the Hundredth Penny Tax was simply not enough to pay for the soldiers, and so despite the agreement of the States General to this tax, Alva still needed to levy the other taxes. As time passed, it became clear that Philip would be unable to visit the Netherlands, meaning that Alva's authority rested on the Spanish soldiers. He knew that his power would be severely weakened if he could not pay them and, thus, was determined to raise the money.

Growing opposition to the Tenth Penny Tax

A similar type of tax to the Tenth Penny Tax was sometimes used in Europe during the early modern period in order to raise emergency funding, but Alva's Tenth Penny Tax was unusual for four reasons:

1 Ten per cent was a high rate of taxation for this kind of tax.
2 Such taxations were usually levied for a brief and limited amount of time. Alva wanted to tax at this rate for as long as he could, and refused to fix an end point. This was a significant increase in the financial burdens of the Dutch people.
3 They were to be collected by a specially appointed group of officials who were not part of the **provincial states** government. This was another affront to Dutch traditional privileges and local autonomy.
4 Alva was not going to seek the approval of the Estates in order to pass the measure confirming the Tenth Penny Tax. He was determined to tax at this rate whether or not he received consent from the Dutch people.

All of these features made the Tenth Penny Tax incredibly unpopular amongst the Dutch. The States General would not consent to the Tenth Penny Tax. They realised that such a tax would mean that the central government would

be able to fund itself and so it would no longer need to seek approval from the provincial states in matters of finance. In turn, this meant that the States General would become the most powerful governing institution within the Netherlands. Although on the surface this might seem beneficial to the States General, it was a political reality that the representatives simply could not support. After all, they were sent to the States General from the provincial assemblies. The representatives at the States General believed that the consequences of the Tenth Penny Tax would completely upset the entire political system in the Netherlands and would result in a loss of those local privileges that each city and province had tried to defend for so long.

When the taxes were not passed by the States General Alva took matters into his own hands and started to collect the taxes without their approval. Alva's refusal to seek consent angered many. It was completely unconstitutional and led to a widespread tax strike.

Conclusion: Alva's rule

When Alva arrived in the Netherlands in August 1567, he took his mission to restore order seriously. He moved swiftly to arrest individuals whom he saw as heretics or rebels because he believed that heretics threatened the realm's stability and challenged Philip's authority. He reinforced the old heresy placards with a new determination. He was afraid that those who had participated in the rebellions would rebel again if given the opportunity. Alva established the Council of Troubles in order to find and prosecute rebels and heretics. Egmont and Hoorn were executed as a way to show what could be done to anyone who resisted the King's authority. The Council of Troubles was viewed by the Dutch as especially cruel. It led to many Dutch people fleeing the Low Countries in order to avoid prosecution. The way Alva relentlessly pursued the Tenth Penny Tax without the approval of the states also damaged his relationship with the Dutch government and people and Alva soon gained a reputation of brutality and tyranny.

> ### Work together
>
> Work in pairs. One of you take the role of Alva and the other the Dutch nobles. Use the material in this chapter to attempt an explanation of the events from each perspective. What else would you need to know to do this better? Consider this in the light of the 'Recommended reading'.

2 Orange's failure

William of Orange fled to his lands in Germany before Alva arrived in the Netherlands. As one of the most vocal opponents of Philip and Margaret's policies, he realised that he would be a target of any retaliation the regime wished to take. Orange remained in Germany and used the time to negotiate with other German princes to raise money and an army. The Council of Troubles issued a sentence against Orange in March 1568. He was condemned as a traitor for his involvement in the Compromise and his lands and wealth that remained in the Netherlands were seized. His palace at Breda was taken by Alva and garrisoned, and its contents were removed and taken to Ghent. Alva's soldiers even kidnapped Orange's eldest son, Philip William, from the city of Louvain and took him to Spain, partly as a hostage and partly to be raised as a suitable Catholic heir to Orange's lands. Furthermore, Orange was furious to learn of the way that Egmont and Hoorn had been treated in their executions. News of the executions encouraged him to launch a revolt against Alva and Philip. This section examines the early stages of William of Orange's invasion. First, it considers the immense power and influence he wielded in the northern provinces before discussing the invasions of 1568. The victory won by the rebels at Heiligerlee are explored next. This section concludes with an examination of Alva's major triumph against the rebels at the Battle of Jemmingen in July 1568.

Note it down

Use a spider diagram (see page x) to explore Orange's power, influence and failure. In the middle of the 'spider' put the topic title 'Orange's failure'. Draw 'legs' for each of the subheadings and place your notes, appropriately subdivided, at the end of the legs. On the back, list anything that you want to find out more about – and consider the 'Recommended reading' as one way to do this.

Orange's power and influence in the northern provinces, 1568–72

Orange's cause faced failures and setbacks in 1568 but by the summer of 1572 the major towns in the northern provinces of Holland and Zeeland decided to support him in his revolt against Alva. This decision was not made instantly. There were several reasons that helped to persuade them:

- The invasions of 1572 and the contribution of the Sea Beggars.

- Orange was a very important person within the social and political elite of Holland. Most of his Dutch lands were located in the province of Holland and he held the prominent political position of Holland's **stadtholder**. He was also by far the wealthiest noble in the Netherlands.
- The people of these northern provinces were encouraged that Orange believed that the Netherlands should have a degree of religious **toleration**.
- They also supported Orange's belief that the Dutch should retain their traditional rights and privileges.
- Following the province's decision to support Orange in the revolt against Alva, Holland gradually became the centre of the revolt.

The invasions of 1568

Despite his exile in Germany, William of Orange was determined to rescue the Netherlands from the tyranny imposed by Alva and Philip. In 1568, Orange wrote and published a series of political writings which were translated into English and French in order to persuade the Protestants in those countries to support the Dutch (see Source A on page 342). In his treatises, Orange argued that Alva, like Granvelle before him, undermined traditional Dutch rights and privileges. Throughout all of his political writings, Orange claimed that he was being loyal to Philip II and rejected the claim that he was planning to place himself on Philip's throne. Instead, Orange repeatedly stressed the traditional rights the Dutch enjoyed, including the level of autonomy in politics, religion, and finance (see pages 314–15). He reminded them of the prosperity they had experienced in the past and of the right of the Dutch to defy any prince who offended their privileges. In effect, Orange's treatises justified an invasion of the Netherlands by the rebels and against Alva and the King of Spain.

In 1568, William of Orange launched invasions into the Netherlands. There were to be three invasions. Orange's brothers, Louis of Nassau and Adolf of Nassau, were to invade the Netherlands through the northern province of Friesland. Jean de Villers would lead an army into the southern provinces from France. French **Huguenots** would invade Artois. Orange himself was to remain in Cleves, in Germany, with a reserve force. This must have seemed like a good plan but in fact it was very difficult to co-ordinate the different rebel armies and made it easier for Alva's forces to defeat them.

Jean de Villers led an army across the River Meuse on 20 April 1568. By 25 April, his army was defeated and his soldiers either butchered or captured. This was a disaster, as not one town had declared for the rebels and Villers betrayed the entire campaign by surrendering the names of those gaining territory for their cause – they failed to capture any cities in Friesland despite this victory.

Disintegration of rebel forces and Alva's triumph

Following the victory at Heiligerlee, Louis of Nassau led his army on to another city in Friesland. William of Orange did not want Nassau to press the soldiers forward because of the military risk this posed, and instead encouraged Louis to retreat to the city of Delfzjil. Louis established a headquarters at Delfzjil on the River Eems and organised a fleet of ships to open up sea access to England. This was temporarily successful, and a Spanish attack on Delfzjil was repulsed on 15 July 1568 by the 'Sea Beggars' under Count Louis' command. Following this Nassau hoped to go on and capture the city of Groningen, but his soldiers were driven back in retreat by Spanish forces. This time, the Spanish army was much larger: they had 12,000 infantry men and 3,000 cavaliers while Louis of Nassau had 10,000 men and a cavalry of approximately 2,000 men.

The Spanish army was led by Alva himself. Alva forced Nassau's army out of Groningen, pushing them into the town of Jemmingen on 21 July 1568. The two armies skirmished for around three hours until finally Nassau's army advanced on the Spanish soldiers. The rebels were outgunned, and began to suffer heavy losses. The advance quickly turned into a retreat, and Nassau's soldiers turned back towards the River Ems and Alva's army drove the rebels into the river. Many rebels drowned and even Louis of Nassau had to abandon his armour so that he could swim across the Ems.

Consequences of the defeat at Jemmingen

The Battle of Jemmingen was a complete disaster for the rebel forces because their army was largely destroyed. With the death of 7,000 rebel soldiers Alva's army had proven its strength to the local Dutch people. The rebels had hoped that their victory at Heiligerlee would encourage ordinary Dutch people in the region to rebel and fight on their side. Instead, the invasions received little support from the populace. As a result of this, Orange was forced to reconsider his tactics. He realised that he and the rebels would have to rely on even more foreign support in order to achieve a successful military campaign. After the disastrous defeat at Jemmingen, Orange and Nassau were reunited and escaped to France, offering their military service to the Huguenots waging war against the French Crown. While there, they sought the advice of the Huguenot leader, Admiral Gaspard Coligny, and tried to improve their connections with other influential Protestants. They needed substantial aid if they were to face Alva's forces again with any success.

who financed the war to the men who interrogated him. The Huguenots fared no better in their invasion attempt. They invaded at St Valery but were defeated there by French royal troops on 18 July 1568. This only left the army led by Orange's brothers as they faced Spanish forces at Heiligerlee.

The rebels' victory at Heiligerlee

The rebels won their first battlefield victory at Heiligerlee in Friesland on 23 May 1568. Louis of Nassau led an army of 3,900 men while his brother Adolf commanded 200 cavaliers on horseback. Adolf's cavalry led the Spanish forces into an ambush near the monastery at Heiligerlee. The two sides were fairly evenly matched in terms of foot soldiers: the Friesland army had 3,200 soldiers but only 20 cavaliers. Despite this, the Spanish army lost between 1,500 and 2,000 men in the battle while the invading forces lost only 50 men, although one of those killed in the battle was Adolf of Nassau. As well as defeating the Spanish army the rebels captured seven cannons to add to their arsenal. The victory was an important one because it showed that the rebels could defeat the Spanish in battle, but it did not lead to them

Conclusion: Orange's failure

Alva relished his victory over the rebels at Jemmingen in July 1568, and melted down the bronze cannons he had captured from the rebels there. Out of this metal, he commissioned a statue of himself that was placed in his citadel at Antwerp (see Source B). The Dutch propaganda that had been published for years in response to the Tenth Penny Tax had pitted Alva against Orange. Armies supported by each man finally met on the battlefield in 1568 and Alva was the victor.

Work together

Using both of your notes, consider the question of Orange's strengths and weaknesses. Divide the work initially so that one of you covers strengths and the other covers weaknesses. Then come together to think about Orange's situation in 1572. Why did Alva win, and what more did Orange need before he could fight more effectively against the Spanish?

3 The role of the Sea Beggars

By the end of the summer of 1568, the rebels had lost large numbers of soldiers and were forced to retreat from the Netherlands. They had to use their contacts in other parts of Europe in order to find the support they needed to meet Alva on the battlefield. They were also able to harness support closer to home, however, and this section examines the role of a rather unlikely source of aid to the Dutch rebels: the Sea Beggars. In early 1572 Elizabeth I of England bowed to Spanish pressure and closed the ports to the Sea Beggars, forcing them to roam the seas. They turned this setback into an opportunity. In search of another safe haven, they captured Brill and Flushing in April 1572. They turned these victories into a bigger success when the provinces of Holland and Zeeland began to support the Sea Beggars and William of Orange. After this point the efforts of the Sea Beggars were transformed into a larger, if initially unexpected, revolt against Alva.

Source B The decapitation of Egmont and Hoorn in Brussels in 1568.

Who is portrayed in Source B? How did it encourage Orange to revolt?

Foreign monarchs and the Dutch Revolt

Why did monarchs like Charles IX and Elizabeth I want to help rebels like William of Orange and Louis of Nassau? There were several reasons that persuaded them that it was important to support the Dutch rebels:

- The monarchs generally wanted to ensure peace in the region at all costs.
- They also viewed Orange and Nassau as fellow princes who they should support.
- It helped the Dutch rebels that these foreign monarchs saw Philip II as a threat to peace in Europe. England, in particular, feared the presence of such a large Spanish (and therefore Catholic) military force near to the English coast. The English government was worried that the Spanish army would be used to attack Protestant England next.
- They wanted to maintain a commercial trading relationship with the Netherlands.
- Alva often intervened in the internal politics of neighbouring countries. He sent soldiers to fight for

the Roman Catholic cause in France and even started a trade war between Spain and England in 1568. Alva was disliked by neighbouring countries just as much as he was disliked in the Netherlands by the Dutch.

These factors meant that the more powerful ruling monarchs felt responsible for helping Orange defeat Philip because it would help their own defence and economic aims whilst also supporting a cause that they thought was just. It led to foreign monarchs like Elizabeth I providing support to the rebels. She provided a refuge for Dutch migrants fleeing the Low Countries during Alva's rule, and allowed the Sea Beggars to operate out of English ports from 1568-72.

The Sea Beggars

The term 'Beggars' was first applied to the rebels by an adviser to Margaret of Parma on the presentation of the Compromise (see page 324) in 1566. It was adopted by the rebels with pride. The Sea Beggars were the rebel naval forces. They were made up of Calvinist pirates, smugglers and rebels who had fled under the Council of Troubles. They were established by Louis of Nassau when he wanted a naval force to protect his supply ships. The Sea Beggars attacked ships of any nation, including a Spanish fleet in 1568. In the later 1560s William of Orange tried to mould the Sea Beggars into a proper fighting force against the Spanish. Their attacks on the Dutch coast were important in establishing rebel control of the northern provinces.

Louis of Nassau (1538–74)

Louis was the third son of William, Count of Nassau and was William of Orange's younger brother. He was important in encouraging the marriage between Orange and Anna of

Saxony. William appointed him as governor of the principality of Orange in 1569, a position of significant responsibility. He was involved in the Confederacy of Noblemen from 1566 and signed the Compromise in that year. He led one of the main invading armies in 1568 and escaped after the defeat at Jemmingen. His Calvinist beliefs provided him with important connections in the search for foreign aid, and he approached several countries with the hope of finding support for an invasion of the Netherlands. He used the lure of territory to try and make this happen. In one plan, he proposed splitting the Netherlands equally between Charles IX of France, Elizabeth I of England and the German Protestant princes, but this did not happen. Nassau fought in several more campaigns in the 1570s and is presumed to have died in 1574, lost in action after being wounded at the Battle of Mookerheyde in 1574.

Louis of Nassau, William of Orange and the Sea Beggars

Members of the Dutch elite were associated with the iconography of beggars thanks to the Compromise (see page 324). This iconography became important once again in 1572. In May 1568, Louis of Nassau searched for ships to protect the men and munitions he brought into the Netherlands. Some ships were hired, while others were supplied under contract by a local pirate, Jan Abels. A year later, in 1569, William of Orange hired more ships in England. By this point the Sea Beggars numbered around 1,200 men with maritime experience and they had a fleet of about 20 ships. They often acted like pirates but equally served as the rebels' navy. William of Orange even used his princely authority to give Calvinist **privateers** letters of marque. These letters enabled the Sea Beggars to attack Spanish ships without facing the charge of piracy by neutral countries. Privateering was an important way for the sailors to support themselves because Orange could not afford to pay them. The Sea Beggars created a blockade in the North Sea in order to hurt Spanish trade and commerce in the Netherlands. The only way they could ensure that Alva remained impoverished was to ensure that their fellow countrymen did not experience economic prosperity either. Many Dutch people disliked the Sea Beggars because of their rough ways and the economic blockades, but they liked Alva and his Spanish soldiers even less.

The closing of English ports to the Sea Beggars by Elizabeth I of England, 1572

Huge numbers of Dutch people had chosen exile in England and Germany rather than certain death at Alva's hands due to their religion or their involvement in the earlier stages of the revolt. Some of these became privateers. England was particularly convenient for ordinary Dutch migrants and for the Sea Beggars. This was because the Dutch already had their own established communities in English cities like London and Norwich. These communities had traded with English cities for generations because English wool had been a key commodity for Dutch clothiers. From 1568 the English government allowed the Sea Beggars to operate out of English ports. These privateers attacked Spanish ships bringing back gold from the New World, which strained already hostile relations with Spain. The Sea Beggars also attacked neutral merchant ships in the North Sea, bringing the stolen goods into England to sell them. Ambassadors from around the North Sea complained to Elizabeth I, arguing that she was giving safety to pirates who were

hurting trade around northern Europe. The merchants were especially upset that the Sea Beggars were attacking neutral ships. England was therefore pressured by allies in northern Europe and threatened by the Spanish. As a consequence, on 1 March 1572 Elizabeth demanded that the Sea Beggars leave all English ports.

The seizure of Brill and Flushing

Expelled from England, the Sea Beggars sailed up and down the North Sea. They had no goods to sell and were safer at sea than in port in the Netherlands because of the threat of capture by Spanish forces, but they needed a harbour in the Low Countries that could be used as a base for their ships. On 1 April 1572, a storm in the North Atlantic drove a fleet of the Sea Beggars to the coasts of Holland and Zeeland. Some of the ships landed at Brill, and when they reached land, they found the town was undefended. Spanish troops were busy putting down riots in Utrecht and most of the local men were away fishing. The Sea Beggars seized this opportunity and conquered the town in William of Orange's name, providing their first territorial victory. Under the leadership of William II de la Marck, Lord of Lumey, the Sea Beggars targeted other ports in Holland and Zeeland and, soon after, other towns in these provinces became loyal to the Sea Beggars.

Alva's impoverished army helped the Sea Beggars turn their seizure of Brill into a success. In early 1572, protection of the coasts became the responsibility of each province. The central government had been responsible for defending the coasts in the past, so Holland and Zeeland asked Alva for help in defending themselves from the Sea Beggars who were preying on merchant ships in order to cause economic damage to the Spanish. Alva responded that such defence was now their responsibility, and that he did not have the money to help them even if he were minded to.

Flushing

One of the towns that became loyal to the rebellion was Flushing. Flushing had hosted Spanish troops in the garrison in 1569 and 1571 but this experience had been extremely bitter. On 6 April 1572, the quartermasters of three Spanish infantry regiments arrived in the town to arrange lodgings for their soldiers. Alva had decided that Flushing would receive a new citadel for fighting the Sea Beggars but the people of Flushing were not pleased. They promised to be loyal to Philip but they also swore that no Spaniard should ever enter their city walls again because of the damage the last garrisons had caused, and the poor reputation of the Spanish soldiers. The city magistrates said that they would accept a citadel in their city but only on the condition that the soldiers stationed there were Dutch. On 8 April Hernando Pacheo, Alva's engineer, landed at Flushing. He carried with him building plans for a new citadel in the town as well as a commission to arrest the magistrates who were opposed to Spanish soldiers. He was furthermore charged with collecting the hated Tenth Penny Tax from the people of Flushing. The local residents were furious and hanged Pacheo. On 22 April, 14 Sea Beggar ships arrived in Flushing. Their resentment of their treatment by Alva and his men led Flushing to join the rebellion and allow the Sea Beggars to set up a base there. Flushing continued to claim loyalty to both Orange and the King of Spain even as they showed their contempt for Alva.

Flushing and Brill became important bases for the Sea Beggars. The unemployed fishermen and sailors from the region joined the rebels' cause in hopes of earning enough money for survival. The Sea Beggars were able to capture more towns along the coast from these two important bases. The men from Flushing even captured two of Alva's naval bases, Arnemuiden and Veere. Along with the towns, they were rewarded with an arsenal including gunpowder and several guns. The success they enjoyed in Holland brought the Sea Beggars other rewards as well. It meant that the English had more confidence in the revolt and they sent financial support. The French were also committed to sending soldiers to help the rebels in Holland and Zeeland. These allies were determined to help the rebels defeat the Spanish.

Development of a general revolt in the province of Holland

The Calvinist Sea Beggars were joined by a number of the populace who were tired of Alva's repression and harsh taxes. In April 1572 these rebels destroyed the part of Alva's citadel at Antwerp that had already been built. They also launched another round of iconoclasm, vandalising churches in Holland and Zeeland. The Sea Beggars were cruel to the local priests, mocking and even threatening to murder them (see Source C). They particularly persecuted Catholic priests because of the Catholicism of the Spanish King and the previous treatment of Calvinists by the Catholic hierarchy. They did not just attack Catholics, however, but any group that did not hold Calvinist beliefs. Their fight for religious toleration only extended to Calvinists, not other Protestant groups. Orange disapproved of such activities. Attacks on churches and priests made the revolt appear to be a religious matter, but Orange continued to argue that the revolt was a response to Philip's disregard of Dutch political rights and privileges. It certainly seems that Philip's policies, and Alva's execution of those policies, led to more and more

> **Source C** From the diary of Master Wouter Jacobsz, Prior of the monastery of Stein, on 4 September 1572. As a Catholic prior he was horrified by the actions against the Church and Catholic religion as well as the violence.
>
> God's temples are despoiled, the holy statues broken, whether God's servants, the priests, religious and upright Catholics, are mocked, driven forth, plundered and miserably murdered … the worship of God and the most holy sacraments are hindered, blasphemed and scandalously abused, being trodden underfoot and brought to nought as they please … They affirm their loyalty to the king, yet dishonour and contradict his edicts. They pretend to be captains and stadtholders of the king, yet they cause havoc throughout the King's realm with their looting, murdering and burning. They wish to restore the ancient privileges and liberties of the province, yet they perpetrate a worse slavery and tyranny than ever before. These men are led to commit such reckless acts to protect their commerce, to rid themselves of the Spaniards and to evade the Tenth Penny. They abandon God for such reasons; they value such matters more highly than the excellent sacraments. They would rather suffer this than receive the assistance of the king's soldiers against robbers and murderers. And what has happened? God has abandoned us.
>
> According to Source C what was the author's opinion on the actions of the rebels? On what does he blame their actions? What leads him to this opinion?

towns in Holland joining the revolt – for political reasons rather than just because of religion.

Reasons for increased support for the Dutch Revolt

Northern Europe had experienced a particularly harsh winter. The harvests in eastern Europe had failed and the trade war between Spain and England had harmed Dutch merchants. Cloth-makers in the Low Countries relied on English wool which no longer reached them. The trade war meant that most people who normally worked in the textile industry were unemployed. Economic conditions around the Netherlands were therefore very bleak in the summer of 1572, leading to desperation. Many people blamed the Spanish and the policies of the King for the problems, bringing more support for the rebels.

William of Orange also used persuasion to gain support of those who were reluctant to support the revolt. The people of Holland and Zeeland were generally Roman Catholic in their faith but the Sea Beggars were committed to Calvinist beliefs. Many inhabitants of the towns and cities in these provinces were afraid of what the privateers might do to them if they did not support the rebellion, but Orange did not want this to be the only reason they joined the rebellion. On 14 April, he printed a protestation against the Spanish. The language he used addressed the merchants and craftsmen, encouraging them to consider joining the rebellion. Orange argued that it was the only way to end Spanish oppression and to restore peace and traditional privileges. This appealed to the economic priorities of the merchants but also called out to their sense of pride in Dutch traditions and customs.

Orange's stress on restoring traditional rights and privileges was especially important in Holland and Zeeland. Only the cities of Enkhuizen and Vlissingen joined Orange's revolt out of a spontaneous rebellion. Most towns and cities joined Orange's cause because of their hatred of the way the Spanish had treated the Netherlands. The rebels were aided when Alva decided to withdraw all Spanish soldiers from Holland on 15 June to take control of a crisis that emerged in the southern provinces. By the end of July, most of Holland and Zeeland were fully in support of Orange and his rebels. On 19 July, representatives from the cities gathered together at Dordrecht in the province of Holland and proclaimed that William of Orange was their true stadtholder. This affirmed their support for Orange and denied that those appointed by Philip were legitimately in charge. Only the cities of Amsterdam and Delft were still loyal to Philip and Alva.

Conclusion: The role of the Sea Beggars

The Sea Beggars were crucial to the later success of the Dutch rebels. William of Orange and his supporters had failed to find additional aid from the Dutch populace when they initially invaded the Netherlands in 1568. When Philip II pressured Elizabeth I to force Dutch privateers out of England's ports in 1572, the Dutch appeared to lose a major source of aid but this action surprisingly led to fortune. When the Sea Beggars landed in the northern provinces of Holland and Zeeland in April 1572, their actions led to a more general rebellion. William of Orange took this opportunity to appeal to the people of Holland, offering a chance to protect the traditional customs and privileges of the Netherlands against the Spanish, who had lost much support with their taxes and the behaviour of their soldiers.

Work together

Work together to produce a profile of the Sea Beggars that will help you in your revision. It should include a definition of who the Sea Beggars were and what their motivations were. A summary of their actions and their role in the Dutch Revolt should also figure.

4 Orange's triumph

Orange gathered an invasion force supported by foreign allies and the Sea Beggars. The intention was to spread the Dutch Revolt beyond its heartlands of Holland and Zeeland. Spain had many enemies, and the authoritarian approach of Philip had not improved this. Motivated by religion and hatred of Alva's rule, the invasion of 1572 was to prove a success. Philip's abandonment of the Tenth Penny Tax won some people back to his side, but not enough and the rebels cemented their control over Holland and Zeeland. After the meeting at Dordrecht Orange had established a stable government. As a consequence, Alva's failure to achieve the aims of his master led to his removal and return to Spain.

Note it down

This section includes many important dates, so make sure that you keep adding them to your annotated timeline alongside short notes on the significance of the events. You should also use the 1:2 method here (see page x) to make more detailed notes on William of Orange's triumph from April 1572 to November 1573.

The invasion of 1572

William of Orange had used the Calvinist Sea Beggars in order to win allegiance to his rebellion. From April 1572, the northern provinces of Holland and Zeeland were in rebellion against Alva and Philip (See Figure 1 on page 348). While the northern provinces revolted, Orange's brother Louis of Nassau led an invasion in the south, hoping to add to the rebels' territory and expand the size of the rebellion against the Spanish.

The French Huguenots provided the military forces the Dutch needed to launch and sustain their invasion. Nassau led his invasion through the province of Hainault, near the border with France and, on 23 May, captured the city of Mons with about 1,500 soldiers. The aid the rebels received from the French Huguenots was essential but they were not the only Protestants who offered help to the Dutch. German princes had provided Orange with an army of as many as 14,000 soldiers and 3,000 cavalry. As Nassau led an invasion from Hainault another Dutch noble, the Count van den Berg, led another invasion into the central provinces. Van den Berg entered the Netherlands from German territories and the rebels therefore also received a large amount of support from their German counterparts. With this help, van den Berg was able to capture the city of Zutphen on 10 June 1572. War now raged in the northern provinces, the central provinces and the southern provinces.

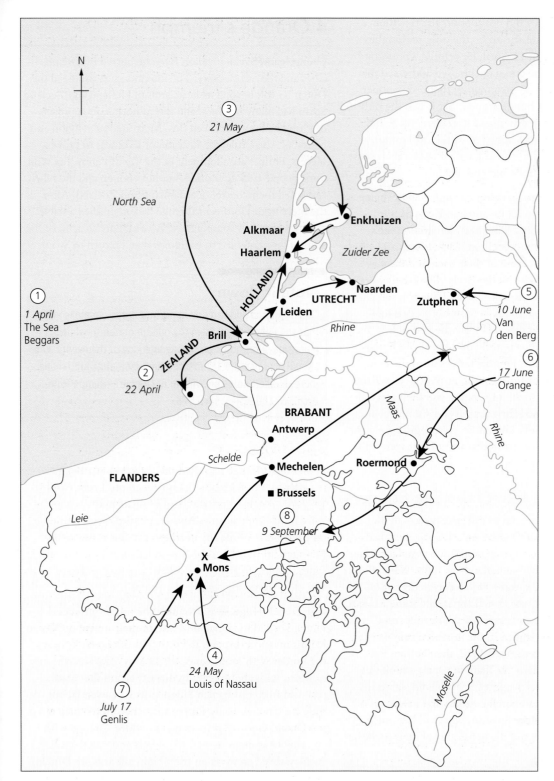

N

1 April
The Sea
Beggars ①

North Sea

③ 21 May

Alkmaar

Haarlem

Enkhuizen

Zuider Zee

HOLLAND

Naarden

UTRECHT

Leiden

Zutphen

⑤ 10 June
Van
den Berg

Brill

Rhine

② 22 April

ZEALAND

⑥ 17 June
Orange

Maas

BRABANT

Antwerp

Rhine

Schelde

FLANDERS

Mechelen

Roermond

Leie

■ Brussels

⑧ 9 September

X
X Mons

④ 24 May
Louis of Nassau

⑦ July 17
Genlis

Moselle

▲ Figure 1: The 1572 invasions

The siege of Mons: a setback for the rebels

The Dutch rebels led an invasion from within France, using Huguenot support to capture the city of Mons on 23 May 1572. This was a huge initial success. The French captain Montgomery sent an additional 4,500 soldiers to Mons but Nassau and Montgomery soon found themselves under siege from Alva and his army as they waited for more French reinforcements. Unfortunately for the rebels, the French Wars of Religion had taken a deadly and violent turn that summer. French Protestants had just been subject to violence in the brutal **Saint Bartholomew's Day Massacre** on 24 August. The Huguenot leader Admiral Coligny had been murdered in the massacre which meant that the French Huguenot forces were unable to relieve the siege of Mons.

By autumn, things had taken a turn for the worse for Louis of Nassau at Mons. Alva's army matched his own in strength and size but Alva's son, Fadrique Alvarez de Toldeo, arrived with an army of 16,000 additional soldiers on 23 June. Toledo laid siege to the city and when reinforcements from France, led by Adrien de Hangest, approached the city they were driven back by the Spanish. Over 2,000 of his soldiers were killed, and

more were captured in the following days. Orange, too, led an army to Mons. On the night of 11 September 1572, the Spanish raided Orange's army. They killed around 600 soldiers, destroyed a number of Orange's supplies and stole some of their weapons. The raid forced the rebel army to retreat to a nearby town and, from there, they returned to the loyal northern provinces. Meanwhile, the siege of Mons continued. Nassau was now isolated from his reinforcements and, with his situation looking bleak, Nassau was forced to surrender the city to Alva's forces on 19 September. This was a significant defeat because it meant that the rebels' goal of expanding the revolt into the southern and central Netherlands had ultimately failed.

Establishing control over Holland and Zeeland

The 1572 rebel invasions into the southern and central Netherlands were initially successful. Ultimately, however, the rebels failed to sustain their early successes because they could not secure the continued support they needed to defeat Alva once and for all. The general populations of these areas did not rise to offer aid to the rebels. The loss of additional help from the French Huguenots was also a serious setback in the rebels' military campaign. The Spanish army proved to be too large and too powerful for them to overcome without any help. Philip II decided in June 1572 that he would no longer pursue the Tenth Penny Tax, perhaps in the belief that this policy reversal would help him win support from the Dutch people. If so, he was correct in the case of much of the Netherlands. The areas that initially revolted against Philip were soon under the control of Alva once again.

In the midst of these setbacks, however, the northern provinces of Holland and Zeeland were the exception. They provided sustained support and a base for the rebels. The people believed Alva was responsible for their troubles. They blamed him for the Sea Beggars' blockade and their loss of business, despised his tax policies and hated the behaviour of the Spanish soldiers. The soldiers were disorderly, got drunk, caused trouble and sometimes mutinied. When mutinying they looted, raped and caused great damage.

The meeting in Dordrecht

The meeting in Dordrecht was as major step in ensuring the stability and success of the rebellion in the northern provinces. In July 1572, Dordrecht's town council invited the rebel cities and towns to send representatives to a meeting of the provincial states of Holland. It would be an important step in creating unification among the rebels.

The representatives gathered on 19 July and were met by William of Orange's representative, Philip Marnix of Saint Aldegonde. Marnix asked that the provincial states recognise Orange as their rightful stadtholder. He encouraged them to fight for the King and to swear not to make peace with Alva or the King without Orange's consent. He asked the provincial states of Holland to pay for the sailors and soldiers fighting against Alva and for the representatives to ensure the freedom of religious worship within the provinces. The provincial states agreed to all these points.

Consequences of the meeting at Dordrecht

William of Orange was able to establish a stable government thanks to the meeting at Dordrecht. After this meeting, he was able to act more like a governor than a military commander. He appointed a committee to find and copy the charters outlining the local privileges. He relied on the advice of the provincial states as he chose new members to serve on their courts and worked together with the estates to find a way to finance their armies and navies. It is important to note that Orange did everything in the King's name. He saw himself as loyally protecting Holland and Zeeland as Philip's representative. Orange's aim, he argued time and again, was to restore and protect the provinces' rights and privileges.

The provincial states of Holland wrote to the States General near the end of 1573 arguing for unity amongst the 17 provinces. They depicted Alva and his supporters as a common enemy that all the Dutch needed to band together to remove. The estates of Holland and Zeeland wrote another document together which was sent to Philip II. The second document reminded the King of his responsibility to uphold the traditional rights and privileges of his Dutch people. Philip was still the King, even if Holland and Zeeland were actively rebelling against his policies.

Alva's failure to reconquer the northern provinces

Alva attempted to reconquer Holland and Zeeland for Philip since it was simply unacceptable for two provinces to leave the Spanish Empire. Orange had taken the city of Mechelen, though the people living there were largely Roman Catholic. Mechelen was an important city in the Netherlands and so Alva sent his son, Toledo, to lead an army into the city to re-take it for the Spanish on 2 October 1572. The people greeted them with chanting and psalms. They were happy to see the army representing the Roman Catholic powers, but Toledo

decided to make Mechelen an example and besieged the city for three days.

The Spanish army also besieged Zutphen (17 November 1572) and Naarden (1 December 1572). In Zutphen, the Spanish killed over 500 people. They cut holes into the frozen River Ijssel, forcing people to drown in the extremely cold river. The city's leading officials were massacred. These actions were repeated in Naarden and other places. In the end, the Spanish soldiers were successful in securing the city but the actions taken by Spanish leaders like Alva did much to tarnish the reputation of the Spanish soldiers and their leaders. They may have won some northern cities but they were losing the war for popular support. Instead of forcing the rebelling people into submission, they became more determined than ever to drive the Spanish armies out of their lands and to restore their rights and privileges. An example of this can be seen in the Siege of Alkmaar. Toledo and an army besieged the city between 21 August and 8 October 1573. The people used boiling tar and burning tree branches to defend their city from the Spanish, and were ultimately victorious.

Alva failed to stop the war in the Netherlands because he created a greater divide between those loyal to the King and the rebels. His brutal tactics, even against loyal Catholic subjects, drove people to the side of Orange and the rebels which made it impossible for Alva to recapture the northern provinces. The fighting was fierce and Alva was also made the subject of an increasingly hostile propaganda campaign which ridiculed him as a weak yet merciless tyrant.

Philip finally grew tired of Alva's failures and, on 29 November 1573, Don Luis de Requesens took over Alva's role as Governor-General of the Netherlands in Brussels. Even as he took up his new role, Philip was uncertain if he wanted Requesens to follow Alva's example or to make concessions to the Dutch people. Alva left for Madrid in December but was not forgotten by the Dutch and continued to be an important symbol of Spanish tyranny and repression as the revolt continued.

Conclusion: Orange's triumph

Victories for the rebel armies, assisted by the Sea Beggars' successes on the waters, helped Orange win support from foreign monarchs. The help they received from the French Huguenots was critical to their battlefield success in the early 1570s. The victories also persuaded Philip to believe that he needed to win popular political support and as a result he suspended the Tenth Penny Tax in the summer of 1572. This plan to completely defuse the revolt failed, although some of the provinces returned to Spanish control. Holland and Zeeland became the centre of the rebellion. They argued that they were loyal to Philip as their King, but they refused to submit to Spanish authority until their traditional rights and privileges were restored. Instead, they began to set up a more stable rebel government which posed a more permanent threat to Spanish control. When Alva was unable to recapture these two important provinces, Philip made him return to Spain.

Chapter summary

- Alva replaced Margaret of Parma in September 1567.
- Alva had two main objectives: to re-establish Spanish control in the Netherlands, and to ensure the Dutch all practised the Roman Catholic faith.
- The Dutch people were angered by the executions of Egmont and Hoorn in June 1568.
- Alva's Council of Troubles was unpopular because it was seen as a very harsh institution.
- The Tenth Penny Tax was extremely unpopular. One reason for this unpopularity was that Alva imposed it without the consent of the provincial states. This tax would become a symbol of Spanish tyranny.

- The initial stages of the Dutch Revolt were very difficult for the rebels as they were matched with Alva's large army and military expertise.
- The Sea Beggars were the rebels' informal and talented navy, and helped them to win many important battles.
- The rebels received crucial military and financial support from Europe's royalty, including Elizabeth I of England, Charles IX of France and a number of German Protestant princes.
- The provinces of Holland and Zeeland were the stronghold of the rebellion against the Spanish forces. Throughout this stage of the rebellion, however, these provinces proclaimed loyalty to Philip II as their lawful king.

Recommended reading

H.G. Koenigsberger, *Monarchies, States Generals and Parliaments: The Netherlands in the Fifteenth and Sixteenth Centuries* (Cambridge University Press, 2007), Chapter 11.

Koenigsberger provides a clear and accessible explanation of the transformations in government in this era. Chapter 11 explains why the people of Holland and Zeeland felt they needed to continue the rebellion. It is about the politics that lay behind the events of this stage of the Dutch Revolt.

Geoffrey Parker, *The Dutch Revolt* (Viking, 1977), Chapter 3.

Parker has written extensively on the Dutch Revolt and this book provides one of the best accounts of it. Chapter 3 is useful because it provides a detailed explanation of the events of the period and how these events affected the opinions of the rebels.

Alva's rule

- Alva was sent by Philip II to restore order and punish heretics and rebels
- The Council of Troubles was used to prosecute rebels and heretics
- Alva became Governor-General after Margaret resigned
- Alva attempted to ensure that Roman Catholicism was the only acceptable religion
- His rule had a reputation for brutality and tyranny
- Thousands of non-Catholics were executed and many fled the country to escape punishment
- Egmont and Hoorn were executed in 1568
- Alva was also tasked with raising taxes and collected taxes without the approval of the States General

Orange's failure

- William of Orange fled Germany before Alva's arrival to raise money and an army
- Orange's writings argued that Alva's actions undermined traditional rights and privileges
- In 1588 Orange launched three invasions into the Netherlands
- The rebels were victorious at Heiligerlee but suffered heavy defeat at Jemmingen

ALVA AND ORANGE, 1567–73

Orange's triumph

- 1572 invasions – war extended to the northern provinces, central provinces and southern provinces
- Rebel invasions into southern and central Netherlands were initially successful
- Holland and Zeeland became the centre of the rebellion
- The Dordrecht meeting in 1572 was an important step in creating unification among the rebels. William of Orange was recognised as the official leader of the revolt
- Alva failed to reconquer the northern provinces.
- In 1573 Don Luis de Requesens took over Alva's role as Governor-General

The Sea Beggars

- The Sea Beggars were rebel naval forces, with around 1,200 men and a fleet of approximately 200 ships
- They were used by Orange to win allegiance to his rebellion
- The Sea Beggars created a blockade in the North Sea
- Queen Elizabeth I ousted the Sea Beggars from the English ports in 1572
- The towns of Flushing and Brill became important bases for the Sea Beggars
- The Sea Beggars found support for Orange and his cause in Holland and Zeeland
- The Sea Beggars were Calvinists and attacked non-Calvinist religious groups. Orange disapproved of this

▲ Summary diagram: Alva and Orange, 1567–73

Section A: Essay technique

Structuring an essay and writing introductions

Well-structured essays are likely to receive higher marks than essays in which the structure is unclear. The structure of your essay should reflect the nature of the task that you are performing. It should, therefore, help you evaluate how far the two sources together are useful to a historian who is investigating a specific topic.

Macro structure

The overall structure of your essay should include:

- an introduction, which focuses on the question and sets out the essence of your answer
- a conclusion that summarises your essay in order to weigh up the extent to which the evidence of the sources is useful, and reaches an overall judgement
- a main body presenting a detailed evaluation of the evidence of the sources.

TIP: Remember, the question asks you to consider the sources *together*. Therefore, a structure which analyses Source 1, and then moves on to Source 2 is unlikely to do well. It would be better to structure your essay in a way that allows you to deal with the sources together.

Micro structure

Each paragraph should set out an analysis of the usefulness of the evidence of the two sources. Therefore, you need to discuss both sources in every paragraph.

TIP: One way of doing this is to make sure that you discuss both sources in almost every sentence.

For example, imagine you are answering the following question:

> **How far could the historian make use of Sources 1 and 2 (page 354) together to investigate the conflicting attitudes to Calvinism following the Iconoclastic Fury of 1566?**

Source 1 An extract from one of the 'Segovia Woods' letters of Philip II to his half-sister and regent, Margaret of Parma, of 31 December 1566. In the letter Philip summarises the situation in 1566 as he sees it and gives instructions to Margaret on how to proceed in relation to the Calvinists.

I am certain, Madame my dear sister, that you can easily imagine the great sorrow this very important matter causes me. What is at stake is on the one hand the respect for our holy Catholic faith which I have always had at heart and furthered with the zeal and in accordance with the obligation I have to maintain it; on the other hand I fear that great difficulties and trouble might come to so many of the honest vassals and subjects whom I have in the Low Countries: I cannot forget the natural affection I have always had and still have for them. In truth I cannot understand how this great evil originated and why it has increased so much in a short time. Since my departure from there, I have not heard of any cruel execution or rigorous prosecution having been undertaken on the strength of the inquisition or edicts, which might account for these difficulties ... The heretics and sectarians who as they daily give to understand in the booklets they distribute, demand absolute religious liberty, will be just as little satisfied as the confederates who, it seems from their petition, have a different end in view and desire that an entirely new edict should be framed on the advice of the States General ... for honest people it is unnecessary to make such or any other ordinance ... It is hoped that the confederation may be broken in this way and those gentlemen to be enabled to deal firmly with the evil-minded.

Source 2 An extract from a pamphlet of 1567 entitled *A true narrative and apology of what has happened in the Netherlands in the matter of religion in the year 1566. By those who profess the reformed religion in that country.* It was written by Philip Marnix, the younger brother of John Marnix of Tholouse, and aims to give a Calvinist view on the events of 1566.

The final point to be considered is the image-breaking, for which the adherents of the new religion are more severely reproached than for anything else. This is interpreted as an act of public violence and as a seditious act clearly intended to disrupt all political order. In short, some think this fact alone is of such a nature that only the ruin and extermination of the greater part of the subjects can represent sufficient satisfaction for His Majesty ... even if breaking and cutting images is the most enormous and capital crime to be committed, yet they do not know whom to blame for it. It is still uncertain who the persons are who did it so promptly and it is still more uncertain who advised them to do it. To accuse the ministers ... or assemblies of those who adhere to the reformed religion, would be shameless, for no one has ever succeeded in extorting a confession from the men executed for this crime, in spite of the torments and sufferings inflicted upon them ... They [the Calvinists] had unanimously decided to send deputies to Brussels to beg Her Highness provisionally to grant them some churches or other public places in which to practise their religion, in order to avoid disturbances and riots. They had great hopes of obtaining this because every one could see that it was the only way to keep the people quiet and tranquil. Would they not damage their cause and fall out of favour with Her Highness, if at the same time they ventured to perform a deed so prejudicial and contrary to their request? Thus it is obvious that they were never of that opinion and intention. I concede that among the image breakers there were people who professed to be of the religion, but I also say that there were as many others who did not make and never made that profession ... There are, however, strong suspicions and clear indications that it was the priests who started this as a device to set the magistrates against those of the religion.

Here are three examples of introductions that could answer this question:

Answer 1

> Source 1 says that Calvinism and the actions of Calvinists are a 'great evil' and describes them as 'heretics and sectarians' who 'demand absolute religious liberty'. This means that Philip II thinks the Calvinists are making extreme demands. He also says that the edicts they were responding to were not new or extreme. It was written by Philip II who was the King of Spain. Source 2 is a pamphlet by Philip Marnix who was a Calvinist. It says that the Calvinists can't be blamed for the image-breaking and just wanted to secure churches to worship in. The sources disagree. The pamphlet was written in 1567, a year after the Iconoclastic Fury.

Answer 2

> Source 1 is useful to a historian because it sets out Philip II's view of the actions and aims of the Calvinists. Source 2 is also useful because it gives the Calvinist view of events.

Answer 3

> Both Sources 1 and 2 are useful to a historian investigating the conflicting attitudes to Calvinism following the Iconoclastic Fury of 1566. Together the sources give an impression of the misunderstandings and suspicions of both sides of the debate. Neither source is wholly unproblematic for the historian to use. Source 1 gives Philip's view but not the view of his regent who was dealing with the problem and was more likely to have an up-to-date view, while source 2 is a propaganda pamphlet intended to persuade its audience of the righteousness of the Calvinists' grievances.

Activity: Analyse the introduction

Having read the three introductions, in pairs consider the following questions:

1 What skills do the different introductions demonstrate?
2 Which introduction focuses most clearly on the question?
3 Which introduction integrates Source 1 and Source 2 most effectively?
4 How could you improve the best of the three introductions?
5 What can you learn from the three samples?

Activity: AS-style questions

1 Why is Source 1 (page 353) valuable to the historian for an enquiry into Philip II's attitude to religion in the Netherlands?
2 How much weight do you give the evidence of Source 2 for an enquiry into the actions of the Calvinists during the Iconoclastic Fury of 1566?

Selecting information

Another skill vital for success in Section A is that of selecting the right information from the sources. So what is the 'right' information?

- Information that is relevant to the question.
- Information that illustrates the main point of the source.
- Information that illustrates the points that you want to make.

In addition to the source material, the exam paper also contains a short description of the source's provenance printed immediately above the source. Selecting the important material from the provenance will also help you do well. You could select information that helps you to evaluate the evidence:

- Information that would help explain the motives of the writer.
- Information that helps explain the purpose of the document.
- Information that helps contextualise the source (see pages 376–78).

TIP: Don't just copy information from the provenance, make sure you use the information to help weigh up the evidence that the source presents.

Source 3 From *The prince of Orange's warning to the inhabitants and subjects of the Netherlands, 1 September 1568*, a propaganda pamphlet distributed on the eve of Orange's 1568 invasion, calling for the Dutch to resist the Spanish attempts to ignore their traditional privileges. He wrote of the repressive anti-Protestant policies of Granvelle before turning his attention to Alva's arrival.

> We see nowadays with great heart-ache, and it is to be feared that if God does not help us ... we may see on an even larger scale, how greatly and grievously all the afore-mentioned innovations, proposals, oppressions, inquisitions, persecutions, murders, seizures, executions and tyrannies have increase and multiplied, and how totally inhuman they have become since the duke (in the name of the king and shielding himself with the king's authority) arrived here with his Spanish soldiers. And we see how these countries have fallen from the greatest prosperity into the utmost misery, how the worthy inhabitants who enjoyed freedom in former times have been brought into unbearable slavery and how piteously the privileges and rights of the country together with the religion of God are lying there oppressed and destroyed.

Imagine you are answering the following question and then carry out the activity on page 356:

> **How far could the historian make use of Sources 3 and 4 to investigate reactions to Alva's Spanish soldiers in the Netherlands from 1567?**

You need think about the focus of the question – here the question is asking you about what these two sources can tell us, as historians, about the differing reactions to the arrival of the Spanish soldiers under Alva in 1567.

Remember the historical context: Alva had been sent from Spain to deal firmly with the situation in the Netherlands, using the soldiers to enforce his rule. In the process of this Margaret of Parma resigned and many were imprisoned.

Source 4 A letter from Thomas Dutton of 7 September 1567. Dutton was an English merchant based in Antwerp. He was writing to Sir Thomas Gresham, an English merchant and financier who had been the English ambassador to Margaret of Parma's court prior to the troubles of 1566, about the situation in Antwerp at that time.

> The Duke of Alva is seated at Brussels and sits every day in council with the other lords. There is Great complaint upon the Spanish soldiers of their horrible living & unhonest dealing in all places where they are. But now there is such sharp orders taken for them that wheresoever they offend they shall suffer according to the Laws of this country and there is already 3 of them hanged at Easter day at Ghent and many of them in prison who shall suffer what their fellows are ... all this week in Antwerp there has been much talk of the King's coming ... here honest & wise men in Antwerp be of the opinion that the King will not come this year ... At this present time Antwerp is in good rest & quietness and the people here are agreeable to the soldiers. I hear no complaint of them and contrarily I do hear out of all places great wonder and complaint of the Spaniards.

Activity: AS-style questions

1 Why is Source 3 valuable to the historian for an enquiry into Dutch responses to the arrival of the Spanish soldiers in 1567?
2 How much weight do you give the evidence of Source 4 for an enquiry into the resolution of Dutch complaints about Spanish soldiers in 1567?

Read the question on page 355 and then the sources.

1 Make a bullet-point list of the information that you would select from Sources 3 and 4 to answer the question.

2 Now turn to page 415 and have a look at an example of the information that you could have selected for Source 4.

3 Check your notes – did you select the same kind of information for Source 4? Look back at the criteria for the successful selection of information. The selected information should all be relevant to the question, not merely giving facts of an event or date, and provide information that would help a historian investigating this issue.

4 Now read over your own notes again. Add anything into your notes on Source 4 that you might have missed, and check that your examination of Source 3 was as thorough. Add any new information you find to your notes.

5 Having read Source 3, and selected pieces of information to use in your answer, consider the following questions with your partner:

a) Did you both select the same information for the source? If not, whose selections were:
   i) most relevant to the question?
   ii) most characteristic of the whole source?

b) Did either of you select any information from the provenance?

c) Did you both select the same information from the provenance? If not, whose selections were:
   i) most relevant to the question?
   ii) most helpful to a historian evaluating the information contained in the source?

d) Did you miss anything?

e) What can you learn from this task?

Having discussed these questions make a bullet-point list of three things that you can do to make sure you answer Section A questions effectively. Review the list with your partner.

Making inferences

Making inferences from sources is one way to demonstrate your understanding of the source and of the period. An inference is a deduction or conclusion that comes from reading between the lines of a source – it's not about what lies on the surface but what's hinted at below. It isn't wild speculation but a conclusion that is drawn from reasoning or evidence. A detailed knowledge of the period is vital to making inferences.

Imagine you are answering the following question:

> How far could the historian make use of Sources 5 and 6 (page 358) to investigate the fears of the Dutch population during Alva's rule?

There is a lot of information in Source 5 which is purely on the surface. But beyond that, you can use your own knowledge, to draw out more complex and insightful conclusions as the annotations on page 357 show.

Source 5 An extract from an account of the disorder at Gouda, a town in Holland, from 10/11 April 1572. It is written by the magistrates of Gouda to Bossu, Philip II's appointee as stadtholder. In it the magistrates tell of the causes of the violence and their actions to restore order.

Rumours had spread throughout the ordinary people of the town.

Certain rumours (to our deep regret) arose and spread through our town among the commonalty around midday. According to these the town of Rotterdam had been seized by troops of His Majesty; there was a great cry that all the burghers of the said town had been miserably massacred by the said soldiers, including the women and children, that people waded in blood up to their ankles and that the heads of children had been thrown over the walls. These reports were spread by some who claimed to have got over the walls and so escaped. These also alleged and spread stories that the soldiers were still continuing with their butchery. This caused a tumult (may God forgive it) to our great dismay among the rabble in our town. Directly after noon on the said day these began to assemble without arms around the townhall of the said town. They let it be known that they would speak with the burgomasters, as they said, because they had understood that some soldiers had also entered the castle of the same town. Some of the stout burghers ... seeing that the crowd was growing and increasing, and being afraid of further troubles, warned the burgomasters of the said town about this. These had gathered in the house of one of the burgomasters to discuss town business and they hastened to the market place around the townhall, where they found the said mob gathered. The burgomasters asked why they had assembled there in such large numbers and the nature of their petition. These replied that they had heard that soldiers had entered the castle and that the town might in this way be betrayed and that a massacre like that which had taken place in Rotterdam, would happen. This they repeated and related, shouting and clamouring, as we have said, and they wanted the burgomasters to carry out an investigation.

The people involved in the violence wanted to speak to the town's governors because they had heard that some soldiers had been allowed into the town's castle.

They were worried that, because the soldiers had been allowed into the castle, it would be easier for them to attack the town and commit a massacre like in Rotterdam.

They kept repeating this fear, shouting and making a lot of noise. They wanted the town's governors to investigate the situation.

Below is an example of how you could develop the inferences annotated around Source 5 into a paragraph in answer to the question on page 356:

The people's fears about the Spanish soldiery (Source 5) were prompted by rumours about a massacre in Rotterdam. The rumours were that the inhabitants of the town had been massacred, and graphic accounts of violence circulated. Their fears were that such a massacre would happen in Gouda too because soldiers had been seen being admitted to the castle. They demanded that their traditional governors stand up to the Spanish soldiers and investigate the situation. The people feared the violence for which Alva's Spanish soldiers had a long-established reputation, and it is significant that they turned to the town's Dutch government to allay their fears. It demonstrates how fear of Spanish violence caused violence from the people, as well as creating increasingly assertive traditional governments.

Source 6 An extract from an address of the states of Holland to the States General, 12 September 1573. Here the states of Holland urge a united front and strong resistance to Alva's rule, warning of the potential consequences of not doing so.

If things remain as they are now and the grim war continues, business will be ruined, sea-borne trade will be stopped, industry will have to close down. As a result the entire country will become so impoverished and disorderly that famine and dearth will inevitably follow and then we can expect revolts and rebellions, severe diseases and plagues, which will completely destroy the country. Furthermore the provinces of Holland and Zeeland and all surrounding countries will be overrun meanwhile by soldiers and completely ruined. Because of this people in Brabant and Flanders, provinces that have also been squeezed by the troopers and soldiers, will no longer be able to get any butter or cheese or other staple food or salt and will necessarily fall into utter distress and misery. As an aftermath of the domestic war all kinds of plunder and robbery will be committed ... if God gives us victory over our enemies, this will be accompanied by frightful massacres of innumerable good inhabitants used by the duke of Alva for his purposes, for as long as he can get money and men, he will certainly not stop trying to extirpate and ruin us completely. So that it will not be possible to overthrow him without horrible bloodshed.

Work together

Having completed the activity 'Inferences', consider the following questions with your partner:

1 Did you both make the same inferences from Source 6?
2 If you differed, look at the source again, discuss your points of view and try and work out which inference is more likely to be correct.
3 How can the inferences that you have made help you to answer the question?

Having discussed these questions, make a bullet-point list of three things that you can do to make sure you use inferences effectively in Section A questions. Review the list with your partner.

Activity: AS-style questions

1 Why is Source 5 (page 357) valuable to the historian for an enquiry into the causes of the violence at Gouda in 1572?
2 How much weight do you give the evidence of Source 6 for an enquiry into the extent of Dutch fears regarding the consequences of a Spanish victory?

Activity: Inferences

Having read the question and example above you can now practise making inferences from Source 6. Remember:

● your inferences should help you answer the question
● inferences should be informed by your contextual knowledge of the period.

Answer the following questions:

1 The states of Holland wrote to the States General on 12 September 1573. From your knowledge of the period and the evidence of Source 6, what prompted them to write to the States General?
2 The states of Holland refer to any success against their enemies bringing 'frightful massacres of innumerable good inhabitants' by Alva. What does this imply about Alva's behaviour?
3 Compare Sources 5 and 6. Together, what do they imply about the fears of the Dutch population in this period?

Section B: Essay technique

Detail and analysis

Paper 2 Section B questions, like Paper 1 Sections A and B questions, need to be detailed and analytical. You may have already read the advice on how to write detailed and analytical essays for Paper 1 (see pages 32 and 64). Now is a chance to practise these skills in the context of the revolt of the Netherlands.

Activity: Detail and analysis

Imagine you are answering the following question:

How significant was William of Orange in the development of the Dutch Revolt from 1563 to 1584?

1 Identify the kind of question (see pages 335–36).
2 Make an appropriate plan: write down the main points of your three or four paragraphs.
3 Next to each of the points add three supporting details – you could use a different colour if you have one.
4 Write one analytical sentence to conclude each paragraph.

Question practice

1 How accurate is it to say that the Sea Beggars were the most important reason for the spread of the Dutch Revolt in 1572? **AS**
2 How far can the continuation and spread of the Dutch Revolt be blamed on Philip II's appointment of the Duke of Alva in 1566?
3 How successful was William of Orange in the period 1566 to 1573? **AS**
4 How significant was the support of the Huguenots in the early successes of the 1572 invasions? **AS**

Working together

Having finished the activity 'Detail and analysis', swap your work with a partner. Consider the following questions:

1 Did you agree on what type of question you were dealing with? If not, discuss it and work out who was right.
2 Whose plan most clearly focused on the specific type of question?
3 Were the details that your partner selected the most appropriate to support their points?

4 Could either of you have used detail that better supports the points that you wanted to make?
5 Were all of your partner's sentences truly analytical?
6 What can you learn from your partner's approach?

Use these questions to feedback to each other and improve your use of detail and analysis.

Key Topic 3 Spain and the reconquest, 1573–84

Overview

By the spring of 1572 the conflict between Philip II's armies and the Dutch had escalated into a full-scale war which continued throughout the 1570s. The rebels won additional support thanks to their military victories, the harsh policies of Alva, and the destructive actions of the Spanish soldiers. As a result, Philip lost confidence in Alva; he was removed from power at the end of 1573 and replaced with Don Luis de Requesens. When Requesens died unexpectedly, the States General ruled the royalist Netherlands for a time, but this kind of government was ultimately unacceptable for Spain, as well as for the Dutch themselves, and a new Governor-General was appointed in November 1576, Don John of Austria. He died in 1578 and was succeeded by the Duke of Parma, Don Alexander Farnese, who led a successful military campaign in the southern provinces. As a result, the split between the northern and southern provinces became more distinct, and the northern provinces became increasingly independent, forming the Union of Utrecht in 1579. They abjured Philip's right to rule in 1581, after he had pronounced William of Orange an outlaw in 1580. This ultimately led to Orange's assassination in 1584. From 1573 Orange looked for foreign allies to provide further support for the revolt in financial, political, and military terms. He sought help from Protestant monarchs and nobles because he believed they were more likely to help the Dutch rebels fight the Catholic King of Spain. The involvement from 1580 of the Duke of Anjou brought support from the King of France, while Elizabeth I of England also offered some aid in the form of money and troops. This support helped to sustain the revolt in the face of attack from Spanish forces which were vastly superior in numbers and experience. The northern provinces also took measures to preserve the progress they had made, by allying in unions such as the Union of Utrecht in 1579. They acted together to try and replace Philip II as monarch of the Netherlands and formed the first step in the establishment of the Dutch Republic.

This chapter examines these issues through the following sections:

1   *The failure of Requesens, 1573–76* explores the problems and military defeats faced by the Spanish government and their impact in terms of mutinies and violence by soldiers. It then examines the consequences of those mutinies for Requesens and the Spanish.

2   *Reasons for the success of Parma, 1577–84* discusses the success of the Duke of Parma in using diplomacy and military skill to regain control in the southern provinces of the Netherlands. It looks at the Union of Arras and the fall of Antwerp in 1584.

3   *Foreign intervention in the Netherlands* examines Orange's search for foreign allies in the period 1573–84. It also looks at the reasons why the Duke of Anjou was chosen as the new ruler of the Netherlands in 1580, as well as the impact that he made, and his withdrawal in 1583.

4   *The growing independence of the northern provinces* looks at the success of the revolt in the north, and the way that this developed from military success to political stability. It examines the political agreements that happened in the period, as well as charting the declining influence and assassination of William of Orange in 1584.

TIMELINE

1573 November	Don Luis de Requesens became the new Governor-General
1574 June	States General summoned
1575 Spring	Peace talks between the King's representatives and rebels held at Breda
1575 September	Philip II issued a decree of bankruptcy
1576 March	Requesens died
1576 November	Don John of Austria replaced Requesens as Governor-General
1576 November	Antwerp sacked in the so-called 'Spanish Fury'
1576 November	Pacification of Ghent signed
1577 September	William of Orange entered Brussels
1577 October	States General formally broke with Don John of Austria
1578	Don John of Austria died, Don Alexander Farnese, Duke of Parma, appointed Governor-General
1579 May–November	Conference of Cologne met to discuss ending war
1579	Union of Utrecht
1579 May	Union of Arras
1580 March	Defection of the Count of Rennenberg
1581 January	Francis, Duke of Anjou became prince and Lord of the Netherlands
1581 March	Archduke Matthias resigned
1581 July	The Act of Abjuration
1583 June	The Duke of Anjou left the Netherlands following his unsuccessful coup
1585 August	Antwerp surrendered to Parma's siege

Note it down

Use the 1:2 method (see page x) to take notes on the causes and consequences of the events within Section 1. Keep adding to your detailed annotated timeline, as you will need detailed knowledge in order to successfully answer essay questions on this topic.

1 The failure of Requesens, 1573–76

Don Luis de Requesens arrived in Brussels in November 1573. He was unfamiliar with the situation in the Netherlands, and relied on Alva for advice about the region and its politics. Although Alva returned to Spain on 18 December, he continued to send Requesens letters of counsel. These advised Requesens on matters of policy. He particularly tried to convince Requesens that the war against the rebels should continue.

The war continued throughout 1574 and the situation was rather bleak for Requesens:

- In January the royal fleet had been defeated in the Scheldt, in the south-west of the Netherlands.
- In February the port of Middelburg in Zeeland fell to the rebels.
- Leiden in South Holland was besieged from October 1573 until April 1574, and again from May 1574 until October 1574.

Philip II doubled his monetary contribution to the war in 1574 and the Spanish continued to find more soldiers to fight. However, neither of these factors seemed to help Requesens defeat the rebels. By 1576, the Netherlands were divided into two distinctive parts which both proclaimed their loyalty to Philip II:

- Requesens governed 15 royalist provinces.
- William of Orange was the clear leader of the two rebelling northern provinces of Holland and Zeeland.

Requesens' problems

Money was a major problem for Requesens as he took on his new role as **Governor-General**. Alva had left him with the problem of paying the soldiers and, in order to solve it, he advised Requesens to attempt to reimpose the Hundredth Penny Tax. This tax was meant to have been a one-time tax (see page 340), but, as Philip was desperate for money, he had no choice but to allow Requesens to summon a meeting of the **States General** in order to approve raising the tax again. They met in Brussels on 4 June 1572 and Requesens asked representatives from each royalist province for additional monetary support.

The representatives took the meeting as an opportunity to make old demands. They asked for:

- the abolition of the Tenth and Twentieth Penny taxes (see page 340)

- Philip II to return and rule over the Netherlands in person
- if that was not possible, they wanted a member of the royal family to return to the Low Countries as regent
- protection from the Spanish soldiers
- the States General to supervise the way the soldiers were paid.

Requesens wouldn't agree to these demand and, therefore, this meeting that was meant to solve some of the realm's financial troubles led only to government stalemate. Outside the meeting, the revolt continued.

The rebel victory at Leiden, October 1574

One key victory for Orange and his rebels was at Leiden. The city was besieged by the Spanish in several stages between October 1573 and October 1574. The city received a break from the siege when the Spanish soldiers were sent to fight the rebels under Louis of Nassau at Mook in April. Nassau had led an invasion into Holland in the hopes of diverting soldiers from Leiden and relieving it from attack. This worked in the short term, but the siege resumed in May after the Spanish won the battle at Mook, killing Nassau and his youngest brother Henry. Around 15,000 rebel soldiers were now in Leiden and, by August, the city's supplies had run out: relief was needed. Orange's rebels broke the dikes holding back the river Maas on 3 August, and the plains around the city slowly began to flood. At this crucial moment, Orange took ill with a fever and attempts to rescue the city were halted until his recovery. The Sea Beggars once again tried to sail into the city on 10 September but were again unsuccessful because the dike they needed to sail through became too shallow for their ships and they ran aground. The rebels' fortunes finally changed on 1 October, when the wind changed and they were able to sail once again. Along the way to Leiden, they encountered the Spanish garrison at Zoeterwoude. The Spanish soldiers fled this fort when they saw the Dutch fleet. The final hurdle to Leiden was the Spanish fort at Lammen. The Spanish soldiers at Lammen retreated overnight on 2 October, and lifted the siege of Leiden as they fled. The Sea Beggars were then able to sail into the city to rescue the besieged rebels on 3 October. They were reinforced the following day, and the rebels were able to feed the starving people herring and white bread. Leiden was finally relieved. As a result of their defeat at Leiden, the Spanish forces left southern Holland.

Peace negotiations, 1575

Following this defeat, Philip commanded Requesens to explore ending the war by negotiating with the leaders of the revolt. Requesens sent a representative, Elbertus Leoninus, who met with Orange in early 1575. He told the rebels that the King would never allow freedom of worship (a key issue for Orange and the rebels in Holland and Zeeland) in any of his realms.

Requesens continued his peace negotiations with the rebels at Breda in 1575. Both sides said that they hoped the political situation in the Low Countries would return to the way it had been during Charles V's reign. In practice, this goal was becoming increasingly impossible to reach because neither side was willing to compromise on the political concerns that mattered the most to them. The rebels insisted that they wanted to have a king, and that the king was a key part of government in the Netherlands. But they also insisted that the States General and **provincial states** were other necessary parts of their political life. They wanted to remind the King that his main role was to uphold their traditional rights and privileges. Under Requesens, as under Alva, the King was firm in his political and religious policies regarding his right to make appointments, raise taxes and implement religious uniformity. The war would continue despite increasing financial problems and the problem of mutinies within the Spanish forces. The King was unwilling to restore the rights and privileges to the provinces and refused to budge on his position that all his territories should practise Roman Catholicism. The seemingly golden days of Charles V's reign could not be restored because neither side was willing to compromise on these points.

Mutinies within the Spanish forces

Mutinies became a common occurrence against the King's army; there were 45 mutinies over the question of payment in the years 1573–1609. In May 1574 soldiers even captured the city of Antwerp and held it under ransom until they had raised enough money to cover their wages. This mutiny foreshadowed even worse events to come.

The mutineers were organised. They elected leaders and drew up lists of grievances. Normally, the soldiers were angry about their lack of pay. However, they also complained about camp conditions, the freedom to change units, or medical services. The mutineers often destroyed the buildings of the city, damaging the cities' civic pride, and symbolising an attack on the Dutch political system. This made the Spanish armies an object of hatred throughout the Low Countries and, by 1576, the Spanish soldiers had become the biggest threat to peace, as each mutiny damaged the reputation of the Spanish and won some support for the Dutch rebels.

Requesens felt defeated by the mutinies. He believed that they were a sign that God had abandoned the Roman Catholic side. Furthermore, Requesens soon realised that Philip could not afford to continue the war effort as, despite the increased financial contribution he had made, the armies still were not being properly paid. Philip's wars in the Netherlands and against the Ottoman Empire in the Mediterranean were financed by credit from bankers in Genoa. The creditors grew impatient with Philip as he was unable to repay and, in September 1575, Philip declared **bankruptcy**. The following year, on 6 March 1576, Requesens died suddenly in Brussels, causing a power vacuum. The **Council of State** was given temporary power to govern.

Despite Spain's bankruptcy, the war continued. The Spanish soldiers were involved in a siege at Zierikzee that had begun in October 1575 and they continued to lay siege to the town despite the bankruptcy **decree**. The town finally surrendered on 2 July 1576. Within hours, the starving soldiers mutinied. They ransacked Zierikzee for months before finally leaving. The mutineers then travelled around the Netherlands.

In response to the mutinies, the provincial states scrambled to raise small armies to protect their towns and people. The royalist provinces decided to meet with Orangeist representatives. Orange also wanted to meet with them. He believed that they needed to find a way to end the war that was destroying the Low Countries. Representatives from both sides first met for negotiations in Ghent starting on 7 October. They hoped to find a resolution before the new Governor-General arrived and they needed to take swift action against the mutinying soldiers, whose reputation was finally destroyed by the Spanish Fury in Antwerp.

> **Source A** A letter from Daniel Rogers in Antwerp to Lord Burghley (lord high treasurer to Elizabeth I of England), 7 March 1576, discussing the impact of Spanish financial problems on the government of the Netherlands.
>
> Surely the Countrie goeth more and more to Ruin, the State whereof is much more miserable, than it was at my last being here with Dr. Wilson. The King's Debts increase daily, and the Soldiers are not payed; the Husbandman in the Country is oppressed, and great Contempt groweth against the Spanyards. Wherefore they scant can conceave any worthie Enterprise, much lesse execute it. Three Weeks past the Commendador [Requesens] had an Enterprise in Hand, against Brill, but because it took not good Effect, the Sickness which he had before, beganne to increase. He was troubled for six Weeks, with a great Itche, which ended at the last into Boyles, and Imposthumes, which broke out under his Armes, and on his Back, in such a Manner, that he died of them the 5th of this Present, about four of the Clock in the Morning, having seen 46 Years.
>
> How useful is Source A to the historian to investigate Spanish problems in the Netherlands? How does it explain Requesens' increasing ill health?

The Spanish Fury of 1576

Sancho d'Avila, the Spanish leader of Antwerp's **citadel**, devised a plan to sack the city in order to seize some of the money that Philip owed them by capturing spoils from Antwerp. The mutineers attacked on the night of 4 November. They ransacked and plundered the city for three days, killing as many as 8,000 people and raping and assaulting its inhabitants. The Spanish destroyed Antwerp's cloth market, completely ruining this industry. This shocking event became known as the Spanish Fury and was a turning point in the relationship between the royalist provinces and their king. As a result of the attack, the States General of the provinces who stayed loyal to the royal government decided that they needed to band together with the rebellious Holland and Zeeland. The two sides began to negotiate an alliance against the mutinying Spanish soldiers. The Spanish Fury had succeeded in uniting the divided provinces of the Netherlands against the Spanish Crown and the result of their talks became known as the Pacification of Ghent.

The Pacification of Ghent, 1576

The Pacification of Ghent was an extremely anti-Spanish document. Three provinces refused to sign the agreement: Luxembourg, Namur and part of Limburg remained loyal to Spain. The Pacification was signed on 8 November. In this document, the provinces all agreed to work together to expel the ruinous Spanish soldiers. The people had simply had enough of their pillage and ransacking.

The main ideas written into the Pacification of Ghent included:

- offences related to the revolt were to receive a general **pardon**
- the Spanish soldiers were to be driven out of the Low Countries
- Alva's **heresy placards** (see page 338) were to be revoked
- religious persecution, against Protestants or Catholics, was not tolerated
- the States General were to determine a religious policy.
- former rights, privileges and liberties were to be restored
- confiscated properties were to return to their previous owners.

The document was printed immediately. It was translated into numerous languages to guarantee widespread publicity. Some Dutch began to view the Pacification as a sort of constitution. It enshrined the

The advance of Calvinism in the southern provinces

One unintended consequence of the Pacification of Ghent was the resurgence of Calvinism in the royalist southern provinces. We have seen that Calvinists fled their homes in the southern part of the Netherlands during the revolt's early days, moving to the more tolerant northern provinces. People who had moved north began to return to the south after the Pacification of Ghent, encouraged by its ideas and believing that religious **toleration** would be experienced throughout the Netherlands. They were also encouraged by the national religious **synod** held at Dordrecht in the summer of 1578. This synod brought order and conformity to the important issues of doctrine and Church organisation.

The States General wanted to remain officially Roman Catholic because they believed that this would help them make peace with the Spanish and end the war more quickly. However,

Calvinist preachers began to gain popularity amongst the common people in the southern provinces once again, winning large numbers of converts, particularly around the city of Ghent. The preachers made and explained a link between true faith and the virtues of participation in local government. They taught that true faith would lead to concord and peace in the Netherlands, believing that peace was the foundation for all government and that religious harmony would be the way that the Dutch could once again achieve peace and unity in their country. They began to influence the decisions made by the States General. Groups like the Calvinists from Ghent and the common people in Brussels were often persuaded to join the Orangeist side. These activities sometimes alienated the Dutch Catholics. The challenge of differences in religious opinion indicates the complex nature of the problem throughout the Netherlands during the revolt.

principles that they valued. It was, in effect, a short outline of the reasons they had originally rebelled against Philip of Spain.

Conclusion: The failure of Requesens

The Dutch faced great horrors from 1573 to 1576. Spanish soldiers added to the problem. They lost the support of the people by their acts of destruction during their numerous mutinies. The Spanish Fury that ransacked Antwerp caused a turning-point in the relationship between the royalist provinces and the two northern revolting provinces. It drove the Dutch together, providing a common enemy that both sides could fight against, despite their religious or political differences.

Work together

This section includes an exploration of the Spanish mutinies, in particular the Spanish Fury. In your pairs, think about the causes of the mutinies and their consequences. Consider other incidents detailed in the previous two chapters where Spanish policies or problems led to political gains for the Dutch rebels. Note them in a table like this:

Event	Causes relating to Spanish policies or problems	Consequences for the Dutch rebels

2 Reasons for the success of Parma, 1577–84

Philip had selected his half-brother Don John of Austria to be the new Governor-General late in the spring of 1576. Don John was a very competent military commander: he was the hero in the Spanish wars in the Mediterranean, had conquered Tunis, and defeated the Turkish navy at Lepanto. He only arrived in Luxembourg on 3 November 1576, having been delayed in coming to the Netherlands by visiting Philip in Spain first. When he arrived he found the royalist States General had decided to meet without the permission of the King and form the agreement with Holland and Zeeland, leading to the Pacification of Ghent.

Don John signed the Pacification of Ghent on 12 February 1577. Once he had done this, the royalist States General accepted him as their Governor-General and began to pay for the Spanish soldiers. The soldiers themselves left the Netherlands, beginning their march back to Spain in April 1577. However, the relationship between Don John and the royalist provinces was strained. Neither side trusted the other. Moreover, the northern provinces of Holland and Zeeland refused to see Don John as their leader and he was unable to establish firm control in the Netherlands. Following Don John's death in 1578, Philip appointed Don Alexander Farnese, the Duke of Parma as Governor-General. This man would prove to be the longest-serving Governor-General in the Netherlands since Alva was forced to leave in 1573.

Re-establishing Spanish rule in the south

Once the States General of the royalist provinces had accepted Don John as their Governor-General, they sent representatives, led by Philippe de Croy Aerschot, to negotiate with William of Orange. The two Dutch groups needed to resolve their relationship with each other and they also wanted to define their relationship with royal authority. Negotiations were hampered by the northern provinces' objection to Roman Catholic rule and their lack of trust of Don John.

Don John's relationship with the royalist provinces was also strained. He retreated to the citadel in the town of Namur and summoned back the troops that had just been sent away. He even wrote to Philip, suggesting that the King find another Governor-General. Instead, Philip gave permission for Spanish soldiers to return to the Netherlands in August 1577. In September, William of Orange claimed Brussels after a triumphant entry into the city, invited by a self-elected Council of Eighteen drawn from the citizens and guilds. The States General broke with Don John on 8 October. The Catholic nobles of the States General sent a secret invitation to a new Governor on 16 October 1577. On his acceptance, they named the 20-year-old Archduke Matthias of Vienna as their new Governor-General. He arrived in the Netherlands on 20 October.

Archduke Matthias (1557–1619)

Matthias was the son of the Holy Roman Emperor, Maximilian II, and was a member of the **Habsburg** family. He was invited to the Netherlands to rule as Governor-General in 1577 aged only 20 years old. His uncle, Philip II of Spain, did not approve his appointment. Matthias was inexperienced and very young, and was easily dominated by more experienced Dutch politicians. He was unable to reconcile the Spanish and the Dutch rebels. After leaving the Netherlands in 1581 Matthias returned to Austria. He became Holy Roman Emperor in 1612.

Archduke Matthias and the States General

Archduke Matthias had one advantage that Don John did not: Matthias had the support of many royalist noble families. Furthermore, he had Orange's support. Matthias made several promises to the States General before they would swear allegiance to him (see Source B).

- He promised to accept the advice of a council appointed by the States General.
- He agreed that William of Orange would be his primary councillor.
- He was to submit all of his policies to the States General for approval before they became law.

The States General also signed an agreement known as the Union of Brussels on 10 December. This document formally identified Don John as an enemy of the Netherlands. In the Union of Brussels the States General also promised to defend Holland and Zeeland if Philip's forces attacked those provinces. Representatives of the royalist States General and the rebellious provinces of Holland and Zeeland were finally satisfied by these agreements. Matthias swore to govern the Netherlands in Philip's name on 20 January 1578.

> **Source B** An extract from the Articles that Archduke Matthias agreed to on 8 December 1577 containing the promises that Matthias made on being accepted as governor by the States General.
>
> ... [t]he governor ... shall be bound to observe all the following articles, and especially to maintain each and all of the privileges, rights, usages and customs of the country and to restore, preserve and keep them inviolate.
>
> IV. The governor shall govern the country with a Council of State, nominated by the States General, made up of men born in the country, capable and qualified, true to the country, without greed and ambition, detached, no longer driven by the passions raised in the party conflicts of recent years, wise and expert in the matter of policy as well as of war.
>
> V. All matters which will be deliberated upon by the said council, shall be decided on and decreed by a majority of votes; the governor is not allowed to conclude matters within other private or secret councils.
>
> What does Source B tell us about the States General's concerns and priorities? Why was Matthias asked to agree to these articles?

The Calvinists continued to gain political power after Matthias became Governor-General. He was an inexperienced young ruler. Many saw him as William of Orange's puppet. All the same, the northern provinces of Holland and Zeeland never recognised Matthias as their Governor-General (see page 370). They preferred to support William of Orange as their Governor-General because they believed he had served them well in that capacity. Furthermore, Matthias was a Roman Catholic. This made the Protestants in the northern provinces suspicious of him from the beginning.

The mistrust between Catholics and Protestants continued to increase in the closing years of the 1570s. Despite a shared common enemy in the form of the Spanish soldiers and leaders, the two groups could not put aside their religious differences. Groups of provinces who shared beliefs began to form alliances with each other. These unions promised mutual support and defence, even though such alliances were against the terms of the Pacification of Ghent (see page 363). The gap between the goals and values of Dutch Catholics and Protestants continued to increase. By 1579, many Dutch Catholics felt isolated by the increased political participation of many Calvinists. Catholics in the southern provinces of Artois, Flanders and Hainault believed that their perspective was dismissed by those in authority. Despite living in the south, Orange had never fully won their trust or support because of his **Protestantism** and his tendency to increase his own power and authority.

Orange in the southern provinces

From 1577 William of Orange began to seek the favour of the common people in the southern provinces, living in Brussels and then in Antwerp, until 1583. Orange understood that the southern provinces resented the power that the northern provinces wielded because of their affiliation with him. He hoped that his presence in the south would appease the people living there. He could show the Dutch living in the southern provinces that he was truly working for the benefit of all the Dutch people by living in different areas of the country. He hoped that he could be a unifying symbol bringing together the northern and southern people.

The Union of Arras, 1579

The Union of Arras, created by Artois, Flanders and Hainault, endorsed Philip and Parma as their political leaders, fully recognising Philip's sovereignty over the Netherlands and Parma as the rightful Governor-General. In creating this Union, they split from the other Dutch provinces; formally splitting the Netherlands into two

divided groups. The Union supported Philip's religious policies and its members could therefore be characterised as Roman Catholic, and opposed to the way that Calvinists had made advances in the southern provinces.

The Conference of Cologne, 1579

The provinces in revolt against Philip were now united together. In 1579, the States General and representatives from Spain began negotiations at a conference in Cologne. The aim of these talks was to find a way to end the war. The Spanish representatives demanded that Roman Catholic worship alone was restored in all provinces. However, one minor victory was that they were open to allowing Protestant worship in the two northern provinces of Holland and Zeeland for a limited period of time. The Spanish also demanded that the political climate of the Netherlands be returned to the way it had been in 1559. This meant that Philip was to have supreme authority in the Netherlands without hindrance from the States General. The Spanish offered pardon to those who had fought in the rebellion in exchange for their conditions.

The Conference of Cologne failed to put an end to the war. Instead, it made the situation in the Netherlands even more complicated. Some of the cities and towns that had been loyal to the Orangeist cause became fearful of Spanish retaliation. They finally declared their allegiance to Spain and the Union of Arras. One of the most important nobles to leave the revolt was the Count of Rennenberg, the **stadtholder** of Friesland, Groningen, Drenthe and Overijssel.

The defection of the Count of Rennenberg, 1580

Rennenberg was the last remaining prominent Roman Catholic noble on the rebel side. He was conflicted about whether to fight with the rebels against the King, or to join the Union of Arras. In March 1580, Rennenberg finally made his decision and declared his loyalty to Philip. He asked the Catholics in the provinces for whom he was stadtholder to rise and restore their Church. They were to acknowledge Philip II as their true king.

Rennenberg's decision to support Philip II was the first major crisis that the Orangeist alliance faced. The Catholics of the northern provinces saw this as an opportunity to show their support for the King and for Catholicism. The results were disastrous. Catholics and Protestants clashed in the streets of many towns and cities. Orange feared that the Catholics would ask Parma to help them fight Protestant forces. Such tactics would simply make the split between the two religious groups even worse. Those who wanted to support Protestantism in the Netherlands would join in the Union of Utrecht (see page 372).

Parma's diplomacy, military tactics and strategy

The continuation of the war allowed the Duke of Parma to bring his military experience to the battlefields of the Netherlands. His soldiers were also experienced. Early in the campaign, his army was mainly comprised of local recruits or German **mercenaries**, but, by 1582, as the size of his army increased to 60,000, many of his soldiers were well-trained, German, Italian, and Spanish professional soldiers. Parma was a much more successful Governor-General and military commander than many of his predecessors. He also used his intelligence and diplomacy to win the southern provinces back over to the Spanish Crown, concentrating particularly on Brabant and Flanders.

Tactics

Parma employed successful tactics and, by January 1581, had devised a plan to defeat the rebel provinces. He knew that the large towns relied on the sea and the rivers (such as the Scheldt) for exporting their goods and for communications. Parma decided that the best way to defeat these towns was to block their access to these important waterways and to the coast. He was one of few Spanish commanders who were able to use the Dutch geography to their own advantage.

Parma also used the split between the northern and southern provinces to his advantage. The rebel provinces were divided into northern and southern sections. Using Artois, Hainault, Namur and Luxembourg as bases for his conquests, Parma drove his army through the middle. As cities and towns like Dunkirk (1583) and Ghent (1584) fell, the divisions between north and south were increased. Parma defeated town after town. Rebel military commanders began to make secret compacts with him, secretly joining his army, and betraying the rebel cause in the process. These included:

- Breda and Mechelen in 1579
- Zutphen and Bergues in 1583
- Nijmegen in 1585.

Parma also bribed some **garrisons** to surrender. For example the English garrison in the town of Aalst surrendered in Februray 1584 in exchange for a payment of 128,250 florins in cash.

Garrisons

Another tactic that Parma used successfully was building garrisons in the Dutch towns he conquered. He redoubled his efforts to create a network of garrisons across the Netherlands from 1585 and along the 'Spanish route' from their lands in northern Italy to the Low Countries. These garrisons were vital fortresses for the Spanish armies for two main reasons. First, they helped the Spanish to maintain order in the areas that they had recently conquered. Secondly, the new garrisons were used as bases for gaining further advancements into the rebelling provinces. Spanish soldiers could be sent to the new garrisons, then move into new territories from the garrisons before finally conquering other areas. The

Alexander Farnese, Duke of Parma (1545–92)

Parma was the son of Margaret of Parma, Philip II's regent from 1559 to 1567 (see pages 318–19). He had been brought up in Spain with Don John (see page 364) and Don Carlos (see page 329). He had fought for Spain in the Lepanto and was an experienced military commander in 1571. Parma spent a number of years at the Spanish court before being sent to the Netherlands in 1577, initially as a military commander under Don John. When Don John was dying in October 1578 he appointed Parma as his successor. Philip II approved his appointment. Parma was a skilled commander as well as a wily diplomat and negotiator.

construction of garrisons was therefore one of Parma's most important and successful military tactics.

Additional soldiers

Philip sent over 11,000 more soldiers to the Netherlands in 1582. This significantly increased the size of Parma's army. These were no raw recruits – they were experienced foreign troops from Spain and Italy. Many of them had served Philip elsewhere, for example against Portugal in 1580 and also in Italy or previously in the Low Countries. They were disciplined soldiers and because they were not local they had no sympathy for the rebels. Parma described his new troops as 'tough, disciplined and born to fight with the people of the Netherlands'.

Additional financial support

Parma's victories were rewarded with additional support from Philip. His finances had improved, thanks to mining in the New World and from the Indies, and he was able to send Parma's army additional monies. In June 1583 Philip sent 1,250,000 florins to Parma. He instructed his ministers to send 200,000 florins more every month. Parma could now ensure his troops were paid regularly to prevent mutinies, employ extra troops, and pay for the building of fortifications as well as bribes to enemy garrisons. Philip's investment in Parma's army proved to be valuable. In just over three years, Parma was able to double the area loyal to Spain. Most of these areas would stay loyal to Philip after that, never again returning to the rebels' side. One of the key cities to fall during this period was Antwerp.

The fall of Antwerp, 1584–85

Antwerp was the largest city in the Netherlands, with 80,000 inhabitants in 1584. It was also a very wealthy city; the cultural and economic centre of that region of Europe. It had long been a centre of Calvinism but did not join the revolt until after the Spanish Fury of 1576 (see page 363). Antwerp joined the Union of Utrecht (see page 372) in 1579 and from that point forward became the capital of the Dutch Revolt.

In the autumn of 1584, Parma's army began to besiege the city. Before this Parma had built forts along the Scheldt River to ensure that the route from the Spanish territories to Antwerp was well protected in order to make sure supplies would reliably and consistently arrive.

Parma's soldiers encircled the city. Then they built a bridge over the Scheldt River. A masterpiece of engineering, the bridge was 731 metres long and rested on pilings driven 22 metres down into the river bed by a specially designed machine. It was defended by 200 siege cannons. The purpose of the bridge was to cut off the city from all supply routes, including the waterways. Inside the city food began to run short as the army intercepted any goods that were shipped to Antwerp. The rebels flooded the river plain, hoping that this would cut off the Spanish army in turn, but the strategy did not work. Instead, the Dutch lost many lives because Spanish munitions ships exploded on the river, causing even more death and mayhem. The city was finally forced to surrender on 17 August 1585. Parma made a point of making moderate demands on the city and ensuring his troops remained disciplined. The Protestant population were given two years to sort out their affairs before leaving the city.

Conclusion: Reasons for the success of Parma

The Netherlands were placed under the authority of many different Governor-Generals during Philip's reign. The Duke of Parma's immediate predecessor, Don John of Austria, was only in power for a very short period because he died before he could establish a firm presence in the Low Countries. He was able to appoint a successor on his deathbed, and Philip confirmed Alexander Farnese, the prince of Parma. Parma proved to be a capable military leader. His tactics were aggressive but successful. The fall of Antwerp was a major victory for the Spanish cause in the Netherlands. This event would ultimately change the shape of the Netherlands forever.

The end of Antwerp's 'Golden Age'

Antwerp was, before the Dutch Revolt, the largest and most opulent economic centre in the north-west of Europe. Its merchants traded internationally and foreign merchants came to its markets to trade. They even had permanent bases there in order to maximise their profits and sell their goods. It sold a huge variety of goods, including beautifully made Dutch tapestries and fine cloth. It was an extremely wealthy and admired city. Although Parma's terms of surrender were moderate, the defeat was to end this 'Golden Age' of Antwerp. Only just over a third of the pre-siege population decided to stay in the city after the Spanish victory, decimating its population. Highly skilled Protestant craftsmen moved to the northern provinces, leading them to economic dominance after they became the United Provinces in 1581. Moreover, Parma's bridge remained and blocked shipping from the Scheldt. Antwerp became an economic backwater and never recovered its wealth and economic dominance.

3 Foreign intervention in the Netherlands

Parma was appointed in 1578 and from that point forward he experienced significant success. Clearly this worried William of Orange. The revolt had not faced such a powerful challenge before. As rebel garrisons in towns and cities across the southern Netherlands fell, Orange looked for solutions that would preserve some of the gains made since 1572. He turned to foreign states for aid. Orange sought help from Protestant England and from the Duke of Anjou, a French prince who had previously aided the Netherlands against Don John.

Orange's decision to seek foreign help

In many ways, the Dutch Revolt was an international war. Philip relied on Spanish soldiers to fight against the Dutch. The Dutch nobility recruited men who owed them fealty. These men could come from wherever the nobles held land, including Germany, France, or even further afield. Orange also hired German mercenaries to fight on his side. Motivated by personal religious ideals, men from throughout Europe joined the fight. All of these men needed to be paid. The rebel provinces did contribute tax money to the armies but the nobility also used their private money to fund the war effort. However, William of Orange needed to ask his allies for aid if he were to defeat the Spanish. Orange had two principal aims:

- To obtain monetary and military support from European governments such as France and England.
- To find a new monarch from amongst European royal families who were friendly to the Dutch cause, in order to replace Philip II as the ruler of the Low Countries.

Monetary and military support

Orange sought help from monarchs and nobles who were known to be Protestants. If they shared the same faith as many of the Dutch people, they were more likely to offer their help. Furthermore, Protestant monarchs were more likely to be opposed to Spain's increasing power.

The Orange family held lands in German territories, and they had numerous Protestant German princes as allies who gave help nearly from the beginning. They had also received support from French Protestants for many years as well. Louis of Nassau had befriended Admiral Coligny, who had encouraged the Dutch in their efforts against the Spanish. Support from the French was invigorated when the Duke of Anjou came to rule the Netherlands in 1580 (see pages 370–71). Anjou appealed to his brother, Henry III, King of France, who sent money and soldiers to the Netherlands to support the cause. Finally, one of the most important sources of foreign help was England. Queen Elizabeth supported the Dutch rebels both informally and officially. One informal way she had helped the Dutch in the past was by providing the Sea Beggars a safe haven in England's ports (see page 344). She sent soldiers under the leadership of some of her best military commanders, including Leicester and de Vere, and also provided money to help pay soldiers. The money that was provided did not satisfy the early expectations of the Dutch, however, and Elizabeth's government took a long time to pay the promised amount. This made the aid less effective, even if the moral support it provided was important.

The search for a new monarch

The revolt had long fought for freedom of worship in the Netherlands. The supporters also wanted the restoration of traditional Dutch rights and privileges. As a result of the Conference of Cologne (see page 366), Orange and his supporters realised that Philip would simply never agree to these two crucial principles. At the same time, Dutch rights and privileges were based on government by a monarch. The Dutch believed that their monarch was the main provider and defender of their privileges and that their government could not operate permanently without the presence of a monarch. Indeed, the States General were not even supposed to meet unless the King summoned them. This is why the rebelling provinces continued to claim loyalty to Philip: they needed him to legitimate their government.

Francis, Duke of Anjou (1555–84)

Francis, Duke of Anjou, was a French prince. He was the youngest son of King Henry II of France and his wife Catherine de' Medici. He became heir to the throne of France in 1574 following the accession of his brother (King Henry III). Francis was alienated by Henry III and joined the Protestant Huguenot rebels in 1575, though he remained Catholic. He was instrumental in the signing of the pro-Protestant peace treaty, the Edict of Beaulieu, in May 1576 and gained the title Duke of Anjou as a result. This treaty ended the fifth of the French Wars of Religion. In 1578 Anjou was recognised as the Defender of the Liberties of the Low Countries. He went to the Netherlands with 12,000 soldiers ready to fight against Don John. He was invited to become the ruler of the rebel provinces in 1580. After he left the Netherlands in 1583 Anjou returned to France, becoming ill shortly after and dying aged 29 in February 1584.

By 1580, however, the rebelling provinces were at a major turning-point. They no longer saw Philip II as their rightful monarch because he refused to defend traditional Dutch privileges. Yet, the Dutch needed to have a prince in order to carry out these rights and privileges. The provinces had no other choice but to search for a new monarch.

The invitation to the Duke of Anjou, 1580

The southern provinces had selected Archduke Matthias to be their new Governor-General (see page 365). However, the northern provinces of Holland and Zeeland refused to recognise him as their leader. Indeed, Matthias resigned from his role completely in 1581. The provinces would have to find a different leader.

The rebel provinces offered their governance to Francis, Duke of Anjou, in January 1580. Anjou would rule over the provinces that had joined with Holland and Zeeland against Philip of Spain: seven provinces in total. These provinces wanted Anjou to agree to specific terms and conditions, mostly regarding the privileges and traditions of the Netherlands, before he was allowed to formally take power. The Dutch believed that this was the only way that they could ensure that their rights and privileges were restored. Their war with Philip would have been in vain if their new monarch would not agree to these terms.

An agreement between Anjou and the provinces, the Treaty of Plessis-lès-Tours, was signed on 29 September 1580. Anjou and representatives of the States General swore oaths in Antwerp on 23 January 1581. Anjou was now the prince and lord of the Netherlands.

The Duke's unpopularity and his withdrawal in 1583

Orange and his supporters hoped that the Duke of Anjou would bring greater unity to the northern and southern provinces of the Netherlands. Parma continued to wage war with them, and he was gaining support. Anjou became increasingly frustrated with Parma's military successes, whereas those loyal to the revolt were frustrated with Anjou's inability to defeat the Spanish; the Dutch had hoped that a new ruler of their choosing would help to bring an end to the war with Spain.

Anjou encountered monetary problems and had difficulty paying the Dutch soldiers, despite asking the States General for additional money and gaining financial aid from Elizabeth in England and his brother Henry in France. This inability to pay the Dutch soldiers hurt Anjou's reputation with the people.

Anjou's religious ideas also caused divisions between him and the people. He had promised not to interfere with Dutch religious matters but was angry when he learned that Roman Catholic worship was banned in the city of Antwerp. William of Orange had to negotiate a compromise between Anjou and the city leaders.

One major cause of resentment was a horrific event that happened on 18 March 1582. It was Anjou's twenty-seventh birthday, and Orange had planned a huge celebration in his honour. As he left the dining table at lunch, a would-be assassin shot Orange point-blank in the face, the bullet just grazing his cheek. Orange survived but many people blamed Anjou for the attack. As a result, his popularity with the ordinary people of the Netherlands continued to fall.

The 'French Fury'

Anjou was an impatient ruler. His style of ruling was incompatible with the expectations of the Dutch people. He had agreed to uphold Dutch rights and privileges but he wanted to rule as though he were in France, and this meant to rule as an **absolute monarch**. This was very different from the representative that the Dutch people, and the nobles in particular, wanted. He did not like the restrictions placed on his authority in Holland and Zeeland and turned to the rebelling provinces of Brabant and Flanders, seeing in them an opportunity to seize power and rule without the limitations his oath had placed on him. In January 1583, in an attempted coup known as the 'French Fury', Anjou seized Aalst, Dunkirk and other places in Flanders. He also attempted to seize Antwerp, which resulted in disaster. The townspeople of Antwerp attacked Anjou's French soldiers, killing hundreds of them. The damage he had done was irredeemable, and Anjou left the Netherlands in June 1583.

Conclusion: Foreign intervention in the Netherlands

Foreign intervention had the potential to be very useful in shoring up the Dutch Revolt against the forces of Parma. Elizabeth's promises of finance and Anjou's potential as a new figurehead could have made a significant difference if they had delivered. Yet the promised English help was minimal and slow to arrive. Anjou did not prove to be the ruler that Orange had hoped, causing more problems and failing to defeat the Spanish. More significant foreign aid was to come after 1584, but was generally counterproductive in the period 1573–84.

Source C A nineteenth-century Dutch engraving of the French Fury.

D'aanslag van den Hertog van Anjou op Antwerpen, in den Jaare 1583. mislukt.

How could the historian use Source C in an investigation of the effect of foreign intervention in the Netherlands?

4 The growing independence of the northern provinces

The Union of Utrecht confirmed the position that Holland and Zeeland had taken in 1572. It extended the principles of the rebellion in those two provinces to the others who joined in the Union. By 1580, rebels in the Netherlands had two centres of power: Antwerp in the south and Amsterdam in the north. The northern provinces of Holland and Zeeland were home to large numbers of Calvinists. The Sea Beggars in particular were opposed to Roman Catholicism in the northern provinces, and even attacked priests and vandalised churches. Orange was opposed to these actions (see page 329). He was in favour of shifting the power base towards the south because he believed that this would balance the radicalism expressed by the northern Protestants.

Orange's hopes did not become a reality. Instead, many of the towns and cities in the south declared their allegiance to Philip. They hoped that Parma would spare them from destruction if they surrendered to the King.

The Union of Utrecht, 1579

Following the Pacification of Ghent (see page 363), smaller groups of provinces began to band together in alliances known as unions. William of Orange was instrumental in the creation of the Union of Utrecht, which brought together the two Orangeist northern provinces of Holland and Zeeland and Friesland, Gelderland, Utrecht, and Ommelanden. This would prove to be an important alliance. By 1581, Antwerp, Brussels and Ghent had come under Calvinist control and also joined the Union.

The Union bound the provinces to a perpetual alliance in which, in terms of warfare, they were to act as though they were one province, promising to fight together until Spain was finally driven out of the Netherlands. The document defined specific policies in which they were to act as one. However, each province was to have control of other policy matters, especially religion. The document became the constitutional foundation for the Dutch Republic.

The royal ban against William of Orange, March 1580

The Union of Utrecht was a blow to Philip II, who had believed that the revolt was nearing its end, because of the actions of Parma. The Union strengthened the rebels' determination to fight and provided a clear political statement of the provinces' unity and co-operation. Philip decided that he needed to deal with William of Orange and asked his old adviser, Granvelle, for advice. Granvelle suggested the royal ban, a mechanism whereby Orange would be pronounced an outlaw with a price on his head. Nobody could trade with him, speak with him, shelter him and his possessions would be forfeited to the Spanish Crown. The royal ban was dated 15 March 1580 but was published in June. It declared Orange a traitor and promised 25,000 Crowns and a noble title to the person who delivered Orange (dead or alive). This caused an outcry in the Netherlands. Orange was provided with a bodyguard. He also published a detailed repudiation of Philip's accusations of treachery which was widely circulated and translated into different languages to ensure a wide audience (see Source D). Orange refuted Philip's accusations and damned them as shameful. It was one of the reasons for the Act of Abjuration in 1581.

The Act of Abjuration 1581 and the establishing of the Republic of the United Provinces

After the Duke of Anjou became the prince and lord of the Netherlands in January 1581, Philip II was still technically the ruler of all the Netherlands. A committee of lawyers drew up a declaration of deposition. This declaration ordered a placard announcing that Philip was no longer the king, his image would no longer appear on the coinage and his name would not appear in the official acts of the States General. In short, the declaration of deposition paved the way to depose Philip as the ruler of the provinces loyal to the Union of Utrecht. The Act of Abjuration was the official act that removed Philip from power in the Netherlands. It solved the problem of removing Philip as the head of state in the provinces that made up the Union of Utrecht. Published on 26 July 1581, the Act declared that Philip was no longer their monarch on the basis that Philip was a tyrant who had failed to keep to his promises and had therefore forfeited all his rights as king of the Netherlands. The Act of Abjuration also contained a list of grievances against Philip. The Act provided another opportunity to remind the Dutch why they had rebelled against Philip in the first place. It was an extremely influential document, the first modern declaration of independence. Some refer to it today as the Dutch Declaration of Independence.

Orange's declining influence and assassination

Orange had hoped that he could influence the southern provinces so moved to Antwerp and Brussels (see page 366). He had hoped that the Duke of Anjou could be the monarch the rebelling provinces needed to bring them closer together. He had also hoped that Anjou's military experience would help the Netherlands finally defeat the Spanish. However, Anjou's failed coup and Parma's continued success brought morale within the Netherlands to an all-time low and discredited Orange.

A sign of Orange's declining influence was his decision to leave the southern provinces in July 1583 and establish his headquarters in a former convent in the city of Delft in Holland. This was partly in despair at the situation in the southern provinces and the failure of his efforts to shore up the revolt there. However, the northern provinces had become more independent from Orange during his years in the southern provinces. They had established their government and maintained it in difficult times without him.

On 10 July 1584, Orange was assassinated on a stairway in his house in Delft. The assassin was a petitioner from the Franche Comté called Balthasar Gerard. Gerard broke into Orange's house and shot him dead. Gerard, young and likely impoverished, was caught as he tried to flee from Orange's house. He was questioned and tortured, dying at the hands of those who examined him. Gerard had committed the world's first political assassination with a handgun but would never collect the bounty Philip had put on Orange's head. The 25,000 gold crowns were eventually given to Gerard's mother.

Conclusion: The growing independence of the northern provinces

The alliances and unions of the 1580s showed that the northern provinces were developing their own distinctive forms of government to replace the Spanish King. This started to put the division within the Netherlands on a more permanent footing. It would have been very difficult indeed at this point for Philip II to regain all of the territory and rule effectively. William of Orange, such a significant figure in the Dutch Revolt since the 1560s, became less prominent from 1583 onwards when he left the southern provinces for Delft. This made his assassination less catastrophic in terms of the stability of the northern provinces but was still a huge loss for the rebels.

Chapter summary

- Alva's replacement, Don Luis Requesens, continued to pursue his policies of winning back the lost provinces and of persecuting those who were not Roman Catholics.
- With the Union of Arras and the Union of Utrecht the Netherlands split into two distinct areas: one area largely Catholic and loyal to Philip; the other was largely Protestant and actively rebelled against Spanish policies.
- The Netherlands were ruled by a series of unsuccessful and short-lived rulers appointed by Philip II.
- Spain was forced to declare **bankruptcy**, which meant that it was unable to pay its soldiers.
- Mutinies amongst the Spanish soldiers were frequent and had a damaging effect on the Dutch people.
- The Duke of Anjou was invited to be the new ruler of the Netherlands in 1580 but was unpopular due to his financial difficulties, religious interference, and impatient and absolutist approach.
- Parma was the most formidable army leader the Dutch rebels faced in many years.
- Parma's military successes drove the northern and southern provinces further apart, and they began to develop different political ideas.
- When the rebels realised that Philip II would never grant their requests, they looked to other European countries for a new monarch.
- The Union of Utrecht in 1579 and the Act of Abjuration in 1581 were two political treaties that laid the foundation for the Dutch Republic.
- In 1584 William of Orange was assassinated after a bounty was placed on his head by Philip II. The revolt needed to find a new leader.

The failure of Requesens, 1573–76

- Requesens took on the role of Governor-General in 1573
- He was faced with difficulties in paying the Spanish soldiers
- Leiden was a decisive victory for Orange and the rebels
- Mutinies of Spanish soldiers meant they were considered enemies of the Netherlands
- Don John became Governor-General in 1576
- The Pacification of Ghent (1576) was an agreement between the Estates General and the rebelling provinces of Holland and Zeeland. The provinces agreed to work together to expel the Spanish soldiers. It also outlined the reasons why they rebelled against Philip II
- Calvinism became more prominent in the 1570s

Reasons for the success of Parma

- The relationship between the States General and Don John was uneasy
- In the Union of Arras (1579) the southern states expressed their loyalty to Philip II and Governor-General Parma. It formally split the Netherlands into two divided groups
- Parma, Don John's successor, was a capable military leader
- Parma managed to win the southern provinces back over to the Spanish Crown
- The fall of Antwerp was a major victory for the Spanish

SPAIN AND THE RECONQUEST, 1573–84

Foreign intervention in the Netherlands

- The Conference of Cologne (1579) failed to put an end to the war
- The rebels looked for a new prince who would allow Protestantism in the Netherlands and support traditional Dutch rights and privileges
- They looked to the Duke of Anjou to rule the provinces
- Anjou became prince and lord of the Netherlands in 1581. He left the Netherlands after a failed coup

The growing independence of the northern provinces

- The Union of Utrecht bound provinces together to fight against Spain
- The Act of Abjuration removed Philip as the head of state in the provinces that made up the Union of Utrecht
- Together, the treaties laid the foundation of the Dutch Republic

▲ Summary diagram: Spain and the reconquest, 1573–84

Recommended reading

Jonathan Israel, *The Dutch Republic: Its Rise, Greatness, and Fall 1477–1806* (Clarendon Press, 1995), Chapter 10.

Jonathan Israel's book provides a comprehensive history of the Low Countries. Chapter 10 focuses on the second stage of the Dutch Revolt and provides details about the growing split between the northern and southern provinces.

Geoffrey Parker, *The Dutch Revolt* (Viking, 1977), Chapters 4 and 5.

These chapters explore the growing divisions between the northern and southern provinces during this period. Parker shows both sides of the story, explaining how the problems caused by the ongoing revolt looked to the Spanish and to the Dutch.

Andrew Pettegree, *Europe in the Sixteenth Century* (Wiley-Blackwell, 2002), Chapter 11.

This chapter places the maturing Dutch Revolt into the wider context of Europe during this period, helping to show its importance and impact on other countries.

Section A: Essay technique

Contextualising the sources

In order to understand the sources properly, you need to place them in the context in which they were written. Specifically, you need to consider the background or environment in which the source was produced. This may sound obvious, but sixteenth-century sources were produced by sixteenth-century people, and therefore reflect their experiences, beliefs and prejudices. This means that sources are never standalone documents – they should be understood within the context of the values and assumptions of the society that produced them.

In essence, your task when contextualising the sources is to try and understand the world in the same way as the writers of the sources. In short, you should try and see things their way.

Understanding the context is an important part of evaluating the evidence that the sources contain.

Imagine you are answering the following question:

> **How far could the historian make use of Sources 1 and 2 together to investigate the reasons for the wider outbreak of violence in 1572?**

You have read about the Tenth Penny Tax and the wider outbreak of violence in 1572 in Key Topic 2. If you wish to remind yourself of the events of 1569–73, re-read the chapter or your notes. This is important before embarking on an exercise about context.

One way to contextualise the sources is to begin by asking the question: what debate is this source contributing to? The reason for this is that sources are written to contribute to ongoing discussions. For example, from 1563 onwards there were discussions in the Netherlands about:

- whether it was legitimate to oppose the King of Spain if he had not kept to his promises made in 1549
- whether there should be religious toleration for the Calvinists and other Protestant groups
- what role the traditional privileges played in the government of the Netherlands
- the importance of trade in making decisions about religion and government
- the extent to which the Dutch nobility should have a say in the government of the Netherlands
- the Netherlands' role within the wider Spanish Empire.

Many of the documents written at the time would have contributed to one or more of these debates. Working out which debate the source is contributing to, and which side of the debate the source is on can help you to evaluate the evidence the source contains. An example of an attempt to put Source 1 in context can be found on page 377.

This letter is dated 16 May 1672. The immediate context was an outbreak of violence and disorder in 1572 prompted by the invasion of the Sea Beggars and their successes at Brill and Flushing in April 1572. Unlike in 1568, a significant number of towns joined the revolt partly because in 1572 Alva had decided to press ahead with the collection of the Tenth Penny Tax, which he had originally proposed in 1570.

This letter is a royalist viewpoint of the causes of the violence, dismissing the tax as a cause. It is from the Count of Boussu who was appointed stadtholder by Philip when Orange was forced to flee. It is to the Duke of Alva, whose idea the tax originally was. Boussu was a Dutch noble, however, so may have had more knowledge or understanding of the concerns of the rebels.

The purpose of this document, a letter, was to try to explain what was happening in the Netherlands. It was a private letter between the two royalist leaders. It was not printed or circulated.

Boussu is probably referring to the actions of the Sea Beggars in **privateering** on the coast of the Netherlands. If so, he blames the Sea Beggars for causing the poverty of the rebels, not the Tenth Penny Tax.

Source 1 An extract from a letter to **the Duke of Alva from the Count of Boussu**, 16 May 1672. Here Boussu gives an alternative explanation for the disorder in 1572.

> Although people here take their impending ruin on account of the Tenth Penny as the sole pretext for the revolt ... the real cause is that there are twenty or thirty thousand men in this province [Holland] whose sole livelihood consists of fishing and seafaring, and, since this has now altogether ceased, and since for some time they have been spending all that they have managed to save in the past, they will eventually be so oppressed by poverty that they will no longer care what price they pay for relief.

The people said their grievance related solely to the Tenth Penny Tax, a sales tax of ten per cent on all sales of goods. This was introduced by Alva as a way to pay for his army. This was necessary because of Spain's poor financial situation, which meant that the soldiers were not being paid. It increased the prices of ordinary goods which meant that more people struggled to afford to buy food and other such necessities.

Boussu warns Alva here that the poor are becoming very desperate, and of the potential for further violence. This was proven correct in the next few years.

The context for Source 1 helps to answer the question in the following ways:

- The document was written by the Count of Boussu, Philip II's approved appointee, to the Governor-General, the Duke of Alva. It is likely, therefore, to reflect the royalist point of view regarding the causes of the conflict.

- Despite this, Boussu was Dutch, and so may have understood the longer-term context of the violence better than Alva.

- However, this source does claim that the actions of the Sea Beggars caused the revolt rather than the Tenth Penny Tax. This suggests that Boussu aimed to blame the rebels for the violence (as might be expected from a supporter of Philip II) rather than the Spanish tax.

> Source 1 is useful to the historian studying the causes of the violence of 1572 because it indicates that the royalist or Spanish view did not credit the Tenth Penny Tax as one of the main causes of the revolt. The fact that it blames the Calvinist Sea Beggars could show a lack of awareness about the people's grievances in relation to Spanish policies. There are limits to the source's usefulness, however, because it just represents one side of the argument. It does not give any information about how the rebels saw this. It is also just one Royalist noble's view rather than that of the poor people he describes.

Source 2 From the Act of Abjuration, 1581, the document by which the Dutch formally deposed Philip II as their monarch. It explains their view of the causes of the revolt. It was composed by the Dutch nobles and representatives in the States General.

[A] great number of other gentlemen and substantial citizens, some of whom were executed, and others banished that their estates might be confiscated, plaguing the other honest inhabitants, not only by the injuries done to their wives, children and estates by the Spanish soldiers lodged in their houses, as likewise by diverse contributions, which they were forced to pay toward building citadels and new fortifications of towns even to their own ruin, besides the taxes of the hundredth, twentieth, and tenth penny, to pay both the foreign and those raised in the country, to be employed against their fellow-citizens and against those who at the hazard of their lives defended their liberties. In order to impoverish the subjects, and to incapacitate them to hinder his design, and that he [Alva] might with more ease execute the instructions received in Spain, to treat these countries as new conquests, he began to alter the course of justice after the Spanish mode, directly contrary to our privileges; and, imagining at last he had nothing more to fear, he endeavoured by main force to settle a tax called the tenth penny on merchandise and manufacture, to the total ruin of these countries, the prosperity of which depends upon a flourishing trade, notwithstanding frequent remonstrances, not by a single province only, but by all of them united.

Activity: Seeing things their way

Now try contextualising Source 2.

Re-read the question on page 376 – remind yourself of the specific task you are focusing on.

1 Ask yourself the following questions and annotate a copy of the source with the answers:
   a) Are there any events that may have influenced the writing of Source 2?
   b) Which debate is Source 2 likely to be contributing to?
   c) This view may reflect the views of a specific group – which group?
   d) Does the source reflect the views of all the groups involved in the conflict?
   e) Who wrote the source?
   f) Why was it written?
2 Next, write a series of bullet points outlining:
   a) the aspects of the source that are useful for answering the question
   b) the aspects of the source that are less useful
   c) a summary of the extent to which the source provides useful evidence concerning the reasons for the wider outbreak of violence in 1572.

Work together

Having read Source 2 and completed the activity 'Seeing things their way', discuss the following questions with a partner:

1 Did you both agree on:
   a) the reasons why the author wrote Source 2?
   b) the debate that Source 2 is addressing?
   c) the extent to which Source 2 might reflect the views of all the groups involved in the conflict?
2 Did you both agree on:
   a) the aspects of the source that were useful for answering the question?
   b) the aspects of the source that are less useful?

   c) the overall extent to which the source was useful to the historian investigating the reasons for the wider outbreak of violence in 1572?
   If you disagreed on the answers to any of these questions, try and work out whose answer was better and why.
3 What else would it be useful to know about the source in order to answer the question?

Use your discussion to make a three-point list of the ways in which you can use contextual knowledge to improve your essay writing.

Activity: AS-style questions

1 Why is Source 1 (page 377) valuable to the historian for an enquiry into the causes of the violence in 1572?

2 How much weight do you give the evidence of Source 2 for an enquiry into the reasons for the Dutch Revolt from 1566–81?

Section B: Essay technique

Overall judgement

An overall judgement is as important to a Paper 2 Section B essay as it is to essays in Paper 1. You may have already read advice about the characteristics of a good overall judgement (see page 74). Remember, good judgements are supported, and the best judgements consider the relative significance of the key factors you have discussed in your essay.

Now you can practise writing an overall judgement to an essay concerning the Duke of Palma.

Activity

Imagine you are answering the following Section B question:

To what extent can Dutch divisions explain the success of the Duke of Parma from 1577–84?

1 Read the question and work out what type of question it is.
2 Make a plan that is appropriate to the specific question. Remember it should consist of three or four main points.
3 Add three pieces of detail to support each of your main points. Remember, use the detail that best supports the points you want to make.
4 Write an analytical sentence to conclude each of your main points.
5 Now write a conclusion to the essay.
   ● Start by asserting an overall judgement.
   ● Support this by weighing up the different main points in your plan.
   ● Summarise your overall judgement in the final sentence.

Work together

Having completed a plan, swap it with a partner. Consider the following questions:

1 Did you agree on what type of question you were dealing with? If not, discuss it and work out who was right.
2 Whose plan most clearly focused on the specific type of question?
3 Did you both begin your conclusion with a clear judgement?
4 Did you both weigh up the different key points to support your judgement?
5 Whose overall judgement was better and why?
6 What can you learn from each other's work?

Use these questions to feedback to each other and improve your essay technique.

Question practice

1 'Requesens' failure was fundamentally caused by the financial troubles of Spain.' How far do you agree with this statement?
2 How accurate is it to say that the Spanish Fury and other mutinies led to the Dutch provinces uniting against Spain? **AS**
3 'The southern provinces signed the Union of Arras in 1579 primarily because of religious reasons.' How far do you agree with this statement?
4 How far did were Parma's military tactics the main reason for his success up to 1584? **AS**
5 'William of Orange was the crucial figure in the Dutch Revolt from 1566 to 1584.' How far do you agree with this statement?

Key Topic 4 Securing the independence of the United Provinces, 1584–1609

Overview

Orange was a stable influence throughout every stage of the Dutch Revolt but his assassination in 1584 raised new questions. Who would lead in his absence? Would the revolt continue? Would Alexander Farnese, Prince of Parma and Spain's chosen Governor-General, finally defeat the rebelling Dutch? The northern provinces of Holland and Zeeland had some experience of autonomy when Orange had moved his headquarters to the south. The rebels were able to rally around Orange's son Maurice of Nassau, whose military successes made him a figurehead (if not a political leader) of the revolt after 1584. The Dutch rebels continued to fight against Spanish repression, facing many of the same troubles of the preceding decades. Foreign support continued to flow into the Netherlands from England in particular, and Philip II's conflicting priorities and commands made it very difficult for his appointees in the Netherlands to succeed in their fight against the Dutch. The provinces continued to grow in independence and strength. The political and economic contribution of Oldenbarnevelt was crucial at this stage. However, peace was not secured until the Truce of Antwerp in 1609. This was nearly 50 years after the troubles took root. It reflected Spain's declining power as much as the success and strength of the Netherlands, but did lead to the recognition of the United Provinces as a separate state from the kingdom of Spain.

This chapter examines these issues through the following sections:

1 *Maurice of Nassau* looks at the impact made by William of Orange's son and heir. It examines his military reforms, victories and work as stadtholder.

2 *Reasons for Spanish failures* examines the different factors that led to Spanish decline in the Netherlands from 1584–1609. It discusses English support, the diversion of troops to the Spanish Armada, and Philip's intervention in France.

3 *The growing power of the United Provinces* explores the reasons why the United Provinces grew stronger in this period. This includes the work of Oldenbarneveldt and the Dutch East India Company. It looks at the growing divergence of the north and south.

4 *The declining power of Spain in the Netherlands* discusses the rapidly proceeding legal separation of Spain and the Netherlands. These include the Truce of Antwerp and the de facto recognition of the United Provinces.

TIMELINE

1584 July	William of Orange assassinated
1585 August	Treaty of Nonsuch
1585 November	Maurice of Nassau appointed stadtholder of Holland and Zeeland
1585–87	Leicester was Governor-General of the Netherlands
1587	Maurice of Nassau took control of the United Provinces' army
1588	Spanish Armada threatened to invade England
1590 July	The United Provinces became the Dutch Republic
1592 December	Alexander of Parma died at Arras
1594 July	Groningen fell to the Dutch Republic
1595	Archduke Albert became Governor-General of Dutch provinces loyal to Spain
1596 November	Philip II again declared bankruptcy
1597	The Dutch victory at the Battle of Turnhout
1598 September	Philip II died; his son Philip III became new King of Spain; Isabella and Albert retained control of the Netherlands
1600 July	Maurice of Nassau suffered defeat at Nieuwpoort
1602	Dutch East India Company established
1609 April	Truce of Antwerp

1 Maurice of Nassau

The assassination of William of Orange in July 1584 changed the nature of the Dutch Revolt and launched Maurice into his military and political careers. Maurice's tactics, his use of siege warfare, and his important victories at Turnhout and Nieuwpoort were incredibly significant for the development of the Dutch Revolt. His successes led him to be appointed **stadtholder** for many more Dutch provinces, and to become a prominent leader of the revolt.

Note it down

Make notes to answer the following questions:
- Why was Maurice chosen as stadtholder?
- What were his significant military achievements?
- What were the consequences of the Dutch victories at Turnhout and Nieuwpoort?
- What was the significance of the declaration of the sovereignty of the **States General** in 1590?

Nassau's military reforms and changes in strategies and tactics

Maurice of Nassau took command of the United Provinces' army in 1587 after the recall of Leicester to England (see page 387). He was now 20 years old and had been stadtholder of Holland and Zeeland for two years. Nassau re-organised the army. One of his major innovations was ordering his soldiers to train. This may seem obvious now but was not standard practice in the sixteenth or seventeenth centuries. Military training was a key part of Nassau's military strategy. It kept the men fit and prepared and also made the soldiers more disciplined. The officers also knew their soldiers better when they both commanded and trained their regiments. All of these changes made the soldiers more efficient in battle.

Nassau was a strategist. He read ancient and modern military theories, for example, the siege theories of Simon Stevin, the writings of the Greek scholar Aelian and those of the Byzantine Emperor Leo XI, and then applied these plans to the military campaigns on the ground. Nassau appointed his former tutor Stevin as a quartermaster general of the army of the States General. Nassau introduced the tactic of using volley fire in battle at the Battle of Niewpoort in 1600. In volley fire, a group of soldiers fired their guns together. This method compensated for the inaccuracy of early modern guns as the soldiers were more likely to hit their targets when they fired as a group. Maurice used cannons extensively – at the siege of Groningen in 1594 his army

fired over 10,000 cannonballs. In 1590, the army built new fortresses in Friesland and he also encouraged the towns and cities to stockpile munitions in preparation for possible sieges. Nassau led a campaign across the River Ijssel in 1591 to reclaim the north-eastern Dutch cities and towns that had been captured by Spanish soldiers in the 1580s such as Zutphen, Deventer and Doesburg. The Dutch Revolt was successful during the 1590s thanks to Nassau's military reforms and leadership skills. He created a well-organised, disciplined and modern fighting force that was better able to succeed against the larger Spanish army.

Siege warfare against fortresses and border towns

In May 1591, Nassau's army besieged Zutphen and after just five days, the town fell. In June, Nassau won the town of Deventer in ten days. These were major victories for the Dutch and was the beginning of a Dutch advancement south into territories held by the Spanish. A change in Spanish priorities also benefited Nassau's army. Following the defeat of the Spanish **Armada** in 1588 (see page 388), Philip began to concentrate his military efforts on supporting the French Catholics, sending additional soldiers to France, rather than the Netherlands. He even diverted some of his armies from fighting in the Netherlands, and sent them to France in the belief that the investment in Spanish armies in France was

Maurice of Nassau (1567–1625)

Maurice of Nassau was only 16 years old when his father, William of Orange, was assassinated in Delft. Maurice was Orange's second son to his second wife, Anna of Saxony. He was a Protestant who lived on his family's estates in Germany at the time of his father's assassination. His studies at Heidelberg and Leiden were paid for by the states of Holland and Zeeland because William of Orange had spent his fortune in support of the Dutch Revolt. Despite his young age when appointed **stadtholder**, Maurice experienced great success. He was a military innovator who paid close attention to new developments in warfare. He was a skilled commander who reorganised the army of the United Provinces into one that could achieve significant victories over the Spanish. The Truce in 1609 was negotiated against Maurice's will, even though the deal was favourable to the Netherlands. Maurice also was politically ruthless, executing Oldenbarnevelt after a rift between them became (to Maurice) irresolvable in 1619. Maurice died in 1625 while once again fighting the Spanish after the Twelve Year Truce came to an end.

a better use of money. This clearly made it harder for his officers in the Netherlands to succeed against the Dutch.

Nassau and Spanish mutinies

In the early 1590s, the Spanish army again ran into financial difficulties and, as they had done frequently in the past, the soldiers began to mutiny. Under Nassau's leadership, the army of the United Provinces was able to take advantage of this situation and as a result recaptured St Geertruidenberg and Wedde. The Spanish army in Flanders mutinied when Philip's nephew, Archduke Ernest, arrived to take charge in February 1594 because the Spanish Crown had just raised the money to pay their army that was mutinying in France – the Spanish army in the Netherlands also aimed to be paid their back pay. Nassau's army lay siege to the city of Groningen as the Spanish mutinied. This was the last city still loyal to Philip in the northern provinces. Nassau's forces were finally victorious on 23 July, partly because the mutineers refused to march to the relief of the city and the Spanish had lost their last loyal northern stronghold.

Success in the border sieges

The strategy of attacking border towns was successful for Maurice of Nassau. He confined the army's fighting to the edges of the United Provinces. The tactic created a border around the United Provinces, operating much like a castle wall. This meant that the towns and cities away from the border were peaceful and with this newfound peace and security, the towns resumed their earlier activities of trade and commerce. The towns and cities of the United Provinces soon became financially prosperous once again, just as they had been before the revolt started so many years earlier. With this financial prosperity, the Dutch were able to invest in their armies, too. Nassau's military tactics therefore led to greater prosperity and an increasing independence in the United Provinces.

Sovereignty of the States General, July 1590

After Leicester left the Netherlands in disgrace in 1587 (see page 388), the States General of the United Provinces concluded that they should not seek a foreign monarch or Governor to rule them. They determined that the best solution to the problem of government was that the States General should become the sovereign authority within the United Provinces. The rebel provinces were already bound together through the Union of Utrecht, and so it was decided that the best course of action would be to stay bound together with the States General ruling the provinces and directing the provinces' military and financial resources. Maurice of Nassau was selected to be the United Provinces' military commander and Johan van

Oldenbarnevelt emerged as the leader of the States General. With these two leaders in place, the United Provinces would pursue two main policies. First, they would do their best to end the war with Spain. Second, they would pursue religious **toleration** in the provinces. By working together as a cohesive state, the United Provinces hoped they would finally be able to expel the Spanish.

The combination of financial prosperity, military leadership, and the increasing confidence of the States General led the United Provinces to declare that the States General were the sovereign institution of the country. This meant that the provinces would no longer be ruled by a king or a **Governor-General**. With this declaration on 25 July 1590, the rebelling provinces had become the Dutch Republic.

The victories at Turnhout, 1597, and Nieuwpoort, 1600

Turnhout

Turnhout was an important town on the border between the southern provinces that were still loyal to Spain and the rebellious northern provinces. Maurice of Nassau led a cavalry attachment into battle at Turnhout on 27 January 1597, meeting a Spanish cavalry group of equal size, commanded by the Count de Varas. Nassau used a concentrated cavalry charge, using cavalry armed with pistols, swords and **arquebuses** rather than the more old-fashioned lance. The Spanish cavalry fled, leaving their infantry to fight the Dutch alone. In this way the Dutch were able to defeat the Spanish cavalry, driving them away from Turnhout. Nassau's army burned the town's castle in response. The battle ended in disaster for the Spanish, with over 2,000 killed (including Varas) and 500 taken prisoner by the Dutch. In comparison, only 12 Dutch soldiers were killed. This battle marked an important strategic victory for the United Provinces, teaching them that it would be strategically better and more effective to capture towns and cities than to attempt victories on the battlefield. Learning from this experience, they would pursue towns in the later stages of the revolt. Moreover, the victory at Nieuwpoort established the reputation of Maurice's cavalry, especially amongst the Spanish. It also gave the Dutch much needed confidence in their abilities to wage war.

Maurice as stadtholder

In October 1589, Count Neunahr, the stadtholder of Utrecht inspected a gunpowder warehouse. It exploded and he was killed. Nassau was elected stadtholder of Utrecht in the wake of this tragedy, aided by the support of Oldenbarnevelt. Nassau's military success while stadtholder of Holland and Zeeland no doubt helped to bolster his cause. He was also made stadtholder of Gelderland and Overijssel. By 1590, then, Nassau was the stadtholder of five provinces in the Dutch Republic (Holland, Zeeland, Utrecht, Gelderland and Overijssel) as well as commander-in-chief of the army and high admiral. As stadtholder of so many provinces, Nassau was able to provide some stability in the republic's political leadership. This stability helped support the Dutch Republic as they began to develop into an independent country.

Death of Philip II, September 1598

Philip II died in September 1598. He was succeeded in Spain by his son, Philip III, but the Netherlands were to be governed by Philip II's daughter, Isabella, and her husband, Archduke Albert. After Philip II's death, Albert earnestly tried to end the war in the Netherlands but the Dutch did not want to create a peace treaty with the Spanish in the Netherlands. Furthermore, the new King of Spain, Philip III, did not trust many of Albert's policy decisions. The Archdukes were forced largely to take the advice offered by the group of Spanish advisers Philip had sent to Brussels. In other cases, the Archdukes were told which policies to implement by Philip himself. The Dutch rebels could not be certain that a peace plan negotiated with the Archdukes would last.

Isabella and Archduke Albert (1559–1621): 'the Archdukes'

Archduke Albert was the fifth son of the Holy Roman Emperor Maximilian II. Aged 11, he was sent to the Spanish court to be educated under the supervision of his uncle Philip II of Spain. He was intended to be a churchman, so was brought up for the priesthood and appointed **cardinal** in 1577. After the union with Portugal, Albert became both viceroy of Portugal and its papal legate. He was recalled to Spain in 1593 and sent to the Netherlands in 1595. He entered Brussels in February 1596. Albert was instrumental in the Peace of Vervins, a treaty between Spain and France. Spain gave up its conquests from France and France pulled out of the war – although it carried on supporting the Dutch. Albert was married to his cousin Isabella, daughter of Philip II of Spain, in 1599. He obtained special permission from the Pope to resign from the College of Cardinals and marry Isabella. Before this Philip II ceded governance of the Netherlands to Isabella and her fiancé. They were to rule the Spanish Netherlands together, until the death of either or both of them. During their rule of the Netherlands they were known as the 'Archdukes'. On Albert's death in 1621 the Netherlands reverted to Philip III's eldest son Philip IV.

Nieuwpoort

Johan van Oldenbarnevelt, the political leader of the United Provinces, devised a plan for Maurice of Nassau to re-capture the important coastal city of Nieuwpoort. By 1600, Nieuwpoort was the last city still under Spanish control that had access to the Flemish coast. Spanish pirates had used Nieuwpoort as a base for conducted raids on Dutch merchant ships, and Oldenbarnevelt hoped that recapturing it would end attacks on Dutch ships. Capturing Nieuwpoort would also disrupt Spanish communications, making it difficult for the Spanish armies located in the southern provinces to communicate with Spain and nearly impossible for them to receive supplies. The summer of 1600 provided a good opportunity for invasion because some of the Spanish troops were mutinying again so their firepower was somewhat diminished. This seemed like a good moment for the Dutch army to advance into Nieuwpoort. Oldenbarnevelt also believed that a Dutch victory would encourage the English to once again invest more heavily in the Netherlands.

On 22 June 1600, Nassau led a sea invasion at Nieuwpoort. He believed that the Dutch people living in this southern area of the Netherlands were tired of the Spanish presence. He thought that the Dutch would be encouraged by his army's presence and would join his fight against the Spanish soldiers, but Nassau had misjudged the sentiment of these people. They were tired of soldiers from the United Provinces conducting raids on their cities and goods, so instead of rising to help Nassau fight the Spanish, they did everything they could to resist Nassau's army. On 30 June, Archduke Albert arrived with an army of 3,000 Spanish soldiers. The two armies met on the battlefield, on the beaches near Nieuwpoort. Though the losses were heavy, Nassau's army was ultimately victorious, charging at the Spanish army when the setting sun was in their eyes. His military innovations also saved the day, with wooden mats allowing the Dutch guns to keep on moving and firing while the Spanish guns sunk into the mud.

Consequences of Dutch victory at Nieuwpoort

The Dutch victory at Nieuwpoort had mixed results. On the one hand, it showed that Nassau was a skilled military leader and won him respect among the princes of Europe. It also showed Nassau that his army would be more successful if they continued to make raids and sieges on border towns. On the other hand, the battle showed that there was little likelihood that the southern and northern Netherlands could be reunited. Furthermore, it damaged relations between Oldenbarnevelt and Nassau because Nassau and his

Source A Oil painting of Maurice of Nassau at the Battle of Nieuwpoort by the artist Pauwels van Hillegaert (1600). He was especially commissioned to paint the scene of this famous Dutch victory.

What can Source A tell the historian who is studying the figure of Maurice of Nassau and his importance in the development of the Dutch Revolt? How has the artist portrayed Maurice and why?

supporters had opposed the campaign, his uncle William of Nassau calling it 'unwise and reckless'. Nassau was bound to obey the orders of the States General, however, so had to go ahead. The struggle of the battle made Nassau even more convinced he was right. The battle had consequences for the Dutch who were loyal to Spain as well. The Dutch living in the southern Netherlands realised that they would have to find a way to finance their own military defence. It was clear to them that Spain did not have enough money to support a full-scale war there. Philip III wanted Archduke Albert to continue fighting for the lost provinces but due to his financial problems could not provide the resources to ensure a Spanish victory.

Conclusion: Maurice of Nassau

Maurice of Nassau was launched into his military and political career after the assassination of his father. It is important to note that these were not positions that were hereditary, but that Nassau became a political leader because the people of several provinces selected him to be their stadtholder. Nassau took command of the army of the United Provinces in 1587, three years after Orange's death. As a military leader, he had some independence

but also closely followed the wishes of the States General. During this period the military fortunes of the Dutch Revolt seemed to change for the better. The provinces also became more confident as they governed themselves. They achieved important military victories against the Spanish, and began to establish more stable governmental institutions to make political decisions. Spain's weaknesses also began to come to the fore in this period. Financial problems led once again to mutinies, and Philip II died. Although Philip II's style of rule had been a significant cause of the Dutch Revolt, his successors did not improve the situation – Spanish power became fragmented and less stable.

Work together

Work with a partner to examine the reasons for Nassau's success. Read through this section and consult the 'Recommended reading' if you would like further detail. When you have finished drawing out the reasons, put them into the following categories: Nassau as commander, Dutch military strengths, and Spanish weaknesses.

2 Reasons for Spanish failures

From 1584 Spain experienced a period of failure and decline in the Netherlands. There were many factors that helped to cause the Spanish failures in this period. Maurice's military capabilities was one such factor (see page 381). The Dutch also received much more substantial support from England after the Treaty of Nonsuch in 1585, however, and this was important in terms of the provision of money and troops. It also, rather ironically, succeeded in distracting Philip II from the situation in the Netherlands. Instead he pulled troops out of the Netherlands and planned an attack on England for supporting his enemies. Following the failure of the Spanish Armada in 1588 Philip turned to France and intervened in the French Wars of Religion in 1589. All of these distractions allowed Nassau to proceed with his military gains with much less intervention from the Spanish army.

> **Note it down**
>
> Use a spider diagram (see page x) to take notes on this section. On the body of the spider write the heading 'Reasons for Spanish failure' and draw three legs – English support, the Spanish Armada, and the French Wars of Religion. Structure your notes using these categories and subdivide them again where necessary.

The Dutch search for a new monarch

William of Orange's assassination changed matters for the Dutch. Orange was regarded as the natural leader of the revolt and in his absence the Dutch once again searched for new leaders. Although Maurice of Nassau was appointed stadtholder of Holland and Zeeland (see page 381), he was as yet inexperienced and lacked the power and authority of a monarch. The rebels first turned to France again before looking to Elizabeth I of England. The rebels in the southern provinces clung to the idea that the Dutch needed to find one leader to replace Orange, and they preferred to be ruled by a monarch.

The southern rebels soon convinced most of their northern counterparts that the most suitable candidate for the throne of the Netherlands was King Henry III of France. Some people were suspicious of Henry because they believed rumours which suggested he participated in the St Bartholomew's Day Massacre in 1572 that had killed Admiral Coligny and so many others. These doubts were cast aside, and an ambassador was sent to Henry's court in February 1585 but Henry was afraid of Spain's immense military power. He was also afraid of the French Catholic League, a militant group within his own kingdom. Religious difference had caused bloody civil wars that still ravished the kingdom and so Henry decided to decline the Dutch offer in order to avoid more bloodshed at home in France.

Support for the United Provinces by Elizabeth I of England from 1584

The States General, meeting at The Hague, were disappointed with Henry III's answer. They next turned to another of Europe's Protestant monarchs: Elizabeth I of England. Like Henry, Elizabeth and her advisers feared the great power of the Spanish military. They were even more afraid of a Spanish victory over the rebels in the Netherlands. This was because:

- Philip II had often declared his intention of ensuring that England would become a Catholic country once again
- the English were worried that a Spanish victory would encourage Catholics in Britain to revolt or assassinate the Queen
- they were also fearful that a Spanish victory would harm the prestige of **Protestantism** in Europe. It would mean that the Spanish had won a better strategic position in Europe
- it would be easier for Spain to attack or invade England from the Netherlands
- it would also be easier for Spain to attack ships coming back to Europe carrying the wealth of the New World.

A Spanish victory in the Netherlands was simply unacceptable to Elizabeth but if she accepted the offer of the States General, she would mark herself as on open enemy of Philip II, the most powerful monarch in Europe at that time.

Elizabeth decided to decline the Dutch offer to rule as their sovereign monarch as it would be too dangerous for English interests. However, Elizabeth decided that she would assist the States General and the rebelling provinces financially and militarily. She demanded that she be allowed to make decisions regarding strategy and finances in exchange for her help. She also wanted to choose the rebels' military and political leader. The States General were satisfied with the arrangements which were made official in the Treaty of Nonsuch.

The Treaty of Nonsuch, 1585

Signed on 20 August 1585, the Treaty of Nonsuch was the first treaty between the United Provinces and another state. The rebelling United Provinces became a protectorate of England. Elizabeth promised to send 6,350 foot soldiers and 1,000 cavalry to fight with the rebelling provinces and would share the soldiers' costs with the United Provinces. The **Governor-General** would command Elizabeth's army and the Dutch army together. The Governor-General would also serve as the United Provinces' political leader. Elizabeth had been granted the privilege of choosing this individual, and she selected Robert Dudley, Earl of Leicester.

> **Source B** From the loyalty oath of the English troops in the Netherlands, July 1585. This was an oath that the English swore to serve first the Queen, then the Dutch. These oaths were legally binding and so were not taken lightly.
>
> 1 They shall swear loyally and faithfully to serve her Majesty as their natural Princess, according to the order given by her Majesty to her general.
>
> 2 Subject to the above homage, they shall swear loyalty to the States General of the United Provinces, their friends and confederates, being of the reformed Christian religion, the Count Maurice of Nassau and the **Council of State** and their officers; and shall be bound to impeach the enemies thereof in the military operations ordered by the commanders: those who refuse to do so, or cause disturbance, to be hung or strangled.
>
> What does Source B tell the historian about the reasons for the English intervention? How valuable is it as evidence and why?

The governorship of Leicester, 1585–87

Leicester was the Governor-General of the rebel provinces from 1585 to 1587. Historian Jonathan Israel has described this brief period as one of the most important times for the Dutch Revolt. Leicester's governorship had the possibility of changing three aspects of political life in the United Provinces:

- The interaction between Holland and the other rebelling provinces.
- The influence of Calvinism on political life in the United Provinces.
- The way the nobility interacted with political life in the provinces.

Interaction between Holland and the other rebelling provinces

During the period of Leicester's governorship, the way Holland interacted with the other rebel provinces and the way political power was distributed through the provinces changed. Holland was the dominant of the rebel provinces, largely because of its size and wealth. The smaller provinces in the north resented the power that Holland exerted over them. The political leaders from Holland

Robert Dudley, Earl of Leicester (c1532–88)

Leicester was an English nobleman. He was Elizabeth I's **favourite** and friend. He was at one point a strong suitor for Elizabeth's hand in marriage but the death of his wife in 1560 led to a scandal which made that impossible. He was condemned to death in 1553 after his father's attempt to put Lady Jane Grey on the throne of England instead of the future Mary I but his actions in the Battle of St Quentin in 1554 against Philip II brought him back into royal favour. He was a soldier, statesman and politician. He was on Elizabeth I's Privy Council and was a major landowner, with extensive lands in England and Wales, especially Denbighshire and Warwickshire. Following his period as Governor-General of the Netherlands, Leicester returned to England and commanded the English army against the Spanish Armada. Leicester was a hardworking privy councillor, a Calvinist, and a consistent friend and adviser to the Queen. His death in 1588 caused her deep sadness.

began to see themselves as speaking for all of the rebels. The problem with this point of view was that they did not always offer the view that everyone shared. Furthermore, they did not always consult with the political leaders from the other provinces, simply assuming that their views reflected the views of all the rebel provinces. The other provinces saw the opportunity to gain greater political power with Leicester as the new leader.

This happened because the arrival of a new Governor-General led to fresh discussions about the nature of political power in the United Provinces. Leicester was not a member of a royal family, and he had no connections to the Orange family who had ruled the Netherlands. Additionally, Leicester believed that he would win favour and support from the people of the provinces outside Holland if he distributed political power equally through the provinces he governed.

Leicester's religion

The second way that Leicester's governorship had the potential to change political life in the United Provinces was through religion. Leicester was a Calvinist and religion was a key component in discussions of political power. The political elite from Holland were opposed to the kinds of Calvinist reforms that many wished to introduce to the Netherlands. The committed Calvinists wanted to strengthen Calvinism, to stop toleration of other religions, and to increase the influence of the Calvinist Church in state and society. They wanted Leicester to convene a synod of the Dutch Reformed Church in the hope that this would clarify doctrinal matters and create better organisation within the Dutch Church's structure. The committed Calvinists believed that these objectives were within their grasp with Leicester as the new Governor-General. This group tried to gain more influence within the leadership of the Dutch provinces.

Changes to the role of the nobility

Finally, the arrival of the Earl of Leicester could have changed the way the nobility acted in Dutch political life. Many of the nobility had faded into the background during the revolt. The nobility had initially been leaders, for example, during the events leading to the Compromise presented to Margaret of Parma (see page 324). In Holland, however, the primary leaders were the wealthy merchants who resided in the cities and towns. The members of the merchant classes took over from the nobility as the political leaders and many of the nobles were unhappy about their loss of political power. Leicester gave the nobility great hope about their political role, leading the nobles to believe that they could win back some of the political prestige and influence that they had lost over the course of the revolt.

Leicester resented the way the Dutch nobles had lost their influence in the northern provinces and was also suspicious of members of the merchant classes who meddled in matters of state. Leicester believed that it was the duty and the responsibility of the nobility to direct political matters. The Dutch nobility of the United Provinces therefore believed that Leicester's arrival would mean that they could claim back some of their former political power and influence.

Leicester in power, 1586–87

When Leicester arrived in the United Provinces in January 1586, a delegation met with him to define the exact nature of his power. Rather than working together successfully, however, Leicester and the Dutch delegation clashed over a number of important issues:

- **The authority to select stadtholders.** Leicester expected that the English would be able to choose stadtholders, but the Dutch argued that this was unprecedented – no previous Governor-General had this power. The Dutch argued that in the absence of a monarch the power belonged to the States General.
- **Leicester's trade embargo**. Leicester prevented the Dutch from trading with regions controlled by the Spanish. This did successfully prevent the Spanish-controlled areas from obtaining food and supplies but it also had a negative financial effect on the rebel provinces. It caused a downturn in trade as there were fewer markets for the rebel provinces to sell their goods. It meant that the economic prosperity of the rebel provinces was greatly affected and so was hugely unpopular.

Leicester returned temporarily to England in December 1586. While he was away, the provincial leadership of Holland set about trying to reclaim the political dominance they had enjoyed in the United Provinces before Leicester arrived. They modified Leicester's trade embargo and introduced new regulations for army officers, whereby officers serving in Holland and Zeeland were only to accept their commissions from the stadtholder. They were also to swear allegiance to the **provincial states**. These activities were meant to undermine Leicester's authority by making the stadtholder the more important figure for the army officers. Furthermore, the Dutch were also tiring of the English presence in their lands. The actions of the provincial leaders helped to weaken support for Leicester.

Leicester's coup, September 1587

The politics of the United Provinces had dramatically changed by the time Leicester returned in March 1587. The Dutch people now hated the English soldiers and the English soldiers had begun to defect. Some of them were now fighting with the Spanish soldiers against the Dutch they were supposed to help defend. Some of the provinces, including Friesland and Utrecht, still supported Leicester but he viewed his situation as precarious. Leicester considered two alternatives:

1 A coup. If he was victorious, he would seize greater power in the provinces he governed. He would be seen as the most powerful person in the Netherlands. He would choose the stadtholders, and make certain that the provincial states followed his policies instead of him listening to their demands.
2 Giving up the role of Governor-General and returning to England for good.

In the summer of 1587, Leicester began to prepare a coup. The coup was launched in September 1587. Leicester sent new soldiers from England into Holland to occupy a few cities and towns in the province. Leicester went into The Hague and attempted to arrest Maurice of Orange along with his personal political enemy, Oldenbarnevelt. This attempt failed. Leicester then tried to gain the support of some of the civic leaders in Amsterdam and Antwerp. Unfortunately for Leicester, they were the merchants who had been hurt by Leicester's trade embargo so this plan, too, failed. Leicester finally tried to invade and take over Amsterdam but when this also failed Leicester returned to England in 1588. Once more the States General were forced to assume leadership.

How successful was Leicester?

Leicester's governorship was unsuccessful. He failed to create political cohesion within the United Provinces that he governed. He also failed to drive the Spanish soldiers out of the Netherlands. English troops remained in the provinces after Leicester left. Some of them made agreements with Spanish soldiers, some defected from their army, and many of them resented being in the Netherlands. The English continued to be involved in Dutch political matters even after Leicester left the country in the belief that the Netherlands were far too valuable as a Protestant entity to leave to their own.

The diversion of Parma's troops to support the Spanish Armada

One reason Elizabeth had selected Leicester to be the United Provinces' Governor-General was because she was afraid of Spain's increasing military power. She hoped that an army led by Leicester would prevent the Spanish soldiers from making further advancements into the United Provinces. The Dutch, too, hoped that a larger army made of both English and Dutch troops would finally force the Spanish to leave the Netherlands once and for all. These hopes were crushed. Parma and his army continued to gain territory in the Netherlands during Leicester's

governorship. They moved into the provinces from the east, the north east, and the south, capturing towns and cities along the way. The Spanish even raided towns in Friesland from garrisons in Gronigen and Steenwijk.

At the same time, however, Philip had decided that he was going to invade England. Parma and Philip both agreed that the Spanish soldiers would not be able to complete the re-conquest of the rebellious provinces if England supported the rebels. The Spanish would have to prevent the English from helping the Dutch rebels by launching a military attack on the English. By 1588, it was clear that Philip planned to send the Armada to England. Now, Elizabeth needed help from the Dutch and their navy and decided to support Maurice as the United Provinces' captain-general. This was a major reversal in English policy.

Philip's invasion plans

The Spanish saw the Treaty of Nonsuch as evidence of firm English support for the rebellious Dutch provinces. They would need to remove the English soldiers from the Netherlands in order to enable the Spanish army to reconquer the remaining provinces. This was why Philip decided to send his Armada into England – to defeat England and prevent her supporting the Dutch. The Spanish navy would need further support for the invasion project and so Philip ordered his army in Flanders to join the Armada. The Armada's commander, the Duke of Medina Sidonia, sailed a fleet of 130 ships carrying 30,000 men from Spain to Flanders. Once in Flanders, the Armada was meant to meet with ships and barges that Parma had under his control. The ships would then carry Parma's 17,000 soldiers to England in an invasion. Once they had landed in Kent, Parma was to lead his army into London and seize it.

Philip hoped that Parma's arrival would lead to one of two situations:

1 English Catholics would revolt against Elizabeth and overthrow her government. A Catholic government, friendly to Spain, would take power and Philip would be able to convince it to take English soldiers out of the Netherlands. Without English support, the Dutch rebels would be forced to surrender. This was the best imaginable outcome for Philip but he also knew that it was unlikely. Philip did not believe that the English Catholics were powerful enough to effectively rise against their queen.
2 Parma and his army would invade, occupy Kent, and seize London. With London and Kent under Parma's control, his soldiers would not try to make further advancements into England but Philip would refuse to remove the Spanish soldiers until Elizabeth agreed to

certain demands. Philip wanted the English to remove their soldiers from the Netherlands. A second condition was that Elizabeth would allow English Catholics to practise their religion without persecution.

Parma was commanded to pursue the second situation because it was the plan most likely to succeed.

The failure of the Armada attack

Due to English and Dutch tactical success, poor navigational choices and bad weather, the Spanish Armada was decisively defeated in July 1588. Most of the ships were wrecked off the western coast of Ireland, dashed into the rocks in the shallow waters. The Spanish lost at least 60 ships and over 20,000 men. This was a turning-point for the United Provinces and the Dutch Revolt.

This was a major defeat for Parma. Parma had won additional support and money from Philip early in his Dutch campaign because he won many battles. Once he began losing, he continued to lose battles, and with each military defeat Parma also lost support and the confidence of the Spanish King. Philip became impatient, and began to question Parma's effectiveness as a military commander.

Parma's first defeat occurred at the Brabant city of Bergen-op-Zoom. His soldiers besieged the city from September until November but they failed to completely encircle the city. Heartened by the victory over the Armada, the Dutch soldiers defending the city fought hard. The Spanish were forced to retreat from Bergen-op-Zoom on 13 November 1588.

The Spanish army began to mutiny as they lost. These mutinies further weakened Parma's army in Flanders. Parma considered resigning from his post as Governor-General of the Spanish Netherlands. Before he took this drastic step, Parma sent a plan for peace to Philip. Philip, however, was committed to winning back the lost Dutch territories, and rejected it.

Intervention in France, 1589

In 1589, Philip decided to intervene in the French civil war which had been raging since 1562. One important reason the war continued was that the Protestant **Huguenots** and French Catholics continued to fight over which religions should be allowed in France. The Protestant King Henry III believed that the way to end the war in France was to encourage religious toleration but he was assassinated in August 1589. Philip wanted to prevent the new Protestant King Henry IV, from gaining support and security. The Spanish King wanted a fellow Roman Catholic to rule France, partly because he was a devout Catholic but also because he believed that a Protestant king in France would help the Dutch rebels in the same way that the English had. In order to support French

Catholics, Philip diverted soldiers away from battlefields in the Low Countries, and sent them to France. The army that Philip had sent to Flanders, which had also supported the Armada's attempted invasion of England in 1588, was once again sent away from the Netherlands. This absence of Spanish soldiers allowed Maurice of Nassau to achieve some military advancements for the rebels. Both the Armada and Philip's intervention in France, therefore, had serious consequences for the Spanish King's attempts to regain his Dutch territories from the rebels.

Conclusion: Reasons for Spanish failures

By the late 1580s, the rebellious Dutch provinces were gradually becoming a strong and independent state. The assassination of William of Orange in 1584 had been a serious blow to the Dutch but it also marked a turning-point in the way that many Dutch people perceived political authority. It forced the Dutch to consider political alternatives and to conduct debates about political authority, finally establishing the States General the governing authority of the provinces.

The terms of the Treaty of Nonsuch confirmed English support for the United Provinces. The Earl of Leicester was installed as the new Governor-General in 1586. Leicester created reforms in the United Provinces but they were unpopular, and he left the country in 1588.

The Treaty of Nonsuch changed the way that Philip viewed the Netherlands. He saw England as a major hindrance to the re-conquest of the rebelling provinces. If Spain were to reclaim these provinces, they would first have to ensure that the English were fully removed from the territories.

Philip's decision to invade England with his Armada proved to be disastrous. When the Armada was lost, the result was to encourage the Dutch rebels even further. Parma's army was divided between England and France and as a result began to lose battles in the Netherlands. Philip also began to direct his attention on France rather than his Dutch realms. All of these elements combined to lead to the beginning of Spanish failure in the Netherlands.

> ## Work together
>
> Together create an annotated timeline for this section. You could do this in a table with three columns: the date; the event; the causes and consequences of the event. Divide the sections between you and then come together to complete your table.

3 The growing power of the United Provinces

The period after Leicester left the Netherlands in 1588 was one of great change in the United Provinces, bringing greater economic and political stability. It also allowed Johan van Oldenbarnevelt to emerge as an important political leader and reformer. He was instrumental in setting up the Dutch East India Company, a crucial development for Dutch economic success from this point forward. The English continued to support the rebels to some degree, maintaining soldiers in the provinces with the purpose of helping the Dutch drive the Spanish out of the Netherlands.

Oldenbarnevelt's reforms

Oldenbarnevelt was a crucial political figure in the Dutch Revolt and was instrumental in ensuring that Maurice of Nassau became stadtholder. Oldenbarnevelt and Leicester had been political enemies because they fundamentally disagreed about where power should lie in the Netherlands. Leicester was in favour of ensuring that the Dutch nobility regained the political authority they had lost to civic magistrates when he served as their Governor-General. Leicester also thought that the Governor-General should be a central authority in the Netherlands. For Leicester, this meant that the Governor-General was the most important political figure. All major decisions could be made by the Governor-General, with or without the approval of other governing bodies like the States General or the General Council.

Oldenbarnevelt also opposed the way Leicester had weakened Holland's power within the United Provinces. He wanted to restore Holland's previous influence. Oldenbarnevelt gained a reputation as a political reformer during Leicester's governorship. He opposed Leicester, and wanted William of Orange's son Maurice to govern the Netherlands instead. Oldenbarnevelt was an instrumental figure in creating unity within the United Provinces. He won important political appointments and combined those political appointments with personal skills to bring about unity in the rebel provinces.

Note it down

Firstly, add Oldenbarnevelt to your collection of index cards (see page xi). Take brief biographical notes as well as those on his actions and significance. Secondly, make a spider diagram (see page x) that breaks down the different actions and policies of Oldenbarnevelt.

Oldenbarnevelt as Land's Advocate (1586–1619)

In March 1586, Oldenbarnevelt became the **Land's Advocate** for the province of Holland and held this position until his death in 1619. The Land's Advocate was the most powerful political position in a province after the stadtholder. He served as the representative of the nobility and had the right to speak first during meetings of the provincial states. Oldenbarnevelt used his role as Land's Advocate to achieve the political reforms that he wished to produce. He was able to wield great power in the States General through the prominence of Holland, and through his political skill and diplomacy was able to benefit Maurice of Nassau. Holland contributed nearly 59 per cent of the funds to the budget of the United Provinces and Oldenbarnevelt was to use that to great effect.

Johan van Oldenbarnevelt (1547–1619)

Johan van Oldenbarnevelt was born in Amersfoort, a town in the province of Utrecht. He was one of Orange's early supporters and was a prominent figure in Holland's provincial government beginning in the late 1570s. He was a trained lawyer and fought for the rebel forces at the siege of Haarlem in 1573 and the siege of Leiden in 1574. Even before he became Land's Advocate he promoted the Union of Utrecht in 1579 (see page 372). He favoured Maurice of Nassau as a leader and military commander and was a determined opponent of the Earl of Leicester. Oldenbarnevelt was intelligent, hardworking and a persuasive politician. He became Land's Advocate in 1586 and also undertook several diplomatic missions for the Republic to France and England. Although Maurice commanded the armies that achieved such success for the Dutch, it was Oldenbarnevelt who co-ordinated the financing and supplying of the forces. Although he was one of Nassau's strongest supporters in the 1580s, they began to drift apart in the early 1590s. This came to a head with the 1606 truce with Spain. After he made a proposal in 1617 for the states of Holland to declare their own sovereignty from the United Provinces Oldenbarnevelt (and his main supporters) were arrested by Nassau. He was tried before a special court, nearly all of whom were his personal enemies. Unsurprisingly the court condemned Oldenbarnevelt. They pronounced a death sentence on 12 May 1619 and Oldenbarnevelt was executed by beheading the day after, aged 71.

Oldenbarnevelt's naval reforms

Oldenbarnevelt reformed the United Provinces' navy. Leicester believed that the province of Holland had become too powerful within the republic and reduced the province's authority by reorganising the navy. He placed naval and other maritime affairs into one single leadership college so that no one province had commanding authority. Oldenbarnevelt negotiated a new agreement concerning naval power. There would now be two maritime colleges, one in Amsterdam and one in West Frisia. The States General, not the Governor-General, would oversee both colleges. Officials from Holland and from West Frisia were happy with these changes.

The Dutch East India Company and the development of overseas trade

The establishment of the Dutch East India Company in 1602 contributed to the financial success of the United Provinces. Oldenbarnevelt was instrumental in creating the Dutch East India Company by bringing together rival companies of merchants into this one company. This company is sometimes considered the first multinational corporation and was also the first company to issue **joint stocks.** This meant that the Company began with a huge amount of financial capital – 6.5 million guilders. Many of the Dutch elite invested in the Company. They reaped huge profits from the goods that the Dutch ships brought back from the East. The States General granted the Company significant powers – monopolies over trade and navigation between the Dutch Republic and the east, authority to build their own armed forces, negotiate treaties with other states and administer justice to its own employees.

The Dutch East India Company was initially established so that the Dutch could participate in the highly profitable business of trading in spices, especially pepper. The Dutch enjoyed great success in their voyages to Asia. Dutch ships sailed to the East Indies, where they bought spices. The ships then came back to Europe, selling the spices at immense profits due to the high demand. Everyone who invested in the ships by purchasing stock then received their portion of the profits. In 1605, the Dutch East India Company conquered territories in the East Indies, in Amboina, Ternate and Tidore. They were gaining more power and influence in the East Indies and would soon develop a monopoly.

The growing divergence of north and south

As the war against the Spanish forces continued to progress, fundamental changes were taking place within the Netherlands. These changes took place amongst the people living in the northern and southern provinces, and would ultimately drive the two sides apart. The northern provinces of the Netherlands predominantly spoke Dutch. Although many people in the north were Roman Catholic, they believed that religious freedom was an important principle to uphold. They valued their traditional rights and privileges above everything, and they saw religious freedom as a critical part of these rights and privileges. As the war progressed, many people living in the northern provinces converted to Calvinism. They began to view their relationship to their monarch in a different light. In the early stages of the revolt, all of the Dutch people were frustrated that Philip II spent such little time in the Netherlands and that he relied on counsellors who knew so little about their country, but they always argued that they wanted Philip to be their monarch. Over time, however, the people in the northern provinces came to see that Philip would not be the monarch that they desired him to be. They searched for other princes within Europe's royal families who could serves as a new monarch for the Netherlands. They explored other forms of government after their attempts at retaining monarchy failed.

Things were different in the southern provinces. The people of the southern provinces were predominantly Roman Catholic. They did believe in religious toleration but fewer southern Dutch people converted to Calvinism. They were more likely to speak **Walloon**, Flemish, or French than Dutch. Their experience of the war was different from that of their northern counterparts. As the landscape of the southern provinces was flat, it was easier for the armies to face each other on battlefields there than in the marshlands of the northern provinces. This meant that the people in the southern provinces suffered the destruction of their houses and cities on a larger scale than in the north. As a consequence, by 1600 they were extremely war-weary.

The key difference between the people of the north and the people of the south was government. The people of the southern provinces had supported the search for a new monarch for the Netherlands in the 1580s and still believed that monarchy was the best possible government for their country. When Philip II died, they were willing to experience the Archdukes as their rulers. As the northern provinces decided to try governing themselves as a republic, the people of the southern provinces maintained their loyalty to the Spanish Crown. The growing differences between the two sets of provinces can be perhaps best seen in the two alliances they formed: the Union of Arras and the Union of Utrecht, each based on a geographical area and a religious ideal. Once these unions were established, the Netherlands were torn apart and never brought together again.

Oldenbarnevelt's success in curbing Calvinist excesses

The issue of religion continued to be a problem even after the Dutch created an independent republic. Calvinists tried hard to ensure that their understanding of Protestantism was made the only official recognised religion in the United Provinces and they succeeded in making Calvinism the official public religion of the provinces. This meant that people were expected to attend Calvinist religious services. Despite this, people who practised other religions were tolerated. Zealous Calvinists believed that the United Provinces' success as a state depended on maintaining their religion. They argued that their Church was older than the state, and had in fact helped to ensure that it became a state. After all, they argued, the Union of Utrecht had written out the basic governing principles of the United Provinces, and was based on the idea that Calvinism was the right religion for the Netherlands. In short, this group was trying to link the revolt with the Reformed Church. The extreme Calvinists clashed with Oldenbarnevelt on this. Oldenbarnevelt wanted to keep the revolt separate from religious ideas. He believed that the way to ensure that the Dutch state would survive was to uphold provincial sovereignty. Provincial sovereignty was also enshrined in the Union of Utrecht. This idea meant that each province would maintain its traditional rights and privileges. Each province could maintain its unique character, and make the decisions that impacted their people. This included religious policies.

The Calvinists were opposed to many of Oldenbarnevelt's policies, and many resented the dominance the province of Holland had achieved within the republic. Leaders of the Calvinist churches urged Oldenbarnevelt to call a nationwide religious synod. The aim of this meeting would be to establish doctrine and a Church hierarchy. They believed such a synod was necessary because religious reforms in the Netherlands were not adopted by the state but rather by individuals. This meant that there was great religious diversity within those who followed Calvinism in the Netherlands. A synod, therefore, would theoretically create religious uniformity. Furthermore, the Church was funded by cities and provinces. Some of the Calvinists hoped that they could receive some monetary support from the States General as well. Oldenbarnevelt resisted the idea of a national synod. He held fast to the idea that the best way to deal with religious matters was to deal with them at the local level, rather than enforcing them either through the States General or nationally. He was afraid that Calvinists would persecute those who practised a religion different from their own because this is what had happened at Antwerp and angered Anjou so much. Religious toleration was one of the hallmarks of traditional Dutch rights and privileges.

Oldenbarnevelt therefore worked to give the right to decide religious doctrine not to the local churches but instead to local governments. This policy was controversial but it was consistent with the original aims of the Dutch Revolt.

Conclusion: The growing power of the United Provinces

The United Provinces took a bold step in July 1590 when they became the Dutch Republic. The States General became more confident as time passed: they had become expert at ruling themselves over the long course of the wars. They made some modifications to the way they operated, such as using the land's advocate as the primary spokesperson for the States General. They also granted Maurice of Nassau, the military commander, greater independence in matters of military strategy. These alterations helped to make the process of ruling the new country run smoothly. Furthermore, they continued to enjoy trade with allies like the English, and developed a new trading venture through the East India Company. During this period, two key figures helped forge the identity of the Republic: Nassau and Johan van Oldenbarnevelt. It became clear to both of these men that the Republic would only truly flourish if the war came to an end.

> ### Work together
>
> With a partner, debate the importance of Maurice of Nassau and Oldenbarnevelt. Which one was more significant in the growth of the United Provinces? One of you will represented Nassau and the other Oldenbarnevelt. Prepare for this by identifying arguments for the significance of each individual, and then an overall argument as to why your chosen individual was *more* important than the other.

4 The declining power of Spain in the Netherlands

The war between the Spanish and the Dutch continued to drag on into the 1590s. Participants on all sides were war-weary. Each side made small advancements but no real victories. As the war continued, it became clear that both sides were at a stalemate. Furthermore, Spanish interventions in the French Wars of Religion revealed that Spain now believed France was to be a more important region than the Netherlands. Spain continued to suffer financially and failed to devise new mechanisms to deal with these financial problems. As had frequently happened before, this had military consequences such as mutiny. This section will examine the declining power of Spain in the Netherlands.

Note it down

Use the 1:2 method (see page xi) to take notes on this section, remembering also to keep adding to your annotated timeline established in Key Topic 1. Put the headings in the left-hand column, such as 'Spain's inability to pay its troops', and the main points in the right-hand column. You could also highlight areas about which you would like to read more. This will be useful in revision.

Spain's inability to pay its troops

Philip II had invested heavily in the Duke of Parma's army earlier in the 1580s. During that decade, Parma had been very successful at advancing into Dutch rebel territories. However, Philip's investment into Parma's army began to fail by 1590. The army suffered many defeats, and Philip began to cut back his financial support. Historian Geoffrey Parker observed that Philip had sent Parma 18 million florins in 1590 but only sent 4.5 million florins in 1592. This cut in funding contributed to Parma's inability to pay the soldiers and led them to mutiny. By 1593, the Spanish army did not have enough money to pay for food or supplies and Philip sent them back to fight in France. New taxes were introduced in the Spanish Netherlands to pay for the war which angered the Dutch because the soldiers were fighting in France, not in the Netherlands.

Spain's financial situation continued to decline throughout the 1590s. Philip's interventions in the Netherlands and in France were very costly. His Italian bankers finally lost confidence in him. Though his navies did seize treasure returning from the New World, this was not enough for Philip's creditors to gain real confidence in his financial capabilities and Philip was forced to declare **bankruptcy** yet again in November 1596. The Spanish soldiers in the Netherlands continued to despair, mutiny, and starve but the situation with the bankers was finally resolved in February 1598, and the battles began anew.

Philip II died a few months later, in September 1598. The Netherlands were to be governed by his daughter, Isabella, and her husband, the Archduke Albert. Albert wanted to end the war in the Netherlands and to make peace with the rebelling provinces, but Philip III, the new King of Spain, wished to continue his father's policy of aiming to achieve a victory over all the Dutch provinces. Like his father, Philip III simply did not have the financial resources to invest in the army in Spain in a way that would ensure such a victory and, on 9 November 1607, Philip III was forced to declare bankruptcy. This provided the necessary circumstances for the armistice concluded in 1607.

The armistice of 1607

Isabella and Albert were eager to ensure peace in the Netherlands and began to negotiate a peace with Oldenbarnevelt in 1607. One key concession the Spanish made was to recognise the independence of the Dutch Republic. On 29 March, an eight-month ceasefire was agreed. The ceasefire would go into effect on 4 May but the Spanish were very unhappy with the terms of this agreement. Isabella and Albert promised that they would make no claims over any territory belonging to the Dutch Republic. In return, Oldenbarnevelt promised to disband the Dutch East India Company, but the agreement was not backed up with a solid plan for the disbandment of the Company. The Spanish were sceptical of whether Oldenbarnevelt would enforce this provision.

Representatives of the Spanish court and the Dutch Republic met at The Hague in February 1608. At these talks it emerged that Oldenbarnevelt had no plans to dissolve the Dutch East India Company whatsoever. Disbanding the Company was impossible for the Dutch: many nobles and elite merchants had invested in the Company. If it were destroyed, the financial ruin would have disastrous consequences for the Dutch elite. The Spanish wanted to destroy the Dutch East India Company because they felt that the Dutch used it to cut into Spanish profits. Dutch competition in the spice trade was unacceptable for the Spanish. The competition between the two groups that had begun in Europe had now spread overseas to Spanish colonies. The question of international trade would prove an ongoing feature of future negotiations, including the Truce of Antwerp in 1609.

The Truce of Antwerp, 1609

The armistice of 1607 was an important step on the way to achieving greater peace in the Netherlands, but negotiations were still necessary if the war was to end permanently. The Spanish had the following aims in the negotiations:

- A promise that the Dutch Republic would ensure religious toleration for Roman Catholics living in the Republic.
- An end to all Dutch trade with the East and West Indies.
- An end to the Dutch blockades of the Scheldt River and the Flemish coast.

These conditions were unacceptable, particularly to Holland and Zeeland. These terms were rejected in August 1608. England and France then stepped into the negotiations, and offered their own plan. This plan would be known as the Truce of Antwerp.

According to the terms of the truce, the Dutch were to stop their plans for creating a new company known as the West India Company. They also agreed to stop attacking the Portuguese in Asia. The Portuguese were allies of Spain, and the Dutch Republic's biggest competition for spices in Asia. In return, the Spanish were to lift trade embargoes they had placed on Dutch goods. The truce was not a lasting peace settlement, but it would end the war between the Spanish and the United Provinces for 12 years.

The terms of the Truce of Antwerp were significantly favourable to the Dutch. Oldenbarnevelt had proved to be a tough negotiator, who would concede little to the Spanish. As a result of the truce, the Dutch had won new markets for trade. They would now be able to sell their products in Spain and Portugal, as well as markets in the Mediterranean. Despite these gains, many people in both Spain and the Dutch Republic were unhappy with the terms of the truce. Nevertheless, Oldenbarnevelt hailed the truce as a major victory for his republic. The truce was signed in a lavish ceremony at Antwerp on 9 April 1609.

Spain's *de facto* recognition of the independence of the United Provinces

In 1609, the Truce of Antwerp established peace in the Netherlands. The terms of the agreement were to last for 12 years, and would then be renegotiated by the two sides. The treaties that arose from the talks between the Dutch and the Spanish showed that the Spanish now saw the Dutch as political equals, rather than as a wayward province that it would destroy. The truce had come from a desire for peace and a recognition that the southern and northern provinces had become very different places. The truce had benefits even if it was meant to be temporary. The United Provinces in the north became their own republic, free from the control of the Spanish **Habsburg** family and the governors they chose. The southern Netherlands remained loyal to the Spanish Crown (see Figure 1). With the peace, the United Provinces had the

opportunity to build their navy. It eventually became one of the most powerful military forces in the early modern world. This time of peace also allowed the Dutch merchants to flourish. The prosperity that was allowed to flourish during the truce would lay the foundations for the Dutch Golden Age of the seventeenth century.

According to the terms of the truce, Spain negotiated with the United Provinces as if it were an independent state. But the terms of the truce led the Spanish to inadvertently recognise that the United Provinces – by this point the Dutch Republic – were an independent country. One way that this *de facto* recognition took place was through the realities of economics. The Dutch were now free to trade with Spanish merchants, and their trade became the envy of all Europe (see Source C). This was an advantage for the Dutch: they still blockaded the Scheldt River, which led to Brussels, so Amsterdam became the port of choice for goods sent north from Spain. The Spanish also recognised that the Dutch were independent through their political declarations over the years. Neither the Spanish nor the Dutch wished to continue the war that had carried on for so many years.

> **Source C** Excerpt from William Carr, *The travellours guide and historians faithfull companion*, 1695. This was a travel guide for English tourists on tours around Europe. It aimed to give some introduction to the history and culture of the Continent. This section focuses on the Netherlands.
>
> > This Commonwealth ... hath worthily bin the wonder of all Europe during this last age, and perhaps not to be paralled in the records of former tymes: for if consider how many yeares it was assaulted by the then most Potent Prince of Europe, who aspired to no less then the Universal Empire, and that how formidable soever he were, yet they onely maintained their pretensions, but with uninterrupted prosperitie and successfulnesse advanced their trade, and spread their conquests in all the foure parts of the world.
>
> According to Source C, what were the achievements of the Dutch? What can it tell the historian about a) the changes between 1563 and 1609 and b) the perceptions of the Dutch Republic?

▲ Figure 1: The Netherlands, 1609

Conclusion: The declining power of Spain in the Netherlands

One of the key factors that led to the decline of Spanish influence in the Netherlands was money. Spain still had a large presence in the Spanish Netherlands, even though it was now ruled by 'the Archdukes', Isabella and Albert. Spanish soldiers were still needed in order to keep the war alive. But both sides were weary of war. In Spain, Philip III had inherited his father's crown. Unfortunately for

Philip, he also inherited his father's money problems. The pattern of Spain's inability to pay the army was repeated again, and the soldiers mutinied in response. As Spain's fortunes fell, those of the Dutch rebel provinces rose. The cities of the Dutch Republic began to flourish, thanks primarily to their ability to trade with a large number of countries in northern Europe. They also began to make money in the New World, thanks to ventures such as the Dutch East India Company. The armistice that was decided upon in 1607 finally became a longer-lasting truce in 1609.

Work together

Together, re-read Key Topic 1. This detailed the situation in 1563 in the Netherlands. Work in pairs to compare the situation in 1563 to that in 1609. What were the similarities? What were the differences? Identify the most significant differences and categorise them.

Chapter summary

- The assassination of William of Orange in 1584 changed the way many Dutch viewed the revolt.
- Maurice of Nassau was a capable military strategist who achieved significant military successes for the Dutch rebels.
- The Dutch felt they could no longer be governed by Philip II but many still wanted a monarch. They made offers to rulers in England and France.
- The 1585 Treaty of Nonsuch established a close alliance between England and the Dutch Republic.
- The Duke of Leicester was the governor of the United Provinces for approximately two years but was unsuccessful, leaving the Netherlands in 1588.

- Spain's interventions in the French Wars of Religion enabled the Dutch armies to win back territories they had lost during Parma's successful military campaigns.
- Johan van Oldenbarnevelt was a key politician whose ideas and policies helped the United Provinces become a modern republic.
- When Philip II died, his territories were divided between his children. Philip III ruled Spain; Isabella and her husband, Archduke Albert, ruled the Netherlands.
- The establishment of the Dutch East India Company in 1602 helped the United Provinces become a major actor in world trade and gave the country financial stability.
- The Truce of Antwerp in 1609 provided an opportunity for lasting peace and the United Provinces were recognised as being free from Spanish rule.

Recommended reading

Peter Limm, *The Dutch Revolt 1559–1648* (Routledge, 1989), Chapters 6 and 7.

These chapters analyse how economic prosperity and religious toleration helped to pave the way for the early success of the Dutch Republic. They also provide a useful analysis of the treaties that helped to establish the Republic as its own entity.

Geoffrey Parker, *The Dutch Revolt* (Viking, 1977), Chapter 6.

An essential text for this topic, chapter 6 includes a good explanation of the consolidation of the new Dutch republic and the role of Oldenbarnevelt.

Marco van der Hoeven (ed.), *Exercise in Arms: Warfare in the Netherlands, 1568–1648* (Brill, 1997).

J. P. Puype's chapter, 'Victory at Nieuwpoort, 2 July 1600' contains an excellent and highly detailed case study of the battle of Niuewpoort, the tactics used and outcomes. The books also includes an assessment of Nassau's use of siege warfare.

Maurice of Nassau

- Maurice was the son of William of Orange
- He took command of the United Provinces' army in 1587
- Maurice was a military strategist and reformed the army which led to rebel success during the 1590s
- By 1590 Maurice was the stadtholder of five provinces in the Dutch Republic

Reasons for Spanish failures

- Queen Elizabeth I declined the Dutch offer to rule as a sovereign monarch but assisted the rebelling forces
- English support was outlined in the Treat of Nonsuch (1585)
- The Earl of Leicester was the governor general of the rebelling forces from 1585–87
- Leicester failed to create political cohesion with the United Provinces that he governed
- He attempted a coup and left the Netherlands after it failed
- The defeat of the Spanish Armada was a turning point for the United Provinces
- Philip also directed his attention to France rather than his Dutch realms

SECURING THE INDEPENDENCE OF THE UNITED PROVINCES, 1584–1609

The growing power of the United Provinces

- The United Provinces became a Dutch Republic in 1590
- Oldenbarnevelt was an important figure in creating unity in the United Provinces
- The establishment of the Dutch East India Company contributed to the financial success of the United Provinces

The declining power of Spain in the Netherlands

- Spain continued to face financial problems in the 1590s and was unable to pay its troops
- Following Philip II's death in 1598, Philip III became king of Spain. The Netherlands were governed by 'the Archdukes'
- The Archdukes began to negotiate a peace with Oldenbarnevelt in 1607
- The Truce of Antwerp (1609) established peace in the Netherlands. The truce was to last for 12 years

▲ Summary diagram: Securing the independence of the United Provinces, 1584–1609

Section A: Essay technique

Evaluating the sources

Evaluating the sources is essential to doing well in the exam. It means working out how far the sources contain evidence that is useful to a historian doing a specific task.

There are different levels of evaluation, which are rewarded to different extents.

Firstly, your source evaluation must be relevant to the question:

- Source evaluation that is not clearly linked to the question will be awarded marks in the lower levels.
- Sources evaluation that is clearly relevant to the question will be awarded marks in the higher levels.

Secondly, there is the issue of the criteria you use to evaluate the sources (see table below).

Level 1	**No criteria** – evaluation is extremely superficial, it does not relate to any criteria.
Level 2	**Questionable criteria** – evaluation is based on a criteria, but the criteria is invalid, simplistic or poorly understood.
Level 3	**Formulaic criteria** – evaluation is based on a discussion of the **nature, origin and purpose** (NOP) of the source.
Level 4/5	**Valid criteria** – at this level responses will use criteria that reflect the kind of source and the kind of specific task that the question focuses on. In this sense the evaluation will be tailored to the question. At Level 4 the criteria will not be applied rigorously. At Level 5 the criteria will be applied rigorously.

Evaluating the sources: The criteria

Imagine you are answering the following question:

> **How far could the historian make use of Sources 1 and 2 to investigate the aims of the Dutch and Spanish representatives in peace negotiations from 1607 to 1609?**

Source 1 A letter from an unknown writer to Count Ernest of Nassau-Dietz on 27 March 1607. He was a military leader who served under Maurice of Nassau. The writer gives details of peace negotiations between the Archdukes and the States General for an eight month ceasefire in order to conduct more permanent negotiations.

Thereafter was sent from Brussels one Vernier Crubbel with a Dr. John Meyen, native of Antwerp, Commissary General of the Friars Minor, Confessor of the Archduke and almoner of the Infanta, who arrived secretly the 13 February, saying that their Highnesses had resolved to treat with this State as a free republic over which they made no pretensions, having commission to treat for a truce or cessation of arms for 8 months, during which neither party should undertake either siege or invasion against the other, to resolve thereafter the matter of peace. The substance of the answer of the Estates (which the monk copied with his own hand to carry away) was: That they should be held by their Highnesses for a free state over which they had no pretensions; that they should treat of a truce by land only and not by sea or by water in rendering or exchanging one to the other certain places for its good performance. They went away and returned the 7th of March to the Hague, bringing the declaration above signed by their Highnesses, except that their Highnesses wish the cessation of arms to be as well by sea as by land, and in Spain and everywhere. And it seems that except for the cessation of arms by sea these Provinces are inclined to conclude the said truce.

Source 2 From an account of the peace negotiations prior to the Twelve Year Truce of 1609. This section deals with the negotiations in September 1608 and was written by Oldenbarnevelt.

> They said further that thy hoped that we would not return to the rigors of war and cause further spilling of blood, calamities and miseries of war, and wanted those who were inclined toward war to think over the matter and to examine in their consciences why they wished to expose the country and its good people to the miseries and calamities of war, and to consider too that they could easily come under accusation and rue a renewal of the war and having broken off this negotiation or caused it to run into difficulty in this way. Our reply was that in so far as they were sorry that the conclusion of the negotiation did not correspond to its beginning, the sorrow of my Lords the States was no less than theirs, for they had hoped to change the war into a good peace and had acted in the negotiation with fear of God, and they too had always tried to achieve this, truly desiring that the spilling of blood and the calamities and miseries of war should cease to the extent that this was in their power; but it was their intention to have their freedom recognized by the king of Spain and Their Highnesses [the archdukes] in proper form, and that without this the whole negotiation would be rejected.

Simplistic source analysis

Having read the sources, it is clear that the Dutch negotiators, including Oldenbarnevelt, prioritised officially recognised freedom from Spain as a demand before peace could be concluded. Therefore, you could say that 'Oldenbarnevelt is biased against Spain'. However, this would be a low level response, because it is not clear why you consider Source 2 biased. Additionally, it is not clear how this statement answers the question.

You could say that 'Source 2 is unreliable because Oldenbarnevelt is only one of the Dutch negotiators and may not have been present all of the time'. However, this is based on questionable criteria: it assumes that only eyewitnesses are useful to historians, which is not true. Additionally, it is speculative about Oldenbarnevelt's presence – so the criteria are not appropriate to the source.

Based on this, here are two basic tips:
- Avoid simply saying 'Source 1 is biased'. Statements like this are very simplistic and are therefore unlikely to get you a good mark.
- Avoid assuming that the only useful sources are eyewitness accounts.

Nature, origin and purpose

One way of evaluating the sources is to ask questions about the nature, origin and purpose of the sources:
- **Nature:** what type of source is this?
- **Origin:** when and where does the source come from?
- **Purpose:** why did the author write the source?

This approach is a good place to start. It is also better than making simplistic statements about sources. However, it can lead to formulaic responses, which are unlikely to gain top marks.

Evaluating sources in their own terms

The best way of evaluating sources is to try and understand them in their own terms. Reading the sources in the context of the time is a good way of evaluating their usefulness. By situating the sources in their context, we can argue the following:

- Firstly, Source 1 describes the Spanish recognition of the United Provinces as a free republic. It was produced in 1607 when there were negotiations between the Dutch and the Spanish for a temporary truce in order to conduct further talks. Source 2 describes the Dutch negotiators' insistence on their independence and freedom. It is an account from 1608, from a time when the final negotiations were taking place for the more long-term Twelve Year Truce of 1609. Therefore, both sources are useful in the sense that they reflect the positions of the two sides at different points in the peace negotiations, telling us of the importance of one of the key Dutch demands.

- Secondly, we know that Maurice of Nassau was opposed to the peace negotiations, and argued with Oldenbarnevelt about it. So it could be argued that these negotiations don't truly represent Dutch feeling on the issues being discussed. However, this would be simplistic. Although Maurice was an extremely important military figure, he did not yet take a strong political role within the States General. The States General were more representative and they were in favour of the negotiations.

- This does not mean that Maurice's views are irrelevant, however, as he was an important figure within the United Provinces. The source is useful in this sense, because it shows the emerging divisions amongst the Dutch even as they were having more success in achieving their aims with the Spanish than ever before.

- Finally, the sources do have some short-comings. Although we know that Oldenbarnevelt wrote Source 2, the author of Source 1 is anonymous. That makes it difficult to draw inferences about his point of view on the negotiations, although we know that Count Ernest was a supporter of Maurice of Nassau. This is important because it means we know a lot more about Source 2 than Source 1.

TIPs:

- Use what you have already learned to help you understand the sources.
- The dates of the sources are often significant. Use what you already know to explore the possible significance of the dates, places and people mentioned in the sources.
- Remember that sources are contributing to a debate. Use your knowledge to situate the sources in the wider debate.

Having read the advice on evaluating the sources, try to evaluate the sources in order to formulate an answer to the question below:

> How far could the historian make use of Sources 3 and 4 together to investigate the influence of Oldenbarnevelt in the growing power and independence of the United Provinces from 1596 to 1609?

Source 3 From a letter of 42 April 1618 from Oldenbarnevelt to Maurice of Nassau, just before Oldenbarnevelt's arrest in 1618. It relates one possible reason why Oldenbarnevelt feels Nassau might be angry with him and attempts to explain his reasons for it.

> Most Serene and High-Born Prince, Gracious Lord, Gracious Prince and Lord, I observe with the most profound vexation that Your Excellency has become totally estranged from me ... Nevertheless, in all sincerity and honesty, I affirm that I do not know when I gave reason for such a change of heart. I have always been and still am Your Excellency's most faithful servant, and with God's grace I hope to die as such. Ten years ago, when we were negotiating for a peace or a truce, I did indeed remark the beginnings of such a change. May Your Excellency be so kind as to recall, however, that I affirmed to you then that my honest and sincere purpose in these negotiations was to serve and protect the country, Your Excellency, and all its good people, and that nonetheless I offered Your Excellency not only to resign all my offices but even to leave the country rather than to remain in office and in the country with Your Excellency's displeasure. This truce [of 1609–21], concluded with Your Excellency's approval, won his satisfaction because it enabled the affairs of Your Excellency, your notable house, and your beloved brothers and sisters to be put in order. During the time it has been in force, this truce has brought the country prosperity, increased revenues, and won for it a lofty and admirable reputation among the greatest potentates, republics, and Cities not only throughout Christendom and even among this country's enemies, but also in other parts of the world as well.

Activity: Evaluating the sources

1. Having read the sources, try and put them in context by answering the following questions:
   a) What events were taking place at the time the sources were written?
   b) What debate are the sources contributing to?
   c) What is the position of the writers of the sources?
2. Now try and evaluate the usefulness of the sources by answering the following questions:
   a) What do the sources tell us about Oldenbarnevelt's contribution to the growing power of the United Provinces?
   b) How similar are their arguments?
   c) How far do the sources reflect the full range of debate about Oldenbarnevelt's influence?
3. Summarise the extent to which the sources are useful to the historian studying the influence of Oldenbarnevelt on the growing power of the United Provinces from 1595 to 1609. Make sure you deal with the ways in which they are useful and their limits.

Source 4 Summary of a letter from Thomas Bodley, the English assistant in the Dutch Council of State, to Lord Burghley on 4 January 1596 describing the pains that Oldenbarnevelt was taking to secure an alliance. This source tells us about the political skills of Oldenbarnevelt.

> His further conversation with Barnvelt [Oldenbarnevelt], who promised to prepare the humours of his fellows, 'which would be the harder because they are' not one man's children, and hardly meet in one conceit in the 'weightiest causes of the country'. The least contributing Provinces, as Gelderland, Overissel, Utrecht, and Groningen, are none of the stiffest in refusing a peace, and have nothing so much feeling of her Majesty's offence as Holland and Zeeland, that stand upon their traffic, and can quickly make the reckoning to how much danger they are subject if her Majesty would be drawn to make trial of her puissance. Nevertheless, because they give the law in a manner to all the rest, Barnvelt will first sound the chiefest of them, and if they will comprehend it, will make less doubt of the residue of the Provinces.

Activity: AS-style questions

1. Why is Source 3 valuable to the historian for an enquiry into the negotiations of 1609?
2. How much weight do you give the evidence of Source 4 for an enquiry into the contribution of Oldenbarnevelt to the independence of the United Provinces?

Reaching an overall judgement

Having understood, contextualised and evaluated the sources, you should finish your essay with an overall judgement. Reaching a supported overall judgement is an important part of doing well in Section A. Your judgement in Section A is similar to the judgement that you should reach in the other sections of the exam (see page 74). However, in Section A, your judgement should be based on an evaluation of the evidence offered by the sources.

Your judgement should:
● clearly answer the question
● be supported by weighing up the evidence of the sources.

In addition to this, the very best essays will distinguish between the levels of certainty of the different aspects of the conclusion.

Imagine you are answering the question on page 400.

Having already read the sources and evaluated them in their context as you did in the activity on page 400, it is possible to reach the following overall conclusion. This is a high level conclusion as it focuses on the question, reaches a supported judgement and discusses the different levels of certainty of the different claims it makes.

This focuses directly on the question.

Contextual knowledge is used to explore the limits of the sources' usefulness.

The sources' limitations are acknowledged.

The limits of the sources are summarised.

> Together, Sources 3 and 4 are of some use to a historian investigating the influence of Oldenbarnevelt in the growing power and independence of the United Provinces from 1596 to 1609. They clearly show that Oldenbarnevelt had a strong political influence in terms of persuading and organising other provinces (Source 4), negotiating treaties and agreements (Sources 3 and 4) and considering the economic condition of the new Dutch state (Source 3). While Source 3 is an attempt by Oldenbarnevelt to regain Nassau's favour and avoid arrest, Source 4 is by an English diplomat who values Oldenbarnevelt's contribution, supporting to a great extent what Source 1 claims. Neither Source 3 nor Source 4, however, looks at a disfavourable view of Oldenbarnevelt or truly considers the extent of his influence in economic, military or religious affairs. For example, Oldenbarnevelt was crucial in setting up the Dutch East India Company in 1602. This brought economic prosperity and stability, enabling the new state to survive. Although Source 3 includes some mention of the economic prosperity brought by the Twelve Year Truce it does not explore the impact of trade. This gives an incomplete picture of Oldenbarnevelt's influence. This limits their usefulness to a historian who is investigating this question, especially as both of the sources have a similar perspective. Nonetheless there is evidence in both sources that Oldenbarnevelt used his diplomatic skill to bring peace, alliances and prosperity to the United Provinces, providing a picture of his power over the other provinces. So, these two sources are of some use due to the detail they provide of Oldenbarnevelt's political and diplomatic skill when the United Provinces was in its early years.

The sources are used explicitly and together.

The extent to which the sources are useful as a description of Oldenbarnevelt's influence is weighed up.

The uses are also summarised, and a conclusion reached which is supported by the rest of the paragraph.

Imagine you are answering the following question and carry out the activity on page 403:

> 'Lutheran negotiation failed primary because of Catholic failure to recognise the popularity of Lutheranism.' How far do you agree with this statement?

Source 5 From *A Defence and True Declaration of the Things Lately Done in the Low Country* – presented to the German Reichstag [parliament] on 26 October 1570 by the rebels as part of Orange's search for allies to support the Dutch cause.

> [O]ur country, namely that part of low Germany that is subject to the most mighty king of Spain, has and especially at this time to their great destruction most miserably suffered. For since that by the most false slanders and other corrupt craft means of the Spanish Inquisitors, this country has, under pretence of **heresy** and impiety, been brought in grievous displeasure with ... Philip, King of Spain and Lord of low Germany, and oppressed with most heinous Edicts about Religion procured by guile and slanderous reporting, and so has of their great truthfulness and obedience to their sovereign Lords now more than fifty years with incredible patience born the Inquisitors' cruel yoke ... It is now come to pass that the adversaries, being grieved to see them aspire to such liberty of religion as by this time flourished not only in Germany but also in France and many other places, have in strange manner and with most earnest endeavour worked, not only to frustrate the hope of the inhabitants, but also, by bringing in a far more grievous tyranny, to pull from them all the residue of their right and liberty that they had remaining. And so to spoil the goods of their wealthy ones, and such noble and mighty ones of their lives, as they saw to be able to withstand their attempts.

Source 6 From the *Prince of Orange's warning to the inhabitants and subjects of the Netherlands*, 1 September 1568. In this pamphlet from Orange to the people of the Netherlands he argues that unless the Dutch defend their privileges and traditions they will be trampled on by the Spanish.

> First we would remind you of something that is clear to everyone, that the Netherlands have always been ruled and reigned over by their princes and overlords with all gentleness, right and reason and wholly in accordance with their freedoms, rights, customs, traditions and privileges, which have always been observed there and were obtained in former times from Emperors, kings, dukes, counts and seigniors by the inhabitants of the country, great friends and supporters of their liberty and enemies to all violence and oppression. The princes as well as the subjects of the country have always had to commit themselves by a formal contract and to swear a solemn oath that they would maintain these rights and realise them. The inhabitants therefore owe obedience to the rulers only on condition that the freedoms are maintained ... Some **grandees** of Spain have been intent on somehow obtaining power to govern and tyrannise over so prosperous a country as they do elsewhere ... It is also only too obvious that Cardinal Granvelle and his adherents took an unfair advantage of the faith of the trustful and good prince [Philip II], and, seeking only to rule and dominate the Low Countries completely in order to satisfy their ambition, avarice and other passions, proposed all those leagues, practices and strange innovations that were to serve as means to ... rob [the country] of all their freedoms, rights, and privileges.

Activity: Write your own conclusion

1 Read the question on page 402, the sources and the information about the sources.
2 Put the sources in context:
   a) What is the significance of the dates of the sources?
   b) What debate or debates are the sources contributing to?
   c) How far do the sources agree on the role of the King of Spain?
   d) Why did the authors write the two sources?
3 Read the question again.
   a) Next, write a series of bullet points outlining:
   • the aspects of the sources that are useful for answering the question
   • the aspects of the sources that are less useful
   • a summary of the extent to which the sources provide useful evidence concerning causes of the Dutch Revolt.
   b) Now write the conclusion, remember:
   • you need to weigh up the evidence, and therefore you should use words that help you to do that such as 'Clearly', 'However', and 'Nonetheless'.
   • You should weigh up the sources *together*, rather than separately. Make sure you use words and phrases that make it clear that this is what you are doing.
   • You should try and specify how certain you are about your various concluding claims. Look at the example of a conclusion you have just read and try and use similar words and phrases to show which of your concluding claims are certain and which are less definite.

Work together

Having completed your conclusion, swap it with a partner's. Consider:
1 How far did you agree on the context of the sources?
2 How far did you agree on the usefulness of the sources?
3 Which conclusion most effectively weighed up the evidence of the sources? How was this achieved?
4 Did both conclusions really consider the sources *together*? How could you improve this aspect of your writing?
5 Which conclusion most effectively expressed the different degrees of certainty? How was this achieved?
6 Which conclusion most effectively focused on the question?

Use this discussion to make notes on how you can improve your Section A technique.

Activity: AS-style questions

1 Why is Source 5 valuable to the historian for an enquiry into how the Dutch attempted to gain allies in their fight against the Spanish?
2 How much weight do you give the evidence of Source 6 for an enquiry into the importance of Dutch customs and privileges as a cause of the revolt?

Section B: Essay technique

Argument, counterargument and resolution

The highest marks in Section B of the exam are available for sustained analysis. One way of achieving this is to write an essay that develops a clear argument, counterargument, and then reaches a resolution. This approach is outlined in the activities that support Paper 1 (see page 176). This kind of structure is equally applicable to Paper 2 Section B.

Activity

Imagine you are answering the following Section B question:

'The arrival of the Duke of Alva was the main turning-point in the development of the Dutch Revolt.' How far do you agree with this statement?

1 Read the question and work out what type of question it is.
2 Make a plan that is appropriate to the specific question. Rather than simply picking four relevant factors, develop an argument, a counterargument and a resolution to the argument.
3 Add three pieces of detail to support each aspect of your essay. Remember, use the detail that best supports the argument you are creating.
4 Write an introduction that sets out the essential aspects of your argument, counterargument and resolution.
5 Now write a conclusion to the essay:
   ● Start by asserting an overall judgement.
   ● Support this by writing an evaluative summary of your argument, counterargument and resolution.
   ● Summarise your overall judgement in the final sentence.

Work together

Having written your introduction and conclusion, swap them with a partner. Consider the following questions:

1 Did you agree on what type of question you were dealing with? If not, discuss it and work out who was right.
2 Whose plan sets out the most compelling overall argument?
3 Which introduction most clearly sets out the key claims of your essay?
4 Which conclusion best summarises and evaluates the argument, counterargument and resolution?
5 What can you learn from each other's work?

Use these questions to feedback to each other and improve your essay technique.

Question practice

1 To what extent was Philip II's decision to attack both England and France the principal reason for the Spanish failures from 1584 to 1598?
2 How far was the English intervention successful in aiding the Dutch from 1584? **AS**
3 'Leicester's period as Governor-General was a complete disaster.' How far do you agree with this statement?
4 How far were Oldenbarnevelt's naval reforms his most important success? **AS**
5 To what extent was the death of Philip II in 1598 the crucial turning-point in the Dutch Revolt from 1566 to 1609?

GLOSSARY

Paper 1 England, 1509–1603: authority, nation and religion

Act for the Advancement of True Religion Restricted the reading of the Bible to clergy, noblemen, gentry and richer merchants. Introduced censorship of books printed after 1540.

Alien A person from a foreign country who is not yet a naturalised citizen of the country where they are living.

Almoner An official distributor of alms, or charity, to the poor.

Amazons Notions of feminity and war, either as female monarch assumed to be a normal woman so having no interest in martial things, or as an Amazon, so obsessed by war and unhinged.

Anticlericalism Opposition to the influence of the clergy, to their behaviour or role in everyday life.

Appeals court A court which hears appeals against judgements in legal cases that have been heard in another, usually lower level, court.

Aragonese revolt A revolt by the Kingdom of Aragon in 1591–92 against changes made by Philip II, King of Spain, that were seen as an attempt to destroy the independence and culture of Aragon by making it more like Castile.

Assize judges Judges at the Assize courts, the court that heard the most serious criminal and civil legal cases in the seven circuits of England and Wales.

Attorney general The main legal adviser to the government.

Bastard-bearing A woman who had produced a child with a man she was not married to (or a man who was married to somebody else).

Bastardised Declared illegitimate.

Battle of Bosworth Field Battle fought on 22 August 1485 where Henry Tudor (afterwards Henry VII) defeated Richard III and became king of England and Wales.

Benefit of clergy A legal provision whereby clergymen could claim that they were outside the jurisdiction of the secular courts and could be tried instead in Church courts.

Betrothed Being legally promised in marriage to someone, being engaged.

Bill A draft of a proposed law that is presented to parliament for discussion, with a view to it passing into law and becoming an Act.

Book of Homilies A collection of authorised printed English sermons by Cranmer that were to be used by parishes to replace the Latin liturgy.

Booty Goods gained through looting or piracy.

Catechism A summary of religious doctrine that was used to educate children about the religious teachings of the Church.

Catholic League An association of Catholics formed by the Duke of Guise in 1576, intended to eradicate Protestantism in France. Played a significant part in the French Wars of Religion (1562–98).

Celtic Church The traditions and practices used in the Irish and British churches but not in the wider Christian world, sometimes seen as a distinct separate Church from the 'Roman' Church established after Augustine arrived in the sixth century.

Chantry chapel A chapel built in a parish church or private chapel for the purpose of masses being said for the benefit of someone who had died, to reduce the time their soul spent in purgatory.

Chastity Sexual purity, not having sex before marriage or with other persons after marriage.

Chivalry A moral system that combined a deep respect for honour and nobility, including courtly manners, a warrior ethos and piety.

Church plate Valuable objects made of gold or silver, generally owned by parish churches for the purpose of collecting money during services.

Classical Referring to ancient civilisations such as Ancient Rome or Greece.

Classical humanist education An education informed by humanist principles which focused on learning the ancient languages of Latin, Greek and Hebrew, and reading the original texts in those languages.

Clients Those who accepted patronage from wealthy patrons.

Colonisation Taking over territory in another country, dominating those who live there already and taking ownership of land off them.

Common law Law created by legal precedent rather than by acts of parliament.

Consort The husband or wife of a ruling monarch. They usually have no governing powers themselves.

Court revels Court entertainers.

Creeping to the Cross A ceremony on Easter Friday where parishioners in churches would make their way in a procession on their knees to a cross and kiss it, to demonstrate humility and respect.

Dearth A scarcity or lack of something, for example food.

Demobilised Ending military operations and taking troops out of active service (usually at the end of a war).

Dynasty A line of hereditary rulers.

Elective monarchy A monarchy ruled by an elected monarch rather than a hereditary monarch, where the throne is passed down as a family inheritance.

Enclosure A process whereby landowners would fence off land that had previously been common land, used for hay or grazing livestock, and restricting it to the use of the landowner or their tenant.

Evangelical reform/reformers A movement initially for reform within the Catholic Church, aimed at stopping abuses and corrupt practices, and creating a purer Church. Began to separate theologically from the Catholic Church from 1519 onwards.

Excommunication An act by the Church to deprive an individual of membership of the Church, and an attempt to place them outside society.

Favourite An intimate companion or close friend of the monarch. Often seen as having undue influence upon the monarch, and rumoured to be having a sexual relationship.

First fruits Payments made by new clerics to the pope of the first year's profits from the territory that cleric now controlled.

Frontispiece A decorative illustration usually facing the title page of a book.

Garrison A body of soldiers stationed in a location (for example a castle) to guard it.

Genealogy The study of families and the tracing of their lineage and history.

Gleaning Collecting leftover crops from farmers' fields after they have been harvested or where it is not economically profitable to harvest.

Glorious Revolution The overthrow of King James II by William of Orange and his English supporters in parliament in 1688.

Gluttony The over-consumption or over-indulgence of food or drink, considered one of the seven deadly sins by the Church.

Government deficit The difference between the government's everyday expenses and its income or revenues.

Great matter The King's need to produce an heir to continue his dynasty.

Groom-porter An officer at the royal court who had responsibility for inspecting the king's lodgings, checking they were sufficiently furnished, providing cards and dice and ruling on gaming disputes. Also had oversight of billiards tables and bowling alleys, gaming houses and tennis courts within the city of London, Westminster and Southwark.

Hanseatic League A commercial and defensive association of merchants and their towns that dominated the coast of northern Europe.

Heir apparent The person first in line of succession to the throne.

Hereditary A role or office that can be inherited, passed down within a family.

Heretics Those who hold beliefs that are contrary to the established Church doctrine or customs.

Holy Roman Empire The territory ruled by the Holy Roman Emperor, spanning much of central Europe or what is now called Germany.

Humanist Someone who studied classical antiquity, its language and literature. A movement that encouraged civic participation, the collection and preservation of ancient literary texts, rhetoric and renewal of the Church.

Hanged, drawn and quartered Those convicted of high treason were fastened to a wooden panel and drawn by cart to the execution site. They were then hanged until they nearly died, had their testicles and penis cut off, were disembowelled and finally beheaded. They were then chopped up into four pieces and the remains displayed in prominent places around the country.

Iconoclasm The deliberate destruction of sacred images, in this period usually by Protestants.

Idols An image that is worshipped religiously, usually seen negatively within most forms of Christianity.

Illegitimate A child born to parents who are not married to each other.

Impeach To charge someone with an offence against the state.

Inns of Court Societies where barristers traditionally trained, lived, and practised law.

Keeper of the rolls The keeper or master of the rolls was initially the official responsible for looking after the records of the Court of Chancery, but from the sixteenth century was also a judge.

King's Book The final official statement of religious doctrine in Henry VIII's reign, issued in 1543, which went back to conservative ways in religion.

Lay persons People who are not members of the clergy.

Legislative Law-making.

Legitimised Made legally legitimate, the status and stigma of illegitimacy removed.

Line of succession The sequence of those who are eligible to succeed to the throne.

Litany A form of prayer used in religious services and processions.

Lord keeper The full title was 'lord keeper of the great seal', one of the great officers of state who had custody of the great seal of England, the seal that symbolised the monarch's official approval of laws or other important state documents.

Lords of misrule An officer appointed by drawing lots to be in charge of Christmas festivities, often including drunkenness and wild parties. Was usually not someone from the top of the social hierarchy, as it celebrated chaos and wildness in contrast to the usual ordered nature of society.

Loyal Catholic   A catholic who remained loyal to the English monarchy rather than obeying the orders of the pope in 1570 to disobey the queen's commands.

Madrigal   A secular vocal musical composition, traditionally unaccompanied by musical instruments.

The marches   The Welsh marches now refer to an imprecisely defined border land between England and Wales.

Masques   A form of entertainment at court involving acting, singing, dancing and music.

Masterless men   Vagrants, men not tied to land by a relationship with a master or lord.

Matriculating   The formal process of entering a university.

The middling sort   A broadly defined social and economic group generally tied to commerce or trade.

Missal   A book containing the prayers said by the priest at the altar as well as all the contents of the mass that are said or sung throughout the year.

Monopolies   Single supplier of a commodity (for example, salt, soap) in this period given permission by the government or ruler, often in exchange for money.

Movable wealth   Property that can be moved and sold, confiscated or bequeathed.

Natural law   A system of law that is deemed to be determined by nature, and so is universal – for example in determining if someone's behaviour is right or wrong.

Neuralgia   Severe pain that occurs along a damaged nerve.

Papal dispensation   The right of the pope to allow for people to be exempted from a particular religious law, for example in relation to marriage.

Papal interdict   The pope's power to exclude individuals or groups from particular rites of the Church, a serious religious and social stigma.

Papal legate   A personal representative of the pope sent on a specific mission to a foreign country.

Parliamentary convention   A political custom in parliament.

Parliamentary time   The amount of time dedicated to a topic or bill in parliament.

Patriarch   A man who exercised autocratic power over an extended family or organisation.

Patron/patronage   Someone who supports (financially, socially or both) a 'client' – in this sense an artist, poet, musician or playwright.

Phantom pregnancy   A condition in which a woman shows signs of being pregnant, caused by a strong psychological belief that they are pregnant.

Piety   Strong religious devotion or spirituality.

Pluralism   A situation where a clergyman is in charge of more than one parish (and receives the income from those parishes).

Polemicists   Those engaged in controversial arguments, in print or in spoken debate.

Polyphonic   A musical composition with more than one line of melody.

Popery   Catholicism (usually used negatively).

Popish   A derogatory term for something deemed to be Catholic.

Popular rebellion   Widespread rebellion rather than one by a small and select group.

Prerogative   The powers that belonged to the monarch alone without consultation of parliament on other bodies.

Presbyterians   Protestants who wanted the abolition of bishops (episcopacy) and the introduction of a system of church elders and regional meetings known as synods.

Press censor   The official responsible for the suppression of books or printed material that are deemed unacceptable to the government. Also approves books or printed material.

Primogeniture   The right of the firstborn male child to inherit all of the family estate.

Privateers   Part of naval warfare, pirates commissioned by states to attack the ships of their enemies.

Royal progress   A royal tour of the countryside or major cities outside London, visiting significant individuals or towns. A ceremonial and festive event.

Protectorate   The period of office of a Lord Protector

Purgatory   In Catholic doctrine, an intermediate state where the deceased's soul goes in order to be purified before entering heaven. It is ideal to spend as little time there as possible.

Queen regnant   A female monarch who rules in her own right.

Real terms   The value of a commodity or amount of money after inflation is taken into account.

Real wages   Wages that have been adjusted for inflation – or in terms of the amount of goods or services that can be bought with the wages.

Recusancy/recusants   Those Catholics who refused to conform to the Church of England and attend Church of England services, penalised financially for their refusal.

Renaissance   A period or movement from the fourteenth to the seventeenth century, beginning as a cultural movement but spreading into politics. Means 'rebirth' or 'renewal' and the word can also be used in that sense.

Rhetoric   The art of persuasion or debate, using written and spoken language.

Rood screen   An ornately decorated partition in a church that separated the area where the congregation sat and that where the priest said the mass at the altar.

Royal arms   The official coat of arms of the monarch, a symbol of their authority and power.

Royal proclamations   An official declaration by the monarch.

Royal Supremacy   Henry VIII's device to achieve the annulment of his marriage by declaring supremacy of the English monarch over the Church of England, replacing the pope.

Sabbath   The weekly day of worship and rest on a Sunday.

Second Coming   The hope of believers that Jesus Christ will return to Earth.

Sedition   Actions or speech seen as disruptive to the established political and social order.

Seminaries   A training college for clergymen (usually Catholic priests in this period).

Sheriff   A legal official appointed by the Crown for each county, traditionally responsible for the maintenance of law and order and for executing royal command, for example in collecting subsidies and taxes.

Spanish Council   A committee of Spanish nobles who advised the Spanish king.

Standing army   A permanent, full-time and often professional army that is not disbanded in peace time. England did not have a standing army until the seventeenth century.

Star Chamber   An English court of law, named after the room in the royal palace of Westminster where it sat. It was a higher court, and became seen as a political weapon under Wolsey against opposition to the king's policies.

Superstitious   Holding irrational or mythical beliefs. Often a derogatory way of describing Catholic practices by Protestants.

Synod   A council of the Church, usually meeting to decide on a point of important religious doctrine or administration.

Tanner   A tradesman who processes animal skins to make leather.

Theology   The study of religion.

Transubstantiation   The religious doctrine according to which the bread and wine used in the mass becomes the actual body and blood of Christ.

Treason   Disloyalty to the Crown, punishable by death.

Treaty of Nonsuch   A treaty signed between Elizabeth I and the Netherlands on 10 August 1585 at Nonsuch Palace in Surrey. Elizabeth agreed to provide troops and money to aid with the ongoing Dutch Revolt.

Tyrant   A cruel and oppressive ruler.

Vagrancy   Somebody without a fixed place to live and without regular work who wanders from place to place and makes a living by begging.

Vestments   Garments worn during religious services, often richly embroidered.

Vicegerent   The official administrative deputy of a ruler, an extremely important official political position.

Virginal   A keyboard instrument of the harpsichord family, popular in Early Modern Europe.

War of attrition   An armed conflict where each side tries to wear down the other by small-scale actions.

Yeomanry   Farmers of small freehold estates.

Paper 2 Luther and the German Reformation, c1515–55

Annates   The first year's revenue of a bishop newly appointed to a diocese, to be paid to the pope on their appointment.

Anticlerical   Opposed to the influence and activities of the clergy.

Asceticism   A way of life that abstains from luxuries and pleasures, generally to attain religious or spiritual goals.

Augustinian   A monastic order living according to the rule of St Augustine. Known for missionary work, living on charitable donations and dedicating their lives to prayer and working in the community.

Autonomy   Self-government or independence of a country or region.

Bigamy   The crime of marrying one person while still legally married to another.

Broadside   A cheap printed ballad, poem or item of news, sometimes with woodcut illustrations.

Canon law   A body of laws made by the Church leadership for the governing of the Church.

Cardinals   The 70 ecclesiastical princes who form the pope's council, and who have the right to elect the pope.

Christendom   All of the Christian countries taken collectively.

Classical world   The ancient world of Greece and Rome.

Communion   Holy communion/mass celebrates Christ's sacrifice and his actions at the Last Supper.

Confession   The acknowledgement of one's sins to a priest.

Contrition   Feeling shame and remorse for one's sins or wrongs. In the Catholic Church it means repenting past sins during confession.

Conversion experience   An experience happening to an individual whereby they are converted to a different form of religion or a deeper sense of religion.

Cortes   A Spanish or Portuguese elected assembly, or parliament.

Curate   A clergyman acting as a deputy or assistant for a parish priest.

Diocese   A district under the care of a bishop, his jurisdiction.

Doctrine   A body of knowledge or system of beliefs taught as the truth.

Ecclesiastical   Relating to the church and religious affairs.

Edict   An official order issued by someone in authority, such as a king.

Envoy   A diplomatic representative or messenger.

Epistle to the Romans   The sixth book in the New Testament, said to be composed by St Paul in order to explain that the gospel of Christ offers salvation.

Excommunication   A punishment inflicted by the Church whereby a person is deprived of membership of the Church and its sacraments.

Factions   A party or group of people who maintain an opinion in opposition to others in an institution.

Flocks   A way of describing a congregation – the priest is a shepherd, caring for his flock of sheep and steering them towards God.

Gulden   A gold coin that was the currency of Germany.

Hanseatic League   A commercial and defensive association of merchants and the towns they controlled along the Northern European coast. Created to protect the trading interests of the member.

Heriot   A death-duty whereby a lord, on their tenant's death, could seize parts of their estate.

Hussite Wars   Also called the Bohemian Wars. Fought during 1419–36 between the Hussites (supporters of Jan Hus) and monarchs who supported the Catholic Church. They aimed to enforce the Church's authority against the Hussites.

Iberia/Iberian   The Iberian Peninsula is a geographical area now comprised of Spain and Portugal.

Late medieval period   Generally seen as comprising the fourteenth and fifteenth century (1300–1500).

Liberty of conscience   Religious toleration, freedom to determine your own religious faith.

Liturgy   A pattern of worship used by a Christian congregation.

Lollards   The supporters of John Wycliffe, a political and religious movement that began in the fourteenth century and lasted in secret until the Reformation.

Margrave   A hereditary title held by some princes in the Holy Roman Empire.

Middle Ages   The period in European history between the fall of the Roman Empire in the West (c500AD) and the fall of Constantinople (1453).

Nationalism   A form of patriotism or allegiance to one's country or region. More extreme forms include a feeling or ideology of superiority over other nations.

Nepotism   Showing unfair preference to a relative when appointing to positions or awarding promotions, for example to illegitimate sons of churchmen.

Oligarchy   Government restricted to a small group of people, generally a wealthy elite.

Papacy   The office or position of pope.

Papal curia   The governing body through which the pope carries out the business of the Catholic Church.

Papal legate   A clergyman sent as a personal representative of the pope to foreign nations or parts of the Catholic Church on matters of faith, diplomacy and administration.

Penance   A sacrament of the Catholic Church whereby a priest hears confession of sins from a parishioner and gives them absolution, meaning their sins are forgiven.

Piety Religious devotion, obedience to God.

Pope The Bishop of Rome and head of the Catholic Church, based in the Vatican in Rome.

Predestination The religious idea that all events have been pre-determined by God. In Lutheranism this includes the idea that the elect (people chosen by God) are predestined to be saved by God.

Purgatory A state between heaven and hell where souls of the dead go until they have been punished for sins that have not been forgiven while the person was alive.

Salvation Being saved from sin and hell. Christians believe that this can happen through faith in God.

Secular rulers Civil rulers, rather than religious ones.

Seminaries A school or college where students of theology are trained to become clergy.

Simony The practice of buying and selling Church positions or promotions.

St Benedictine An order of monks who lived together in monasteries under the rule of St Benedict, which emphasised spiritual growth, community life, and prayer.

The creed A formulaic statement of shared belief often repeated during religious services.

Vulgar tongues The native language of a country, area or language (as opposed to Latin, which was used amongst educated and bureaucratic classes across Europe).

Woodcut An image created using a printing technique whereby an image is carved into a block of wood, which is then covered in ink and pressed onto paper.

Worldly Behaviours more appropriate to the secular world rather than the ecclesiastical.

Paper 2 The Dutch Revolt, c1563–1609

Absolute monarch A king or queen whose political powers are unrestricted.

Archbishoprics The office or position of Archbishop, or the province that he is in charge of.

Armada 'Armada' is the Spanish word for naval fleet, the Spanish Armada is the name given to the failed Spanish invasion of England in August 1588.

Arquebus An early muzzle-loaded firearm, a forerunner of the rifle. It was used from the fifteenth to seventeenth centuries.

Authoritarian A regime that demands complete obedience to authority, with the threat of punishment to reinforce those demands.

Bankruptcy The state or condition of being bankrupt.

Bequeath To leave some money or property to somebody in your last will and testament.

Bishoprics An area controlled by a bishop, otherwise known as a diocese.

Cardinal A senior churchman, a bishop of the Catholic Church, nominated by the pope.

Citadels A fortified area within a town or city.

Consecrated When someone or something is declared sacred by the Church. In terms of Church appointments it means being ordained to a sacred office.

Council of State The advisory body to the government, traditionally consisted of the most important and powerful Dutch nobles.

Decree An official order that has the force of law.

Duchies Areas or provinces ruled over by dukes or duchesses.

Embargo A ban on trade with a particular country or group of countries.

Favourite In this sense, the intimate companion of a ruler – who people often thought had a sexual relationship (although it was not necessarily true).

Fealty A formal acknowledgement of a person's loyalty to a lord.

Governor-General The representative of the Spanish Crown in the Netherlands, had (in theory) day-to-day responsibility for governing the Netherlands.

Grandees Person of high rank, in this case the Dutch nobles.

Habsburg A royal house of Europe, were frequently Holy Roman Emperors but members also ruled Austria, Spain and colonies in the New World in this period.

Herald-at-arms The chief herald, responsible for granting new coats of arms, recording pedigrees and registering flags and other important symbols

Heresy laws/heresy Laws enacted in defence of the religion of the state against heresy, any belief or theory that is contrary to the established beliefs – in this case, the Catholic Church.

Heretical beliefs Beliefs that are contrary to those of the established Church.

Huguenots A religious group, members of the Protestant Church in the sixteenth and seventeen centuries in France.

Humanist education An education on humanist principles – including Latin and Greek languages, concentration on classical texts in vernacular languages, and liberal arts (for example, history, philosophy, rhetoric, maths, poetry, music). Had the goal of fitting gentlemen for active participation in public life.

Iconoclasm The destruction of images or hostility towards visual images, particularly religious or sacred images. A strong feature of more radical Protestants during the Reformation.

Immovable goods Property that cannot be moved without destroying or altering it. Includes buildings or land.

Imperial election The election of the Holy Roman Emperor, who ruled the lands now known as Germany.

Inquisition An institution within the Catholic Church set up to combat heresy.

Joint stocks A business where shares in ownership are sold and can be owned by individuals or companies, known as shareholders.

Land's Advocate Chairman of the States of Holland the most powerful political position after the stadholder.

Mercenaries Soldiers hired and paid to fight for an individual or state.

Movable goods Property that can be moved, for example livestock, clothing, household goods.

Order of the Golden Fleece An order of chivalry founded in Bruges by the Duke of Burgundy, Philip III, in 1430. Became one of the most prestigious orders in Europe.

Papal bulls A charter, order or decree issued by the pope.

Pardon The forgiveness of a crime and the cancellation of the punishment, usually granted by the head of state.

Placards Public announcements of the laws in the form of a notice or sign, for example those against heresy.

Prelates High-ranking clergy within a church, for example archbishops and bishops.

Primate A bishop or archbishop who is the highest ranking in a province or country.

Principalities A region or state ruled by a prince or a monarch with a different title (for example, margrave, count).

Privateers A ship that is commissioned by a state to fight or attack enemy shops.

Protestantism A form of Christian faith that originated in the Reformation begun by Martin Luther, originally a movement for reform of the Catholic Church but soon split into a permanent division.

Provincial states The states of the individual provinces, for example, Holland, Zeeland.

Saint Bartholomew's Day Massacre Targeted assassinations, followed by mob violence, against the Protestant Huguenots of France beginning on 24 August 1572 and lasting several weeks. Estimates of the dead range from 5,000 to 30,000.

Schmalkaldic War Short period of war from 1546 to 1547 between the forces of the Catholic Emperor Charles V and the members of the Schmalkaldic League.

Stadtholder Originally one appointed to rule a province on behalf of the king, but after the Dutch Revolt a local ruler who acted as the highest official appointed by the states of the province.

States General A political assembly made up of deputies of the provincial states. They originally existed to co-ordinate tax assessment for the Crown but became the government of the Dutch republic.

Synod A meeting of a church and its representatives.

Toleration The practice of allowing or tolerating other views, especially those on religion.

Walloon A form of French spoken by those living in the region now known as Belgium but formerly in the Netherlands.

The Publishers would like to thank the following for permission to reproduce copyright material.

Photo credits: pp.2–3 © World History Archive / Alamy; **p.5** © World History Archive / Alamy; **p.6** © Georgios Kollidas/Fotolia (top and bottom); **p.7** © Georgios Kollidas/Fotolia; **p.14** © Georgios Kollidas/Fotolia; **p.20** © Photo by The Print Collector/Hulton Archive/Getty Images; **p.25** © Georgios Kollidas/Fotolia; **p.27** © Niday Picture Library / Alamy; **p.28** © Georgios Kollidas/Fotolia; **p.29** © Georgios Kollidas/Fotolia; **pp.33–34** © The Art Archive / Alamy; **p.37** © Photos.com/Thinkstock; **p.39** © Georgios Kollidas/Fotolia; **p.41** Author's own; **p.46** © Georgios Kollidas/Fotolia; **p.47** © The Art Archive / Alamy; **p.60** © World History Archive / Alamy; **p.68** © Rischgitz/Getty Images; **pp.76–77** © Jupiterimages/Thinkstock **p.80** © Jupiterimages/Thinkstock; **p.88** A beggar is tied and whipped through the streets, c.1567 (woodcut) (b/w photo), English School, (16th century) / Private Collection / Bridgeman Images**; p.95** © British Library Board / TopFoto; **pp.106–07** ©TopFoto; **p.111** Universal History Archive/ UIG via Getty images; **p.119** Author's own; **p.122** © Mansell/The LIFE Picture Collection/ Getty Images; **p.135** ©TopFoto; **p.136** © jamiehink/Fotolia; **pp.142–43** Photos.com/Thinkstock; **pp.211–12** © Christopher Bradshaw/Fotolia; **p.224** © INTERFOTO / Alamy; **p.238** Floriano Rescigno/Thinkstock; **p.243** © INTERFOTO / Alamy; **p.246** © INTERFOTO / Alamy; **p.260** © Heritage Image Partnership Ltd / Alamy; **p.271** © ullstein bild/ullstein bild/ Getty Images; **p.273** © nickolae/Fotolia; **p.274** © Georgios Kollidas/Fotolia; **p.293** © World History Archive / Alamy; **pp.309–10** © HildaWeges/Fotolia; **p.316** © The Art Archive / Alamy; **p.322** © Peter Horree / Alamy; **p.328** © The Granger Collection / TopFoto; **p.338** © Peter Horree / Alamy; **p.343** © World History Archive / Alamy; **p.344** © PAINTING / Alamy; **p.367** © Classic Image / Alamy; **p.371** © World History Archive / Alamy; **p.384** © liszt collection / Alamy; **p.386** © Georgios Kollidas/Fotolia.

Paper 1 England, 1509–1603: authority, nation and religion

Acknowledgements: p.149 David Armitage, Conal Condren and Andrew Fitzmaurice: from *Shakespeare and Early Modern Political Thought* (Cambridge University Press, 2009); **p.149** Jim Sharpe, 'Social strain and social dislocation' from *The Reign of Elizabeth I: Court and Culture in the Last Decade,* ed. John Guy (Cambridge University Press, 1995); **p.151** Susan Doran: from *Elizabeth I and Foreign Policy, 1558–1603* (Routledge, 2001); **p.151** Anna Whitelock: from '"Woman, Warrior, Queen?' Rethinking Mary and Elizabeth" from *Tudor Queenship: The Reigns of Mary and Elizabeth*, eds. Alice Hunt, Anna Whitelock (Palgrave, 2010); **p.155** Paul E. J. Hammer: from *Elizabeth's Wars, War, Government and Society in Tudor England 1544–1604* (Palgrave, 2004); **p.155** Carole Levin: from *The Reign of Elizabeth I* (Palgrave, 2002), reproduced by permission of the publisher; **p.156** John Guy: from *The Tudors* (Oxford Paperbacks, 2010); **p.156** Ian W. Archer**:** from *The Pursuit of Stability: Social Relations in Elizabethan London* (Cambridge University Press, 2003); **p.159** John Guy: from *The Tudors* (Oxford Paperbacks, 2010); **p.160** J. B. Black: from *The Reign of Elizabeth 1558–1603* (OUP, 1959); **p.163** John Neale: from *The Elizabethan Political Scene* (G. Cumberlege, 1949); **p.163** Paul E. J. Hammer: 'Patronage at Court, faction and the Earl of Essex' from *The Reign of Elizabeth I: Court and Culture in the Last Decade,* ed. John Guy (Cambridge University Press, 1995); **p.163** Natalie Mears 'Regnum Cecilianum' from *The Reign of Elizabeth I: Court and Culture in the Last Decade,* ed. John Guy (Cambridge University Press, 1995; **p.167** Wallace T. MacCaffrey: from *Elizabeth*

I: War and Politics, 1588–1603 (Princeton University Press, 1992); **p.167** Paul E. J. Hammer: from *The Polarisation of Elizabethan Politics* (Cambridge University Press, 1999); **p.170** John Guy 'The 1590s: the second reign of Elizabeth I' from *The Reign of Elizabeth I: Court and Culture in the Last Decade*, ed. John Guy (Cambridge University Press, 1995); **p.170** Susan Doran and Paulina Kewes: from 'The earlier Elizabethan succession question revisited' from *Doubtful and Dangerous: The Question of Succession in Late Elizabethan England*, eds. Susan Doran and Paulina Kewes (Manchester University Press, 2014); **p.175** Paul E. J. Hammer: from *The Polarisation of Elizabethan Politics* (Cambridge University Press, 1999); **p.175** John Guy 'The 1590s: the second reign of Elizabeth I' from *The Reign of Elizabeth I: Court and Culture in the Last Decade*, ed. John Guy (Cambridge University Press, 1995); **p.177** Carole Levin: from *The Reign of Elizabeth I* (Palgrave, 2002), reproduced by permission of the publisher; **p.177** Janet Dickinson: from *Court Politics and the Earl of Essex* (Pickering and Chatto, 2012); **p.181** John Neale: from *Elizabeth I and her Parliaments, 1581–1601* (Cape, 1953); **p.181** Wallace T. MacCaffrey: from *Elizabeth I: War and Politics, 1588–1603* (Princeton University Press, 1992); **p.182** David Dean: from *Law Making in late Elizabethan England* (Cambridge University Press, 1996); **p.182** T.A. Morris: from *Europe and England in the Sixteenth Century* (Taylor and Francis, 2002); **p.184** Wallace T. Mac-Caffrey: from *Elizabeth I: War and Politics, 1588–1603* (Princeton University Press, 1992); **p.184** Christopher Haigh: from *Elizabeth I* (Taylor and Francis, 2014); **p.186** Michael A. R. Graves: from *Elizabethan Parliaments* (Taylor and Francis, 1996); **p.186** John Guy 'The 1590s: the second reign of Elizabeth I' from *The reign of Elizabeth I: Court and Culture in the Last Decade*, ed. John Guy (Cambridge University Press, 1995); **p.186** Carole Levin: from *The Reign of Elizabeth I* (Palgrave, 2002), reproduced by permission of the publisher; **p.190** G. R. Elton: from *Studies in Tudor and Stuart Politics and Government* (Cambridge University Press, 1981); **p.191** Paul Johnson: from *Elizabeth I* (Little, Brown Book Group, 1976); **p.193** John Guy: from *The Tudors* (Oxford Paperbacks, 2010); **p.193** Roger Lockyer: from *Tudor and Stuart Britain: 1485–1714* (St. Martin's Press, 1964); **p.196** Peter Clark: from 'Popular Protest and Disturbance in Kent, 1558–1640' from *The Economic History Review* (Wiley, 1976); **p.196** Jim Sharpe, 'Social strain and social dislocation' from *The reign of Elizabeth I Court and Culture in the Last Decade,* ed. John Guy (Cambridge University Press, 1995); **p.196** Ian W. Archer: from *The Pursuit of Stability: Social Relations in Elizabethan London* (Cambridge University Press, 2003); **p.198** Steve Hindle: from 'Poverty and the poor laws' from *The Elizabethan World*, eds. Susan Doran and Norman Jones (Taylor and Francis, 2014); **p.198** Ian W. Archer: from *The Pursuit of Stability: Social Relations in Elizabethan London* (Cambridge University Press, 2003); **p.202** Jim Sharpe, 'Social strain and social dislocation' from *The reign of Elizabeth I Court and Culture in the Last Decade,* ed. John Guy (Cambridge University Press, 1995); **p.202** Peter Clark: from 'Popular Protest and Disturbance in Kent, 1558–1640' from *The Economic History Review* (Wiley, 1976); **p.207** David Dean: from *Elizabethan Government and Politics* (Wiley, 2008); **p.207** Joseph P. Ward: from 'Metropolitan London' from *A Companion to Tudor Britain,* eds. Robert Tittler and Norman Jones (Wiley-Blackwell, 2008), **p.210** John Guy: from *The Tudors* (Oxford Paperbacks, 2010); **p.210** Jim Sharpe, 'Social strain and social dislocation' from *The reign of Elizabeth I: Court and Culture in the Last Decade,* ed. John Guy (Cambridge University Press, 1995)

Paper 2 Luther and the German Reformation c1515–55

Acknowledgements: p.215 From an account by Quirini, Ambassador of Venice (1509); **p.221** B. Ann Tlusty: from *Augsburg During the Reformation Era: An Anthology of Sources* (Hackett Publishing Co., 2012); **p.223** Aleander on the anti-papal sentiment in Germany (8th February 1521); **p.225** G. Elton: from Reformation *Europe 1517–1559* (Fontana Press, 1963); **p.236** Martin Luther: from a letter to his father Hans, from the dedication of 'On Monastic Vows', about his decision to become a monk and his father's reponse to that (1521); **p.240** Johann Tetzel: from 'Sample Sermon for Priests Selling Indulgences' (c1517); **p.245** Extracts from Luther's cover letter to the Holy Roman emperor and the nobility of the German nation, enclosing his Address to the Nobility of the German Nation (1520); **p.249** From Martin Luther's letter to the Archbishop of Mainz (1517); **p.251** Martin Luther: *Address to the Christian Nobility of the German Nation* (1520);

p.251 Berardo Navagiero: from a letter to the Doge and Senate of Venice (July 1546); **p.253** Martin Luther: from a letter to Christoph Scheurl (5 March 1518); **p.253** Martin Luther: from a letter to Pope Leo X (30 May 1518); **p.254** Johann Eck: from a letter to his colleagues at Ingolstadt University (1 July 1519); **p.254** Petrus Mosellanus: eyewitness account of the Leipzig Dispute (July 1519); **p.259** Martin Luther: from a report of his statement of beliefs at his trial at the Diet of Worms (1521); **p.267** Count Philipp von Solm: from report to his son Reinhard of the aftermath of the Battle of Frankenhausen (16 May 1525); **p.268** Martin Luther: from *Against the Robbing and Murdering Hordes of Peasants* (1525); **p.268** Hermann Muhlpfort: from a letter (4 June 1525); **p.275** Martin Luther: from a letter to Philip Melanchthon (29 June 1530); **p.279** From the introduction to The Twelve Articles of the Swabian Peasants (27 February–1 March 1525); **p.280** From a letter from the peasant army of the Black Forest to representatives of the City of Villingen (8 May 1525); **p.285** From the protestation (1529); **p.289** From the preface to Luther's Articles of the Schmalkaldic League (1537); **p.297** From the *Consilium* (1537); **p.303** Andreas Carlstadt: from *On the Removal of Images* (1522); **p.303** Martin Luther: from the Invocavit Sermons at Wittenberg (12 March 1522); **p.304** Cardinal Lorenzo Campeggio: from the description of the attitude of the people of Nuremberg (March 1524); **p.304** From an account of the religious practices issued by the Diet of Nuremberg; **p.306** Luther to the Pope (3 March 1519); **p.306** Martin Luther: from *Babylonian Captivity of the Church* (October 1520)

Paper 2 The Dutch Revolt, c1563–1609

p.315 From a short exposition of the rights exercised by the knights, nobles and towns of Holland and West Friesland (1587); **p.319** Philip II: from a letter to Margaret of Parma (17 October 1565); **p.319** John Marnix of Tholouse and Louis of Nassau petition presented to Margaret of Parma (5 April 1566); **p.328** Account of a nun in s' Hergotenbosch (23 January 1566); **p.332** Philip II letter to Margaret of Parma (17 October 1565); **p.333** Excerpt from the Compromise of 1566; **p.342** William of Orange: from *Faithful exhortation to the inhabitants of the Netherlands against the vain and false hopes their oppressors hold out to them* (1568); p.346 Master Wouter Jacobsz: extract from his diary (4 September 1572); **p.349** William of Nassau from a propaganda pamphlet (1572); **p.352** Philip II: from one of the 'Segovia Woods' letters to Margaret of Parma (31 December 1566); **p.354** Philip Marnix: extract from a pamphlet entitled *A true narrative and apology of what has happened in the Netherlands in the matter of religion in the year 1566. By those who profess the reformed religion in that country* (1566); **p.355** From: *The prince of Orange's warning to the inhabitants and subjects of the Netherlands* (1 September 1568); **p.355** Thomas Dutton: from a letter to Sir Thomas Gresham (7 September 1567); **p.357** Magistrates of Gouda: from an account of the disorder at Gouda (April 1572); **p.358** Extract from an address of the states of Holland to the States General (12 September 1573); **p.363** Daniel Rogers: extract from a letter to Lord Burghley (7 March 1576); **p.365** Extract from Articles that Archduke Matthias agreed to (8 December 1577); **p.373** William of Orange: from *Apology or Defence of His Serene Highness William by the Grace of God, prince of Orange etc. against the ban or edict published by the king of Spain* (1581); **p.377** Count of Boussu: from a letter to the Duke of Alva (16 May 1572); **p.378** From the Act of Abjuration (1581); **p.386** From the loyalty oath of the English troops in the Netherlands (July 1585); **p.394** William Carr: from *The travellours guide and historians faithfull companion* (1695); **p.398** From a letter to Count Ernest of Nassau-Dietz (27 March 1607); **p.399** Oldenbarnevelt: from an account of the peace negotiations prior to the Twelve Year Truce (1609); **p.400** Oldenbarnevelt: from a letter to Maurice of Nassau (April 1618); **p.400** Thomas Bodley: summary of a letter to Lord Burghley (4 January 1596); **p.402** From *A Defence and True Declaration of the Things Lately Done in the Low Country* (26 October 1570); **p.402** From the Prince of Orange's warning to the inhabitants and subjects of the Netherlands (1 September 1568).

ANSWERS

Answers for Selecting from the Sources on page 253

Paper 2: Luther and the German Reformation, c1515–55

1 To counter 'malicious, heretical lies'.
2 Implied to defend 'your Holiness [the Pope's] name'.
3 To deal with complaints about 'the greed of the priests'.
4 To defend 'the honour of Christ', because of his 'zeal for the honour of Christ'.
5 To 'draw the attention of some prelates to the abuses' by 'throwing doubts upon their doctrines'.
6 To prepare for a debate.
7 To throw down 'a gauntlet to the learned by issuing my theses'.

Answers for Selecting from the Sources on page 356

Paper 2: The Dutch Revolt, c1563–1609

1 There were complaints about the Spanish soldiers upon their arrival for their dishonesty and way of living.
2 Alva put strict orders in place to punish them for this kind of behaviour.
3 The people in Antwerp are now reasonably quiet and happy with the soldiers.
4 There are many complaints about the Spanish from elsewhere.

culture
architecture 136–7
art 132
drama and theatre 106, 132–4
education 106, 120, 122, 127–30
Gloriana, cult of 137–8
music 106, 134–5
overview 106–7, 138–9
poetry 135–6
printing press 128, 130–1, 213, 218–19, 240
and religious change 131–2, 134

deserving and undeserving poor 86–7
Devereux, Robert, Earl of Essex 147–8, 153–4, 163–7, 171–2
de Villers, Jean 341–2
Diet of Regensburg (1541) 285–6
Diet of Speyer (1526/ 1529) 284–6, 288
Diet of Worms (1521) 212, 258–60
dissolution of the monasteries 39, 45, 86, 89, 106, 118–20
Don António, of Portugal 145–6
Dordrecht meeting (1572) 349–50
Drake, Francis 113, 145–7
drama and theatre 106, 132–4
Dudley, John, 1st Duke of Northumberland 6–7, 42–3, 168
Dudley, Robert, Earl of Leicester 13–14, 386–8
Dutch East India Company 390–1, 393
Dutch Revolt 112
Armistice 393
Battle of Heiligerlee 342
Battle of Jemmingen 341–3
Battle of Nieuwpoort 382–4
Battle of Turnhout 382
Brill and Flushing, seizure of 345–6
Calvinism, influences of 325, 329–30, 364, 366, 387, 392
and Catholic reforms 321–4
Compromise 324, 339
Confederacy of Noblemen 324
Conference of Cologne 366, 369
contributory factors 319–22
Council of Troubles 338–9, 338–40
and de Requesens 360–4
Dordrecht meeting 349–50
and Duke of Alva 337–40
and Duke of Anjou 369–71
and Duke of Parma 364–8
Dutch Republic, recognition of 393–5, 397
and Earl of Leicester 386–8
Fall of Antwerp 368
foreign support and intervention 145, 310, 343–7, 369–72, 385, 389
French Fury 370–1
Grandees, opposition from 321–5
heresy persecutions 323–4, 326, 338–9
Iconoclastic Fury 326–9
and Joan van Oldenbarneveldt 310, 382–3, 390–1
leading figures 321–2
and Maurice of Nassau 310, 381–4
overview 309–11, 331, 337, 352, 360–1, 376, 380, 397
Pacification of Ghent 363–4
peace negotiations 362

rebel invasions 341–3, 347–50
rebel tactics 381–2
Sea Beggars 342–7, 362
Siege of Leiden 362
Siege of Mons 349
Siege of Zutphen 350
and Spanish Armada 388–9
Spanish counter-tactics 367–8
Spanish decline 392–6
Spanish Fury 363
Spanish mutinies 362–3, 382, 393
Tenth Penny Tax 339–40, 349
Union of Brussels 366
United Provinces, governorship of 385–8
United Provinces, growing power of 390–2, 394–5, 397
and William of Orange 309–10, 321–2, 324, 339, 341–3, 345–52, 362–3, 365–6, 369–73, 385

Eck, Johann 242–4
economic change
and exploration 106, 112–15, 118
in Germany 217–21
and immigration 110
overview 106–7
and social distress 143
Edict of Worms (1521) 284–5
education 106, 120, 122, 127–30
Edward VI 5–7
place in succession 9–10
principal ministers 25
Protestantism under 68–9, 72
rebellions against 42, 98–100
religious changes 39–44, 52, 55
Elizabeth I 8
accession to throne 13
Attorney General controversy 166
and Burghley 164–5
Catholic plots against 56–7, 61, 101–3, 169–70
claims to throne of 169
court co-operation and conflict 164–6
crisis of government under 142–3, 149–50, 205
cult of Gloriana 137–8
death 172
economic and social crisis 154, 192–7
and Essex 164–5, 171–2
excommunication 59
and factionism 142–3, 161–73
France, war with 148, 150, 194
gender, relevance of 13–14
image 14, 132, 137–8
Ireland, war in 151–6, 167, 171
legitimacy 8–9
marriage proposals 13–14
military crisis 151, 156
Netherlands, war with 150–1, 194, 343–5, 369, 385
and Parliament 19–20, 143, 178–87
Parliamentary speeches 179–80
place in succession 9–10
principal ministers 29–30, 164–5
Privy Council 164, 180